THE KINGDOM OF ART

The Kingdom

of Art:

UNIVERSITY OF NEBRASKA PRESS · LINCOLN

*Selected and edited
with two essays and
a commentary by*
BERNICE SLOTE

WILLA CATHER'S FIRST PRINCIPLES AND CRITICAL STATEMENTS
1893–1896

Publishers on the Plains

UNP

Manufactured in the United States of America

For
Mrs. George Seibel
and the late Elizabeth Shepley Sergeant—
two friends of Willa Cather
who have been friends of this book.

Preface

✳ ✳ ✳

As Willa Cather said of the development of the singer Thea Kronborg in *The Song of the Lark*, there is "the play of blind chance," there are the "fortunate accidents" that determine our way. This book about Willa Cather's own beginning as a writer is the result of one of those accidents. While I was working on another project, and purely out of curiosity about some minor point, I began to read in the Lincoln, Nebraska, newspapers of 1895–1896. There I found the unexpected. Willa Cather's weekly column on the arts, which had appeared in the *Nebraska State Journal* during her last two years at the University of Nebraska, had not stopped at her graduation in 1895, as biographical statements have indicated: the column and other critical writing had continued in Lincoln papers for another year. Eventually, after a score of astonishments and a good deal of detective work, I had a body of writing which nearly doubled the number of items given in existing bibliographies of the Nebraska years, including forty-four additional weekly columns, many more play reviews, and some unexpected biographical facts to piece together. The supposed year of inactivity and silence before Willa Cather left Nebraska for Pittsburgh in June of 1896 did not exist, and the gap between her journalistic writing as a student and the signed columns she sent back to the Lincoln papers from 1896 to 1900 was filled with material that made a continuous, interrelated sequence of comment on the arts. Moreover, the articles of 1895–1896 were of unusual interest, directly related to Willa Cather's own art as a writer. As well as defining one artist's development, they also revealed in frank, full statements a little more of the way of creativity, with all its errors and problems and quick, sharp illuminations. But not only was there another year of writing to consider: another person stepped out of those pages, a Willa Cather at twenty who at every turn seemed to be more prolific, more engaging, more full of surprises than old Herrmann the Magician on the Lansing Theatre stage. By the time all of the pattern came clear, it was not only a writer's first statements about art that might be important, but a young woman of consequence; a lively, funny, remarkable girl; a little more of the truth. These things I hoped to present in a small book on what Willa Cather thought of art and the artist when she left Nebraska in 1896.

THE KINGDOM OF ART has twice been delayed. Twice new material has developed, and it had to be set somehow into the mosaic. Constantly, new directions and lines of relationship have emerged, and if the book stops where it does, it is not because the story is complete or because all the problems have been solved. I have not attempted to present all of the material, only that relating to Willa Cather's ideas of art. Nor have I tried to make a definitive bibliography. That work is still to be done—if it ever can be, for the field sometimes seems made of quicksilver. A good part of my work has been to establish connections between the early unsigned pieces and the later signed columns and fiction. Here there are literally hundreds of close links, references, and developments of style or material. Another task has been to try to suggest a little of the context of the 1890's, for the newspaper writing is personal, occasional, informal, and needs to have a contemporary frame. But even the texture and tone of life as Willa Cather knew it in the 1890's is important to a full understanding of her mature work.

The plan of THE KINGDOM OF ART is to give a summary of the first, elementary principles on which this one writer based her art, and then to present a collection of critical statements—personal and occasional as well as theoretical—that seem to give a realistic view of Willa Cather as she was in the years 1893–1896. The summaries in the two essays, "Writer in Nebraska" and "The Kingdom of Art," were written after the completion of Part II, five groups of critical statements. As I see it now, I would leave out some selections that do not hold up in interest, though it may be just as well to have a reminder that these pieces are not essays, not formal statements or finished writing. They are the materials of an artist in motion. The reader may have the pleasure I have had—to find in them some definitions of a writer's beginning and the sound of a voice that is real, alive. But even these things would be unimportant if the broken pieces given here did not increase our understanding of the final work of a writer and its full significance. I believe they do help us to know a little more about Willa Cather's art, which has been called elusive, subtle, complex. There has always been something more beyond the pages, something we could not quite put our fingers on, or define. There still is, for that matter.

PREFACE

In acknowledging the help I have received in the preparation of THE KINGDOM OF ART, my first and deepest thanks are to my publishers, whose patience and understanding have been more than any book deserves. I am also grateful to other scholars who have waited patiently for its completion. My greatest debt for material is to the Nebraska State Historical Society, whose resources have been used relentlessly and whose staff members have been unfailingly helpful: among them particularly Dr. Donald Danker, State Historian; Mrs. Opal Jacobsen and all who have assisted in the newspaper room; and the staff of archivists who have made research possible. Thanks for material and assistance with research also go to the University of Nebraska Library, especially Mr. Eugene M. Johnson and Mrs. Charity Greene; the Newberry Library; the Carnegie Library in Pittsburgh, especially Mrs. Julia Cunningham in the Pennsylvania Room; the Willa Cather Pioneer Memorial in Red Cloud; the Bennett Martin Public Library in Lincoln, especially Miss Bernice Kaufmann, former reference librarian; Mrs. Mildred R. Bennett, who was the first to study and collect materials of Willa Cather's Nebraska; Dr. James R. Shively, whose 1949 study reached in general many of the same conclusions about Willa Cather and the University which I have presented; the University of Nebraska Research Council for grants for material and typing; Mrs. Judy Young Hamilton and Mrs. Betty Hoyenga for help with the manuscript. I owe an unusual debt to several persons who contributed in especially individual, important ways: to Mr. and Mrs. Philip (Helen Cather) Southwick and Mr. Charles Cather for their encouragement and their help with materials; to the late Elsie M. Cather, whose words are in this book, and not always in quotation marks; to the late Elizabeth Shepley Sergeant, who told me I was on the right track, that the Willa Cather I found in the nineties was the one she knew later; and to Mrs. George Seibel, who at ninety-three gave me more life of a good past than I can say.

BERNICE SLOTE

University of Nebraska

Contents

✵ ✵ ✵

Preface · vii

PART ONE: FIRST PRINCIPLES

WRITER IN NEBRASKA · 3

THE KINGDOM OF ART · 31

PART TWO: CRITICAL STATEMENTS

THE INDIVIDUAL TALENT · 115

The Great Ones · 115

Bernhardt and Duse: A Duel of Genius · 116 Alexander Salvini: Hero of Old Romance · 121 Richard Mansfield: A Master · 122 Clay Clement: A Beginner · 124

Limitations and Distinctions · 127

Mounet-Sully's Classic Acting · 127 Nat Goodwin's Comedy · 128 Four Singers: Tavary, Doenhoff, Melba, Lussan · 131 Kinds of Opera · 134 Kinds of Realism · 134 The Sledge and the Rapier · 135 Some English and French Performers · 136 Judith Gautier: The French Quality · 138 Voices of the Stage · 139

The Making of Artists · 141

The Rights of Genius · 141 A Talent for Living · 142 Intellect in Art · 144 Prodigies: The Dovey Sisters · 145 The Child and the Artist · 148

The Personal Side · 150

The Good and the Proper · 150 The Effect of Evil · 151 The Privacy of Art · 152 Renunciation · 154

CONTENTS

Lives and Deaths · 160

Rubinstein · 160 Carvalho · 161 Mascagni · 162 Paganini · 164 Campanini · 165 Ambroise Thomas · 167 The Author of "Kathleen Mavourneen" · 168 Clara Wieck Schumann · 169

THE WAY OF THE WORLD · 171

Art in Philistia · 171

Philistia · 172 The Lansing Drop Curtain · 172 Dress at the Concerts · 176 Moral Music · 177 The Literary Life · 179 Winners and Losers · 181 Parlor Critics · 186 The *Ladies' Home* · 187 The Queen's English · 189 "We Pay" · 194 Responsibilities · 198

The Relations of Things · 205

The Band and the Building · 205 Building a Ruin · 207 The Dislocated Arts · 207 Ingersoll's Prose · 210 The Poetry of Football · 211 Opera: Scenes and Music · 214 Arts of the Stage · 215 Views in the Haydon Art Club Exhibit · 217

A Sense of History · 220

Classical Plays in Nebraska · 220 History in the Arts · 221 Yvette Guilbert: Image of France · 225 Natural Justice · 228 A Primitive Force · 229 On Nature and Romance · 231

DRAMA · 235

The Playwright and His Craft · 235

David Belasco · 237 Charles H. Hoyt · 240 Henry Guy Carleton · 243 Dumas *père* and Dumas *fils* · 246 On Revising a Play · 249 Observations on Craft · 251 The Playwright's Intention · 254

Drama Critic · 256

The Gallery Gods · 256 The Highest Kind of Criticism · 257 The *Journal* Critic · 258 The French Ideal · 260

A Round of Reviews · 262

Clara Morris in *Camille* · 262 The Signed Reviews · 263 Plays with Craigen and Paulding · 265 *She* · 267 *Uncle Tom's Cabin* · 268 Robert Downing in *The Gladiator* · 270 Another *Friends* · 272 *Yon Yonson* · 273

CONTENTS

The Black Crook · 273 The Spooners in *Inez* · 275 Roland Reed in *The Politician* · 277 Variations on *Faust* · 278 *The Wife* · 281 *Fleur de Lis* · 282 Richard Mansfield in *A Parisian Romance* · 284

Shakespeare on the Stage · 286

A Man of the Theatre · 286 *Henry IV*, with Frederick Warde and Louis James · 288 Playing the Histories · 290 Cleopatra at the Funke · 291 Rosalind at the Lansing · 297 *Othello*, with Louis James · 298 *Hamlet*, with Walker Whiteside · 304 "That Greatest Drama" · 305

LITERATURE · 309

Romance · 309

Stevenson: "The King and Father of Them All" · 310 Go Back, Mr. Kipling · 316 Anthony Hope: Modern Times in Zenda · 318 Stanley Weyman: The Anglo-Saxon Manner · 322 Defense of Dumas · 324

Fields of Vision · 326

Coppée · 326 Anatole France · 327 Hall Caine · 329 James Lane Allen · 330 Eugene Field · 332 Amélie Rives · 334 Mystery Stories · 335 Children's Books · 336 Scottish Novelists: A Limited Landscape · 338 Burns and Others · 341

Poets · 345

Christina Rossetti · 346 Sappho · 349 Swinburne · 349 Whitman · 350 Carman and Hovey · 353

Novels and Novelists · 357

Hardy · 358 James · 360 Du Maurier's *Trilby* · 362 Pierre Loti's *Romance of a Spahi* · 365 Zola's *The Fat and the Thin* · 367 Mrs. Burnett and Thackeray · 371 Mrs. Humphry Ward and George Eliot · 374 Tolstoi · 377

The Life, The Art · 380

Poe · 380 Wilde · 387 Verlaine · 393 Byron · 398 Ruskin · 399

IMPROVISATIONS TOWARD A CREDO, 1894–1896 · 405

Commitment · 406
The Demands of Art · 408
The Artist's Life · 410
A Mighty Craft · 415

[xiii]

CONTENTS

APPENDICES

I. The 1891 Essays · 421 II. An Uncollected Story · 437 III. From *The Roman and the Teuton* by Charles Kingsley · 442 IV. Early Interviews · 445

A Note on the Editing · 453
Bibliographical Note · 455
Index · 479

A picture section follows page 18.

Part I

FIRST
PRINCIPLES

✤ ✤ ✤

Writer in Nebraska

❖ ❖ ❖

When Willa Cather went from Nebraska to Pittsburgh in June of 1896 to begin editing the *Home Monthly* magazine, she was no country girl, shyly bemused by city marvels and overawed by the worldly East. She was neither unaware of culture (she could read five languages, including Latin and Greek, and had reported the arts for three years), nor unprepared for her new job (she had edited or contributed regularly to five publications in Lincoln). Nor was she unknown: At twenty-two, Willa Cather was a formidably brilliant, determined young woman, charged with talent—a widely admired newspaperwoman in her own state, and recognized in theatrical circles throughout the country as one of the leading drama critics in the West.

We have not known the extent of Willa Cather's early accomplishments, partly because she did not talk about them. An experienced writer does not boast of routine publication, or even remember it all. And for her, as time went by, it became unimportant to talk of past successes when greater ones were at hand. But she was also reluctant to speak of practice sketches that had developed into major fiction. As she saw it, one's several careers could be separated and only the chosen be remembered; yet in the work she did first—especially the journalistic writing of 1893–1896—are important elements that redefine her total achievement. In the perspective of history, the world-renowned novelist that Willa Cather became must be joined with the young Nebraska newspaperwoman.

For context, there are new biographical findings to consider. As her college friend Louise Pound was fond of saying in later years, there was a good deal of myth about Willa Cather. The standard biographical sketch begins with the untutored western girl running wild on her pony and talking to old Bohemian women on the Nebraska Divide, and continues with the abrupt transformation of the undergraduate amateur writer to the Eastern editor to the serene novelist for whom books almost wrote themselves. Like most dramatizations of history, the story is not as good or as exciting or as relevant to her novels as the way things really were. And it does not explain some apparently illogical acts: Why should a Pittsburgh publishing firm pluck an inexperienced girl from the Nebraska prairie and put her in full charge of a new magazine? Or why should she be called back from a Nebraska vacation in 1897 for a full-time job on the Pittsburgh *Leader* while men journalists at hand were out of work? A thorough study of the newspaper writing and other accounts of 1893–1896 gives some answers to these and other questions. For example, though it has always been known that Willa Cather wrote drama criticism in Lincoln, we have not realized that in production and distinction she was the equal of metropolitan critics. That she was of their stature is easy enough to prove: Only a few months after she reached Pittsburgh in the summer of 1896, and even while she was beginning her work as editor of the *Home Monthly* (and writing most of several issues herself), Miss Cather was also writing the lead drama reviews for the city's largest paper, the *Leader*—and using, when she could, parts of the reviews she had published in Lincoln.[1] We have also believed that during the year after her graduation from the University in 1895, Willa Cather sat at home in Red Cloud, doing no writing and fuming while the world passed her by. On the contrary, we find that she was editing a newspaper part of the time, writing for at least one and sometimes two papers all year, going to balls and the theatre in Lincoln, giving speeches, and receiving an unusual amount of public recognition.

The 1893–1896 writing also redefines Willa Cather's relation to her art and to criticism in general. Though admired in later years for her subtle, meticulous craftsmanship, Miss Cather rarely consented to discuss her work, and so her few brief essays on the arts and writing (like "The Novel Démeublé" and "Escapism") have been treasured. Yet as early as 1896 Willa Cather had written nearly a half million words of criticism, self-analysis, and explorations into the principles of art and the work of the artist. The fact is, she had said it all so many times in the beginning that

1. Although it has been assumed that Miss Cather's reviews for the Pittsburgh *Leader* began in the fall of 1897, she was writing drama criticism for that paper a full year before she joined its staff. I have noted twenty signed reviews between November 24, 1896 and June 1, 1897 (see Bibliography). The first (November 24) was signed "Willa," the others "Sibert." At least six unsigned pieces can be identified as Miss Cather's by their relationship to the Lincoln reviews. For example, the unsigned September 22, 1896, *Leader* review of Roland Reed in *The Wrong Mr. Wright* uses passages from accounts of two Roland Reed appearances in Lincoln, published in the *Nebraska State Journal* (hereafter cited as *Journal*) when Miss Cather was its drama critic: *The Woman Hater* (September 13, 1894) and *The Politician* (September 5, 1895).

the 1920 and 1930 essays seem like afterthoughts or absentminded repetitions of the obvious. Particularly in the criticism of the "lost year" of 1895–1896 we find a constant concern with literature and its craft, and in the whole view of Miss Cather's work, this series may be the most valuable of all her critical writing. It is in effect the journal of a writer discovering her art; a journal made out of life, in the act of its own living, not at all recollected in tranquillity. Unorganized and irregular, with fragments both flashing and dull, here is at least a beginning of a documentary on the creative process. All of it relates to, changes, and illuminates Willa Cather's writing career.

It is ironical that the novelist who in later years made conspicuous efforts to discourage all inquiry into her apprentice work (as Willard Thorp has said, "to dictate to posterity what we may know of her struggle for mastery"[2]) should leave behind one of the most complete and personal records of a writer's desires, delights, and agonies we have in modern literature. Except for the letters of Keats, I know of no comparable body of personal writing that shows so much of the creative process itself, or enables us to see it working out in the created thing. Willa Cather's 1893–1896 articles, many of them lying unread for nearly seventy years, return like the voice of beginnings, unexpectedly fresh and new. They comprise a marvelously authentic portrait of the artist as a young woman.

Because we are used to thinking of Willa Cather as the novelist of pioneers and the wild land, biographical interest has always focused on the country places where she spent her childhood. True, in speaking of the sources of her material, Miss Cather often singled out the years from eight to fifteen as the important ones. At first, however, she used a longer time-span, saying that "all the material for her writing had been collected before she was twenty years old."[3] Since it was during her twentieth year (1893) that she started to write regularly for the newspapers, perhaps she came to think of it as the boundary line between the gathering and the shaping of her material. It is certain at any rate that the Lincoln and university period of 1890–1896 (six of her thirteen years in Nebraska) was one of special significance in her professional career, and we need to see her in that urban setting.[4]

2. Statement accompanying a letter to the publisher, October 28, 1965.

3. Stated in an interview included in "Lincoln Girls Who Have Been Successful in Literary Work," *Journal*, October 24, 1915.

4. In the following pages, biographical details concerning Willa Cather, sketches of her contemporaries, and accounts of Lincoln and the University of Nebraska in the 1890's

Lincoln in the early 1890's was a little more than twenty years old—a city of about 30,000 laid out on the open prairie in a straggling north and south rectangle a couple of miles long and a mile wide. In the center was the state capitol. A dozen blocks away business jammed Haymarket Square, ran up and down Eleventh Street where University Hall presided at the north end, ran east and west on O, a wide street with horses and buggies scrambled irregularly along the sides. In town the buildings stood out—bald, giant-sized among new trees—but a few miles away in outlying Hawthorne, one writer looked back over the circling wooded creeks and found it beautiful: "the rambling prosaic town of Lincoln at that distance is dissolved into mere patches of color, red, gray, smoke, opal and purple. . . . I never knew there were so many trees about Lincoln or that their tinted foliage could be so effective until I looked out of those studio windows." That scene should awaken "anyone's artistic sensibilities, even if they have been sleeping the long sleep of a western small town for years." 5

In the very nature of things, the first generation or so of a frontier capital city like Lincoln must have a transplanted culture. There is no time to grow up from roots; a city must be created now, at once; one must have a place in which to set down civilization. The process is a little like building a movie set. And among the firstcomers were families of education or money or both, bringing along their tapestries and oriental rugs, their fine linen and china, pianos and libraries. They trampled through the tall grass and sunflowers, criss-crossed a few square miles of mud and dust with streets (like cutting a plate of fudge), and built houses—the first large ones like blunt exclamation marks against bare earth and sky. And along with smaller boxes were great houses of brick or wood in chaste and

---

are based largely on my own study of newspapers, maps, pictures, records, letters, books, and other documents of the period, as well as interviews and conversations with a few people who were there. (See Bibliography for particular sources.) All factual statements regarding Willa Cather are based on published accounts that may be found in newspapers and other records of the period, on later interviews and reminiscences, or on primary accounts. Citations will be given only when references would be useful to verify new findings or to check details that differ from those in the established biographical sources: E. K. Brown, *Willa Cather: A Critical Biography* (New York: Alfred A. Knopf, 1953); Edith Lewis, *Willa Cather Living* (New York: Alfred A. Knopf, 1953); and Mildred R. Bennett, *The World of Willa Cather*, New Edition with Notes and Index (Lincoln: University of Nebraska Press, 1961).

5. The [Lincoln] *Courier* (hereafter cited as *Courier*), October 5, 1895. Like numerous other articles which appeared in the *Courier* while Miss Cather was on its staff (see below, pages 23 ff.), this piece suggests her hand, though there is no positive evidence for attribution.

classical lines, or spun wonders of Victorian Gothic. They moved in, took out their white kid gloves, subscribed to *Century*, shipped in oysters frozen in blocks of ice, and tried to keep life very much as it had been in Ohio, New York, Illinois, or Virginia. It took a while for the smell of the prairie, the wild blue power of the sky, the hard cold and the dry winds to shake the city into roots through sunflowers and red grass.

These were the pioneers not of land but of commerce and the professions: judges, lawyers, merchants, publishers, railroad builders, professors. There were also the exploiters, the boomers of paper towns and promoters of wildcat banks. But good or bad, they did not come to Nebraska to build a different world; they wanted the kind of society they had always considered desirable—but they wanted it here, where success (so they thought) was quick as a grasshopper, almost sure as the wind.

On some levels, life in Lincoln was not at all primitive, nor did it seem very different from life elsewhere—only a little harder to conduct with proper standards. There were social clubs and calling cards (though some people still lived in dugouts just east of town). Lincoln had a library, a university, and five private schools; about as many saloons as churches; and five major hotels (the Arlington, Oscar Wilde had said, was "the best hotel west of the Mississippi, not even excepting those in San Francisco"[6]). Travel was constant—to Chicago, to Europe; or you could take the electric streetcar to Lincoln Park for light operas, dancing, acrobats, balloon ascensions; or at Burlington Beach, cruise over Salt Lake in the fifty-passenger steamer. The main streets of Lincoln were paved with cedar blocks, and before hard times and weather made them buckle and bump you might watch cyclists whirl down Eleventh Street, or, after a good snow, see the dashing Latta girls flash by—red sleigh and white horses, bright feathers, and silver bells.

Lincoln's greatest cultural distinction was its professional theatre. On the main rail lines between east and west, the city became a regular stop for touring metropolitan companies. Most of the time Willa Cather was in Lincoln there were two large, luxurious theatres—the Funke Opera House (1885) seated 1,200; the Lansing Theatre (1891), 1,800. When both theatres were running there were approximately one hundred dramatic companies a year, sometimes five or six plays a week, and stars as good as Julia Marlowe, Helena Modjeska, Margaret Mather, Richard Mansfield, Joseph Jefferson, the Drews, Otis Skinner—as well as orchestras conducted

6. Lowry Charles Wimberly, "Oscar Wilde Meets Woodberry," in *Prairie Schooner*, Spring, 1947, p. 108. Wilde was in Lincoln in 1882.

by Anton Seidl or Theodore Thomas; opera stars like Nordica, Scalchi, and Campanini.

In Lincoln there were opera cloaks and oysters in ice, but always in spring came the smell of burning prairie grass, for this was still the edge of the frontier, and the frontier still had teeth. Some summers, grasshoppers stripped the newly planted trees; and one winter after a blizzard, just outside town a man was found sitting straight up in the middle of the road, frozen to death. And yet in 1893, after bank failures, panic, and drouth, a pre-theatre reception on the night Clara Morris played in *Camille* had a menu of twenty-four items, from "Blue Points on Shell" through "Fillet of Beef aux Truffles" to "Charlotte Russe" and "Cafe Noir."[7]

The University of Nebraska campus—four square blocks defined by a high iron fence—was by 1892 neatly laid out with grass, walks, young trees, and four buildings. The oldest (1871), and the center for classes, was an ornate red brick structure with red mansard roof and square bell tower. In all the early pictures University Hall looms up from nothing like a great red rock. But it was mortal, everyone knew—its delicate bones shored up with braces, and a perpetual leak in the chapel ceiling. Here Willa had come in 1890 as a "second prep" (Red Cloud's school was rated high enough to exempt her from the usual first year of college preparatory work). When she was a freshman in 1891–1892, there were between three and four hundred students (plus another hundred preps); by the time she graduated, three times that number were choking for space. The library was housed in two cluttered, creaking, shadowy rooms on the second floor of University Hall. A new library, begun in 1893, was still four weedy, half-grown walls that had stopped when the money did, waiting until the 1895 legislators could give it a roof and insides. These were physical realities of another frontier which students like Willa Cather knew beyond illusion.

Like the transplanted culture of Lincoln, the learning of the University came from other places—the East and Europe. It was an immigration of ideas as mixed as the nations and languages of those who came for the black soil. The very differences stretched the mind. For example, take three men who taught there when Willa was in school: A. H. Edgren from Sweden, translator of Sanskrit, former Rector of the University of Gothenberg, became in 1893 the first dean of Nebraska's Graduate College. James T. Lees, who taught Greek, was "a magnificent scholar. British born, with British conservatism dyed in his wool, educated at Johns

7. *Courier*, November 25, 1893.

Hopkins under the great classicist Basil L. Gildersleeve, passionate admirer of Paul Shorey, Platonist, despiser of his times and particularly of anything savoring of democracy."[8] Herbert Bates came to teach English in the fall of 1891. He was a young man just a year out of Harvard, a capable poet and short story writer. During his nearly five years at Nebraska—and in spite of his nervous manner and his sarcastic remarks on themes—he became a popular and influential teacher. It was Bates who most helped Willa Cather in early publication and serious writing. Though he may always have felt himself an exile in the West, Bates came to believe that western universities were the equal of the ivied eastern schools, especially in the vigor and accomplishment of their students. [9]

Bates had a high opinion of his students, as well he might. The University of Nebraska in the early 1890's was itself a little Renaissance world—almost a real community of scholars. On the campus with Willa Cather were people who would in extraordinary proportion become distinguished novelists, poets, editors, professors, jurists, governors; one would be Dean of Harvard Law School, one the Head of the New School for Social Research, another the President of the Modern Language Association; one would be General of the Armies and Commander of the A.E.F. in 1917; two would win Pulitzer Prizes, two would represent America at the 1918 Peace Conference. They were people like Dorothy Canfield, Hartley Burr Alexander, Alvin Johnson, D. N. Lehmer, William Westermann, Lieut. J. J. Pershing, and the legendary Pounds— Roscoe, Louise, and Olivia—all scholars, teachers, writers. The talents they exhibited in the 1890's seem already prodigal. Dorothea Canfield (still in prep school) was both fencer and violinist; Lehmer was a composer as well as mathematician; Louise Pound was a scholar in Anglo-Saxon, but also pianist, wheelwoman, and tennis champion; Roscoe Pound, the future jurist, skimmed over the campus, teaching botany and law, reporting the football games, and raising money for the team. Many students did come to school unused to books and the ways of learning, and some of them achieved in spite of it. But most of those named here belonged to families who, like Aeneas, had brought their culture, their household gods, to the new land. The old and the new together had a strange, individual alchemy. Willa Cather herself, even by her twentieth year, had more than a glint of the fabulous, for in her particular

8. Alvin Johnson, *Pioneer's Progress* (Lincoln: University of Nebraska Press, 1960), p. 87.

9. Useful notes on Herbert Bates appear in the *Hesperian*, December 24, 1896; and (after his death) in the *English Journal*, September, 1929. See also his article, "A Western University," in *Outlook*, February 27, 1897.

background the disparate pieces of tradition, eccentric interests, emigration, chance encounters, tough frontier, and haphazard education fall into an almost perfect example of the humanistic ideal, as it was bred through centuries of literary gathering and selection. Something elemental and firm, that did not think a leaking roof was sky.

Possibly there was never a time when Willa Cather "started to write," or even when she "learned to write." She was born to language, and she rode its rhythms as a dolphin takes the sea. And from her first year in Lincoln she was published and recognized: her class theme on Carlyle (which had been passed on to the *Nebraska State Journal* by her teacher Ebenezer Hunt) was in fact printed twice on March 1, 1891—in the Sunday *Journal* (signed "W. C.") and also in the university paper, the *Hesperian* (unsigned). An editorial note in the *Journal* commented on what seemed an astonishing combination: the strong, sonorous, darkly poetic Carlyle essay and its author, a "second prep" at the University. In a picture of that year Willa Cather looks small and boyish, shining, eager, very young —but she was ready for the world of print.

Her freshman year began well: another signed publication in the *Journal* ("Shakespeare and Hamlet," November 1 and 8, 1891), and a new venture on the campus. The first issues of a small magazine, the *Lasso*, appeared anonymously in October and November; in December the masthead identified the staff as James B. McDonald, proprietor and managing editor; Willa Cather and Louise Pound, associate editors. The *Lasso* was published only that one year, and Willa's name was on the masthead only the first semester, but it took her inside university journalism.

On the campus in the nineties, publications were combined magazine-newspapers, owned and operated by individual students or organizations. The oldest was the *Hesperian* (once called the *Hesperian Student*), normally a sixteen-page semi-monthly, conducted by the literary societies (Union, Palladian, Delian). The editorial staff was elected by the membership of the societies, the position of managing editor rotating among the three organizations. Early in the fall of 1892, Willa (a Union) was elected an associate editor (the staff included a managing editor and eight associates). She is listed on the masthead as "Literary"—and certainly she conducted a superlative department that year. A number of her own signed stories appeared the first semester, but nothing was signed during the last part of the year—either she wrote less or had invoked an increasingly familiar editorial anonymity. But she was often in print, by name or reference.[10]

By the spring of 1893, Willa Cather was a well-known campus figure. During the year she had won modest fame in two productions given by the new dramatic society: Reviews admired her Lady Macbeth in *Shakespeare Up to Date* (given November 22 and 29, 1892), a farce in which Shakespeare's characters accuse him of falsifying their true natures. On December 10, 1892, as a benefit for the Athletic Association, the dramatists gave *A Perjured Padulion*, a five-act "emotional tragedy" and takeoff on university life written (so the newspapers said) by Louise Pound, though in after years she would never quite admit it. Willa played the role of Diamond Witherspoon, who presumably causes the difficulties of everybody else. The part also allowed her to give her famous reading of "Curfew Must Not Ring Tonight."[11] Willa was also elected literary editor of the 1894 annual, the *Sombrero* (published by the class of 1895), and she was made managing editor of the *Hesperian* for 1893–1894.

In the first issue of the *Hesperian* with "W. Cather—Managing Editor" on the masthead (September 27, 1893), a "Salutatory," obviously by the editor, states the program "in plain, unornamented language which anyone can interpret without the aid of a handbook of mythology or a dictionary of similes." The paper will center on college affairs, and "If there is any fighting to be done, we will be down in the line fighting on one side or the other, striking out from the shoulder. If we err, we will err through bad judgment, not through lack of enthusiasm." Some statements are especially characteristic: "If a man says that the earth is flat, if he slanders a great book or writes an absurd one, we claim the right to pummel him as much as we please; it is within the province of liberal education and legitimate journalism. As to dictating whether our neighbor shall wear jewelry or not, we think this is none of our business." We begin, says the editor, with our own worth: "It is absurd to spend one's time dying for the principles of a paper when the paper itself is perishing

10. For one example: After Willa Cather's story "A Tale of the White Pyramid" was published in the *Hesperian* (December 22, 1892), the *Nebraskan* (January, 1893) ran the following poem: "A student sat in his attic story, / Conned the Hesperian from lid to lid; / In his eye was the light of seraphic glory, / As he read o'er the story of 'The White Pyramid.' / Hours thus he sat in sweet contemplation, / Never a word, like one inspired— / Then down dashed the book in wrathy d—nation, / And murmured, 'These cuts make me tired.'"

11. *Nebraskan*, January, 1893. The Hitz Collection of Cather material at the Newberry Library has correspondence and other information on *A Perjured Padulion*.

for want of a little proof reading. . . . We are not going to work with a lance or sword, but with a good stiff stub pen."

The editor worked hard. "The truth is," a staff member recalled in later years, "the *Hesperian* was Willa practically."[12] (Perhaps the pattern is significant: she not only *could* take over a project or write most of a magazine, but it was in her nature to do so.) The *Hesperian* that year had a flair and freshness unequalled in other volumes of the magazine. Even pieces signed by others had strong, easy writing; the content was varied, often unexpected. Fewer stories appeared under Willa Cather's byline than in the previous year, but we hear her voice in many paragraphs and columns—comments on those who talk incessantly in Shakespeare class without knowing the subject, on football and art, or on student fiction writing: "We believe that literature is so great and grand an art, so infinitely above all other arts, that even if one never takes a master's degree, its apprenticeship is worth its labor and its cost."[13] As an editor she won particular praise for the 32-page Charter Day issue on February 15, 1894, commemorating the Quarter-Centennial of the University and including a history of the institution. With its full range of commissioned articles and pictures, this issue of the *Hesperian* was one of Willa Cather's major productions at the University.

Even while she was editing the *Hesperian*, Willa Cather was also learning practical journalism (always in her mind distinguished from literature) by working for the city press. At least we become aware of her in the *Journal* during the winter of 1893–1894 when, on November 5, she began a Sunday column and in the same period put her stylistic mark on a number of play reviews. In 1893 the *Journal* was the largest and most substantial of Lincoln's five major newspapers. A morning and Sunday paper, it was founded and published by Charles H. Gere, whose family had been Willa's close friends since she first came to Lincoln. Will Owen Jones, an imaginative and energetic young man still in his twenties, had been managing editor since January 1, 1892. Other dailies were the *Evening News*, owned by the Westermann family (also friends of Willa, they are described as the Erlichs in *One of Ours*), and the *Daily Call* (originally the *Daily Democrat*). Two weeklies were the *Herald* and the *Courier*, whose part-owner and editor since May, 1893, was W. Morton Smith. Willa Cather was to write for the *Courier* as well as for the *Journal*.

12. Quoted in Brown, *Willa Cather*, p. 57; the statement is in the correspondence of Flora Bullock and Benjamin Hitz (Hitz Collection, Newberry Library).

13. *Hesperian*, December 19, 1893.

All of these Lincoln papers were interesting and well conducted. All used some syndicated material. The *Journal* had excellent Sunday literary and feature sections: for example, a new Stevenson novel serialized, a story translated from Turgenev, poems by Kipling, and a good deal of locally written material. Important staff columnists on the *Journal* were A. L. Bixby with humorous comment on the local scene, and Walt Mason, who included in his "Important If True" the kind of prose poem Miss Cather assigns to Scott McGregor in *The Professor's House*. All the papers had contributors from the University, among them Lucius A. Sherman, chairman of the English department, who did a book column for the *News*, and Herbert Bates, who wrote music criticism for the *Courier*. Will Owen Jones of the *Journal* worked especially to develop new writers among the students. He organized an informal journalism club during the first semester of 1893–1894, through which some newspaper writing could receive credit in regular English classes, and he volunteered to teach a class in journalism for the second semester.[14] The *Journal*, the *News*, and the *Courier* had regular reviews of plays, concerts, and other entertainment, and often a weekly summary of theatrical news. It was such a column in the Sunday *Journal* that in 1893–1894 Willa Cather took over, developed, and made notably her own for nearly seven years.

Willa Cather's column of sketches, observations, and theatrical and literary comment began in the Sunday *Journal* on November 5, 1893, appearing under various titles until in July, 1895, it was permanently named "The Passing Show." As "The Passing Show" it was a more or less regular feature of either the *Journal* or the *Courier* until the spring of 1900. That it was continuously Willa Cather's column even in the early years has been affirmed by Miss Cather herself and by her contemporaries. It was, in fact, her professional property. When she was ill it did not appear.[15] When she went to another local paper, she took it with her. When she sent the column back from Pittsburgh for the first time (December 6, 1896), she started to sign it.

Although the beginning of Miss Cather's weekly column can be dated, the time when she began to review plays is not so precisely marked. Eventually, of course, she was both admired and notorious as "the *Journal* critic" and was repeatedly and explicitly singled out and identified. Short

14. Noted in the *Hesperian*, November 15, December 1, 1893; March 10, 1894.

15. "Those who read the Sunday *Journal* missed the dramatic criticisms from Miss Cather in last Sunday's paper," Sarah B. Harris wrote in the *Courier* on March 30, 1895. "Many of us read her columns first and always with pleasure, though sometimes we do not agree with her, which is of little consequence."

of being on the masthead—and not even the editor's name appeared there —Willa Cather was the official *"Journal* critic." The period usually designated for her work on the *Journal* is that of her junior and senior years at the University. She may have begun early in the 1893–1894 season (her junior year), for two years later—in August and early fall of 1895—it is reported that Miss Cather has been the *Journal's* drama critic "for the last two years"; in June, 1896, the paper itself says "more than two years." 16 The first reviews in the fall of 1893, however, are mostly routine and without a distinguishable style. Willa Cather's touch is more apparent in the November reviews, but her first official appearance is on December 14, when two reviewers comment on the play *Friends*; one of the pieces is signed "W. C." By then it is possible to trace some developments in Lincoln dramatic criticism as the *Courier*, like a mirror, reflects the scene.

The *Courier* complained in December, 1893, that local dramatic criticism was "a dreary waste of undiluted mediocrity," and that except for "Toby Rex" on the *News*, Lincoln's critics were "wooden men" who complimented everyone alike. ("Toby Rex" was Dr. Julius H. Tyndale, a relative of the Westermanns, who had come from the East earlier in 1893 to practice medicine. He was fifty, had theatrical connections, experience in criticism, and a very personal style—humorous, cocky, a bit malapropish.) The *Courier's* continued comments referred to developments in the *Journal*—Jones and his "immature dramatic critic"; the curious business of all those pairs of signed reviews (there were several more in January); in March and April, mock despair about disagreements with "the effusive dramatic critic of the *Journal*"; finally, a compliment to the *Journal* and its new "sprightliness." 17 Most interesting in both the newspaper talk and the dramatic criticism itself is the sharpening focus: from mid-February—exactly when the Charter Day issue of the *Hesperian* was completed—some *Journal* reviews lengthen to essays; columns and reviews swing clear in the same orbit. There is no doubt about the identity of the reviewer. If others have been helping, they fall away before the clear-cut authority of the *Journal* critic—described later that year as "a young lady with a level head and bright pen." This was Miss Cather, and she would rule the field until she left in 1896. She would also be the prime reason the Des Moines *Record* could say in June, 1895: "The best theatrical

16. *Courier*, August 3, 1895; *Journal*, June 17, 1896.

17. The *Courier* sequence includes the issues of December 2 and 9, 1893; January 13 and 27, February 17, March 24 and April 14, 1894. "Toby Rex" is identified from numerous references in the Lincoln newspapers, as well as Dr. Tyndale's comments in the *Journal*, July 24, 1927.

critics of the west are said to be connected with the Lincoln, Neb. press." [18]

It may be natural to wonder about beginnings, motivations, influences. Although Willa Cather's recognizable—perhaps official—beginning as drama critic in February and March, 1894, coincides with the journalism course given by Jones at the University during the second semester, and for which Willa was enrolled, it would be misleading to say that her dramatic criticism began as class work. The reviews of 1894 are major efforts. They show experience, authority, and knowledge of the theatre. Although Willa was a quick study and preternaturally observant, such skill could not come automatically. There had been a preparation, for how long it is hard to say. Although she almost immediately outshot his range, she certainly learned about the stage and reviewing from Dr. Tyndale, who became her lifelong friend. She might have been involved in the journalism club during the first semester, but more likely as initiator than as follower. As the leading campus journalist, author of a number of published stories and poems as well as three signed articles in the *Journal* itself, she was even then long past the need for either suggestion or opportunity. But we can find an earlier, more probable beginning. Willa might have learned something about dramatic criticism from George W. Gerwig, a young insurance man and law student with an M.A. in English from the University, who—said the *Lasso* editors in December, 1891—had contributed the column of drama news to the paper. Gerwig, all signs indicate, was then the *Journal's* dramatic critic, for while he was in the East during January, 1892, the usual Sunday columns of theatrical news were sent from New York, signed "G. W. G." His style is also recognizable in the reviews of that period. Gerwig was then and continued to be a good friend of Willa Cather, and considering her own developing interest in drama, he might well have let her help occasionally. In the light of later events, other facts about Gerwig are relevant: In 1892 he left Lincoln for Allegheny, Pennsylvania, and the adjoining city of Pittsburgh. Shortly after he was settled there, he was elected secretary to the Allegheny Board of School Controllers, a position he held many years. [19] George Gerwig's career and Willa Cather's cross at other times, as we shall see.

18. The comment on Miss Cather is from a note which first appeared in the *Nebraska Editor* in late 1894 and was reprinted in the *Journal* on January 6, 1895 (see also note 34, below). The Des Moines *Record* article was reprinted in the *Courier*, June 29, 1895.

19. George W. Gerwig (1867–1950) was for fifty years the secretary of the Board of Education in Pittsburgh, for thirty years secretary-treasurer of the Frick Commission, the author of a number of books. See also a note in the *Courier*, August 11, 1894.

For influences one might also note some qualities of the newspapers themselves—like Lincoln, a combination of sophistication and crudeness, music boxes and mud: individualistic, outspoken, romantic. Two local columns, Mason's "Important If True" in the *Journal* and J. D. Calhoun's "Nothing But Lies" in the *Herald* had a style that was frank, personal, humorous, biting—the same qualities which in sharper tones of sarcasm, personalities, and political anger often touched western journalism. To the modern reader, the editorial tone of the Lincoln papers seems literate and controlled, but there are enough blunt shockers to remind us that we are still close to the frontier where some of the truth is not at all civilized. The papers are outspoken even in reporting the news: a divorce is granted because of a husband's "general good-for-nothingness" (not "incompatibility"); a man is openly called "a noted drunk"; and in the account of a girl in labor who could not get help, the names are given of the doctor who would not go on the call, and the doctor who wanted his one dollar first. Call it crude or call it honest, this was the hell-cat tone you sometimes heard in the newspapers of the nineties, and it was a natural sound. If it did not determine the way the *Journal*'s drama critic was to write (and nobody could), at least it suggested a climate in which no one needed to pull his punches.

After the spring of 1894 and the conclusion of her work on the *Hesperian*, Willa Cather worked mainly for the city papers. That summer she wrote a number of signed articles[20] and reviews for the *Journal*, and began immediately in the fall with redoubled energy and assurance to justify a reputation already established. We have some portraits of Willa Cather at work in this period[21]: John M. Thompson, a *Journal* reporter, remembered "the terrible scrawl which she made when using pen and ink and there is a legend about the office that her spelling was not exactly up to date." Shakespearean, he added—never the same from day to day. Will Owen Jones recalled in 1921 that "she wrote dramatic criticisms of such biting frankness that she became famous among actors from coast to

20. These articles and extensive material not in the scope of this book will be included in the forthcoming *The World and the Parish: Willa Cather's Articles and Reviews 1893–1903*, selected and edited with a commentary by William M. Curtin, to be published by the University of Nebraska Press in 1967.

21. Quotations in the following two paragraphs are, successively, from Thompson's "'Confessions' of a Reporter," *Journal*, July 24, 1927; an editorial note by Jones, *Journal*, November 1, 1921; Ella Fleishman (quoting Abbott), "Willa Cather, Former Nebraska Girl, Puts Prairie in Literature," Omaha *World-Herald*, February 1, 1920; William Reed Dunroy, "Literary Lincoln," *Courier*, June 1, 1895; an editorial note by Walt Mason, Beatrice *Express*, reprinted in *Journal*, December 25, 1894.

coast. . . . Many an actor of national reputation wondered on coming to Lincoln what would appear the next morning from the pen of that meatax young girl of whom all of them had heard. Miss Cather didn't stand in awe of the greatest actors, but set each one in his place with all of the authority of a veteran metropolitan critic." And Keene Abbott, who followed her as critic on the *Journal*, said that when he tried to write the same kind of scathing review, Jones called him on the carpet. "It's no worse than those Willa Cather did," said Abbott. "Well," Jones replied, "but that was Miss Cather!"

Part of it was indeed Miss Cather. She wrote like nobody else, and her pen—for all its inky scrawl—was brighter than any of the calcium lights she had to strike through. One journalist at the time described her as "a strong writer. . . . As a critic she is fearless, and has the knack of seeing things as they really are." But even some of her supporters, like Walt Mason, thought she roasted more than she praised. He wrote in 1894 that theatre people "speak very bitterly concerning the criticisms that appear in THE LINCOLN JOURNAL. Some of the actors have cause for complaint, and others would be wise to take their medicine and profit by it"—the old barnstormers, for example, who would victimize the West by exchanging tickets for flattery in the papers. They had been given far too much of that kind of taffy, he said, but he thought the *Journal* threatened to go to the other extreme: "Its critic has rare intelligence and a most entertaining way of crucifying ambitious actors and actresses, but he (or she) is never so quick to give credit for good work as to offer denunciation for poor work." (The critic also kept score. In her column of November 18 she had reported fifteen companies praised, fourteen damned —so far that season.) But it was not always the barnstormers who needed to be exposed. Even the companies sent out in every direction by the big theatrical managers, the Frohmans, varied widely in quality—and some poor ones had been in Nebraska. Toward the end of January, 1895, Gustave Frohman came through Lincoln—among other things, to check on the Frohman companies then under attack in the city, and to talk with Miss Cather. They sat in the loge of the Lansing—Willa, Dr. Tyndale, and the manager from the East—and discussed "honest criticism," the high quality of Lincoln reviewers, and the possibilities of the theatre in the West. There is no sign in the interview that Willa had softened.

If Willa Cather had a reputation as the incomparable roaster, the "meatax young girl," it was partly because she liked a good fight. The tone of her *Hesperian* "Salutatory" was true and prophetic: she often let go with her stiff stub pen in haste and later agonized for its errors on the field. One of her student pieces, a characterization of Roscoe Pound in the *Hesperian* column, "Pastels in Prose," brought the Pound house down around her ears and drew a counterattack in the rival student paper, the *Nebraskan*. Some statements in the fall of 1894 about the overweening pride of the University were called "an overflow of bile" by the *Hesperian's* new management; and remarks about ladies' clubs brought Mrs. James H. Canfield, wife of the chancellor, to write an article in rebuttal.[22]

Willa's conflict with Professor L. A. Sherman was less dramatic but more extended, and it has enough larger significance in her work to justify some detail. Minor skirmishes came between Sherman's book column in the *News* and Willa's in the *Journal*, as when Sherman called *Trilby* immoral and Willa rejoined with several eloquent defenses of both book and principle. But chiefly she opposed his efforts to make the study of literature and language scientific, a purpose he stated and demonstrated in his *Analytics of Literature* (1893). Sherman was not all bad, even for Willa; in the *Analytics* are many insights that obviously influenced her. But some attitudes seemed to her both ignorant and ruthless. Often his scientific method came down to mere word-counting: judging by published examples, he and his students had counted words of nearly a hundred thousand sentences in works of seventy authors from Spenser to Henry James. Half of *Analytics* is devoted to such analyses of sentence length, comparative predication, and ratios of force, with charts, diagrams, formulae, and equations.[23] Willa wrote a number of satires on Sherman's analytics, recalled one of her friends, including some poems on the "counting" assignments. Though unsigned, the "count" poems in the *Hesperian* are easily recognizable. For example, on December 1, 1893, there was "He Took Analytics":

22. The sketch of Roscoe Pound, identified in later years by Louise and Olivia Pound, appeared in the *Hesperian*, March 10, 1894 (pp. 4–5). The other exchanges of criticism ran in the *Hesperian* and the *Journal* during October and November, 1894.

23. "In the *Count Gismond*," he wrote, "the sum of emphasized words to the whole number is as 449:865, or not far from 1:2. In the prose passage from Carlyle there is more than seventy per cent of emphasis, but the force-ratio of the present paragraph and the next is 25:45, or only fifty-five per cent" (*Analytics*, p. 18). Results of the "counting" research are presented in two Nebraska monographs: L. A. Sherman, "On Certain Facts and Principles in the Development of Form in Literature," *University Studies*, Vol. I, No. IV (July, 1892); and G. W. Gerwig, "On the Decrease of Predication and of Sentence Weight in English Prose," *University Studies*, Vol. II, No. 1 (July, 1894). Willa Cather's "counting" satires were identified by friends, as quoted in Marjorie Wyman, "Willa Cather, Novelist, Was Modern Flapper at Nebraska U," Lincoln *Star*, June 29, 1924. One poem named was "Count Gismond," *Hesperian*, December 19, 1893.

The University of Nebraska Campus in 1892

Willa Cather as a "Second Prep," 1890-1891

Photograph from the Pound Collection, courtesy of Nebraska State Historical Society.

Willa Cather in June, 1894

Photograph courtesy of Bennett Martin Public Library, Lincoln, Nebraska.

Faithfully yours
Willa Cather.

Photograph courtesy of the Cather family.

Willa Cather in June, 1895

Photograph courtesy of the Nebraska State Historical Society.

The Lansing Theatre in November, 1891

I am dying, Egypt, dying,
　　Ebbs the crimson life-tide fast;
And the dark Plutonian shadows
　　Gather on the evening blast;
Ah I counted, Queen, and counted,
　　And rows of figures massed
Till e'en my days are numbered,
　　And I'm counted out at last.

Although they were not stressed in her columns, some events in the winter of 1894–1895 (her senior year at the University) are important in our view of Willa Cather, at that time and later. Drouth and famine may not have been appropriate in a feature which thrived on the arts and gave some richness to the air which then blew thin and bitter over the plains. Nebraska had endured two summers of almost literal hell—hot winds, no rain, no crops. Writers seemed unable to avoid terms like "desert," "skeleton," and "hot blasts from a fiery furnace," clichés most irritating to those who insisted that views of the land were being distorted. But by December, 1894, some parts of the state were devastated by stark cold, famine, and death—for persons and animals alike. Relief programs were set up and contributions came in from distant states—carloads of food, fuel, and eventually seed. This was the time Willa Cather described in 1921 as "the lean years in the nineties," when "the ghosts walked in this country."[24] In December, 1894, articles reporting observations in the disaster area appeared in the Omaha *World-Herald* (then edited by W. J. Bryan), but the *Journal* and others angrily accused the rival paper of sensationalism. Eastern papers reprinted the accounts, sometimes with variations and additions of their own. The story—a mingling of rumor, fiction, and fact—seemed important enough to one Eastern agency to warrant special coverage.

Stephen Crane arrived in Lincoln on February 1, 1895, sent by the Bacheller-Johnson syndicate to report conditions in the drouth-stricken areas of Nebraska. Papers welcomed Crane not as a literary man but as a journalist "representing a large syndicate of newspapers of national reputation and influence," and business interests were confident that he would find the truth less lurid than earlier reports printed in the East. Crane would also have been known to Nebraskans as the author of *The*

24. Eleanor Hinman, "Willa Cather, Famous Nebraska Novelist," Lincoln *Star*, November 6, 1921.

Red Badge of Courage. An early shortened version had run in six install-
ments in the *Journal*, December 4–9, 1894. During his stay in Nebraska
Crane interviewed officials, visited the disaster areas, experienced the
violent blizzard of February 6, and had finished his work by February 14.
His article appeared as a syndicated feature in the *Journal* on February 24,
under the head, "Waiting for the Spring." Willa Cather may have met
Stephen Crane in Lincoln (it would seem likely that she did, since she
was often at the *Journal* with copy and he received mail in care of Will
Owen Jones), but her article "When I Knew Stephen Crane," published
shortly after his death in 1900, cannot be used as proof or as biographical
fact. It is fictional in a number of details. Most striking is the time of
Crane's visit as it is represented in the article—not the actual bitter-cold
February, but late spring, "oppressively warm" with a dry wind blowing
up from Kansas. And Crane is represented as a romantic but indigent
wanderer, with no mention of his serious, even demanding, assignment in
Nebraska. Nor was Crane mentioned in the columns and reviews of
1895.[25]

A pivotal experience for Willa Cather that season was a trip to
Chicago with her friend Mary L. Jones (then acting librarian at the
University) to attend grand opera during the Metropolitan season. They
were gone for the week of March 10, conveniently a time when both
theatres in Lincoln were dark. In the columns after Chicago one may sense
a new kind of vitality, often freer, more ecstatic language. She knew that
the best was real, and her own independence and authority in the arts
could be based on that knowledge.

Willa Cather graduated from the University on June 12, 1895. She
was generally considered brilliant in literature and writing, independent
in college activities. She belonged to a Lewis Carroll club, and held
several offices in the Union Literary Society. In later reminiscences her
fellow-student Ned Abbott said that she belonged to the English Club
(organized in the spring of 1894), though I have not found her name in
any contemporary list of members or report of a program, or that she

25. Circumstances of Crane's trip west are established from *Stephen Crane: Letters*, ed.
by R. W. Stallman and Lillian Gilkes (New York: New York University Press, 1960),
pp. 48 ff.; the *Call*, February 2, and the *Journal*, February 2 and 14, 1895. It is important to
note that although "When I Knew Stephen Crane" appeared in the *Courier* under Willa
Cather's own name (July 14, 1900; reprinted in *Prairie Schooner*, Fall, 1949), it was first
published in the *Library* (June 23, 1900) as by "Henry Nicklemann," a frequently-used
Cather pseudonym of that period. "Henry Nicklemann" as the narrative voice in "When
I Knew Stephen Crane" is not bound to factual autobiography, and may be a precursor of a
later persona like Jim Burden in *My Ántonia*.

was connected with the *Nebraska Literary Magazine* which the English Club sponsored in 1895–1896. Her name does come up in reference to other organizations. Illness kept her from speaking on "English and German Homes" to the Haydon Art Club on February 27, 1894 (Will Owen Jones substituted). And presumably she did some debating, for a poem by A. L. Bixby a few years later laments the passing of the stars of the Girls' Debating Clubs that flourished in the "Arcadian days of old"— "Those palmy days," he concluded, "when 'Lizabeth Field / And Billy Cather, too, / Could chew the parliamentary rag / Till there was none to chew."[26] She was fond of arguing—in or out of formal debate—and was able to make the last meeting of the United Literary Societies in 1895 something to remember.

On Saturday evening, June 8, the three literary societies ("barbs") met in the chapel for a program which included an oration on "The Fate of the Greeks" by Hugh Walker (Palladian) and an essay on Poe by Willa Cather (Union). Walker's oration roasted the Greek-letter "frats" to extremity, with some disregard for personal feelings. When Willa rose, instead of presenting Poe she tore into an extemporaneous denunciation of Walker's attack on the Greeks and its lack of humanity and maturity— she "pretty vigorously contested some of Mr. Walker's statements," said the *Journal*. Then she turned to her own manuscript. "Her essay on 'Edgar Allan Poe'," continued the newspaper account, "was a most excellent and interesting article and was read in a very earnest and effective way." Ned Abbott, who arranged the program, wrote to his mother that he had been "the recipient of roasts, countless in numbers and most brilliantly hued in color (sort of Joseph-coat order) ever since the unfortunate program was rendered. To begin with, Walker opened up with an invective against fraternities. It was too partish [*sic*] and misleading to accomplish any good. Then came Willa Cather, a Union, for whose position on the program, I was responsible. Unbeknown to me, she has become a sympathizer of the frats and waded into Walker with an improvised roast. I was now between Beelzebub and the wine-colored ocean and wanted to roast both roaster and roastee. Afterward the partisans of both lammed me for letting them be on the program. Oh, it was glorious!"[27]

26. References to Carroll Club: *Hesperian*, March 1, 1892; English Club: *Nebraskan*, May 12, 1894, also N. C. Abbott's unpublished "Children's Book" (MS 2626, Nebraska State Historical Society); Haydon Art Club: *Nebraskan*, March 2, 1894, and see "Critical Statements," pages 217 ff.; Bixby: *Hesperian*, October 29, 1897.

27. N. C. Abbott, letter to his mother, June 16, 1895 (MS 2626, Nebraska State Historical Society). The *Journal* account is June 9, 1895.

It was glorious all right—youth and the bright tongues of fire—but the incident reveals some subtle distinctions. By that time Willa was of course a famous roaster (the *Nebraskan* had saluted her on February 14, 1895, with a sketch of a smoking pen and the lines, "This is for 'Billy' of journalist fame, / Who writes her roasts in words of flame / And gives it to everyone just the same"), and she could talk as well as she could write. But at least by the end of her senior year the attacks were mostly on aesthetic or ethical grounds rather than on personalities—she had made some enemies herself on that score. At the literary society meeting her argument was for "humanity" and in defense of persons who were not there—many of them her close friends. At this distance it also seems like irritation with collegiate bickering over artificialities. This side of Willa Cather needs to be held in view along with her combativeness, for it coincides with other deeply felt judgments of her as she was in the years just after college. "She was not one to criticize others," Mrs. George Seibel told me, speaking of her friend Willa Cather as the Seibels knew her in Pittsburgh in 1896 and after. "No," she said, "Willa was always looking for the motive behind the action instead of criticizing the action—always. That was something that was rare in people. That was Willa Cather. I never knew her to gossip about people. . . . She really was a rare person. There weren't many like her."[28] Whatever else Willa Cather had learned by 1895, she had developed, too, in a certain kind of human sympathy. It was evident in the Poe essay she read that June night as well as in the unexpected roast.

After her graduation in 1895, Willa spent a year in Nebraska—but one neither lonely nor unproductive, as it has always been described. Accounts of a "fallow" period in Red Cloud have overlooked a great many facts that were never concealed in the early years, even by Miss Cather ("In the fall of 1895 I was connected for several months with the Lincoln *Courier*," she wrote in 1900[29]), though later they were minimized. As it happens—and the record is plain to read in a dozen periodicals of the 1890's—Willa Cather wrote for both the *Courier* and the *Journal* that year, was in Lincoln more than half of the time, and had a rather glittering

28. Talks with Mrs. George Seibel were in New York, July, 1965.

29. From *The Class of Eighteen hundred and Ninety-five: 1895–1900*, a record of class news compiled by Olivia Pound and printed in Lincoln in spring, 1900. Also pertinent: a biographical sketch of Willa Cather in *Poet Lore* (Winter, 1903) which states that after her first two years at the University she worked for the *Journal* and the *Courier*; and a note in the *Nebraska Alumnus* (April, 1914): "After her graduation in 1895, she stayed in Lincoln for one year, writing for the *Courier* . . . ."

life of it, both professionally and socially. Of course she wanted to get away to the big things, and she was often restless (though in fact it took only a few days away from Lincoln to make her write of Red Cloud as "Siberia" and "exile"), and she was, most of all, unsettled about the future. But even a general chronology of the months from June, 1895, to June, 1896,[30] shows that she was rarely quiet and her pen hardly ever dry: in 1895 Willa Cather was in Lincoln during June and part of July, in Red Cloud to the last week in August. She worked on the *Courier* as associate editor from August 24 to the end of November, with two recorded visits to Red Cloud. At the same time, she wrote play reviews for the *Journal* and in December, after she left the *Courier*, she brought her column, "The Passing Show," back to the *Journal*. Though she lived in Red Cloud after the first of January, she returned to Lincoln periodically, writing play reviews whenever she was in town. There is proof that she was in Lincoln for substantial periods in late January and early February, in late March, and during the first part of June. Letters and other circumstances of the spring suggest that there also might have been short visits at the middle of March, in April, and again in May. In mid-June she had a job in Pittsburgh.

The *Courier* chapter of the 1895–1896 story began officially on August 3 with the announcement that the Courier Publishing Company would be reorganized: Miss Sarah B. Harris had purchased the interest held in the paper by Charles L. Burr. (The editor of the *Courier* at this time was the other part-owner, W. Morton Smith—not Miss Harris, as biographies have usually implied.) The article in the *Courier* continued: "Miss Willa Cather who for the past two years has been the dramatic critic and theatrical writer for the *Journal*, will become a member of *The Courier* staff. Miss Cather's reputation extends beyond Nebraska. She is thoroughly original and always entertaining. Her writing has a piquant literary flavor, and her services are a valuable acquisition to any paper." Although the Beatrice *Express*, in commenting on the *Courier* change-over, said on August 15 that Miss Cather ("the unusually bright young woman who has for a couple of years written the dramatic criticisms for the Lincoln *Journal*") had invested money in the paper, she was not officially listed as an owner. On August 17 the *Courier* noted that next week "Miss Harris will assume her duties as associate editor of *The Courier*, and Miss Cather

30. Based almost entirely on items in Lincoln and Red Cloud newspapers, with some reference to letters written to Mariel Gere and her family (Nebraska State Historical Society collection).

will commence her contributions to the theatrical and other departments of the paper." The masthead of the *Courier* for August 24 is new:

W. MORTON SMITH	Editor and Manager
SARAH B. HARRIS	Associate Editor
WILLA CATHER	Associate Editor

And so it remained to the end of November, 1895.

Who were they—Willa Cather's co-editors? Sarah Butler Harris was thirty-five, the literate, energetic, and solvent daughter of the George S. Harris family, pioneer railroad builders. She had graduated from the University in 1888, was interested in the arts, had written for several newspapers in Lincoln, and in the preceding year had had a number of signed articles in the *Courier*. Hospitable and warm-hearted, Miss Harris was an honest, outspoken, independent woman of integrity and strong feminist principles. An early picture of about 1890 shows her as dark, round-faced, vivid, attractive—looking not a little like Willa Cather. Mrs. Olive Watson, who wrote society news for the *Courier* in the late 1890's, remembers Miss Harris as "not beautiful—but attractive, *whole-some*-looking."[31]

W. Morton Smith was in his mid-twenties—an experienced, capable newspaperman primarily interested in politics and public affairs, though he could write well on almost any subject. Smith had come to Lincoln from Pennsylvania in 1888, working for the *Journal* as a legislative reporter, associating with the Omaha *Republican* for a time, and serving on Governor Thayer's staff. From late 1891 to spring, 1893, he was editor of the Lincoln *Evening News*. He then bought a half-interest in the *Courier*, which he developed from a "society" to a discussion paper. From August, 1894, to the spring of 1895, in addition to handling the *Courier* he was also part-owner and manager of the *Daily Call*. Morton Smith is described as a tall, handsome, rather dignified man with a fine black beard ("umbrageous and murmuring whiskers," wrote Walt Mason in 1893). There is no indication in anything I have read that there was either special friendship or particular antagonism between Morton Smith and Willa Cather, but he came nearer than anybody in Lincoln to being a real professional rival. Perhaps that is his particular significance, but one must also consider the events of 1896 and 1897. In the summer of 1896, Smith was often away, writing of political conventions and campaigns. (That was

31. A conversation with the author, November, 1965. Miss Harris later married Dr. Alvin Dorris. When she died in 1918, articles concerning her appeared in the *Star* and *News* on April 11 and in the *Journal* on April 12.

the summer of Bryan and his famous "Cross of Gold" speech in Chicago.) In the fall Smith sold his interest in the *Courier* to Miss Harris (who only then—September 19, 1896—became its editor) and went to New York to take a position in the financial department of the *Mail and Express*. From October, 1896, to the following June his column of comment and news about New York appeared nearly every week in the *Journal*, often just across the page from Willa's "Passing Show" sent from Pittsburgh. Then, on June 13, 1897, Lincoln learned that Morton Smith had drowned in the Hudson River—his catboat had been hit by a sudden squall and capsized. "A clean and accurate writer," the *Journal* said of him. "He invested everything he touched with something of his own personality."[32]

In the reorganization of 1895, the editors planned to make the *Courier* a paper of substance and sophistication. According to the announcement, "The Passing Show" and the theatrical columns can be officially credited to Willa Cather, but obviously she did much more. Some paragraphs in "Observations," a feature similar to the *New Yorker*'s "Talk of the Town," are directly related to her other writing, as are portions of other columns. She had one signed piece in a symposium, "Man and Woman" (September 28), in which the participants discussed whether the Bible teaches that woman is subservient to man. ("The Bible undoubtedly teaches that woman should be subservient to man, but does it say that she was, is, or ever will be?" wrote Miss Cather, concluding: "Woman may be man's inferior, but she makes him pay for it.") As owners, Smith and Miss Harris had managerial problems as well as writing to consider. Occasionally Sarah Harris was gone—the week she went to Chicago for the German opera the paper (of November 23) is particularly Catherian. And Smith was concerned as always with political attacks and exposés, which took him away from the office. Willa Cather's name last appears on the masthead on November 30, 1895, but whatever the reason for her leaving—money, politics, personalities—or whatever tension might have existed at the time, by January 11 there could be a complimentary paragraph in the *Courier* on Willa's story, "On the Divide," just out in the *Overland Monthly*.

After November 30, Willa returned to the *Journal*—though in fact she had never left it. A note in that paper on August 29 made clear that she was still the *Journal* critic: "Miss Willa Cather, dramatic critic of THE

32. *Journal*, June 14, 1897; also the *Courier*, June 19, 1897. Among the many earlier references to Smith are notes in the *Courier*, May 6, 1893, August 11, 1894, May 4, 1895; and in the *Journal*, December 17, 1893.

JOURNAL, has returned from her summer vacation, spent with her parents."
Thus she had been doing double duty on play reviews all fall (two visits
to Red Cloud in early October and early November were timed, according to her usual careful planning, for periods when no plays were at the
theatres). On December 8 the *Journal* announced that Miss Cather would
visit her home in Red Cloud that week, and next week (December 15)
"she will begin her regular contributions to the Sunday *Journal.*" "The
Passing Show" was then continuously in the *Journal* to the following
June 14. The column was a valuable property, and the *Journal* advertised
it in January at the head of its special features: "The Passing Show / always
telling and interesting." But by then Miss Cather had found that she
would have to return home for a time. She visited friends during Christmas holidays, finally moved her trunk, and—said the Red Cloud *Chief* on
January 3—"spent New Years at her home in this city."

Of course the "*Journal* critic" couldn't review plays when she wasn't
there, and by January anyone can notice a difference—and a revealing
pattern—in the Lincoln papers. From late December to along in the spring,
the *Journal* had virtually no reviews of plays except when Willa Cather
was in town. Then they appeared with a flourish of old times. From
January to May, many important plays and popular actors came and went,
with no notice at all in the *Journal* and often none in the *Courier*. Only
"Toby Rex" kept things going at the *News*. All of this suggests that
Willa may have been not only the *Journal*'s drama critic but also the
director of the whole operation, in charge of arranging substitutes and
"seconds" when they were needed. Certainly nobody else did it when
she was gone.

By early 1896, Willa Cather was in the confusing position of being a
star without a firmament. Greatness had been prophesied for her with the
utmost consistency: "A literary woman of distinction" . . . "at the head
of Lincoln writers" . . . "her dramatic work compares most favorably
with the work of like nature on the great Chicago papers and without
doubt she has a great future before her."[33] But the highest compliment
was to be recognized in the *Nebraska Editor* as one of the state's chief
newspaperwomen. In an article in the fall of 1895, Mrs. Elia W. Peattie,
columnist for the Omaha *World-Herald* and a nationally published fiction
writer, described Miss Cather as "a young woman with a genius for
literary expression. Although not an editor in the correct sense of the

33. Quotations from the Red Cloud *Chief*, August 17, 1894; William Reed Dunroy,
"Literary Lincoln," *Courier*, June 1, 1895.

word, yet her work is editorial and it has made the *Courier* the brightest paper in Nebraska, regarded from a literary point of view. Her criticisms, both literary and dramatic are clever, original and generally just. But above all they are clever and full of "ginger" . . . . She keeps in touch with whatever is newest in literary work the world over, and writes her opinions freely and one may say—gaily. If there is a woman in Nebraska newspaper work who is destined to win a reputation for herself, that woman is Willa Cather. She has great capacity for study, and is sure to grow from year to year in knowledge of her work and in felicity of style. . . ."[34]

Late in January Willa Cather came to Lincoln to attend the meeting of the Nebraska State Press Association.[35] On Friday morning, January 31, she spoke to the Nebraska newspaperwomen (both active journalists and the wives of newspapermen). Sarah Harris was chairman and gave an address of welcome. Miss Cather then read a five-minute paper on "How to Make a Newspaper Interesting." Even from the *Journal*'s summary one may catch her tone: "She thought that it was not enough for a newspaper to deal with facts. It should present them in the most interesting form. A paper can afford to let each writer handle the line of work he is best able to do. If a newspaper man rides a hobby, the theatre or boxing, he will have a host of followers. A neutral newspaper is an abomination. The newspaper should be personal." The women had intended to form their own organization. Perhaps they made their point by having the meeting, for almost immediately they received an invitation to join the previously all-male Press Association.

The following week in the Beatrice *Weekly Express*, an article about the Press meeting in Lincoln spoke of Miss Cather as "a young woman who is rapidly achieving a western reputation, and who will soon have a national reputation. She is one of the ablest writers and critics in the country, and she is improving every week." And Walt Mason stated flatly: "She is unquestionably destined to be among the foremost of American literary women." This was a familiar prophecy, but it was not

34. Although the original issue of the *Nebraska Editor* has not been available, Mrs. Peattie's article "Newspaper Women in Nebraska" was reprinted in Henry Allen Brainerd's *History of the Nebraska Press Association* (1859–1923), II, 23–32. Portions of the *Nebraska Editor* were also quoted in the *Journal* from time to time. The *Nebraska Editor*, says Brainerd (p. 23), was published by Fletcher N. Merwin, editor of the Beaver City *Times* and also secretary of the Press Association for several years.

35. Accounts which follow are from the *Journal*, January 31 and February 1, 1896; and the Beatrice *Weekly Express*, February 6, 1896.

undiscriminating. Nobody else in Nebraska received that kind of praise. And it was given on the spot, without hedging—except that Mason did say "literary *women*."

Willa Cather's name also appears quite consistently that year in the Lincoln society news. She was frequently the guest of the Patriarchs, the city's most exclusive social club. She went to one of their parties on November 15, attended the Charity Concert on December 17 in one of the boxes taken by the Patriarchs for the occasion, and put on her masquerade for the Patriarchs' Ball on February 7. We can even see how it was that night: Lansing Hall was decorated with bunting and Japanese lanterns, masks and posters, for a "weird Aubrey Beardsley effect." There were over seventy-five masked dancers. Among them "priests and monks mingled with giddy worldlings and demure nuns waltzed with court gentlemen of Louis XIV." So complete were the disguises that people "sought for their own kinsmen and found them not." In the long list of detailed descriptions of the dancers we find Mariel Gere as a colonial dame in pink silk and white chiffon fichu, and Ellen Gere as an Italian peasant girl. Willa's brother Douglass came, too—as a tennis player. And there are the *Courier* trio: Sarah Harris as a Lutheran sister, Morton Smith as a priest, and "Miss Willa Cather as folly was in pink and silver, with silver bells and a harlequin hat and staff." [36]

Spring came, and real frustration. In February Herbert Bates had resigned from the University faculty, and Willa had tried unsuccessfully in March for the appointment to teach his classes. [37] But when she came to Lincoln June 6 for Commencement, her name was in interesting company on the cover of the *Nebraska Literary Magazine*: "Professor L. A. Sherman, Chancellor Geo. E. Maclean, Hon. Wm. J. Bryan, Miss Willa Cather." Inside was her story of colonial Virginia, "A Night at Greenway Court." [38] Then on June 17 the *Journal* announced: "Miss Willa Cather,

36. *Journal*, February 9, 1896.
37. Bates left to be music and literary critic for the Cincinnati *Commercial Gazette*. The *Hesperian* on February 28, 1896 said that he had resigned "two weeks ago." See Brown and Bennett for accounts of Miss Cather's application for a teaching position.
38. There is at least a possibility that Willa Cather was already extending her publishing range. If "Clara Wood Shipman" is to be regarded as one of Miss Cather's pseudonyms, as suggested by John P. Hinz in "Willa Cather in Pittsburgh" (*New Colophon*, 1950)—and it seems to work out that way in 1900 in the *Library*, for which Miss Cather was a principal contributor—we must also consider that the story "A Loyal Traitor" by Clara Wood Shipman published in the *New England Magazine* that same June, 1896, might also be by Willa Cather. Certain elements favor the supposition: Though "A Loyal Traitor" is a Civil War incident, its setting, like that of "A Night at Greenway Court," is the Lord Fairfax region of Virginia; and it has several passages that sound familiar to those who have read

who has served the *Journal* so acceptably as dramatic critic and special writer for more than two years, has been called to do some special work for the *Home Magazine* [*Monthly*] of Pittsburgh, Pa., for a couple of months. She will go to Pittsburgh in about two weeks and will remain there until early in September." That same day Willa returned to Red Cloud. In less than ten days she was ready. The *Journal* reported on June 28 that during the week Miss Cather had passed through the city on her way to Pittsburgh, "where she will do literary work during the summer."

Temporary or not, Willa Cather's job as managing editor of a new magazine projected by publishers Axtell, Orr and Company in Pittsburgh may seem unusual—young people more often tried for New York, even Chicago. Miss Cather's later explanation was that she went to Pittsburgh because she had warm personal friends there.[39] Though it has been suggested that she got the job by meeting one of the publishers—Charles Axtell—at the Geres sometime during that year, I have found no mention of such a visit. But there was a visitor from Pittsburgh who might have been an intermediary—a friend who knew Willa Cather's work, who was himself a writer (he would appear in the *Home Monthly* almost from the beginning), who was interested in publishing and active in educational circles. George Gerwig had been in Lincoln at the end of March, 1896, a time when Willa Cather was also in town.[40] Perhaps there were several connections with Pittsburgh through the Geres and newspaper interests. But it was Gerwig and his bride who were to be Willa's most helpful friends during her first months in Pittsburgh.

So it was that Willa Cather left Nebraska for the East. In 1896 she was a girl who could stop national dramatic companies in their tracks, who could write for two or more papers at the same time (words to fill a page, earn a dollar, sometimes mark the heart); a girl who did not need to sign her work. A certain kind of writing, she knew, was like talk— voices disappearing on the air—but talk that often changed to the texture of the slower, deeply felt, created thing that is art.

Willa Cather's 1893–1896 writing. The logic of the pseudonym is clear to me, though not as the transposed initials of "Willa Sibert Cather" as Hinz suggests, for she did not use "Sibert" as a middle name until 1900. But "Shipman" is a distinguished Virginia name, good for one who should know about the South; and Willa was also interested in a popular author of the period whose name would be certain to engage her fancy—Mary Hartwell Catherwood. It is not far from "Cather wood" to "Clara Wood."

39. A statement in the biographical sketch in Knopf's pamphlet of the early 1930's: *Willa Cather* (New York: Alfred A. Knopf, n.d.).

40. *Journal*, March 31, and *Courier*, April 4, 1896.

The Kingdom of Art

✳ ✳ ✳

To Willa Cather in 1896 the kingdom of art was clearer far than the land she was leaving, more precisely marked than the lines of earth and sky in Nebraska. She had described it in more than three hundred separate pieces in newspaper columns and reviews, through more than three years in which all the weathers of her mind and belief were marked, and in which she set down those principles of art which she finally considered to be absolutes. What she did not see so clearly was her own place in that world of art. To those who know how the tale did end, a look at the way it was with the young Willa Cather will be a flashback in an old story-telling tradition. It may also be an illumination, and a quite different beginning for the Cather story.

What was she like when she left Nebraska? The young Willa Cather —as she is revealed in her writing of the mid-nineties—was primarily a romantic and a primitive. That she was eventually to be called a classicist, a Jamesian sophisticate, and the reserved stylist of the novel démeublé, may be one of the great jokes of literary criticism, for even if the novelist at fifty was different from the beginner of twenty, the critical tags of the years between tended to obscure the reality of Willa Cather's work, what was constant in her from those earliest years. Reading her statements of 1893–1896, one expects to find in them a deep seriousness, a love of beauty, dedication, and a belief in the greatness of art. They are all present. What one does not expect is the vivid argument for passion, the feeling for romance, and at the same time, the dogged insistence on a kind of elemental reality (reality, however, quite different from the currently fashionable "realism"). Neither does one quite expect the literary interests that emerge. With Willa Cather at twenty-two it was Stevenson, not Henry James; Daudet and Dumas *père* rather than Flaubert. Even with Flaubert, it was the fiercely romantic *Salammbô*, not the colder, harder *Madame Bovary*. And she liked the sweep of Tolstoi more than the precision of

[31]

Maupassant. These were not unusual preferences in the 1890's; it was a spirited time, and the romanticists had it out with the realists on fairly even terms. Since then we have forgotten that whole group of Continental romanticists from Dumas and Daudet to Pierre Loti and Heine—yet they influenced other writers than Willa Cather. To see her plain and to recognize the temper of mind and feeling that determined her primary attitudes toward art and the artist, we will need to draw closer to those lost books and years.

Willa Cather's kingdom of art lay in the context of the 1890's, a time as distractingly, glitteringly "modern" as any time is when its years are new and change is more noticeable than permanence. But this "modernity," in particular, had that end-of-the-century, hectic flush that seemed part promise and part disease. It eloped in terms of "the Decadence," "Bohemianism," Philistinism; in continuing games of Wilde's lily and sunflower, living pictures, Beardsley's cartoons; a widening range of magazines from the more ponderously serious *Century* to the special elegance and color of the *Yellow Book* and the *Chap Book*, the flashing new *McClure's*, and the hundreds of plain and puritan home journals. The literary world was handsomely illustrated, described, and discussed in the *Critic*. "Modern" writers were still Arnold, Ruskin, and Browning, as well as Shaw, Verlaine, Ibsen, Kipling, and Hardy. From it all Willa Cather took what she wanted (though primarily for allusion and illustration rather than the formation of principles): Populism and silver-tongued orators? A little, not much. *Fin de siècle?* A joke, only. The new science, sociology, and "cosmic philosophy" of Herbert Spencer and John Fiske? A touch, though more likely in summaries than in the original heavy-handed tomes. She changed "Art for Art's Sake" to "Art for Life's Sake," in the sense of Shelley's *Defense of Poetry*. About theories of art or ideas of culture she was not particularly fashionable; she was on the side of permanence, and she had a habit of looking shrewdly (even with startling prescience) underneath new names and fascinating differences. Bohemianism, for example: It came from youth and lack of money, she said; things belong to the organized forces of the world.[1] Because she could see through the surface, there is little of the pale-handed weariness or elegant posturing of the Decadence or of *fin de siècle* madness, smartness, and cleverness in the young Willa Cather. Instead, there is an insistence

1. Citations in footnotes will be given only for quotations which do not appear in Part II or the Appendices in this book. Other quotations and substantial paraphrases (such as the statement above) may be located by referring to the index supplement.

on the shine of things, the reality of the good and the hopeful, and the necessity of delight. But she also had a wild, sharp tongue, a fearless independence and honesty based on her conviction that she was right (which she usually was). Her cynic's lash is more like Swift than Wilde—a serious buffoonery directed against pretentions and false elegance. Was she modern? "Up-to-date" in matters of general information on the arts she certainly was. In theatre matters, especially, she was like the fanciers of baseball statistics and could cite names and performances and the latest stories with perfect assurance through any number of columns. The same about books and writers—who wrote what in the latest magazines, quotations by rough memory from Shakespeare to Oscar Wilde to Howells to Sappho, an apparently unlimited and unorthodox range of inquiry and absorption. She found details of stories on every street corner. This is to say that she was no dreamy-eyed recluse, was quite alive to her own time, smart, advanced, eager to achieve. And yet, we may well ask, what in 1896 was her fundamental attitude toward her own present and historical past? No reader can escape the nostalgic aura of some of her greatest novels. Did she then, even at the beginning, look back with regret to a past of vanished glory?

Willa Cather had by 1896 gravitated to a fundamentally primitivistic position—historical, cultural, human. The world was haunted by a divinity, there were forces on the earth and in heaven greater and more mysterious than man could interpret. She chose action and power; emotion, sympathy, and life. She rejected whatever was effete, over-refined, or delicate. She rejected, too, whatever was hard and intellectually inhuman. These elements are clear and fairly consistent in her attitudes. To the question of nostalgia, the answer is by no means simple, and one might cite passages in equal number as proof of either yes or no. Actually, the dominant impression of Willa Cather's several hundred pieces is that of brilliance, vigor, and buoyant youth; of energy and keen desire. Yet in a great many comments—perhaps more than one expects for even the universal anger of youth—one hears an elegiac tone compounded of the ordinary rituals of primitivism (one always *says*, at least, that the golden age was long ago) and what may be more personal—a recurring melancholy, a sense of loss in the sad (but dramatic) ironies of life. So many pieces commemorate the dead, so often there is mourning for lost chances —childhood gone, the death of a young poet, the brave gauds that came to tinsel. But much of this tone is there because, more than most writers, she had a strong bent for rhapsody, a style usually given to praise, glory,

hope, and desire, though in the swing of high feeling rhapsody is appropriate to the intensity of sorrow as well as the intensity of joy. It is the
nature of the instrument. But as most writers know, it is harder to speak
well of delight than of tragedy. Willa Cather's approach to experience
was always poetic: with high feeling and wonder, whether of darkness or
light, her language even in newspaper writing becomes incantation, evoked
by something beyond the ordinary. And the extraordinary thing was
often a sense of greatness, past or possible. The litanies of Père-Lachaise
(and she did often write of cemeteries and the buried, living dead) are
therefore as much praise for the greatness of the dead as laments for their
loss. In these ways, one must modify the view of the elegiac statements as
pure nostalgia and the rejection of the present. But even with modifications, there are sufficient statements on a feverish, diminished world to
justify a qualified yes: Willa Cather did, even in 1896, have some tendency
to look back with nostalgia, but it was a tone rather than a theme.

More important than her statements of primitive regret, are the more
active, determining forces they point to. The world is diminished, but she
gives a reason. It is lessened by our failure to aspire and in "these days of
pigmies" no one seemed to be attempting greatness in literature, the
"Wagnerian flashes and thunders and tempests of Carlyle and the lofty
repose and magnificent tranquility of Emerson." But it is worth noting
that even Emerson is described with words that denote no ordinary
serenity but greatness achieved—*lofty* repose and *magnificent* tranquillity.
The same piece on Emerson and Carlyle observes that the world has lost
real joy and honest laughter: we are frolicsome only, and there is no
mirth in us. These statements touch on two familiar concepts in Willa
Cather's early writing: First, that the measure of reality is how deeply we
are involved with elemental things; if we are out of touch with that reality,
the age is then a painted age, a paper world. Second, that our most
frightening (though perhaps inevitable) loss is our diminished sense of
wonder—wonder at greatness, beauty, and the mystery of things. She
included both of these elements in a comment on Ruskin, who was, she
said, out of sympathy with his time: he belonged "to the age of epics
and Ionian columns, of marble and fine gold, not to this pâpier-maché
civilization." Joy and real laughter are linked with mornings, youth,
freedom, and the freshness of pagan delight. Poets like Byron and Moore,
for example, were "bohemians" who worshipped beauty without a
creed. "They were the last of their school; the world has grown graver
since then." Such gravity may be a part of maturity, but it is just as much

a loss of something more important to man than his own ingenuity—the loss of the gods themselves. She returned again and again to the theme of lost divinity, or lost belief. She liked to refer to Heine's *The Gods in Exile* and, more indirectly, to the twilight of the Gods. Certainly, to Willa Cather some of these elements of man's dilemma were more than the traditional agony of youth and their statement more than the forms and rituals of primitivism. She quoted from Alfred de Musset's *Rolla*: "They have destroyed the terrible idols of old, / But they have also frightened away the birds of heaven." Part of her eventual effort was to bring the gods home from exile, and to welcome again the birds of heaven.

To understand Willa Cather's principles of art as she expressed them in the 1893–1896 period of furious public writing, we need to see them in another more personal context—her own private past of the imagination. By what way had she come to this place? It is not my intention to review the events of her childhood, even those relating directly to art, but to look at the stream of experience most central to her own creativity— books and the reading of books. When Willa Cather's own statements of this early period and later are combined with the accounts of those who knew her,[2] and the sometimes surprising witness of the books themselves, we can see quite accurately the road she followed and to what end.

From the beginning, as if by inheritance, Willa Cather absorbed the Bible and *Pilgrim's Progress*. Their presence in her writing is constant, insistent, pervasive. Indeed, they made allegory familiar and natural to her, so that she *thought* allegorically (or symbolically), as these early critical pieces make very clear. The central concept of the kingdom of art itself is allegorical, though if there were a term like "broken allegory" it would more accurately describe the effect—a style of mingled allusiveness and symbolism over a groundwork of fixed, related metaphors. She did not need to contrive the metaphor and its extension, nor (at this time, at least) did she think to examine it logically, to correct roughnesses and omissions and even contradictions. This was simply the way one talked.

In her childhood, too, she learned the heroic literature of Homer, Virgil, the Norsemen. She knew the great epics so well that all the seas and islands of the ancients were living and real, crossed perpetually by strong

2. Most of the information on Willa Cather's early reading comes from her 1893–1896 writing, plus other comment throughout her later work. I have had other valuable help from many conversations with the late Elsie Cather, including a television interview in July, 1962. See also E. K. Brown, *Willa Cather: A Critical Biography* (New York: Alfred A. Knopf, 1953); Edith Lewis, *Willa Cather Living* (New York: Alfred A. Knopf, 1953); Mildred R. Bennett, *The World of Willa Cather* (Lincoln: University of Nebraska Press, 1961).

men who suffered and dared to act. With the epics she joined the actual histories—the conquests of Alexander, the grandeur and tragedy of Rome, and the golden journeys of the Spanish explorers. There were Grimm's *Fairy Tales*, *The Arabian Nights*, and the stories and figures of Greek, Roman, and Germanic-Norse mythology—the latter a body of reference that has scarcely been recognized in Willa Cather's work. Throughout her writing, however, in addition to the classical allusions there are strong uses of Teutonic myth as described in Carlyle's *Heroes and Hero Worship*, in a number of books by Charles Kingsley, in Jacob Grimm's *Teutonic Mythology*, and possibly in a small, poetically written book of *Norse Stories* retold from the Eddas by Hamilton Wright Mabie.[3] Especially in her early writing, there are tones of many passages in *Norse Stories* as she speaks of the cold north, the polar seas, the Norns, and the Northmen. And surely from that same book the mighty tree of Ygdrasil, kept ever green by the Norns who each day sprinkled it with the water of life, and under whose branches "browsed all manner of animals; among its leaves every kind of bird made its nest" and whose leaves " told strange stories of the past and of the future"—surely Ygdrasil grew straight into the Christmas tree of the Burdens in *My Ántonia*, which was "the talking tree of the fairy tale; legends and stories nestled like birds in its branches."[4] Finally, in Willa Cather's background of classics, Shakespeare had roots deep as any tree of life. Her references to him are both direct and indirect; quotations are ready on the pen, casual, almost ritualistic, as when she would set down "The rest is silence."

When Willa Cather began her continuous journalistic writing in 1893, this early reading was deep in the grain of her thought and style. But along with the primary substance of Bible and Shakespeare, of epic, allegory, and myth, she gathered familiar pages of Longfellow and Lowell and Poe. She had already studied a good many nineteenth-century classics (the comparative "moderns") with some intensity: the great essayists Carlyle, Ruskin, Pater, Arnold, and Emerson, writers whose beliefs and whose rich, incantatory, or elegant styles certainly touched her own. She read many of the standard classics in fiction long before she went to the University, and there is abundant evidence that by the time she began writing for the papers, Stevenson, Dumas, Daudet, George Eliot, and Thackeray were old favorites, as were Keats, Shelley, Byron, Tennyson, and Browning. With these writers (Browning is perhaps the best example)

---

3. *Norse Stories* was first published in 1882 by Roberts Brothers. I have used an edition edited by Katharine Lee Bates (New York: Rand McNally & Company, 1902), p. 26.

4. *My Ántonia* (Boston and New York: Houghton Mifflin Company, 1918), p. 94.

we move into the range of reading in her University years, where study and personal choice are most noticeable.

We know the courses Willa Cather took in college and many of the textbooks she used,[5] but it is apparent from the network of literary references in her columns of 1893–1896 that they would account for only a fragment of her reading in those last years in Nebraska. Most interesting are the personal choices and directions which can be traced in the columns; to give them the right emphasis and proportion, however, it is necessary to remember that her knowledge of mature literature had been full and constant since childhood. Thus the effect of books and writers she knew first is often submerged, used in whatever way might be natural—sometimes with passionate interest, sometimes by a glancing allusion, sometimes by only an undersong in a line. Concerning the new writers, the later discoveries (or distractions), she is more explicit. Taken together, the old and the new, the sum of her reading seems formidable, and, more important, it is curiously personal. Why Dante rather than Pope? Or Heine's *The Gods in Exile* rather than *Paradise Lost*? In the end, Willa Cather's formal education does not explain how she happened to know what she did. Moreover, it is difficult to understand her independence or realize the implications of what she says in her critical statements unless we know that books and reading were among the most personal and necessary things in her life.

One individual pattern of choices and discoveries in books is her reading of modern Continental literature. Dorothy Canfield Fisher has spoken of Willa Cather's passionate interest in French writers during her university years,[6] and her friends George and Helen Seibel, whom she knew in Pittsburgh beginning in the fall of 1896, have both described their evenings reading and translating Heine, Alfred de Musset, Verlaine, Flaubert, and many others. "During that first year," Mrs. Seibel has told me, "we all read *Salammbô* in French. It was Willa's favorite."[7] Something

5. I have given some of this information in "Willa Cather and Her First Book," *April Twilights (1903)* (Lincoln: University of Nebraska Press, 1962), pp. vi–viii.

6. "She amazed and sometimes abashed some of her professors by caring much more fiercely about their subjects than they did. Especially French. There seemed to be a natural affinity between her mind and French forms of art. During her undergraduate years she made it a loving duty to read every French literary masterpiece she could lay her hands on." ("Daughter of the Frontier," New York *Herald Tribune*, May 28, 1933, pp. 7, 9.)

7. The best account of Willa Cather's reading tastes just after she left Nebraska is George Seibel's "Miss Willa Cather from Nebraska," the *New Colophon*, II, Part Seven (September, 1949), pp. 195–208. In a number of conversations with Mrs. Seibel I have learned more of the literary interests of the Seibels and Miss Cather, who were good friends from her first months in Pittsburgh in 1896.

of what came before is suggested in the articles of 1893–1896. Willa had started reading translations of Continental literature quite early. As she says herself, she knew the Dumas heroes of *The Three Guardsmen* in childhood, plus *The Count of Monte Cristo* and a cluster of other romances. Friends say that she was introduced to both French and German classics by the Wieners, the Jewish-German neighbors of the Cathers who were particularly valued by Willa and described with admiration and sympathy in "Old Mrs. Harris." Some of her family believe she got a good many of her modern favorites like *Anna Karenina* at the drugstore in Red Cloud long before she went to Lincoln. From letters of the period we know that she owned and valued a copy of Daudet's *Sapho* as early as 1891.[8] George Sand was also a young enthusiasm, for by 1895 Willa had passed by far enough to make some dispassionate judgments. This first reading was in translation. After she began to study French in 1893, the references to French writers and her almost awed excitement increased. Her favorites were always nineteenth-century Romantics—Dumas, Hugo, George Sand, Pierre Loti, Alfred de Musset—though she also wrote about Zola, Dumas *fils*, Verlaine, and others. But not only French literature: Heine was a favorite in her University years, and she knew something of Goethe, Ibsen, and Turgenev.

By temperament and habit (and perhaps by genius), Willa Cather was never a classroom reader. It was her pattern to study for herself and not for assignment, to take in omniverously whatever captured her imagination. The evidence in her early writing is that she read enormously more of almost everything than one might expect, given the generally non-academic nature of her later novels; and, as occasional mystifying allusions will show, she explored without logic, and sometimes without discrimination, the remote, the popular, the obscure, the unimportant, the rare, the good, the trashy, even the ludicrous, in anybody's writing. This eclectic, perhaps unorthodox, personal range of reading is physically matched by the very human miscellany of books familiar to Willa Cather in her own home.[9] Among the Cather books which have been preserved are some complete editions of the standard nineteenth-century English and American classics—Dickens, Scott,

8. A volume of *Sapho* is mentioned in letters of July 16, 1891, and January 2, 1896, from Willa to the Gere sisters (Nebraska State Historical Society collection).

9. By courtesy of the Cather family I have been able to examine a collection of books from Virginia and Red Cloud which were in the home of Miss Elsie Cather at the time of her death. This portion of the Cather family library includes some of Willa Cather's books (see the discussion below).

Thackeray, Poe, Hawthorne, Ruskin, Emerson, Carlyle. There are volumes of Shakespeare and Bunyan, anthologies of poetry, the works of Campbell and Moore, a few translations of Greek and Roman classics, some general histories, a number of miscellaneous religious books (many from Virginia), books on the Civil War, home-bound volumes of the *Century* and ladies' magazines of the eighties. There were also a good many popular romances around the house (Willa's mother enjoyed them for light reading)—novels by Marie Corelli, Ouida, Sarah Grand, Richard Harding Davis, and dozens of now forgotten names. When Willa spoke of these books in her newspaper columns, she knew what she was talking about. If she was often flip or furious about them, it was usually because they were not the highest kind of art, or even art at all—not because she scorned to look at one or even read it. The fact was, she probably read everything, and she knew very well what the world was like for both writer and reader; she could afford to be passionate about her own choices.

Willa also had her own collection of books. In some period in the late 1880's she organized some volumes into her carefully labeled "Private Library." Many of them are numbered (according to the prevailing nineteenth-century habit) and inscribed "Wm Cather Jr," a signature she affected for a time in her childhood and into her freshman year at the University. Some of the books are stamped several times with "Willie Cather" (the family version of her name) in small formal script.

The earliest dated book in the group I have seen is a small, very worn copy of the *Iliad* in Pope's translation, volume I of a three-volume edition of Homer published by Harper & Brothers in 1846. On the flyleaf is inscribed in her hand, "Wm Cather Jr / Red Cloud / 1888." At the top, "Private Library / No 70" is partially erased. "Willie Cather" is stamped twice on the lower half of the page. According to the handwriting, two other books of the same period, when she was around fourteen, are Jacob Abbott's *Histories of Cyrus the Great and Alexander the Great*, marked "Private Library / No 71 / Wm Cather Jr"; and a fat blue volume of Bunyan's *Pilgrim's Progress* ("Private Library No 14"). In 1888 Willa was given George Eliot's *Spanish Gypsy*, inscribed in another hand, "Miss Willa Cather's / Christmas—1888." As the "Private Library" signature changes slightly to "W. Cather Jr" with a less curly, more upsweeping initial "W," it included books like Carlyle's *Sartor Resartus* (a red-bordered white sticker is marked "37") and Alexander Winchell's *Sketches of Creation* ("42"). A paperback of *Antony and*

Cleopatra in the Elzevir Library series has "William Cather" inscribed on the cover, and "Willie Cather" stamped there three times. In her later University years, "Private Library" is dropped and the signature is an efficiently scrawled "W. Cather" or "Willa Cather." A few inscriptions add "State University, Lincoln, Neb." We can sample her classical development: A Greek text, dated in her handwriting "Dec. 1892," is the *Odyssey*, Books I–XII, edited by W. W. Merry. It opens to its most worn passages in Book 5 (subtitled in English, "Athena in Olympus complains of the hard fate of Odysseus"). Her *Selections from Lucian*, with introductions and notes by Charles Richard Williams, is dated "April 1893." Bearing these later signatures are also Thackeray's *Henry Esmond*, an edition with illustrations by the author; Meredith's *The Egoist*; Marie Corelli's *Barabbas*; and Cassell's National Library paperback editions of *As You Like It* and *Prometheus Unbound*. One of her Shakespeare books is a record of growth and continuity. On the flyleaf of a volume (IX–X combined) of Clark and Wright's edition of the *Works* (containing *Romeo and Juliet, Timon of Athens, Julius Caesar; Macbeth, Hamlet, King Lear*), the name "William Cather" has been erased and "Willa Cather" written over it. The upper right corner has one of the old red and white stickers, numbered "19." On the title page, but erased, are some doodlings in Greek characters. One passage marked on a torn page in *Julius Caesar* is Brutus's comment on Cicero: "For he will never follow anything / That other men begin"(II.i.151–152). In *Hamlet*, a box is drawn around a favorite line—"The rest is silence." Even this rough sampling will show that Willa Cather's own books were the literal foundations of her kingdom of art.

On the basis of her library and her articles, can one then determine Willa Cather's chief literary influence? Such nominations are interesting, though not very important if we go no farther than a name. My answer, of course, has already been given, and I would not care to separate the strands. It is fairly easy to find in her early writing certain positions of Carlyle, especially from *Heroes and Hero Worship* and *Sartor Resartus*; but Emerson is also strongly echoed (it seems so, at least at certain moments), as well as the judgments and spirit of Henry James (especially in *French Poets and Novelists* [1878] and *The Art of Fiction* [1884]), and Stevenson, and Arnold, and Swinburne, and Ruskin, and Shelley; to confuse us, there are tones of both Pater and Whitman. We are speaking of directly stated critical judgments, which are more easily removed and reattached than the rather more subtle glances of poetry or fiction. If all could be counted, there would be hundreds of other influences. For illustration, let me cite from these early years two very simple but real parts of her store of imaginative experience. I have never heard either of the writers given as an "influence" on Willa Cather, yet their works have genuine if not always surface relationships with her way of seeing things. Both are related to the early interests in the Cather home.

Willa's younger sister, the late Elsie Cather, has told of her father's custom of reading to the children. One of his favorites was Arnold's *Sohrab and Rustum* (which Willa also read to the young children when she was an adult). Other favorites were the poems of Thomas Moore and Thomas Campbell. One small, much-used volume in the Cather library was an 1859 edition of *The Complete Poetical Works of Thomas Campbell.*[10] Now Thomas Campbell was a poet of various interests, many of them similar to Willa's—heroic song, folk stories and ballads with a bit of celtic wildness and magic, Greek echoes in translation, Gothic tales. The Cather volume of Campbell has paper markers and dog-ears at "Lord Ullin's Daughter" (p. 154) and between "Lines, / Written on Visiting a Scene in Argyleshire" and "The Soldier's Dream" (pp. 160–161). "Lines" describes a lonely, grass-covered road traveled by few, a wilderness; in this scene, the "desolate heart" is urged to "Be strong as the rock of the ocean that stems / A thousand wild waves on the shore!" and to have courage "Through the perils of chance." The last line of the poem states a theme which runs through Willa Cather's later accounts of the pioneers and the ancient people: "To bear is to conquer our fate."

Willa Cather had also grown up with a special interest in writers of the South, her family's ancestral Virginia with its tradition of war and the romance of the Old Dominion. Of all the Virginia writers of the time, the best known and most prolific was John Esten Cooke (1830–1886) who, like the Cathers, came from the Winchester area. (His name was given to Willa's youngest brother Jack, named John Esten Cather in 1892.) In his thirty-one novels and constant periodical articles, John Esten Cooke became the almost official chronicler of the Civil War, at least from the Southern point of view. There are enough reminders of him, particularly in Willa Cather's early writing, to suggest that she knew his work fairly well. Her own occasional tone of rhapsodic lament is very near to his. In several pieces of the 1890's she writes variations on Cooke's theme of the sledge-axe and the rapier, two forms of warfare described metaphorically in his *Hammer and Rapier* (1870). Though quite different in plot from anything Cooke wrote, her story of June, 1896, "A Night at

10. With a Memoir of His Life (Boston: Phillips, Sampson and Company, 1859).

THE KINGDOM OF ART

Greenway Court,"[11] is set at Lord Fairfax's estate in Virginia, which was described by Cooke in a number of magazine articles and in the book *Fairfax* (1868).[12] Another Cather story of 1896, "The Count of Crow's Nest," with its group of boarding-house transients suggests the situation in Cooke's *The Virginia Bohemians* (1880), in which a group of strangely assorted travelers stay in a house called the Crow's Nest.

I have given this much of Willa Cather's literary background in 1893–1896 to suggest that she knew literature, great literature, in a personal, continuous, and living way, through all of her life, and in a relatively grand design. Occasionally she talked off the top of her head, it is true, but we can be sure that she knew better. It is also true that every account of backgrounds and books read—in general, the literary influences and sources of a writer's work—has its own seeds of disaster, for the bare alignment of book, time, and person says little of the interplay and transformation when the particular ingredients are combined. A miscellany of school texts in Homer, drugstore novels, concealed *Saphos*, paperback Shakespeares and Shelleys, Doré's Dante, the works of Thackeray, Carlyle's *Heroes and Hero Worship*, the poems of Verlaine, *The Prisoner of Zenda*, Virgil, Keats, and Emerson meet in one person, who made of them something new. Explaining Willa Cather by the nineteenth-century novel (or even the early Henry James) and even more blandly by the nineteenth-century essayists whose ideas on greatness, goodness, and beauty, on the soul and the oversoul, on sweetness and light, or on man's nobility must (we think) have certainly formed her attitudes—this will simplify her creative art straight out of reality. She was different from all of them, as the totality of her writing will show. She took what she could use, and what suited her temper. For example, she used a good deal of substance from the serious work of the passionate idealists like Carlyle and Ruskin and Emerson—but with a brilliant personal transformation. She was like them, but her passion was charged with "barbaric pearl and

---

11. *Willa Cather's Collected Short Fiction, 1892–1912* (Lincoln: University of Nebraska Press, 1965), pp. 483 ff. "The Count of Crow's Nest," mentioned below, is on pp. 449 ff. Hereafter this volume will be indicated by CSF.

12. Among the articles are "Greenway Court," *Putnam's*, June, 1857; and "Greenway Court," *The Southern Literary Messenger*, April–December, 1859. In *Hammer and Rapier* (New York: Carleton, Publisher, 1870), after describing Lee's rapier and Grant's sledge-hammer in battle, Cooke writes at the end of the Wilderness chapter: "In the gloomy depths of the Wilderness thickets lay thousands of corpses in blue and gray—that was all. The whippoorwill was crying from the tangled underwood. The war-hounds had gone to tear each other elsewhere" (p. 244). See also Willa Cather's "The Sledge and the Rapier," page 135.

gold," and her idealism grew physically out of the earth and into the sun. She had joy in glitter and plumes, in the strong arm, in the wide seas. There is a poetic, cosmic character in her imagination, something almost celtic in the melancholy abandonment to fate, to the mysteries of things. With that, she is observant, curious, shrewd, practical, determined, and stubborn. And she feels to extremity. In 1896 Willa Cather is a particular person, working out her own principles of art, perhaps trying to understand her own beliefs. For a most general description of her critical and creative position at that time, I would say that she stands somewhere between Shelley and D. H. Lawrence. But above all, she is Willa Cather, and she should be listened to for exactly what she says.

"Genius means relentless labor and passionate excitement from the hour one is born until the hour one dies."[13] Willa Cather knew that when she was twenty, and there is no sign that she ever changed her mind about the total commitment and the mingled dullness and glory of the creative life. During the next few years, as she worked out in language the forms of her ideas about art, the standards of belief and action for the artist, she touched on myriad variations of her theme. Yet, at the end of this period the central concept was unchanged. A few months before she left Lincoln she wrote, "In the kingdom of art there is no God, but one God, and his service is so exacting that there are few men born of women who are strong enough to take the vows." In this statement we have the motif for Willa Cather's first principles of art: a religious-chivalric framework, with belief stated allegorically in terms of the Bible, *Pilgrim's Progress*, myth, and romance; and like any allegorical structure, its dimensions and degrees existed solely to make the spirit visible.

From the beginning Willa Cather joined art and religion, not only in the allegorical kingdom of art but in her primary belief that man's creation shares in some divine power. God in creating the world was the "Divine Artist"; the human artist serves and worships, becoming both the priest and the translator of God. If the God of art can also be a temporal ruler, vested with power and demanding worship, service, or renunciation from his subjects, the artist in turn has "that kingly dower which makes men akin to the angels." The revelation of divine things is through inspiration and the gift of genius; the artist with individual talent gives back "what God put into him." She used the God-priest metaphor in various ways: In this age "many of the seers and prophets have been

13. *Journal*, February 11, 1894.

musicians. . . . If we believe that the Lord takes any interest in human affairs at all we cannot suppose the music of Mozart and Handel and Bach and Beethoven accidental." Speaking of Teutonic art: "Someway the artists of the north seem to get so much nearer God. They are not crafts-men, they have no law but inspiration, they are priests in verse and proph-ets in stone."

Various images form a shifting montage of Christian, pagan, and worldly ritual. The one God may be also the Muse, who is also Our Lady (Our Lady of Art, Our Lady of Beauty, Our Lady of Genius); we may worship at the altar of Artemis and listen to the oracle of Apollo. But the kingdom of art, like a medieval seignory, has a hierarchy of nobility. Shakespeare and Thackeray are the "two King Williams"; Henry Irving is a knight, and Campanini "a prince of artists"; she saw the great 1895-1896 cast of *The Rivals* as "spurred knights" and "crowned kings."14 At its simplest, the function of a mortal is to serve—with "relentless labor" and vows of commitment. But one must worship, too, and in Willa Cather's comments there is always a sense of the magic, the mystery, the awesome beauty and power of whatever spirit is invoked. Worship is still tinged with frustration, for neither labor, nor prayers, nor reason can obtain for man the immortal touch. Rewards are by fate, in almost the Calvinistic sense of election ("the shadow of God's hand as it falls upon his elect"), though often they seem like part of a cosmic joke, the favors of a La Belle Dame sans Merci or a willful Lady in a medieval Court of Love: for the Transcendentalists, "she only laughed her scornful laughter, that deathless lady of the immortals." Sometimes "the muse plays queer tricks with men, and she can only be courted, never com-pelled." Art can be "a treacherous mistress, who betrays a hundred lovers for every one she crowns"15; or "she is fickle as Cleopatra, knows her lover but once and then throws him to the crocodiles."

Within this realm of chance and order, of rituals and mysteries, where knights may do heroic deeds for ladies who smile as they will, where power and glory are matched by stern humility, where every true artist "cannot do what he will, but what he must," Willa Cather visualized the artist at work. In another sense it is Willa defining herself, and in these sketches of the framework of her ideas we can observe some characteristic qualities. She works by telling a story, by translating figures to symbolic

14. *Journal*, May 10, 1896. The cast included Joseph Jefferson, Julia Marlowe, William Crane, Nat Goodwin, and a number of other very good actors.

15. *Journal*, March 4, 1894. On Steele Mackaye.

positions, with a short cut of images and allegory. She does not think in abstractions, yet she insists on the immediacy and the wonder of the invisible, using phrases with an almost primitive picture-making quality to dramatize and condense the idea: once she remarks on "those shadowy ideals that watch us out yonder in the big dark." The world, seen and unseen, is alive with forces; there is indeed a thing beyond, something more than men. But all of this she needed to put into a visible form. Seeing how naturally she turned to the rituals of chivalry and the church, it is not surprising that she could later be at home in the historic Catholic worlds of *Death Comes for the Archbishop* and *Shadows on the Rock*.

The allegorical rituals of the kingdom of art appear and reappear through these early Cather pieces, but as in Keats's "The Eve of St. Agnes" the darker, more ascetic shapes of vows, prayers, altars, anchorites, incense, labor, loneliness, and the danger of the quest only intensify the bright color and passionate excitement of the central drama—the divine act and joy of creation. As she wrote in one 1894 piece, God as the artist of creation made the world with that same joy: "the tropics were made in exalted, exuberant passion, passion that overflowed and wasted itself, made in all the divine madness of art. Forests, where the tiger crouches in the bush, deserts that the sun laps like fire . . . ."[16] From the beginning she linked art and religion, but art that praised by its own being, and religion that was neither stiff-necked nor solemn, that would let the world be crimson and turquoise, let us ride in music with flags on the yellow-wheeled carriages.

A summary of Willa Cather's first principles of art may suggest an orderly system which in fact did not exist. But I believe it is possible to draw from her writing in 1893–1896 certain primary assumptions or points of reference toward which her ideas would habitually bend. If detours, distractions, and contradictions must be omitted, they have their own life in the full story of those years. In general terms, I see as the most important informing or governing principles those of *life* (or the life force), *degree*, the *ideal*, and *duality*. These are not new or uncommon in an artist, but I believe that they are stronger and in some ways more individual with Willa Cather than with most others.

Like Keats's "O for a life of Sensations rather than of Thoughts,"[17] statements in Willa Cather's 1893–1896 writing that "to feel greatly is

16. *Journal*, October 7, 1894. On God as "Divine Artist."
17. Letter to Benjamin Bailey, November 22, 1817, in *The Letters of John Keats*, edited by Hyder Edward Rollins (Cambridge: Harvard University Press, 1958), I, 185.

genius and to make others feel is art," or "to know is little and to feel is all," are likely to send the worried modern critic scurrying to prove that such a naive and anti-intellectual attitude certainly did not exist. Luckily one does not need to go far to see in perspective that "feel" is Willa Cather's shorthand note for the living experience of art. As a pinprick can separate the living from the dead, so feeling is the simplest evidence of some reality created through the imagination. The absolute necessity in art is the personal encounter. The artist or the work of art succeeds if something works—if there is a response. As she said of Bernhardt's performance in *La Tosca*, "It is all a thing of feeling, you cannot apprehend it intellectually at all. What do you know of a grief till it is in your heart, of a passion till it is in your veins? But if you have seen her you know not only her but many other things. Yes, you know though you cannot tell others." If you have seen her you know—that is the crux of Willa Cather's argument about art, not only about the receiver but about the creator who must himself have looked on the real thing. In the artist, "feeling" means both intensity and a personal, authentic involvement with his material. She called it "sympathy," in the nineties as well as later. The critic who writes of a play, for instance, must try to capture its physical reality, its emotional aura, in a review which has "the glare of the footlights and the echo of the orchestra in it .... It is not a matter of judgment, but of sympathy." The novelist writes neither history nor science; his art is "not to dissect the dead men of old, but to vivify them, and that ... is a greater art then to analyze a whole nation of buried heroes."

In one way or another, she had always been concerned with the implications of life and art—how to vivify, how to evoke emotion and the sense of reality. At first, in the fall of 1893, she leaned heavily on the idea of art *as* nature: "Nothing can be more natural than nature, more lifelike than life. There are heights beyond which even art cannot rise." But in the same review she has a critical beginning : on the great individual creation "we build a whole philosophy of art"—we study how the artist does it. As she was to say many times later, the first fact is that it *is* individual, it is his own. By the spring of 1896, in one of her last play reviews in Lincoln, she speaks of causes and process—"the primary causes and impulses of artistic creation," concluding that the "creative laws of art are as merciless, as savage, as blind to human good [as is] nature, their great prototype." Art is no longer nature, but is created according to the *laws* of nature. This bond of art and nature draws together the strong primitivistic elements in Willa Cather's writing of the period.

In a primitive view of the world—and of art—there is in the beginning a life force, the desire and passion of creation; from this mysterious movement all other things come. Life is earth-centered, physical, starred with sense, instincts, and passions; these are the first materials of art. So the artist must go to the source, as nature taught Bernhardt "the few elemental, fundamental facts upon which life rests, by which life rules. She has that old and deep knowledge of a very few things . . . ." Repeatedly Willa Cather returned to this theme in her columns and reviews, praising an actor or a writer for that "old and deep knowledge" of the few elemental facts of human life; or the use of the primary, universal themes of birth and death, love and hate; or the deep passion which informed his art. Possibly this belief in the ancient, elemental principles had something to do with her impulse in later years toward condensation and with the value she placed on the old things. In these early years the primitive leaped out in more primary colors. She believed that poetry and art must come from the elements nearest to that first fire—physical things, action, emotion (grammar and mathematics will not do it). She stressed the excitement of animal courage. She called Alfred the Great "that old bearded giant" of "that age of heroic savagery." The primitive is also the passion of myth, and in one description Willa Cather puts herself on the side of the gods, before their exile. Nature in the summer, she says, is like "the reckless old pagan that she is," and the green world shouts the Dionysian cry, "'Evoe, Evoe'; the old cry that calls youth to life. . . . We are all pagans in the summer time." Put together, these almost apocalyptic incantations of the primitive may be the purple flurry of youth. But their very strength in these early pages is a sign of their primary importance in Willa Cather's view of the nature and direction of creative work.

With her physical, passionate sense of the basis of life, she understandably saw purely mental qualities of art as secondary. Good plays had action rather than talk, she said (speaking as a Romantic rather than an Aristotelian, I am sure, but she did have the Greek on her side). She discounted Wilde's skill with epigrams (and poked ruthless fun at such "epigrammatics"), for wit would not save a play with stick figures, and Wilde's characters had no body or passion at all, she said. Cleverness, language for its own sake, conversation, problem-solving, and argument —these are not so good as character. Character in action is what the life principle implies. She said many times that the subject of art must be humanity, that the artist must write not as a sociologist but for the curious wonder of man himself. His subject should be the fundamental, underlying forces of life. "His business," she wrote in 1894, "is to make men and women and breathe into them until they become living souls. . . . Other men may think and reason and believe and argue, but he must create." If he does not create men and women, he will produce something like *A Lady of Quality*, in which the characters are only masquerading: "A few obsolete words and a satin waistcoat and powdered wig cannot give a picture of the last century"; in comparison with *Henry Esmond* the book is "a wraith, a shadow."

To have "living characters" is not a new principle for writers or even actors. More interesting here is the way it worked for Willa Cather. The creation of life was fundamental in art, and of course everything came from that primeval fire. But the principle of physical, breathing, moving wholeness turned itself into constant variations of metaphor that included even the instruments and works of art, and the artist himself, in one stream of life. Sometimes books no longer seem "art" but "life" itself: "A great book is a creation, like a great man; you can acknowledge its power and influence without cherishing any personal fondness for it." Eugene Field in *Love Affairs of a Bibliomaniac* "does not write of books as 'art,' but as personalities." Because the art of singer and actor was directed to an audience (and perhaps because it was more physical and sensory than the art of language) the voice of the performer had a special human quality for Willa Cather. Melba's voice is "an individual living thing" that can feel and act: "Those vibrant tones can plead and thrill and suffer, can love and hate and renounce of themselves, alone, without aid of any kind." She recalled Margaret Mather's performance in *Romeo and Juliet*, and the actress reading Juliet's line, "Believe me, love, it was the nightingale"—"I can hear the despair and pleading of that great voice now. It was a voice that throbbed and pulsed with feeling, that waxed and waned, that fell upon those who heard her like the warmth of a living touch."[18] She conceived of the performer's own body and passion as the literal instrument of his art and used metaphors of quickening, awakening; the creation of art, in both the artist and the receiver, is described in terms of conception, birth, and growth. The absence of life is coldness, sleep, and death; its presence, bloom and fire. If a performer is called "cold," as she said of Mary Anderson, it means that "the power in her was not applied; that genius was asleep. It was never awakened," the "quickening power" never came. So Mary Anderson "has not and never had that mysterious 'madness of art.'"

18. *Courier*, October 19, 1895. Margaret Mather played in *Romeo and Juliet* in Lincoln, November 30, 1892.

Like all primitive mysteries, the end of art is named only by indirection—cryptic suggestions of the "something else" which is perceived, or the veiled confusions of words like "beauty," or the trials of metaphor. Imperfect and indefinite—yet all the pieces wheel like a constellation around some core of light. Whatever its physical sign—color, word, song, or motion—the truth of art is intangible as spirit though caught for a time in human sense. While the "great imagination" can be a "spiritual force" which "may rise to snatch for us the blue from heaven and the fire from the sun," the gift it brings is not an idea. Great themes in a play do not insure the sublime; the test is between actor and audience, who must be uplifted by "transfiguring emotion" (ecstasy is to the soul what passion is to the heart). One of her best descriptions of this ultimate mystery is in a note on music: "When a singer can feel strongly and make others feel, then her voice is merely an instrument upon which a higher thing than even melody does its will." Whether the "higher thing" is the god himself or simply the fact of creation felt in the blood and the spirit, certainly the awakening, the quickening, the very incarnation of art in human feeling and belief, make the "higher thing" possible. Zola, for instance, though one of the "strongest craftsmen of his time," could not accomplish "that which is the end of craft." The life of his work is sluggish: "you never feel in it that thrill as of a soul that wakens and expands before the sun. You may heap the details of beauty together forever, but they are not beauty until one human soul feels and knows. That is what Zola's books lack from first to last, the awakening of the spirit." Beauty is the sense of life and the awe one has in its presence. The life principle means that art is based in the physical, ends in the spiritual. What is accomplished between is the literal enactment of creation and birth. In primitive, magical, and mythical terms, it is the ceremony of creation, the ritual of the human discovery of the divine. Nowhere is Willa Cather's central religious orientation in the kingdom of art made more clear.

Given the view of art which she held in these years, Willa Cather's vendetta with the forces of intellectuality is understandable. She merely believed that some things were extraneous to the life quality, the *fact* of the *experience* of art. Facts themselves had nothing to do with the matter, and by implication, neither did analysis, dissection, and all the other *outward* examinations of art. It was better to have the experience with literature (to enjoy, to feel, and therefore to realize a higher truth) than to criticize it or explain it or give knowledge *about* it. This was not the entire story, for Willa Cather herself did a great deal of analysis in thinking through techniques and characteristics of art; moreover, she was dogmatic and violent only when comparative values were concerned. And I would guess that like most writers, even in these first practice years, she knew personally that what she was trying to do, even in an imperfect way, was more complex and more mysterious than she could understand or explain, or that others who had never tried, could know. Therefore her distrust of the counters, the analyzers, the explainers, even the scholars (as distinguished from teachers, who illuminated experience), and what to her seemed like authority based on very thin knowledge. The substance of a thing was in the spirit, and the spirit was in the experience. She obviously resented attempts to make art itself lower than theory. Neither was it a vehicle for the teaching of morality, for propaganda or reform, or for the giving of information. Facts that remained facts were like buckets of rattling marbles; to be art, they must be part of a body that could move and touch you, could stand with a personal presence. Art, it remained, was the experience. What one must learn was to create life.

The implications of this strong central principle are many. In these early years—to go no farther ahead than 1896—they come in themes of life and energy versus sterility and defeat; elements of magic and alchemy; images and symbols of water and dust, sea and desert, bread and stone. The savage barbarian is matched (often to his advantage) with the over-refined mentalizers. Divisions are made in striking terms between the blood and the intellect. She summarized these contrasts in her evaluation of George Eliot and Mrs. Humphry Ward in the spring of 1896: Mrs. Ward is mental, literary, special; George Eliot more earthy and universal. Mrs. Ward appeals to the intelligence rather than to one's sympathies, writing admirable but not lovable books. George Eliot is concerned with "those simple, elementary emotions and needs that exist beneath the blouse of a laborer as well as under the gown of a scholar," she knows "the red blood of common life," but "there is no corner in Mrs. Ward's well regulated heart where that hot, imperious blood of the street beats and throbs and battles for its rights. She understands it, but she can never know it." Mrs. Ward is skillful; George Eliot is vivid.

A curious parallel to the analysis of George Eliot and Mrs. Humphry Ward is Burton Rascoe's 1922 comparison of Edith Wharton and Willa Cather.[19] Saying flatly that Miss Cather, not Mrs. Wharton, is "first among the women writers of America," he makes much the same kind of distinction between them that Willa Cather had used in 1896: "The difference between Mrs. Wharton and Miss Cather is largely a difference

19. Burton Rascoe, "Mrs. Wharton and Others," in *Shadowland*, October, 1922.

between fine workmanship and genius, talent and passion, good taste and ecstasy. It is, essentially, that Miss Cather is a poet in her intensity and Mrs. Wharton is not. . . . Mrs. Wharton gives us correct pictures; Miss Cather gives us life and the poetry and beauty of its emotions." He was talking about Willa Cather the novelist—but she was also the writer who had made inescapably clear before 1896 that her central elements of art were those very qualities of genius, passion, and ecstasy; "life and the poetry and beauty of its emotions."

In some lights the kingdom of art is a contour map of several dimensions in which elements are ranged from high to low, from stage center to the wings. The nearest thing to a system in Willa Cather's first ideas of art is this hierarchy of talent, achievement, and values—a system of degrees that assumes the possibility of greatness. There are the "highest kinds" of art or talent, and there are others. Lowest and most infuriating is the commonplace—not the common, which may be universal and therefore important, but the flat deadliness of things without individuality or significance. Saddest is the middle ground of mediocrity, to be fairly good, for as she said of one actor, "There is no known means by which one can pass out of the carefully imitating sphere into the creative. Mr. [Lewis] Morrison stops just where elocution ends and acting begins."[20] She continued to elaborate on the imperceptible boundaries of talent: The French critics "know where training stops and art begins, where the imitative verges into the creative, where endeavor becomes inspiration, where talent becomes genius." The real things and the best things were not easy to distinguish.

Willa Cather's view of art in these years was both exclusive and inclusive. She believed in the aristocratic and she believed in the common, but with qualifications: the first may die from over-refinement, the second from dullness and vulgarity. The most vital kind of aristocracy, in art or in life, was that of greatness and excellence. Although she said more about the elect of the kingdom of art, or about the aim of one who hoped to be chosen, she was certain too that the world of art was complex and varied. One had to recognize all variations and degrees, distinguish between purposes, allow for limitations, and define greatness in many ways. One early definition was that "the highest kind of art, whether in comedy or tragedy, has lofty types and conceptions back of it, . . . is elevated by high artistic sincerity, warmed by a genuine love for all things human,

20. *Journal*, March 25, 1894.

stimulated by some great belief."[21] Yet this is pretty much of an abstraction for Willa Cather, almost a listing by rote. More personal and intense are the explorations of the particular qualities of greatness she placed first.

In her last year in Lincoln, she suggests that a great performance of Shakespeare would have "the transcendent emotion, the inspired enlightenment, the complete majesty of the highest art." Louis James as Othello, alas, is admirable and earnest, intelligent and dignified—exactly in the dull pale country of mediocrity. And what did he lack? Willa Cather's answer brilliantly illustrates what has just been said about her deep commitment to the principle of life as central to art and links it to her concept of greatness: the portrayal of Othello, she said, lacked only one thing—genius. "Mr. James is too civilized; he cannot reach the intensity of those few simplified and terribly physical and direct emotions which make up [the] life of the barbarian." His blood is cold, he lacks force and power, and he lacks "those qualities of body and soul which enable men to wrestle with great emotions, to conceive of great passions." Art includes both the strong and the delicate, but her theme throughout the early writing is that strength, power, and passion are the primary elements of greatness. This emphasis comes directly out of her vision of art as a living act, and from the value she placed on primitive and elemental things. She hated languor as much as mediocrity or sham and cheapness. Action and energy were life qualities. In her principles of art, then, largeness, intensity, strong feeling, and great effort counted far more toward greatness than did the perfection of prettier but colder forms.

During her first winter of column-writing she attacked drawing room critics "who sneer at the great and the powerful, and adore the clever and the dainty." People who cannot stand the large strokes, even excesses, have "a poverty of emotion and imagination." The great things cannot be accomplished by slender means. Scottish writers Crockett and Maclaren, for example, have not reached the highest art—"pathos in itself is not greatness," and, she added, "I doubt if local color alone ever gave real greatness to any man." Neither can charm make a great singer. She often compared or characterized performers as to their power, and the difference is caught in her own style.[22] She described Signor Tamagno's

21. *Journal*, December 9, 1894. On William Crane in *Brother John*.

22. On Tamagno: *Journal*, December 22, 1895. On Nordica: *Courier*, September 21, 1895. Willa Cather heard both in Chicago in March, 1895: Tamagno sang Othello March 12 and the matinee of March 16; Nordica sang Valentine in *Les Huguenots* March 11 and March 16.

"fire and fury, the passion and tenderness" of his role in Verdi's *Otello*:

> In that first love duet on the Island of Cyprus he is as violent in his love as he is later in his hate. He sings of love until he falls back on the garden seat gasping "Il Bacio!" and his very eyes seem to burn with flame. In the last act he is like a beast of prey. When finally he strangles [Desdemona] he seizes her in his arms and rushes across the stage like a beast that is mad with pain, and literally flings her upon the bed.

Then there is Madame Nordica. She is robust, with a constitution of iron, but also invulnerable, phlegmatic, and calm:

> I shall always think of her as she appears in the last act of the *Huguenots* singing that magnificent duo, wringing her hands and laboring like a stroke oar to work up a little emotion, and shyly taking the hair pins out of her back hair until it wriggled down over her shoulders in order to look grief stricken and woe begone. . . . Anyone who could sing "Ah Raoul, my despair," with unperturbed calmness will always enjoy good health.

A more detailed comparison occurs in a series of reviews and articles on Clara Morris and Julia Marlowe.[23] She admired them both, but thought Clara Morris was great, an actress with passion and power; that Julia Marlowe had beauty, art, delicacy, and grace, but not "power, passion or intensity." Her quality is the beauty of "glimpses from certain old pictures and lines from certain old pastorals," all very winning and beautiful but "not the highest kind of art":

> Mr. Whistler's nocturnes in color are ravishingly beautiful things, but they have not the power or the greatness of the old faded frescoes that told roughly of hell and heaven and death and judgment. After all the supreme virtue in all art is soul, perhaps it is the only thing

23. Willa Cather reviewed Clara Morris in *Camille*, November 23, 1893 (see pages 232–233), and had probably seen her the previous year in *L'Article 47*, January 16, 1893. Her review of Julia Marlowe in *The Love Chase*, March 1, 1894, was admiring; the only criticism was that Marlowe could not do powerful, passionate roles. In her column of March 4 she said again that Marlowe had beauty but not passion, recalling her performance in *Twelfth Night* on January 3, 1893. In answer to an article of protest—"Clara Morris and Her School" (*Journal*, March 18)—she wrote on March 25 in defense of Morris's loudness and against Marlowe's charm. Later comments are from the *Journal* columns of September 16, 1894; July 21, 1895; and May 12, 1895.

which gives art a right to be. The greatest art in acting is not to please and charm and delight, but to move and thrill; not to play a part daintily or delightfully, but with power and passion.

Although one would not want many Clara Morrises on the stage, Miss Cather defended her kind of talent:

> Clara Morris is undoubtedly a loud actress; she uses freely both noise and intensity; but she plays only loud and stormy roles. . . . She has always impersonated women who live harder, love harder, hate harder, and die harder than the women of our world. She is coarse grained mentally and spiritually. She dresses gaudily and in bad taste. She is rather awkward; her favorite literature is the heavy, massive school of Tolstoian realism. Like George Sand, she has the temperament of an unbalanced woman and the imagination of a great artist.

As for Marlowe's being "charming" (as another writer had said), that is "the final word of doom to any great artist. One could not breathe that fatal word 'charming' anywhere near even the pictures of Siddons, Modjeska, Rachel, or Bernhardt. In literature, painting or acting charmingness means agreeable mediocrity."

Later she wrote again on Julia Marlowe—"as cold as she is bewitching, as heartless as she is dainty. She knows nothing of the stronger, coarser emotions, 'the ungovernable fury of the blood,' with which high tragedy deals." In the summer of 1895 there were several notes on Clara Morris's power to make you forget her age and ugliness, and on "her thunder-bursts of passion and pain" ("A cataract has a right to roar"). And nostalgically, "the fire was there once, the real fire that is stolen from a better world than this." It was Clara Morris in all her imperfections who could move and thrill, who could reach the soul.

Strength, power, and the concept of art as action (moving, causing to feel) emerge in a related metaphor. Willa Cather also thought of the artist as a conqueror. Images of combat, heroes, and victory charge her pages with the power and the glory of the strong arm or the winner of souls. "O yes, art is a great thing when it is great, it has the elements of power and conquest in it, it's like the Roman army, it subdues a world, a world that is proud to be conquered when it is by Rome." In these terms, the work of the artist may seem less ascetic and more temporal than it was with God or Our Lady and their servants who take vows of devotion. But all sides were in Willa Cather in these years. There were passion and desire and exaltation in art, but also Duse on the stainless icy heights of reserved dedication, and Victor Maurel who had risen to heights beyond criticism.[24] And it could be Bunyan's Holy War as much as Napoleon's.

If on the one hand she believed in the aristocrat, the elect, the hero, the great man, or the divine artist, and on the other sympathized and identified with the ordinary person, her use of the term "art" is also a little ambiguous. Sometimes it means only the highest kind, at other times it includes all the forms that appeal in a human way. She had moods when she thought it pretentious to talk about "art" all the time; many who did so knew little about it. She was also a practical girl. Obviously one could not ignore everything but the heights, and the truth is she enjoyed a good deal along the way. There was much to delight her in the color, physical presence, and quirks of humanity: She liked to watch DeWolf Hopper, not for his acting but for himself, "his big, genial personality," she wrote in the fall of 1895 after a production of *Wang*. "I like to watch him when he is not doing anything in particular, when he is just riding his elephant and awaiting the will of providence to dismount, when he is waltzing with the children, or getting married and rocking himself to and fro in helpless despair." And she liked seeing Bella, the chambermaid in *Our Flat*—"none shone like the faithful Bella, Bella of the psyche and the scarlet hose, Bella with the feather in her hair."[25] She enjoyed good farces as well as tragedies, light verse along with Shakespeare, but she had a stern sense of what was appropriate: one keeps distinctions clear. Barrack-room ballads are all right for Kipling, but not good enough for a poet laureate. In her own case, she quite clearly did not think of her newspaper writing as "art." One revealing point is that she never once spoke of the stories she was writing and publishing; even the problems of writing are usually discussed in general terms. Skillful journalism had its own place in a system of degrees and distinctions, as did the arts of the people.

In comment, Willa Cather is often irate about the unfeeling, unseeing public. At the same time she makes a real effort to defend the people's choice. If the lowest kinds of art are not very far within the boundaries of the kingdom, at least they have a right to that much of its air. In a way,

24. *Journal*, March 31, 1895. Describing Victor Maurel in *Falstaff*, seen in Chicago, March 14, 1895.

25. On DeWolf Hopper in *Wang*: *Courier*, November 2, 1895. On *Our Flat*: *Journal*, May 14, 1895.

this was Willa Cather's manifesto on the rights of man. Even in Philistia she argued that the amateur should not be judged as a professional. Her own reviews of such performances were usually reasonable and sympathetic; there was no gushing, but neither did she use the lightning bolts and hammer of Thor that she often threw at clumsy "professional" performances. She also argued for the rights of the unfamous, ungreat—like young Cecil Spooner, ingenue of perpetual local repertory: "When one can dance and is graceful one does not have to be a great actress."[26] Sometimes she praised a bit actor or an unknown who had the spark. Or there were those like Nat Goodwin, who "has the rare gift of reaching out to the people and appealing to them, and he can delight you a whole long evening so thoroughly that you almost forget that his art is not of the highest kind, for it is not." In his sphere he is an artist. Moreover, "he belongs to a clan that is a very real part of American life and that has a strong influence in the moulding of American society, and it has a right to a representative in the great legislature of art." Her defense of Americans was often in that vein. If Americans like Hoyt's kind of comedy, let them have it—"in spite of their nibs, the critics."

For Willa Cather, taking the side of the people against the critics is part of her general tendency to invest the common man with instincts of appreciation and knowledge that are in many ways superior to those of the learned—superior, that is, in being closer to the "real thing" of authentic response. It may also relate to her distrust of the scholarly pontiff who asserts laws of literature by count and abstraction. So she did join the Philistines on occasion, even if it might be to unite with an enemy to defeat a mutual foe. "The people of this century have a right to demand something that is close to them, something that touches their everyday life. The drama is not for nor supported by students of literature."[27] She also defended *Trilby*: "It has done what art and correct style frequently cannot do; it has appealed to the human in humanity; it has won for itself a place in the hearts of the people. Most of us would write books if we could do that." None of this is to say that she denied her own ideals of excellence or the high vocation of the artist; or that she saw any virtue in a public art that was conventional, imitative, and vulgar. Rather, she emphasized the positive side of commonness and praised whatever form of experience touched on the reality of art. There were also some good ways to combine the aristocratic and the common—the integrity of the artist and the universality of the art.

26. *Courier*, September 14, 1895.
27. *Journal*, December 16, 1894.

Integrity means, first of all, that an artist must use his individual talent. If he recognizes what is his own, and at the same time knows his limitations, he has at least an authentic art. Others have pleasure in his individuality. Clara Morris, for example, "was one of those exceptions who cannot be explained or analyzed, she is great, original and inimitable, even in her decline." One may not want a "school" of Clara Morrises, and—"A school of Kipling would be tiresome, but Rudyard himself is very otherwise." An artist should not try to do everything; a good comedian need not play Shakespeare. Even in comedy one could make distinctions. Roland Reed, although a "skilful and finished light comedian," with "the naturalness and spontaneity necessary to all good comedy," is "not an interpretive actor"; his is "not the comedy of a man who analyzes character and motives or who sees far into life. . . . Refined farce seems to be his limit."[28]

The only morality in art, she said, is the morality of excellence. In the artist, goodness is partly integrity; sin is the waste of genius. She has some vivid comments on what she considered artistic immorality. The actor Thomas Keene wasted himself in ranting and barnstorming, yet once in a while one still gets the ring of genuineness. "Mr. Keene might have made a good actor, but he has sold himself for the beloved dollar of his country. He has aimed too high, not at a star, but just three flights up. He has lost his head, not in the clouds, but in the third gallery." And again she said, "I suppose the curse of having sold one's self is that one is always branded with a trade mark and can never escape from the habits of his vice. Truth once betrayed tracks the betrayer to his grave."[29] For one does have his choice, especially the artist who is given more than others. She thought of Wilde as this kind of sinner: "To every man who has really great talent there are two ways open, the narrow one and the wide, to be great and suffer, or to be clever and comfortable, to bring up white pearls from the deep or to blow iris-hued bubbles from the froth on the surface . . . when a man who was made for the deep sea refuses his mission, denies his high birthright, then he has sinned the sin."

In smaller ways the artist can distort and therefore sin against art. To be unnatural is the greatest of all literary faults, and one can't write decently without clear vision or without common sense. The sin might be insincerity ("A man who founds his art upon a lie lives a lie") or

28. On Clara Morris: *Courier*, September 28, 1895, and *Journal*, March 25, 1894. On Roland Reed (in *The Woman Hater*): *Journal*, September 13, 1894.

29. On Keene: *Journal*, March 25, 1894. The second comment refers to F. Marion Crawford: *Courier*, September 21, 1895.

artificiality, like the "sawdust people" in Belasco's play: "Most of us find an honest vice more endurable than an affected virtue." She was often in a fury about tastelessness, stupidity, or mawkish disregard for the good things; she was often weary of what she considered gratuitous attention to the other kind of sin in the current plays; but she could also strike an amused and sophisticated tone. "Without the nude," she said about that universal problem, "art could not exist; but nudity is not necessarily artistic, nor is it the end of art. . . . In art, Apollo Belvedere is most proper nude, but Quasimodo must keep his clothes on." (One must know his limitations.) On the whole, her principle was to defend art that was done well and seriously, no matter what the subject. Even wickedness must be made interesting, as she said in a perceptive and very human paragraph on the seeming return of a gossip sheet called *Vanity Fair*, an on-again-off-again local publication. "The latest startling thing in the sensational field of Lincoln journalism," she wrote in the fall of 1894, "is an ominous resuscitation of *Vanity Fair*. If it were possible to run a sheet with just enough vanity it might be a good thing; it would keep the animals stirred up and the donkey from dozing." But the sensational papers defeat their own ends by "being coarse where they should only be suggestive. A *Vanity Fair* might be published which even people of culture would like to read, even though they would hide it under the sofa pillow when the doorbell rang. It is too bad that when there are so many clever ways to say wicked things, people will insist on using the most offensive."[30]

Willa Cather did not praise the common man for being common, but for being human and himself; thus he could touch the universal and achieve another kind of excellence. As she said of a play she liked: "It does not deal with the impossible, the unusual or the bizarre, but with the common, universal impulses of humanity which all really great men find quite strange and wonderful enough." She admired William Crane in *Brother John*: "It is a high and noble art to so take the scales from men's eyes that they can see the good that is near to them." In this century, the truest artist is the one "who can distill poetry out of the commonplace."[31] Because the most commonplace and universal element is man himself, his character and his feeling, art is great when it gives us characters "to whom one's heart can go out in either love or pity."

In linking the great and the common, Willa Cather was no Great Commoner, Thomas Paine, Lincoln, or Wordsworth. She did not

30. *Journal*, October 14, 1894. Directed to articles in the *Courier*.
31. *Journal*, April 5, 1894.

campaign for the people. Moreover, she always had more to say about the hero of the arts than about his common followers. Yet of the seven signed stories published in these three years, only one ("A Night at Greenway Court") deals with a literal aristocracy while four are down to earth stories of farmers—early settlers—on the Nebraska plains: "Peter," "Lou, the Prophet," "The Clemency of the Court," and "On the Divide." Her first newspaper sketches in the fall of 1893 deal with obscure, unnamed people. In these years Willa Cather was herself linked by feeling to many more of the commonplace things than her idealistic, passionate devotion to the "highest kind" of art would suggest.

One paragraph written during her last year in Lincoln summarizes, I think, all of her feeling for the great common things. In a notice of a charity concert of December 17, 1895, praise is modest ("many meritorious performances"), and even ambiguous ("If you wish to have a realizing sense that art is long you should attend a charity concert, for in that respect all charity concerts are alike"). The language is lyrical only when she comes to an example of music that is old, familiar, and always new—"the immortal serenade of Schubert's, against which time and custom have done their worst and failed. For that can never really become hackneyed. It is like the moonlight which comes to us every night and yet has never lost its poetry, like the nightingales that sing every summer and yet are not less sweet for that." People may call it a "chestnut," she concludes, "but everyone knows it is not. It is no more a chestnut than the thing for which it stands . . . ."[32]

I have said that Willa Cather in these years was a passionate idealist. Neither the kind, form, substance, nor principles of art would matter if there were not the "other"—the high, rare, splendid ideal that justifies the quest and the devotion. What she worked for was the sense of goodness or perfection, the linked and interchangeable "Beauty is truth, truth beauty," or even what seems to be a mystic insight. The ideal is more often directly expressed as an earthly pattern or achievement, but the human which approaches the divine is enough reason for reverence and passionate excitement. Greatness is also splendor—something half the ideal of heaven and half the power of human excellence. Splendor in art gives the impulse to transfigure, lift, shine, and make more than ordinary. The greatest artists, then, become as the gods, and the highest arts are holy ground.

32. *Journal*, December 22, 1895.

Among artists, Shakespeare is accorded the highest position. Emperor of literature, he is the almost unbearably rich, godlike creator, king of language and the imagination, who must be worshipped and loved. Beethoven is the Shakespeare of music. Music itself has a special significance: "Good music is just a little above anything else that ever honors any stage. . . . Music calls for the best of everything." Though literature and language became Willa Cather's permanent choice in the arts, the experiences of the theatre often had in these early years the most intense and directly powerful hold on her emotions. In drama, "tragedy remains the highest form of art. It speaks most deeply to the soul of man." But she warned poetically that tragedy can be dangerous; in its sacred realm an actor may fail if, like the sons of Aaron, he "carries in his censer only earthly fire." Any of these choices might be studied in greater detail. In this study I have taken for illustration two ideals that I believe are importantly related to all of Willa Cather's writing, though without her first critical statements their significance would not be realized. These are the ideals of French culture and the literature of romance.

Willa Cather's wide reading in French literature and her continued study of the French writers she admired have been mentioned by her friends. There are other proofs, such as the portrait of George Sand she hung over the mantel in her apartment,[33] and the prints of Flaubert and Pierre Loti she brought to the Seibels from Europe.[34] But only in these first newspaper accounts do we learn how intensely she admired France itself, or more exactly, the idea of French culture. Some of her attitudes surely have implications for *One of Ours* and *Shadows on the Rock*.

Remarks during the summer of 1895 will illustrate her judgments. She believed, for example, that French literature was great and universal, that "in these days it is as necessary for a literary man to have a wide knowledge of the French masterpieces as it is for him to have read Shakespeare or the Bible. What man who pretends to be an author can afford to neglect those models of style and composition?" She names particularly Daudet, Maupassant, Hugo, and George Sand.[35] In the novel and the drama, especially, French writers have the central position. But—even more appealing—in France art and artists are treated with understanding,

33. Elizabeth Shepley Sergeant refers to the portrait of George Sand by Coutoure in *Willa Cather: A Memoir* (Lincoln: University of Nebraska Press, 1963; first published 1953), pp. 124, 202, 252. It is also described by Elizabeth Moorhead in *These Too Were Here* (Pittsburgh: University of Pittsburgh Press, 1950), p. 56.

34. Mrs. Seibel showed me these prints in the summer of 1965, saying that Willa had been so pleased to find them in a bookstall in Paris, during her first trip to Europe in 1902.

35. *Journal*, May 5, 1895.

respect, and sympathy: "The French have a talent for appreciation. In matters dramatic they have an unerring instinct"; and she stresses the nicety of popular taste: "Every man is a critic; his judgment is crude but just," and critics themselves are wise and respected. In France, play-making is in the hands of men of letters. Paris is "where the great heart of the world beats," where Frenchmen remember genius. This sounds like some Utopian land, but it is not far from the aura of tradition and quality that led many an American to Europe. Willa Cather did not admire French culture because it was elegant or sophisticated, but because it had standards, excellence, warmth, and color.

Because she was most interested in the French Romantics—and, we might add, in the Latin-Romanic world throughout history—she thought of the French in the exotic, Oriental light of the Mediterranean South rather than in the sharper climate of reason and prose that other critics defined. After reading Gautier she wrote: "The great passions never become wholly conventionalized in France. . . . Beneath that most polished suavity in the world there is always something of the savage. It comes from the South . . . . There are sentences that ring out like the clank of golden armor, chapters that are embalmed in spices and heavy with the odors of the vale of Cashmere." This passage is not only a suggestion of Willa Cather's view of the French but a condensation of important elements in her relationship to art, as if she had given bodily form to a personal ideal. In that land the great passions are real, primitive violence is combined with controlled form (the savage under the suave); in the allusive imagery the feeling of page and language is vivified into chivalric "golden armor" and medieval knighthood, into the rare, remote, perhaps sacramental beauty suggested by the "embalmed spices" of Cashmere.

The ideal of French culture which rings through her own pages in 1893–1896 is in many ways Willa Cather's positive image set against much that she found negative in America. Around her the world was diverse, unsettled, full of unresolved differences; France had unity, repose, and assurance, and its long tradition of art represented achievement. France had standards, and in France artist and public were one. In America nobody cared, or tried; America had no standards, and the artist worked against odds in a careless and unappreciative society. In a more personal sense, France may have been to her the detailed equivalent of her generalized but primary feeling about Virginia, with its structured society, its sense of past and continuity, its richness, elegance, and romance (all qualities of the South she mentions in these articles). Before her, there was the unfinished face of a new world. But reading chronologically, one does notice a change—more frequent comments on what she does not like in modern French literature (crude realism and smart language), and in criticisms of American culture, often the urgency of a prophet who feels that great things are possible. The high culture of France was marred by its decadence; the inadequacies of the New World were balanced by its possibilities.

Another important ideal was romance and the literature of that tradition. "Romance is the highest form of fiction," Willa Cather wrote in the fall of 1895. She placed it on a highly poetic, mythic, and even immortal plane—"it will never desert us . . . . It will come back to us in all its radiance and eternal freshness in some one of the dawning seasons of Time. Ibsens and Zolas are great, but they are temporary. Children, the sea, the sun, God himself are all romanticists." Elegiac in the tone of "Adonais" (The One remains, the many change and pass), haunting the mind like Keats's lines on the Elgin Marbles (A sun—a shadow of a magnitude), this passage is more a statement of belief in certain values of life and art than a lament for a kind of literature that seemed to be out of fashion. What, then, did she mean by "romance"?

Her statements on romance were part of the long-standing debate by writers, critics, and public on whether or not "realism" was a way of art superior to all others—an argument which continued into the 1920's and through changing, individual definitions of both terms. In the context of the 1890's, it was not a question of "reality"—both realism and romance were for *that*—but specifically a difference in the definitions of reality and the techniques of achieving it. In general, she did not have much use for realism—whether of Ibsen, Zola, or Howells—or its country cousin, local color. To set down a multitude of exact details about the physical and actual world would not in itself give a sense of life, nor would a concern for social problems insure reality. The work of the current realists often did little more than wallow in ugliness and end in the hopeless gloom of man's incapacity to rise from the mud. When one spoke of realism and romance in 1895, it was, in the largest sense, to set up a counterpoise of good and evil, dullness and excitement, ugliness and beauty, idealism and despair.[36] Willa Cather's choice of romance took in these elements and some individual qualities as well.

36. Willa Cather wrote in a review of *Brother John* (*Journal*, April 5, 1894): "In this wicked and perverse generation plays like *Brother John* and actors like William H. Crane are restful and wholesome. They are realistic with the realism of good and remind one that realism after all may not be an absolute synonym for evil."

The men she spoke of most directly as writers of romance were Dumas *père*, Hugo, Daudet, Stevenson, Kipling, Stanley Weyman, Anthony Hope. Books of romance included *The Count of Monte Cristo*, *The Three Guardsmen*, *Kings in Exile*, *The Prisoner of Zenda*—but also *Treasure Island* and *Soldiers Three*. What these books have in common is first of all a physical brilliance—color, action, narrative speed—the obvious structures of exciting play that Willa Cather called in a 1913 interview "the games that live forever." They also show before our eyes the strange and far away and long ago. And they give us heroes, in heroic action. All these qualities are suggested in a comment on the actor Salvini in *Count of Monte Cristo*—he has "the sparkling dash and brilliancy of the heroes of old romance." She obviously liked these patterns of romance, whatever the story. On another level, as her comments show, romance exalts courage, honor, daring, love, and all the emotions she considered ennobling; it also represents the creative, exploring truth of the imagination.

Romance is significant because it demonstrates heroic action. The hero is the exemplum of courage, daring, and the strong passions that give life purpose and strength. Stevenson wrote of the glory and the hope of effort and of the completeness which a man's work gives to his life. He could not conceive of a futile passion. His books are not lazy. Such heroic action is the imaginative antidote for a civilization that has become fearful of any risk; it might cut through the "hundred little precautions with which we have hedged ourselves about to make life easy." One important theme in Willa Cather's writing in these early years is that the heroic impulse, fulfilled in danger—even war—is linked to ideals. If war would materialize, it might give us the heroic impulse again. "Too much security and comfort in living begets a sort of apathy toward the heroic, and an unconsciousness of those shadowy ideals that watch us out yonder in the big dark." Romance also extends our world. Its imaginative experience is what we do not easily have in our ordinary life. So Stevenson gave the world an outlook beyond the rigid horizons of social life— something new, fresh, unheard of, full of brilliant color and rugged life; and she exhorts Kipling to tell us of things new and strange and novel, love and war and action, the boundless freedom that we do not have. Even more daring and remote were the explorations of another world, Poe's "voyages into the mystical unknown, into the gleaming, impalpable kingdom of pure romance."

To summarize, "pure romance" as much as anything in fiction is the unconfined but self-contained realm of the imagination. It exists by its own vivid life, it is not a lesson in sociology. In fact, romance has the primitive virtue of being in the imaginative world as nearly a *new* creation as it is possible to make, one not subject to the laws of ordinary life. Like poetry it heightens the color and rhythm of its material, places events (like images) in unexpected juxtaposition. Like poetry, romance is also a kind of bardic incantation, invoking through ritual phrases and objects the powers of courage and wonder.

If one lists say a dozen of the nineteenth-century (or reasonably modern) writers for whom Willa Cather had some special feeling, whom she quoted or referred to or used in some way, except for Browning, George Eliot, and Thackeray all the rest would be Romantics: Keats, Shelley, Heine, Musset, Poe, Pierre Loti, Daudet, Dumas *père*, and Stevenson. And this list omits Anthony Hope whose *Prisoner of Zenda* became a very great favorite, the early Tolstoi, and the early Henry James—who, as William Dean Howells pointed out in 1882, was also a Romantic when he wrote the stories of *The Madonna of the Future*.[37] Perhaps Willa Cather's statements on romance should therefore be placed in the context of Romanticism as a whole: She did not merely like the *stories* of romance; she believed in the central *principles* of Romanticism, or at least moved to that side. Her feeling about romance and realism relates primarily to the great value she gave to imagination. In context, her distinctions would be something like this: Romance is pure literature, an imaginative creation that is a body, not a container for information or a weapon for social action. Realism means writing for a cause outside the work. Romance is idealistic, realism is brutal. Romance is a release: it has something to do with distances (place or time) and in it the movement of the imagination is outward. It allows praise and glory, and shows the distance between greatness and the commonplace. Realism is a constriction, a drawing in. With realism the imagination is bound—at least until it can be released in the opposite direction, going through the looking glass to find a world in a grain of sand, or, as she said Zola very nearly did, to find splendor in vegetables that were no longer ordinary.

In Willa Cather's writing, romance is often identified with children, or the feeling of wonder and belief that is more common to children than to adults. Children "are not realists as yet and exult in the imagination

37. Howells said of James: "His best efforts seem to me those of romance; his best types have an ideal development, like Isabel and Claire Belgarde and Bessy Alden and poor Daisy and even Newman," and he mentions particularly the stories of *The Madonna of the Future*. "Henry James, Jr.," *Century*, November, 1882, pp. 25–29.

their elders have lost." The qualities of wonder and imagination link child and artist—"An artist is a child always, but a child is not always an artist."38 And the child is closer to nature. His feelings are more direct and complete; he is in harmony with the physical, elemental world. It is in this direct, pure, and positive sense that she could link all cosmic forces with romance—"Children, the sea, the sun, God himself."

"The highest cannot be spoken," she said, quoting Goethe. It was the mysterious origin of genius, that "one lambent flame" in which all power is distilled; it was the ecstasy of the spirit, the beauty which is the end of craft, the ideal of creation achieved. But to describe the highest ideal of the artist in more exact words was not possible at that time, or perhaps ever. It had to be said by indirection and in ritualistic invocations. Late in the spring of 1896, only a few weeks before she left Nebraska, Willa Cather summarized Ruskin's creed—"roughly and somewhat vaguely"— but in terms that seem appropriate to her own ideal as well: Ruskin, although a scientist, knew that "art is supreme," the highest and only expression of divinity in man; the end of man is to create, or to see, beauty. There is an interesting inflection of the lines from Keats—"That beauty alone is truth, and truth is only beauty." But this is Willa Cather's rhapsodic style—ritualistic, incantatory, as if it were the expected ceremonial music (one thinks of her comment that "singing is idealized speech"). All that she had written before this spring gives body and human force to that rough vagueness of "beauty and truth." In the same Sunday column, along with the piece on Ruskin is one on Tolstoi in which she defines in another way the ideal of art: Art is "the highest moral purpose in the world"; paradoxically, the real beauty and truth which serves God is the indirection and earthy glory of *Anna Karenina* rather than the didactic morality of *The Kreutzer Sonata*. "If God is at all a literary God *Anna Karenina* will certainly do more toward saving its author's soul than all the prosy tracts he had written since." Ruskin knew that, too—and that "the spiritual force of a nation immortalizes itself with the spirit of beauty," in monuments of art. (Tolstoi rather than stone, she might add.) Ruskin's truth was that "All sciences, discoveries, systems, which did not tend to increase the aggregate sum of beauty could not increase the sum of human happiness. They were merely wheels within

38. Cf. "The Treasure of Far Island" (*CSF*, pp. 265 ff.): A child's normal attitude "is that of the artist, pure and simple"; "'whenever I look back on [childhood], it is all exultation and romance'"; "'To people who live by imagination at all, that is the only life that goes deep enough to leave memories. We were artists in those days, creating for the day only; making epics sung once, and then forgotten.'"

wheels, like the prophet's vision." Of course all of this had been said before. The young Willa Cather was simply taking her position.

Like the goddess of triple sight, three-fold Diana who rules three realms—"*Terret, lustrat, agit, Proserpina, Luna, Diana, | Ima, suprema, feras, sceptro, fulgore, sagitta*," as it is quoted in Lemprière—the artist is not only himself but also man and god. As we see it in Willa Cather's pages, the kingdom of art is poised, with intricate balance and mingling, between two other worlds. The artist may look to the kingdom of heaven, and sometimes the gods come down; but on earth he is caught in time, living at once in two worlds and with two selves, a duality even the gods would find hard to divide. Of all the dilemmas which appear in Willa Cather's frank statements during these first years, none is stronger or with more permanent implications than this one of artist and person. It is one form of the duality of self which was to appear in many guises through her yet unwritten pages.

On the relationship of the two worlds of earth and art she was quite explicit and, in the end, consistent. To look at it one way: the world of actuality is on the whole a dull and common world, placed well this side of romance; it is bound by conventions and burdened with trivialities. For this dimension of the world, the function of art is to intensify experience. So we go to the theatre, where "the stage is the kingdom of the emotions and the imagination." Here, cluttered with all the machinery and distractions of earth (hard chairs to sit on, people who eat in theatre boxes, a lurid drop curtain to look at, hoots from the gallery), one still may enter that other world. It gives what the everyday world lacks— strong emotions and experience to warm and uplift, sharpening what custom or caution obliterates. On the stage, then, "let people love and hate each other to the death. Your drivelling lover and hater are not worth an actor's exertions. . . . behind the footlights let people love with kisses and suffer with tears." In the fall of 1895 she said it even more directly:

> Certainly we go to change our atmosphere, to get for a moment into the atmosphere of great emotions that are forbidden in our lives. I hope that the stage will [keep] its illusions, that the footlights will always be a boundary line beyond which men will deign to feel and dare to love. I want them to be the dead line of the practical. The dress circle, the parquet, the orchestra chairs—that is all the dead world of fact; but right beyond that line of lights are the tropics,

the kingdom of the unattainable, where the grand passions die not and the great forces still work.[39]

The kingdom of art is therefore an intensification, an expansion, a change from sterility into life.

In almost the opposite direction, she saw art as a harmonizing and quieting force. Here it is directed to "this time" rather than "this world": the age was hectic and shrill, its temper was neurotic, its people all nerves and tension, but in the eternal quiet of great art one might find another kind of satisfaction. Willa Cather also had a Virgilian kind of primitivism, with its pastoral ideal of simplicity and harmony. In Arcadia (which at this point looked a little like Scotland) one could simplify, become as a child. Art returns us to realities that are more basic than social science or the polished complexities of civilization.

These views of the relation of art to the ordinary world are not necessarily in conflict. In the first, art is to intensify, to counter the world of fact. In the second, art is to simplify, to counter the world of confusion. But these divisions involved intricate juggling of values and considerable simplification. This world is not always dull; as she often said, in the eyes of the artist it was the rich and only source of art, "a bit of the 'Comédie Humaine,' which, up to date, is the greatest comedy on the boards, and the hardest to enact."[40] Life is not only the material of the artist but also his teacher, for in humanity and nature he finds the elemental forces and the laws of art. This brings us to the more specific problems which had to be worked out, both theoretically and emotionally.

Willa Cather had a great respect for nature—"jovial, robust old nature" whose virtues include common sense ("if one does not see at least a few things as they are by the time one is twenty, then one never sees them at all"). Nature is also a notable debunker. At twenty, or thereabouts, Willa Cather likewise viewed the ordinary world with a steady eye. That she could be realistic, even flatly cynical, is shown in a round of biting criticisms of the ways of the world (or Philistia) in 1894. But although these comments were in the person's voice, they had predominantly the artist's point of view and values. Increasingly, however, the

---

39. Cf. Willa Cather's review of *The Prisoner of Zenda* (Pittsburgh *Leader*, October 19, 1897), in which she calls the footlights "the boundary line beyond which dreams come true and lost illusions live on, forever young"; and "'A Death in the Desert'" (*CSF*, pp. 199 ff.): "The footlights had seemed a hard, glittering line drawn sharply between their life and his; a circle of flame set about those splendid children of genius."

40. *Journal*, October 9, 1894. Reviewing *Gloriana*.

world obtrudes into the ideal of art. In her last year in Nebraska, she is noticeably aware of the misuse of "art" and "artist." She is disenchanted with actors, irritated with the failures of writers, and perhaps worried about her own place in it all. About actors, for example: in 1894 when the great ones were perfect, she said they did not have conceit but standards; by the fall of 1895 she had met plenty of them whose ignorance and conceit seemed boundless. Should Calvé leave the stage for a chicken farm? "If she prefers the chickens let her have them and warble Bizet's impassioned measures to them until they become very nightingales. Perhaps she can even train a rooster orchestra. If she loves chickens better than two thousand a night let her have them." Should Maude Adams sacrifice her love to her art for the world's sake? "Bah! the world can do without Miss Adams' art." In fact, the people of the theatre seemed as much a threat to its art as Philistia could be—the actresses who couldn't pronounce "Ibsen," the advance man who was sure that Cleopatra was a good and proper housewife and married lady. The value of the stage was clearly secondary to Willa Cather's primary interests: "I think the stage is a great act," she said in the fall of 1895, "but I think literature is greater." Yet she was not blind to the defects of writers. "It is gravely to be feared that literary people are rather mean folk when you get right down to the selfish little pericardiums that lie hidden behind all their graceful artistic charms. They love humanity in the abstract, but no class of men can treat the concrete individual more shabbily." And, she added, "too often they hate each other like rival chorus girls."[41] It was possible for her to stand on the other side, in the other world, looking into the kingdom of art.

Often in this last year "art" has a bemusing strangeness and even unreality. Little things slip out to suggest that the conflict of worlds was a very practical one. In a review of *Our Flat* in the spring of 1895 she notes that the main characters (a playwright and his wife, the daughter of a rich old Philistine) "go on kissing and writing tragedies, living on love and high art until they get thin. Finally Margery decides to abandon art for the same reason that many of us abandon it—because her clothes wore out." About the career of an actress from Kansas City: "Geography is a terribly fatal thing sometimes." By the following spring of 1896: "It is a bitter task, that of living by one's wits and amusing the public, and none too inviting to a strong man's spirit." And of the ways one might have to take: "Journalism has its faults and they are many, but it is considerably

41. On Calvé: *Courier*, September 7, 1895. On Maude Adams: *Courier*, October 5, 1895. On "literary people": *Journal*, June 7, 1896.

nearer to the living world than a university and it has this great merit, that it speedily kills off inferior talent and brings the real article to the front."[42]

During the fall of 1895 she had written of the stage as the tropics and "the kingdom of the unattainable," the footlights as the dead line of the practical. In early June of 1896, just two weeks before she left for Pittsburgh and journalism, she returns to that idea in a paragraph of rather more complexity than its crisp, bright tone would suggest. Calvé, one hears, can't ride a bicycle—she is too clumsy. Well, says the *Journal* columnist, "Volcanic emotions are all right on the stage, but they don't go on a bicycle. Bicycles are not to be wooed by languorous glances or guitars or the Spanish melodies of Bizet; they are stiff and formal and uncompromising; they stand for the age of steel in which Carmens and Calvés belong not. A bicycle insists upon being treated coolly and respectfully and bitterly resents ardorous advances."[43] Whose side *is* she on? "The age of steel in which Carmens and Calvés belong not".... Was the boundary line between past and present already so sharp? Or was it a habit of melancholy? or frustration at the conflicting demands of two worlds? or even a more subtle meshing of voice, image, and metaphor? Miss Cather could handle a wheel, it is true, even in a world of rough reason and practical commitments, but she was not about to give up guitars.

From the first essays of 1891 to the last columns of 1896 Willa Cather talked of the difficulties of art, its exacting and even cruel demands, and the necessity of the artist to endure loneliness, self-abnegation, and sacrifice if he is to choose and serve the god. At first her statements have a youthful idealism and generality ("Art of every kind is an exacting master".... "a man must be willing to be poor and despised for its sake"[44].... he should be "in the world but not of the world"), a proverbial tone which changes sharply during the last year and a half of her writing to more detailed, realistic, and—many times—impassioned statements of personal importance.

As the problems of the artist's life and work seem to narrow to her own particular questions, she is concerned first of all with the woman as artist. Can a woman be a great writer? Or is she bound by some limitations of sex and temperament to a narrower kind of achievement? The

42. The review of *Our Flat* and the comment on journalism appeared in the *Journal* on May 14, 1895, and March 8, 1896, respectively.

43. *Journal*, June 7, 1896.

44. *Journal*, December 16, 1894.

question comes like a refrain through many of the articles in which she considers Christina Rossetti, Elizabeth Barrett Browning, George Sand, George Eliot, and a lesser galaxy of popular names. If it is possible for a woman poet or novelist to widen her subjects and strengthen her style (for yes, there *is* sex in art),[45] what then shall she do with nature? Wherein lies happiness? It must be remembered that when these questions were asked, only a few women had careers and public opinion was sure that marriage must come first. So the problem of artist and person was compounded when one was a woman. In any case, Willa Cather put great value on the human side of the ordinary world—the desires and passions, the elemental facts of existence, from which art took its life. When the actress Réjane sacrificed for her child, she "possibly also knows that there are other things on earth than art, things higher and more sacred."[46] Of George Sand—"sometimes the workman is above his works." And "Ruskin's work, great as it is, is a little thing compared to the mind that produced it." But she also considered how the personal self might endanger the artist.[47] Marriage was one hazard ("domestic and artistic life do not mix well and . . . in art there is no compromise. . . . Liberty and solitude, they are the two wings of art"); pleasure was another. One talented actress "never rose to the place Booth marked out for her, because she cared very much more for Pearl Eytinge than for all the laurels in christendom. Pearl Eytinge the woman slew Pearl Eytinge the artist years ago." The woman slew the artist—that was one way of putting it. Could the artist also destroy the woman?

If Willa Cather had not resolved the conflict of selves in her own life by that summer of 1896, at least she had recognized the problem—and its drama. In an essay on Mary Anderson's marriage and retirement from the stage she had also tried to weigh the elements. On one side is the passion for art ("the beauty of good work") and the statement of what perfection means—"what labor, what suffering, how one must pay for it in blood." On the other side is not only the woman Mary Anderson, but an artist who is falsely self-satisfied and content, uncommitted to sacrifice; she is not a great artist but a great and happy woman. She was lucky, says Willa Cather: "Art touched her life without consuming it, and the flame did not blacken the brand." And surely for a woman this is right. But no,

45. *Journal*, March 15, 1896.
46. *Journal*, April 21, 1895.
47. The two comments which follow are from the *Journal*, April 7, 1895, and January 26, 1896, respectively.

there were Sappho "and the two great Georges" for which nothing but art would do. As she had said a month earlier on Bohemianism, "the business of an artist's life is . . . ceaseless and unremitting labor," and the man who writes of great men's feats has little time to do them. Although she did not go so far as to reverse the metaphor of "the woman slew the artist," she began to say it in other ways. She quoted Coppée, that a poet's life consists of ink and reams of paper. Perhaps Mary Anderson *was* lucky.

In the argument of life and art, person and artist, Willa Cather came to some bitter convictions during her last months of writing in Nebraska. She had to say, for example, that in the end the artist does put his work first; he does not care about the world. Artistic pursuits, or "intellectual passions," are "personal, intense, selfish. They are more violent than the loves of Helen, more lasting than the spell of the rare Egyptian. . . . They are not to be acquired by any labor, any worth, any effort, and once possessed they are not to be lost." These are the passions and desires that are real for the artist. Yet she saw the paradox: "Fools say they will live for art and they never know its face. Artists say they will live with men, and they go back to their shadows, which to them are real."[48] And speaking of some personal tragedies in the lives of successful artists— "That's the curse of glory; that it comes too late, when we have an open wound that it cannot heal and hearts that it cannot mend. Most men desire one thing above all things, they don't get it, not even the great ones. That is why life grows pretty distasteful after awhile. We want one thing, desire one thing, demand one thing, and that life kills."[49] If one studies the map of desire and glory, it seems certain that the way does not follow the life: "We are always trying to see in a man's life the cause for his work, to trace in his blood and environment the reason for his genius. That has so little to do with it." Rather, the choice is made by "Our Lady of Beauty," and who knows "why or how this goddess of created things moulds a man to her will"? Our lady, as Willa Cather astutely observes, is *both* woman and goddess.

In almost every column and review of the 1893–1896 period Willa Cather dealt in some way with the elements of art in general, or those principles of material and technique which might be applied interchangeably to performer, composer, painter, and writer. But there is no doubt that eventually all of her observations converged in one great

48. *Courier*, November 9, 1895.
49. *Journal*, December 15, 1895.

question: How is it done? or, How am I to do it? For neither can there be any doubt that she was trying to discover—by observation, comparison, analysis, and repeated experiment—the central principle of the writer's art.

In her three years of argument with herself and others, changes of mind, restatements and revisions, the elements of art she considered fall into two general categories: first, those intangible qualities, personal or god-given, which make up or determine the internal substance of art—intuition, inspiration, feeling, emotion, idea, experience; second, the body of the work itself—form, craft, technique, language, and, as the determining force, the labor of creation. Now each of these elements, in some degree and relationship, was always a part of Willa Cather's concept of art; the problem was to refine and evaluate, placing each element in its proper light. Some things of course are constant: the touch of divinity, the fearful necessities of fate and genius, the magic of words, the elemental mysteries. But even assuming these things, one still must make some choices.

In the first years Willa Cather seemed to be on the side of feeling, of content rather than craft: "The less craft and cult there is about literature the better," she said in the fall of 1894; the "talent for writing is largely the talent for living, and is utterly independent of knowledge." The danger she saw then was that the writer might think success comes from knowledge and cleverness rather than from his human experience, his imagination. Moreover, style for its own sake is not enough—neither epigrams nor inimitable phrases can create art, for one must "paint with emotion, not with words." She respected craft—"a man who can't draw can't paint, and a man who has not had good instruction can't do either." But also, the "cleverest stagecraft is all wrong when it is at war with the eternal truth of things"; a play is "organically false" when it "moves upon not the hearts, but the nerves" of an audience. In the same winter of 1894–1895 she commented on the Russian novelists, whose "amazing fecundity" is often combined with the "unfortunate disregard of perfect finish" (she excepted Turgenev). The composer Rubinstein, for example, lacked "the discipline and patience that enables a man to labor over one theme until he has exhausted all its possibilities. He had too many ideas to be constant to one; the very richness of his imagination was perhaps his worst fault."[50] Neither will inspiration do without labor, material without craft.

50. *Journal*, November 25, 1894. On the death of Rubinstein.

Without drawing any sharp lines to suggest periods, one still notices a strong reversal in the spring of 1895. Feeling and knowledge are put in more balanced relationship: the heart must humanize the brain, she says, but unless the artist has understanding "the inner courts of his art are forever closed to him." Furthermore, in a creative artist "the much talked of emotional qualifications are only the beginning of true greatness. It requires a master intellect to apply strong emotions, or it is the feverish, meaningless passion of a child." The artist "should give his emotions an anchor that will reach down into the very depths of the very nature of things and hold him to the truth." She assumes the necessity of technique: stage people forget that to use the pen even moderately well "requires a study and inspiration and mastery of technique almost as great as that of their own art." And she assumes the necessity of hard work: Stevenson had that enormous discipline and effort—no one will know what his chapters cost him as he drafted, wrote, destroyed, and wrote again.

During this period she also tried to distinguish between language used for itself and that used as an instrument of art. In some ways, style needed more attention: "We are losing all understanding of the power of language in the theatre," she wrote. We should be back in the Elizabethan Globe, "driven once again to the resources of human speech and to the naked strength of words." But words were strong when they had the power to move; language was right when it became the living body of art. So she admired the suggestive "inner harmony and kinship of words," and lines in drama "that haunt one's memory, words that have an especial fitness for each other." Perhaps her best attempt to suggest the subtlety and wholeness of style is her comment on Verlaine: "His verses are like music, they are made up of harmony and feeling, they are as indefinite and barren of facts as a nocturne. They tell only of a mood. . . . He created a new verbal art of communicating sensations not only by the meanings of words, but of their relation, harmony and sound."

Early in 1895 and again in the spring of 1896 Willa Cather stated in balanced key phrases the combination of both substance and execution as forces in art: *Camille* "unites in itself those two affinities so seldom mated, measureless feeling and perfect form." (What she meant by "perfect form," however, was not style but logical construction—one grand motif, nothing accidental, all inevitable.) Nearly a year and a half later, in the spring of 1896, she restated the proposition: Tolstoi "possessed all the great secrets of art once, an inimitable craft and power unlimited." The change in language here is informative. *Feeling* and *form* pertained to the play, the work itself; *craft* and *power* pertained to the writer and his way of accomplishing the work of art. Increasingly, Willa Cather was interested in what the writer himself must do. In both pairs the conception extends to mysteries: *measureless* and *unlimited, perfect* and *inimitable*. But the last combination seems stronger and more exact: *inimitable craft* and *power unlimited*.

In the winter of 1895–1896 Willa Cather wrote two essays in which, it seems to me, she articulates not only the debate of craft and power but also the pull of forces in herself. Her pieces on Henry James and Walt Whitman are counterpoints of yes and no, so finely balanced as to leave some doubt about which side she was really on.

She calls Henry James "that mighty master of language and keen student of human actions and motives." His stories are models with a perfect framework and flawless polish; but though perfect, they are "sometimes a little hard, always calculating and dispassionate." She admires his style—"the mere beauty of his sentences." James controls, unifies: "He never lets his phrases run away with him. They are never dull and never too brilliant." This sounds like very much of a middle ground for one who often found art to be passion and ecstasy. With James "you are never startled, never surprised, never thrilled or never enraptured." On the other hand, you are always delighted. By what? by the style again—"that masterly prose that is as correct, as classical, as calm and as subtle as the music of Mozart." But this was Willa on one of her Apollonian days. As she often said, "There are others."

When she wrote of Whitman the pull of forces is even more apparent. (Did she, perhaps, mute her style for James and color it for Whitman?) She is caught between her distaste for Whitman's disorderly, unfinished work (surely he could not be a poet) and her own pleasure in his "joy of life." She says both yes and no to Whitman, in a succession of turns like a Greek chorus, rejecting, returning, unable to let him go. Whitman, she says, was a mixture, neither good nor bad, undiscriminating, enjoying everything "with the unreasoning enthusiasm of a boy," writing "reckless rhapsodies over creation in general" that are "sometimes sublime, sometimes ridiculous." He is reverent toward the world, but he has no principle of selection or relationship—and yet (she becomes rhapsodic herself about Whitman's joy of life, sounding like her other less Apollonian, more primitive self) "there is a primitive elemental force about him. He is so full of hardiness and of the joy of life. He looks at all nature in the delighted, admiring way in which the old Greeks and the primitive poets did. He exults so in the red blood in his body and the strength in his arms." He has a passion for warmth, dignity, all that is natural—exactly the primitive virtues that she often urged on the world. He is like the old barbarians. But though Whitman accepted and glorified the world, he is limited to the physical. Though there is an undeniable charm about "this optimistic vagabond" who revels in "sunshine and the smell of spring fields," whose "good fellowship and whole-heartedness" and veneration for the world make you want to be like him, she concludes that "keen senses do not make a poet," that spiritual perceptions must be a part of sensuous verse. Certainly she was herself torn between instinct and law. And the judgment of the centuries (she thought at this time, as she shows in other articles) is by no means clear. Both the primitive virtues and the learned systems have power. She knew what she ought to like, but she was not at all sure that she did.

We might note that the comparisons in the James and Whitman pieces are exactly opposite: Whitman communicates personal joy, but without order; James has the order of Mozart, but with him you must be content with quiet delight, and live without rapture.

During her last months in Nebraska, a time when she was concentrating most on writers and books, Willa Cather predominantly spoke of the ways and means of the artist. The question of how it is done and what to put first is obviously a practical and personal one. Three statements in columns of late January and early March, 1896, are remarkable for their sense of fresh personal conviction and their evidence of some real effort to combine and balance the various elements in art. The first (in the same column as the essay on Whitman) is an unadorned literal observation on the psychology of the artist: "No artist does a thing because it is noble or good; he does it because he can do it well, because his mind is so made that perfection in something or other is his chiefest need." A week later she gave her best account of the relationship of the two halves of art, here described as inspiration and technique (technique, that is, which implies hard work and effort). Under Bernhardt's emotional power and physical impact is a "perfect art," the result of rigorous training: "technique that in itself is enough when for a moment her inspiration fails. . . . The training that she carries so lightly that one seldom thinks of it, has killed the originality in a hundred lesser artists . . . . under all those thousand little things that seem so spontaneous there is a system as fixed and definite as the laws of musical composition." In this statement is the full and direct application of what she had said about intelligence,

[75]

knowledge, and understanding (others must feel, but the artist must know), but she also clearly implies the dangers of either inspiration alone (it may fail) or technique alone (it may ruin). In other words, neither genius nor skill can make an artist. But the paradox exists: Craft may be the very arm of power itself. Structure, system, and order are not captivity but release.

Finally, in her column of March 1, 1896, she comes to her most impassioned realization of the meaning of art, as it was to lie in her own hands. Here, I think, for at least this moment she saw clearly the figure of her own artist-self and made her commitment to a principle of art which was neither form-craft-technique nor feeling-power-inspiration, nor even hard effort, though it included all three and something more—an order of priority.

The crucial element in art, she says, is action, but she puts it another way: What is god-given must come first—feeling, power, and thought; what the artist must attend to is therefore his craft: the *process* of creation.

> Art is not thought or emotion, but expression, expression, always expression. To keep an idea living, intact, tinged with all its original feeling, its original mood, preserving in it all the ecstasy which attended its birth, to keep it so all the way from the brain to the hand and transfer it on paper a living thing with color, odor, sound, life all in it, that is what art means, that is the greatest of all the gifts of the gods. And that is the voyage perilous, and between those two ports more has been lost than all the yawning caverns of the sea have ever swallowed.

The context is an article on Edgar Saltus, a writer who, she thinks, fails to achieve art; though he has the power of language—a "fervid and ardent English"—he does not have lofty ideas or substance. If we call a man an artist, we thereby imply that he does have "ideals and . . . human worth," and has conceived "lofty things." These are the first gates of art, and Mr. Saltus has not passed through them. Though his work has all the perfection of sound, style, and form—"the craft of exquisite speech" ("clever stagecraft" she had called it a year earlier)—the substance is not there. To turn it around: assuming that a man *has* all the substance of feeling and idea, *then* he may build the ship of his craft, and that is the critical moment of art. For great thoughts and great feelings are possible to all men; the journey of creation is given only to the artist. "There are a thousand people who see in *Carmen* all that Calvé does. There are a thousand who have dreamed *Alastors* and *Endymions*, but, ah, to sing it, to say it! It is an awful and a fearsome thing, that short voyage from the brain to the hand, and many a gleaming argosy of thought has gone down in it forever." To bring the life of the self into the mold of another life is all of creation compact, and the gift of the gods is the power to accomplish that labor. This is the "mighty craft" of literature.

The last part of the essay rises again with the poetry of religious incantation and the artist's passion: he is the pilgrim-knight who goes through the desert of himself to find the holy sepulchre. Only a few can take that journey:

> There were other crusades many centuries ago, when all the good men who were otherwise unemployed and their wives and progeny set out for Palestine. But they found that the holy sepulchre was a long way off, and that there was no beaten path thereto, and the mountains were high and the sands hot and the waters of the desert were bitter brine. So they decided to leave the journey to the pilgrims who were madmen anyway, without homes; who found the water no bitterer than their own tears and the desert sands no hotter than the burning hearts within them. In the kingdom of art there is no God, but one God, and his service is so exacting that there are few men born of woman who are strong enough to take the vows. There is no paradise offered for a reward to the faithful, no celestial bowers, no houris, no scented wines; only death and the truth.

So in the elemental and archetypal figures of water and desert, voyage and quest, Willa Cather sets down the first principle of art, and with it a pattern of choices. The personal metaphor which was to haunt her all her life is here: "all the way from the brain to the hand," ... "that short voyage from the brain to the hand." The hand is the ultimate port, the instrument of birth, the ship of impossibilities. She had used the image before, writing of Stevenson and "the truly great, whose minds have so much more power to conceive than their hands ever have strength to execute, whose work is so far below the level of their dreams," and she would use it again.[51]

51. This article identifies Willa Cather as the author of "A Philistine in the Gallery" (signed "Goliath") in *The Library*, April 21, 1900, pp. 8–9. Arguing that the Philistine as well as the art student has a right to like certain paintings, and describing vividly some paintings of a marshland, of a "little low-browed peasant girl who speaks all the tragedy of her people," of "the work-a-day Palestine, the place where men plowed and sowed and prayed," and remarking that "Tanner's insistent use of the silvery green of the olives, of the yellow of the parched clay hills of Palestine . . . reminds me of Pierre Loti's faculty of infusing absolute personality into environment," that the painter William Chase has

Here, too, in compact allusion is a company of passionate pilgrims—
the poet of *Alastor*, Endymion, Bunyan's Pilgrim himself, the knighthood
of Malory's world, Odysseus, the anchorites of Browning's "A Death in
the Desert"; here are the Castle Perilous, the perilous seas in Keats's faery
lands forlorn. It is a violent, mythic world for a journey—wilderness and
mountain, yawning sea caverns to swallow the voyager, water that turns
to brine, fire in the desert. Is this, then, "the greatest of all the gifts of the
gods"—to endure that danger? But only in such a world can the voyage
perilous—from the brain to the hand—be true *epic* danger: a task neither
frivolously nor egotistically chosen, but which becomes portentous and
magical, sometimes preserving the sacred fires.

In March of 1896 Willa Cather had set down the poetic vision of art.
But like the strange illuminations of dream, it did not solve the problems
of the waking world. She still debated the two selves of art—body and
soul, order and spontaneous feeling. Because the practical need of expression was both a way to do it and hard work besides, she says more on
workmanship—"work poorly done is very seldom interesting," or a
"book that is never rewritten is seldom reread."[52] But like a reprise for
the Whitman she liked comes another note on poets—"poetic form seems
to be almost common property when compared to the rarity of poetic
feeling"—that "joyousness, that glad pleasure at the mere existence of
things . . . . to like the sun just because it shines." Yet she does hold to her
principle that art has an order of events; poetic feeling is called the *causal*
force, and after the "causal force" of feeling, then comes "expression,
expression, always expression." In May, a curious grace note: Burns sang
in the "spontaneous metres which the larks taught him"—a paradox, for
learned metres are not spontaneous. Was Burns then like Bernhardt, who
had under what seemed so spontaneous "a system as fixed and definite
as the laws of musical composition"? There were other complications.

"marvelous facility and craft, and it ill becomes folk with large ideals and scant technique
to belittle him," the writer concludes: "Technique is the base of every art, and the noblest
sentiment may be shipwrecked in the perilous voyage from the brain to the hand. A pretty
little girl, daintily posed in a studio, painted with a beautiful refinement of color, has as
good a right to exist in the catholic kingdom of art as the pale, primeval shades of Puvis de
Chavannes." Some of the same article was used in a signed piece in the *Courier*, August 10,
1901.

The hand-brain metaphor (though not "the voyage perilous") relates to Henry James's
"The Madonna of the Future" (1873), in which the artist Theobald speaks of transposing
his ideas for a masterpiece "into some brain that had the hand, the will"—his hand is
paralyzed; he has Raphael's brain, needs only his hand.

52. *Journal*, May 10, 1896. On F. Marion Crawford's boast that he never rewrote.

That same month she implied that one might have in him the possibilities of power but never be awakened to its full realization. "Expression" as art was a complicated organic thing.

Miscellaneous details of Willa Cather's observations on technique are scattered throughout her early writing. Most of these seem to bear on two ways by which an artist might bring disparate elements into a whole: simplification and contrast. To simplify was also to concentrate, unify, get rid of clutter—a need she may have first observed in some long evenings at the theatre. In reviews she often said that plays have too many characters, too many plots for their scope, too much stagecraft and not enough play. She quoted Dumas, who said that to write a play he "needed only four walls, four boards, two actors and one passion." For stories, it was Poe's "one vivid impression," and she admired the French writers' skill in grasping the heart of a situation, making details look after themselves, and "making one critical episode tell a life and analyze a character." Novels must have proportion and harmony, keeping the end in view. The other deliberate technique was contrast, which "rightly used, gives the tone and shading to every artistic creation. It is the laughter and reckless gaiety that make the first act of *Camille* so horribly pathetic, the seriousness of the poor inventor that makes *The Poor Relation* so funny."[53] In one of her last columns she describes what she had learned about Irving's staging of *Godefroi and Yolande*; a morbid play, it is saved by the gaiety and splendor of its setting—"that telling element of contrast."

Both simplification and contrast are basic in achieving a sense of body and form. Willa Cather often admired an actor or a writer for combining the two in some variation of paradox—achieving a mood or a characterization with greater intensity by first establishing the opposite effect. An actress in *Lady Windermere's Fan*, for example, heightened the sympathy for Mrs. Erlynne in the third act by making her revolting in the second. This was "the negative method, which means so much in any art."[54]

53. *Journal*, December 9, 1894. On Crane in *Brother John*.

54. This comment in Willa Cather's signed review of *Lady Windermere's Fan* (*Journal*, June 5, 1894) has relationships with both earlier and later drama criticism. In the student magazine *Lasso* for April 1, 1892 (Willa had been an associate editor the first semester and it is likely, though not sure, that she helped as drama critic that spring), the column of dramatic criticism said that Modjeska, who had been in Lincoln on March 23 in *As You like It*, used the "negative way of characterizing." In her signed column sent from Pittsburgh to the *Journal*, March 28, 1897, Miss Cather writes of Olga Nethersole, who "by a negative process . . . achieves a spiritual result." This, she says, is spirit born of the senses—what Browning does so often, and Bernhardt, and Sappho.

Also, by understatement, restraint, and controlled force one can accomplish more with less apparent effort, suggest by what is not said, and gain power or significance. She defined "ranting": "an actor only rants when he does not make the effort to control himself; after that effort is once made every inch that an actor's emotion overflows its barrier is his gain."[55] She was quite clearly aware of the need to anchor emotion in a formal way, and at the same time keep the creation warm-blooded and alive.

To mention these techniques at all is merely to suggest the directions Willa Cather had in mind in 1896. She said enough about simplification later in "The Novel Démeublé" to mark it indelibly as one of her critical principles. But according to the 1893–1896 articles, "that telling element of contrast" might be equally important in all of her work, both as a deliberate technique and as a natural, perhaps unconscious embodiment of other dualities. We might note some reasons.

One cannot read very far into Willa Cather's writing of these early years without feeling that he is in some Elizabethan landscape of paradox and the play of elements, or in the Romantic world of oppositions and identities. Part of it is style. She liked doubleness and alliterative play—in fact, she could do a Swinburnian swing with *élan*—and a considerable Catherian bite. Commenting on Bernhardt's supposed admiration for Julia Marlowe: "I should not exactly call it the yearning of the star for the moth, nor yet the passion of Heine's palm for the pine, but rather the longing of the range for the refrigerator."[56] But even here, in casual writing, and with some ungainly images, there is an instinctive pairing of the major dualities with conflicts within conflicts. No, it was not simply a matter of style; she thought this way, in doubleness and contrast. (Was it, then, a primitive way of invoking the whole by naming elemental opposites?) We recall the ambiguity of her response to both James and Whitman; the arguments of craft and power, the great and the common, the person and the artist. The turns and counterturns of style and theme are implicit in her vision.

More dramatic than any of the plays at the Funke or the Lansing are these alternations of symbols and desires, with their sometimes agonized encounters, moving openly across the pages. They are struck off in primary colors and elemental symbols of North and South, desert and sea, flame and snow; passion is given more body and color by the counter play of chill remoteness, the withdrawing voice, the secret light. Willa

55. *Journal*, March 25, 1894.
56. *Courier*, November 30, 1895.

[80]

Cather in those years was caught in that ancient pull of the gods, torn between the Dionysian and Apollonian forces of rapture and repose, release and containment. That conflict was at the very center of her creative will. She wanted both in one. Sometimes she achieved wholeness, as in the temporal-sacred metaphor of art, or even in the figure of the "voyage perilous," in which were joined both brain and hand, power and craft. But much more was unresolved. That story is harder to tell, for never again after this summer of 1896 would Willa Cather speak so frankly of what she desired, feared, and worshipped in the kingdom of art.

The critical writing of 1893–1896 not only becomes a part of Willa Cather's literary biography (she would say that no other kind is really important), but inevitably it changes the proportion, balance, emphasis, and interpretation of the body of her work, as if a curtain, opening a little wider on a stage, gave us windows and a landscape. The room is larger than we thought, the design grander. To adapt her phrase—the writer's craft seems infinitely more complex, individual, mysterious, inimitable; the power is more richly felt, like the touch of a living hand. In context, as these first critical statements join the imaginative action of her total art, it is possible to see some unifying principles. Three of the most illuminating might be called *continuity, absorption,* and *memory.*

That there is continuity of an unusual kind in Willa Cather's work has been noted—continuity as the simple recurrence of image and symbol and as the rising development I have elsewhere called incremental repetition. New materials or studies always seem to deepen the road or extend the design. Those who read the direct, personal writing of her first newspaper columns and reviews will be likely to wonder first of all about a new kind of continuity—if the girl of 1896 is still there when fame drops down, if somewhere in the later years one might hear an echo of that imperfect, young, and passionate voice. If the girl we know is writing those novels, we can read them again with primary knowledge, as from the beginning, before criticism.

Reading the interviews of Cather the novelist in the period after *O Pioneers!* is to meet an old friend after distance and separation. In 1913: "Art ought to simplify—that seems to me to be the whole process"; on the "intellectual excitement" of the artist's discoveries, feeling, and desires (is this the same as the "intellectual passion" of 1895?)—"it is the story of the man-eating tiger over again—no other adventure ever carries one quite so far." In 1915: "Writing is a personal problem and must be worked out in an individual way"; a writer must sacrifice extravagant language, "just as a great singer must sacrifice so many lovely lyrical things in herself to be a great interpreter"; no writer "without a good ear can write good fiction," and it is essential "to be sensitive to the beauty of language and speech"; "it is the longest distance in the world between the artist and the near-artist"; the artist "must strive untiringly while others eat and sleep and play"; and writers "must care vitally, fiercely, absurdly about the trickery and the arrangement of words, the beauty and power of phrases," but they must "get more out of life itself than out of anything written." In 1921, it is the same voice saying, "Art has nothing to do with smartness. Times may change, inventions may alter a world, but birth, love, maternity and death cannot be changed"; and in 1923, "Directly [a novelist] takes himself too seriously and begins for the alleged benefit of humanity an elaborate dissection of complexes, he evolves a book that is more ridiculous and tiresome than the most conventional cold cream girl novel of yesterday."[57]

Willa Cather's first convictions and principles of art were unchanged through the years, down to the fundamental religious metaphor of art. She had written in 1894 of the artist's special election ("The Lord has so revealed himself to man through music") and that music demands reverence and ceremony ("It is worth while to dress for a concert on the same principle that it is worth while to dress for one's wedding"). And half a lifetime later we read in a newspaper report of her lecture at the Institute of Modern Literature in Brunswick, Maine, on May 13, 1925, the following:

> Back in the beginning of art, when art was intertwined insepar-
> ably with religion there had to be great preparation for its cere-
> monials. The creature who hoped for an uplifted moment often
> endured privation in preparation for that moment. I do not think
> we should sit at home, in the clothes in which we have been working
> all day and turn on the radio to hear the Boston Symphony. I think
> something more than passivity should be expected of the recipient
> of any such bounty as Brahms.

57. For the 1913 and 1915 interviews, see Appendix IV. The last two quotations are from the report of a lecture to the Omaha Society of Fine Arts on October 29, 1921 ("Flays Nebraska Laws 'That Regulate Personal Life,'" Omaha *World-Herald*, October 31, 1921, p. 1), and an interview, "To-Day's Novels Give Much Hope to Miss Cather" (New York *World*, Paris dateline of May 20, [1923]).

Even as late as 1936 in "Escapism," like a deep chord of affirmation: "Religion and art spring from the same root and are close kin. Economics and art are strangers."[58]

Certain images or metaphors have particular emphasis through repetition. For example, at the end of "The Novel Démeublé" is that well known statement of a passage from Dumas which has become identified with Willa Cather's critical principles: "The elder Dumas enunciated a great principle when he said that to make a drama, a man needed one passion, and four walls."[59] This principle was first quoted directly in Willa Cather's Sunday column of February 9, 1896, as a part of a longer passage from Dumas in which he said that for effects, "I needed only four walls, four boards, two actors and one passion." Her comment adjusts the language to the writer: "All ye young writers of plays, there is a precept for you. 'I needed only four walls, four boards, two characters and one passion.'" With variations and different contexts, the Dumas principle is restated throughout the next twenty-six years. For example, reviewing Belasco's *The Wife* in the Pittsburgh *Leader*, November 23, 1897, she wrote, "Once, when the elder Dumas was asked what were the materials he required to make a play, he replied: 'A stage, four walls, two characters and one passion.'"[60] Some weeks later in her signed column sent from Pittsburgh to the Lincoln *Courier* (January 1, 1898) she expands the idea:

Dumas said only one thing was necessary to a great play—a great passion. I think Ibsen has extended that definition to a great passion or a great truth. Pinero, on the other hand, claims that only a great

58. The 1925 lecture at Brunswick, Maine, is reported in the *Christian Science Monitor*, Boston, May 15, 1925, p. 5. "Escapism," a letter to the *Commonweal* (1936), is reprinted in *Willa Cather on Writing*, with a Foreword by Stephen Tennant (New York: Alfred A. Knopf, 1962), pp. 18–29.

59. "The Novel Démeublé," *New Republic*, April 12, 1922, pp. 5–6. Reprinted in *Not Under Forty* (New York: Alfred A. Knopf, 1936), pp. 43–51.

60. Belasco is several times associated with the Dumas principle in Willa Cather's writing. Long before she quoted it in 1896, she said in a review of Belasco's *The Charity Ball* (January 6, 1895) that perhaps there will be in America a playwright "who will take one living, fearless passion" and work it through, as the French have done. The review of *The Wife* in 1897 combines the Dumas material with the substance of a longer criticism of Belasco's plays she wrote in 1895 (see page 238), and draws in the element of the "over-furnished" stage—or novel. After mentioning "A stage, four walls, two characters and one passion," she says, "If Mr. Belasco had been limited to such slender resources, I fear he would never have written plays at all. No man needs so many accessories, so many irrelevant characters, so many effects of stage carpentry."

problem is essential. One thing is certain, if a play is truly great, if it appeals to those higher sensibilities which are only roused by the *fortissimo* passages of life, if it is to move one like poetry or music, it must have at least the character who is submerged, absorbed by and identified with some great emotion or purpose.

And again in the *Courier* for August 10, 1901, reviewing Eden Phillpotts' *Sons of the Morning* (signed "Willa Sibert Cather"): "Old Dumas said that to make a play he needed but four walls, two people and one passion." But these are enough examples to show the pattern and that "Old Dumas," with his wilderness of romance, was in fact the first architect of the novel démeublé.

Sometimes we find in 1893–1896 the seeds of later work. In 1896 did the newspaper account of Baron Constantine de Grimm, which appeared in May, suggest the character of the Count de Koch in "The Count of Crow's Nest," a story published in September? Both the Baron and the Count were Europeans in America, had known royalty, and had won the iron cross on the field of Gravelotte.[61] Or, because we learn that Willa Cather knew and quoted certain books and writers, can we find in them some other links in the creative process? She quoted at length from Daudet's *Thirty Years in Paris*. If she liked this volume of recollections, no doubt she read others, and some passages stayed with her—lines like his description of Provence (Willa Cather called it "Daudet's country" when she was there in 1902) as the South of platforms and plumes; its people family-loving, tradition-ridden, inheriting from the Orient loyalty to the clan or tribe; "the cajoling, cunning South," eloquent, luminous, with "those glaring Provencal roads, bordered with tall reeds, covered with hot, snow-white, crackling dust." From *Notes on Life*, did she somehow carry over to the unfurnished room of "The Novel Démeublé" the comment by Daudet: "The French language to be compared to an old salon: the pieces of furniture are the words"? Or to her interpretation of *Othello*, his note: "Othello is not a jealous man—he is ingenuous, a passionate primitive"? And this paragraph: "Something fine to make out of 'War.' State of mind of a young man of the Second Empire, whose life, day in and day out, left no room for upward strivings, knew no standard of duty. Illuminated suddenly, he understood life, one long night of guard, while great flames mounted silently over the woods

61. On Baron de Grimm: *Journal*, May 3, 1896. "The Count of Crow's Nest" appeared in the *Home Monthly*, September and October, 1896 (*CSF*, 449 ff.)

of Malmaison."[62] Surely Daudet had something to do with *One of Ours*.

To understand Willa Cather we will have to study the French Romantics. For there is also George Sand. Her novel *Antonia*, I think, gives an additional dimension, even illumination, to Willa Cather's *My Ántonia*. George Sand's book[63] is in part about an old horticulturalist, Antoine Thierry, who wants to develop a lily surpassing all others, to be named *Antonia Thierrii*. One day he finds that an unknown bulb had put forth sturdy shoots; when a bud opens, it displays "a corolla soft as satin, of an incomparable sheeny white, with bright red stripes." This will be his lily—but before it can be christened, the stalk is broken by someone else in a careless, impassioned act and pushed back into the earth. A few months later, Monsieur Antoine gathers a group of people around a large table, in the center of which is a tall object, "concealed under a great bell of white paper." This, he says, is at last the incomparable lily— exceeding all others in size, fragrance, and splendor. It is his "*individual*." The paper is raised: the *Antonia Thierrii* stands like a miracle—fresh and blooming. A second shoot had blossomed into a flower more beautiful than the first. Quite aside from the name there is something singularly right in using the *Antonia Thierrii* as a symbol for Ántonia's earthiness, endurance after defeat, and creative glory—this rooted bulb growing in spite of neglect and destruction to great beauty, placed in the center of a circle of people, and given a special name. There is even more personal evidence. When *My Ántonia* appeared in 1918, Elizabeth Shepley Sergeant recalled that in the spring of 1916, when they were talking of form and technique in the novel, Willa Cather had set a Taormina jar filled with orange-brown flowers "in the middle of a bare, round, antique table" and said, "I want my new heroine to be like this—like a rare object in the middle of a table, which one may examine from all sides."[64]

Seeds, roots, organic growth—these are all particularly evident in Willa Cather's body of work; for it is a body, having all the mysteries of any life but with also the visible connections and evolvements. We see

---

62. The Daudet passages may be found in an English translation, *Novels, Romances and Writings of Alphonse Daudet* (New York: Fred DeFau & Company, 1899, 1900), VIII, *Memories of a Man of Letters*, pp. 34, 38; *Notes on Life*, pp. 183, 227, 245.

63. The following passages may be found in George Sand, *Antonia*, translated by George Burnham Ives (Philadelphia: George Barrie & Son, 1901), esp. pp. 46, 51, 75–76, 284–285. Several translations were available earlier.

64. *Willa Cather: A Memoir*, pp. 138–140. As another footnote: Could the Thierry family have anything to do with the Thierault family associated with Godfrey St. Peter in *The Professor's House*?

this if we place *The Song of the Lark* in a new country, the kingdom of art as Willa Cather described it before 1896. *The Song of the Lark* grew out of those first principles of art, all of the elements dramatized or vivified in the body of an imaginative work. Although many circumstances in the book are taken from the career of Olive Fremstad (as well as from the early life of the author herself), the singer Thea Kronborg is not the portrait of any individual. She is years of performers whom Willa Cather heard or whose art she studied—Melba, Nordica, Helena von Doenhoff, Zélie de Lussan, Marie Tavary, Margaret Mather, Bernhardt, Rachel— but she is even more the embodiment of a personal belief about the way of art. The design of Thea Kronborg had been set down twenty years before the book. Perhaps the futility of assigning fictional characters their prototypes in the real world has never been better illustrated.

 The Song of the Lark is filled from first to last with details and restatements of the material in Willa Cather's 1893–1896 writing, including the themes she stated in her 1932 Preface: "a young girl's awakening to something beautiful," the paling of the personal life "as the imaginative life becomes richer," and the escape from commonness.[65] I can show here only the most important relationships with the kingdom of art: the opening motifs of myth and metaphor, and the central idea of art as creation and quickening, as a living thing of body and passion.

 From the beginning *The Song of the Lark* has a mythic aura, as if to make us at least look toward the gods. "Kronborg" is a Scandinavian name, but does it not also suggest Kronos (or Saturn), ruler of the elder gods and king of the Golden Age of the Titans? "Thea" is identified in Lemprière as the daughter of Uranus (the most ancient of all gods) and Terra. In Keats's *Hyperion* Thea is called the "tender spouse of gold Hyperion" (l. 45), the sun god of the Titans. That Thea's first teacher and motivator is named Wunsch deliberately places the story in Teutonic myth as well as Greek. Wunsch is the god Wish or Desire, defined by Carlyle in *Heroes and Hero Worship*, and more completely in Grimm as "god of bliss and love, who wishes, wills and brings good to men," who creates and imagines: "There is about Wish something inward, uttered from within."[66] Professor Wunsch thinks of his hopes for Thea: "It was

---

65. *The Song of the Lark* (Boston: Houghton Mifflin Company, 1963), pp. v–vi. I have used this edition—the 1937 revised form of the novel—unless otherwise stated. Hereafter, pagination will be given in parentheses in the text whenever possible.

66. Jacob Grimm, *Teutonic Mythology*, translated from the fourth edition by James Steven Stallybrass, 4 vols., IV (London: George Bell and Sons, 1883), 1328, 1330.

long since he had wished anything or desired anything beyond the necessities of the body," but now "he was tempted to hope for another" (37). He says to Thea, "There is only one big thing—desire" (95). The music Wunsch gives to Thea as a special sign of his hope for her is from Gluck's *Orpheus and Eurydice*.

The primary metaphors and images developed through Willa Cather's 1893–1896 articles include Dumas' "four walls and a passion," or the self with its powers of genius and its limitations and confinement; the mythic journey, which begins in the service of the god in the kingdom of art and has the bodily involvement of "the voyage perilous" from the brain to the hand; and success in terms of awakening and quickening, and also conquering by opening gates and breaking barriers. All of these thematic metaphors are stated in the opening chapters of *The Song of the Lark*; they are then used in three key passages which represent the stages of Thea's awakening.

Themes of awakening and movement are suggested by Wunsch's teaching and the trip outside Moonstone that Ray Kennedy arranges for Thea and her mother. Then we see Kennedy's notebook of "Impressions," whose pages "were like a battlefield; the labouring author had fallen back from metaphor after metaphor, abandoned position after position." This was the "treacherous business of recording impressions, in which the material you were so full of vanished mysteriously under your striving hand"(146). But it is Ray Kennedy whose desire for Thea's future is fulfilled, his death the instrument of her beginning in art. The periods of her development are marked symbolically in the scenes of her room in moonlight, of Panther Canyon, and of the stage and her triumph as Sieglinde. These scenes of awakening have several things in common: each one has a physical confinement (the room, the canyon, the stage); each is an extension of Thea's powers, a quickening; each has a movement or journey outward; each has both mythic overtones and deep physical involvements.

The first passage is tentative, desire in its first motion. When Thea lies on the floor of her childhood room on summer moonlight nights in Moonstone her body pulses "with ardour and anticipation"—life seeming to rush in upon her through the window. Actually the movement and power come from within, says the author, for every work of art was once contained "in some youthful body." On such nights, Thea learned "the thing that old Dumas meant when he told the Romanticists that to make a drama he needed but one passion and four walls" (177). Immediately after the passage we are told of Ray Kennedy's death, and the events of the story move outward and away.

In Panther Canyon, Thea's awakening is to a sense of history and personal heroism, a physical involvement (animal and wild, as the name of the canyon suggests) with the ancient people, the primitive past, all elemental things, and man's passion to endure and create. She finds music in "a sensuous form," thinking becomes sustained sensation, identity with lizards, stones, the sound of cicadas, the simple primitive force of life: sensation first, then attitudes of body, then passion. The eagle—bird of Jupiter and Odin—sails into the canyon and mounts "until his plumage was so steeped in light that he looked like a golden bird." Thea salutes it —"endeavour, achievement, desire" (398–399). And then there is the journey upward and outward as Fred (like Orpheus) leads her out of the canyon through the storm and darkness.[67]

A transitional scene with Thea and Fred in Central Park some ten years later links Thea again with primitive, animal forces.[68] She is in furs "like some rich-pelted animal, with warm blood, that had run in out of the woods." In this passage, the original uncut version of the book (1915) clearly identifies the stage with the canyon and Thea with the panther: Fred observes that she is as much at home on the stage as in Panther Canyon—"as if you'd just been let out of a cage."[69] When Fred asks if she didn't get some of her ideas there, Thea answers, "For heroic parts, at least." Also omitted in the 1937 revised edition is her clarifying comment that the ancient people must have been reserved, somber, "with only a muscular language, all their movements for a purpose; simple, strong, as if they were dealing with fate bare-handed." Then it is that she says she learned in the canyon the hardness of human life— "And you can't know it with your mind. You have to realize it in your body, somehow; deep. It's an animal sort of feeling."

When Thea sings in *Die Walküre*[70] her former teacher Harsanyi

67. In Gluck's opera, the gods take pity on Orpheus at last and permit him to have his Eurydice.

68. The quotations in this paragraph are from *The Song of the Lark* (Boston and New York: Houghton Mifflin Company, 1915), pp. 462–463.

69. The deliberate identification of Thea and the panther may be related to an early description of Rachel. George Henry Lewes, in *On Actors and the Art of Acting* (London: Smith, Elder & Co., 1875), begins his chapter on Rachel with the following: "Rachel was the panther of the stage; with a panther's terrible beauty and undulating grace she moved and stood, glared and sprang. There always seemed something not human about her. She seemed made of different clay from her fellows—beautiful but not loveable" (p. 23).

70. Subsequent quotations in the paragraph are from the 1937 version of *The Song of the Lark* (see note 65, above), pp. 567–568, 571.

watches, "his one yellow eye rolling restlessly and shining like a tiger's in the dark." Then, in the moonlight, her voice like the spring "blossomed into memories and prophecies." Thea as Sieglinde rises "into the hardier feeling of action and daring," to "strength and hero-blood," and to victory. The house applauds savagely, fiercely. When Harsanyi is asked her secret, he says, "Her secret?... passion. That is all." Passion—and Harsanyi meant just what he said. Not something safely abstract, but emotion and power; something vibrant, yearning, physically alive. As Willa Cather said a hundred times in her early articles, it was that old fire and intensity, primitive, physical. That was the point of the mythic awakening in Panther Canyon, to become one with nature and the deepest sense of life. The description of Thea's success uses the other familiar metaphors: she "came into full possession," "entered into the inheritance." Before, she could not break through, but now "the closed roads opened, the gates dropped." The moment is described as if to identify with the writer (who creates from the brain to the hand): "What she had so often tried to reach lay under her hand. She had only to touch an idea to make it live." Her body was "absolutely the instrument of her idea.... All that deep-rooted vitality flowered in her voice, her face, in her very finger-tips. She felt like a tree bursting into bloom."[71]

In these ways Willa Cather dramatized the life of art. If *The Song of the Lark* is primarily directed to power—the primitive, physical, and emotional involvements of art—it is craft which placed these elements in the marvelously related sequence of scenes, metaphors, and incremental repetition.

By the 1930's Willa Cather was a past master of adjusting style to subject and audience (this was, after all, implicit in the concept of "expression"). So when we recognize in her later writing some familiar details, symbols, and attitudes—the old passion with a new grace—we may give them a different emphasis. For example, since there has been a critical consensus that *Madame Bovary* was Willa Cather's chief delight and first influence, it is interesting to turn again to "A Chance Meeting" and hear the girl of 1896 come vibrantly through the lines. As Miss Cather tells the story of her meeting with Madame Grout, Flaubert's niece, she

71. Cf. Miss Cather's 1896 versions of "the closed roads opened, the gates dropped": The girl in Henry James's *The Tragic Muse* "beats and beats upon those brazen doors that guard the unapproachable until one fine morning she beats them down and comes into her kingdom, the kingdom of unborn beauty that is to live through her" (see page 361). Of Mary Anderson: "There was one gate between her and the kingdom of unattainable things that was never broken down" (see page 157).

evades answering when the Frenchwoman asks if she does not like *Madame Bovary* best. Later in the sketch she writes that it is *Salammbô* which "is the book of Flaubert I like best. I like him in those great reconstructions of the remote and cruel past." That night the full moon is the moon of *Salammbô*. She then recalls how young readers (like herself) begin with Balzac when they first read the French writers (coming on them accidentally and not in classes). And when they try *Madame Bovary*, "they resent the change of tone; they miss the glow, the ardour, the temperament." She speaks then of the time one "first began to sense the things which Flaubert stood for, to admire (almost against one's will) that peculiar integrity of language and vision, that coldness which, in him, is somehow noble—"[72] *Almost against one's will*—and you recall the divisions and pulls against her will in those early James and Whitman pieces of 1895–1896.

The presence of the young Willa Cather and her world is felt even more strongly in her essay of the early 1930's on Thomas Mann's *Joseph and His Brothers*. In only the first few pages we have these reminders: a description of *Salammbô* again ("horrors and splendours"), a reminder of legends from the most ancient periods of life, the "dreamy indefiniteness" and deliberate slow tempo of pastoral life as compared with "this age of blinding speed and shattering sound" (in 1896 we were feverish, pitched too high), phrases like "the strong feeling under the strong hand" and the "undecipherable riddle of the old legends," songs we sang in Sunday school, the effect of the King James Bible on English prose, a dig at the routine scholar and his "cheerless road of reference reading." One comment on the deep-rooted, primary quality of Mann's use of the great past of literary and human consciousness is a very nearly exact description of her own position in 1896, and when she began to write. We begin the book, she says, "with the great imaginings and the great imaginators already in our minds—we are dyed through and through with them."[73]

Of great significance, I think, are the correspondences between the first things Willa Cather wrote and some of the last. In one of her most poetic and impassioned essays of the early years, an article on *Hamlet* in the fall of 1895, she describes the people in the wilderness of Sinai, "journeying to an undiscovered country"; in their camp was a tabernacle, with a court inside for the priests to perform holy offices, and within it another chamber "where only the high priest might enter, who carried

72. "A Chance Meeting" (1933), in *Not Under Forty*, pp. 17–18, 22–25.
73. "'Joseph and His Brothers,'" in *Not Under Forty*, pp. 96–103.

God's fire in his censer." This she parallels with her own people, journeying into something better but dim and undefined, beyond the peaks of Sinai: "And with us we carry all that has been most worthy in our race, the memory and work of the great." Our holy fire is *Hamlet*. After more than thirty-five years, *Shadows on the Rock* (1931) shows another people in the wilderness, preserving, as Cécile's mother had done, "a feeling about life that had come down to her through so many centuries and that she had brought with her across the wastes of obliterating, brutal ocean. The sense of 'our way.'" Later in the book, recalling Aeneas, "*Inferretque deos Latio*. When an adventurer carries his gods with him into a remote and savage country, the colony he founds will, from the beginning, have graces, traditions, riches of the mind and spirit."[74] Just after the publication of *Shadows on the Rock*, Willa Cather commented on the book in a way that seals the link between it and the *Hamlet* essay: "Those people brought a kind of French culture there and somehow kept it alive on that rock, sheltered it and tended it and on occasion died for it, as if it really were a sacred fire."[75] God's fire in the wilderness—from the Children of Israel to the English "memory and work of the great" to French culture or "feeling about life"—this concept of preserving through history some sacred fire, of carrying it through ocean and savage wilderness, is again the quest and the voyage perilous. For Willa Cather it was an absolute, lifelong vision.

Something like the commitment to preserve the sacred fire is a vow both stated and implicit in the early writing, a vow of belief and delight in the cosmic movements—the exquisite order of the heavens, the cycles of birth and death, hard fate and eternal beauty. These are the most ancient of all ways, and the most youthful. Once in the winter of 1896 she wrote about the renewal of summer, "the reckless old pagan that she is," when "the whole glittering green world shouts, 'Evoe, evoe'; the old cry that calls youth to life." And another universal promise: "nor while there is June will the daughters of the sea foam be forgotten." The daughters of the sea foam—Venus, Aphrodite, the immortal conception. At the end of her career we come to Willa Cather's story "Before Breakfast."[76] And there, after whatever perilous voyages to all those islands of morning and beginnings, there she is, the daughter of the sea

74. *Shadows on the Rock* (New York: Alfred A. Knopf, 1931), pp. 25, 98.

75. "On *Shadows on the Rock*" (Letter to Governor Wilbur Cross, *Saturday Review of Literature*, October 17, 1931), in *Willa Cather on Writing*, p. 16.

76. Published posthumously in *The Old Beauty and Others* (New York: Alfred A. Knopf, 1948), pp. 141-166.

foam, like a sign to old Henry Grenfell, watching from the headland. Below at the water's edge, a girl in a pink bathing suit sheds her grey and white robe (the figure described with some humor as if she really were Venus-on-the-halfshell), swims into the cold summer sea to a rock, and out of the sea again. In the bright shock of life re-enacted, Henry Grenfell sees some absolute sense in it all—the planetary movements, geologic ages, illimitable time, and one man's imperfect moment. This was a pagan sacrament, perhaps, but as in the ordered church, taken before breakfast. As a summary story (or perhaps poem), with its intricate weaving of symbol and fact, "Before Breakfast" is one of the most remarkable things Willa Cather wrote: at the end, a re-affirmation of the beginning.

In the process of absorption, what is plainly on the surface and directly stated in the early writing is gradually taken into the substance of new work until it can no longer be easily identified. Conversely, what has been only an undercurrent rises to clear definition. The articles of 1893–1896 can be viewed as the raw material of the later fiction, but it is indeed a wilderness of allusion, reference, the combination of unexpected elements. (Although most of its references skim along in full sight, already certain uses—of the Bible and myth, for example—are subtle, assuming other forms.) In some of the early stories (even those in *The Troll Garden* in 1905), Willa Cather transfers this body of comment to function thematically, but the material is very nearly plucked from the articles whole. Reading "The Count of Crow's Nest" (1896) or "Eric Hermannson's Soul" (1900), one may think he is still in the familiar world of the newspaper columns.

Because of her *Journal* experience, Willa Cather, unlike most beginning writers, was used to handling a kaleidoscope of reference, and she continued to work with it in fiction, mingling names, references to books, characters, paraphrased quotations, sudden unexplained phrases, in a glittering and allusive texture. As a matter of fact, at the turn of the century she was using—though irregularly—the same technique that Pound and Eliot used in poetry a dozen years later. Furthermore, as one is able to study the early material and the process of its absorption into the fiction, it becomes increasingly clear that in the later writing a body of reference and allusion still exists, molded into a style so compact and unobtrusive that on one level, at least, nothing is outside the work. What would happen if Miss Cather's writing were given the same kind of textual attention that has been given to Eliot, Pound, and Joyce I can at this point only conjecture. For although she disliked explanations and analysis and wanted the experience of literature to be absolute and real (she would not think that conscious recognition of allusions would always be necessary), Willa Cather also liked symbols, magic, suggestion, and myth. There is enough evidence to suggest that she did try some complex and subtle designs in her fiction, usually giving clues in names, places, details, quotations. No allusions were irrelevant. It was not a puzzle (though she was not averse to games) but a way of simplification and concentration. As she became more skilled in handling references and symbols, the early material became understated, absorbed, so smoothly integrated that *The Waste Land*, by comparison, is indeed rough terrain. To illustrate this process of absorption, I can trace in part two major themes which recur in the 1893–1896 critical writing: the historic cycles of dying civilizations and barbaric conquest, and the myth of Endymion and Diana.

By the time she put together *The Troll Garden*, Willa Cather was skilled enough in construction and allusion so that she might expect the two epigraphs to suggest its theme. The lines from Christina Rossetti's "The Goblin Market" gave little trouble, but the key epigraph (the book's title came from it) was merely signed "Charles Kingsley," and according to published comment on the book, no one placed it in the context of its source—the first chapter ("The Forest Children") of Kingsley's *The Roman and the Teuton*, given in Appendix III. The Trolls in their fairy palace are the Romans—inside the garden and the palace, rich, busy, experienced, materialistic, ruthless; the Forest Children are the Teutons or Barbarians—outside in nature, strong, barbaric, innocent, and desiring the wonders of the Trolls. When the Forest Children enter the realm of the Trolls, some are lost forever, others return to the forest. Eventually the Children conquer the Trolls. How important this idea was to the young Willa Cather we could not know until, reading her first pieces, we find numerous variations of the theme, especially during her last year in Nebraska. In the spring of 1895 she discusses over-refinement in families, who go back "to first principles by the lightning express" when the tiger breaks out "in the hot blood of some descendant." In November there is a nearly explicit statement of the Roman-Barbarian conflict: When the Roman world became corrupt, then the barbarian races came down "to destroy and renew," bringing "the snows of the Danube to cool the heated blood of the south, and the great hammer of

Thor to crush the defiled altars of Aphrodite into dust." She linked the over-intellectualization of man and all artificialities to the decadence of Rome: Perhaps eventually "the savage strength of the Slav or the Bushmen will come upon us and will burn our psychologies and carry us away into captivity and make us dress the vines and plow the earth and teach us that after all nature is best." In the spring of 1896 she is still speaking of "the days of the final decadence of the Roman empire, when old things, outworn and corrupt, were giving place to new, when nature was revenging herself." Throughout her comments on this theme, there is a kind of delight in the barbarian, in savage strength and the dramatic movements of conquest and decay throughout history. In her favorite *Salammbô*, Carthage did withstand the Barbarians; but the wild people of the North (Goths, Saxons, Teutons) were more nearly her own, and they may have had an even deeper, more primitive fascination. If she also believed in Rome, it was the Rome which was strong and powerful and creative. The truth of history was that one does fall from original strength and goodness (as one form of primitivism asserts), and inevitably forces and civilizations exchange positions. For this, the conflict of the Forest Children and the Trolls is symbolic.

Even as she was writing about the theme of Rome and the Barbarians in her newspaper columns, Willa Cather used it in a story, "On the Divide," published in January, 1896. Canute Canuteson, a huge, silent, lonely Norseman on the prairie, captures and carries away the teasing girl he wanted to marry: "even as his bearded barbarian ancestors took the fair frivolous women of the South in their hairy arms and bore them down to their war ships." The soul gets weary of conventions, and "with a single stroke shatters the civilized lies," the "strong arm reaches out and takes by force what it cannot win by cunning." In a more complex way, the material is used in "Eric Hermannson's Soul" (1900). Here the West is clearly the land of the Forest Children in the best sense of primitive reality. Margaret Elliot comes from the effete life of the city and the East to have a brief encounter with the force and passion of nature. Eric is "a giant barbarian" whose "arm could have thrown Thor's hammer out in the cornfields yonder." In Margaret's presence "he felt as the Goths before the white marbles in the Roman Capitol, not knowing whether they were men or gods . . . . Away from her, he longed to strike out with his arms, and take and hold." The parallels with the early critical statements are clear: feeling, action, and elemental truth are contrasted with a world of lesser reality. A passage from the April 28, 1895 column (slightly revised) is used in the story: Nature says, "I am here still, at the bottom of things, warming the roots of life; you cannot starve me nor tame me nor thwart me; I made the world, I rule it, and I am its destiny." Margaret, "on a windmill tower at the world's end with a giant barbarian, heard that cry."[77]

The conflict of Teuton and Roman also explains Willa Cather's comment in her travel article on Arles and Provence in 1902. She feels the presence of Rome still in the land and the look of the people (the women who used to make vows to Venus to gain their beauty, the children who have the old clear-cut Roman profiles). But Rome's destiny, out of its "self-devouring and suicidal vastness," was also the doom of its descendants, those Latin races in all their beauty who "must wither before the cold wind from the north, as their mothers did long ago.... one knows that this people face toward the setting, not the rising sun."[78]

This chain of reference and fictional use leads directly to *The Troll Garden* in 1905. To Kingsley's allegory of Trolls and Forest Children are added the "poison fruit" of "The Goblin Market" and the idea of contrasting double selves (one sister tastes and the other one saves). In the nature of things, poison and corruption are built into the magic, and though the cycles may be inevitable, they can be qualified by the integrity of those who refuse the forbidden fruit, or saved by those who sacrifice and love. The stories of *The Troll Garden*, as E. K. Brown observed in his analysis of the industrious Trolls and the evil-working Goblins, are clearly arranged in alternation and contrast.[79] I would suggest a slightly different symbolism: By the direction of the epigraph and the title of the book, we must consider the basic contrasts to be the Trolls inside and the Forest Children outside, the Romans and the Barbarians, Palace-Garden and Wood-Country, and the cyclic movements of decaying civilization and reconquering nature. Playing through these primary contrasts and alternations are the extensions of the theme to the less literal innocence and experience, those who have and those who desire. For unlike the contrast in "Eric Hermannson's Soul," the values in *The Troll Garden* are not simply the city-East and the country-West; the greedy and insensitive are everywhere, and even in art there are both Trolls and Forest Children (the over-refined versus the genuine, the real desire versus the false). In brief, *The Troll Garden* is about corruption, the distortion of

77. "On the Divide," *CSF*, pp. 493 ff.; "Eric Hermannson's Soul," *CSF*, pp. 359 ff.
78. *Journal*, October 19, 1902, p. 9.
79. Brown, *Willa Cather*, pp. 113 ff.

values; in every human sense there may be goblin fruit to desire, and Trolls who guard their riches. All of these themes are mingled with considerable complexity in *The Troll Garden*, within the stories and through the arrangement.

Although it is not appropriate here to discuss the details of structure and interpretation of *The Troll Garden*, it is important to note that in the context of the 1893–1896 articles and the more plainly stated contrasts of "On the Divide" and "Eric Hermannson's Soul," Willa Cather's first book of short stories has absorbed the original pattern and at the same time evolved some new themes from Kingsley and Rossetti. Remembering, too, her habits of allegory and contrasting statement (love and hate, North and South); her interest in rituals, hierarchies, and degrees; her awareness of the many dualities of human life; and her frequent mention of contrast as a deliberate technique—it is easy to believe that whatever design seems to be there was put there by the author. For example, in "On the Divide" one curious detail is that Canute has made rude carvings in horizontal panels on window sills and boards, all designs of a Dance of Death in formal symbolic absolutes: "the men were always grave and were either toiling or praying, while the devils were always smiling and dancing." The carving, we can see, is a medieval Gothic motif that links the story with that earlier Barbarian world. It is also the author's deliberate composition of opposing forces into a formal, linear design.

One way to look at the *Troll Garden* stories[80] is to arrange them in a similar composition of seven panels (a variation of the septenary) in which successive stories are associated and contrasted, and in which several combinations of the figures are possible. To give one example only: "'A Death in the Desert'" might be considered the central panel (a story with all of the themes from both Rossetti and Kingsley and something, too, from the Dance of Death). On either side the stories fall into related but contrasting pairs: "The Garden Lodge" and "The Marriage of Phaedra" (on marriages, with women in different relationships to the work of an absent artist), "The Sculptor's Funeral" and "A Wagner Matinee" (exactly reverse movements between life and sterility). The opening and closing stories, "Flavia and Her Artists" and "Paul's Case" (the first so obviously false desire and the other a genuine if excessive feeling for art)—these two particularly suggest contrast and design.

"Flavia and Her Artists" has an air of allegory, as if it were the set

80. The text of *The Troll Garden* used here is that of *CSF*. Quotations in the following paragraphs are from "Flavia and Her Artists," pp. 149 ff.; and "Paul's Case," pp. 243 ff.

piece and presentation. The time is 1900 and the place Westchester, but the story is permeated with allusions to the Rome of the Flavian emperors, and with its atmosphere. Flavia's "House of Song," which is her "temple to the gods of Victory, a sort of triumphal arch," might be a sybaritic villa in the Sabine Hills, with its polyglot swarm of servants (six languages spoken in the kitchen) and its assortment of pampered artist-guests (among them the epigrammatic M. Martel—to remind us of Martial?). And there are ironic allusions to "the Mother of the Gracchi," and, at the disastrous end, to the Roman general Caius Marius who was comforted for his own vicissitudes when he sat among the ruins of Carthage.

In "Paul's Case" the theme of Troll Garden and Palace is specifically restated. Paul is a Forest Child who desires things rare and strange, but to excess and with no one to help him (as did the sister in "The Goblin Market" and the husband of Flavia). When he goes to the Troll Garden of New York to take for himself, all around him are creatures hot for pleasure, and on every side "towered the glaring affirmation of the omnipotence of wealth." In his room he surrounds himself with warmth and flowers, covers himself with a Roman blanket. He wanders through rooms and corridors of the hotel "as though he were exploring the chambers of an enchanted palace, built and peopled for him alone." His last moments are in the country. (Does the snow he picks up to cool his mouth come from the snows of the Danube which the Barbarians brought to cool the heated blood of the South?) As always, it is nature in her inexorable way which will not be cheated. The last statement of "Paul's Case" involves not only the eternal cyclic rise and fall, interchange, and contrast of nature and man, but also the *idea* of structure and pattern: with his death before an oncoming locomotive, "Paul dropped back into the immense design of things." When we look again at the first story of *The Troll Garden* and read the first sentence, "As the train neared Tarrytown ...," the suggestion of design is inescapable.

The second example of absorption is the career of the moon-myth. One of the most deeply affective and complex symbols in Willa Cather's writing, the moon is the goddess Diana, the desire of Endymion, the queen of witches, the cat-goddess, or the pagan goddess of all motion. Like any writer who uses myth organically, Willa Cather had some habitual emotional values for particular stories or figures, and by the invocation of a name could gather in the whole body of associations. The moon is generally seen as some high, illimitable beauty; the sign of yearning and desire; the radiant or mysterious illumination of darkness; and the sign also of the voyage perilous (anyone can dream *Endymion* but only the artist can create it).[81] In the 1893–1896 writing, however, she refers often enough to three literary sources of moon symbolism to suggest that their individual qualities might be important. We assume the moon of romance in *Romeo and Juliet*; in addition there were Keats's *Endymion*, Heine's *The Gods in Exile*, and Flaubert's *Salammbô*. From the overt and plainly marked allusions in the early years, we can see how the elements blend and are absorbed into the whole texture of the work.

The Diana-moon (or Cynthia) of Keats's *Endymion* is loved by the enchanted shepherd youth who goes on a perilous quest through underworld and heavens to find her. The moon in Keats signifies desire, yearning, and magic. She is also the sign of an impossible ideal, for Endymion could not have Diana in her own eternity. But even the gesture of yearning and the journey itself are links with the goddess. It was in this sense that Willa Cather quoted Stevenson, "Although the moon should have nothing to say to Endymion, although he should settle down with Audrey and feed pigs, do you not think he would move with a better grace and cherish higher thoughts to the end?" This idea stayed with her, and she paraphrased it in several later reviews and articles.

While Keats's treatment mythologizes the self, Heine's *The Gods in Exile* humanizes the divinities. Heine's account places them on earth after Christianity, often in disguise to hide from persecution. They travel the usual roads, almost inseparable from man, and though they still have some of the old power it often becomes demonic. The gods in exile are signs of the passing of former beliefs ("Once we believed in the moon, but now we believe in it no longer," as Heine quotes the saying of an old man in Greenland)[82] and the remnants of old pagan beauty destroyed by the Christian's gloomy zeal for destruction. *The Gods in Exile*, like *The Roman and the Teuton*, suggests the periodic rise and fall of human

81. Since *The Song of the Lark* was also about the voyage perilous, we might note that it has a striking series of moon images: The town is called Moonstone; the scenes of desire and fulfillment in Thea's childhood room and finally on the stage are in moonlight; she sings at the Mexican dance in bright moonlight, with moonflowers of "an unearthly white" blooming on the vine and the moon a "great pale flower in the sky" (291–292); in Panther Canyon Thea recalls the moonflowers—"it was as if she had been that vine and had opened up in white flowers every night" (374). The last metaphor in the scene on the stage is another example of the interwoven image: As she sang Sieglinde, Thea's vitality "flowered," she "felt like a tree bursting into bloom" (571).

82. *The Gods in Exile*, in *The Works of Heinrich Heine*, translated by Charles Godfrey Leland, Vol. VI, *Germany* (London: William Heinemann, 1892), p. 296.

and divine orders. The loss of the gods is linked to the passing of the Hellenic world of serene, less fearful art.

We have observed that Flaubert's *Salammbô* had a lifelong meaning for Willa Cather. If she still thought of that moon of Carthage when she wrote "A Chance Meeting," it had a special power. Flaubert's moon is cosmic. "The moon was rising just above the waves"[83]—so begins the third chapter of his novel, and Salammbô herself ascends to the terrace of her palace to perform the rituals of the night. She looks at the polar star, salutes the four points of heaven, and prays with all the names of the goddess. Then, "By the hidden symbols,—by the resounding sistra,—by the furrows of the earth,—by the eternal silence and by the eternal fruitfulness,—mistress of the gloomy sea and of the azure shores, O Queen of the watery world, all hail!" She later salutes the moon as goddess of all forces, causing the winds and rain, and "According as thou dost wax and wane the eyes of cats and spots of panthers lengthen or grow short. . . . Thou formest the pearls at the bottom of the sea!" She is the causer of all things, fertility and decay. She is fearful and beautiful—"white, gentle, luminous, immaculate, helping, purifying, serene!"—but also a terrible mistress whose eyes can "devour the stones of buildings . . . ." She changes form, slender and curved "like a mastless galley," then a shepherd keeping his flock, or "Shining and round, thou dost graze the mountain-tops like the wheel of a chariot."

In the early stories[84] as in the first articles, moon references are direct and usually in single aspects. The story of Diana and Actaeon is mentioned in "The Treasure of Far Island" (1902) as Douglass, watching Margie, thinks how "Diana's women sped after the stag down the slopes of Ida, with shouting and bright spear." Later on Far Island, "out of the east rose the same moon that has glorified all the romances of the world." The moon also shone in "Eric Hermannson's Soul," full in the moment of deepest longing and realization. But in "The Enchanted Bluff" (1909) there is the real moon of *Salammbô*, more fierce than benign, and governing both the island world and the imagination. The parallel is deliberate, even to the ritual of marking the North Star and the diagrams of the heavens. Then the moon comes up "as big as a cart wheel" ("the wheel of a chariot" in *Salammbô*). "We all jumped up to greet it as it swam

83. Gustave Flaubert, *Salammbô*, in *The Complete Works of Gustave Flaubert*, Bouvard Edition (New York and London: M. W. Dunne, 1904), I, 51–55, 91–93.

84. "The Treasure of Far Island," *CSF*, pp. 265 ff.; "Eric Hermannson's Soul," *CSF*, pp. 359 ff.; "The Enchanted Bluff," *CSF*, pp. 69 ff.

over the bluffs behind us. It came up like a galleon in full sail; an enormous, barbaric thing, red as an angry heathen god." Though the talk changes it to an Aztec moon, the world invoked in the imagination is ancient, pagan, splendid—a world of quest and discovery, enchantment—and like Carthage, once caught in the turning of history.

The most intricate use of the moon-symbol is in *Alexander's Bridge* (1912). Here are combined all three literary antecedents—the yearning, desire, quest, and ideal of *Endymion*; Heine's human embodiment of the gods and the cyclic rise and fall of history (or human life); and the cosmic moon of *Salammbô*—plus the Greek story of Actaeon's change to a stag when he viewed Diana naked, and finally Stevenson's comment on Endymion. Not only is there a remarkable compacting of all of those qualities that interested Willa Cather in her 1893–1896 writing, but they are laid out, plotted, and ordered as if to insist on the reader's attention to the associations of myth. Now of course Miss Cather was not retelling any one myth in *Alexander's Bridge*; to the contrary, she mingled a half dozen or more.[85] She was using associations, and in a much more indirect way than in "The Enchanted Bluff."

The basic moon-myth used in the story of *Alexander's Bridge* is that of Endymion and Diana—desire and inevitable loss. As Endymion yearned for the moon, so Bartley Alexander desired the magic of youth and its representative in Hilda Burgoyne, who thus becomes Diana (or Cynthia). The scene in which Bartley Alexander watches Hilda on the theatre stage is a brilliant example of Willa Cather's skill in compact allusion—in part, perhaps, a kind of magical game. Hilda like Diana is in another world, the stage and the play. She is performing in *Bog Lights*, a fairy story. Like a goddess disguised, she is playing a part, is a country girl (like Audrey?).

85. As far back as 1956 Virginia Faulkner pointed out to me and others that *Alexander's Bridge* repeats in several ways the story of Paris, the nymph Oenone (his wife), and Helen of Troy, and that the characters in the Cather novel—Bartley Alexander, Winifred Alexander, and Hilda Burgoyne—share the elements of the original triangle. The crucial fact in identification is that Paris is also called Alexander: in fact, he is repeatedly referred to by this name in the Greek text of the *Iliad*, beginning with the first description of him (Book III, ll. 15 ff.): "Among the Trojans there stood forth as champion godlike Alexander, bearing upon his shoulders a panther skin and his curved bow, and his sword . . ." (The *Iliad*, translated by A. T. Murray, 2 vols. [London: William Heinemann; New York: G. P. Putnam's Sons, 1925]). Among the striking connections between *Alexander's Bridge* and the Paris-Alexander story are the parallel scenes in which the bereft wife mourns by the body of her husband (see Lemprière for the account of the death of Paris). As another example of Cather's use of myth as structure, Miss Faulkner also mentioned the Pyramus and Thisbe parallel in *O Pioneers!*—the tragic death of Marie Shabata and Emil Bergson under the white mulberry tree.

Like an invocation out of *Salammbô*, she sings "The Rising of the Moon." And she makes a ring of primroses for her donkey (a surrealist tie with Stevenson, whose comment on Endymion and Audrey was in *Travels with a Donkey*). Later scenes with Hilda are often in gold. Once in her primrose satin gown, she sits on the edge of her chair, "as if she had alighted there for a moment only," and in the same scene Bartley says that he has been "mooning about." Hilda answers, "Mooning! I see you mooning! You must be the busiest man in the world." Stevenson comes in again when Hilda describes her role as not a dress-up part: the director does not fancy her in fine feathers: "He says I ought to be minding the pigs at home, and I suppose I ought." Near the end, Bartley (or Endymion) makes the Diana-Cynthia role of Hilda very clear as he also becomes Actaeon: "And what have you to do, Hilda, with this ugly story? Nothing at all. The little boy drank of the prettiest brook in the forest and he became a stag."[86]

"The Bohemian Girl," written immediately after *Alexander's Bridge*, incorporates a number of elements from *The Gods in Exile* (principally, the pagan deities in disguise among the earthbound mortals). It is based on a story mentioned by Virgil in the *Georgics* (III. 393–396):

> Arcadian Pan, if ancient lore be true,
> Lured thee, O goddess moon, to be his love,
> Then won thee and embraced. To wild wood shades
> He called thee, and thou didst not scorn the call.[87]

Nils Ericson—restless, ruddy faced, carrying a flute—suggests Pan. Clara Vavrika (Olaf Ericson's wife) suggests Diana—the huntress riding at night, uneasy in domesticity, sitting in a white dress with a black cat at her feet. Clara's father suggests Bacchus—convivial, drinking rare wine, keeping a tavern. These affirmative and life-loving creatures are sharply distinguished from the stolid earthbound farmer lot of the Divide. One is not surprised that Diana and Pan escape. Another curious parallel is that the Ericson dance in "The Bohemian Girl" resembles the situation in one scene of Heine's ballet "The Goddess Diana" (a sketch which follows and is associated with *The Gods in Exile*)[88] though with the position of

---

86. *Alexander's Bridge* (Boston and New York: Houghton Mifflin Company, 1922), esp. pp. 32, 54, 55, 73, 130.

87. *The Georgics and Eclogues of Virgil*, translated by Theodore Chickering Williams (Cambridge: Harvard University Press, 1915), p. 87.

88. See note 82, above, pp. 383 ff. "The Bohemian Girl" is in *CSF*, pp. 3 ff.

the lovers exchanged: in Heine it is the Knight who is married, Diana who lures him away. The second tableau of "The Goddess Diana" is in the Great Hall of a Gothic Castle, where a Knight and his wife entertain at a ball. Among the visiting masqueraders is Diana, who reveals herself to the Knight and urges him to follow her to Venusberg. Then we see "a pas de deux in which Greek and heathen divine joyousness dances a duel with German spiritual domestic virtues." In the final tableau, "Diana and the Knight kneel at last at the feet of Lady Venus .... Magnificent transfiguration." The elopement scene in "The Bohemian Girl" is in almost supernal moonlight with music felt though unheard. Clara like Diana the huntress rides mysteriously out of the darkness, under the full moon.

Two examples from Willa Cather's later novels will illustrate the absorption of the myth and the moon's symbolic elements.[89] For what is *A Lost Lady* about if not the old pattern of yearning for the beauty which is impossible to hold? There are no obvious clues, only an image placed with exact and delicate precision. Niel recalls first seeing Mrs. Forrester in her carriage, dressed in black hat and dress, carrying a parasol with a curved ivory handle. She gets out of the carriage with "a black, shiny slipper" thrust out of "a swirl of foamy white petticoats" and goes into church. Niel is proud that he recognized her "as belonging to a different world from any he had ever known." He pauses at the lane's end to look up at a bare poplar: "just above its pointed tip hung the hollow, silver winter moon." Only the curved ivory handle, and the final sharp tracing along a skeleton tree to the moon. In *My Mortal Enemy*, the narrator, Nellie Birdseye, describes the end of a New Year's Eve party at Myra Henshawe's apartment. Outside, Madison Square is white with moonlight. Within the room shadowy and thick with plum-colored hangings, the actress Helena Modjeska (looking no less queenly than when Nellie had seen her as Marie Stuart, and as Katharine in *Henry VIII*)[90] is seated near the window, her cloak draped over her shoulders, moonlight falling across her knees. One of the group sings the aria from *Norma*—"Casta Diva," Queen of Heaven. Beginning "like the quivering of moonbeams on the water," the song "grew and blossomed like a great emotion." The

89. *A Lost Lady* (New York: Alfred A. Knopf, 1923), pp. 42. *My Mortal Enemy* (New York: Alfred A. Knopf, 1926), pp. 57–61.

90. In Lincoln, Willa Cather had seen Helena Modjeska as Rosalind in *As You Like It* on March 23, 1892, and as Katharine in *Henry VIII* (with Otis Skinner) on March 18, 1893. In her *Journal* column of March 10, 1895, she recalled Modjeska as "fit for those lofty and heroic impulses which belonged to the days when women were saints and queens."

aria is identified with something felt in Myra that was "compelling, passionate," which was "audible, visible in the air that night." "*Casta Diva, casta diva!*"—to Nellie it could always "recall powerfully that hidden richness in her." The scene itself is rich, blossoming, passionate, sensuous, alive, mysterious, majestic—like that of the half-hymned invocation to the pagan moon of Carthage. *My Mortal Enemy* has the moon of *Salammbô*—called "Queen of the watery world," the fierce and splendid goddess of cosmic motion and changing forms, the mother goddess Tanith robed with a mantle of purple and gold.

With only the moon for a guide, is it not possible to see in these two exquisitely skillful scenes the two different thematic forces which initiate the conflicts in *A Lost Lady* and *My Mortal Enemy*? They are also the same dualities we have been finding in Willa Cather herself as early as 1896— the high secret snows of the ideal, the blood and wine of the body. Nothing could be clearer than the skeleton tree in one book, and the blossoming song in the other.

Willa Cather often spoke of using the materials of memory, her early experiences, because they had primary associations, color, feeling, personal life. But these materials were not only details of place and person; they were also the ancient ways of the imagination: What she knew and how she thought in those formative years were as much a part of memory as the Bohemian people and the red grass of the Divide. At some point around 1908—very likely at the time when Sarah Orne Jewett reminded her of what she had always known (for it *was* a reminder rather than a revelation, as the early writing shows)—Willa Cather seems to have made a deliberate effort to use primary experience in a mythical or allusive structure. In the dissembling of myth (and myth fragmented, changed, slanting into other forms) one may both extend and mask his original material. "The Enchanted Bluff" (1909) is primarily recall and the logical restatement of literary allusion; "The Joy of Nelly Deane" (1911) uses a combination of *fata*[91] and Norns—in Norse mythology, the three who tend Ygdrasil, the tree of life (note, for example, how Mrs. Spinny, Mrs. Dow, and Mrs. Freeze hover over and care for the girl, how they are entrusted with Nelly's children after her death). The first novels have a more elaborate structure of mythic allusion, but in O *Pioneers!*

91. I am indebted to Richard Giannone (whose *Music in Willa Cather's Fiction* will be published by the University of Nebraska Press) for the suggestion that the three women in "The Joy of Nelly Deane" represent the three Fates.

there is also the clear emergence of the strain Willa Cather found to be most in her "life line"—the poetic evocation of landscape and her own past. This use of memory—complete in itself except for the special light of distance—seemed to be the one best way to combine her own passion and vitality with the immemorial richness of art. Was this use of memory a special mark of Willa Cather's genius, the individual talent which made her unlike any other? Or was it something she learned to do when she was forty? Here the early writing of 1893-1896 can give an important answer.

Readers familiar with Willa Cather's complete published works have inevitably wondered why she waited until *Sapphira and the Slave Girl* in 1940 to use the material of her Virginia childhood—the stories and scenes of the Back Creek and Timber Ridge areas of the Shenandoah Valley where she lived until she was nine. But she did in fact write about her Virginia childhood as early as 1893, in the story "The Elopement of Allen Poole" (Appendix II) which appeared in the *Hesperian* on April 15 of that year. Although it is unsigned, "The Elopement of Allen Poole" is unquestionably by Willa Cather, identifiable by circumstance, style, and—most strongly—the material itself. For the story contains nothing less than a capsule description and recreation of Willa Cather's Virginia home, paralleled in almost every detail by passages in *Sapphira and the Slave Girl.*[92]

The landscape in "Allen Poole" (here called Limber Ridge) is the same as in *Sapphira*: the distant mountains of the Blue Ridge; the nearer mountains of pine woods, chestnuts, and laurel; the valleys with fields of wheat and corn; the creek which "wound between its willow-grown banks." Laurel, "just blushing into bloom," is described in *Sapphira* as "drifts of rose and peach and flesh colour." In "Allen Poole" we see the "wavering line of locust trees"; in *Sapphira*, "the locusts look yielding and languid," or as Till looks across the creek she sees "the wavering slopes of the North Mountain."

The scene in "Allen Poole" of reapers at work in the valley, "the mowers swinging their cradles and the binder following close behind,"

92. Firsthand descriptions of the Cathers' Virginia home of Willowshade and its surroundings are in E. K. Brown's *Willa Cather*, Edith Lewis's *Willa Cather Living*, and Mildred Bennett's *The World of Willa Cather*; in recollections of Virginia people and life in Willa Cather's 1900 story, "The Sentimentality of William Tavener" (*CSF*, pp. 353 ff.); and throughout *Sapphira and the Slave Girl* (New York: Alfred A. Knopf, 1940). The quotations which follow are from *Sapphira and the Slave Girl*, pp. 172, 117, 73, 101, 103, 273 f., 277, 123. Brown's account of Mrs. Anderson is in *Willa Cather*, p. 21.

is repeated in the hay-cutting sequence of *Sapphira*. In "Allen Poole," the creek lane goes by a family burying ground, with "white headstones, tall, dark cedars, and masses of rosemary, myrtle and rue," a graveyard surrounded by a stone fence. This is the Cather—or Colbert—burying ground described in *Sapphira*: a wall of "flat slabs of brown stone laid one upon the other," headstones of marble or slate, mounds "covered with thick mats of myrtle"; the master and Nancy talk "behind the dark cedars just outside the stone wall." But the most startling identification is the description of the unique wooden footbridge, or suspension bridge, which crossed Back Creek near the Cather home. In "Allen Poole": "Across it [the Creek with willow-grown banks] was the old, black, creaking foot-bridge which had neither props nor piers, but was swung from the arms of a great sycamore tree." In *Sapphira*: "But the wooden foot-bridge over Back Creek hung just as it did in the Colberts' time, a curious 'suspension' bridge, without piles, swung from the far-reaching white limb of a great sycamore that grew on the bank and leaned over the stream."

"The Elopement of Allen Poole" is about the people of the Gap, and the dialogue recreates their speech. Here is the familiar "Bethel camp-meetin'" mentioned in *Sapphira* ("picnics and camp-meetings in summer," and "meetin's . . . at Bethel Church"). The episode of Allen Poole and the revenuers could well be mountain lore Willa Cather learned from Mrs. Mary Ann Anderson, the woman of the Gap whom she often visited as a child. According to Brown, Mrs. Anderson had a great gift for telling stories—"She knew the histories of all the families in the region, rich and poor, and all the dramatic events that had become legends among the country people. Her talk was full of wit and fire, it was shot through with the vivid native idiom; and the stories she told, Willa Cather remembered all her life."

A few other details of "Allen Poole" are important for their relationships with Willa Cather's work, both earlier and later. The ending of the story—"the rest is silence"—picks up the *Hamlet* quotation she often used and even parallels a closing passage in her 1891 essay, "Shakespeare and Hamlet" (Appendix I). In the story, the feel and smell of the country ("that odor of indescribable richness and ripeness which newly cut grain always has"), the image of the "red harvest moon" just rising, the white mystery and tragedy of the moonlight night, are all familiar Catherian motifs. And Allen's "irresistible impulse to pick Nellie up and carry her" suggests the central episode of "On the Divide" and, in

O Pioneers!, Alexandra's dream of being lifted high and carried away. When Allen, waiting for Nellie, hears the whippoorwill in the locust trees, its song throbbing through the summer night, his "heart went out to the heart of the night," and in his own whistling "he broke out in such a passion of music as made the singer in the locusts sick with melody" —as when Nils (in "The Bohemian Girl") waits for Clara in the moonlight field, "deaf under the waves of a great river of melody." A symbolic shaping of the landscape is suggested by the scene of harvest in the valley, shadowed by an occasional cloud, crossed by the running creek, combined with the youth's feeling of high permanence above the changing scene below: "Above it all were the dark pine-clad mountains, in the repose and strength of their immortality." One of Willa Cather's poems in the 1903 *April Twilights*—"From the Valley"—can be placed in this very context: "Toward the heights the pines climb row on row," and on those heights "The elder gods, implacable, austere, / In their imperishable seats and high, / Behold the valley where our days go by / Like shining water, coming not again."[93] That "repose and strength" which Allen Poole felt above the changing world of ripeness and cut grain, of the whippoorwill's music heard momentarily in the darkness and joined with the human, whistled melody of youth—these Keatsian elements were part of Willa Cather's vision from the beginning.

It is interesting of course that Willa Cather did write of her Virginia childhood so early, and also that she wished to claim none of that writing until the personal and historical summation in *Sapphira and the Slave Girl*. But it may be even more important to compare the story and the novel, knowing all that went between. In 1893, Virginia is a place and a feeling remembered, and the strokes of memory must paint the primary images; in 1940, in *Sapphira and the Slave Girl*, the writer could embody the smallest details, freshly observed and minutely recorded. Yet there are lines in the early story that suggest more of the intensity, the evocative simplicity of Willa Cather's style in her other great books of memory— *O Pioneers!* and *My Ántonia*—than one finds in *Sapphira* ("... the Blue Ridge lay against the sky, faint and hazy as the mountains of Beulah Land"). "The Elopement of Allen Poole" is therefore a remarkable piece to consider in any study of her creativity, one of the first creations— lovingly done—of the things that haunt the mind.

Willa Cather wrote lyrically of the Virginia landscape when she was in Nebraska. Before 1896, her stories of the western country and people

93. *April Twilights (1903)* (see note 5, above), p. 45.

do not have a similar sense of place; their interest is in character, conflict, intensified emotions, and dramatic ironies. "On the Divide" has a feeling of the wild and awesome spaces, but in neither the fiction nor the articles do we seem to find the pull of the land she described later in *My Ántonia*— that violent, absorbing love for the red grass and the great western sky that were so like illimitable oceans. Of course it takes a while for the mind to be haunted; meanwhile, the scene is often commonplace and even funny, like the ghost town she described in a play review: "where the rain never falls, and they have to set traps for the rattlesnakes and keep the thermometer on ice." The play's scenery, "to anyone who has had the misfortune to dwell in a small Nebraska town, [was] painfully reminiscent. There was a saloon, a Keeley institute, a real estate office, a peanut stand, the office of the Rush City Bazoo and a well equipped public cyclone cellar."[94] The familiar places were ordinary and undramatic—"our peaceable and rather inoffensive country."

Yet the pull of the land *was* there in 1893–1896, revealed in other forms: the strength of ancient things, the elemental things, the mysteries of all that was unexplainable (fate and the strange ways life went); her passionate excitement, feeling for individuality, sense of drama, even exaggeration; the joy in battle, power, and achievement; all primitive fires of feeling and language. It was a protean flow of memory. The pull of the land can be found in mirrored images. She liked to read of exile and space—the lonely ice of northern seas, or the desert, or islands—and describe those scenes which have a noble melancholy mixed with wildness, mystery, magic. She liked Pierre Loti's desert, "which the ancients quaintly called a sea," and his *The Romance of a Spahi*, a book with simple language "intense as the savage emotions it portrays." She called it "a tragedy of environment and the bitterness of exile." In Hall Caine's Iceland—"a country beyond the end of the world, dark and remote"— there is fate personal and relentless, reminding the world that "under us all there is still nature, uncontrolled, unsubdued, inexplicable," nature who does not make heroic men, but heroes. Sometimes the images come directly home: one painting of a western scene is too tame and gentle— "not the fierce, white, hot sunlight of the west. Sunlight on the plains is almost like sunlight on the northern seas; it is a glaring, irritating, shelterless light that makes the atmosphere throb and pulsate with heat." But with the sweeping contrasts and mysteries, we can also read of the physical joy in "the glittering green world" of summer, in all country

94. On *Rush City: Journal*, October 14, 1894.

places of rich color and growth, and feel "the high noon meridian ecstasy that Keats and Shelley knew how to breathe into song." She once commented on how strange it is that Russia—"that great barren, barbarous country"—brings forth "mighty geniuses." When she added: "Left to herself in the wilderness with the mixed blood of strange nations nature will do wonderful things sometimes"—was she perhaps thinking of her own hope for the wild land she knew?

In the context of Willa Cather's writing of 1893–1896, the unifying principle of memory in her whole work becomes a larger force than simple recall and recording; it is a source, a technique, and a belief. Her first articles show overwhelmingly that even by 1896 her set of mind was to the elemental things in man's nature and experience, to the distances of history and primitive knowledge, and to the Biblical, mythic, and allegorical expression of such truth. The two motifs which we have traced briefly in her work—the conflict of Roman and Teuton and the symbolic imagery of the moon—suggest the psychological movements that seem to concern her most. The cyclical rounds of rising and falling civilizations, of waxing and waning moons, of Roman and Barbarian, of desire and loss; the contrasts of old gods and new, of exile and home— these become a cosmic pulse or rhythm throughout everything she wrote. For Willa Cather, personal memory is also the memory of the race. Though she may not have used the word, she dealt with the archetype— the inescapable human experience.

In her own life and immediate memory the contrasts had been violent and sharp. How violent it was, at nine, to change from green-mountained Virginia and the Shenandoah waters to the obliterating landscape of Nebraska is revealed in her 1913 account (see Appendix IV) of the wagon trip from Red Cloud out onto the prairie: "I would have got on pretty well during that ride if it had not been for the larks. Every now and then one flew up and sang a few splendid notes and dropped down into the grass again. That reminded me of something—I don't know what, but my one purpose in life just then was not to cry, and every time they did it, I thought I should go under." Homesickness and the sense of exile were emotional realities, and so was the swing back to the creative excitement of new people, new land.

In 1933, Dorothy Canfield Fisher made a perceptive and I think important analysis of those early years in Nebraska—the eighties and nineties—as they would have affected Willa Cather. In the first years of settlement, wrote Mrs. Fisher, it was a "stirring drama of hope," since nothing had been done, "everything was still possible," and the settlers were "half drunk with the exquisite and unforgettable elixir of frontier hopefulness." In the mid-eighties, the tide was already turning, and disappointments increased in the next decade. So until she left Nebraska in 1896, Willa Cather lived "in the midst of one of the greatest disillusions the American pioneer movement has ever known. . . . She had lived through years of hope so blinding that the defects of frontier life could not be seen; she had lived through years of reaction so bleak and black that its fine qualities were invisible."[95] Willa Cather knew pioneer life in both the dark and the light of the moon, and she wrote of both sides. More important, she was used to living in rhythms of exile and return, conquest and defeat. They were the inevitabilities of life. Is it possible that she wrote less to lament the old order than to embody—vivify—that inescapable experience? It was indeed one of the fundamental facts on which life rests.

At the close of *My Ántonia* Jim Burden comes upon the old road which once ran "like a wild thing across the open prairie," now "mere shadings in the grass." There in the night he could close his eyes and "hear the rumbling of the wagons in the dark," feeling again that old "obliterating strangeness" of the new land. As at the end of the voyage perilous, "I had the sense of coming home to myself, and of having found out what a little circle man's experience is . . ." (418). The rounding of experience was more than a motif in Willa Cather's creative life; it was a fact, a great parabola seen in completion only from the vantage point of 1896. For almost as if there *were* a design, the line of her creative will curves out from the first years, turns, and comes home.

In its first fifteen years, to about 1908, Willa Cather's fiction runs in a jagged line of experiment and losses: stories of simple power; others with an open, glittering texture of reference and allusion; *The Troll Garden* with its complex, symbolic design; and a pause from 1905 to 1908, with stories that diverge to the very psychologies and talk the writer once scorned. Beginning with "The Enchanted Bluff" there is genuinely Willa Cather's own material (meaning not only the Nebraska experiences but her kind of mythic, archetypal, even magical vision), and through the next dozen years to *One of Ours* (1922) a gradual development from the carefully structured mythic or symbolic pattern (as in *Alexander's Bridge*) to the use of people and the land remembered, a free dependence on personal materials, ideas, and feeling as their own patterns.

95. "Daughter of the Frontier" (see note 6, above).

The recognizable kingdom of art has gone from surface allusion to organic principle (as in *The Song of the Lark*). In the three problem or conflict novels of the 1920's—*A Lost Lady*, *The Professor's House*, and *My Mortal Enemy* (that curious triptych)— the 1893–1896 material virtually disappears from view.

At this point and with Willa Cather's early writing in mind, the old definitions of her work which began with *Alexander's Bridge* in 1912 (and cut off twenty years of a writer's career) must be revised. *Death Comes for the Archbishop* and *Shadows on the Rock* do not in fact continue the parabola outward into distances of space and time but bring it home, returning straight into the kingdom of art, and with a richer load than one would have believed in 1896. They have the old elements of gods and devotions, hierarchies, stages, romance, sacred fires, heroic journeys, an ideal France, gods in exile—but with something more. One is not quite sure whether these books are the kingdom of art vivified, or a rich spiritual achievement explained in primary terms, like a parable.[96]

Death Comes for the Archbishop is told as if it were a romance, with a prologue on the stage of Rome, "an Odysseus of the Church" in the cast, and a ritual beginning: "One afternoon in the autumn of 1851 a solitary horseman . . . ." The "solitary horseman" pricking o'er the plain has the courtesy of Spenserian knights ("a man of gentle birth"); like a motif of chivalry, "periodically the plumes of poplars flashed like gracious accent marks . . . ." We see the town of Santa Fe set like a lighted stage in "the amphitheatre of red hills behind." In this physical and romantic book the movements of air and earth are one, forms changing in the liquidity of light and a most supple language: physical, pagan, devout, transfigured. There are so many of the old themes and even cadences: "no man born of woman," "the Kingdom of Heaven," "fulfil the dreams of one's youth"; "how it was of the South, that church, how it sounded the note of the South!"; in his last weeks, all of the Bishop's "former states of mind" were "within reach of his hand"; "the world one actually lived in, was the sky, the sky!" Again, the changing of gods as the Navajos were driven out—"they believed that their old gods dwelt in the fastnesses of that canyon," in the white houses on the cliff "which were older than the white man's world." And there are the significant names for a Pilgrim's Progress: Father Vaillant and Father Latour.

96. Quotations in the following discussion are from *Death Comes for the Archbishop* (New York: Alfred A. Knopf, 1927), pp. 3, 14, 16, 19–20, 218, 219, 263–264, 272, 293, 235, 296, 298, 303; and *Shadows on the Rock*, pp. 280, 170, 172, 137.

Vaillant is plain, but does Latour mean *tower* or *turning* or both? Do we have again the cyclical round, and a subtle irony? For it was not Father Latour but Father Vaillant who was the young man "being torn in two ... by the desire to go and the necessity to stay."

And *Shadows on the Rock*? Here, too, is the stage—the tableau of a crèche, as in the first pages Willa Cather directs us to see it, a tableau romance a little apart from history: "here where nothing changed," as the last pages say, and where the death of a king would never touch the people of Quebec. That we know more than Auclair about the changes of history will not disturb this moment of art; within itself it *is* complete. Like a bright stage divided from the common (and even fearful) world of the ordinary (the other side of that line of lights that marks the dead line of the practical), Quebec can attend to the rituals of human and sacred devotion. Here are people like Pierre Charron, who even looks like Salvini and the "heroes of old romance"—he is "quick as an otter and always sure of himself," with "the good manners of the Old World, the dash and daring of the New." He had "a fine bold nose, a restless, rather mischievous mouth, white teeth, very strong and even, sparkling hazel eyes with a kind of living flash in them." Here are the Count with his blown glass from the South of France, the secret silent devotions of the veiled Jeanne, and miracles that are like the blossoming of art and emotion: "In them the vague worship and devotion of the simple-hearted assumes a form. From being a shapeless longing, it becomes a beautiful image; a dumb rapture becomes a melody that can be remembered and repeated; and the experience of a moment, which might have been a lost ecstasy, is made an actual possession and can be bequeathed to another." Pervading *Shadows on the Rock* is a sense of the highest kind of excellence—what in the family, and in the place made in a wilderness, is kept of traditions, culture, the household gods that Aeneas so long ago felt also compelled to deliver into a new world: in short, the sacred fires of a people.

To see *Death Comes for the Archbishop* and *Shadows on the Rock* in the context of romance, the French ideal, and the drama as Willa Cather had spoken of them by 1896 does not lessen their spiritual force, or the truth of their Catholic worlds. For all of these elements were from the beginning the highest kind of art for Willa Cather, and with a religious significance. It seems to me inevitable that she would try to convey her deepest and most profound convictions in something like these forms, which were as natural to her as breathing, and so return a little of the kingdom of art to the kingdom of heaven, from which it came. It was as if the rough and broken sketches of a creative world which she envisioned in 1893–1896 had come into a body "with color, odor, sound, life all in it," an art which is a blossoming of spirit. If *The Song of the Lark* was the embodiment of the way of the artist, *Death Comes for the Archbishop* and *Shadows on the Rock* are embodiments of values and the way of men.

From *Lucy Gayheart* on through *Sapphira and the Slave Girl* and the last stories, we leave the formal framework which suggests the allegorical kingdom and turn to a deeper personal landscape of reprise, definition, summary, and illuminations. The movement is irregular, like the first experimentation. Does "The Old Beauty" sound a little like those early essays on the lives of artists, or the loss of greatness? and Cherry Beamish a little like the *Journal* critic herself? Is *Lucy Gayheart* perhaps the most perilous voyage of all, a Pilgrim's Progress in which no one except the book itself reaches the Celestial City? It all fits: even *Sapphira*, with a lifetime load of unwritten, cancelled Virginias, comes back across the prairies to both beginnings, the life and the art.

Some works and lives fall into a design of such logical wholeness that one can only be baffled, as if by some other kind of art. In Willa Cather's work, nothing was frivolously done, and—as the later books show—least of all her first plain statements of what she was and what she discovered in the kingdom of art by 1896.

Part II

CRITICAL
STATEMENTS

�֍ �֍ ✖

The Individual Talent

❖ ❖ ❖

The great enjoyment that makes the theatre
worth while is in seeing individual talent,
in watching a man give back what God put
into him.

THE GREAT ONES

*In the Kingdom of Art there was for Willa Cather a natural nobility—the
aristocracy of genius in all its bewildering variety, color, and degree; genius
(which is of God) made complete through human achievement, in the particular
human accent of body, voice, hand, or word. She was ready to give passionate
devotion to all artists who touched that peak of greatness; she lived intensely in
the experience they made possible. But she was also a close observer of every
nuance and every gesture that would help to define an artist's particularity and
the exact quality of his achievement. How else should one learn greatness except
by studying the human forms of such magnificence?*

*Willa Cather's first and perhaps most eloquent considerations of great
artists were of actors and actresses, singers and performers, for they could demon-
strate personal accomplishment in the most immediate and human way. Night
after night beyond the calcium lights a glory was attempted, and sometimes won.
When an actor did succeed, he was there in person, the artist in the very act of
performing the miracle of creation. She liked strong characters, those who could
capture and convince. And she admired the skillful ones who, like Tolstoi, could
match unlimited power with inimitable craft. So the quality of greatness is not
fixed. In the world's rich beauty there are ranges of fire and ice; there are pulses,
tides, and various winds; and some artists, like Bernhardt and Duse, seem to
embody those elemental oppositions. Willa Cather's comments on those two
artists in 1894–1896 comprise a key statement of her own principles of greatness
and the individual talent.*

Bernhardt and Duse: A Duel of Genius

When Sarah Bernhardt played Sardou's La Tosca *at Boyd's New Theater in Omaha on February 22, 1892, Willa Cather was there.[1] It was a glittering occasion. An audience of two thousand crowded in from the winter night (five hundred had stood in line for tickets during the morning); Governor Boyd sat in his box of red plush and gilt; and—a lesson in pioneer sophistication—the performance was given entirely in French. For years Willa Cather thought of the flame-like Bernhardt as the prototype of the great artist. Duse, however, did not perform in Nebraska, and what is said of her comes from Willa Cather's reading—that other reality of imaginative recreation and colorful narration so characteristic of her newspaper columns. Her representation of the "duel" of Bernhardt and Duse—a duel both actual and symbolic—is also characteristic: she delighted in the vitality of argument and the play of forces, in differences, in particular individual genius. The duel was of course an elemental contrast—body and spirit, heart and soul, passion and restraint. It is easy to see which artist Willa Cather thought victorious; but the winner in a larger and more personal sense, even she did not yet know.*

Since the academy will have none of Zola,[2] let Paris give honor where honor is due. Let it give Bernhardt her cross. She is typically and entirely French and is worthy of the honor of her country. She has done what Zola has never done, she has given France and all the world unlimited pleasure, unlimited raptures of passion and power. That is what we honor artists for, anyway, for kindling the latent warmth in us, putting around our weary workaday life that brightness and halo which only genius can give. Otherwise they would have no right to fare sumptuously while the thousands starve, to take from us by song what we earn with aching muscles, by the sweat of our brow. They deal in wares which are as necessary to us as the bread we eat. Whole nations have died from spiritual famine as well as from a famine of corn. The world must have ideals and emotions and it cannot always make them for itself. It will pay any price for them, risk any peril for them. They come to us, these actors and poets and painters and singers of sweet music, from somewhere out of the region of the vast unknown, and we give them food and raiment, the best the land affords, and in return they give us our dreams. Most of us are

---

1. "Miss Willa Cather went up to Omaha on Feb. 22 to hear the world-renowned Bernhardt in *La Tosca*" (*Lasso*, 1 [March, 1892], 70). The account of the performance is in the *Omaha Daily Bee*, February 24, 1892, p. 2.
2. Zola had been denied a chair in the French Academy for the fourteenth time.

willing to live and toil and die in our allotted place that from our nations and our people one great teacher and consoler of men may be born. We are willing to furnish the physical basis upon which one spiritual force, one great imagination may rise to snatch for us the blue from heaven and the fire from the sun. Somehow it seems as if Bernhardt atones and compensates for all the toil and suffering of those swart, misshapen peasant women Millet used to paint. The many must suffer that the one may rise. It is the old law. If every man were something of a poet, something of a musician, something of an actor, then there would be no great names in art. If all men were happy, refined, cultivated, then society would be a monotonous plane—there would be no mountains.

Journal, December 30, 1894, p. 13.

The summer that is just ending has been a most eventful one in the theatre. Among the other great presentations that ran through the hot months were the two great London seasons of Bernhardt and Duse. William Winter accuses the American people of having a sneaking admiration of Madame Bernhardt's personality. Well, there are some things about her that compel admiration. All artists who have the supreme assurance and strength of their art command admiration. Early in the summer Signora Duse went to London, playing *Camille*, *La Tosca* and *Fédora*, the plays that for so many years have meant Bernhardt. Duse is a great artist, altogether original, altogether modern. London went wild, that is, as wild as London ever gets. The delicacy and power of the woman enchanted the critics. They thought these lofty and spiritualized passions infinitely grander than the fierce and fiery ones of the old Frenchwoman. We always think the higher and colder passions better when the warmer and lower are away from us; it's one redeeming trait in human nature. One morning the London papers said unanimously that Duse was greater than Bernhardt. Bernhardt was over in Paris recalling old days with Sardou, using unrepeatable language to her creditors and reading everything in the world, as she always does. At last the growing rumble of a great fame reached her, a fame that was not hers. For the first time in her life she had a rival, a woman young, modern and indisputably a genius. Bernhardt is old, nearing sixty now.[3] She never was beautiful, and London said that she belonged to a school that is growing passé. It was generally supposed that she would realize that her star was setting and would quietly yield. But she never was a woman to yield anything. Her age and

3. Sarah Bernhardt (1844–1923) was actually fifty; Eleonora Duse (1859–1924) was thirty-five.

wrinkles did not trouble her, she never had any beauty to depend on, nothing but her whirlwind of passion and her flawless art. She read those London papers through and when she had finished her cigarette she telephoned for her manager. She cancelled her Paris engagement, sent her fond adieux to her despairing creditors, packed up her son and grandson and boa constrictors and in a week was in London. She rented the biggest theatre and began playing her rival's plays in her rival's very teeth. She had none but the kindest feelings and the most appreciative words for and of Signora Duse, but she had been challenged and came for war. It was simply a duel of genius, not pique or vanity, but an artist's defense of her self-respect and her art. Madame Bernhardt has seen a good deal of men, individually and collectively, and she doubtless knew from her very vast and varied experience that loyalty once reconquered is all the stronger for a little unfaithfulness, because it has the spur and sting of remorse. That is true, even in phlegmatic London. Before a week was over the great London public had surged back to the feet of its premier amour. It repented and apologized, it wondered and marveled and was amazed. Why, this woman was sixty and the old irresistible magnetism was there still, the mighty force that seemed to go back and awaken the primitive elements in man and analyze things into their first and simplest constituents. All who have felt it remember it too well. It is like red lava torn up from the bowels of the earth where the primeval fires of creation are still smouldering. With all the coquetry and Parisian capriciousness, it is still a force which has in it something of the savagery of the stone age and arouses in the individual the forgotten first instincts of the race. London went from intoxication to delirium. It published her picture, it raved over her as it did years ago when she was young, it declared that she alone was great and that there was none like unto her. Then, having made her honor clean, Bernhardt went back to Paris to her wine cellar and her creditors.

Surely in all the category of stage women none has had power and magnetism like hers. It is almost probable that her greatness will not die with her, that generations unborn will feel the thrill of her presence, the magic of her power, just as we feel Cleopatra's. Bernhardt is more like the royal Egyptian than any other woman ever was, and it is not unlikely that future generations will associate them together.

Journal, October 14, 1894, p. 13.

. . . If [Duse] is well enough she and Bernhardt will both play *Magda* at the same time in London. There will be two schools of art for you.

Hermione and Cleopatra, Lucretia and Messalina. Signora Duse has always played with the highest, noblest qualities of her soul, with what was best and liveliest in her, and that wears an artist out quickly. Her acting has been done in marble just as Bernhardt's is done in color. Upon the stainless heights of art she has dreamed and created, the heights on which it is not given to a mortal to live long. Some women act with their senses, some with their soul. The soulful ones burn out the quickest. It is a bad thing for an actress to be too sensitive. Bernhardt's acting is a matter of physical excitement, Duse's of spiritual exaltation. Bernhardt enjoys Camille, but Duse pities her with all her infinite compassion and all her divine woman-hood. She takes her work too hard. Art is Bernhardt's dissipation, a sort of Bacchic orgy. It is Duse's consecration, her religion, her martyrdom.

Journal, June 16, 1895, p. 12.

. . . Signora Duse is dying of her own peculiar kind of emotion, the kind that has made her great and unique in art. Other actresses of the emotional school are demonstrative and impulsive. They suffer and they vent their suffering. Their methods are simple and transparent; they pour out all their self-inflicted anguish, and when it is all over they are merely tired as children are after excitement. Their emotions are wondrously simple and they go no deeper than those of a child. . . . Signora Duse is as well bred on the stage as she would be in her drawing room. The losing of herself in her part is only the half of her work. Keeping her part within herself is her individual and self-imposed task, the art that is all her own. . . . In this generation, when so many of us live altogether upon the false and artificial, when all life is tuned an octave higher than nature, there are a few souls to whom the truth is necessary and all-important, for nature evens herself out after all. Eleonora Duse is one of these. She suffers as the women of her time have learned to suffer, in secret and in silence. The great art of other women is disclosure. Hers is concealment. She takes her great anguish and lays it in a tomb and rolls a stone before the door, walls it up and hides it away in the earth. And it is of this that she is dying, this stifled pain that is killing her. As I said once before, it is hard upon a woman when she acts with her soul. That wears out so much sooner than the senses.[4]

Courier, September 21, 1895, p. 6.

4. The expression "As I said once before" refers to the *Journal* column of June 16, 1895 (see above), and portions of the later article were used two years afterward (*Courier*, July 31, 1897) in the signed story "Nanette: An Aside" to characterize a prima donna, Tradutorri. (*Willa Cather's Collected Short Fiction, 1892–1912* [Lincoln: University of Nebraska Press, 1965], pp. 405 ff., esp. 408. Hereafter this volume will be indicated by CSF.)

[Bernhardt] is with us again, the triumphant, the unvanquished, the ancient of days, and with her she has brought her wonderful Hindoo play, *Izeyl*. We are to see her once again, and wonder once again, and pity the generations yet unborn who will never hear that voice of gold. It's queer, but the very arrival of Bernhardt brings about a sort of quickening of the spirit in matters dramatic. It reminds one that the drama is not all rot after all, that it's really an art. It would be rather nice to be in New York now, just to watch the straggling public that has gone daft over Duse and Nethersole rally back to the old standard, kindle anew with the old reckless irresistible enthusiasm that only one woman in all the living world can inspire; just to watch this Circe, this dread goddess of mortal speech, pour out her wine and make men what she wills. O yes, art is a great thing when it is great, it has the elements of power and conquest in it, it's like the Roman army, it subdues a world, a world that is proud to be conquered when it is by Rome.

It is amusing to have people ask you what there is about Bernhardt, and it is hopeless to try to tell them. Is it her art, her perfect technique? No, not exactly that. Is it her tremendous emotion, her whirlwind of passion? Yes, partially, but other women have had that in less degree. Is it her deftness, her intuition, her perfect understanding and sympathy with all the endless details and minutiae of the part she plays? Yes, but more than that. It is all these things plus the most perfect voice that ever spoke through a human throat and something else beside, for which language has no name. Bernhardt is a good deal like certain human emotions that everyone studies and reads about and theorizes on, and then, when they once actually experience them, they are knocked senseless. What do you know of the sea till you have seen it, what can you know of Bernhardt till you have heard her? Who can tell you of the meaning in one gesture, of the anguish in one cry, of the longing in one look, of the love song in one tone, of the power of life and living that is in the woman? It is all a thing of feeling, you cannot apprehend it intellectually at all. What do you know of a grief till it is in your heart, of a passion till it is in your veins? But if you have seen her you know not only her but many other things. Yes, you know though you cannot tell others, if you have heard her shriek while her lover is being tortured in *La Tosca*, if you have seen her, in the fourth act of *Camille* when she meets Armand once again, catch his hand and pass it swiftly over her face and arms, draw one quivering breath and then take his curses in a silent stupor, like a thirsty man who drinks and dies; and under it all there is that perfect art, the result of the most rigorous training of the most rigorous masters of France, technique that in itself is enough when for a moment her inspiration fails, if it ever does fail. The training that she carries so lightly that one seldom thinks of it, has killed the originality in a hundred lesser artists. She never fails or disappoints you because under all those thousand little things that seem so spontaneous there is a system as fixed and definite as the laws of musical composition. Her very enunciation, which baffles all the artists of her country in its perfections, is the work of years of labor, her every tone is not only beautiful, but correct.

Journal, January 26, 1896, p. 9.

Willa Cather admired many performers for many different reasons—Clara Morris, Julia Marlowe, Joseph Jefferson, William H. Crane, Victor Maurel, a cluster of unknowns—but two actors seemed to her to have achieved a special kind of perfection: Alexander Salvini and Richard Mansfield. Salvini was like Bernhardt in his physical power and impact. Chief player in romances like The Three Guardsmen, *the "games that live forever,"* [5] *he charmed as much with the joy of swift movement and physical vitality as Bernhardt did with strong emotion. Willa Cather saw Salvini at least once in Lincoln—*The Three Guardsmen, *May 3, 1894—though he was also there in D'Ennery's* Don Caesar de Bazan *on September 26, 1892. Richard Mansfield was the great master of intelligent, controlled, skillful acting. If he was not as colorful as Salvini, he was more subtly authoritative, interesting, and complex. Willa Cather saw him twice: in Clyde Fitch's* Beau Brummell (*also spelled "Brummel"*) *on April 23, 1894—a performance, she wrote on April 29 in her column, so great that it was a fit honor for Shakespeare's birthday—and in* A Parisian Romance, *March 28, 1896. One new actor she nominated for success was Clay Clement, who played in* The New Dominion (*also called* Baron von Hohenstauffen) *on March 1, 1895. She recognized in him many of the Mansfield traits: intelligence, honesty, understatement, and especially the authentic achievement of character. He was a beginner who had the qualities that make greatness.*

Alexander Salvini: Hero of Old Romance

... There can be little doubt that Alexander Salvini is one of the greatest romantic actors of his generation. He has all the qualifications for that position, ambition, personal attraction, all the vigor of youth and all the enthusiasm of art. His vivacity is without limit, his surprises without number. His D'Artagnan is thoroughly French and entirely a cavalier.

5. See the 1913 interview of Willa Cather, Appendix IV.

He lives life joyously and faces death fearlessly. He fights half a dozen duels on his way to dinner, drinks half a dozen bottles of wine at dinner and after dinner kisses half a dozen women on the wing. He could not resist a cry, a quarrel, a kiss—or a window. His little feats of fenestration were almost alarming. Whenever a new set of scenery came on the stage one looked at it with passionate anxiety to see if there were even the smallest kind of a window in it, knowing that if there were the irrepressible D'Artagnan would be out of it before many minutes. Signor Salvini's forte is in his agility, his activity and his charming audacity. He is everywhere at once and he carries everything by storm. He might challenge the king or kiss the queen or waltz with the cardinal and his audience would not be much surprised. He has an almost Mercutio-like buoyancy; indeed, he is the one actor who could do Mercutio's fencing lines beginning "More than the prince of cats." As a tragedian it is doubtful if Signor Alexander could add anything to the great name of Salvini. He was not made for great stage loves or great stage sorrows, but for the sparkling dash and brilliancy of the heroes of old romance which all the world loves and admires. He is a whirlwind of good humor, bravado and smiles.

Journal, May 4, 1894, p. 6.

Richard Mansfield: A Master

... Mr. Mansfield is one of the few actors who do not use their voices very much. He does not have to, he can make the silences speak. His Beau Brummell is a masterpiece of fine toning and shading. There are no sensational climaxes that show up like great dashes of color. The whole creation is like a picture in soft color, whose strength and delicacy is not easily appreciated by an untrained eye. A character like Beau Brummell takes one into the sharps and flats and intricate modulations of art. It is not easy to give a role foolishness and foppishness and with them elegance and manliness. In some way Mr. Mansfield always makes one side of his nature suggest the other. When he is manicuring his nails one always feels that he can do something better because he does that so well, and when he sacrifices his love and prosperity it seems perfectly natural that he should brush the dust from his sleeve while he does it. The thing that ennobles Mansfield's Beau and makes him more than a cad or a fop is the wonderful preservation of the type. There is never a suggestion of affectation, or of assuming airs, because he never drops them. He is the same elegant gentleman to himself and to his own mirror, one knows that he even sleeps with elegance and grace. If it is a role, he never drops it and he wears the mask starving. It is not the cheap bourgeois elegance that is pinned on and laced on and tied on with strings; it fits him as easily and lightly as his own skin. His foppery is his personality. If Beau were a coal heaver he would be Beau still, would handle his coal gracefully and never blacken his hands. It was the preservation of the type that made the last two acts so pathetic. The highest kind of nobleness is when a type can survive the things that seem necessary to it, when a man can be lord of an attic as though he were lord of a manor and be luxurious without luxury. It is this strange, consistent correctness that makes him burn the letters which would blast the reputation of men and women [who] have deserted him, and keep his honor as immaculate as his hands.

Journal, April 24, 1894, p. 5.

. . . It is easy to see that Mr. Mansfield is an intelligent and educated man. Any actor with an emotional nature can play roles in which the emotions are simple and decided. He has only to work himself up and let himself loose. Thomas Keene, by limping and leering and hissing, manages to make the public believe he can play *Richard III* because the popular conception of Richard is only that he should be as wicked and disagreeable as possible. Robert Downing deludes people into thinking he can play *Virginius* because he is fat and oratorical.[6] Hate, love, nobleness in the theory and the abstract are easy things to enact. But the emotions in the role of Beau Brummell are delicate, complex, negative, almost contradictory. It requires as much intelligence and insight as Hamlet. Most very good actors would be vulgar fops in the part; it requires a scholar and a gentleman to portray it, it takes culture of mind and delicacy of instinct to comprehend it. There is but one living novelist who could handle the character in a novel, George Meredith; but one living actor who can act it, Richard Mansfield. The two men suggest each other in many ways, though perhaps it is only because they are two of the very few serenely great in this troubled, feverish century.

Journal, April 29, 1894, p. 13.

6. Thomas Keene played in *Richard III* on September 19, 1891, and on November 22, 1892. Robert Downing played in *Virginius* on November 29, 1893. In her column on December 3, 1893, Willa Cather wrote: "Every actor has his forte. Mr. [James] O'Neill's is his diamonds, Mr. [Sol Smith] Russell's is his sublime ugliness, Mr. Keene's is the strength of his voice, but Mr. Downing's is in his neck. Mr. Downing is a conscientious actor and he believes in giving the public their money's worth, and as he has very little else to give them, he gives with royal bounty the beauty of his physique" (*Journal*, December 3, 1893, p. 13).

Clay Clement: A Beginner

People who go to the theatre night after night, like the Athenians of old, ever watching for something new, find it tiresome and disappointing work sometimes. The only really lofty pleasure to be got out of the drama is the detection and recognition of individual merit. An even and well balanced company of conscientious mediocre actors is no unpleasant thing to see, and heaven knows they are sufficiently rare to make them novel. But the only real aesthetic pleasure to be got out of the theatre is that which we experience when we can say of a play that it is not like other plays, or of a man that he is not like other actors. It matters not in what school of drama or in what class of actors; the comedienne who has the real twinkle in her eye, or the tragedian who has in his face the dark contradictions of tragedy. The great enjoyment that makes the theatre worth while is in seeing individual talent, in watching a man give back what God put into him. It is this pleasure that one feels in a considerable degree in Mr. Clay Clement's work. There are no heavy climaxes in the *Baron von Hohenstauffen* [*The New Dominion*], as they would be entirely inconsistent. From seeing Mr. Clement in that play alone it is impossible to judge whether or not he could rise to a great occasion. He had no opportunity for any great flashes of transcendent power, for the white heat of passion, only the genial, constant warmth of a generous and charming personality.

In the matter of physique, which is a matter of considerable import- ance after all, Mr. Clement is able to assume the worthy baron with very little disguise. It is worth while to say that he grows that remarkable hair himself. He has some German blood in his veins and a great deal of German character in his face. In more than his face; one feels that he is the Baron Hohenstauffen under his clothes, the very play of his muscles, the carriage of his shoulders, are interpretative of his part, and as for his walk, that is Hohenstauffen himself. Mr. Clement puts his bone and muscle as well as his heart and mind into the character. It is more than skin deep. On a one night's seeing one can hardly say that Mr. Clement is a great actor, but that he is a great Hohenstauffen is evident enough.

Journal, March 3, 1895, p. 13.

... The thing which is most hopeful and full of promise in Mr. Clement is his deliberateness. He knows the value of silence. Nervous haste is the curse of half our younger actors. An actor must have his work and himself well under control before he can afford to be slow. To say goodbye to one's sweetheart and rush precipitately off the stage at the left centre is one thing, and not a very difficult thing, either. To stop and think, to remember, to tell by look and gesture all that has been and will be, to meet temptation and fight it out, to be weak and then to be strong, to look once more over the James River to the hills to stamp them forever into the memory, all this without a word, without a sound, that is acting. To do it requires the depth and deliberation of an artist.

The play is Mr. Clement's own. It is cleverly and in some parts strongly written. In plot it is entirely simple and unassuming, in language chaste and dignified. It is not a great play, but it is a strong and original one. Back of it one can detect the same calm sincerity and intelligence that permeates that Baron von Hohenstauffen. We can recognize any vestiges of an intellect on the stage. A great many actors have emotion, some have real feeling, and a few, a very few have intelligence. That one thing is the difference between the creator who discerns and penetrates and the hectic emotionalist who fights his way in the dark.

Journal, March 2, 1895, p. 6.

Willa Cather's final comment in the mid-1890's concerning four of these artists makes another index of her fundamental concerns with human personality and human life. By the summer of 1896 Clement seemed to be advancing in his career, a success (at least at that point) she said. But as in many other statements in that unsettled spring before she left for Pittsburgh, Willa Cather emphasized the truth within rather than the outer accomplishment. Clement is a greater man than his success: "He has that delicate balance of imagination and sympathy which external powers cannot help or hinder much." He has "that conscious truth which to an artist means so much more than success. . . . He has the pearl that is priceless, the thing sought for, the kinship with art. He was a great man long before the world ever knew it" (Journal, June 7, 1896).

Salvini's greatness ended with the poignant, dramatic irony of his death in 1896. In her signed column "The Passing Show," sent from Pittsburgh and published in the Journal, Willa Cather wrote of him (December 27, 1896) in much the same terms she had used a year and a half earlier: "It is hard to realize that Alexander Salvini is dead. He was such a magnificent young animal; such a buoyant, effervescent fellow. He had the physique of the Faun of the Capitol and seemed unable to contain his spirited health. He completely captured the stage in a whirlwind of good humor. He was everywhere at the same minute, on the chairs, under the table, vaulting out of the windows. His high spirits were cyclonic. It doesn't seem possible that such a perfect physical specimen as Salvini can be packed away in a vault in Florence. That nimble D'Artagnan, that reckless Don Caesar, that virile Ruy Blas seemed the last man likely to die in his youth."

With Bernhardt and Mansfield, Willa Cather inclined more and more to distinguish between the artist and the person. She never changed toward them as artists, yet as she became more knowledgeable she admitted freely that there were elements of personal clay in most idols. Mansfield became rather unattractive in his public life, could be described as "the irascible, the eccentric," but still "the great" (Journal, December 15, 1895). Bernhardt with her dogs and her publicity was surely something of a harlequin. Yet Bernhardt, the human artist, had—or perhaps represented—what to Willa Cather were the old, eternal, primitive powers of life, and this was a greatness that could not be dimmed.

Bernhardt has the intensity of the East, she wrote early in 1896: "Yes, she is of the east, the old, old east, where the sun himself is born and all things glorious and refulgent. Where else can one find that sinuous motion of hers? Only in the jungles or the harems of the east. Her voice is one with which a fire worshipper might sing his triumphant chant to the sun, or a snake charmer put his serpents to sleep. She has the fierce flame-like beauty of the old Jewish women" (Journal, February 16, 1896). In this spring Willa Cather believed that Bernhardt would never play men's parts—"she knows so well the power of sex in art." Ages ago when the pyramids were young, "nature taught that old and oft transmitted soul of hers the few elemental, fundamental facts upon which life rests, by which life rules. She has that old and deep knowledge of a very few things that sufficed the Hindoo philosopher under his banyan tree. You feel it when you see her; 'O, the gulf that there is between me and thee!' The mummy of a daughter of the Pharaohs is not more remote from all things modern than this woman" (Journal, March 29, 1896). The aura of Bernhardt was truly one of those things that haunt the mind. Later that year in Pittsburgh Willa Cather saw Fanny Davenport in La Tosca, but wrote in "The Passing Show" (Journal, January 31, 1897) that there keeps coming to you a vision of "a figure slender, spirit-like, impalpable, a face of flame that is now all love, now all jealousy, now all hate, and you keep thinking of Sarah."

LIMITATIONS AND DISTINCTIONS

In the Kingdom of Art are many mansions. Willa Cather felt strongly from the first that an artist must recognize his own particular talent and not try to do the work of others: his limitations may also create his individuality. In some of her specific statements, she pointed out that the classic tragedian Jean Mounet-Sully and the popular comedian Nat Goodwin both have a place in the Kingdom; in her notes on four women singers, she observed how some qualities of temperament may limit or release a talent, how the art itself becomes one with the singer. Particularly significant, she thought, were the limitations and distinctions of national character, and she reiterated what she considered a basic difference between the English (cold, proper, and stiff) and the French (warmly emotional, with exotic grace). It is interesting to note that while Willa Cather was probably aware of W. C. Brownell's French Traits (1889)—some terms are reminiscent —she followed him only in some remarks on the French epigrammatic style. For his basic French traits of reason and intellectuality, she substituted grace, wit, and "the hot blood of the South."

Mounet-Sully's Classic Acting

Mounet-Sully's season [1894] in New York has begun with curious effect. The critics and public are divided over him, and the factions in warring with each other very nearly forget the great Frenchman. It seems that Mr. Mounet-Sully is especially billed for Greek and is at his best in translation of Sophocles. It must be a wonderful thing to see a Frenchman of this century who can play the stern classic roles of old Greece well. It is hard to see how a Frenchman could be severe and simple enough to play *Oedipe Roi*. It is almost a revival of the age of great sculpture. The New York critics say that his every pose is a sculptured god, that his emotion is simple, direct and rises perfectly to the climax of universal woe and bitter fate which is the key note of all Greek tragedy. If M. Mounet-Sully plays Creon and Oedipus so well it is easy to see why he does not make any astounding success as Hernani. A Lincoln dramatic said truly when he said that versatility is a nightmare. Mr. [E. S.] Willard seems to be able to play *Hamlet* one night and *The Silver King* the next and could probably play the *Police Patrol* the next, but not many men can wear the cap and bells and the tiara with equal grace, much less can they combine the classic and romantic. If M. Mounet-Sully has sufficient statuesqueness to impersonate such characters, he will only lower his tone by attempting romantic drama. He can never attain the warmth and complex sympathies of Ruy Blas or Don Roderique, he must keep himself like the cold classic literature and the shapely marble gods of the language he adores. He has a grand serenity that is almost a reproach to the fret and fume of modern art. He has dignity and beauty of person and mind. He belongs to an age when men hewed out lofty ideals in white rock and embodied in literature only what was noblest and purest in life. His acting belongs to the time when man's only enemy was fate, when he was strong against his doom, before he feared his own weakness and was his own foe. The Greeks lived just at the balancing period when mind and sense were equally active and were not ashamed of each other. Man was a healthy animal with a healthy mind, he succeeded or he failed, all his emotions were positive. He lived while he could for he knew that the fates would trick him and thwart him, that the Eumenides would torture and laugh at him. He had only one fear, the fear of fate and the inexplicable vengeance of the heavens. Such life was all action and swift motion in white sunlight with night and the sea for a background. The great French tragedian can suffer as Oedipus or meet black doom as Creon, but the suffering is all inflicted upon him, he cannot suffer from himself. He cannot know the success of Faust which was failure, the failure of Hamlet, which was success. He has the chisel of Praxiteles, he must forge[t?] the brush of Murillo.

Journal, April 8, 1894, p. 13.

Nat Goodwin's Comedy

... As to Mr. Goodwin himself [in *A Gilded Fool*], well, he is just Mr. Goodwin, jolly, easy-going, clever Nat Goodwin. A good deal of a Bohemian, considerable of a chappy, something of a vagabond, and just enough of an artist to redeem all the other ingredients. It is true that Mr. Goodwin only plays one role under many names, but in that role he is a clever and skilful actor. It is true that his personality and peculiar temperament limit him rigidly, but if they make certain lines of comedy entirely impossible for him, they also especially fit him for others. The coarser phases of his role seem to come to him just a little too easily, so easily that they jar on one at times. Yet when he was serious last night it was with effect. He tore that rose to pieces like a man who could feel, and he said his "thousand years of life and sunlight" line like a man who had a little of the poet in him after all. He gave that long and difficult monologue about his mother and his youth without being prosy, and if he did not put real feeling into it then he can imitate feeling wonderfully well. Mr. Goodwin is not of the highest order of artists who can shake off the fetters of the flesh and set aside the limitations of temperament; who can "rise on stepping stones of their dead selves to higher things." Mr. Goodwin has not crucified his "self." It is very much alive and it is his limit. But within that limit he is all that any man could be. He belongs to the great majority of good actors who cannot escape from their own shadows. The actor who can be other and greater than himself is the rare exception.

Journal, December 4, 1894, p. 8.

There has been a good deal of excitement lately over Mr. Nat Goodwin and his future career. Mr. Goodwin's successful work as David Garrick has stirred up the dear old classicists who are forever trying to force every young man of promise into classic comedy. Mr. [Elwyn A.] Barron, the talented and eminently just critic on the [Chicago] *Inter-Ocean*, has fallen into a bad habit of discovering genius. He has laid genius up against Mr. Goodwin and declares that he has given the American public a pledge which he must redeem; that the seal of greatness is upon him, and that he must begin to fast and pray and play Shakespeare. Now, why in the name of the sacred nine should Mr. Goodwin play Shakespeare? Just because he is a thoroughly modern spirit, because by personal tastes and sympathy he is peculiarly fitted to represent one of the most amusing, if not one of the most elevating phases of modern American society, why should he be relegated to the shades of classic comedy? Mr. Goodwin has no particular love for Shakespeare and he is honest enough to admit it. His literary tastes are not much above Bell's life. He belongs to the rapid, sporty set of young men who have more vivacity than brains and he is the artistic exponent of his class. This is no discredit to Mr. Goodwin. He is to be respected because he has recognized his limitation and has not essayed Orlando or Bob Acres. In his sphere Mr. Goodwin is an artist. The American public has need for him and love for him. It is true that he can only impersonate one type, but that type happens to be very much in vogue. All his acting is strongly colored by his own personality, but he belongs to a clan that is a very real part of American life and that has a strong influence in the moulding of American society, and it has a right to a representative in the great legislature of art. Mr. Goodwin represents it on the stage very much as Mr. Richard

Harding Davis does in literature, and he does it just as well. There is no reason why Mr. Goodwin should draw a long face and confine himself to hardtack and congress water to become an indifferent impersonator of classic roles. If only the dear critics would permit a man to be great in his own way and the way nature intended for him. Most of us would be rather sorry to see Mr. Goodwin a better man than he is or even a more serious actor, for it would unfit him for just the class of work that no other man can do so well. He has his sphere, a sphere of human interest, and he fills it well. In art that means success. He is not a perfect workman, and never will be. He jumps from pathos to comedy, where a man of finer grain would glide so subtly that you could never tell just where the transition took place. But the public does not demand perfect work; it only asks for something that every other actor cannot do. Mr. Goodwin has the rare gift of reaching out to the people and appealing to them, and he can delight you a whole long evening so thoroughly that you almost forget that his art is not of the highest kind, for it is not.

Journal, December 9, 1894, p. 13.

So New York has discovered that Nat Goodwin cannot play *David Garrick*. . . . Now how could the jovial and frivolous Mr. Goodwin play a part requiring such careful study and fine character work? Study of any sort is not a weakness of his. He has the artistic makeup and he picks up readily and easily, but there are some things in the world that refuse to be picked up, that cannot be learned from a cigar, or a glass of brandy, or even out of a pretty face. . . .

Where has Mr. Goodwin ever had time or inclination to even prepare to play *Garrick*? What does he know of that time, those conditions, of how it feels to be in earnest even? David Garrick was a peculiarly complex man and lived in a peculiarly complex time, a time that was still full of the influence of Fielding and Goldsmith and Johnson. One would have to simply be permeated by the literature and atmosphere of that time to play the part, as Thackeray was in *Henry Esmond*, as Mansfield is in *Beau Brummell*. They say that Mr. Goodwin does the drunken scene better than any of the others. That's just it, he can play Garrick's weakness, but not Garrick's strength. He can be Garrick the rake and Garrick the drunkard, but not Garrick the artist and lover.

For several reasons it is perhaps a good thing that Mr. Goodwin did not succeed so brilliantly as Garrick. Mr. Goodwin's laxness in his living is his own business, but his carelessness in his work is the public's affair.

The young actors of America need an example. They need to learn that there is a great difference in degree as well as in kind between a character actor and even the best of the low comedians. That there are reasons why a man who speaks Henry Guy Carleton's lines perfectly [in *A Gilded Fool*] may not read Shakespeare passably. That after all one may not serve God and the Other Fellow, even though he serve the Other Fellow passing well.

The truth is, that if Goodwin were not so delightful he would be a great pity. For under all his vagabond ways nature really gave him some of the stuff of which the great are made. But the world has given him too much else, too much flattery and pleasure and encouragement of his weakness. And then the man never had any conscience or sense of responsibility. Now he must be content to lie on the sunny side of the apple tree and take it easy. He is the prince of good fellows and must let it go at that. It is a good thing to be a graceful vagabond, and he is that. We are always glad to laugh with him, but we must weep with other men. Goodwin has no sincerity. That says all there is to be said. A man may have every thing on earth but that and still have nothing. Sometimes, indeed, sincerity makes fools of shallow men, but without it they are always fools, "gilded fools."

Courier, November 2, 1895, p. 7.

Four Singers: Tavary, Doenhoff, Melba, Lussan

Madame Marie Tavary and her opera company presented Il Trovatore *in Lincoln on December 8, 1894. In the company was Helena von Doenhoff, whom Willa Cather interviewed, quoted, and often admired for the very passion and feeling that she found wanting in Tavary. During the week of March 10, 1895, Willa Cather went to Chicago for the opera, hearing Nellie Melba (who sang in* Les Huguenots *and* Roméo et Juliette*) and Zélie de Lussan (who sang in* Falstaff*).*

¶ [Mme. Tavary in *Il Trovatore*] has grace and finished technique. She has all the things which accompany and attend great feeling, but of feeling itself, of consuming passion, never a spark. For this she very largely atones by earnest endeavor and a voice which is remarkable for its power and sweetness.

Madame Helena von Doenhoff has real dramatic fire. She has a strong and deep contralto voice which was just a little "catchy" in her first scene, but she soon had it completely under control. To speak of

Madame von Doenhoff's voice alone would be manifestly unfair, for she has something higher. When a singer can feel strongly and make others feel, then her voice is merely an instrument upon which a higher thing than even melody does its will. [*Journal*, December 9, 1894, p. 4]

¶ Mention should again be made of Madame Helena von Doenhoff whose vigor and abandon were so plainly manifest in the mountain scene, as was her deep and vibrant contralto voice in "Home to Our Mountains." She has all the fiery intensity and the genuineness of emotion which seems to particularly belong to the contralto temperament.

The convent scene was a beautiful one, although Madame Tavary did not lay aside her diamond rings with the vanities of the world. But in that scene she certainly sang with feeling and came nearer than anywhere else to perfect freedom and ecstasy. She seems to portray the anguish of love better than its delight. Those spontaneous bursts of feeling, those flashes of great exaltation which belong to great passion, either Madame Tavary never had or they have burned themselves out and left something of languor and melancholy. [*Journal*, December 10, 1894, p. 8]

¶ "Yes," said Madame Helena von Doenhoff, of the Tavary Opera Company, as she bustled wildly about her dressing room, speaking of music in general, "to always want to sing, to be always young and in love, to keep up the enthusiasm, to sustain the ecstasy, that is what it means to be a singer. Of course Tavary and I are no more sixteen, but," as she gave her satin slipper an impatient toss, "art does not come at sixteen." [*Journal*, December 16, 1894, p. 13]

¶ Mme. Melba, not content with the most wonderful voice and perfect execution in the world, is hard at work cultivating the dramatic possibilities of her roles. . . . But if she stood perfectly still, if she never moved a muscle while she sang she would still be a great actress. Her voice can act just as it can do everything else. Those vibrant tones can plead and thrill and suffer, can love and hate and renounce of themselves, alone, without aid of any kind. She swells a B flat that is all the triumphant anguish of resignation, she runs cadenzas that are the very swooning ecstasy of love, sings allegros that are the black bottom of hopeless despair. Most great singers follow the score with their voices and libretto with their gestures. Melba's voice does both. It is not like other voices, it is an individual living thing which can feel and exult and experience. One never thinks about Melba's acting, it is all in her voice. [*Journal*, June 9, 1895, p. 12]

¶ Miss Zélie de Lussan who is this season trying to twinkle among the serene great lights of grand opera, is a striking example of how comparatively futile is vocal talent without creative power or what for a lack of a better name we call the "artistic temperament." Mlle. de Lussan is a graceful and charming little actress with a sweet and bird-like though rather light voice. It would be difficult to recall a more winning personality or a more delightful stage manner. But charm cannot make a great singer. The truth is that Mlle. de Lussan has not the first conception of the meaning of the role. No one in the world could teach her what it means to be Carmen. She is not especially cold like Mme. [Emma] Eames, she is just trivial and painfully limited. She can be quite ardent in a way, but it is such a pretty Sunday-school-picnic sort of ardor, like that of a girl just from boarding school who kissed a young man on the chin and thinks she has done something awful and is quite a woman of experience. Mlle. Zélie tries to be passionate, but she is only sentimental; she simulates abandon, but it is only giddiness. When she tries to be naughty she is simply ludicrous. Some one has said that it takes a large woman to sin gracefully. Mlle. de Lussan has not sufficient width of chest. Yet for all this she is a very dear little person, the sort of woman that one would be willing to have one's younger brother marry, even if she had been "on the stage," the sort of woman who could teach the banner class of a Sabbath school admirably, but scarcely the sort of woman who could create a role in a great opera. [*Journal*, April 7, 1895, p. 13]

> *The next fall Willa Cather repeated her judgment of Mlle. de Lussan, who was then doing* Carmen *abroad. She began by quoting from the Dublin* Times, *which said that "Mlle. de Lussan was always a darling, delightful and charming Carmen; but to this she has added an audacious suggestiveness and an almost unlimited abandon...." This was too much for Miss Cather. She continued:*

The Dublin *Times* man has lost his head. It simply is not possible. Mlle. de Lussan is a nice little person with a nice smile and an angular form without a single natural curve on it. The only kind of abandon she can simulate is a sort of giggling school girl abandon that might do for the Three Little Maids of the *Mikado*, but is pretty light diet for Carmen.... Why she is as sweet and innocent as a new born babe, and very nearly as artless. Imagine a thin Carmen with a Band-of-Hope smile and engaging Y.W.C.A. manners and slender Sunday school arm. Bah! [*Courier*, September 28, 1895, p. 7]

Kinds of Opera

Light opera in any form is popular in America and is becoming more so every year. The Germans are built for heavy music. In an opera they demand music pure and simple. The prima donna may be as old as the "hills" and as uncomely as those withered dames Hans Holbein drew, but if she can sing the Germans will not only forgive her, but in their artistic enthusiasm and naive simplicity they will fancy her an Aphrodite rising from the waves. But the Americans, like the French, prefer action to music. They can understand and feel and enjoy more readily through action and sound. This is not a depravity of taste; it is merely a temperamental difference. In grand opera Americans prefer singers like Calvé, who have magnetism as well as voice. In light opera voice is the least consideration and, alas, action is not the greatest. The one thing which a light opera singer cannot do without is beauty. Either she must possess the genuine article like Lillian Russell and Della Fox and Pauline Hall, or like Marie Tempest she must possess such, have such an elusive and fascinating sort of homeliness that she can make the public believe it is beauty. This is not a repetition of the adoration of the chappies; it is an indisputable fact, and perhaps it is not a fact to be proud of. No woman who did not possess unusual physical charms has ever succeeded in light opera. The result of this is that the American stage is always crowded with women who can neither act or sing and who do not even make an honest endeavor to do either.

Journal, November 25, 1894, p. 13.

Kinds of Realism

It is not enough that Ibsen's plays have been thrilling and chilling us for so long, the professional people are threatening to run in a Russian social ethics drama upon us, written in the most blood-curdling style of the most blood-curdling Russian. The play, *The Thunderstorm*, was written by Ostrovsky.[7] Katherine, the heroine, is a girl of a sensitive and enthusiastic temperament, and is tyrannized over by her mother-in-law, who even forbids her to kiss her husband. Finding no sympathy in her own home Katherine seeks it outside. In her husband's absence she yields to her lover, Boris. During a terrible thunderstorm she confesses to her

7. The Russian dramatist Aleksandr Ostrovsky (1823–1886) wrote a variety of plays, such as *Poverty Is No Crime* (1854), *The Forest* (1871), and *The Snow Maiden* (1873). *The Storm* (1860) was later used as the basis of the opera *Katia Kabanova* (1921) by the Czech composer Janacek.

husband, whose only care is as to what his mother will say. When she tells Boris that they are discovered, he also trembles at the thought of the mother-in-law. Finally Katherine drowns herself in the river. We have stood the awfulness of French realism very patiently, but we must draw a line at the Russian. French anguish isn't so bad after all, it's such a self-satisfied, intentional, stagey kind of anguish, while the anguish of the northern people is such a dumb, brutal, helpless sort of suffering. When the French lover commits suicide he does it artistically and dramatically with a fan in his pocket, a neat epigram on his lips and a rose in his button-hole. The northern man does it in an awful disgusting manner like Ibsen's Lövborg. When Frenchmen go insane it is always a beautiful, fanciful insanity like that of Guy de Maupassant, who in his madness thought his fancies were big red and white butterflies and spent his time catching them. When a man of the north goes mad it is the madman of *Brand*. It doesn't pain one to see the French heroes die, because they either die to the flourish of trumpets or smothered with kisses, while Ibsen's heroes crawl off and die disgustingly like beasts. Ibsen has already sent a shiver over the bare shoulders of the theatrical world. When Mr. Ostrovsky's plays are staged we will have to go to see them muffled in furs like Greenlanders.

Journal, February 25, 1894, p. 9.

The Sledge and the Rapier

The Green Carnation [by Robert Hichens, 1894] is both a clever and an inane book. Clever in that it is a bright satire, inane in that it devotes itself to parodying a school almost wearisome to parody. It is not immoral as the publishers for business reasons have advertised, mere epigrams cannot be immoral. The book is a collection of epigrams on and off the subject. It certainly ought to succeed in disgusting people with Mr. Wilde's epigrammatic school once and for all. It turns and twists those absurd mannerisms and phrases of Wilde's until they appear as ridiculous as they really are. The hero thinks jam must be immoral because it is so good; his friend thinks deviled kidneys must be wicked because they are so beautiful. So the book strings on from driveling effeminacy to maudlin-ness. In a sense it is a timely book for the English-speaking world needs prodding in the matter of epigrams. There are a number of really talented young writers who are sacrificing the strength, vitality and common sense of their style in straining after the epigrammatics. So far as the writer remembers no really great English author has ever been epigrammatic. It's not in the blood—or the climate. The Frenchman is born with an epigram on his lips. He uses them unconsciously. When he is a child and fights over his marbles he disputes in epigrams. The peasants speak in epigrams. But the English were made for slower, heavier speech. The Frenchman cuts like a rapier, but the Englishman crushes like a sledge.[8] If he studies French word-fencing he only makes a clown of himself. He can never apply his power through a slender blade, and he is at best only a poor imitation. The affectation poisons his style, his vigor and his whole personality. He loses not only his art but his manhood. The Anglo-Saxon must be content to plod heavily along as his fathers did before. He can be good or wicked or great whichever he chooses, but he cannot be all three at once. He cannot discuss art and vice in the same breath. The Frenchman may live *en concubinage* with his muse, but the Englishman must live in wedlock, chaste and holy and devoted, "forsaking all other and clinging to her only." He may be basely, sordidly, contemptibly wicked if he wishes, but he can never be gracefully or artistically wicked.

Journal, November 4, 1894, p. 12.

Some English and French Performers

In three items in the Journal *during the season of 1894–1895, Willa Cather notes again the individual ways of nations and their people. From her reading in the theatrical papers, she knew that critics had been praising the new English actress Olga Nethersole as a great Camille—and that raised a question. She could speak more definitely about the performers she saw in Lincoln. Her comparison of Dorothy Morton's work in* The Fencing Master *with that of Marie Tempest (who had appeared in the same play the year before, April 3, 1894) is one of dozens of such tries at distinguishing and evaluating the qualities of separate stage performances. Willa Cather saw some plays three or four times during her Lincoln years, and as a reviewer she characteristically tried to note just where and in what degree one production differed from another. Some lecturers also came often. "Max O'Rell" was the pseudonym for Paul Blouet, a Frenchman who (like a small corps of others) capitalized by lecture tours and books on the desire of the American people to be told about themselves. He was in*

8. Although W. C. Brownell in *French Traits* (1889) speaks of the "rapier" of the French, Willa Cather's phrasing here is more suggestive of John Esten Cooke's *Hammer and Rapier* (New York: Carleton, Publisher, 1870), comparing Generals Lee and Grant: "The rapier had been tried for three long years.... One course alone was left him [Grant]—to take the sledge-hammer in both hands, and, leaving tricks of fence aside, advance straightforward, and smash the rapier in pieces, blow by blow, shattering the arm that wielded it, to the shoulder blade" (p. 230).

Lincoln on February 9, 1892, lecturing on "America As Seen Through French Spectacles," and again on February 11, 1895, speaking on "Her Highness, Woman."

¶ Miss [Olga] Nethersole is of a nation which is not productive of great tragediennes. Her nationality is heavily, heavily against her. She comes from a country that is shut out from the sun's face all the year around by clinging clouds of wet mist. A country where society is entirely formal, where coldness is esteemed a virtue among women, and where demonstrativeness is almost a crime. It may be highly to Miss Nethersole's credit that she "is an Englishman," but it is certainly a disadvantage to her art. However, nationality is not always fatal. It influences and limits physique, character, temperament, talent—everything but genius. If Miss Nethersole can either rise above or sink below the conventional standards of her country's art, she is indeed a great actress. . . . if Miss Nethersole can play the Camille of the first act, can overcome her traditions, nationality, instincts, and be thoroughly and entirely a French coquette and a woman of the demi-monde of Paris, then she has the ability to take unto herself the spirit of all times and lands, the power to "live in all lives that are and love in all loves that be." Let us hope that in this instance the critics are right, that Miss Nethersole is all this, and that the world is richer by one genius more, for with all its splendor and magnificence this world would be very poor were it not for the memory of its great. [November 11, 1894, p. 13]

¶ Miss Dorothy Morton [in *The Fencing Master*] makes a thoroughly blonde and placid Anglo-Saxon Francesca. Her vocal qualifications are unquestionable and she puts into a single solo more music than ever [Marie] Tempest had in her treacherous, tricky little throat. But her movements are heavy. She lacks those undefinable little graces of person that Tempest brought back with her from Paris that were as fascinating as they were artificial. She is much more earnest and conscientious in her work, but in opera conscience is not always a saving grace. She plays the part with rosy-cheeked, Anglo-Saxon good nature. Tempest played it with a dainty foreignness and inexplicable caprices of posing that were like fantastic phrasing in music. It is not unjust to Miss Morton to say that she is blonde and English and is entirely without local color—no reflections at all on her make-up. [March 3, 1895, p. 8]

¶ It has been a long time since we have encountered anything more thoroughly enjoyable than the lecture of Max O'Rell, or to be more exact, than the lecturer Max O'Rell. One does not go to hear him for his lecture, but for his personality. It is not what he says, that has all been said a great many times before, but it is the incomparable way in which he says it. He is of a nation of actors and his manner, it would be absurd to call it a "delivery," is thoroughly and unconsciously dramatic. His words amount to very little, but his presence, his gestures, that little pucker of the eyebrows and inimitable shrug of the shoulders, amount to a very great deal. That little shrug, by the way, is the index of the cynicism and skepticism of the Frenchman. It is his way of saying that he is not to blame for his own sins or anyone's else, that he is not at all responsible for society. That significant gesture is the ever-living Voltaire of the French. [February 24, 1895, p. 13]

Judith Gautier: The French Quality

Mme. Judith Gautier has written a new Hindoo play called *Aspara* for Bernhardt. Mme. Gautier, it will be remembered, translated from the Japanese *Heart of Ruby*, the play that failed at Daly's last year because it was too poetic to succeed. Mme. Gautier is the daughter of Théophile Gautier, the author of those luxuriant oriental studies *Fortunio* and *Une Nuit de Cléopâtre*. The French are full of oriental feeling. Those hot winds that blow up from Provence carry the odor of citron and orange groves even to Paris. Said Daudet, "O wind and fire of the South, ye are irresistible." French art is full of them. The great passions never become wholly conventionalized in France. Every year that hot blood and ardorous enthusiasm from the south pour into Paris, into Parisian life and Parisian thought. Beneath that most polished suavity in the world there is always something of the savage. It comes from the South, with the poets and the orators. In the last forty years a whole oriental vocabulary has crept into the French language. Half of the best novels, the greatest pictures, the most perfect music are oriental in theme and treatment. Last season Bernhardt played *The Earthen Chariot*, a Sanskrit drama four thousand years old. No one imbibed more of this oriental atmosphere than Gautier. He stands next to Flaubert in handling oriental color. There are pages in his oriental sketches that seem to palpitate with heat, like a line of sand hills in the South that dances and vibrates in the yellow glare of noon. There are sentences that ring out like the clank of golden armor, chapters that are embalmed in spices and heavy with the odors of the vale of Cashmere. Judith Gautier has followed her father's eastern studies and gone beyond him. The Academy of France never questions her translations from the Japanese, Sanskrit and Hindoo. She is a linguist, an ety-mologist, a poet, a novelist and a dramatist. She has literally "ransacked the ages, spoiled the climes," [9] and yet she is a Parisienne. They are strange people, those women of Paris; they are so versatile and they can touch upon so many extremes. They are, on a general average, about the most learned women in the world, and yet they are never "digs" like other learned women. Study never takes any of the vivacity out of them. They learn a language as they learn a dance.

Courier, September 28, 1895, p. 7.

Voices of the Stage

Among all the rich evidences of Willa Cather's habit in these early years of observing closely and recording exact details of looks, manners, dress, speech, gesture, and movement—all the minutiae that can be used to draw the lines of living character—some Journal *notes on voices will illustrate not only the precision of her ear but also a style that fits itself in language and rhythm to the particular tone she is after, lilting or melancholy or plainly deliberate. Perhaps one can also catch an undercurrent of fun, a kind of amazed pleasure at the absurdity and wonder of things.*

¶ Mademoiselle Celeste [in *Count of Monte Cristo*] is a dream of beauty. There are few handsomer women to be found in either the higher or lower walks of the profession, but her acting is weak, insipid and pointless. She is innocent of all art or even of a clever imitation of it, and her voice was a continual and painful surprise. It rather startles one to hear the tones of a cavalry officer issue from such very bewitching lips. . . . It is certainly strange that the leading lady of the romantic drama should always be so atrociously bad when she has nothing under heaven to do but wear gorgeous apparel with moderate grace and scream "Edmond!"—or whatever his name may happen to be—with moderated tenderness. [January 26, 1894, p. 6]

¶ Miss [Effie] Ellsler [in *Doris*] is a well meaning little woman with an impossible little nose, an irritating placidity of manner and a shrill domestic little stage shriek that is suggestive of mice. She delivered the most histrionic lines with correct elocution and unalterable calm, just as though she were ordering clam chowder and baked whitefish. [April 25, 1895, p. 8]

¶ Mr. [J. K.] Emmett [in *Fritz in a Mad House*] is by no means a heavy comedian, not even a very finished or magnetic one. But he has a sort of

9. A line from Browning's "Evelyn Hope" which Willa Cather quotes several times.

nonchalant mirth about him that is unmistakably refreshing. His part is light and his voice is light, his step is light and his laugh is light. He skims gaily along the surface of a part which is mostly surface. He is at his best when he is playing with the baby, waltzing with his coat tails spread and blowing bubbles which are as airy and unsubstantial as he is. [January 26, 1895, p. 6]

¶ And then of course there was DeWolf [Hopper in *Wang*]. DeWolf the tall, of the talented legs. No one has ever been able to say quite what it is that makes Hopper so funny. It may be those expressive paws of his, it may be those enormous and shapely limbs, and it may be that voice which forever cracks with anguish and quivers on the ragged edge of utter despair that passes despair and begins upon a tragic resignation. It's the kind of voice a man might have who had lost his last collar button, or smoked his last cigar, or arrived late at his wedding. There are times in life when one feels like that voice. [October 25, 1895, p. 6]

¶ It is a strange fact that people on the stage can't talk the English language like their fellow mortals. In these days there is a regular stage dialect, just as pronounced and set a dialect as any other. If in the real world anyone should gurgle the word "innocence" in the sensational actress manner, he or she would be sent to the first asylum that would risk receiving such a dangerous case. If any daughter should cry, "Me father!" in the fetching tone of the stage the frightened parent would most likely box his deluded darling's ears.

There is a peculiar difference in the way in which different actresses say the words "My God!" When Cora Tanner says them they are painfully suggestive of swearing; Margaret Mather says them daintily enough, but she is rather too conscious that she is saying them nicely; Edna May and Cecil Spooner shriek them as though the person addressed were deaf; Julia Marlowe says them very quietly, as though she did not want to say them at all and was trying to keep them back. Modjeska says them as Saint Ursula or Jeanne d'Arc might have said them, with wrapt belief and lofty conviction. It is as good as two or three sermons to hear the great Pole say those words. Clara Morris says them with terrible agony, like a woman in her extremity. Bernhardt says them—but who can say how Bernhardt does anything? But we think that the lips that speak must be a great deal naughtier than even those of the little Frenchwoman for the Deity to be wholly deaf when Bernhardt says "Mon Dieu!" [January 21, 1894, p. 16]

THE MAKING OF ARTISTS

The individual talent is a pleasure to observe, but if one is on the inside trying to find his own, it can also be a problem. When it comes to making an artist—if it can be done at all—Willa Cather's comments are often contradictory or extreme. Perhaps this is because they were often written out of disappointment, exaspera- tion, or passionate desire. What she felt at one moment she said with conviction, and no doubt she felt that every hazard in the way of a possible artist was her own. What does make an artist? Exactly how can one create the creator? This was something she would very well like to know. It seemed that a person must do the work of genius by himself, alone; and yet he must live fully and know the world. Logic and reason were silly crutches, and yet knowledge and intelligence were necessary guides in the darkness. What is the relation—and the comparative importance—of the gift of genius and the long years of learning to use it? Willa Cather has a few answers.

The Rights of Genius

A good many actors are breaking away from old ties and leaving their old managers this season and the said managers are loudly wailing of their ingratitude. The fact is the actors are not much to blame. It is so seldom that an actor gets an understanding manager, and most actors are too much managed. Over-management has broken down many a good actor. Every actor has some instinct of what he is fitted for. He gets a manager, a man without an artistic temperament, without ideas of art, who decides that he is fitted for something entirely different, and who in all kindness sets about melting the actor down and casting him over. The only thing left for the actor is to politely but firmly refuse to be melted. Take the case of Bernhardt alone. One manager declared she must be a singer, which would have been bad. Another insisted that she must be a comedienne, which would certainly have been worse. When she was fifteen her parents and uncles and aunts decided that she must go into a convent and be a nun, which, heaven knows, would have been worst of all.

It is laughable, this passion the canaille have for running a genius. Almost every butcher and baker and candlestick-maker has discovered some little genius and is endeavoring to develop him. Of course, as a rule, his genius is not a genius at all, and his swan is only a goose with its feathers rumpled. But if he happens to be something of a genius the case is even more absurd. Here is a man essentially commonplace, who has the common needs and the common desires and lives the common life, attempting to manage and control a man who is not of the common, whose every strength lies in the fact that his needs, desires and life are different from those of every other man on earth. He decides to generously find time to manage this genius. This artist shall paint the pictures he would paint if he could, write the books, act the plays that he would act. This artist is a Bohemian and wears a blouse. He will put clean linen on him and make him a gentleman. He desires him to be popular—that is his idea of greatness—to have nothing ill said about one. Now the artist, poor fellow, has but one care, one purpose, one hope—his work. That is all God gave him; in place of love, of happiness, of popularity, only that. He is not made to live like other men; his soul is strung differently. He must wander in the streets because the need of his work is with him; he must shun the parlors of his friends and seek strange companions, because the command of his work is upon him. Conventions which are necessary to other men suffocate him and bring upon him the deathly sickness which warns him. He needs ceaseless variety and change, a thousand complex inexplicable things, whereas his manager needs only beefsteak. If he has the courage he throws off the yoke of management; if not the strength to work leaves him, and he drifts on,

> Doing the work of all his several friends
> And serving every purpose except his own.

The fewer friends he has the better; every friend means one more manager. Friends demand weekly dividends on the interest they invest in one. When a man has nothing on earth but a purpose people might hold their tongues and leave him alone with it. Leave him to fail alone with it if God shall put upon him the chagrin of failure, to succeed alone with it if God has reserved for him that fulness of joy. He cares only for that purpose. They might leave him that.

Journal, October 21, 1894, p. 13.

A Talent for Living

It is a strangely significant fact that the book which is unquestionably the great book of the year [*Trilby*, by George Du Maurier] should be the work of a man who never wrote a novel until he was fifty. The practice of youthful novel writing has done as much as any other one thing to weaken and vitiate literature. The notion seems to have gone abroad that a man can write before he has lived; that he can project his personality before he has any personality to project. Literature is generally regarded as a craft which anyone who has a thorough classical education and a dictionary of synonyms can practice at will. The talent for writing is largely the talent for living, and is utterly independent of knowledge. The less craft and cult there is about literature the better. There is nothing more fatal than the habit so cultivated by young authors of seeing things in a "literary" way. There is only one way to see the world truly, and that is to see it in a human way. The scientist who sees the world as a collection of atoms and forces, the political economist who sees it as a set of powers and federations, sees falsely. They see facts, not truths. The only things which are really truths are those which in some degree affect all men. Atoms are not important; the world would be just as happy if we did not know of their existence. The ultimate truths are never seen through the reason, but through the imagination. The litterateur who reduces his work to a craft makes the fatal mistake of regarding success as the sum of his knowledge and cleverness, whereas in reality it is the result of his living.

The young writers who spend their time in making epigrams, who rack their brains for clever comparisons, who torture their tiny imaginations to find a new figure to fit the "golden leaves of autumn" or the "moaning of the surf" are all on the wrong track. It may be well enough to describe a daisy in an inimitable phrase, but daises play such a small part in the real life of the world. Word artists have had their day of greatness and are rapidly on the decline. We want men who can paint with emotion, not with words. We haven't time for pastels in prose and still life; we want pictures of human men and women. We are not even satisfied with ideas; we want people. Even the great essayists are not read much now, because the nineteenth century demands humanness. There are requisitions in all arts, and in literature there is one that is inexorable: An author must live, live deeply and richly and generously, live not only his own life, but all lives. He must have experiences that cannot be got out of a classical dictionary or even in polite society. He must know the world a good deal as God knows it, in all the pitiable depravity of its evil, in all the measureless sublimity of its good.

Journal, October 28, 1894, p. 13.

Intellect in Art

The matter of intelligence has been so abused on the stage and off of it and the importance of intellect in art has been so grossly exaggerated that it rather tends to produce a reaction and make us underestimate the necessity of high mental qualities in an actor. In traditional roles and imitative acting the mind plays a very little part. Superficial people with marked hist[rion]ic talent, like Margaret Mather and Robert Mantell, have known periods of great temporary popularity. But their career has always been a flash in the pan. Such lights fail in a very little while. The oil is exhausted and the wick burns out. They may have every talent under the sun, but if they lack the mental weight and seriousness to sustain an ever-rising ideal, the high perceptions to realize the awful seriousness and dignity of art, their limitations are invincibly fixed, and their star will set where it should begin to rise. It is true that some actors have been over refined, that they have been spoiled by too much learning, but very many more have been spoiled by too little. The heart must be big enough to absorb and humanize all that a man holds in his brain, but unless he has that motive power which is in understanding alone, the inner courts of his art are forever closed to him. An actor must be able to live the common life, to mean something to the lowest intelligence in his audience. He must make other men feel, but he himself must know. He must live their life before their eyes, but he must live it understandingly where they live it blindly. He must not only reproduce, he must interpret. An actor can never know enough. He can never afford to give up the study and contemplation which give him his insight back into the sources of things and which keep him unspotted from the world. They are his only safe-guards against flattery and egotism, the only things which can keep an artist's soul simple, and pure, and strong. In a creative artist the much talked of emotional qualifications are only the beginning of true great-ness. It requires a master intellect to apply strong emotions, or it is the feverish, meaningless passion of a child. Into his own art an actor should bring the spoils of every other art on earth, and above all the arts of living and loving. He should give his emotions an anchor that will reach down into the very depths of the very nature of things and hold him to the truth. An actor's imagination is his genius; it should be fed upon whatever is best in science, letters or art. He should know how it felt to be an Egyptian, sunning himself on the marble steps of the temple at Elephan-tine, how it felt to go up to the Acropolis on a blue spring morning in old Athens, how it feels to be a thirsty Bowery boy, hesitating between a free lunch of pork and beans or corned beef and cabbage. He should know how a king ascends the steps of his throne and how a peasant scrapes the mud from his wooden shoes. Potentially he should know all manners, all people, all good and all evil. The effects of this complete knowledge a gentleman more wise than holy once summed up by saying, "And ye shall become as gods." That is, ye shall create.

Journal, March 10, 1895, p. 13.

Prodigies: The Dovey Sisters

One of the most remarkable accounts in these early years is that of the Dovey sisters and their family, easily recognizable as the source for the characters and situation of Willa Cather's story "The Prodigies," first published in the Home Monthly *for July, 1897 (reprinted in* Collected Short Fiction, 1892–1912, *pp. 411 ff.). At the ages of ten and twelve, Alice and Ethel Dovey were singing prodigies of a kind, children from Plattsmouth, Nebraska, who had been trained abroad to use their fine voices with premature skill. In the fall of 1895, the Dovey sisters sang at a private performance in Lincoln on September 10, and at a more formal concert at the Funke Opera House on October 16, assisted by their teacher, Miss Lillian Terry. The girls did the balcony scene from* Roméo et Juliette, *the gypsy duet from* Il Trovatore, *"Suanee Ribber" (in a trio with Miss Terry), and a dance—"La Lucrece." Alice Dovey sang the waltz song from* Roméo et Juliette, *and Ethel "The Green Tree" by Balfe. In the story, "The Prodigies," the children become Hermann and Adrienne Massey, a little older than the Doveys (about fifteen and fourteen, though small for their age). Adrienne, like Alice, sings Gounod's "Waltz Song"; but instead of the balcony scene, the Massey children do the even more mature and tragic parting scene from* Roméo et Juliette. *Both accounts stress the children's phenomenal "method" and correctness, their seriousness, and their strangeness. In "The Prodigies" the pathos and fragility of the children have been intensified, especially by concentrating on one, the girl Adrienne, described as stooped and weary but perfectly taught in both her tones and her assumed, mechanical gaiety. In the reviews of both Lincoln appearances there is no real sign of what in the story would become a tragic theme—the heavy burden of premature and thoughtless (or even ruthless) manipulation by adults. But even in 1895 there is some feeling that the child-genius is unnatural, with a strangely inhuman magic. By the time she wrote "The Prodigies," Willa Cather had decided that the magic was black, not white.*

It was whispered about Tuesday [September 10, 1895] that Misses Ethel and Alice Dovey, the two wonderful little daughters of Mrs. George Dovey of Plattsmouth were in town. They have recently returned from Madame Cellini's school of music in London where they will take up their musical studies again next year. Through the kindness of several persons I had an opportunity to go and hear them Tuesday afternoon, and I went.

Not that I expected to be entertained, O, dear no! I have no weakness for prodigies. I had never heard a child who could sing and I never expected to hear one. The misguided infants with white dresses and blue sashes and golden curls who sing at Sunday school concerts were never dear unto my soul, and their curls never atoned for their sharp rigid little voices. When I saw the little Dovey girls I was still more discouraged, not but that they were pretty enough, but they were *so* little. I had heard they were young, but here were two tiny little things, ten and twelve years old, and small for their age. They were both charming little people, but there are so many charming people who are not great. Ethel has the real tragic eyes, the big gray eyes set deep and shaded by long lashes. That was the only ray of hope I saw. After a while the little girls quietly took their place by the piano and began to sing. It was some old English song that begins "I know a bank where wild thyme grows." It was simply wonderful. That is all I can say. It was the singing of children, and yet not of children. It was the child idea glorified, like the music of young composers and the songs of young poets. So far as I could see, though so little, they were both almost perfect in method. The little soprano, the youngest of the two, has a voice of wonderful flexibility, and sang beautifully in a spirit wholly childish. But the little alto is not a child in musical feeling. It was beautiful, the way she would take up her sister and strengthen and sustain her with those deep true tones. Then they took up from the pile of music that time-honored duo "Home to Our Mountains" from *Il Trovatore*. I was scarcely ready for that even then. One has a natural horror of trusting music of sentiment in the hands of children, no matter how gifted, and that duo has suffered enough abuse, heaven knows. The other was only a child's song, suited to children, but this was one of Verdi's most beautiful arias. But that little alto did not disappoint us. Under the childish accents there were the deep full tones, and there was feeling, real musical feeling, the thing that cannot be made or aquired, that gold dust and star dust cannot buy. That little voice rang full of yearning and those big gray eyes looked with dreamy intensity away from the music, away from us, beyond us all somewhere—I wondered at what. There was no doubt about it any longer. She had it, *the* thing, the thing of things, as much as a child could have it. Then came a solo, a lullaby, and then that old duo, "Hear me, Norma," all sung with that indefinable sympathetic and imaginative quality that is great in a woman, but is glorious in a child. Older people try their strength and make their mark, and we know their limit, but for a child we may plan so much, hope so much.

. . . The little Dovey girls will return to [Mme. Cellini's] school next year. It is this magnificent training, begun so early, that makes me so hopeful for these children. Most singers spend years of their lives unlearning the things they have learned wrong. There is talent enough in the world, and there is training enough too, but talent dies unknown and unrecognized by the wayside every day, and training is wasted upon lay figures and creatures of wood. They so seldom meet, but when they do they shake the stars sometimes. There is an explosion somewhere when those two get together. Of course even Mme. Cellini's word can not insure Mr. Dovey's little girls or anybody else's little girls a future. They have the great hope, the rest depends on many things.

Mrs. George Dovey, the mother of the inspired youngsters from Plattsmouth, is the daughter of Mr. Charles Dawson, for fifteen or twenty years storekeeper for the Burlington road at Plattsmouth. Mr. Dawson is an Englishman of the rotund, clean shaven, Pickwickian type. The children get much of their love of Shakespeare from their grandfather. He has been a student of the master all his life. The man is an artist to the ends of his tapering delicate fingers. He understood from the first that these children were not as other children are, and insisted that they be put under the best teachers. Their grandmother took them to London. In an American dentist's office, where the children's teeth were being treated, Mrs. Dawson met a wealthy lady who was the manager of the American booth in a charity fair managed by Society. The lady was bewailing her lack of two little girls to sing American airs in front of her booth. The dentist told her he knew of two little American girls who sang like larks. He brought them in. They sang for her. She was enraptured. Henceforth they sang to the oldest and noblest of the English nobility. Madame Cellini, who occupies the same place in London that Marchesi does in Paris, offered to teach them for nothing. Their reception in England was a tribute to their powers. When the children arrived in Plattsmouth they were met by "the band" and the people took the horses out of the carriage and dragged it themselves.

Courier, September 14, 1895, p. 7.

... The singing [of the Dovey sisters in their concert at the Funke on October 16] was remarkable, when judged as the singing of children ten and twelve years old. It was wonderful because it was simple, artistic singing, without the affectation and the straining of voices that almost invariably accompany such efforts. It is doing these little ones an injustice to say that they are sure to be among the world's great artists. All that we know now is that they have extraordinary talent. Its development depends upon so many things that it seems unfair to assume that their future is assured, that it is not necessary for them to leave the usual years of childhood free for the building of bone and muscle and the accumulation of vital forces. It is as unfair to expect them to become famous right away as it was to compare them last night with mature singers. They are children. Their charm lies in their beauty, their simple behavior, and the sweetness and accuracy of their singing. ...

The accompanist had the disadvantage of using a piano that was out of tune. It was necessary to play softly or create heavy discords, and a little tinkle was all the support the singers could receive. The dancing in the closing number was marred by the inadequacy of the music. The piano had a highly polished case, but there was no music inside of it.

Journal, October 17, 1895, p. 2.

The Child and the Artist

Writing about Josef Hofmann in the Courier *a week after the Dovey concert, Willa Cather makes a clear distinction between a child's talent and the real thing, for "the very things out of which an artist is made do not come to a man before he is twenty." Although she later said on numerous occasions that all of her material was gathered before she was twenty (after 1921 she said "before fifteen"), the statements do not conflict. The materials of art, yes—before twenty or before fifteen—but not the materials of the artist. These are the matters of experience, knowledge, the practiced hand.*

Josef Hofmann,[10] the young pianist, is to travel this season. Some musical critic has beautifully said of him that though the prodigy is gone the wonder is still there. Young Mr. Hofmann is to be congratulated that the wonder is still within him, but he is to be doubly congratulated upon the demise of the prodigy. As long as he was a prodigy he could never be an artist, indeed not a musician even. There have been certain great men,

10. The Polish-American pianist Josef Hofmann (1876–1957) was still under twenty in 1895. He had toured Europe as a child prodigy, making his American debut in 1887 at the age of eleven.

Mozart and Paganini chief among them, who have been able to live down the fact that they once were prodigies, but they had to be great indeed to do it. It may not really hurt a child to be a prodigy, but it hurts him very much to be told so. There is no more pitiful sight on earth than a passé prodigy whose life is outgrowing his art, who still wears yellow curls about a face that is no longer childish and tries to disguise the lengthiness of his growing limbs by stockings and knee breeches.

But in music the prodigy is more hopeful than on the stage. The boy who is the coming Booth at ten is generally property man at thirty. What becomes of them all anyway, those advanced young people who have brilliant careers from eight to twelve and then are heard of no more, Wallie Eddinger, Elsie Leslie Lyde and all the rest of them? Nothing great, so far as I can learn. They go too soon into an artificial atmosphere, an atmosphere where there is no time for silence and reflection and in which study is unknown. It kills them, that is, figuratively. For the boy who plays the Roman populace, helps the property man, does a song and dance and has big dreams there is hope, but I doubt if the tragic muse herself could make an actor out of the infant who is starred before he is in long trousers. So long as a child does only children's roles he is endurable, but when a child recites *Hamlet*, *Lear* and the much abused *Richard III*, it is the torture of the Spanish Inquisition to hear him. It is simply terrible to hear a child who ought to be reading fairy tales or sound asleep in his bed, mouthing the most perfect poetry in the world and cheerfully chirping with the wrong inflections words that represent the *governing* forces and impulses of the world. It's sacrilege to childhood and it's blasphemy to art. As Helena von Doenhoff once said to me: "Art does not come at sixteen." [11] No, verily, it does not, and those who have touched even the hem of its garment by the time they are twenty-six are blessed by God. Why, everything that a child creates is laughable, beautiful, only because of its naive imperfections. All childish creations lack anything beyond promise and mild merit, from the school boy verses of Byron to those peaceable little sonatas of the baby Beethoven. Thank heaven Shakespeare's earliest productions are not extant, he knew enough to burn them. The very things out of which an artist is made do not come to a man before he is twenty. While other boys are growing to be men he grows to be a creator. An artist is a child always, but a child is not always an artist.

Courier, October 26, 1895, p. 7.

11. See page 132 above.

THE PERSONAL SIDE

The relation of the man or woman to the artist in him was a problem that concerned Willa Cather for years after 1896. Perhaps it was more exactly the problem of division within one, the pull of separate motions and the result of some inevitable imbalance. How shall we then know the dancer from the dance? In these early years the fact of her statements may be more important than their conclusions, which are generally yes and no: "Good" and "evil" depend on their definitions. What a person is, does and does not affect his art. One's personal life is and is not more important than one's art. As a girl turning twenty, she tempered her own judgment about the balance of "life" and "art" quite noticeably between the first buoyant optimism when everything was possible, through times later on when she quite literally did not know what way she would take, to the final more complex distinctions in her last essays. But in several statements given here (and in the essays on writers in " The Life, The Art," pages 380 ff.) one point comes through: In the really great, art is supreme. Nothing will or should touch it, for it is in a firmament outside the usual rise and fall of human ways. In lesser ones the life encroaches. Duse could create the highest kind of art; Mary Anderson could not. Yet greatness comes to men and women as well as to artists.

The Good and the Proper

... How long will it take the public to find out that [in acting] the righteousness of the woman cannot save her art?[12] That many good and noble women are sad bunglers, and that many delightful ones are consummate idiots. People go to the theatre to see good acting, they should be satisfied with nothing else. The personal character of the actor is none of their business and should not enter into the question. ...

No one wishes to disparage goodness in an actress. No thoroughly evil woman could ever act. Acting postulates an appreciation of goodness, greatness and truth. But with all great actors goodness is a matter of impulse rather than of principle. An actress should be good, but not necessarily proper. How often have we gone to see an American Juliet or an English Camille, and left the theatre feeling the need of a bracing stimu-

12. Apropos of a report that the English actress Katharine Kidder would play Sardou's *Madame Sans-Gêne*. Miss Cather did not feel that Miss Kidder (a notable Christian woman) was up to it.

lant. The little women try hard enough, but it is like a schoolgirl trying to play a nocturne of Chopin's, or a glow-worm trying to give back the fire of the sun.

Journal, February 24, 1895, p. 13.

The Effect of Evil

Occasionally the stage affords a moral object lesson and on such occasions the people who write about the stage generally take occasion to preach a little. One can't blame them. They have to write so much that is very other than sermonizing that they ought not to be denied the privilege of a sermon now and then, just by way of a change. The latest occasion for moralizing is Mr. Robert Mantell's[13] failure as Romeo, and it is a pretty plausible hook to hang a sermon on. The public has no particular right to criticise an actor's private life until it affects their work; then it has a right to speak. It has been demonstrated a hundred times that a mediocre actor cannot play the son of the Montagues. An actor must have grace, abandon and the inward fire to even attempt the role. There was a time when Mr. Mantell could play Romeo, imperfectly, but with a promise which he has never fulfilled, which now he never will fulfil. Now, by a peculiar little touch of irony which the gods are rather fond of giving human life, Miss Behrens can play a better Juliet than Mr. Mantell's Romeo. That must make Mr. Mantell smart a little if he remembers the time when his managers and friends besought him to drop Charlotte Behrens at least professionally, and to get a leading lady who could properly support him. Mr. Mantell's friends knew well enough that she must either rise to his level or he must sink to hers. And they knew she could not rise. What is that old line that we used to read before "Locksley Hall" grew trite?

> Yet it shall be; thou shalt lower to his level day by day,
> What is fine within thee growing coarse to sympathize with clay.

In this case it was the man who lowered. It is difficult to say [at] just what point evil affects and weakens art. Some artists have been able to stand a good deal of it. Most great artists have had rather imprudent flames, but they outgrew them. Mr. Mantell has not outgrown his. Schiller and Goethe and the rest of them had their temporary weakness, but they were more faithful to their work than to the woman in the case.

13. Robert Mantell (with Charlotte Behrens) had played several times in Lincoln: *Monbars*, September 17, 1890; and *The Face in the Moonlight*, October 18, 1893.

That was rather heartless, but in keeping with the unwritten laws of art. Faithlessness to art is only fatal when it becomes habitual. Mr. Mantell allowed his to become so. There is a certain servitude which no soul can give to another and live. A book much more frequently quoted than followed remarks: "The soul that sinneth shall die." There is something in it. The Hebrews knew a thing or two. They had Solomon's glaring example before them. A more modern way to put it would be, "The soul that abases itself shall die." It does not matter much in what way, whether it is through whisky or frivolity, the yoke of social bondage, general indolence or Charlotte Behrens, it all amounts to the same thing. This peculiar balance of the vital forces, this unison of all one's powers into one lambent flame which men call genius, is such an exceedingly delicate thing. When the fire is out once, only God Himself could relight it. No one can say just how or when the change comes, any more than they can say how the light fades from an opal. In some undiscernible way the elusive quality of value goes and what was precious becomes common clay.

. . . In stories painters and musicians who have wasted their lives die painting or playing divinely, but in life things don't go that way. No, there are no deathbed repentances in art. It takes a whole long life not only of faith but of works to give an artist salvation and immortality among his kind. For the prodigal in art there is no return. A man cannot spend his life or even a few years of it among the husks and the swine and then go back clean and upright to his father's house. Neither can he call on a dozen young ladies and the wine houses in the same afternoon or reach the temple of fame by walking the Rialto in creased trousers.

Journal, December 2, 1894, p. 13.

The Privacy of Art

It is a peculiar fact that Signora Duse has never allowed her daughter to enter a theatre or to see a play. It is another evidence of how vastly Duse differs from all other women of the stage. The love of admiration, of homage, of publicity, the warm fellow feeling for others of the same profession, the genuine affection for the very outside of a theatre which are the almost inevitable accompaniments of an actress' life, seem never to have touched her. She has moved through the crowd of babbling Thespians without seeing or hearing them, she has worn the motley as though it were a nun's hood, she has gone from theatre to theatre as though she were going from shrine to shrine to perform some religious worship. Of her own personality, of her private life, the public has never had a glimpse;

we know as little of it as we know of Shakespeare. The most enterprising reporters have never been able to interview her, her answer has always been the same, "I cannot see what the public wants of one off the stage, I am not beautiful and I am ill." Even the most imaginative newspapers cannot say what wines she drinks, what books she reads, or who are her friends. In this respect she is greater than any other woman who has ever been before the public. She has kept her personality utterly subdued and unseen and spoken only through her art. It is like the music one hears in a convent where the tones awaken and thrill, but the singer is hidden behind the veiled grating of the choir. No one knows what manner of woman it is that this music comes from. Apparently she has no confidential friends, there is no man whom she loves, no woman whom she trusts. She is utterly alone upon the icy heights where other beings cannot live. She is an actress, yet not of "the profession." In a calling that is the least austere she leads the life of a nun. . . .

Journal, November 4, 1894, p. 12.

Six months later the Dramatic Mirror *published a long letter from Duse to the Italian author Matilde Serao. Willa Cather quoted and commented on it, with particular reference to Duse's insistence that "I am what I am," that explanations of one's life are futile, and that one cannot tell the curious public what he fears to tell himself. Miss Cather continued:*

. . . You are right, Signora Duse, keep your secrets, you might tell us all and we would never understand. Only souls like your own could do that, and we have only our senses and our conscience. There is something wonderfully beautiful in that letter, it is so full of the loveliness and lovelessness and desolation of art. Of the isolation of Balzac and Shelley and de Musset and of all creative genius. Of the loneliness which besets all mortals who are shut up alone with God, of the gloom which is the shadow of God's hand consecrating His elect. Truly, it is fortunate that genius is not often laid upon men, for how many are strong enough to endure its anguish? Solitude, like some evil destiny, darkens its cradle, and sits watching even upon its grave. It is the veil and the cloister which keep the priesthood of art untainted from the world. . . .

It is not well to know how the beautiful things of this world are made. It is not well to know of the pearl fisher gasping on the sand, of his heavings in the great deep. It is better not to think of the single drop of blood, dug fresh from a dove's breast, by which every great ruby is tested. The tears of the weaver should not dim his cloth of gold. It is better that we do not know what the last chapter of *Père Goriot* cost Balzac, what the third chapter [act?] of *Phèdre* cost Rachel. We see only the fair complexion and divine perfection of creation, we never know the tears and failures and human weakness out of which it is wrought. But let us honor and reverence the creators who have the supreme agony and the supreme happiness. Honor them as the Greeks honored the women who bore their deliverers, the sons of Jupiter.

Journal, June 16, 1895, p. 12.

... [Duse] knows what the true dignity of art means; how completely it should absorb and drown and hide a life, how it should exclude all trivialities, all phantoms of a day. This woman lives among us, in our own time, in our own land, yet we know as little of her as we know of Shakespeare. We know where she was born, whom she married, and that she has a child, but more than that we know not. In this age of microscopic scrutiny and X rays to have maintained such absolute privacy is little short of genius in itself. Her great contemporary [Bernhardt] has given herself body and soul to the public, but Duse has kept her personality entirely free, her relations with her public are of the most self-respecting and platonic character. That is the difference in the women. She is like some veiled sister of the church whose good deeds are known to many, but whose face no man sees. If the insatiable curiosity of the public were granted, if it were permitted to inspect every detail of this woman's daily life it would be none the wiser and very much bored for its pains. For the world in which Signora Duse dwells when off the stage is not one that the dear public could breathe in or even see, and those with whom she speaks are voices invisible, like those which whispered long ago to the peasant girl of France. Mr. Barron did more than invent an alliterative phrase when he called Duse a "daughter of Dante," for if ever the spirit of Gothic art spoke through a woman's lips and out of a woman's face it does from hers.

Journal, March 22, 1896, p. 9.

Renunciation

In the summer of 1895 it was announced that Mary Anderson was writing her memoirs. Willa Cather, recalling the retirement of the great American actress at the time of her marriage in 1890, commented on that personal drama of renunciation. Almost a year later, in 1896, Miss Cather reviewed the published book, considering thoughtfully not only the division of the artist and the woman but also the drama of the artist's struggle, growth, and achievement. This was a theme that would recur many times in her work, with its most complete development in The Song of the Lark *(1915).*

. . . . To aspire and create and conquer, to strike fire from flint, to compel the worship of an indifferent world, to make the blind see and the deaf hear whether they will or no, to win the world's highest honors and noisiest fame, that is great. There is only one thing greater—to give them up. Many have been bold enough to win glory, but few have been strong enough to renounce it. Having won the best the world has to give, then to quietly put away all the glamour and brightness and intoxication of it because there is still a higher life unfilled, to have been a queen and then to be merely a woman, that is indeed greatness. It was Anderson's greatest creation.

Journal, July 21, 1895, p. 9.

It is noticeable that in the recently published volume of Mary Anderson's memories [*A Few Memories*, 1896] she does not state an absolute and definite reason why she left the stage. The most conservative of New York newspapers has recently published an account of her retirement by a gentleman who professes to understand what he is talking about. Of course one cannot declare it absolutely authentic, but here it is for what it is worth. There lived in Louisville an editor with a genuine love for the theatre and rare taste and judgment in dramatic matters. He was Mary Anderson's first artistic admirer and friend. He saw the marvellous talent in the raw undeveloped girl and encouraged and directed it. He was with her constantly while she was preparing for her first performance, and was present at her debut. He criticised her severely and praised her sincerely. He devoted his newspaper to helping and advertising her, his earnestness drew to her the attention of all the critics in the country. He prophesied for her greatness of the highest kind, of a new kind—if she would work. He said that she had the pure tragic fire of the heroines of the Grecian dramatists, of Electra, of Antigone, of Phaedra. That he saw in her the tragic spiritual force unweakened by sensual things, the force that could conceive and portray a great purpose, a great sacrifice, a great denial. He said that she might be greater than Bernhardt—if she could forego temporary success, if she could withstand the glittering temptations of immediate and unsubstantial fame, if she would work. He was not in love with his young protégée, he would willingly have sacrificed the girl to the artist. Indeed he was not a man of love affairs at all, and his one and only passion was for art, the beauty of good work. He saw in the girl his dream of dramatic perfection and he worshipped her for the possibilities within her. When Mary Anderson left Louisville he watched every step she took toward fame and was grieved that they came too fast. He knew what perfection means, what labor, what suffering, how one must pay for it in blood.

He knew that she got too much praise; that she was gauging her efforts by the standards of the hour, not by the standards of all time; that she played for Daly and William Winter, not for the Muse of Tragedy. When, years afterward, she returned to Louisville fresh from all her European triumph, he went to call on her. He found not the eager, wistful little girl he used to know, whose high desire almost burnt out her frail body, but a placid, self-satisfied woman who had satisfied the world of her generation. Great men had told Mary Anderson that she had sprung into the world full-armed and needed no improvement and she had taken them at their word. That night her friend, the journalist, went to the theatre to study the result. He sat in a box close by the stage and never took his eyes from her. He caught every gesture, every attitude, every intonation. He left the house overwhelmed by a great disappointment. The world had spoiled the woman, his ideal would never come to pass. The next morning all the papers in Louisville were full of Mary Anderson, her triumph and her "success." All but one, that represented by her oldest and staunchest friend, and it contained a whole page of the saddest, bitterest and yet soundest criticism ever written by any man in any language. That much of the story is bona fide at least. I have seen and read that paper, and it contains the most perfect expression of the dignity of dramatic art I know. If you had never heard this story you would know that critique was not written by an enemy or a man who wrote merely to have something to say, but by a man who cared, and cared greatly. It is full of the earnestness and sadness of a man who has awakened from a long dream to find that the feet of his idol are clay. It was a tragic thing, that criticism, and lingered long in my memory before this story ever came out. But to continue the story. A few days after its appearance it was known that Mary Anderson was ill with nervous prostration and had cancelled all her dates. That feuilleton cut deep.

The actress knew this man's sincerity, knew his great interest in her. She knew he was not jesting. Perhaps it recalled some half-forgotten dream of her youth, perhaps it made her think that, after all, her success had been superficial and her real advancement small; perhaps it brought back the glow of that virginal enthusiasm, that yearning passion for perfection, she had felt when she had talked of the future with that man years ago. At any rate, she became ill and nervous, and declared she would leave the stage. At this juncture Antonio Navarro came to Louisville. He had pressed his suit in vain for two years and in this fit of discouragement he saw his opportunity. He was accepted, and since then "our Mary" has been ours no more. As for the critic, he declared himself well contented with this; it was better that Arachne should leave her loom than pervert the gifts of God. One who was meant for the highest and was content with less had failed, and in art no bread was better than half a loaf. Then he sank into ignominious silence. He may be dead now; he may still be weeping over the frivolous decadence of art. He tried to make a Duse before her time and before the world was ready for her.

That there are some errors in the above story is evident enough, for Miss Anderson's last appearance on the stage was in Washington City. She made no farewell tour or public farewell; suddenly and seemingly forever, she left the stage. Perhaps in good time, perhaps not so. New methods have come into vogue since then, better methods; and whether she could have coped with a woman like the great Italian, no one can say. Probably not. Let that be as it may, she was a very great actress; she brought to the Americans only dignity and honor and no reproach of any kind. To a great extent, she was artificial and superficial, but when she left her work she was only thirty. Bernhardt was never at her best before her fortieth year. Mary Anderson was too young in art to be judged absolutely. She had all the faults of her countrymen; she grew up in a breezy, busy, confident, unartistic atmosphere; she never saw deeply and seriously into the awesome mystery of creative art. There was one gate between her and the kingdom of unattainable things that was never broken down. Everyone who saw her act knew and recognized that she had genius, but they did not feel its indescribable thrill, so they said she was "cold." Which meant the power in her was not applied; that genius was asleep. It was never awakened. Mary Anderson never had the art to draw the soul out of herself, but there are few people who doubt that it was there. Her admirers waited long for the quickening power, but it never came. Probably it never would have come. In her memoirs Mme. Navarro says that now when she goes up to London and sees *A Winter's Tale* or *Juliet* enacted she enjoys them, but it seldom occurs to her that she once played those roles. That is the whole explanation of her career and its strange contradictions. She is a sane, normal, and highly gifted woman; she has not and never had that mysterious "madness of art." Do you

suppose Rachel could have heard *Phèdre* without her very soul catching
fire? She says, furthermore, that she has very little recollection of how she
herself acted the details of these roles, and when she sees other women
play them, could not easily say wherein her own acting differed.
This shows only too plainly how little of deep study, how little of
intellectual and spiritual concentration Mary Anderson gave to her roles.
Do you suppose an artist who had spent days and nights on the interpretation of a single phrase could forget the glad knowledge of the truth that at
last came to her? She might forget the mother who bore her, but never
that!

Madame Navarro has, perhaps, much to be thankful for. Art touched
her life without consuming it, and the flame did not blacken the brand.
She had a touch of that fatal malady, was moonstruck, indeed, but it was
only a girl's aspiration, a midsummer night's dream, not the lifelong madness of Endymion. Yet Mary Anderson was a great woman; one must be
great to achieve her success and greater still—how much greater—to
renounce it. To win the praise and admiration of all the world, to have
fame and flattery and the most intoxicating of all successes, that is much.
But to keep through all this a clear vision, a pure and untrammeled taste,
to estimate all these things at their true value and turn one's back on them
and live one's life, that is vastly more. For what shall it profit a woman if
she gain the whole world and lose—what she wants? It was this clear
vision, this correct estimation of the values of things that ennobled her
as a woman and sadly limited her as an artist. With her, art was unconsciously a means, not an end; a stepping stone, not an altar. She was
meant to be Mme. Navarro, not Juliet or Hermione. If all artists could
end so it would be happy indeed for them, but sad, sad for art. For a
woman it is plainly the proper consummation—and the happy one. Has
any woman ever really had the art instinct, the art necessity? Is it not with
them a substitute, a transferred enthusiasm, an escape valve for what has
sought or is seeking another channel? But no, there was Sappho and the
two great Georges [Sand and Eliot]; they had it genuinely; they tried
other things and none could satisfy them. The closing words of Mme.
Navarro's book are beautiful in their directness and modesty and simplicity: "The following November (1889) I became engaged to Antonio F.
de Navarro, whom I had known for many years, and in June of 1890, at
the little Catholic church at Hampstead, London, we were married. Many
and great inducements have since been frequently offered me to act again,
but—

'Il en coute trop cher pour briller dans le monde,
Combien je vais aimer ma retraite profonde;
Pour vivre heureux, vivons cachés.'"

What does that French mean? Read Browning's "Love Among the Ruins," that's what it means. This book of "Memories" is so frank and simple that it is a valuable contribution to literature, not because it is at all literary in itself, but because it is human experience, from which all literature is made.

Journal, May 3, 1896, p. 13.

LIVES AND DEATHS

From the beginning of her newspaper column in 1893, Willa Cather had been sketching the human face—sometimes in the traditional seventeenth-century "character," sometimes in a portrait-sentence to catch the eye, sometimes in a brief biography that held the spirit of a life. In her last year in Lincoln she included a number of vignettes of those artists whose lives in some way touched her sympathy, wonder, or respect, and whose success or failure seemed to embody the principles of human endeavor. Her tone in these pieces is often elegiac; some of them (here and elsewhere) form a litany of Père-Lachaise, that cemetery in Paris which seemed to focus for her the continuity of history and the elemental cycles of life and death. In her "lives" she marked, too, the ironies and curious dramas of particular human experience—a gallery of scenes and characters to compose her own comédie humaine. Above all, she paid attention to people, and to what they might become.

And so the habit of belief in greatness, of praise for the individual talent, began early with Willa Cather. It was an affirmation to think of those who were truly great, who, as Stephen Spender wrote many years later, "traveled a short while towards the sun, / And left the vivid air signed with their honor." Or as she herself said in the same Promethean terms (writing of Bernhardt, December 30, 1894): We desire that out of the ordinary earth "one great imagination may rise to snatch for us the blue from heaven and the fire from the sun."

Rubinstein

Whom the gods love die young, at least before their failures find them out. It is a well established fact now that the colossal production of Rubinstein's [14] colossal sacred opera at Bremen, Germany, is an artistic failure. The reasons for this are many and varied, some of them are very deep and obscure, some of them very evident. To begin with there is the enormous length of the work. It has a prologue, an epilogue and seven acts. The seventh act representing the crucifixion of Christ has been cut out entirely, and still it takes five hours and five minutes to produce it. A man might have considerable music in his soul and still become weary long before St. Paul sings the credo of love under the cross in the epilogue. Then there is all the ponderous and pretentious scenery that the marvelous nature of the opera demands, and the delicacy and sublime unap-

---

14. Anton Rubinstein (1829–November 20, 1894). His last work was the oratorio *Christus*.

proachableness of the theme—unapproachable to Rubinstein at least. It is a peculiar fact that no Jew has ever successfully treated the Christ theme in art or in literature. It is not a prejudice, but an inability. The Nazarene is not without honor among his own people, but to this day it does not understand him. That is the secret weakness of Rubinstein's *Christus*. Besides being almost entirely lacking in the element of climax, deficient in emphasis, decision and the dramatic quality, the opera lacks the fervor, the emotion, the mysticism and spiritual ecstasy that the theme demands. . . . *Christus* is a beautiful idea, lofty, intellectual, cold. It came to Rubinstein when he was old, when he had neither the fecundity of invention nor the spiritual intensity to attain to it. Yet the man who wrote the "Ocean Symphony" and that beautiful little melody in F, died thinking that *Christus* was his great work, the work by which he should live and which posterity would couple with his name. It is well that dreams of this kind should not be broken. Most composers have had a pet great failure to which they have clung with pathetic constancy. Very few men live by their greatest efforts, but by their lighter and more spontaneous work. The world will read *Pauline* longer than it will analyze *Sordello*. Boccaccio spent all the strength of his maturity writing ponderous Latin tomes upon nobody knows what, but he is immortal through a book of licentious tales written in his youth to please a princess who was none too delicate, which is all but another illustration of the fact that every true artist is in the hands of a higher power than himself, that he cannot do what he will, but what he must. Effort and conscientious labor count for nothing against that inspiration which is not of man.

Journal, June 30, 1895, p. 12.

Carvalho

There is another grave up in the part of Père-Lachaise where the people of Paris put their geniuses for their last long sleep. This time it is the great Madame Carvalho,[15] for years one of the first singers of France. Although Madame Carvalho's name has not been upon the play bills of late years, she has been, since her retirement from the stage, one of those inspiring teachers, one of those just and thorough critics, one of those tireless enthusiasts and deep and potent forces that have always wielded such an influence over French art. In Paris the day of an artist's greatness is by no means over when she leaves the stage. In a certain sense it has only

15. Marie Miolan-Carvalho (1827–July 10, 1895). A noted French operatic soprano, she was particularly distinguished for her Marguerite in *Faust*. She retired in 1885.

begun. Then she has the authority of a career that is complete, a work that is finished, a destiny that is fulfilled. She is the guide of young artists and the defender of the old. She is consulted by dramatists, prima donnas, composers. She is a link between the old art and the new. She laments the dead and calls the living. There are many of them there in Paris, these aged artists, these magnificent wrecks in whom the soul has outworn the body and they are honored and beloved and not forgotten. Old singers and authors and conquerors of all nations drift there, where the great heart of the world beats. Frenchmen are fickle in some things. They forget quickly the names of their queens and kings and quicker the names of their sweethearts, but they remember genius.

The funeral services of Madame Miolan-Carvalho took place in the chapel of St. Augustine at noon. All the great of Paris were there, all the young men whom she had aided, all the old men whose youth were full of memories of her song, Sardou, Dumas, Lemaître, Massenet and a hundred others. Saint-Saëns himself played the prelude, the church scene from *Faust* and the sleep scene from *Juliette*, the deep, calm sleep that came after the turmoil and passion of living and loving were over. The great singers of Paris sang her requiem. And so it is over with her, whose action was tragedy and whose voice was love.

Journal, August 11, 1895, p. 9.

Mascagni

Whatever the future holds for Mascagni,[16] he has always that one opera [*Cavalleria Rusticana*]. Most of us would be content to have written just that and then cease to be. There are parts of it that will "Die not till the whole world dies." There is the Seduction song we heard Scalchi sing three years ago, that would seduce the archangels themselves as in the days when the sons of God saw that the daughters of men were fair. Then there is the Intermezzo, yes there is the Intermezzo. It would be worth writing a whole opera for that alone. It is unique in music as *The City of Dreadful Night* is in poetry. With its bass that labors and fails and struggles, that suffers and protests in its black despair; its treble that never yields, never falters, dips sometimes toward the lower octaves like a bird that is faint with its death wound, and then flies on, flies on. That treble that knows and

16. Pietro Mascagni (1863–1945), Italian composer, whose *Cavalleria Rusticana* was first performed in 1890. A memorable concert performance was given in Lincoln by the Nordica Operatic Concert Company on March 2, 1893, with Nordica, Scalchi, Engel, Campanini, and Del Puente.

sees the hopelessness of all things and yet never wavers; love betrayed that still loves on, hope deferred that still hopes on; it is the despair which passes despair, despair sublime, impersonal, and full of awe as though it comprehended universal futility and universal doom.

They say that Mascagni is at work on a new opera. The news is not entirely welcome for ten chances to one it means another disappointment. It has been several years now since the advent of *Cavalleria Rusticana* and yet Mascagni has done nothing worthy of himself since then. People have begun to doubt whether he will ever again equal those magnificent measures that hunger and poverty and despair drove him to, or whether that opera will stand as his one witness to the world as *Carmen* stands for Bizet. So often these peculiar and unique works of art are without successors. Not every composer can be like Verdi, great a hundred times. There is a kind of musical genius which rather lacks musical intelligence, a sort of emotional tone fury which expresses itself once and dies. The muse plays queer tricks with men, and she can only be courted, never compelled. She is all things to all men. Sometimes she is as constant as Penelope, as she has been to Verdi for these eighty years. Sometimes she is fickle as Cleopatra, knows her lover but once and then throws him to the crocodiles. And if she happens to be in a cruel mood she lets him live, to wander over the world dreaming of her face, to be scorned and mocked of men.

> As if a blacker night could dawn on night,
> With tenfold gloom on moonless night unstarred.
> A scene more tragic than defeat and blight,
> More desperate than strife with hope debarred,
> More fatal than the adamantine never.
>
> The sense that every struggle brings defeat
> Because fate holds no prize to crown success;
> That all the oracles are dumb or cheat
> Because they have no secret to express;
> That none can pierce the vast black veil uncertain;
> Because there is no light beyond the curtain;
> That all is vanity and nothingness.[17]

Courier, September 7, 1895, p. 7.

17. From James Thomson's *The City of Dreadful Night*, XXI, stanzas 9–10. The exact reading is as follows (according to the London edition of 1922, published by P. J. and A. E. Dobell, p. 47):

Paganini

There is such a thing as fatality, an influence which guides a man all his life, that sticks to him closer than a brother, that sits above his grave when he is dead. Paganini's [18] bones have been exhumed for the fourth time since his death. Paganini died unreconciled to the Roman church and bitterly hostile to the priests. His body was not allowed to rest in consecrated ground and for years was moved about from one place to another until his son at last obtained special permission from the Pope to bury his father in a cemetery. About two weeks ago it was moved again, and to the astonishment of all present at the opening of the tomb that great demon face was in an almost perfect state of preservation, those features worn by genius and sin were still the same. It is strange that he cannot rest even in death, that great restless soul who wandered the world over frightening and enchanting the nations. Now fleeing from his own great career and lounging in the villa of his Tuscan Princess, a riband in his coat, twanging a guitar to accompany a woman's singing. Now silent and gloomy, living the life of a monk of the fifth century. Always from one extreme to the other. Always dreading loneliness, yet always tiring of love, weary of his roses before they were withered, sick of his wine as soon as the chalice had touched his lips. He hated Italy, yet was unhappy out of it, he distrusted men, yet was driven to seek them. He never found rest on earth except during those long heavy slumbers which followed his concerts. Even then perhaps his soul was out on the wings of the tempest, with the demons of darkness and spirits of storm. When he grew tired of the Grand Duchess

---

But as if blacker night could dawn on night,
  With tenfold gloom on moonless night unstarred,
A sense more tragic than defeat and blight,
  More desperate than strife with hope debarred,
More fatal than the adamantine Never
Encompassing her passionate endeavour,
  Dawns glooming in her tenebrous regard:

The sense that every struggle brings defeat
  Because Fate holds no prize to crown success;
That all the oracles are dumb or cheat
  Because they have no secret to express;
That none can pierce the vast black veil uncertain
Because there is no light beyond the curtain;
  That all is vanity and nothingness.

18. Nicolò Paganini (1782–1840), Italian violin virtuoso. His skill was so incredible and his appearance so bizarre that some credulous persons believed Paganini to be the son of the devil, whom he was supposed to resemble.

of Tuscany and neglected her and insulted her beyond all forgiveness, she said to him, "It is your game here, God only knows why women love you, but they do. Here great women lose their souls for you and you trample them like dirt. But in the next world it will be ours. Those of us who are in Heaven will never let you enter there, and those of us who are in Hell for you will stand all day at the gates infernal and hold them shut against your soul." It looks as though the Duchess' rhetoric were coming true, and that great Frankenstein cannot rest even in the grave.

Courier, October 5, 1895, p. 7.

Campanini

They do say that old Campanini[19] is exceedingly hard up these days, that he is glad to sing small concert engagements and cannot get enough of them. Sacred lyre of Apollo! and has he come to this, Campanini, the bosom friend of old Verdi, the knave of hearts and the prince of song, the Rhadames who wore golden armor, the tenor who threw money at the birds, Italo the magnificent? Why, time was when he had to devise ways and means to spend his money and when he couldn't his friends obligingly spent it for him. But he was a prince in his day and a prince of artists at that. Few people who had the pleasure of witnessing it will ever forget that first American production of *Aida* by the Mapleson opera company with Campanini as Rhadames, or that scene in which he was borne in on a shield resting on the shoulders of six Abyssinian slaves, clothed in golden armor, naked sword in hand like a statue of victory, while a chorus of six hundred priests and soldiers sang the great triumphal march to the accompaniment of golden trumpets. However poor Campanini may be now he must have priceless memories. He was reckless and prodigal and a good deal of a sybarite. He liked beauty of every kind and that is the most expensive thing in the world, for it is the product of man's most perfect work and God's divinest moods. He had it and paid for it. But the great bulk of Campanini's fortune was lost on the first American production of *Otello*. He went abroad and got Verdi's help in the matter and brought it out with all due magnificence. He was an Othello indeed, and he sang

19. Italo Campanini (1845?–1896), Italian tenor whose remarkable voice decayed early, though even after 1888 when his singing was no longer dependable he continued to tour in America and Europe. His first appearance in Lincoln was a disaster. Scheduled to sing three nights at the May Festival of the Lincoln Oratorio Society, May 16–18, 1892, he managed only the first performance, in the cantata *Sleeping Beauty*. Even for that he had to appear on crutches because of rheumatism—and without his dress suit, lost with his trunk somewhere along the line. Illness kept him in bed the next two days. Campanini sang much more successfully the following year with the Nordica company (March 2, 1893).

that famous love aria at the end of the first act as no one has sung it since. When he dragged Desdemona about by her hair the matinee girls used to say they envied her. But Verdi's *Otello* is more of a play than an opera. The composer became enamored of Shakespeare before he was through and he rather neglected his arias and choruses in his enthusiasm for the sweeping dramatic action and all through the opera the English dramatist stands out head and shoulders above the Italian composer. People who wrestle with Shakespeare are very likely to get the worst of it and even Verdi was not so great as in other compositions. So *Otello* failed, collapsed totally, and with it Italo Campanini's gold. He still held his place as a leading tenor for some years, but after a time age and high living and a great deal of whisky told on him and his voice lost in quality and there was a very audible "crack" in it. He began singing in concerts then, big ones at first, then smaller ones. And now he wears last winter overcoats and hats of seasons gone by, and more provident tenors smile at him indulgently. It is the old story of La Cigale. But who shall say that it is not better to sing for a summer than to build ant hills for a century? The winter doesn't count anyway, one might as well freeze as anything else then, and to have been an ant in June is decidedly worse than to starve in December.[20]

Journal, January 12, 1896, p. 9.

A little while ago a man who had once years ago, saved [Lily] Langtry's life, was found dead. In his vest pocket was found Langtry's card, so worn that it was almost illegible. There are the materials for a story if you care to write it. Langtry is neither good nor great, but this poor devil probably went through life with the sublime conviction that he had saved an angel and an artist unaware. It is peculiar, and rather pathetic, that tendency that the lowly have to revere the great, and it is one of the encouraging traits of humanity. It shows that the general aspect of the world toward achievement and perfection is right. If we fall down sometimes and reject good work and accept bad, it is from stupidity, not from intentions. We all reverence power and in a way those who possess it, whether it is power of wealth or beauty or genius or simple goodness. And that reminds us of a story of a little girl. Once, when Campanini was on his way to California, he was snowed up in a little western town. Every morning when he took his usual walk to get the air and curse the blizzard,

20. Much of this article was used, some passages word for word, in "Italo Campanini," an unsigned piece in the *Home Monthly* for January, 1897, when Willa Cather was managing editor of the magazine and writing a good portion of each issue herself. Campanini died on November 13, 1896.

this enterprising maiden, then about eleven, would take her sled as a pretext and drag it after him for miles, following him at a safe distance and never daring to speak to him any more than she would have addressed Olympian Zeus. She had never heard him sing a note, but took upon herself this bleak pilgrimage merely because he had one of the greatest voices in the world shut up in his larynx, and when the divine Italo condescended to throw a snowball at her, she felt honored for life and somewhat apart from other mortals. Snowballs are perishable souvenirs, or she would probably have preserved that one between the leaves of her Shakespeare. It's the same old instinct that makes the little boys follow the band wagon.[21]

Journal, January 19, 1896, p. 9.

Ambroise Thomas

The last five years have gathered to their rest most of the surviving composers of the past generation. Ambroise Thomas,[22] the composer of *Mignon* and *Hamlet*, died in Paris February 15. . . . That a composer should live in one of the musical centers of the world for eighty-five years and have but one, or at most two, operas to show for it, tells its own story. There have, indeed, been other composers of one opera; there was Georges Bizet, than whom no man ever promised greater things, but he was cut down in his glorious prime and died three months after the production of *Carmen*. Yet as an exponent of sentimentalism in music Thomas holds a high and an honored place and the grace and poetry of his *Mignon* do much to redeem a career that would otherwise have been sterile. There is deep regret in Paris now that another of the old time landmarks is gone, and there is in Père-Lachaise another of those mighty graves marked by a single name of which poor Balzac, in his hungry and desolate youth, said: "Surely the noblest epitaphs are single names; La Fontaine, Masséna, Molière—names that tell all and make the passer dream."[23]

21. Whether Willa Cather is recalling her own experience or not, it is true that Campanini did tour in the 1880's, and Willa Cather's home town of Red Cloud, Nebraska, was a railroad division point on the main line between East and West.

22. Charles Louis Ambroise Thomas (1811–February 12, 1896), French composer.

23. Balzac wrote in a letter to his sister, Laure de Balzac, in 1820. "Décidément il n'y a de belles épitaphes que celles-ci: *La Fontaine, Masséna, Molière,* un seul nom qui dit tout et fait rêver!" (*Correspondance* 1819–1850 [Paris: Calmann-Lévy, n.d.], *Oeuvres complètes de H. de Balzac*, XXIV, 48). In a later *Journal* article (September 14, 1902) written from Paris after she had visited the cemetery, Willa Cather quoted again: "It was Balzac himself who used to wander in the Père-Lachaise in the days of his hard apprenticeship, reading the names of the tombs of the great. 'Single names,' he wrote his sister, 'Racine, Molière, etc.; names that make one dream.'"

And thirty years later Balzac himself was laid there, on the highest spot of that great cemetery where it overlooks Paris, having won his longed for chrism, a grave marked by a single name. What a great harvest field of death it is, that Père-Lachaise! If, indeed, "Death keeps his count" anywhere, it must be there. More than anything else that field and its names make France great, that and the tomb of Napoleon. And the epitaph of them might be written in the words of a modern poet little known as yet, but for whom the future certainly holds such a crown as no man wears today:

> Men's eyes, once seeing
> The broken isolated beauty turn
> Back to God's work and find it there forever.
> So God makes use of poets; teach me then,
> To fashion worlds in little, making form
> As God does, one with spirit—be the priest
> Who makes God into bread to feed the world.[24]

Journal, March 1, 1896, p. 9.

The Author of "Kathleen Mavourneen"

It is curious to notice how much public sympathy has been excited by the fact that the old author of "Kathleen Mavourneen"[25] is ill and in poverty. There are hundreds of old men who are just as ill and just as poor, and when all is said "Mavourneen" is not a great song nor strictly original. But we all of us have that peculiar reverence even for the merest camp-followers of an art, and in spite of our own better judgments and of his failure we respect him for the sake of what he was once, of what he longed to be sometime. For we know that at one time he has had the courage of a great resolve and has set himself to run with the swift runners. No matter in what straits or in what darkness we find him we know that once, long ago, he looked up at the sun and set his purpose as high as heaven. The glory of

24. From Richard Hovey's *Taliesin: A Masque* (*Poet Lore*, VIII [February, 1896], 71). The passage, slightly paraphrased here in the first lines, is part of a statement on the work of the artist, who takes apart the harmonies of design and color, which,

> shown to men, their eyes, once seeing
> The broken beauty isolated, turn
> Back to God's work to find it there forever;
> So God makes use of poets. Teach me then . . . .

25. Frederick Nicholls Crouch (1808–August 18, 1896). Belonging to a distinguished musical family in England, Crouch had a miscellaneous career, chiefly playing in orchestras, both in Europe and America, but also composing operas and once serving as a trumpeter in the Confederate Army.

one such minute hallows a life forever. Age, poverty, disease and dissipation can never quite blot out from a face the stamp of such an aspiration. Even the memory of it is a holy thing; it has followed many a man to his grave, the only spark of manhood he had left in him. You see this strange something in the face of men every day, most often in the faces of actors who intended to be great and are not. A great man once wrote of an old stranded player he met at Précy: "If a man is only so much of an actor that he can stumble through a farce, he is made free of a new order of thoughts. He has something else to think about than the money box. He has a pride of his own, and, what is of far more importance, he has an aim before him that he can never quite attain. He has gone upon a pilgrimage that will last his life long, because there is no end to it short of perfection. He will better himself a little day by day; or, even if he has given up the attempt, he will always remember that once upon a time he had conceived his high ideal, that once upon a time he fell in love with a star. Although the moon should have nothing to say to Endymion, although he should settle down with Audrey and feed pigs, do you not think he would move with a better grace and cherish higher thoughts to the end?"[26]

Journal, April 19, 1896, p. 13.

Clara Wieck Schumann

May 21 Clara Wieck Schumann[27] died in Frankfort-on-the-Main. She is almost the last survivor of the golden age of music. She could remember a time when all the great composers were doing their work; when she herself was young and gifted and worshipped by them. And she was one of the most brilliant pianists in the world. Yet her execution was not brilliant; that is not the word. Those who heard her say that it was everything that it should be but that. However, that part of her career does not concern us much; it was not as the virtuoso Clara Wieck that she desired to be remembered, but as the widow of Robert Schumann. "So doth the greater glory dim the less," the higher life transcend the lower. She was Robert Schumann's sanity, the last thing to which his

26. The "great man" is Robert Louis Stevenson, and the passage is quoted from "Précy and the Marionettes" in *An Inland Voyage* (*The Travels and Essays of Robert Louis Stevenson* [New York: Charles Scribner's Sons, 1909], pp. 126–127). In this edition the first sentence of the quoted passage reads "But if"; the second sentence reads "beside the money-box"; the fourth sentence reads "last him his life long"; and the line "'Tis better to have loved and lost'" comes between the fifth and the sixth sentences.

27. Clara Wieck Schumann was born in 1819 and died on May 21, 1896. She married Robert Schumann in 1840; he died in 1856.

failing reason clung. Almost all of his best work is dedicated to her. In that mighty disordered brain of his she was the causal force of production. During the four years when Clara's father refused to let her marry Schumann, they were both at their best. They had the anticipation of that most alluring prologue without the dreary monotony of the inevitable, unavoidable five acts. She was giving triumphant performances in Vienna and Leipzig; he was writing the most beautiful of his melodies. A note from the fair Clara was the provocation of a song for immortality. Such little things affect fine temperaments so . . . . An exquisite temperament needs subtle excitement, and Schumann was all temperament. He had one need, and Clara Wieck filled it. She had all a magician's power over that erratic mind of his; until the last hopeless wreck of his faculties she kept it in its delicate poise. Wives are not generally helpful to musicians. This case is wonderful, because of its rareness. After his long and ardent wooing Schumann married Clara Wieck. The first work he produced after his marriage was his symphony in B flat, which has been called the happy symphony. Has any woman living more to show for herself than that? Schumann's works are among the best edited, because when he lost his reason his scholarly wife edited them. He was, although for six years insane, almost the only one of his contemporary masters who did not die in poverty, because his talented wife supported him. Clara Schumann was one of the few women since time began who loved an art and an artist unselfishly, and who have understood and cherished a genius. There is no higher wisdom, no holier tenderness. The women who have tortured and ruined musicians have been hundreds; the women who have helped them, how few. Perhaps, in the great account book of heaven, what Clara Schumann saved may balance what George Sand destroyed.

Journal, June 14, 1896, p. 13.

The Way of the World

She is a Spartan mother, but she has unruly
sons to handle.

ART IN PHILISTIA

*Philistia is usually The Place Where You Live—Eleventh Street in Lincoln,
or this side of the footlights. Bohemia is somewhere else—that desert kingdom by
the sea, or the Paris of Henri Murger's* Scènes de la vie de Bohème. *Yet
Willa Cather with her customary good sense made no such arbitrary distinction.
Philistia was a chameleon country which included Europe as well as America,
Buckingham Palace just as surely as a western town, salons as much as Sordello
Clubs, and—alas for Bohemia—the artist as well as the audience. Queen
Victoria was there, with New York theatre managers, editors of popular
magazines, and makers of church hymnals; the Poet Laureate was there, and the
heavyweight champion of the world, and the painter of the Lansing curtain. But
though Willa Cather was eclectic in naming the monuments of Philistia, she
was single-minded in her reason for attacking them. To many the problem of art
in society is the alienation of the artist. Willa Cather, however, was less concerned with the artist as an outsider than with society as second rate—with
anything second rate. Philistia is primarily a state of mind, a human failure to
choose the real thing. In one sense Willa Cather did think of the artist as a lonely
worker, dedicated and separate. But as a newspaper columnist who was speaking
out a dozen times each week she was also very much a part of the world. She
liked being involved, but she also saw what was wrong or inadequate and she had
to speak out against it. Partly it was youth that made her such a fighter, but it
was also her own honor: one could not smile and smile at villainy. So with a
strict, thorough, and fearless intelligence she sorted out and attacked whatever
was makeshift, imitative, shoddy, pretentious, cheap, and phony. The tone is
uneven and personal—sometimes a comic despair, sometimes reckless exaggeration*

or anger, sometimes a cool, logical authority—but she did not pretend to be writing anything but personal comment on a passing show. And perhaps nowhere is the hand of Willa Cather, girl journalist, more humanly felt than when she uses her strong and sputtering pen to dash black ink all over Philistia's lovely white false front.

Philistia

Artists, great and small, leaders and camp followers, have the credit of being the most conceited set of people who walk this unworthy planet. But that is a mistaken conception. The colossal egotism of the world is in Philistia, not Bohemia. The Bohemians make large pretentions, it's a part of their business. But they have great standards, that saves them. The most exalted leading lady after she talks about Duse twenty minutes is humble. In Philistia there are no standards and no gods. Each house has its own little new improved portable idol and could never be convinced that it was not just as good as any other idol. Here the great standards of art avail nothing, for these people patronize art. Every Philistine thinks he could be a greater actor, a greater painter, a greater poet than any Bohemian if he chose to soil his hands with art. It is no wonder that men like Mansfield and Salvini grow bitter and resentful toward this mighty Philistia which patronizes and criticises and ridicules art, but which is itself above criticism, beyond ridicule, sacred, exalted, holy, "like a city set upon a hill."

Journal, November 18, 1894, p. 13.

The Lansing Drop Curtain

The new Lansing Theatre, rich with rose plush and gold, opened in the fall of 1891, but it was several months until the old drop curtain was replaced. On March 11, 1892, came the unveiling, along with James O'Neill in Count of Monte Cristo. *According to a story in the* Journal *that day, the painting on the curtain depicted Ponce de Leon's search for the fountain of eternal youth. The description was explicit: "In the left foreground, hovering over a small fire, whose feeble warmth does not suffice to dispel the chill from her blood, sits an old woman. Benumbed by cold and worn with age she falls asleep and dreams. Before her appears a beautiful fountain, rising out of crystal waters which sparkle in the sunlight. Playing in the water are a host of nymphs, who tauntingly beg her to join them. Half afraid and with incredulous eyes she does so, when suddenly she is transformed into a lovely young lady and joins her lover and companions on the*

*other bank." Willa Cather may have overlooked this explanation, but she
could not overlook the curtain. In due time, as an editor of the* Hesperian,
*she opened fire with a comment that is obviously from the pen of the same
journalist-crusader who developed the theme in two* Journal *Sunday
columns. The sketches below are details of the Lansing curtain, apparently
drawn for the occasion by a* Journal *artist, and reproduced here exactly
as they appeared in "One Way of Putting It," January 28 and 21, 1894.*

Ruskin said that bad art is only permitted to exist in countries where
there is bad taste, and that bad taste is only found in countries where bad
morals prevail. If this is true, it does not look well for the morality of
Lincoln that such a piece of atrocious painting as the Lansing drop curtain
is allowed to exist. The curtain is certainly one of the most pitiable attempts
at art that can be seen anywhere. There is absolutely no perspective, the
anatomy is all wrong, the groupings are anything but beautiful, and the
coloring is simply maddening. At the bottom of the curtain is this elegant
though rather startling bit of Latin, "*Somnium: Fons Vitales.*" I defy any
classical scholar to translate it.[1] If such a piece of canvas had been hung in
an Italian town during the Renaissance, the most ignorant of the peasant
folk would have turned from it with loathing, or, more likely, they would
have torn it to shreds. It is almost time that the Americans should discover

1. "A Dream; the Fountain of Life" was the *Journal* rendering (March 11, 1892).

that a man can lie and cheat and sin with his brush as well as with his pen or tongue, and that distorted art is an insult to nature and to humanity.

Hesperian, March 15, 1893, p. 3.

He sits there. His head is thrown back; his eyes are raised to hers; his face is drawn and pointed as though he were suffering. He has sat there now some three years, and every night the hundreds of people assembled before him have suffered with him. His misery has not been without company. He is leaning upon something, no one knows upon what. Some have thought it a stone, some an altar; some have thought it a table and some a little hand organ. His sweetheart has a wreath of flowers about to crown him; he is looking up at her. When one realizes that he has had to look at her face for almost three years, one does not wonder that he is delicate and has to lean upon something. Many people have hated this youth, but he seems an object of pity rather than hatred. When one thinks of the ugly little imps beneath him who proudly show those three words of Latin, and the awful strains of that awful medley that have floated up to him year after year, we ought to have charity for him. We, thank heaven, can go out and forget the anatomy of the naiads in front of him and the impossible architecture back of him, but he, poor wretch, must stay there always. And yet, it is not our fault that he is there, we would gladly dispense with him; we know of no good reason for his existing. Perhaps, when the world has found out which are Tintoretto's pictures and which are not, and when we discover what the frieze of the Parthenon means, then we may also know why he sits there and upon what he is leaning.

The artist who painted the drop curtain in the beautiful Lansing Theatre was unique. In art, to be unique is to be great. It is not every man who could paint so many yards of anatomy as are bathing in that weird *fons vitalis* and not have one square inch of beauty in it all. I do not know where one could turn to find ten such ugly women as the ten who are guilelessly disporting themselves in the middle of that picture. Without the nude, art could not exist; but nudity is not necessarily artistic, nor is it the end of art. To paint draperies and ribbons may be frivolous, but to paint human flesh indifferently is desecration. One had better paint badly shaded draperies than badly shaped limbs. When an artist has no more beauty to show than Mr. Kettler exhibited in his naiads, he should veil his figures in something more substantial than mystery. In art, Apollo Belvedere is most proper nude, but Quasimodo must keep his clothes on.

It must have required an exceptional man to have painted so many pictures without once evincing the slightest knowledge of form or the slightest feeling for color. Mr. Fred Kettler has not even followed the lower French school; he was not even artist enough to make his naiads wicked; he has made them great, loosely stuffed, staring-eyed, doll babies and one expects to see the sawdust come pouring out at any time.

There was and may be still just such a drop curtain in the new Boyd [in Omaha], but the manager had a neat little device of covering it up with a white canvas every night, until the oculists of Omaha bribed him not to cover the curtain any more, because times were hard and in Omaha people's eyes did not wear out fast enough in the natural way.

Journal, January 21, 1894, p. 16.

If it took Ruskin six months to interpret Turner's "Garden of the Hesperides," surely a person who is totally ignorant of the technical laws of art may be allowed several weeks to struggle with the Lansing drop curtain. I have been suffering acutely from that curtain for two long years, and sometimes I have longed for artistic knowledge, that I might understand and appreciate it better, but recently an artist told me that I was enviable because of my ignorance, that art could not help one with that curtain, for the more one knew of other pictures the less they knew of that. I begin to believe his statement, for I have found art books as powerless to help me with the anatomy as classical lexicons are to throw light upon that abominable Latin. "Somnium Fons Vitales." I wonder how many people have been able to translate it? Lincoln is full of colleges and ought to contain a good deal of classical learning, but the lore of this generation has not got as far as "Vitales." Most freshmen try to construe

[175]

that Latin. The world looks very bright to a freshman and he has the fond complacency to try anything from discovering a new element to translating the *Iliad* in blank verse. He goes to the theatre saturated with Horace and he gazes on that mystic sentence and tries to read it. When he fails he is chagrined. He swears that, when he is a senior he will translate those words. But when he is a senior he does not look at it any more. By that time he has learned the lesson of his own littleness and his own helplessness. He knows then that genius is something more than eternal patience after all, and that even were he the proverbial patience on a monument he would never write a *Hamlet* nor discover a new planet nor construe the Latin of the Lansing drop curtain. He goes out into the world to live his life and leaves the task to mightier men than he.

After all, the sad, sad thing about that curtain is that it should be such a contrast to the rest of the house, which is really in very good taste. The drapings of the boxes, the color of the seats, the frescoing, the woodwork, are all very artistic and the harmony of colors is perfect. Very few theatres in the west can boast of such elegant interiors. It seems like those gauzy women in front had got in the wrong place some way. Perhaps, after all, there is method in the manager's madness, and the curtain is there to make us more keenly conscious of the artistic settings of the house itself. We should be sorry to interfere with any deep laid scheme like this, but aren't the managers bearing down a little hard on us? Wouldn't a fifteen-minute exhibition of that curtain every night do? We would all promise to look and suffer and get it over with. Then they might cover it up in some way and let us enjoy ourselves for the rest of the evening.

Journal, Janury 28, 1894, p. 13.

For a period in the fall of 1894, Willa Cather looked closely at things around home and found reason to observe in her columns that what was good could be better, and what was bad was both awful and funny. Mostly, it was the group actions of Philistia that she found dismaying: wherever people gathered—at concerts, at the theatre, in church, on the campus, in clubs, in libraries, at fairs, and at prize fights—there was public evidence that the risks of art were very great indeed. With only a few exceptions, the pieces which appear in the next five sections—until we turn to the Ladies' Home—*are from 1894, and most of them from the fall of that year.*

Dress at the Concerts

... Lincoln has gradually worked up a great deal of musical enthusiasm, which is certainly genuine, even if it is not all of the very highest order.

A great many people are willing to pay $2.50 to hear two hours of good music. And now it is about time that the matter of evening dress should be agitated. It is one of the few good features of the western theatre-going public that it insists upon its right of going to the theatre in negligee costume. Nobody cares to wear out very many pairs of elbow kids in applauding Corse Payton or *The Hustler*.[2] But a concert is a different matter. Good music is just a little above anything else that ever honors any stage, and everyone owes it a certain respect. The traditions of concert dress are rigid. It is always and invariably bad form to go to a concert in ordinary street costume. It is no more trouble to put on a dress suit than anything else and in a civilized community every man ought to possess a dress suit. . . . It is worth while to dress for a concert on the same principle that it is worth while to dress for one's wedding. Music calls for the best of everything. . . .

It is probable, though, that we will go on as we always have done; that the youths will go to concerts in striped shirts and scarlet neckties and the papas in dressing gowns and skull caps and the ladies muffled to their ears.

Journal, October 21, 1894, p. 13.

Moral Music

During the last few years a most commendable change has taken place in the church choirs of Lincoln. The Episcopal and Congregational churches at least, perhaps others, dignify and sanctify their services with music. But there are still too many churches who profane the sanctuary with music that would not be endured from a musée band. It is probably a terrible thing to say, but it is a fact that the much venerated Gospel Hymns have driven more people of good taste from the churches than Robert Ingersoll and all his school. It is strange that in this age, in which music has developed so rapidly, in which so many of the seers and prophets have been musicians and in which the Lord has so revealed himself to man through music, the churches should cling to the old whining psalm of the Puritans. If we believe that the Lord takes any interest in human affairs at all we cannot suppose the music of Mozart and Handel and Bach and Beethoven accidental. The Lord has made his own musicians and his own music, but the churches give him "Let us Scatter

2. "Corse Payton and His Merry Company," as the advertisements said, came to Lincoln periodically. *The Hustler* was a farce that played there at least once yearly, and was soon due again.

Seeds of Kindness" and "Pull For the Shore, Sailor." He must be a very loving and patient God indeed to endure such music.

It is peculiar, this idea people have of everything colorless and spiritless being sacred. It is strange how we object to giving beautiful things to God. He must be very fond of beauty Himself, He never made an unlovely thing any more than He ever made a "moral" thing. In nature God does not teach morals. He never limits or interferes with beauty. His laws are the laws of beauty and all the natural forces work together to produce it. The nightingale's song is not moral; it is perfectly pagan in its unrestrained passion. The Mediterranean at noonday is not moral, the forests of the Ganges have no sermons in them. . . . The world was made by an Artist, by the divinity and godhead of art, an Artist of such insatiate love of beauty that He takes all forces, all space, all time to fill them with His universes of beauty; an Artist whose dreams are so intense and real that they, too, love and suffer and have dreams of their own. Yet when we come to worship this Painter, this Poet, this Musician, this gigantic Artist of all art that is, this God whose spirit moved upon chaos leaving beauty incarnate in its shadow, we bring the worst of all the world's art and lay it at His feet. Of all the innumerable human absurdities that have been committed in religion's name this is the most absurd. In the general crash and destruction of things, when the Potter tries His vessels by fire and every man and every artist is judged not according to his piety or according to his morality, but according to his works, when the Master Workman selects from this world the things that are worthy to endure in the next, it is not likely that He will take Baxter's *Saints' Rest*[3] or the Gospel Hymns, or bound volumes of the sermons of great divines—for in the next world we won't need any sermons. Please God, we will be wise enough then to be taught by beauty alone. He will probably take simply the great classics and the things which should be classics, and the paintings that will make even heaven fairer, and the great tone melodies that must make even His angels glad, and the many lives that in themselves are art, and the rest will perish in the void "as chaff which the wind driveth away, or stubble which the fire consumeth."

Journal, October 7, 1894, p. 13.

3. *The Saints' Everlasting Rest* (1650), by Richard Baxter (1615–1691), English Puritan divine. The Cather family owned an edition combining two of Baxter's works: *Call to the Unconverted* and *The Saints' Everlasting Rest*, abridged by Benjamin Fawcett (Hartford: Silas Andrus and Son, 1854).

The Literary Life

Ladies' Clubs

Whatever else Lincoln is or is not it is certainly a much beclubbed town.[4] It is particularly rich in ladies' literary clubs. All week long the intellectual female may be seen haunting the public libraries, stretching the seams of her best black silk handling massive volumes and writing unreadable notes with her kid gloves on. About once a week the literary ladies meet together and mingle the "glories that were Greece and the grandeur that was Rome" with tea and muffins and Saratoga chips. These club meetings are highly beneficial in many ways, and particularly so in the pleasure and sense of self-satisfaction they give the participants. But the idea of women's clubs is just a little ludicrous. In the first place women have no particular talent for good fellowship. They can't leave their family affairs behind them and can't resist declaiming upon the faults of their last maid or the high marks their daughters get at the high school or university. Now a man who went to [his] club and discussed his family affairs would be promptly and violently sat down upon. Of course, if we may trust the dialogue of the club scene in *Lady Windermere's Fan*, men frequently discuss worse things than their family affairs. It is decidedly to the credit of women that their interests are concentrated where their affections are; a woman whose interests are not is distasteful, even to one of her own sex. But this sort of concentration is almost laughable in a club. Women have no talent for good fellowship. Most of them acknowledge it. The only woman of this century who has been noted for that talent is Miss Trilby O'Ferrall, and she had no family affairs, at least none to speak of. It is this same capacity for friendship and companionship that makes some women think her so shocking.

Ladies' literary clubs are particularly funny. Family matters mix so strangely with Kant's philosophy or Ruskin's theory of art. If the good ladies made their assemblies entirely matters of novels and recreation they ought to get a good deal of pleasure and even profit out of them. But they

4. In the fall of 1894 one reads miscellaneously of Lincoln social clubs like the Patriarchs, the Empires, and the Ravolas; there were the Pleasant Hour, Wednesday Afternoon, Century, and Cheese and Cracker Clubs; Sorosis, W. T. G. Cooking Club, P.E.O., and the Club of Clubs. Among the study groups, Century had papers on Charlemagne; Hall in the Grove dealt with both "French History" and "Socialism"; and P.E.O. was studying the Homeric Age. A newcomer in town was the Bryant Matinee Literary Society, composed of sixth-graders from Bryant School.

are too desperately learned. They read all the dryest books in the world because they are the most scholarly and endure a great deal of chaff to get a very little wheat. Now, outside of a university or a laboratory, Kant's philosophy is not half so enjoyable or beneficial as a novel by Thackeray or Meredith, or even the mild though undoubtedly great Mr. Howells. This world is not a scholarly world, and it is perhaps better that it should not be. Self-improvement is so often gone at in the wrong way and a little of it so often makes bores of very nice people. After all this life is so short we do pretty well if we get through it comfortably at all, with or without "self-improvement." If we are the happier for Kant's philosophy, by all means let us have it; if we are not it is doubtful if it is worth while stopping for.

Of all the ladies' clubs the Sordello clubs are undoubtedly the funniest. Sordello doesn't seem to mix well with tea and muffins, though perhaps he had too many of them when he was hanging around Verona after his debut and that was what was the matter with him. At any rate he was never a ladies' man and he always appears uncomfortable amid roses and ices and gold-rimmed nose glasses. "Sleep and forget, Sordello." [*Journal*, October 28, 1894, p. 13]

The Use of Libraries

One of the most touching phases of human generosity and un-selfishness is the habit of marking the books of the city library. It is sweet to know that there are so many people who think so constantly of others that they carefully draw a line about every paragraph which strikes them as good. But the unbridled generosity of the human heart frequently leads to error. The fact is nobody has a right to mark a book that other people are going to read. It is enough to prejudice one against a book forever to open it and find "Splendid!" "How true!" pencilled all along the margins in a delicate female hand. Then it is rather courageous to appoint oneself a sort of running commentary on Browning or Tennyson and pronounce verdict upon their work. It takes considerable assurance to write "This is a gem" over *Sordello* or "a dainty little poem" over *Maude*. It is quite a study in psychology as well as literature to read the remarks written upon the margins of books of [the] city library. One of the most refreshing commentaries is written in the front of one of George Meredith's novels, "I don't understand this book at all; it don't say whether he married her or not.—H. G." H. G.'s comment is the most sensible one this writer has yet seen. If people must mark books, if they can't sleep well without it, they should mark only their own and hide those in their most secret chamber. It is too great a burden for anyone to assume to direct the taste of the great public. [*Journal*, September 23, 1894, p. 13]

... It is almost laughable in this century, when the best talent has almost all gone into the novel, that people should be ashamed to put Meredith or Balzac on their book shelves. It seems that illustrated books are considered frivolous and that ponderous volumes with formidable bindings and uncut edges and paper labels are the correct thing. Libraries should be only exhibition rooms filled with matter to impress the beholder with the rigid intellectuality of the family. . . . Yet many of these same people, who talk like the data of ethics, who dance like the origin of species, who wear their hats in a Holy Roman Empire sort of way, will go down to the city library and draw out the works of Mary J. Holmes and Augusta J. Evans[5] and read them with gusto and delight. [*Journal*, November 11, 1894, p. 13]

Reputations

Zola is coming over too, and people who have never read *La Terre* and never heard of *Nana* will flock to look at the great Émile, invite him to their homes and make him the king of the animals. That is a characteristic American habit, to adore authors with whom we are acquainted only through the book reviews. But then one of the advantages of being great is that the world accepts your reputation without examining your claims.

Authors should not feel hurt when they find their books uncut upon the shelves of their friends. That is proof that they are great enough to go unread and unwatched. It is the little fellows we must reach, the little fellows who would be always sneaking into notoriety if we did not keep them in their places. [*Journal*, July 21, 1895, p. 9]

Winners and Losers

The vagaries of popular taste fascinated and provoked Willa Cather as they have social observers before and since. Regardless of the old adage, accounting for some tastes was not difficult. For example, the public's passionate

5. Light novels by Mrs. Mary Jane Holmes (1825–1907) and Mrs. Augusta J. Evans Wilson (1835–1909) were extremely popular at the end of the century. Mrs. Holmes began with *Tempest and Sunshine; or, Life in Kentucky* (1854) and continued with more than forty novels. Of all the ladies' books, however, the only one still in the Lincoln City Library is *St. Elmo* (1867), by Augusta J. Evans.

interest in the Corbett-Mitchell fight for the heavyweight championship of the world on January 25, 1894, in Jacksonville, Florida, could be explained in terms of elementals—of primitive instincts. (" The Battle Brief but Bloody" headlined the Journal's *story of Corbett's victory by a knockout in the third round.) And the exhibit given over to the arts at the Nebraska State Fair (the week of September 10, 1894) offered evidence that man, the clever ape, found it at least as admirable to imitate as to originate: although the entries included many original paintings with western subjects—cornfields, a cowboy, a sod house—an astonishing number of "copies" showed up in the lists of awards. As for the popularity of the Intermezzo from* Cavalleria Rusticana, *it appears from Miss Cather's comments that even in pre-Madison Avenue days a public that did not know much about art could be brainwashed into knowing what it liked.*

At last it is over, thank heaven. Thursday was a day of suppressed excitement. Every man you met looked as though he were going to be married the next hour—until the first telegrams came, and then some of them looked like they had recently been made widowers. Everyone talked about the fight, and everyone hung around the telegraph offices, everyone except the ministers and they kept the telephones redhot all day, firing in questions on the city editors. Nothing but a prize fight or a presidential election could have aroused such interest. If Gladstone and Bismarck had been having a joint debate in Jacksonville, no one would have waited for the telegrams. If all the great poets and painters in the world had assembled there to vie with each other in great creation, the milkman would not have driven a bit faster to get an evening paper. Young man of talent, the arts don't pay. If you want to be beloved by your countrymen, if you want to draw near to the hearts of the people, be cherished with their household gods, remembered in their prayers, if you want to be truly great, there are but two careers open to you—politics and the prize ring. It has been so ever since men were men. The old sports of Athens were much more interested in the victorious *athletae* than the bards who meandered about with the laurels on their heads. People come to the state fair to see the horse racing, not to gaze upon Mrs. So-and-So's crayon work or silk crazy-quilt.

The struggle of brawn with brawn seems to appeal more strongly than anything else to the great mass of the people, and it seems that all the primitive instincts have not died out of the world. Civilization is a very large boast. Like Eli Perkins, it has a greater reputation than it can live up to.

"A man's a man for all 'o that" and will be for some years to come. Civilization has not destroyed the needs or passions of men's lives; the former it has only exaggerated and multiplied, the latter it has alternately whetted and drugged and drained into a thousand aimless, frivolous channels which nature knows naught of. [*Journal*, January 28, 1894, p. 13]

What would happen in this world if a state fair should ever rise to the lofty dignity of hanging only original paintings in the art department? That state of things will probably never come about, but if people will exhibit studies they might at least give us the study itself first hand and spare us the copy. Now and then you can find a copy that has merit in it. One of the best pictures at the fair was a copy of a Corot by Miss Parker.[6] Sympathy with a great master means something, but the better one imitates a chromo "study" the worse painter he is. The fact is that half of the crazy stuff that is sent about to state and county fairs is just a kind of fancy work on canvas, with which dear old ladies are wont to console their loneliness, when they had far better employ themselves with poodle dogs and parrots. The fact must be forced upon the dear people some day that a man who can't draw can't paint, and a man who has not had good instruction can't do either. [*Journal*, September 16, 1894, p. 13]

Lincoln has been greatly agitated for the past year over the Intermezzo from *Cavalleria Rusticana*. Everyone who can play the piano at all plays it; and a great many people who cannot, play it just the same. Any piano rendition of it is bad enough, so that really doesn't matter much. Most people seem to think that the Intermezzo is a complete composition in itself, a sort of sonata or nocturne or funeral march under another name. Just now the Intermezzo and Rubinstein's "Melody in F" seem to enjoy the entire favor and patronage of this musical centre. It is unfortunate that the great northman is dead and that Mascagni is in Italy. They would be so pleased and flattered if they could only know. Three or four years ago Lincoln had the privilege of hearing *Cavalleria Rusticana*, the Intermezzo included, splendidly rendered. The Nordica concert company gave the opera entire, with Nordica as Santuzza, Scalchi as Lola, and Campanini as Turiddu. On that occasion the opera and even the sacred and holy

6. Miss Cora Parker, who taught art at the University, had loaned rather than entered her copy of a Corot painted from the original in the Louvre.

Intermezzo did not seem to please Lincoln half so much as a very trivial little song about "Love May Go Hang,"[7] which Mme. Nordica would not have dared sing east of the Missouri unless it were in Council Bluffs. The music dealers say that they never sold a copy of the Intermezzo until two years afterward when people had been reading about it in the "patent side" [syndicated material] of the newspapers. The singers rendered the opera in concert dress and for that reason the greater part of the audience did not consider it an opera at all, but thought it was an oratorio or something. Next day there was a good deal of complaining about the second part of the programme being "monotonous." All the young ladies who play the piano and those who do not were there, and they did not even discover the Intermezzo. They went away blissfully unconscious that there had been an Intermezzo. And yet today they spatter it over the keyboard in ecstasy and admiration. Queer world this, anyway. [*Journal*, December 15, 1895, p. 9]

Who or what made the local audiences laugh was analyzed by Willa Cather with particular reference to Anna Boyd and Mamie Mayo, two good comediennes who had been in Lincoln several times. Miss Mayo had just appeared in The Hustler *(October 24, 1894), in which she sang "The Bowery Girl"; Anna Boyd had played* A Trip to Chinatown *earlier in the year (January 19) and was remembered as a "matchless" performer. The following piece is only one of many Willa Cather wrote on the tastes and rituals of audiences—hats worn in the theatre, chatter, meaningless applause, roughhouse in the gallery, laughter at tragedy, and all the other familiar manifestations of Philistia.*

There is one peculiar feature about the Lincoln theatre-going public, or rather there are a good many, and one of the most peculiar is its cold reception of all comediennes, from soubrettes up. A man with a genteel face and a painted abdomen causes deep and lasting joy. The dress circle waxes glad and the gallery waxes loud. But the prettiest, the cleverest, the wickedest soubrette finds dead silence in the house. The spectators unanimously give her ice. It is not from conscientious reasons, either, for if a skirt dancer stands on her head the fact at length dawns upon them that

7. The first half of the concert by the Nordica company on March 2, 1893, was a group of solos by the principals; the second part was a concert presentation of *Cavalleria Rusticana*. More literally, Mme. Nordica's encore songs were entitled "When Love Is Kind," by Lehmann, and "She Is Fooling Thee." The *Journal* account (March 3, 1894, p. 8) said that "in the encore songs her piquant manner was irresistible."

that must be rather naughty, and that therefore they ought to laugh. New York has been raving all summer because its population is not yet educated out of its overweening weakness for pretty actresses who cannot act, but we, alas, have never even got educated up to that ordinary point. On the Lincoln stage a homely man takes better than a pretty woman, which is an unusual and unnatural state of affairs. It speaks of a liking for coarser comedy and a certain obtuseness for more delicate fun. Not that it is any better than any other audience, O, no, but it likes to hear coarseness boldly stated rather than delicately insinuated; it likes the little element of poesy and beauty, which is the only redeeming element about many stage practices, left out. Even Anna Boyd, whose magnetism and catching eyes are almost irresistible, failed to arouse the audience when she was here with *A Trip to Chinatown* last season. The other night Mamie Mayo, who is almost Anna Boyd over again on a little lower scale, met with the same chilly reception. It may be bad taste to like the delicately suggestive, but it is still worse taste to like the distorted and grotesque. If people have no taste for champagne they might at least drink a respectable brand of whisky.

"Is there no way in which I can rouse this house? I have exhausted myself on them. It's like running up against a stone wall," groaned Mamie Mayo as she was getting off her "Bowery Girl" make-up.

"Oh yes, if you put on a red wig and stick on a red wax nose over your own pretty one and go on and be as generally disgraceful as possible, you'll wake them up." [*Journal*, October 28, 1894, p. 13]

Philistia was not one of the countries explored by the Orientalist and author Sir Richard Burton, but his widow—though "considered very liberal-minded"—was governed by its values, as Willa Cather regretfully noted.

The death of Lady Isabel Burton recalls the loyal, though rather undiscriminating devotion which she bestowed upon her learned husband. She followed him for years in all his dangerous and trying travels in the Far East, aided him continuously in his exhausting literary labor, only at last to destroy, after his death, the most cherished of his manuscripts, his translation of *The Scented Garden*, from the Persian of Saadi, because she considered it unfit for publication. The amusing womanishness of the action was almost enough to compensate for the very great loss that English literature sustained in the destruction of so valuable a work. A man would have felt in duty bound to publish the work which had cost his friend so many years of unremitting labor, and fit or unfit would have sooner cut off his own right hand than destroyed so great a monument of man's scholarship. But not so the estimable Lady Burton. Her husband's respectability was of more importance than his erudition or all the learning of the orient. She would destroy his life work rather than have people make unkind remarks about him. How exceedingly like a wife and like a woman! And yet Lady Burton is considered very liberal-minded—for a person of her sex. Nevertheless she placed the unquestioned home-and-fireside respectability of Richard Burton and wife above all the poetry of Persia. Byron's mamma said she wished he had been a fool and respectable. Well, we have still some things to be thankful for. Sir Richard did succeed in publishing his matchless translation of those glorious Arabian romances, *The Thousand Nights and a Night*, that brought the strange sound and color of the east into our tongue as Félicien David brought them into music.[8] Had he not published them himself the manuscript would probably have fallen victim to his good wife's over-whelming sense of propriety. [*Journal*, April 19, 1896, p. 13]

Parlor Critics

In the spring of 1894 the point of view of "the Journal critic" was challenged in an article "As to Clara Morris and Her School" (Journal, March 18, 1894) by "Jane Archer," who may have been Miss Sarah B. Harris, later to be Willa Cather's good friend and co-editor on the Courier. The writer (and no doubt others) preferred Julia Marlowe to Clara Morris, and thought Miss Cather too energetic in defending the "emotional school." As Miss Cather saw it, objections to emotion, power, and unconventionality were symptomatic of one of the worst faults of Philistia—its pale, fearful prudery.

The curse of every school and phase of modern art is the guild of drawing-room critics; critics who sneer at the great and powerful, and adore the clever and the dainty. They refuse to read anything more stimulating than Howells' parlor farces, and to hear any play more moving than *The Rivals*. This race of critics has declared Ruskin and Wagner and Turner and Modjeska blasé and have taken unto themselves new gods in the very airy and fragile shapes of Whistler and Jerome K. Jerome and

8. The French composer Félicien David (1810–1876) used, for example, Arabian melodies in his oratorio *Le Désert*. Of his five operas, the best known is *Lalla Roukh* (1862), based on the work by Thomas Moore, a poet Willa Cather much admired. Burton's sixteen-volume translation of *The Thousand Nights and a Night* is dated 1885–1888.

[Reginald] De Koven and Julia Marlowe. They take the books that look well on their tables; the music that is not too loud for their parlors; the pictures that hang well on their walls; the actresses who most gracefully adorn their receptions, and say, "This is art, and these are artists; everything else is overdrawn, coarse, stagey, unnatural." It is no new phase of criticism for people with a poverty of emotion and imagination to say that everything more pronounced is overdrawn and unnatural. Whatever they cannot feel, they claim is beyond the range of human feeling; and whatever they have not experienced, they claim is beyond the limit of human experience. These critics have had a wonderful effect upon the authors and playwrights of the nineteenth century. A playwright cannot write without presenting emotions any more than a painter can paint without laying colors. The world in which playwrights are born has no emotions; it furnishes its parlors in dull grays and cold blues and has society and guests to match. Following the creed of realism, the playwright can no longer create knights and ladies, but tells of the things that are. Artists of every nation have escaped from the chilling atmosphere of their own world, and have gone to the so-called crust of society[9] for types which at least have the all-redeeming virtue of sincerity. The greatest play that has been written to amuse society is *Camille*; the greatest book that has been written to instruct it is *Anna Karenina*. One would think Mephistopheles' sides would ache with merriment over the satire of it.

However, the parlor people have a right to run their parlor world the way they want to, but let them leave the stage world alone. On the stage let people love and hate each other to the death. Your drivelling lover and hater are not worth an actor's exertions. On the stage friendship must be something more than "intellectual sympathy"; hatred something fiercer than a lack of affinity. Make your own world as moderate and proper and conventional as you wish, but behind the footlights let people love with kisses and suffer with tears.

Journal, March 25, 1894, p. 13.

The Ladies' Home

That organ of exquisite literary culture, the *Ladies' Home Journal*, has added ex-President Harrison and Madame Melba and Mary Anderson to its collection of contributors which has so long been headed by that

---

9. An allusion to the play *The Crust of Society*, a version of *Le Demi-Monde* by Dumas *fils*. It had been presented in Lincoln twice the previous season, March 1 and May 2, 1893. For the other plays mentioned: *The Rivals*, with Joseph Jefferson, had been given on November 30, 1891; *Camille*, with Clara Morris, on November 22, 1893.

shining literary light Ruth Ashmore.[10] The standards of popular journal-ism in this sweet land of liberty have always been a little bit peculiar, but the *Ladies' Home Journal* can certainly claim the honor of having first reached the line of complete literary emancipation. Over most other periodicals there has hung a dim superstition that literature was a craft apart and by itself and that not every one who runs may write. But not so with the *Ladies' Home Journal*. It is devoted exclusively to the interests of the great and to the unknown wives of the great; to how Henry Ward Beecher liked his mutton chops, to how Paderewski ties his shoes, to how "The Duchess" wears her back hair. Any "famous person" whatsoever may enter the paths of literature through the *Ladies' Home*. It matters not at all what their especial line of distinction. Cissy Fitzgerald may write a chaste and classic history of her celebrated winks, Corbett may write articles on physical culture, Buffalo Bill may write on the financial aspect of the new west. The *Ladies' Home* is democratic and all-embracing. It has a department in which we are told of the beauties of Shakespeare and Dante, and another in which we are told that bonnets and elaborately trimmed toaks [toques] will be worn for the theatre this winter; a depart-ment in which we are told the history of Beethoven's sonatas and another in which we are told whether it is proper to kiss a young man good night after returning from a party.

Above all, the *Ladies' Home* covets articles from actresses, prima donnas and eminent divines. We all know what pure and exquisite English prima donnas write. There have been foolish men like Stevenson and Thackeray and George Meredith, who considered literature a craft and an art, who labored and sweated for years to learn just the elementary principles of style and form. What labor lost! Here Mme. Nordica and ex-President Harrison and Mrs. Henry Ward Beecher and Dr. Charles Parkhurst can just blossom out into literature off-hand. We do things rapidly in this end of the century. Probably it's the influence of the bicycle and locomotive. It would not be at all surprising if Carmencita should

10. In the December 1895 issue of the *Ladies' Home Journal* appeared "This Country of Ours," by the Hon. Benjamin Harrison; "My First Appearance on the Stage," from the memoirs of Mary Anderson de Navarro; and in the announcements for future issues, "Madame Melba will write of 'The Voice.'" Ruth Ashmore's contributions as a staff member were "Side-Talks with Girls" and "The Girl Who Is Employed." Among other subjects and contributors: "The Duchess" probably refers to the pseudonym of Mrs. Margaret Wolfe Hungerford (1855–1897), Irish novelist whose works were currently popular; The Reverend Charles H. Parkhurst, New York minister and reformer, began a series of articles in February, 1895 ("Marriage and Its Safeguards," "The True Mission of Woman," etc.).

write the important novel of the age, or if New York's chief of police should compose a symphony after office hours.

In looking over the *Ladies' Home* table of contents for December you will see many noted names. Among them Ruth Ashmore on "Girls," Margaret Simms, on "New Designs in Knitting"; Emma M. Hopper, on "Holiday Gowns," and Patty Thumb on "Marking Initials." Now we all know Ruth Ashmore and Margaret Simms and Emma M. Hopper, their glory has bestrode the morning light and flashed upon the uttermost parts of the earth, but in the name of the venal vampire and the great primeval mystery, who, who is Patty Thumb?[11]

Journal, January 12, 1896, p. 9.

The Queen's English

To the girl in Nebraska, Philistia could stretch as far and as high as the British throne itself. With Queen Victoria solidly installed as the guardian of bad taste, there was always the problem of how much approval one ought to accept from the Establishment. Should Henry Irving—already a knight in the Kingdom of Art—kneel to receive knighthood from Queen Victoria? And there was that matter of the laureateship. The court had gone bardless since Tennyson's death in 1892, though many successors were mentioned (Willa Cather, like others, thought Swinburne was the only real poet among them), and now the laurels were given to the docile, prolific, and more than undistinguished Alfred Austin (1835–1913). The choice was, perhaps, predictable in view of the Queen's taste in literature: it was said that her favorite novelist was Marie Corelli (1855–1924), whose many easy books were embellished with what Willa Cather called "alliterative sky rockets" (Journal, November 4, 1894). The Queen's English had all the accents of Philistia.

The Knight: Henry Irving

The knighting of Henry Irving has been world talk for at least two weeks. All of Sir Henry's friends have had something to say about it and all of his enemies, and the people who know nothing whatever about Sir Henry or his work have said a great deal. On the whole, though the

11. Since the spellings "Simms," "Hopper," and "Thumb" appear twice, they are left here as they were intended. They should read "Sims," "Hooper," and "Thum." The first two are often in the magazine, but "A Set of Marking Initials" does seem to be Patty Thum's solo appearance.

public seems to approve and to think that the court of England has not done anything so sensible for some time past, there is, of course, always that question as to whether a man who has risen to greatness without the aid or prestige of any temporal power should bend to receive its recognition at last, whether a man who has been the knight-errant of fortune all his life should kneel for any other knighthood. There are plenty of Irving's friends on this side the water who would have been glad to see him quietly refuse the proffered honor and remain titled only among his fellow players, a lord only in his own domain. But Sir Henry Irving is only mortal after all and the day of art's imperial defiance is dead.

There were many and weighty reasons why he should permit the doughty queen to dub him knight. In the first place, Irving is distinctly an English actor. He has done more than any other Englishman to create a national dramatic taste in England and to give the theatre a high and individual place among the arts of his country. He has left no way untried to appeal to the sympathies and even to the egotism of his cockney public. He has touched the British in their vulnerable spot through historic plays that proclaimed the gentleness of English traditions and the divine descent of English kings. While his big theatre with the pre-Raphaelite scenery and its elaborate customs and its mechanical effects is rather laughable as the work of a great actor, yet it is a serious and effective factor in English life. It is a part of the daily routine of the respectable British subject. Before Irving's time no player and no theatre ever succeeded in arousing national sentiment or national support in England. There was but one way left for him to get any nearer to his public and to stimulate appreciation among the English people and effort among English actors and that was to bring to the English stage the recognition and support of the English crown. Then it was an act of charity on Irving's part toward the English nobility to bring into that august body one man of talent, just as it was charitable of Tennyson to sacrifice himself that his country might boast of one poet laureate who was a poet. Sir Henry Irving can do more for the cause than Mr. Henry Irving ever could, had the gods blessed him with twice his ancient greatness. The cockney who knows very little of Irving's work and cares less, will take it for granted that he is a great man, that the theatre is a great institution and that acting is a great art. It is the bitter truth that in England a title can do more to "elevate" the stage than a genius.

It is rather amusing that Irving should be playing "Don Quixote, the Knight of the Sorrowful Countenance" just at this particular time. Last week when he came to those lines, "Knighthood sits like a halo around my head" the pit rose up like one man and clamored for more air.

It is whispered about the inner circles in London that Mr. [Herbert] Beerbohm Tree would have been knighted along with Irving were it not for the risqué nature of some of his plays. We are informed that the court is very strict about such matters, and as long as Mr. Tree persists in playing such roles as Loris Ipanoff to Mrs. Pat Campbell's Fédora, it will be impossible for the court to recognize him. O dear, dear! That much boasted morality of the court of England! The world is sick of it. We have been hearing about it ever since the fall of the Stuarts, when the crown went into the hands of Dutch grandfathers and grandmothers.... What an exemplary lot Queen Victoria's offspring have been to the exemplary British nation. How often we have heard how all her little princesses in their youth were initiated into all domestic duties, how they had to make their own little beds and cooked their own little pies and watered their own little flower gardens. How her little princes were never permitted to play cards or to smoke, and drank only lemonade colored with cochineal—it would have saved her royal highness a good many thousands, by the way, if Wales had been taught to play baccarat in his early youth; he might make a better stagger at it now—how they were only allowed to read [Fénelon's] Télémaque and Maria Edgeworth's moral tales and to see only expurgated Shakespeare or "Punch and Judy" at the theatre. Probably even now the queen mamma would think twice before she would permit Wales to see Camille or Gismonda.

Well, let Mr. Tree do without his title. Now that Irving has sacrificed himself—at least it is nicer to put it that way and to think that he cared nothing for the title for himself—and the English stage is saved, let Mr. Tree be free and be an artist. Let him be an artist only, and an artist all the time. He can dispense with the solemn annual old ladies' tea at Windsor palace and the crest on his letterheads. Life has larger things for Mr. Tree than those. It was Mr. Irving's duty to bring to the English stage the recognition and reverence of English authority. It is Mr. Tree's duty to see that the flattering patronage of aristocracy does not weaken and hamper and stunt its development. Let Mr. Tree play Fédora, let him play French plays, Italian plays, Russian plays, let him shock old England to its centre. Perhaps if England were shocked deeply enough and violently enough it might awaken from the sleep of centuries and look about and see God's world.[12] [Journal, June 30, 1895, p. 12]

12. Sir Herbert Beerbohm Tree eventually received his title in 1909.

The Laureate: Alfred Austin

Mr. Alfred Austin, the new poet laureate of England, is eminently the man for the place; partially because he is a politician, partially because he is a conservative, partially because he is nice looking, but principally because no one has ever heard of him and he is not a poet at all. The problem of that laureateship has always been to secure a man who wrote verse and was not a poet. The queen has solved it in the admirable and deft manner in which she always does things. Anyone who has done the penance of reading *Savonarola; a Tragedy*, or *The Golden Age*, knows that if the nine muses with lyric Apollo at their head should conspire together, they could never make a poet of Mr. Alfred Austin. Of course, the only living English poet who really deserves the laureateship, unless it were William Morris, is the man who wrote "Atalanta in Calydon." But Swinburne would be shut out on erotic grounds, and then, too, he is a genius, which would be fatal. The author of "The Praise of Venus" ["Laus Veneris"] could never be trusted to write odes when cunning princesses are born or laments when dissipated young princes die. He could not condole with May of Teck for the loss of her sweetheart one year and congratulate her upon her marriage to his brother the next without perceiving the satire of it.[13] Then Swinburne has done great things in English verse and has achieved the impossible in English meters, even if Dr. [Max] Nordau does call him a degenerate; and he has not deserved that England should ridicule him by giving him the laureateship. *Bothwell* is glory enough for him, and perhaps succeeding generations will know more of him than we do, and they will wonder why and how he and Rossetti managed to live and sing in this commercial age of commercial, industrial, domestic old England. [*Journal*, January 19, 1896, p. 9]

So England is not overly pleased with her new poet laureate, nor with his first effort during his laureateship, a poem written on the situation in the Transvaal, which he calls "Jameson's Ride." Certainly it would be hard to find a more commonplace piece of verse. It is nothing more nor less than a feeble drivelling imitation of Rudyard Kipling's sturdy, though scarcely classical, verses. "Barrack Room Ballads" are right enough from a newspaper man and a writer of romance, but from the man who

13. A reference to the late Queen Mary, who was first engaged to the Duke of Clarence, eldest son of the Prince of Wales (later Edward VII), and on his death was engaged to and married the next son, George, later King George V.

is filling the seat of Tennyson and Dryden they sound rather out of place, and yet it is just such men as this Alfred Austin that England is eternally exalting while men like Addison and Dryden are left to starve or beg their bitter bread from the hands of patronizing nobility. It is strange that England should ever have produced any great poets when the discouragements to lofty verse are so many and the price set upon commonplaceness so great. And yet she has had them. . . . Of all the men who have ever worn England's guerdon of honor, Chaucer, Spenser, Dryden and Tennyson are about the only ones to whom the fatal title of poet could ever be applied. And we may rest assured that their countrymen did not recognize the fact or they would never have been laureates. Of all the divine rights of olden times, divine rights of kings and popes and priests, the poet's is the only one which has lasted. An army may make a king, a faction may make a pope, anything may make a priest, but up to date God alone can make a poet. So after all the laurel matters very little; the only laurels that mean anything are those that a man's descendants place gratefully upon his tomb a hundred years after he is dead. [*Journal*, February 9, 1896, p. 9]

Mr. Alfred Austin has published a sorry dramatic poem in innumerable acts and scenes on Alfred the Great, and the title, *England's Darling*, is the sorriest part of it all. It is hard that that mighty Saxon king should have lived so well and fought so valiantly only to be called a "darling" at last. Think of it, that giant who fought with sea kings, who smote the Danes north and smote them south, who transformed England from a barbarous community to a civilized state, who stands with Shakespeare as the embodiment of all that is greatest in English character, a "darling"! What a picture it calls up of that old bearded giant, toiling in his study to translate Latin books for his illiterate people, leading his half-savage soldiers through the stagnant Fens, driving back the pirates of the north from his barren coasts. If you want to read a poem full of the spirit of that age of heroic savagery try Swinburne's *Locrine*. [*Journal*, March 22, 1896, p. 9]

The Litterateur: Marie Corelli

Marie Corelli, the "queen's favorite novelist," who had the temerity to write a novel of the Christ, has published her new book, *The Sorrows of Satan*, and no doubt if that unhappy gentleman were compelled to read it, it would add considerably to his eternal woe. Why doesn't someone introduce the queen to the classic fiction of "The Duchess" or Mary

J. Holmes? It would open a new world to her and solace her declining years. With Alfred Austin for her poet and Miss Corelli for her novelist, the queen ought to become very literary in time. "Ouida"[14] in her wildest freaks, Augusta J. Evans in her most rampant moods, grow pale and colorless before the hot glow of Marie Corelli's pages. To them it was at least given to write grammatical and sometimes coherent sentences, but not to Marie. Her mission, like Browning's, is to write that which passeth understanding, though their methods are somewhat different. All minor authors have their specialties, which are the fulcrum of their power. Miss Corelli's are the dash and the exclamation point. When you first glance through one of her books you think that the compositors have made chopsticks of it and that the proof was never corrected; then it dawns upon you that all this is "art"—alas the hour! If anything more maudlin, more sensational, more trashy than *The Sorrows of Satan* was ever written one would not know where to turn for it, unless, perhaps to one of Miss Corelli's other works. She calls them her "works," people of her stamp always do. Sensationalism and aggressive cynicism are hard enough to endure when they are coupled with great talent, but without it they are simply unbearable. Why such people find publishers and readers is the difficult thing to understand, but whether it is understood or not, Marie Corelli will continue to produce literature for the news agents to sell long after people of respectable ability have abandoned literature because their clothes are worn out. So far as material gain goes, Miss Corelli's work is considerably more lucrative than that of George Meredith, or the late Mr. Stevenson. There's the justice of literature for you! [*Journal*, February 23, 1896, p. 9]

"*We Pay*"

> In her last year in Lincoln Willa Cather became increasingly aware of the economics of art—mainly, that the quality of the work has little to do with the payment or recognition the artist receives. In a deeper sense, however, she was concerned about the moral effect of wealth on individuals or nations: if one has the ability to buy, will he cease to create? Like Emerson, Thoreau, and Whitman before her, she was especially eloquent on the subject of America's "brutal, barbarous adoration" of foreign artists. Part of the piece

14. "Ouida" was the pseudonym of Marie Louise de la Ramée (1839–1908), whose Victorian-Gothic prose was used most famously in *Under Two Flags* (1867), *Tricotrin* (1868), *Ariadne* (1877), etc. For the other popular writers mentioned here, see notes 5 and 10, above.

of June 14, 1896, in which this characterization of our attitude appeared, was used in an unsigned article, "Prodigal Salaries to Singers," in the Home Monthly *for October, 1896.*

In speaking of the coming musical season in America the [Berliner] *Tageblatt* says: "Paderewski, 100 evenings; Rosenthal, fifty; Ondricek, fifty. Paderewski gets $1,000 a night, Rosenthal $800, Ondricek as much. Add Albani, Calvé, Melba, Trebelli, Sucher, Tamagno, Plunket Greene, Masini and Leoncavallo—and sigh. Poor Europe!"

Yes, America is a strange country. It doesn't make, but it buys. Having no very great painters it buys all the greatest pictures in the world. Having no poets it is the first to recognize and honor the poets of other countries. Having no Paderewski, no Calvé, no Melba, it hires them all, pays them so magnificently that the poor kingdoms of Europe, who gave them birth and whose tastes and traditions made their art, scarcely ever catch sight of them. There was another nation once that made nothing, yet had all; the poets of Greece, the harpers of Ionia, the purple of Tyre, the gold of Africa, the scholars of Egypt, the warriors of the north, and loved its gladiators better than them all. A nation that gleaned the world and gathered into its colossal city everything that was worth loading on its galleys—everything but taste; whose emperors offered a kingdom for a single native artist—and never found him. Great statesmen, great generals, rich merchants, not one singer, one painter, one master of marble. A populace that hurried past the libraries plundered from Alexandria, the Sphinxes brought from Memphis, the marbles stolen from Greece, to see the Nubian lions fight with bears from the German forests. A nation that cooled its wines with snow from the frozen Rhine, spiced its food with aromatics from the Ganges. A nation that owned the seas, conquered the lands, ruled the whole earth and finally, through Peter's chain, usurped the supreme dictatorship of hell and heaven, and yet out of it from beginning to end not one artist. But this sounds entirely too much like Nordau. Perhaps, though, if we should become poor, we might have art of our own. Meanwhile we buy. The Prince of Wales' motto is "I serve." We should elect a Prince of Commerce, and his motto should be, "We pay." [*Journal*, August 11, 1895, p. 9]

So Felix Morris will quit starring this year. Well, that's another misfortune in a world of trouble. It's a misfortune to Mr. Morris, for when an actor once tries to stand on his own name and fails, it generally finishes him for the future, it writes his destiny for him—and reads it. It is a misfortune to the general public, but the public will never know that. Felix Morris is one of few artists in this country. One of the few men who have depth and seriousness. His work in *The Old Musician* [15] was in its way almost perfect. No one-act piece on the modern stage is more finished except Beerbohm Tree's *Ballad-Monger*. Having had the best possible training in leading business Mr. Morris undertook to star. But the public does not want Mr. Morris. It has Eddie Foy and Tim Murphy [16] and a dozen other burning and shining lights. It refused to patronize him. He was praised indeed, by the few whose praise is worth while, and appreciated by fewer still, but man cannot live by praise alone and the money in this world unfortunately does not belong to the appreciative souls. At any rate it did not come Felix Morris' way. He has gone back to leading business.

All this may sound very simple and commonplace, but it's a tragedy in its way just the same, and the worst part of it is that it's only a tragedy of money after all. It is always doubtful whether it is wise for a man of talent to attempt to star in this country. He may strike it indeed, and if he does there's millions in it, but his chances are equally good for a bitter and humiliating failure. In France, in Germany and even in England there is a code and a measure for success. There are men whose power is absolute and whose word is law. They represent the taste and culture of the nation and their judgments are just. If they proclaim a man an artist his future is assured. But in this country there is no court of appeal, nothing but the erratic impulses of the crowd that is too lazy and too good-natured and too ignorant to judge at all. The highest salaried man on the American stage is Eddie Foy, and the way that Eddie Foy became the people's idol was this: One night during the World's Fair a young man who had rather more aboard than he could comfortably manage was making an exhibition of himself in the street. A theatrical manager who was passing that way stopped and asked who the fellow was and found he was a pork-chopper in a Chicago packing house. Now the manager knew his business. A pork-chopper from Chicago who could be as vulgar as that; who could twist his mouth into so many shapes—he ought to make a hit,

15. Felix Morris played in *The Old Musician* in Lincoln on November 6, 1893.

16. These two comedians had both played in Lincoln. Eddie Foy was with the American Travesty Company in *Off the Earth*, February 21–22, 1895 (cf. Bibliography). Tim Murphy made famous the role of Maverick Brander in the farce comedy *A Texas Steer*. His several appearances included October 13, 1893.

he ought to achieve greatness and leave a name to posterity. In two years Foy was drawing the highest salary of any American actor, more than Henry Miller, more than Henry Dixey or Maurice Barrymore. Nowhere does the great American people show its originality of taste as it does in the theatre. [*Courier*, August 31, 1895, p. 6]

Abbey and Grau have failed, just as all other American operatic managers have failed, just as all others will fail, so long as the present exorbitant salary system continues and America is the gold field of European artists. This is not meant as a defense of America or American taste. American audiences are for the most part snobbish and stupid and vulgar; they deserve to be "worked" and cheated as much as they have been and more. But it is unfortunate that the managers should be the men who really suffer from this worship of the golden calf. Now, this is the situation exactly: The grand opera stars exact five and six times the price from Americans that they do from any other people on earth, and they do not do as good work. Here are the actual figures: Melba sings in Paris for $200 a night; in America she demands and gets $1,600, just eight times as much. Jean de Reszke gets $1,250 a night here; in London he is glad to sing for $500, and seldom gets more than $200. We pay Calvé, Plançon, Maurel, Nordica and Eames five times the salary they command in Europe. Now, why? The whole attitude of flippant contempt which foreign artists have toward us may be explained by this: It is a grovelling acknowledgment of our conscious inferiority and lack of taste. It is simply the destruction of our operatic managers; it has driven them all to bankruptcy and despair. Not that the artists themselves are to blame for despising America and Americans and demanding more money here than elsewhere. How could they help despising a country where the amount of their salary is a more effectual advertisement than the perfection of their art? Actually it is a fact, that fully one-half of us go to hear Melba simply because she is paid $1,600 a night and for no other reason. No, nobody blames the singers; but perhaps twice, or, at least, three times the salary they receive in Europe would tempt them to endure us for a few months each year. There is no use in simply burying them in gold. It is not for their good any more than ours; it lowers the standard of work and belittles the dignity of it. It makes a fortune hunter of an artist. In Europe these prima donnas are singers living that they may achieve; in America they are adventuresses singing to make a fortune.

Our brutal, barbarous adoration has broken more than one of those frail musical glasses, crushed the finer essence from more than one great soul.

Our own position in the matter is supremely ridiculous and humiliating. At present it is impossible for any man to attempt operatic management in this country and live. Jean de Reszke's word goes in the Metropolitan; he selects the singers and repertoire; the whole future of American opera for the next few seasons seems to be in his hand. We have made such ever-blooming fools [of] ourselves, ungracefully gambolling in our adoration before these foreign gods and goddesses that they despise and flout us and tell us to our faces that they only endure us for our money, and still, like some maddened senile gallant who would buy his lady's favor, we pay and pay and always pay. We are very like a certain dotard monarch enamored of a fair captive, and she, when he even gave her his crown, only laughed at his bald head. We have taken it upon ourselves to make these singers wealthy, and they only hate and scorn us, as well they may. In our present attitude toward foreign art there is neither good taste nor self-respect. [*Journal*, June 14, 1896, p. 13]

Responsibilities

Though art in Philistia has its eternal problems, Willa Cather regularly pointed out that there were responsibilities on all sides. The critic, for instance, should remember that the failure to recognize is also the power to destroy. Her example here is the young playwright Henry Pettitt, but she also had in mind (if mistakenly) the examples of Keats and Chatterton, "and the rest of them who were put upon the altar and sacrificed and no angel intervened, though the thickets were full of stupid sheep whose death would have been quite as effectual" (Journal, June 7, 1896). But the artist, too, has a responsibility to his audiences—to give value without patronizing. Though she generally liked Sousa, she thought that one of his concerts (May 4, 1894) underestimated the audience. It is only fair to recall that Willa Cather often accused audiences of more than a lack of appreciation, but by her standards it was even worse for an artist to do less than he could. In the theatre she saw the chief need as good management—not great actors but intelligent managers who knew and valued good literature (who could, for example, recognize the difference between Goethe's Faust *and the half-dozen parodies of it on the American stage), managers who would not put profit totally above artistic achievement. But always, and above all, there is the responsibility of the public to see the artist and his cause for what they are. She was young enough to believe it could be done.*

Critic and Artist

There has been another case of Keats in England. The critics said that Mr. Henry Pettitt could not write plays, and Mr. Pettitt foolishly went off and died. People should not take critics too seriously; they should remember that because of the necessity of eating, critics have to say something and that they can't always say the same thing. But, to speak seriously, the English stage has lost in Mr. Pettitt a promising playwright. He was not a man of this generation, and he was not at all a realist. He was intoxicated by the rich and lavish color of the orient and could not work in half tones. His work lacked the ingenuity of more modern plays, but it had in it a great strength and vividness and awful sincerity that the plays of today lack altogether. The English critics are so horribly merciless and stony, and they have such an injudicious way of turning their thumbs down on everything that is youthful and hopeful. It is all right to be satisfied with only the best work, but there is no use in eternally damning genius because it is unnatural and good work because it has flaws. The British public is never really enthusiastic, it never has been, there never was a spark of enthusiasm in their old mud bank except what the Normans brought over when the gallant William landed, and the climate was too foggy for that to live very long and it died centuries ago. The English people have never been excited since they began, probably that is why they have kept going so long. The French are so constantly wrought up that they wear themselves out every generation or two and go all to pieces and have to make a new government, but the English have expended so little vital force that they will live on centuries after they are dead inside, like the Chinese. When there is really a great genius in England, the people are never enthusiastic, they remain perfectly deaf and stolid until years after he is dead and then it is too late for any emotion except respectful reverence. They are very economical of their praise, but it wasn't poetic economy to kill Keats, it wasn't dramatic economy to kill Pettitt. It is strange how much finer work the critics condemn than they ever do. [*Journal*, March 11, 1894, p.13]

Artist and Audience

A large audience—much larger than one would expect at a Friday matinee—gathered at the Lansing yesterday afternoon [May 4, 1894] to listen to Mr. Sousa's band. Many of them were music lovers, drawn by the hope that, at last, the time had come for a real treat. And they got very near to the promised land. They saw before them a large body of accomplished players and a conductor energetic, gifted and graceful in every movement; and they heard one good overture and three inspiring marches. But there their pleasure stopped. Beyond that there was only a dreary waste of musical jugglery. Mr. Sousa has, it seems, a very low opinion of the appreciative calibre of a Lincoln audience. He did not want to take any risk of casting pearls before swine. Apparently he and his orchestra were here for the twofold purpose of earning money and of resting from any violent musical exertion. One thing is certain, that in New York or Philadelphia he never would have dared to present so trite a hash of musical commonplaces. He cannot claim the exemption of the pianist who was "doing his best."

The concert really does not call for much detailed criticism. The opening overture, "1812," by Tschaikowsky, was effectively rendered, as effectively as it could be by a band. Of course it lacked the incisive strength of the strings and had the reedy sleekness that the absence of these is sure to give. The "Musical Critic's Dream" should have been called a nightmare. The parodies it involved were ingenious, but it is venturesome for a man to mingle "Annie Rooney" and the *Tannhauser* march. There is a vulgarity of incongruity that, in audacity, approaches genius. The suite called "Scenes at a Masquerade" was simply wearisome. It belongs to the great class of band music that is neither good enough to be impressive nor bright enough to be amusing. One wishes for something better than long-drawn clarionet warbles, punctuated with tinkling of the triangle and intermitted by occasional causeless exhibitions of dynamics.

The trombone solo by Mr. Pryor showed a fine command of technique and a deplorable lack of taste. Mr. Pryor is too fond of sounding certain impossible notes at the bottom of the compass of his instrument. The result is not music, but sounds that make angels—and certainly did make some babies—weep bitterly. Miss Mecusker was not particularly pleasing, even as a soubrette, a role which her encore decidedly suggested. Neither her singing nor her costume showed any particular respect for her audience. Her rendering of "Where are you going, my pretty maid?" was at least unique. The speaking voice in a song has occasionally, as in the case of Lottie Collins' "Marguerite,"[17] a good effect, but the result of Miss Mecusker's attempt was a rather insipid cheapness. As to the "Clock

17. In *A Naughty Substitute*. Lottie Collins (1866–1910) was most famous for her singing of "Ta-Ra-Ra-Boom-De-Ay." She played in Lincoln with Mrs. Leslie Carter in *Miss Helyett*, March 13, 1893.

Store" and the "Good-Bye" the less said the better. The latter is bad enough with a small band, but when one has to sit waiting while one by one some sixty musicians straggle off the stage and back, one feels that patience is really ceasing to be a virtue. This trick is too old.

Mr. Sousa's own marches were some compensation. Probably no band, in this country at any rate, can play marches better. The trouble was that the appetite was spoiled by the cloying mess in which they were served. If the program had contained nothing but the "Overture" and the three marches, "The Liberty Bell," "The High School Cadets" and "The Washington Post," the total impression left by the concert would have been infinitely better. For in these the sharpness of precision, the delicate shading, all told perfectly. Mr. Sousa has a wonderful perception of rhythm, a perception that he embodies well as conductor. His motions are peculiar but wonderfully sympathetic with the spirit of his marches. He seems so ideal a leader that it is sad to think of the treat he might have given us if only he had seen fit. It is pathetic to see so gifted a musician go chasing after the false gods of cheap popularity. [*Journal*, May 5, 1894, p. 2]

The American Theatre: Standards and Support

. . . In America we do not seem to have the faculty of developing great actors. We have no great national schools of acting like those abroad, where the severe training mercilessly divides talent from vain assumption, giving to the great man all the secrets of art and putting the little men where they belong. We have no managers who have elegance of taste or fine discrimination; who are actors, playwrights, critics, artists all in one; who can select the gold from all that glitters and purify and chasten it. It is an art to manage an artist, and our managers are for the most part guiltless of all art, heaven knows. Then we have no precedent. In this country whosoever wills and can find a backer may star, may even rent a big theatre and play to the metropolis, yes and receive respectful attention and consideration as if they had a right to be there. With us training is not requisite to a "star," to say nothing of talent; only "nerve" and money. Of course in spite of all this we have had some great actors, men in whom the God-sent madness of genius raged so riotously that they developed without our help, in spite of us, in defiance of us, were their own school, their own managers and their own traditions. But we have had many more . . . who go very well until they reach the point where they need the guiding discipline of the strong arm and do not find it. [*Courier*, September 7, 1895, p. 7]

... With a few gentlemanly exceptions, American managers are the scum of the earth boiled down and scented with musk and lager beer. The men who manage our "shows" and theatres are generally all-around sports, without ordinary intelligence, much less any notion of art. Gentlemen whose ideas of literature are limited to the *Police Gazette* and whose taste in art runs entirely to living pictures. Actors, the very greatest of them, are helpless in the hands of these men, who direct the theatrical taste of America. If the public only knew it, it is just as harmful and dangerous to have an ignorant and dissolute man in the box office as in the pulpit. He directs the taste and thought of the growing generation more than the minister. [*Journal*, December 22, 1895, p. 9]

Oscar Hammerstein, formerly a cigar-maker, now manager of the Olympia music hall, has written a new version of *Faust*. The new opera will be run on the "Twelve Temptations" plan and will be plentifully supplied with dancing and living pictures. The plot is refreshingly novel, in that Faust marries Marguerite and they live together happily ever afterwards. It is about time there was a new *Faust*, and after the usual production doubtless even Mr. Hammerstein's would be refreshing. Of course *Faust* the opera is great enough, but *Faust* the play, which the malicious American public charge to Goethe, is enough to make that unfortunate poet writhe in his grave. It is to be hoped that Mr. Hammerstein has at least omitted the garden scene; living pictures are preferable and less demoralizing. That scene has made the public suspicious of all garden scenes and gardens. We have all seen lackadaisical Fausts and matronly Gretchens play hide and seek about an incandescent rosebush until we shudder at the mention of gardens.[18] We can forgive Mr. Hammerstein almost anything if he only won't come out into the garden, Faust. There is only one thing in the world that can compensate one for sitting through *Faust* the play, and that is to read *Faust* the poem.

How strangely fitting it is that an American cigar-maker should rewrite *Faust*, to "utilize its opportunities," as the professional phrase runs. Some American syndicate is going to build a big machine shop over Niagara Falls to utilize its opportunities, too. We never let things go to

18. Various adaptations of *Faust* had been playing regularly around the country—Irving's *Faust*, Morrison's *Faust*, Griffith's *Faust*. For accounts of these productions and the illuminations of garden and Brocken, see page 278. Steve Brodie, mentioned below, won fame (and a theatrical career of sorts) by jumping off Brooklyn Bridge.

waste in this country, not even if we have to shroud with a factory one of the greatest spectacles on earth. But on the matter of Mr. Hammerstein's *Faust*, it would not be at all surprising to awaken some morning and find that Steve Brodie had "improved the opportunities" of *Hamlet*. While the management of almost all provincial theatres and many metropolitan ones rests in the hands of ex-bartenders and cigar-makers, we may expect almost anything. What the American theatre needs is not great actors, we have them, but managers whom heaven has seen fit to bless with some faint glimmerings of intelligence and a moderate ability for speaking the English language. [*Journal*, February 23, 1896, p. 9]

The season of '95–'96 will long be remembered in the "provinces," that is away from the larger American dramatic centres, for the general worthlessness of its theatrical attractions. The managers have their old and partially valid argument that the people want trash and refuse to pay for first-class entertainments. That they refuse to pay for them is certainly true, not because they do not care for them, but because just now the dear people are horribly and desperately poor. Managers are hasty in their conclusions. It is not so much a lack of taste that keeps the multitude away from the first-class performances as the want of money. In New York the situation is just the same. We read every day of the immense sales for Duse's performances in Washington, but how many of the "respectable poor" or even the common people do you suppose those great audiences include? In Paris all the people go to the best theatres, and the street sweepers may see Bernhardt and Mounet-Sully if they choose—and they do choose—for the government has bound the theatres to admit these people for what they can afford to pay. At stipulated times each theatre must give its best performances free to the poor of Paris. In America the poor take what they can get, and that is vaudeville, generally. Mr. How-ells, in an excellent editorial in *Harper's Weekly*, suggests that the board of education should take this matter in hand and give the people a chance. This year all the greatest artists of foreign lands are among us, artists whom to hear and see is an education, yet the pleasure and profit of seeing them is confined almost entirely to people from Wall Street and Fifth Avenue, people who are neither serious nor earnest nor artistically inclined, while the struggling, ambitious youth of the country is practically shut out. That even art should be restricted to the men of dollars is one of the most bit-terly unfair things in a very unjust state of affairs. Until there is some means devised whereby the young men and students of America will have at least occasional admission to the best theatres, there will never be an elevated theatrical taste.[19] [*Journal*, March 8, 1896, p. 13]

The Public and Heine

The city fathers of New York have decided that they will not allow the "German element" to erect a statue of Heine in Central Park. Their argument is that the park already contains the statues of too many foreigners. That is a seemingly valid reason. New York is certainly the most American of American cities, and Central Park is the very heart of New York. If there is any one spot on the continent that ought to represent American characteristics and sentiment, it is Central Park—after Wall Street. But since one of the principal and most individual American characteristics is the liberal purchase and patronage of foreign art and foreign artists, the proposed statue could not be so very much out of place after all. America is an appreciative rather than a creative nation. There is only one thing we make here—fortunes, a few of us. And with them we buy the wares of the world. Our theatres are filled with foreign players, our concert halls with foreign singers, our galleries with foreign pictures, our libraries with foreign books. When Hall Caine is the lion of New York drawing rooms why should Central Park be denied to a man infinitely greater, and who is besides dead and much less dangerous?

Then there are other reasons. If the statue of any one foreigner could be appropriately placed in Central Park it would be that of Heinrich Heine. If ever there was a republican spirit it was his; if ever there lived an admirer of America and Americans, a lover of a free people and a free land, it was he. He was a much better American than many of us. He was a republican among tyrannies, a poet of liberty among the flatterers of kings. Until we have great poets of our own, surely no man has more claim upon our reverence than he who said: "Among all the gods I prefer to worship Jesus Christ, not because He is the royal born Dauphin of heaven, not because He is the heir to a million worlds, but because He is the republican God of the republican many, because the gifts of kings cannot move Him more than the prayers of peasants."[20] [*Journal*, December 15, 1895, p. 9]

19. In the same issue of the *Journal*, an editorial (p. 12) advocated a series of endowed theatres in America; philanthropists could remove the theatre from commercial pressures as they had done with art galleries and colleges. Howells had written twice in *Harper's Weekly* protesting high prices in the theatre (February 22 and 29, 1896).

20. From Heine's *Die Stadt Lucca* (1830). The context is a conversation about paintings, including "The Marriage of Cana" and others with figures of Christ. The passage quoted here may be found (in another translation) in *Poetry and Prose of Heinrich Heine*, ed. Frederic Ewen (New York: Citadel Press, 1948), p. 598.

THE RELATIONS OF THINGS

One of the world's old ways is to speak to its poets in metaphor. The doubleness of things is of course primarily in the observant, imaginative mind; but metaphor is also proof of elemental order, and the game of creation is to articulate some version of it. To Willa Cather, finding the relationships in the passing show was obviously a delight, a revelation; a way of intelligence and understanding; a more intense reality than a catalogue could ever be. And so she looks at a building and discovers a band, translates music into living moments and speech into music, sees poetry in football. All of the arts are one art, and the body of the world can blossom out of metaphor. But part of the pleasure we have in observing a young writer in action as she begins to collect, measure, and pattern her materials, is to note just where she stops joining and begins to pinpoint. For relationships are also made by precision, contrast, separation, clarity. Let us be honorable about distinctions, she might say. A blur is not a metaphor. Let us see, for example, the differences in novels and plays, in acting and writing; just what qualities persuade in a man like Ingersoll; what distance does to a painting; where a thing exceeds and where it misses the mark. She was a little like Browning, perhaps, and a bit more analytical than she thought. Anyway, she worked a good pattern with the figures in the passing show.

The Band and the Building

When Willa Cather was a student at the University of Nebraska, she lived on L Street, midway between Tenth and Eleventh Streets. If she walked to the right and then north six blocks on Eleventh to the University, she would pass a miscellany of frame and brick buildings and houses, including the Masonic Temple and the Odd Fellows Hall. Maps do not show just where she paused to look and wonder. If she walked to the left and then north four blocks on Tenth (on the way to the Journal), she would pass the brick building of the Bohanan Brothers, livery men and operators of the popular dime musée, a place of sideshows and varieties for family entertainment. It was called variously the Eden Musée, the Lincoln Dime Musée, and—as she saw it, perhaps even with her family on earlier trips to Lincoln—the Wonderland Musée.

The men in red coats sigh and brace themselves for the struggle. They lift the battered brass instruments that are so old and dented one might think they had played for the original Light Brigade or sounded the charge of the Old Guard at Waterloo. But they didn't; they have never served any more martial purpose than to herald the arrival of Jo-Jo, the dog-faced man, or to conduct the Lilliputian queen through the streets and play sweet symphonies before the Wonderland Musée. The men get their pieces in position and send forth a burst of music—minus its charms. Yes, it is the same strain we have heard these last five years; it has the same ambitiously high note and there is the same cracked, wheezing cornet that never reaches it. Every time, that cornet nerves itself hopefully, dashes ahead of the rest, leaps and grasps at the air; but it never gets anywhere. It has been leaping to reach that note every day for five years that I know of; it is strange that it does not grow weary of the utter futileness of its pursuit. It is said that practice makes perfect; if so, this Wonderland band should long ere this have attained perfection. Strauss's orchestra could not practice more steadily and patiently, yet so far as one can tell they are not one whit nearer the right time than they were five years ago. And still we live and breathe and have our being.

It is a building on the corner of L and Eleventh Streets, and it has been written up by a mightier hand than mine, but because I have had to look at it a great deal I desire to humbly express my wonder at it. It started out in life on a narrow scale, but when it grew to the second story it widened out and became twice as wide as its first story; then it repented of its expansion and narrowed again, narrower than ever. It has an overhanging balcony like old houses in Antwerp, and it has a facade which must have been modelled from the famous one in Venice. It has a very modern bay window and beside it a little diamond-paned window which might have been at home in old Puritan houses. The architecture is partly Roman and partly Gothic, and partly Greek and largely kinds that are not spoken of in books and were not eulogized by Ruskin. It is partially of brick and partially of wood, parts of it are painted one color and parts another. It don't look as though it had ever been built, it looks as though it had just happened. It not only has not unity, there is positive discord about it, it looks as though its members were warring together like Saint Paul's. Either the architect had gone mad or he needed the Keeley cure.[21] Madame de Staël says that architecture is frozen music, if so then that building is the musée band congealed.

Journal, January 21, 1894, p. 16.

21. A cure for alcoholics, using bi-chloride of gold, as devised by Leslie E. Keeley, (1832–1900).

Building a Ruin

There is a lonely brownstone ruin on Fourteenth and P Streets. It is not the relic of a lost civilization, its mutilation is not the work of Goths and Vandals, its future is entirely behind it, its history is already written in the great annals of the mortgage record in the county clerk's office. It is a monument not of blasted hopes or crushed ambitions, but of wind that went down and cheek that was smitten both upon the left and the right. The building has never grown beyond the first story, yet it is as complete as the builder thereof ever meant it to be; it has no roof, but the builder never intended it should have, he built it to be a ruin.

He built the building to help his credit and he built it on credit—credit which stopped at the first story. It is becoming quite an art in Lincoln to build ruins to boom credit. Some men have only had to dig foundations, but this gentleman had too large a past to bury in a foundation hole, so he really had to pile some bricks together. It is a strange thing to contemplate that a ruin should be built for ruin's sake and so fulfil its purpose. It is a degradation of architecture that must make the old architects restless in their graves. It is a thing that could have happened in just no other age or civilization or nation. In these times it is very much better to be born cheeky than rich.

Journal, January 21, 1894, p. 16.

The Dislocated Arts

In the 1890's, as always, the arts of others sometimes looked easy, and another's product looked better than one's own—at least if it were successful, for success breeds its own imitators in the arts as elsewhere. It was true that one art might teach something about another art, and that in every created work there must be some transmuted elements; yet it seemed to Willa Cather that the exchange had been overdone. One cannot write just because he can sing, or act because he has won a prize fight. Nevertheless, as she said at various times, fame makes all things possible: Magazines like the Ladies' Home *(see page 187) publish the writing of Melba and Mary Anderson, and theatre managers put the impassive John L. Sullivan and Jim Corbett on the stage as if they were actors: "Sometimes it looks as though the theatre were going to descend to the level of the old gladiatorial shows again" (Journal, December 16, 1894). If the arts can be thus dislocated, so can the works of art. Good novels and plays will inevitably have their "adapters," who turn them into something else in order to make art do several duties. Perhaps occasionally there would be an actor who could write, and a book that would make a good play, but in general the arts would flourish only if the individual qualities of a skill or a genre were understood and respected.*

Lillian Russell recently wrote a rambling and rather irrelevant article for the Chicago *Times-Herald*. It treats of woman, the stage and of course man and marriage. Miss Russell states that "no matter how fortunate or favored a woman's situation in life may be, she is always more or less dependent upon and ruled by man. Without his guidance and counsel in the affairs of life most women are like a vessel at sea after the rudder has been battered into uselessness by the fierce waves and the compass has been washed overboard." . . .

From a literary standpoint, or even a newspaper standpoint, Miss Russell's article is very great rot. It is loose, disjointed, disconnected and full of atrocious metaphor. She talks about "women who have paddled their own canoe down the stream of time, without even asking the tyrant man to lend a hand at the oar, but all such women are mere drops in the great sea of humanity that roars about them." It is interesting to think of a drop paddling a canoe down the stream of time. Her remarks about "woman leading the orchestra in the great symphony of life," are almost as ridiculous. No, Lillian's vocation is not literature. Like most stage people, she makes a great fool of herself when she attempts it. They are well enough attired in blue tights, smiling like so many Aphrodites newly risen from the sea and singing like the angels of paradise, but to converse with them often breaks the charm, and to read what they write always does. Why, even Madame Melba, who sings like all the morning stars, who is "il bel canto" come to earth again, cannot write.[22] It is amusing, the candor and self-complacency with which these great artists of song take up the pen and write upon any subject under heaven, forgetting that to use that inoffensive article even moderately well requires a study and inspiration and mastery of technique almost as great as that of their own art. [*Journal*, May 19, 1895, p. 12]

Odette Tyler has left *The Gay Parisians* at Hoyt's, where she was drawing a big salary and no end of admiration and gone down into Vir-

22. Although Willa Cather does not mention a particular performance, it is certain that she heard Melba during the week she attended opera in Chicago in March, 1895. Melba sang in *Les Huguenots* on March 11 and in *Roméo et Juliette* on March 13. In the *Courier* (September 14, 1895) Miss Cather speaks of Melba as Juliette and in other parts, and quotes Philip Burke Marston's sonnet "To a Voice" ("that most magic voice"). See also the description on page 132.

ginia to write a novel. O, why, why is it that all persons theatrical, from soubrettes to prima donnas, insist upon trying the mightiness of the pen? Why, even Sarah Bernhardt and Mary Anderson can't do it successfully. Take, for instance, Mary Anderson's memoirs, very interesting lucid accounts they are, but the literary quality is altogether absent. That is just a little bit surprising, too, for it would seem that just to play the parts she played as she played them, would be literary training enough. [*Journal*, February 23, 1896, p. 9]

The dramatization of a novel is not so easy as it looks. *She* [by H. Rider Haggard][23] was a very successful book, but it does not even make a fairly successful play. Of course the fact that the dramatization was made by an illiterate man must be considered, but even more offensive than the style of writing is the strained and undramatic tone of the piece. A play that is spread out over several thousand years and several continents is apt to lack unity. A heroine who is several thousand years old and who was the wife of Pericles of Athens is apt to lack human interest. One can read such things in a novel and, if the style is good and the tale well told, not mind them or notice the inconsistencies to any painful degree, but when people see absurdities represented in flesh and blood before their eyes it is another thing. The chief trouble with *She* as a play is that it lacks human feeling. The heroine is not a woman, her passions are not those of a woman. There is no one character to whom one's heart can go out in either love or pity. The only dramatized novel which has been played successfully is Dumas' *Dame aux Camélias*, and that the author himself dramatized. [*Journal*, April 22, 1894, p. 13]

Elwyn A. Barron, formerly critic on the *Inter-Ocean*, is now dramatizing George Eliot's *Romola* for Julia Marlowe. Mr. Barron is not a particularly successful playwright. He is a reflective man who writes very decidedly in the essay style and is sometimes a little given to fine writing and sophomoric figures. His paragraphs are graceful and poetic, but he seems to lack the power to work up definite and strong action. His only former attempt at a drama, *When Bess Was Queen* [1894], was rather a story in dialogue than a play and did not outlive a dozen performances. It is pretty safe to say that in *Romola* he will not do much better. *Romola* is the most tedious and impossible as it is the most studied of all George

23. *She*, adapted by Richard Barbour, had just played in Lincoln, April 19, 1894. See the review, pages 267–268.

Eliot's novels. It is great in its way, but not as a novel. Then what will it be as a play? There are playwrights who could divest the plot of the awful results of Mrs. Cross' devoted study of Florentine history, oil it up a little and make it alive. Tito Melema could be made quite a fellow if he were not so learned and even Romola herself might be persuaded to care more for her husband than for Theocritus, but Mr. Barron is scarcely the man to persuade her. He will devote himself to the cameos and old parchments and Savonarola, all of which the theatre-going public cares very little about. When the gentle and reflective Mr. Barron gets through with *Romola* it will be a choice addition to Miss Marlowe's collection of un-playable plays. *Chatterton, Peg Woffington, Colombe's Birthday, Blot in the 'Scutcheon* and *Romola*. Great arms of Juno, what a repertoire! If Miss Marlowe would only revive *The Jew of Malta* and Wycherley's *Love in a Wood* and a few of the miracle plays she would be perfectly consistent. [*Courier*, September 7, 1895, p. 6]

... Was there ever such a season for dramatizing novels? *The Prisoner of Zenda* and *The House of the Wolf* and *Romola* and *Chimmie Fadden* and a dozen others. Now they have gone a step further and are turning novels into operas. Gaétano Orefice has actually turned *Consuelo* into an opera. How much of *Consuelo*, pray, how many of its thousand pages and how many threads of its complicated plot does the opera pretend to handle?

By the way isn't George Sand just a little passé now? She was great, great as no other woman has been or will be, but who would now wade through the nine hundred and nine pages of *Consuelo* and its interminable sequel for all her greatness. Myself, I prefer her *Histoire de ma vie*. It isn't always frank, but if one reads between the lines one gets near to a wonderful personality, much greater than any she ever created in her books, and like Chopin I can forgive her her *Consuelo* for herself. Of course the novels are all masterly and the pastoral ones supremely beautiful, but sometimes the workman is above his works. [*Courier*, September 14, 1895, p. 6]

Ingersoll's Prose

On November 29, 1894, the atheist and freethinker Robert G. Ingersoll lectured in Lincoln on his view of the Bible. The previous year, on October 25, he had delivered a particularly eloquent speech on Shakespeare.

What's all this row about Ingersoll being converted at Kalamazoo, Michigan, and the churchmen of that worthy city praying for him? Converted from what to what? He is not a man to change his opinion lightly.

His answer to these prayerful people is that he thanks them for their interest. It's too bad that Ingersoll ever got mixed up with the church one way or another. His magnificent talents as an orator have really been greatly against him, for they have made him popular and that is the greatest calamity that can befall a man of bold and original thought. If he had only written those melodious sentences instead of speaking them the great majority of the militant churchmen would never have read him at all and he would be considered as a philosopher and a writer of polished prose, rather than an enemy of religion. And still who would miss the pleasure of hearing him? Henry James writes somewhere of a great speaker whose conversation reminded one of a great pendulum of luminous crystal plunging through the air.[24] That's a good deal like Ingersoll. When you hear him on Shakespeare, for instance, you think of the old days before written characters when men talked their poetry instead of writing it. The beauty of his language has never been fully realized and perhaps never will be for a century. Then he will certainly stand as one of the first prose writers of this epoch. If he were a Frenchman now, how different would be our attitude. We would regard him as a man of letters and a savant, much as we do Renan, a better philosopher though not so strong a writer, for whom the church militant never prayed though he attacked Christianity much more violently than ever Ingersoll has done. In France he would be called the man of letters. In this country he is merely "an infidel," as though infidelity were a sort of profession like medicine or the law. This sort of cheap popularity that the public has thrust upon him has been bad for Ingersoll. He has been superficial where if he were addressing thoughtful men and learned contemporaries he would be accurate. He has often done his worst work instead of his best because to be the "enemy of religion" is much easier than to be a philosopher.

Journal, February 9, 1896, p. 9.

The Poetry of Football

Willa Cather's poetic view of sports may be colored by her feeling for Greek art and heroic literature. But it is not hard to see that there was

24. Although I have been unable to find this description in James, there is a remarkable parallel in Emerson's essay on Carlyle, which begins, "Thomas Carlyle is an immense talker, as extraordinary in his conversation as in his writing . . . ." His "tone and talk and laughter" make him "a trip-hammer with 'an Aeolian attachment.'" And, Emerson says, England keeps Carlyle as a national figure, "a sort of portable cathedral-bell, which they like to produce in companies where he is unknown, and set aswinging . . . " ("Carlyle," in *Lectures and Biographical Sketches* [Boston and New York: Houghton Mifflin Company, 1887], pp. 455-456).

*something else, too—something less academic and more of the spirit that
was in the beginning, the same living power that has itself determined the
course of legends. She wrote on football in 1893–1894 because the argument
raged both locally and nationally on the question: Is football brutal, and a
dangerous sport?*

It makes one exceedingly weary to hear people object to football
because it is brutal.

Of course it is brutal. So is Homer brutal, and Tolstoi; that is, they
all alike appeal to the crude savage instincts of men. We have not outgrown
all our old animal instincts yet, heaven grant we never shall! The moment
that, as a nation, we lose brute force, or an admiration for brute force,
from that moment poetry and art are forever dead among us, and we
will have nothing but grammar and mathematics left. The only way
poetry can ever reach one is through one's brute instincts. "Charge of the
Light Brigade," or "How They Brought Good News to Aix," move us
in exactly the same way that one of Mr. Shue's runs or Mr. Yont's[25]
touchdowns do, only not half so intensely. A good football game is an
epic, it rouses the oldest part of us, the part that fought ages back down in
the Troad with "Man-slaying Hector" and "Swift-footed Achilles." We
still have the old instincts in us, and it is well for us that we have. Poetry
is great only in that it suggests action and rouses great emotions, and all
great emotions are essentially animal. The world gets all its great en-
thusiasms and emotions from pure strain of sinew. Gothic art, the greatest
art of all time, has been going for centuries just on the brute momentum
it got when the old Goths used to throttle polar bears with their naked
hands.

Hesperian, November 15, 1893, p. 9.

Apropos of football, it seems to be one of the very few thoroughly
reputable and manly games left in the nineteenth century. It is one of the
few games which offer no particular inducement to betting and which
are not conducive to strained or unnatural excitement. It arouses only the
most simple and normal emotions. It requires strength and skill and
courage, attributes which no young man can afford to be without. In
answer to the old objection that many young men of leisure go to Yale
only to play football, it is certainly true that football is the most whole-
some and reputable of all the many diversions of young men of leisure.

25. Shue and Yont were student players in the days when players were students.

The extreme popularity of the game and the ambition to be on the "first eleven" has done more to purify the living of young men in the larger colleges than all the precepts of their instructors. The average public can hardly appreciate the value of keeping gentlemen of leisure under rigid training for four months in the year. The necessity of eating plain food, of sleeping eight hours, of abstaining absolutely from tobacco and stimulants and other things more or less harmful for four months is a novel experience to most young men of the "fast set," and an experience which cannot be other than beneficial. There is another thing. Athletics are the one resisting force that curbs the growing tendencies toward effeminacy so prevalent in the eastern colleges. Football is the deadliest foe that chappieism has. It is a game of blood and muscle and fresh air. It renders distasteful the maudlin, trivial dissipations that sap the energies of the youth of the wealthier classes. It is all very well for old grandmothers over their tea to sigh at the cruelties of the game. But it is not half so dangerous as many other things. It doesn't do Cholly or Fweddy any harm to have his collar bone smashed occasionally. He is better off than his soft-handed, soft-headed friend who, for reasons not very creditable to himself, could not play on the eleven if he wanted to. Anything is worthy that encourages a young man to keep his physical manhood perfect. The field is the only place that some young men ever know anything of the rough and tumble of life. Like the fagging system at Eton it is good because it lays the mighty low and brings down them which were exalted. Neither his bank book nor his visiting list can help a man on the eleven, he has nothing to back him but his arm and his head, and his life is no better than any other man's. It is well for the gilded youth to be placed in that position occasionally.

Taken as a game, it is a royal one. It is one of the few survivals of the heroic. It is as strictly Anglo-Saxon as fencing is Latin. It is founded on the bulldog strength which is the bulwark of all the English people. It has in it something of the old stubborn strength that goes clear back to the days of the Norman conquest. The descendants of King Harold can never be entirely gentlemen; there must always be a little of the barbarian lurking in them somewhere. When the last trace of that vital spark, that exultation of physical powers, that preference of strength to dexterity, that fury of animal courage dies out of the race, then providence will be done with us and will have some new barbarian people ready to come and conquer.

Journal, December 2, 1894, p. 13.

Opera: Scenes and Music

When Willa Cather attended the opera in Chicago during the week of March 10, 1895, she heard Verdi's two most recent works: Otello *(1887) and* Falstaff *(1893).*[26] *The "individual talent" that most impressed her was Victor Maurel, who played Iago and Falstaff, but the great joy of the opera was its mingling of the arts.*

¶ There was a time, when Greece was young, when art and athletics went always together and perhaps it is coming again. If you have ever seen Victor Maurel you have hoped so, for you have seen how glorious a thing grace can be, and you have beheld the whole poetry of motion. Not in vain does he fence and wrestle and box and spend half his time in his gymnasium. When he strikes an attitude as Iago the Apollo Belvedere is not in it, and the Faun of the Capitol is a farmer, that's all. But to say that he strikes an attitude is a gross falsehood. He never does, he glides imperceptibly from one to another, he is all attitude. That man has resurrected the virile grace of the Greeks. His gestures are as perfect as the sculptured poses of the Athenians. It is a privilege and a lasting joy just to remember him as he defied God, looking up and shrugging his shoulders while he sang, "And Heaven, an ancient lie!" Or as he stood over Othello after he had fallen in a swoon from rage and despair, stood looking down at him with the complete satisfaction of an artist who sees that his work is good, and cries with holy pitying irony, "Behold the Lion of Venice." O, the evil grace and accursed triumph of that pose! [*Journal*, January 5, 1896, p. 9]

¶ In Verdi's youth he was accused of light and superficial orchestration, but certainly his last opera, a crowning glory in more senses than one, once and forever refutes that charge. It is a wonder, a marvel, a miracle of clever orchestration. Beside the wonderful beauty of the central themes and the still more wonderful management of them there are a hundred little things, like the prodigious sigh of satisfaction among the wind instruments every time Falstaff lifts a cup of sack to his lips, the

26. She probably saw *Otello* at the matinee of March 16. In her *Journal* column of March 31, 1895, Willa Cather describes the Desdemona of Mme. Emma Eames, who sang the part at only the one performance. The *Falstaff* she saw in Chicago was the fourth American production of the opera, on March 14, 1895. Other singers mentioned particularly as from personal knowledge are Tamagno, who sang Othello on both March 12 and March 16; Melba (see note 22, above); and Jean de Reszke, who was Romeo with Melba in *Roméo et Juliette* and Raoul in *Les Huguenots*.

lively crescendo when fat Sir John is dumped into the moat, the monotonous mezzo forte of the orchestra as Falstaff runs over the items of his
bill at Garter Inn and then, when he reaches the total, suddenly forte!
The second part of the third act opens with some of the most beautiful
lyric music Verdi ever wrote, music breathing all the witchery of a
summer night, of moonbeams and uncertain shadows, of fairy festivals
and of elfin trumpeters. And then those rare mellow strains of which the
opera is full, now racy, snappy and piquant as one of Sir John's jests which
were best not told before ladies. Now blood-stirring, amorous to
grotesqueness, with a sort of yearning sensuousness like the naughty
dreams which flitted through the fat knight's tipsy slumber. Tantalizing
strains of reeling, sweeping sweetness that were rudely broken off before
they were half begun, that pleased and excited and irritated and went to
one's head like champagne, and over and over again came that royal
laughter of the king of jolly good fellows; now crashing out of the whole
orchestra, now picked lightly upon the strings amid the chatter of
women, now sighing from the wind instruments in the summer breezes
of Windsor Forest, now chuckling in the bellies of the big bassoons,
repeated in every kind and degree of mirth, the ribald laughter of Sir
Jack Falstaff. [*Journal*, March 31, 1895, p. 13]

¶ Maurel, they say, is Verdi's favorite singer. I can well believe it.
There are great singers on the stage today, like Jean de Reszke, and great
actors like [Francesco] Tamagno, but the two together are so hard to find.
Maurel is both. He is the only man I have ever seen to whom I felt that I
could apply without reservation that much abused word, "Artist."
Verdi has the dramatic instinct almost as strongly as the musical one. I
suppose that Victor Maurel more nearly embodies the old man's ideal
heroes than any other living singer. No wonder he is dear to him, since
he makes the dreams of his youth live before him. [*Courier*, November 9,
1895, p. 7]

Arts of the Stage

¶ An actor is no longer looked upon as an imitator, but as an author
who writes a book every night, an artist who every evening paints a
picture in the gaslight.... An actor's life is the hardest of all the hard
lives men lead for art's value. Other men can do their work and forget
the travail in success. But an actor's creation must be born again every
night out of his own brain sweat. He should have all working while he

lives for when he dies his work dies with him. Poets can die trusting their work to the appreciation of the future, but an actor's greatness dies in him, as music dies in a broken lute.[27] [*Journal*, April 8, 1894, p. 13]

¶ Staging is to a play what style is to a book, what color is to a picture, what beauty is to a woman. No one can feel at all the beauty of a play unless it is well staged. That is half of it, the color, the background, the thing that captures the eye and sets the imagination to work. Suppose in the case of *A Gilded Fool* what would become of that telling first act if Goodwin had only a stuffy little barrack to do it in? Suppose that great supper scene in *A Parisian Romance* was done about a measly little table of stage viands without the flowers and crystal glasses? Half its impressiveness would be gone and that telling element of contrast would be wholly lost.[28] [*Journal*, May 31, 1896, p. 13]

¶ To one who did not understand Greek, spoken or chanted, the real beauty of the Greek play[29] lay in two things; the music one heard and the colors one saw. The music was twofold, first the rich harmony of Mendelssohn, second, but none the less beautiful, the speech itself, the "vowelled Greek." One often hears it said that Greek is more musical than Latin, but to realize this properly one must hear, as he might last night, Greek following Latin, like music following speech. [*Journal*, February 24, 1894, p. 6]

¶ Henri Flacke the great French pianist says that Sarah Bernhardt's declamation taught him more about phrasing music than all the music teachers he ever went to. That's just what Bernhardt does anyway, she phrases her lines as if they were music. [*Journal*, August 11, 1895, p. 9]

¶ A change from concert work to opera is always a perilous venture; it's like when a successful novelist undertakes to become a playwright. A concert singer must have voice and magnetism, an opera singer must have voice and magnetism and a powerful dramatic instinct and must be altogether an artist. An opera singer must have more dramatic power

27. To see how Willa Cather put a personal mark of style and interpretation on a common idea, cf. the *Journal*'s editorial on the death of Edwin Booth (June 11, 1893): "An actor's art is peculiar. It dies with the actor or at most with those who have seen him. There is no way in which the magic effect of his voice or the play of his features can be conveyed to one who has not seen him. Descriptions are powerless. His name is perpetuated but it is almost an empty name and the power that once was behind it is gone forever."

28. Nat Goodwin appeared in *A Gilded Fool* on December 3, 1894, and Richard Mansfield in *A Parisian Romance* on March 28, 1896.

29. Student productions of parts of *Antigone* and *Elektra* in Greek, the *Captivi* in Latin, on February 16 and 23, 1894. See also pages 220 f. Miss Cather herself knew Greek, but was able to generalize on the effect.

than an actress. Singing is idealized speech, and, in order to preserve the proportion and harmony between words and action, the acting which accompanies it must be ideal. A singer is on the stage before her audience less than an actress, and she must do more when she is there. She must do in one gesture what the actress of spoken words does in many. . . . Concert singers should all come from Boston; they should all be able to sing chro[mat]ic scales and do problems in calculus. The field of concert work is largely intellectual. . . . The stage is the kingdom of the emotions and the imagination. Literature, painting and even music are all more or less stilted by pedantry and technique, but on the stage skill counts for nothing. The theatre is patronized and supported not by people who think, but by people who feel. A singer might have as many tones as a piano, but lacking the power to make men have great experiences she would sing to an empty house. The author and the painter send their work out into the world and the critics tell the people what its merits are. But in the theatre the people are their own critics. The action speaks directly to them viva voce and it must rouse their strongest emotions, stir their holiest memories. The artist whom the people love must feel, interpret, create. [September 30, 1894, p. 13]

Views in the Haydon Art Club Exhibit

Willa Cather stopped in several times at the midwinter show the Haydon Art Club had arranged on the campus. In the Armory building were one hundred pictures on loan from an exhibit of American artists at the Chicago Art Institute, plus some work by local artists. Looking at the pictures in different lights, from different distances, she found in both portraits and landscapes some clues to the most tantalizing riddle of all—the relation of beauty and truth.

The most attractive landscape in the collection is certainly Theodore Robinson's "Scene on the Delaware and Hudson Canal." That picture is full of air and sunlight, its abundance of clear atmosphere gives it a bracing, exhilarating effect. One instinctively takes a deep breath as one stands before it. Better sky effects are not often seen. The sky actually arches and recedes. The horizon seems incalculably far away. The clouds are such as might float and the thinner ones have a suggestion of rapid motion. It is plainly a morning picture, a few hours later than the misty time that Corot loved to paint, done when the sun is well up in the sky and the world is high and dry and the life and work of the world has begun again.

[217]

In sharp contrast to this wonderfully airy picture of Robinson's is Charles Corwin's "St. Joe, Michigan," which looks as if the atmosphere had been exhausted with an air pump. It has the dead, lifeless effect of a scene worked upon tapestry.

Richard Lorenz's "In the West" is at once strong and disappointing. The worst thing about it is the title. It is a western subject and a western man placed in an unwestern atmosphere. The position of the man, his bronzed, rugged face, his sun-browned beard, the way his hair grows, or rather does not grow on his head, that arm and hat and buckskin glove leave little to be desired. But for all that the picture is not western. The impressionists say it is "keyed too low." Whatever that may mean, the lights are certainly at fault and the color is too tame. The sunlight is gentle, not the fierce, white, hot sunlight of the west. Sunlight on the plains is almost like sunlight on the northern seas; it is a glaring, irritating, shelterless light that makes the atmosphere throb and pulsate with heat.

Turning to the western wall again there is Thomas Noble's sermon, "Idle Capital," an "unprotected furnace in Alabama." Though it is perhaps the most correctly and skilfully drawn of the collection it is an irritating and unpleasant picture. It tells the story too plainly and too well, and it was done too much for the story's sake. It is a picture that ought to delight Hamlin Garland. The secret of the jarring effect is that like too many novels and pictures of the hour it was not done with an artistic motive. That furnace was not painted because it was beautiful or touching, but because it was a stern, ugly lesson in political economy. In the spectator it appeals to the matter-of-fact, not the artistic sense. There is no artistic merit in painting a subject merely because it has a sermon in it. A run on the bank has sermon enough, but it is not an exalted thing to paint it. Some people have tried to make political economy out of Millet's picture, but there is none there. There is only the poor pathos of labor and poverty. Millet painted for the sake of the people who suffered, never vexing himself about the cause of it. There is no humanness in "Idle Capital." The earth and air about Millet's laborers is filled with a sad poesy which is the painter's own. There is no poetic medium between you and that furnace of rusted iron. It would fascinate a mechanic and repel a poet.

In literature and painting there is no such thing as sacrificing art for truth. Perfect art is truth, truer than any science, even political economy. It is unfortunate that the economic sciences cannot keep to their place, but insist upon overrunning and coarsening everything else. We shall be hearing economic symphonies and sonatas next. . . .

As to the impressionism in general, it is natural enough. The treating of phases and moods and incidents becomes more popular in every art. It should not occasion any very bitter warfare with the more conservative school. While Mr. [Frank Weston?] Benson's "Firelight" does not at all put Rubens and Rembrandt to shame it is an excellent picture in its way. If a picture is good it does not denote whether it is done with a pin point or a palette knife, whether it must be seen through the big end or the small end of an opera glass. If a man gives good work to the world he should at least be allowed the privilege of choosing his own method. Beauty is not so plentiful that we can afford to object to stepping back a dozen paces to catch it.

Journal, January 6, 1895, p. 13.

A SENSE OF HISTORY

Willa Cather did not study much formal history, but she had a strong feeling for the reality of the past. To feel history may be better than to know it, according to her principles. There is little question that she was realistic, almost matter-of-fact, about the inexorable changes of time and place—as in the succinct account of the Greek plays in Nebraska. She knew what was modern—not that she particularly liked it, but that one must know where he is. If she was exasperated by the state of contemporary art, it is hardly unusual. In all periods there is the question: Who will be the new Alexander Pope, or Ben Jonson, or Henry James—or Faulkner, Eliot, Browning, Poe? The difference in Willa Cather is that she was sure that greatness—inevitably, in the nature of things—would come again. It was just hard to wait.

Classical Plays in Nebraska

Charter Day for the University of Nebraska—and its twenty-fifth birthday —came on February 15, 1894. As a part of the week's celebration, students presented a program of classical plays at the Lansing on Friday, February 16. Portions of the Captivi *were performed in Latin; a part of Sophocles'* Antigone *and a chorus from the* Elektra *were given in Greek. Willa Cather represented Electra in a tableau, a scene inside the palace with Aegisthus, Electra, and her sister gazing at the slain Clytemnestra. The classical plays were successful enough that the program was repeated the following Friday, February 23, but the audience then was small.*

It was, perhaps, but natural that the scenes from the Greek and Latin plays interested only a small public, and interested them but little. Detailed scenes, even from Shakespeare, are usually pretty dull affairs, and detailed scenes in a foreign language are, to the ordinary mortal, still duller. It is true that great actors can overcome the obstacle of speaking in a foreign tongue—that we can feel the fire and pathos of Bernhardt's French, or the majesty of Salvini's Italian. But, in spite of the very good work that the students did, they were very far from actors of this surpassing type, and could not quite reach us through the unfamiliar medium of the dead languages.

One thing that the scenes from the Greek plays did bring out was the immense distance, not only of time, but of nature, of emotional habit, that divides us from the Greeks. The Latin comedy was a little nearer to us. Comedy is universal and eternal. But in tragedy ideals have changed. We cannot appreciate the Hellenic love for calm, for dignity, for sorrow that is majestically self-contained. We want people to weep, to sob, to throw their arms about, and to faint gracefully backwards. It is true, people in real life go through very considerable griefs without doing these things, but we are determined that, whatever real people may persist in doing, our actors shall be sorrowful or despairing according to our own traditional expectations.

But then, too, in real life we are a little more emotional, some of us, than those old peoples, who set up for their ideal a calm, contemplative self-development to an absolute human perfection. "In nothing go too far," that was their motto. They went through the world—the philosophers among them—grandly self-restrained, every passion in vain, every ardency subdued. But that is not the way with us, at least not with most of us. We like enthusiasm, and like it most where the Greek liked it least, in our religion—and in our theatres. We have prayer meetings, we have the Salvation Army and we have the "emotional actress." And all these are very well, but they set us infinitely far from the old majesty of the classic drama—as far as the modern waltz is from the minuet that our stately great-grandfathers danced.

So Greek tragedy does not move us much, especially when presented in disconnected scenes by people we know in a place we know. To a few of us, to those that have imagination, it may speak more. Some may forget the cushioned seats of the Lansing, and the horrible figures on the curtain, and see in fancy the white curving seats of the Greek theatre, the marble stage beyond with blue sky blazing above it—and there, in such majestic setting of open nature, our heated drama would be out of place as the antique is behind our glaring footlights.

As it was, the antique was exhibited only as a curiosity, like the whale that is carried about in a freight car, and it was just as much out of element. It is not our day or generation. Whether for better or for worse the world has changed, and changed irrevocably.

Journal, February 25, 1894, p. 9.

History in the Arts
Descent

The Lady of Venice [30] is by no means a financial success, indeed it is very otherwise. The play has thrilling situations. The actors are good, the

30. A play of 1841, originally called *Nina Sforza* (and acted by Macready at Drury Lane), the modern production starring Katherine Clemmons as Nina lasted from mid-February to early March, in New York. It was backed by Buffalo Bill.

scenery and costumes are beautiful. The play is highly romantic and in blank verse. The trouble is that the world doesn't want romance on the stage now. It is tired of armor and helmets, it likes dress suits and silk hats better. Of course from a sense of duty we still go to see Shakespeare and *Virginius* and a few time honored plays of a romantic and historical nature, but we go because our fathers went and because it is traditional. We have put the historical play and the historical novel on the shelf, they have seen their day. The public demands realism and they will have it. They want plays with modern wit and modern sympathies and modern emotions. [*Journal*, March 11, 1894, p. 13]

. . . There was a time when people read Carlyle and Emerson, but nowadays if one pretends to half way keep up with current fiction he has absolutely no time for anything else. If you did a thorough job on it you would not have time to sleep. And the worst of it is that most of these thousands of novels are good and none of them excellent. Perfection seems to have ceased to be a standard even to be dreamed of. Today an author knows that one good chapter will save his book. Formerly he knew that one weak one would damn it. It's a strange thing, this descent of literature. I picked up an old American periodical last week. Among the contributors were Dickens, Thackeray, Emerson, Lowell, Longfellow and Hawthorne. Heavens, what names to stir the hearts of men! Now we have Kipling, Hope, Weyman, Hamlin Garland, Zangwill, Richard Harding Davis and Mrs. Burton Harrison. Our essays are never anything heavier than the pleasant little chats of Andrew Lang or the "smart" paragraphs of that Idle Fellow, Jerome K. Jerome. As to poetry, no one ever attempts anything loftier than the erotic verses after the style of Bliss Carman. The Wagnerian flashes and thunders and tempests of Carlyle and the lofty repose and magnificent tranquility of Emerson seem to have gone out of the language. In all the literature of the last ten years I have not found one burning conviction, one new and really confident truth wrested from the concealing elements. All our makers of literature are asleep or playful. They have all with one accord come down from smoking Sinai with its jealous, tyrannical and never satisfied God, and are dancing a frolicsome two-step about the golden deity in the valley. To dance is easier than to play, and they do it. All our litterateurs are frolicking and doing the kindergarten act. Frolicsome literature was all very well in the youth of the nations, when every man was a sort of Donatello and had nothing better to do than to toy with Amaryllis in the shade. But after all the spiritual warfare of the centuries it is so grotesque for the grave Anglo-Saxons to begin doing the desperately frivolous. It's like a dance of the gnomes. And the dire thing about all this frivolity and froth is that it is so sad. There is not a gleam of the old time mirth of Fielding or Smollett in it. It makes one think of Nordau and his "Dusk of the Nations."[31] It is like Anacreon who when the women told him he was growing old and that his locks were white beneath his crown of roses, said, "The nearer I draw unto the gates of the grave, the more will I dance, and my lyre shall ever ring of love until I tune it to the mournful numbers of the choir below" [Ode IV]. [*Courier*, November 16, 1895, p. 6]

In the West

The Kansas Populists are having a play written to expose the infamous corruption of the Republican party. Several scenes will be devoted to last year's legislative warfare.[32] The Pops expect to stage the play next year and send a company out to do missionary work. Undoubtedly they will assign the role of leading lady to her masonic majesty, Mary Lease,[33] and let her represent their ideal of womanly virtue and sweetness. For the leading man, they cannot do better than send over the line and borrow General Van Wyck to play the embodiment of manhood and honor. The only trouble with such a company would be that the theatre would scarcely be holy enough for them, and they would probably have to play in the churches. [*Journal*, March 11, 1894, p. 13]

Be it known that a new play has been written for Gladys Wallis by Franklyn Lee and the title thereof is *Nebraska*. Just what there is in this particular part of the universe to make a play of it is difficult to say. Probably the drama will deal with "barren, wind swept prairies; fields of stunted corn, whose parched leaves rattle like skeletons in the burning

31. "The Dusk of the Nations" is the first chapter in Nordau's *Degeneration*.

32. Because of four disputed seats in the Kansas legislature, both the Populists and the Republicans claimed a majority in the lower house; both elected chairmen and a full quota of officers. Before the "legislative war" was settled, the governor had to order out the militia. (John D. Hicks, *The Populist Revolt* [Lincoln: University of Nebraska Press, 1961], pp. 275–281)

33. One of the most effective campaigners for Populism, Mrs. Mary E. Lease reputedly declared: "What you farmers need to do is raise less corn and more *Hell*" (Hicks, p. 160). Charles H. Van Wyck, mentioned below, who had commanded a regiment in the Civil War, was U.S. senator from Nebraska (1881–1887) and the unsuccessful Populist candidate for governor in 1892.

south wind," and all that sort of rot which Mr. Hamlin Garland and his school have seen fit to write about our peaceable and rather inoffensive country. [*Journal*, April 14, 1895, p. 13]

Destiny

... The public seem to think they have only to name [Edwin] Booth's successor to cause him to appear, that if they only give an actor permission he will straightway go and be Booth. Now the truth is the public needn't trouble themselves for it won't do any good. If, after Shakespeare's death, the learned English doctors had got together and elected another Shakespeare, much use it would have been. We can elect Benjamin Harrisons and Grover Clevelands any day, but Booths and Shakespeares have to be balloted on in heaven. We will just have to patiently wait until God and nature are pleased to give us another Booth, and it may be a long old wait, for we can't hurry the tide of destiny. [*Journal*, March 11, 1894, p. 13]

If anyone is inclined to doubt the fact that Napoleon was considerable of a fellow, the late Napoleonic revival certainly proves to the contrary. Bonaparte had ceased to interest the practical world and had become pretty much of a myth to everyone except school boys, when suddenly he becomes a potent, living reality again. All the magazines and news-papers are full of him, Richard Mansfield and Madame Rhea are playing him and all the painters in Paris are painting idealizations of him. Fame has its regular orbit and it comes and goes in cycles. Napoleon will always have his worshippers. This planet has a great and overwhelming respect for any man who is able to play football with it and has always enjoyed being "taken in."

The renewal of enthusiasm is perfectly natural in France; indeed, enthusiasm never dies there. The French have the most remarkable talent for embalming their great and trotting their mummies out to every feast. France is the most adoring of nations. It arises at 7 and says early mass to Molière until 10, then worships Victor Hugo until noon. Then it bows at the shrine of Balzac and Racine and Dumas until night, then it goes into the theatre and worships a ballet dancer until morning. [*Journal*, November 11, 1894, p. 13]

Talk about musical criticism, we will have some that we can depend on now. Monsieurs Binet and Lund have invented a machine which will register on paper an entire performance, the duration of notes, vibration of touch and everything. Now we will have some criticisms that cannot be disputed. This is becoming such a terribly mechanical age that pretty soon we may have a little ticker that will keep correct count of our deeds done in the body and estimate the exact state of our souls and save St. Peter the trouble. [*Journal*, May 26, 1895, p. 12]

It seems that the age of romantic conquests is not yet dead. A month or two ago there came to Berlin a young Russian, Alexander Petschnikoff, who played the violin. He was horribly poor, had been brought up in the most remote corner of the world, and had never had instruction of any sort except at the musical conservatory at Moscow, which, as everyone knows, is beyond the reach of civilizing musical influences. Nevertheless with the extreme candor of youth this boy went into Germany and played. Today he is king of Berlin. Musical Germany, and all of Germany that is not philosophical is musical, has literally gone mad over him. He came a beggar, he will go away a prince; they have anointed and crowned him a king of music. It is strange what mighty geniuses that great barren, barbarous country of Russia brings forth. It seems to be the way the country gets even for all its misery and unhappiness. Left to herself in the wilderness with the mixed blood of strange nations nature will do wonderful things sometimes. After France, Russia is the most promising art country on earth and it looks as though most of the great artists of the future will be Slavs. In fifty years it will be Paris and St. Petersburg. [*Journal*, February 9, 1896, p. 9]

Yvette Guilbert: Image of France

The pride of Montmartre, recognized even by us in a later day as the flame-haired, black-gloved woman in the posters of Toulouse-Lautrec—Yvette Guilbert (1868–1944) was the French singer of the demi-monde who suggested to Willa Cather the difference between the present and the past, a past when France was personified by the great tragedienne Rachel (1821–1858). Though Guilbert was a superlative artist, after her fashion, she was precisely the image of all that was confusing and ominous in the course of history. Laying aside the highest values with a smooth negligence, a nation like France might surely deliver all of its beauty to the beast.

She has done it, as we knew she would. Yvette Guilbert has conquered New York. She came out on the stage of the Olympia, not the

Greek Olympia, but the New York one, where the chappies and the Johnnies flock to hear the very modern muses, came out in her black gloves and virginal simplicity, and sang of the half-world, and New York apparently understood. It even caught on to her great word, regret, not remorse nor repentance, but regret, a reminiscent, indolent sort of regret, the regret of the man who wakes up with a headache and who means, if he lives, to have a worse one tomorrow morning. The regret of wasted lives that have enjoyed the waste, and of worn-out rakes whose only sorrow is that dissipation has lost its first sweetness. And the charm of her seemingly is that she sings the street songs of Paris daintily, merely touches their vulgarity with her finger tips, hints at their grossness; she keeps herself above them all the time. She sings very much as Mr. Paul Bourget[34] writes, using loud colors and coarse suggestions merely for artistic effect. This is a new thing on the lyric stage. Of course, there have been coarse women, dancing girls and variety singers who have sung coarse songs, but they had nothing to do with art and did not pretend to have. The object of all lyric singers has always been to keep the romantic uppermost, to idealize human emotion of every kind. But here is a singer who is a realist, who simply knocks the varnish off, who tells the truth, and the most brutal form of the truth at that. She sings of the streets and cafes and dance halls, of drunkenness and vice and dishonor. Not a very noble thing to do, perhaps, but she does it well, and that, once and for all, is the *raison d' être* of art. No artist does a thing because it is noble or good; he does it because he can do it well, because his mind is so made that perfection in something or other is his chiefest need. That is why Mlle. Guilbert sings and why people who care for perfection technically, merely as perfection, love to hear her.

In the Lycée in Paris Mlle. Guilbert's picture hangs beside that of Rachel. Yvette says that it is typical, that she represents the art and philosophy of this generation, as Rachel did those of yesterday. If this be true, may God have mercy upon the art and philosophy of this generation. If we have descended from the tragic muse to a grisette it is time to reflect. But there is more truth in Mlle. Guilbert's statement than one realizes at first thought. In a way she does represent an undesirable phase of modern French society, and above all a type of the eternal feminine in Paris. The life and tragedies of the half-world are no longer individual

34. Paul Bourget (1852–1935), member of the French Academy since 1894, was primarily a novelist of the psychological-romantic school—a recent book was *Cosmopolis* (1893)—but as a social commentator he attracted attention with *Outre-Mer* (1895), in which he gave his impressions of America.

matters. The curse has become national and it is a standing menace to French society. It was of this that Dumas *fils* spoke in the preface of *La Femme de Claude* when he speaks of the modern Beast of the apocalypse[35]: "This Beast was like a leopard; its feet like the feet of a bear; its jaws like the jaws of a lion, and the dragon gave it its power. And the Beast was clad in purple and scarlet and adorned with gold and pearls and precious stones. Her hands were white as milk and in them she held a golden vessel full of the abominations of Babylon, of Sodom and of Lesbos. At times this Beast, which I believe was the same that St. John saw, exhaled from its body an intoxicating vapor, in which she shone like an angel of God. ... The Beast was never satisfied. She crushed her victims with her paws, tore them with her claws and ground them in her teeth and stifled them against her bosom. But they were the most fortunate, they were to be envied. ... The seven heads of the Beast towered above the highest mountain tops, like an immense coronet skirting the horizon. Its seven mouths, always half open and smiling, were red as coals of fire. The eyes were as green as the waters of the ocean. Below each of the ten diadems, among all sorts of blasphemous words, gleamed this word, larger than all the others, 'Prostitution.'"

That is pretty pointed rhetoric and it made a stir in Paris when it first came out twenty-three years ago. Dumas went on to speak of the superior morals of the Germans and of the curse that loose living had been to the French army. Some of his words are darkly prophetic of the future of France. The French had war and debt and poverty and danger, but "still the Beast shakes out her locks, moistens her lips, holds out her arms and offers her breast, murmuring, 'You must suffer, you must hunger, you have been betrayed; you have been brave, you are vanquished, you need rest, diversion, joy. Come to me! I am the immediate sensation, I am the pleasure of all time, I am the intoxication eternal, I am forgetfulness, I am the greatest proof of life, I am love.'" But the man hesitates; on the wall of the feast Germany has written these four words, "Five millions of debt." The Beast points out to him the Jew who on the other wall has

---

35. The preface is Dumas' reply to M. Cuvillier-Fleury, editor of *Les Débats*, who had denounced the play. In his letter Dumas defends his theories and his right to judge and attack the evils of a social order in which the laws of indissoluble marriage encourage adultery, and in which woman has become man's adversary. The woman-beast described by Dumas represents the adulteress or prostitute who may devour France or make her powerless against the attack of Germany. The passages quoted here may be found in the edition of *La Femme de Claude* published by Calmann-Lévy, Paris, 1906, pp. xxviii–xxix, xxxiv–xxxv.

written these magic words, "Forty-two millions of credit." She answers him, "You see, you are as rich as ever. There is nothing to fear, you have the sympathy and confidence of the whole world. Come, let us be gay, let us love, joyously we will repeople the earth." And ninety-nine out of a hundred reply, "That is true. Let us be gay." And they make up for lost time. They wed the Beast upon the first night and upon the second night are *in extremis*. And when they discover that in spite of everything they do not die fast enough, they kill themselves. On the other side of the Rhine stands a man, bare-headed, with a thick mustache, his grave eyes fixed and unfathomable, his lips cold and smiling, with muscles of steel, a will of iron, an enormous stomach and a powerful chest. And this man of genius who has conquered and utilized the Beast, foreseeing the future, rubs his hands and says to his false master, "Your majesty can have his eye on the orient now, there is nothing to fear from the west, they are dead there."

Journal, January 19, 1896, p. 9.

The way of the world must be the way of nature. The following selections invoke a deep and primitive power that underlies the surfaces of things. Whatever man does, Willa Cather says in various ways, there is a force that eventually brings him home to a kind of cosmic balance.

Natural Justice

Another instance of the short mutable reigns of these women who travel only on their beauty and wardrobes and unenviable reputation is the inglorious fall of Lily Langtry. . . .

Ten years ago this woman, who could not act, who could not even read her lines properly, was called a genius by an infatuated rabble. Today even the rabble has other things to think about . . . .

All of this must be particularly gratifying to the people who have given the strength and effort of their lives to a despised and thankless profession. The public is easy to deceive and slow to comprehend, but it understands at last. The heathen do not always rage, they are sure to recover their normal sanity some day. The whole American public gets on a metaphorical drunk occasionally, a champagne drunk, and requires a great many bottles of congress water to get over it. But it sobers up at last and sees with merciless clearness. For the favorites of its aberration this is tragic enough, for it means annihilation. From this court there is no appeal. The public is stupid. It can be tricked and duped and made to dance like a bear by a beautiful woman. But when it turns it is pitiless and it spares not.... Yes, in the long run, society is just. It does not mean to be or try to be, but somehow in the course of events, in the very nature of things, it stumbles upon justice.

Journal, November 25, 1894, p. 13.

... About a week ago [in New York] some very good ladies, lacking something to do, having neither husbands nor children nor enough literary clubs to employ their time, organized a crusade against "living pictures." They wrote long articles for the newspapers and they made public speeches. Now two weeks ago the "living picture" business was a losing one. People had forgotten that they were entrancingly wicked and only remembered that they were stupid and uninteresting and had quit going to see them. Last week they appeared to crowded houses and are making money. It is a pity. "Living pictures" are indecent and senseless and a grotesque travesty on the paintings they claim to represent. Their influence is evil and is unmodified by any kind of good or any wholesome pleasure. When they were dead it was too bad to revive them. Very often in this world, evil is its own doom and carries its own death with it. As Napoleon once said, the person who made the universe was clever, whoever he was. Whoever made human nature understood his business. There are so many seeming paradoxes in human society that will explain and rectify themselves if the reformer would only give them time. The planets continue to travel in their appointed courses without assistance, and so would human society if reformers would not attempt to hurry nature and to aid providence. For every ill in human life God made a cure, and it would all work out right some day if the reformer will only let it.

Journal, December 9, 1894, p. 13.

A Primitive Force

In one of her Sunday columns in the spring of 1895, Willa Cather discussed Marie Wainwright's production of The Daughters of Eve, *as reported by a Lincoln woman who saw it in St. Louis. The concluding portion of that article is given below. Miss Wainwright had been in Lincoln in* The School for Scandal *on May 25, 1893. She particularly interested Willa Cather because the Wainwrights, like the Cathers, were Virginia people. Commodore Wainwright, father of the actress, had been killed in the bombardment of Galveston, and her grandfather was Bishop Wainwright, "one of the most respected and beloved of the clergy of the south." Miss Cather's comment is important because it is one of the few times she refers to her own knowledge of Virginia, her early home. It is important, also, because here and in the following article, "On Nature and Romance," we have the most direct statement of themes which began in myth and heroic literature, took focus in Kingsley's* The Roman and the Teuton, *and entered deeply into Willa Cather's later fiction, particularly* The Troll Garden.

. . . For generations the Wainwrights have been among the first families of Virginia and the Wainwright women have, for their graces of person and sweetness of character been supreme in a land that is full of ideal women. Down there a woman of Wainwright blood could not live just like other women, she must have a special code of her own. She must be very much better than Caesar's wife. She must not only be thoroughly good, but thoroughly in good taste. Their birth and name imposed upon them duties and considerations above those that belonged to newer names. Except for her culture and intellect and brilliant conversation Marie has nothing whatever in common with the women of her father's house. Her life has been an entire revolt against their traditions. It is almost as though she has been giving the devil his dues that her ancestors neglected to pay. Almost all particularly correct and distinguished families end in this way. A house may set up for itself household gods greater than those of other men, it may distort life by super-refinement as much as other men brutalize it by vulgarity, it may be rigid in its life and merciless in its judgment and go on so for years, being more correct than nature and more proper than God. But at last there comes into the world some scion who reverses all this dreary artificiality and goes desperately back to the native. He is unable to bear the burden of his spotless name, the whiteness of his own escutcheon dazzles his eyes, and his memory is not long enough to hold all the countless things that it has become necessary for the men of his family to do. Then he—or she—goes back to first principles by the lightning express, and he doesn't stop half way either. After all nature revenges herself. We cannot with impunity rise entirely above her any more than we can sink below her. She turned upon Jerusalem after a time just as she had turned upon Sodom. She revolted upon Saint Anthony in his desert just as she did upon Nero in his seraglio. That is why all particularly exquisite families have their black sheep at last. They may tame the tiger for centuries and think they have made a kitten of it, but in the hot blood of some descendant it breaks out sooner or later and cries, "I am here still, you cannot thwart me nor starve me nor tame me nor stultify me, I am here always, at the bottom of things; I made the world, I rule it and I am its destiny."[36]

Journal, April 28, 1895, p. 14.

On Nature and Romance

Of all the "attractions" that are running in New York just now, it is *The Prisoner of Zenda* that is turning away people every night because the Lyceum Theatre cannot hold all the people in New York at once. We seem to be drifting back to the older and more healthful style of drama in which men act instead of talking about the futility of action, in which men have hearts and hands instead of nerves and inherited tendencies. Things look a little black for the stage now and then when plays like *The Second Mrs. Tanqueray* get the upper hand. The critics get blue and say that all the strength and sincerity are going out of the drama. Just now, when the "end of the century" feeling has its undoubted influence, both literature and the drama look discouraging. But the critics need not lose sleep over it. Such things have been in the past and will be in the future, and humanity will always go back to the best. Even if one has not much faith in men individually one should believe in them collectively. Truth has such a confirmed habit of prevailing that it is not going to fail us now. Humanity has always recovered itself, after its maddest debauches, after most austere asceticisms; and whatever a man's faith may be, he cannot doubt the wisdom of that great hand that shapes the destiny of the nations. We say, "But if these things go on, if all women and all men look at morality as merely a relative thing and at virtue [as] a myth or a fable, what will become of the world?" If——but they will not. Humanity is always rushing to its own destruction, but it never quite accomplishes it.

In Rome, at one time, it looked as though marriage and the family were things of the past. Later, in the first exaggerated zeal of the church, when St. Ursula alone had forty thousand virgins in her convents, it was

36. This passage, revised and adapted to a new context, reappears in Willa Cather's story "Eric Hermannson's Soul," first published in *Cosmopolitan*, April, 1900, and reprinted in CSF, pp. 359 ff. In "Eric," western people are strong, while Margaret Elliot, the girl from the East who briefly visits the West, is said to belong to an "ultra-refined civilization" which tries to cheat nature: "Cheat nature? Bah! One generation may do it, perhaps two, but the third—Can we ever rise above nature or sink below her? Did she not turn on Jerusalem as upon Sodom, upon St. Anthony in his desert as upon Nero in his seraglio? Does she not always cry in brutal triumph : 'I am here still, at the bottom of things, warming the roots of life; you cannot starve me nor tame me nor thwart me; I made the world, I rule it, and I am its destiny'" (p. 377).

thought that the race would die out altogether. In the days of the robber
barons men said that chaos had come to stay. But none of these things was
true. We are always taking temporary tendencies of humanity and regarding them as final. But the final tendencies and destiny are in the keeping of
a greater hand than ours, of that great intelligence who—when the Roman
world had corrupted the civilization it had made, enslaved the state it had
freed, grown monstrous in its pleasures—had the barbarian races ready to
destroy and renew, brought down the snows of the Danube to cool the
heated blood of the south, and the great hammer of Thor to crush the
defiled altars of Aphrodite into dust. Humanity cannot utterly blast itself,
even when it tries. Some day, perhaps, when our civilization has grown
too utterly complex, when our introspection cuts off all action, when our
forms have killed all ambition, when sincerity and simplicity have utterly
gone from us and we are only a bundle of nerves, then the savage strength
of the Slav or the Bushmen will come upon us and will burn our psychologies and carry us away into captivity and make us dress the vines and
plow the earth and teach us that after all nature is best. God's scheme is so
big, his resources so many.

Humanity is always so much of a child, its digressions and sins are
always more pitiful than terrible, and it always, when its small boy
pranks are done, some way comes back to its mother, whose forgiveness
seems to be without end. Nature is pretty rough on the individual at
times, but to the type she is wonderfully kind, and her mercy is from
everlasting to everlasting. When she has one nation that is wholly abandoned and given over to its emotions, and another that analyzes more than
it feels, she puts them together and lets them fight it out and they strike
an equilibrium somewhere. She is a Spartan mother, but she has unruly
sons to handle. We are growing too analytical ourselves, and we need
young men like Rudyard Kipling and Anthony Hope, not because of the
greatness of their talent, but because of the sincerity of their motive,
because the atmosphere of their work is one in which men may love and
work and fight and die like men. Because in their own small way they are
carrying out the task of their great master and chief [Robert Louis Steven-
son] who died down in the blue Pacific last winter when the winds of
December were covering us with snow. We owe him much, that great
master of pure romance, even his death blessed us, for it drew the world's
attention to his work and the greatness of it, to his faith and the sublimity
of it, showed us how vast was the future for work like his. Living, he
enriched us by his life; dying, by his death. Romance is the highest form

of fiction, and it will never desert us. If Stevenson did not accomplish its revival, some other man will. It will come back to us in all its radiance and eternal freshness in some one of the dawning seasons of Time. Ibsens and Zolas are great, but they are temporary. Children, the sea, the sun, God himself are all romanticists. Clouds cover the sun sometimes, and there is darkness upon the face of the deep, and God hides his face from us. But they come again, and with them Romance, as fair and beautiful and still as young as when it came with the troubadours to the springlit fields outside Verona where the Dukes held their Court of Love. As the old French song says,

> The swallows that winter scatters
> Will come again in the spring.

Courier, November 2, 1895, p. 6.

Drama

> The dress circle, the parquet, the orchestra
> chairs—that is all the dead world of fact;
> but right beyond that line of lights are the
> tropics, the kingdom of the unattainable,
> where the grand passions die not and the
> great forces still work.

THE PLAYWRIGHT AND HIS CRAFT

*Many years after she had left Lincoln, and the Lansing and the Funke had long
been dark, Willa Cather recalled how much the living stage had meant to her,
even as a child. "We hear the drama termed a thing in three dimensions," she
said, "but it is really a thing in four dimensions, since it has two imaginative
fires behind it, the playwright's and the actor's."*[1] *She began to see the playwright's fire during the years in Lincoln, when she learned through all the hours
of play-going and review-writing that the drama shone in vastly different lights.
When she began to measure the quality and kinds of playwriting, to formulate
some principles of effective stagecraft, she worked as inductively as anyone could—
seeing the plays, feeling what worked in them, testing by her own reactions. No
doubt she knew something of Aristotle, she spoke sometimes of the unities, and
she occasionally quoted other critics like Francisque Sarcey or William Winter;
but on the whole her comments on drama were firmly based on the plays themselves—as she saw them. Reading through the columns and reviews of three
years, one can see that the technical observations increase in both number and
authority. They lead to the concept of a tight, logical, swift-moving play, in
which action is more important than talk, feeling greater than argument; in
which language is literate and moving, and the characters alive in their own*

1. "Willa Cather Mourns Old Opera House," Omaha *World-Herald*, Sunday Magazine
Section, October 27, 1929, p. 9.

dimensions. She did not like artificial manipulation or obtrusive stagecraft, but she enjoyed the visual harmonies of good staging, the style *of a play.*

In the 1890's, the state of drama in America was about the same the country over. You elbowed your way through a vast ten-cent carnival of farces, melo-dramas, and music hall varieties; but there was always the splendor of Shake-speare, on a hill beyond. Between were a good many ordinary and easily-forgotten plays of high and low society. The important dramas were either the old English favorites like Sheridan's The Rivals *and* The School for Scandal, *Bulwer-Lytton's* The Lady of Lyons *and* Richelieu, *and Knowles's* Virginius *and* The Love Chase, *or the countless translations and adaptations from the works of the French writers, notably Dumas père, Dumas fils, and Victorien Sardou. On the horizon were the new playwrights: Willa Cather read Ibsen, perhaps Shaw; she attended plays by Pinero and Wilde (and had doubts about both writers—one was all social problems, the other epigrams without a heart). Most of the drama, then, came from England and the Continent; the American stage looked like a foreign country. As Willa Cather (and many others) observed, in America there was very little use of native materials; but even worse, very few playwrights were seriously attempting to write good plays out of any kind of material. " Most of our charming dramas might have been written in a ballroom on the back of a program, or on a lady's fan, for all they amount to," she remarked in the* Journal *for February 2, 1896. Some plays of American life, like Bronson Howard's* Shenandoah, *Denman Thompson's* The Old Homestead, *and James A. Herne's* Shore Acres *(all familiar on the Lincoln stage), she thought were good but not great. Better plays by Americans were Clyde Fitch's* Beau Brummell *(an English period piece) and Steele Mackaye's* Paul Kauvar. *A good historical drama, Paul Kauvar was "in spirit, in rapid movement, strong action and ringing phrases almost the equal of the stirring romantic dramas of the elder Dumas," and "the one serious American drama in which men did things instead of saying them" (*Journal, *February 26, 1895). But Steele Mackaye was dead, and the present was not filled with golden triumph.² When she looked at two of the most prominent American playwrights, David Belasco and Charles H. Hoyt, she had some serious reservations; the possibilities of American drama were better suggested by the work of a man like Henry Guy Carleton. Nevertheless, all drama had to be measured by the truly great, and those were the great Frenchmen.*

2. Steele Mackaye's death in 1894 at the age of fifty-two was a real loss to the American theatre, for he was not only a playwright but an imaginative producer. Ironically, the play which Miss Cather was reviewing when she commented on Mackaye was a distorted production called "The New *Paul Kauvar*" in which all of the good dramatic action she had admired is merely reported.

David Belasco

As a play-maker and producer, David Belasco emphasized spectacular and astonishing scenic displays, the kind of realism that ran to replicas, and the unrelenting use of "comic relief." By January, 1895, when he was in his mid-thirties, he was successful enough to have a number of plays on the road, and in that one month three of them came to the Lansing—not for the first time. Two were collaborations with Henry C. DeMille: The Charity Ball *(about a social mixup), which played on January 5; and* Men and Women *(about a banking scandal) on January 21. The third play, for which Franklin Fyles contributed the story, was* The Girl I Left Behind Me *(about an Indian uprising in Montana), performed on January 26. Following are some excerpts from the reviews in the* Journal, *with Miss Cather's summary of the Belasco world.*

The Charity Ball itself, like most American dramas, is only the shadow of a play. It employs more characters than it has actual need for, which is always a mistake, and worse still it employs them too much.

Of what use to the plot are Mr. Betts, Cain or Mr. Creighton? They stroll through an act or two and are seen no more. "They came like water and like wind they go." Superfluous characters are fatal to a play, no matter how well they are enacted.

Then there is that constant dilly-dallying with situations, that bringing two lovers together and having the family come in and part them, repeated over and over again. Belasco has a trick of taking up a situation and putting off its consummation, laying it aside until it gets cold and loses its edge before he takes it up again. Climaxes like those at the end of the second and third acts are strained and instead of being powerful they are only *outré.*

Perhaps some day there will be born in America a man who can forbear wasting a play on half a dozen lukewarm salad-day love complications, who will take one living, fearless passion and, losing himself in the greatness of his theme, will work it through to its consummation without faltering, as the French have done. Then the history of American drama will begin. [January 6, 1895, p. 6]

One would not care to see many of Belasco's plays in a season, not even if the players were Booths and Janauscheks. This play [*Men and Women*] is a better play than *The Charity Ball,* as in this the characters all at least have a speaking acquaintance with each other and are not so utterly irrelevant to the plot. But the same unnatural, strained elements are there, the same incongruous sequence of events. His "Men and Women" are only stage puppets and the wires which control them are not even concealed. Not only is there no attempt at character drawing and development, but the characters do not live. The "Men and Women" have anatomy, but not life. The cleverest stagecraft is all wrong when it is at war with the eternal truth of things. The only great effects produced on the stage are those which grow out of the consequences of individual character as opposed to circumstances, not those which are produced by the howling of the wind or the effect of an organ voluntary or uncalled for references to *Les Misérables*. The only good tragedies are those whch come about so naturally, so inevitably that everyone who sees must shudder and say: "That might have happened to me." Then a play means something to an audience. [January 22, 1895, p. 8]

> *The review of* The Girl I Left Behind Me *says that it "shows the touch of a firmer hand" than either of the others. "It is not nearly so pretentious, but it tells its story with fewer unnecessary convolutions and there is more directness and sequence in the plot. Besides it only handles three loving couples, which is a decided improvement on four." However, it has the same tacked-on comedy: "Mr. Belasco is intensely ashamed of seriousness, and when he permits any of it he always immediately apologizes by hurrying in the youth and maiden, who are supposed to be the personal representatives of the muse of comedy" (January 27, 1895). On another page of the* Journal *for January 27, Willa Cather presented in her Sunday column some conclusions about the Belasco plays.*

Within the last few weeks we have had the somewhat doubtful pleasure of witnessing three of Mr. Belasco's plays. As all of them were well enacted, they were all enjoyable, but even the most enthusiastic and uncritical soul must have felt in some degree the false and jarring note which predominates in everything Belasco ever touched.

Mr. Belasco is a master of stagecraft in its lower sense. No one ever denied that. Apparently he thinks of a number of bizarre and unusual situations and climaxes and then strings them together with an indifferent plot and impossible characters. His range of imagination is not great. In both the two plays we have just seen there was the same fidgety old gentleman enamored of the same dashing widow, the same youthful relative who plays tricks on the aged lover, the same bashful youth and coquettish maiden, the same fond mother of the hero, the same wind storm, the same preposterous——³ of a novel to preface some startling announcement.

The sameness of all these things is by no means their worst feature. It is the unnatural things that the characters are made to do that stamps the play as weak and inconsistent. What self-respecting man would sit down and tell the story of his crime in the maudlin, sentimental way of Governor Rodman [in *Men and Women*]? Why should Miss Rodman make special arrangements with the stage hands and scenic painters to leave an open door through which she could watch her lover's face during his interview with her father? Why should Mr. Belasco arrange with the regulator of the universe to have the sun rise at just the right moment to light up the figure of the Christ over the hero's repentance? All these things are merely stage claptrap, not natural, human actions. The art of such plays rests mainly with the stage hands and property man.

The highest dramatic art is that in which the minor characters develop the major ones and at the same time are essential to the plot. Mr. Belasco does not develop his characters at all, and fully half of the personages introduced have nothing whatever to do with the plot. They enter from the unknown and exit into the unknown and are seen no more.

The severest criticism that can be passed upon any play is to say that it is fundamentally and organically false. No plays merit that charge more truly than those of David Belasco. His only aim is to bring a "hand" of applause. His heroes make love not because they love, but to arouse a clapping of hands. His plays lack any great emotion. He moves upon not the hearts, but the nerves of his audience. He simply takes one's nervous system and thumps and bangs at it as though it were a pianoforte. He would probably excuse his timid little Sunday school emotions by saying that they are realistic. Well, that sort of Howells realism goes very well at home in a wrapper and an easy chair, but we need something more vivid to recompense us for sitting three hours in a cramped opera chair with our tight clothes on.⁴

Mr. Belasco's philanthropic women are even worse than his sentimental men. They talk so incessantly. They are not ministering angels,

3. In the newspaper text of this article a rule has been printed to show an omission from copy. The sense is probably that the plays all have irrelevant allusions to novels, like the "uncalled for references to *Les Misérables*" mentioned in the review of *Men and Women*.

4. If anyone doubts that a woman is writing these articles, he has only to consider this statement. There is, of course, no attempt to conceal the person of the writer in Willa Cather's early journalistic pieces; in fact, the personality is made as explicit as a signature. But this offhand glimpse of a young woman squirming on an opera chair recalls an unintentional slip into a feminine point of view in *My Ántonia*, when the narrator Jim Burden, recalling his room in Lincoln while he was attending the University, speaks of "the great walnut wardrobe which held all my clothes, even my hats and shoes. . . " (p. 293).

but itinerant preachers. A preaching woman has no place behind the foot-lights. If she has that tendency she should confine herself to the Salvation Army. On the stage a woman has but one business, to be in love, and to have it mighty hard.

"Yes," said Miss Bernice Wheeler, the leading lady of the *Men and Women* company, as she began making up for the last act, "all that you say is true enough. The falseness and absurd lack of consistency in the characters cramps us terribly. I felt it more as Ann Cruger [in *The Charity Ball*] than I do as Agnes. There were plenty of good lines, but there was no particular reason why they should be said, and it was very hard to say them as if there were. It is very trying to attempt to do an unnatural part naturally. One gets weary of false roles just as one does of people who are not genuine. The construction of the plays is clever, but all the time we, who enact them, feel the lack of the strong hand of the master playwright. We are like sheep without a shepherd. We wander through our parts and do our best, but we are all the time feeling the lack of a cause or an end. We have little spasms of joy and little spasms of pain, but we cannot be strong or really powerful because there are no sustained emotions. We never feel ourselves driven along by an irresistible current. We are half the time fighting in little whirlpools and half the time drifting in the shallows." [January 27, 1895, p. 13]

Charles H. Hoyt

Like Belasco, Charles H. Hoyt was in his mid-thirties, a successful theatre man with a knack for making farce-comedy out of nothing, using everyday events in American locales (Texas, San Francisco, New England). The Hoyt plays blew in and out of Lincoln, light as down and always popular. Willa Cather's comments on them in a group of reviews and columns were consistently favorable, for like any talent which is good in its own way, Hoyt's was skillfully handled and unpretentious. A Texas Steer (*about a Texas congressman*) *and* A Hole in the Ground (*life in a railroad station*) *had been in Lincoln several times.* A Trip to Chinatown (*wherein there is no trip at all*) *played on January 19 and October 31, 1894; and* A Contented Woman (*who runs against her husband for mayor of Denver*) *on October 9, 1895.*[5] A Temperance Town (*all of Hoyt's titles began with*

5. Play lists based on first New York performances (for example, Arthur Hobson Quinn, *A History of the American Drama from the Civil War to the Present Day* [New York: Harper, 1927], II, 255 ff.) give 1897 as the date of *A Contented Woman*, but it was on the road before that. The advance notices in the fall of 1895 said that it was Hoyt's new play, written for his wife, Caroline Miskel Hoyt.

"A") *was somewhat different. It played on February 6, 1895, the day of that year's great blizzard, and in her* Journal *review on February 7 Willa Cather wrote that it was of Hoyt's earlier period, before he ran exclusively to farces. An anti-prohibition play, it was still fair to both sides—one act in a bar room, the next in a church. She quoted Hoyt's definition of a prohibitionist:* "*Investigate a prohibitionist and at the bottom you will find that he is either a crank or a man with an axe to grind.*" *On the following Sunday she wrote, "A Temperance Town is one of Mr. Hoyt's mistakes. . . . No, Mr. Hoyt should try nothing but farce. We would rather have him coarse and natural than stilted and artificial. We would rather have old Ben Gay's long wait in the private supper room than all the long lost sons in the world"* (Journal, *February 10, 1895). She thought he was funny, but in a more serious vein she always returned to Hoyt as an imperfect but possible beginning on American subjects and humor. The following excerpts from one year of the* Journal *reviews and columns repeat some ideas, but are useful for that very reason: they show that there is but one hand at work.*

¶ *A Trip to Chinatown* is just as absurd, as plotless and as funny as it was last year and the year before that. There has been a good deal of talk about Mr. Hoyt lately, most of it unjust and uncalled for. The critics have declared that Mr. Hoyt is immoral and indecent. Ten years ago, when Mr. Hoyt's success was not quite so sure as it is now, these same critics went to see him play and laughed as hard as anybody and kindly allowed him to amuse them. But now Mr. Hoyt has become a greater man than they gave him permission to be, and with the critics that is the one unpardonable sin. They demand that whom they bind shall be bound and whom they loose shall be loosed. Now the critics may bind and loose at will in the next world, but in this rocky and sordid sphere they can't keep the American public from liking Mr. Hoyt. Mr. Hoyt's great hold on the people of this country lies in the fact that his humor is thoroughly American, just as much as Mark Twain's. It is not borrowed from England or stolen from France. It comes right up from the streets and the shops and the everyday life of the American people. His satire is appreciated and understood because it is directed against the simple everyday matters that everybody understands. Coarse it may be, but Mr. Hoyt is almost the first really American satirist, and the early comedy of all peoples has always been blunt, from Aristophanes and Plautus down. No one pretends that Hoyt is artistic, least of all he himself. No one pretends that he will rank with Molière and the immortals, but sometimes jolly, ordinary little men are awfully comfortable, just by way of a rest from the immortals. Hoyt will not be played in fifty years from now; he will be unintelligible to another generation. He is like a daily newspaper, like oysters, like champagne that has been uncorked; he won't last forever, but he is mighty refreshing while he lasts. [November 1, 1894, p. 2]

¶ It is useless to go squirrel hunting with a cannon, and it is useless to level the guns of serious criticism at anything written by Mr. Hoyt. Mr. Hoyt is not a scheming villain, or a corrupter of public morals; he is simply a very pleasant, clever, brainless man who is exceedingly wise in his generation. Mr. Hoyt does not know a great deal, but he knows the American public better than any other man connected with the stage. The one thing about him worthy of respect is his staunch Americanism. He is really and sincerely American. He is really the exponent of the average American's taste in the matter of comedy. Of course the public taste will some day outgrow *A Trip to Chinatown* and *A Hole in the Ground*. It will some day be able to feel the more delicate humor which cuts cleaner and deeper, but at present it certainly is not. One charm about Mr. Hoyt is that he is so very unpretentious, anything will serve him for a theme, any little existing annoyance that we have all felt and fretted over. His plays can't last long because their interest is entirely local, but he is not writing plays for posterity, but for the living present and the box-office receipts of the living present. [November 4, 1894, p. 12]

¶ There are some people, first-rate people, who do not think Hoyt funny. They are generally of foreign blood or tastes. Hoyt's fun is strictly American; to a European it is as incomprehensible as the fascination of Wall Street. The French and Germans have a deeper kind of comedy, they must always have passion of some sort at the bottom of it. Nothing but a contortion of serious emotions is funny to them. They can see the comedy of a man's flirting with his own wife at a mask ball, but the comedy of a country railway station, of a prohibition community, of a Texan in politics are to them trivial nonsense, things for peasants to laugh over. Mr. Hoyt's comedy is a little broad and it is rather coarse, but as yet all American standards are coarse. We have yet to learn that there is nothing excruciatingly funny in a dozen people falling down stairs without any particular cause. We have not yet found out that a clean comedy is almost impossible and that the highest kind of comedy must be spiced with sin just as the highest kind of tragedy must be darkened by it. But give us time, we will learn to appreciate a more delicate and insinuating class of comedy, the comedy which is not content with burlesquing politics, railroads and prohibition, but which denies love and mocks at honor. We will grow to their elevated comedy in due time. Just now the American public is a big, restless baby which likes the color of pretty costumes, the noise of loud laughter, the music of very limited composers. It likes Hoyt, and it likes Sousa's "Liberty Bell," and it will continue to do so in spite of their nibs, the critics. Let it alone, it will grow old and nasty tempered soon enough. [February 10, 1895, p. 13]

¶ Mr. Hoyt is, on the whole, a satisfactory writer of farces. Indeed the only American farces worth hearing at all are those Mr. Hoyt has written. He never soars very high, but he never falls very flat. You can depend on him to be jolly and entertaining. He pleases the American people without being absolutely vulgar, and that is an exceedingly difficult thing to do. Whatever Mr. Hoyt is or is not, he is candid and honest. He never tries to be what he is not. He does not affect vast culture or work over situations from foreign plays. He is an American, as American as a cocktail, and he has the monumental pluck and nerve of his people. [October 10, 1895, p. 5]

Henry Guy Carleton

Although he wrote good plays, Henry Guy Carleton had only moderate success in New York, and mostly with The Butterflies (1894), *which starred John Drew, Olive May (Mrs. Carleton), and Maude Adams. The year before there had been a history play,* The Lion's Mouth. *But the one which Willa Cather noted especially was* A Gilded Fool, *played with considerable success on the road by the comedian Nat Goodwin (see page 128). In the summer of 1895, Mrs. Carleton was visiting her sister in Beatrice, a town near Lincoln, and Willa Cather tells in her column of August 4, 1895, about meeting the actress there. The article on Carleton as a dramatist appeared in the same column. Because it is partly an occasional piece, perhaps it should be seen not as a real judgment of Carleton but as a chance for Willa Cather to summarize the elements she thought important in playwriting.*

It is to be sincerely hoped that Nat Goodwin will see fit to journey westward this season and that we will have an opportunity to see him in Mr. Carleton's new play [*Ambition*]. American plays as a rule are not much to be proud of, but certainly the author of *A Gilded Fool* has reason more than any of his contemporaries to be satisfied with his work.

We have plays that deal with the war, with the navy, with Indian outbreaks, with society and even with undertakers, but very few that condescend to deal with men and women. It is to Mr. Carleton's great honor that he has never written what polite critics call a "timely play"; that is he has never dramatized a popular novel or worked temporary political or social complications into a play for the ostensible purpose of making a hit. Neither strikes nor hypnotism nor horse races nor the stars and stripes have ever formed the central point of his plays. He has never baldly taken advantage of popular sentiment to make a popular play.

Anyone who remembers *A Gilded Fool* will recall how genuine and moving it is. There is not one line of bombastic eloquence, not one improbable situation in it from beginning to end. It does not deal with the impossible, the unusual or the bizarre, but with the common, universal impulses of humanity which all really great men find quite strange and wonderful enough.

Contrast the play, for instance, with Belasco's *Charity Ball* or *Men and Women*. If in either of Mr. Belasco's indisputably clever plays there is one impulse or action that an ordinary man or woman would be capable of we failed to find it. If you had the misfortune to know such sawdust people you would slash them off of your visiting list quickly enough.

On the other hand if you knew Charley Short[6]—particularly Nat Goodwin's Charley Short—you might resolve every day of your life to cut him, but you never would. You might even meet him when he was tipsy and you would speak to him just the same.

After all, behind the footlights or in the world, the only unpardonable sin is artificiality. It is very doubtful if it is wise to assume a virtue if you have it not. Most of us find an honest vice more endurable than an affected virtue. That is why we like Charley Short "the morning after," disheveled and crumpled, with a sore head, better than Mr. Belasco's drivelling clergymen and white-winged cherubs of Wall Street. Perhaps we will all be angels some day. We hope so, but "meantime we are men and women."

Mr. Carleton seems to be able to get along without much aid from mechanical accessories. Not only has he never advertised a great spectacular scene, but he never resorts to organ voluntaries played at inopportune moments by characters who have nothing whatever to do with the play,

6. The cast of characters for the New York production gives the name as "Chauncey Short." (George C. D. Odell, *Annals of the New York Stage* [New York: Columbia University Press, 1949], XV, 305)

lamps shining from a parsonage window, sunlight breaking through a stained glass picture of the Christ, and those everlasting wind and snow storms that howl through Mr. Belasco's society dramas. Mr. Carleton's characters are human enough and likeable enough to excite and sustain interest of themselves. His plays are dramas of character and not of accident or environment. When they are over it is always a surprise to think how little happens and how much is felt and enjoyed.

He has stuck to the good old method of limiting his *dramatis personae* and does not attempt to introduce the entire population of New York into a society drama to be "realistic." He concentrates his strength and his hearers'. With the exception of Clyde Fitch, the young author of that admirable play *Beau Brummell*, he is about the only American dramatist who has the slightest regard for unity of action, cause and effect, or character consequences.

Perhaps the most peculiar thing about Mr. Carleton is the fact that he is a literary man. Most American dramatists are not. In France play-making is in the hands of men of letters; in America it is in the hands of men of the theatre. Daudet wrote his first play when he was almost entirely unfamiliar with the theatre, but it had genius enough to save it. The dramatic instinct is necessary, of course, but absolute greenroom knowledge and experience counts for much less than one thinks.

In this country every "old timer" who has seen all the ins and outs of the theatre and knows half a dozen members of the ballet thinks he can write a play. Unfortunately many of them do. To the average American playwright a play is merely a thing of "situations," beauty of language has nothing to do with it. In this country there has always been too wide a gulf between literature and the drama, so much so that our novelists are as dramatically impossible as our dramatists, and plays by Howells and Henry James[7] are as laughable as plays by the property man. Just as our novels lack the dramatic element so our plays lack literary perfection. Their ways are far apart.

The traditions of our stage are distinctly unliterary. When a French-man talks to us about beauty of diction or about an actor sustaining the

7. Willa Cather's information on James and Howells as dramatists came almost certainly through reading. She might have seen James's published dramatization of *Daisy Miller* (Boston, 1883); or the plays in *Theatricals: First Series* (London, 1894) and *Second Series* (London, 1895); or read about productions of *The American* (1891) and *Guy Domville* (January, 1895). She followed Howells rather closely through the magazines and made frequent comments on his work. "A Masterpiece of Diplomacy" appeared in *Harper's* in February, 1894. Howells also had had numerous plays in print and on the stage.

strength of a line we have not the wildest conception of what he means. To us "lines" mean nothing, it is all "climax" and "situations." We have grown so dense in these matters that we even allow Mr. Daly to re-write and adapt Shakespeare for us.[8] Shakespeare's diction, which the French consider his greatest beauty, means nothing to most of us. We only rave over his "scenes"; the "balcony scene" and the "tomb scene." We cannot understand why lines 220 and 381 of Hugo's *Hernani* at the first representation drove all conservative classics out of the house and almost ruined the play, though all the author's friends were there, headed by Gautier in his memorable red waistcoat.[9]

We are losing all understanding of the power of language in the theatre. It is enough to make one wish that our calcium lights and re-volving scenery and all our thousand and one mechanical myths were abolished and that we were back in the Globe Theatre, driven once again to the resources of human speech and to the naked strength of words.

Among the younger American dramatists there are very few who begin to have that feeling for language, who have begun to write lines that can stand alone. Mr. Carleton is certainly foremost among them. There are lines of *The Lion's Mouth* and *A Gilded Fool* that haunt one's memory, words that have an especial fitness for each other. Mr. Carleton is not a poet, but he is a man of literary knowledge and ability, and after Belasco and [Paul M.] Potter, Hoyt and Bronson Howard that means a great deal.

Journal, August 4, 1895, p. 9.

Dumas père *and Dumas* fils

With the two Dumas, father and son, there was no question: one had written the great romances, the other Camille. *Though Willa Cather was not eager to praise Dumas* fils *for his later social dramas, such as* Le Demi-Monde

8. The next spring Willa Cather noted that the producer Augustin Daly and his star Ada Rehan were planning to present "Daly's *Midsummer Night's Dream*"—a risky thing, she said. "It is dangerous to let assertions like that pass in a world where a lie can run a mile before the truth can get its boots on. In a hundred years they will be printing it in the school books that Daly wrote *Hamlet*" (*Journal*, March 1, 1896).

9. Victor Hugo's *Hernani* was the focus for the battle of the Classicists and Romanticists in French drama. From the very first night—February 25, 1830—performances of the play caused an uproar of hisses, laughter, argument, shouts, and showers of torn paper at the Comédie-Française. Hugo had ignored classical rules, using free caesuras and enjambement instead of the strict Alexandrine, changing forms of words for the sake of rhyme, and ignoring at least the two unities of time and place. The Classicists had organized to defeat the play.

(played throughout America in several adaptations) and L'Étrangère, *she could recognize a master playwright.* Camille, *of course, she saw in November, 1893.*[10] *Other Dumas plays she read, translating and quoting, for example, from the preface to* La Femme de Claude *in an essay on Yvette Guilbert. When she found that the plot of Henry Arthur Jones's* The Case of Rebellious Susan *was a version of Dumas' Francillon, she wrote: "Is there no one in all this densely populated world who can write plays but that one white-haired little Frenchman? It seems not, certainly. . . . M. Sardou has written very playable and effective plays, but they have not the vital significance of Dumas' dramas" (Journal, January 27, 1895). With Dumas père she was no doubt more interested in the novels, but the play* The Three Guardsmen *was an old favorite, and she particularly liked Alexander Salvini's performance of May 3, 1894. Writing in the Journal about Dumas père and Dumas fils, Willa Cather reveals some important recognitions.*

¶ *The Three Guardsmen* makes a strong and effective play. Its art is not perfect, but its interest is, and that is much more practical and necessary. It was as Frenchy as need be; in the first act there were three intrigues and five duels, and in the other four acts these of course multiplied as the play approached its climax. The play follows the novel very closely. The novel is a great romance of a dissolute age, the work of one of the most clever though erratic geniuses of France. It is strong in plot and execution, candid in wickedness and egotism. It is only natural that if the father wrote *The Three Guardsmen* the son should write *Camille*, both masterpieces of art and immorality, but with the art and ethics of different epochs. [May 4, 1894, p. 6]

¶ Dumas has written the one great drama of the century, the one which will go down to all time as a classic in literature, a criterion in dramatic art, by which every young actress for centuries to come will measure and prove herself. A young dramatist could do no better thing than to learn *Camille* [*La Dame aux camélias*] by heart. He will find it the compass and square of the technique of the drama. It unites in itself those two affinities so seldom mated, measureless feeling and perfect form. It has only ten characters, only one love story, no comedy appearances. It moves entirely upon the strength of one great seriousness, one grand motif. Its pathos is never accidental, its tragedy is as inevitable as doom.

10. For other comments on *Camille* and the plays mentioned below, see pages 262–263; 227–228; 121–122.

It depends less than any other play upon accessories, it might be enacted without costumes or scenery or the tremolo agitations of an orchestra. There is only one great tragedy in life, the tragedy of sin, and no play has told it better than the lady of the camellias.

Then that is not the only one, there are *L'Ami des femmes*, *Le Demi-Monde*, *L'Affaire Clémenceau*,[11] *Le Père prodigue*, *L'Étrangère* and a dozen others. Some of them are impossible in America, but in France all things are possible. [January 27, 1895, p. 13]

¶ Whether Dumas' treatment of ethical problems was discreet or practical is an open question. But there is no doubt that his name is written under at least a dozen of the greatest plays of the century. *L'Étrangère* and *Le Demi-Monde* probably contain his most perfect work, but it is through *Camille* that his name will endure. He handled that subject once and for all. No matter how much the literature of the world advances, that play will never lose its vital interest. It has a greater defense against oblivion than even its author's genius; like the *Decameron*, it is the reflection of a time and a people. It will live as a master study of an epoch and a phase of life. Its influence upon literature has been incalculable. Half of the novels and plays of the last fifty years have taken their suggestions from *Camille*. Even operas are not above taking the hint. When old Massenet found that his bank account was growing short a few years ago and his creditors pushed him, he said, "Then I will write an opera of a courtesan, that will save me." He wrote *Thaïs*.

During the last five years of his life Dumas was at work upon one drama which he said he would make absolutely satisfactory or never produce it at all. Several of the more ambitious actors of France grew old while they were anxiously waiting to "create the leading role." But Dumas was in no hurry. It is not often that circumstances allow an artist the luxury of working for perfection. Dumas knew what that privilege was worth and he meant to enjoy it to the full. He had reared his family and put money in his purse and was released from his obligations as a man. He had written much for the world and now he was writing for himself. A few months ago he said that if he died before the play was finished he desired to have it burned after his death. It is to be hoped that his executors will have mercy upon the world and disregard his request. *The Road to Thebes* will never be finished now, for its author has gone upon a much

11. The play *The Clemenceau Case* (1890) was by William Fleron, and was only "derived from" Dumas' novel *L'Affaire Clémenceau*. A recent Lincoln performance was by Corse Payton and his company on January 26, 1894.

longer and darker road, whose end is beyond the compass of mortal measurements. And now when he has done his work and earned his star he has taken his place among those other immortals of the higher academy, where the shades of the great sit apart on the mountain in the light of their own glory, where Homer and Dante and Shakespeare and Keats and all the rest of them sit singing always for pure delight, and Tacitus and Gibbon and Fielding and Balzac tell each other stories of all lands and of all people. Where they run over the history of things from the beginning down to the end and beyond, and know and understand and read the mighty purpose in it all. Where, in that brotherhood of genius they interpret all life to each other, and one is all and all are one. [December 15, 1895, p. 9]

¶ Of all the many articles that have recently been written upon Alexandre Dumas *fils* there is none so just and comprehensive as the one his own father wrote about him thirty years ago and published in a now forgotten magazine. Incidentally he characterizes himself as well as his son and compares the romantic and realistic drama.

"When Alexandre first began to devote himself to writing for the stage, his task was by no means easy. Victor Hugo and I, who were practically in possession of the theatre at that time, represented schools that were widely different. Hugo was lyric and theatrical; I was dramatic. Hugo required for his effects the introduction of organ music and chorus, of tables covered with flowers and black draped coffins. He needed elaborate scenery, costumes, stage effects, secret doors and stairs, rope ladders and traps. I needed only four walls, four boards, two actors and one passion. . . ."[12]

All ye young writers of plays, there is a precept for you. "I needed only four walls, four boards, two characters and one passion." That is the stuff of which great plays are made. No "comedy element," no soubrette, no snow storm, no organ accompaniments, no unnatural scenic effects, two characters and one passion. When will we have a playwright who can take those things and make of them a great drama? [February 9, 1896, p. 9]

On Revising a Play

By the end of 1894, Willa Cather could settle down to some specific notes about play-construction and strategy. The occasion was Daniel Sully's own

12. This is the first appearance in Willa Cather's writing of the passage from Dumas which has become identified with her own critical principles. See pages 83 ff.

play, O'Neil, Washington, D.C., *presented on December 14, 1894. O'Neil apparently sank without a trace—there is no mention of it in the standard theatrical records and histories—but the advertisements in 1894 say it is a play "depicting the social, political and military sides of life at the national capital." We are urged to " See the Man-o-War Model. Startling Electric Effects." This (perhaps secret) model and its inventor seem to be O'Neil's central figures.*

. . . Mr. Sully is a good actor and has an unusually strong company. They are worthy of a better play. *O'Neil, Washington* has a practicable plot and strong situations but it is in very crude shape and needs a thorough over-hauling. The play does not realize or improve its own possibilities. That first act is wearisome enough to prejudice an audience against the entire performance. On the stage, time is everything; it is priceless. A play must not amble or stroll, but gallop toward its goal. All that is done in that first act could be done in ten minutes. First acts are generally bad, but they are necessary evils and should get all the characters well understood and some of the most difficult parts out of the way. The first act of *O'Neil* does nothing. Nothing happens, and it has not even an apology for a climax. There are too many interruptions and irrelevant conversations by the cook, the neighbors and other unimportant people. If the model is to be tampered with it should be done in the first act to give a strong and vital interest to the play.

It is entirely a misconception that first acts are merely to introduce characters. The French, who are the acknowledged masters of stagecraft, plunge at once into the main part of the story. A play with a melo-dramatic plot like this one cannot afford ten lines of unnecessary or uninteresting conversation. Its object is not to divert the listener, but to interest and concentrate him. What business has a play with a moving plot to give the dimensions of a box by telephone, like every farce comedy on the road? When a man writes a play that has a story to tell, his mind should be filled and dominated by one great idea, one chief motif, his eyes should be dazzled by one great situation so that he is blind to all unimportant and trivial detail. The trouble with most American play-wrights is they lack that enthusiasm for their subject, that infatuation [with] their own idea which seems so natural to the Frenchman. In melodrama everything which does not help hinders. Every pound that is not of service should be got rid of. The accoutrement should be light, but deadly. The introduction of such characters as Sheridan, who have nothing to do with the plot, does not, as the author intended, give the play an air of naturalness, but of weakness and insufficiency.

The two succeeding acts are much better than the first. Cut out the conversation of Sheridan and strengthen the climaxes and they would do well enough. They need higher color and general toning up. They would be strong enough in a novel, but to make a good play they must be intensified. The inventor should have a harder time finding his cylinder and draw a little more on the sympathy of his audience. Let him lock his door and tear off his coat, handle his forge and begin to make his cylinder, hammering the metal against time. Let the curtain fall before the audience is sure of his success. Let his magnificent determination, not a lucky chance, be the finale. Discard the idea of having a baby bring about his success, a baby cannot bring about the climax of a strong play. That has been tried before. Save the appearance of the Lilly Phillys for the climax of the last act, then let the perfected model close the play. Let it end with the work as it began.

This is not an attempt to rewrite Mr. Sully's play for him, but it is irritating to see the way that clever actors and strong situations go to waste in that play. Mr. Sully himself really has great possibilities as a comedian of the warmer and more human kind. He can be simple without being trivial and he can dispatch a climax with naturalness and strength. If he finds the right play there is no reason why he may not be better known than he is.

Journal, December 15, 1894, p. 2.

Observations on Craft

Ideas came from both the stage and the page. Following are a few excerpts from Willa's reviews and columns in the Journal.

¶ *The Voodoo*, like all farce comedy, is an exaggeration; the only difference is that it is a little less clever and a little more loud than most of them. More than that, "Voodoo" wit is a little stale. In wit and women we can pardon every sin but age. Reigning comedies like reigning belles may be as shallow, as frivolous, as wicked even, as they please, but wrinkles and gray hair are forbidden them. The world not only wants to laugh, but it wants to laugh at something that it has not laughed at in its youth. There is no possible excuse for a comedy-farce being stale. Tragedies must be more or less so, for there is only a limited number of ways of killing men after all. Dramas are apt to be, for love is pretty much the same the world over. Operas are sure to be, for there are only a certain number of tones and combinations of tones in music. But farce-comedy deals with the follies and wickedness of all creation, and these are without number and are always fresh and inspiring. The assortment of nonsense and wickedness in the booth of his satanic majesty is so large and varied that there is no excuse for a playwright selecting naughty jokes that have been used and returned to the second-hand counter. [March 22, 1894, p. 6]

¶ [A Summer Blizzard] is the work of a man who believes that a company and a little scenery and considerable nerve are the only requisites for a play. If there is any evil in the Hoyt school of farce it is that the opinion has gone abroad that a little horse-play and half a dozen songs are all a play really needs. The play is loosely written and coarsely acted. There is not a man in the company who is not knocked down in the first act and kicked down stairs in the second.

The comedy is all of a crude, clownish sort that hinges on sounding blows and the physical degradation of the actors. It is a pity, for most of them seem to be bright young people and deserve a better play. This one could only run successfully in Zululand or the Cherokee strip or among the cannibals of the upper Congo. [December 5, 1894, p. 3]

¶ In point of construction there are many commendable things about the comedy [A Jolly Good Fellow]. First and chiefly it only pretends to handle one hero and one love episode and subordinates everything else to them. Secondly, the comedy element does not depend on any one or two characters, that is, there are no labelled clowns whose mere appearance is supposed to be a cue for laughter. The serious people are sometimes funny and the funny people are occasionally permitted to be serious, as funny people have a way of doing in this world. The comedy is nicely distributed throughout the play and is not bestowed upon the public in indigestible chunks. [January 11, 1895, p. 8]

¶ The play [The Spider and the Fly] is one of those combinations of circus and very light opera which seem written especially to give employment to ring contortionists and trapeze performers during the season when the canvas is too breezy to exhibit their skill. Light operas are supposed to be light, but this one came nearer an absolute vacuum than any play we have seen lately, except the Hendrick Hudson of Sweetie Corinne. In fact, the whole thing was merely "atmosphere trimmed in blue ribbons." . . . There was very little heart or mirth in any part of the play or the action. Some plays, like the people who habitually visit them, in their great desire to be sufficiently wicked lose even the pretext of mirth and have only the raw material left. Spectacular plays as a rule are written for people who are too far gone to laugh normally or naturally. [February 9, 1894, p. 6]

¶ Of course the great dream of every playwright is to introduce an absolutely new situation on the stage. It is for this that race horses, police wagons, fire engines and all such abominations are introduced behind the footlights. Mr. John Stevenson in his new play, *Nobody*, has achieved a hitherto unheard of situation, but it is so colossal that he is likely to have brain fever from the worry of it. If his novelty were only an earthquake or a cyclone or a storm at sea it would be easy to manage, but Mr. Stevenson's ambition demands that a soubrette shall milk a real cow on the stage. The situation is, of course, idyllic, but the distracted playwright cannot find in all America a soubrette who can milk a cow—nor a cow who will be milked by a soubrette. [April 22, 1894, p. 13]

¶ Of plot [in *The White Squadron*] there was enough and to spare, so much indeed that the average hearer occasionally wondered if the hero himself had not got the two girls mixed. He, the hero, was a good, substantial fellow, very unsailorlike for a naval officer, able, however, under all circumstances to call down the gallery by a spirited appeal to the "star spangled flag." There was an abused slave, two villains (both foiled) and a number of brigands, not to mention the very dingy and disreputable persons who posed as the admirals of various fleets. The story set all these people at work with kisses and curses and pistols and cutlasses and denunciations and explanations, till finally everything cleared up and things went universally well to the tune of "Hail Columbia." [March 16, 1894, p. 3]

❖

¶ There are some stage questions which have never been solved yet. Among them are why the maids always wear red dresses and always dust the same piece of furniture through the whole play; why the villains always wear silk hats and smoke cigarettes; why the leading lady always wears black in the fourth act and faints in the fifth. [October 21, 1894, p. 13]

¶ The principals of the play [*Shenandoah*] are given more to do than to say, which is an excellent plan, and they are none of them allowed to practice oratory at the expense of the audience. There is no excuse for a man's rhetoric being florid just because he dies for his country, and when a soldier's bosom swells with patriotism, there is no reason why his head should proportionally swell. If he must die, let him perish like a hero, not like a sophomore. [April 17, 1895, p. 5]

¶ The art of writing dialogue is at a rather low ebb just now. Probably the rapid increase in play-writing has done as much as anything to weaken it, for as a rule plays contain the worst dialogue in the world. The neatest little bit of dialogue work since Anthony Hope's *Dolly Dialogues* appeared in the last *Cosmopolitan* [February, 1896] under the title *The Charm*. It is by Walter Besant and Walter Pollock and it has a quaint poetic sort of flavor that quite smacks of Goldsmith. It is not strictly a playable piece, because it has more poetry than action, but it is certainly fitter for the stage than many of the one-act pieces running today that have all of its monotony without its poetry. If it were played properly it would be good to see the two faded belles before the transformation receiving the homage of their ancient vassals, and then the two courtly old men in their wigs and paint and padding, kneeling at the feet of the heartless beauties who are young and do not remember. Then that touching little scene, there at the end with the princess playing her cracked spinet and singing in her high, tremulous voice, the song of vanished youth and perished love. It's so neat to leave them there with their cards and gossip and stories and memories, these beaux and belles of eighty years. Someway it makes one think of Thackeray, probably only because all the best things make one think of him. [February 23, 1896, p. 9]

The Playwright's Intention

There is an amusing "scrap" going on in New York just now between Richard Mansfield, actor, and G. Bernard Shaw, playwright. Last summer Mr. Shaw wrote a play which he called *Arms and the Man*, and Mr. Mansfield played it. Mr. Mansfield thought the play was a satire and played it as such with magnificent success. Everyone else thought it was a satire and the critics heaped unconditional praise upon the head of Mr. Shaw, saying that such a piece of audacious cynicism had not been flung at the world for years. They called Mr. Shaw the master cynic since Juvenal. Well, now after this realistic masterpiece has run for a whole year as successfully as any masterpiece or work of merit can ever run in New York, and after Mansfield's impersonation of the hero, Captain Bluntschli, has become a byword for delicate irony Mr. G. Bernard Shaw says that Mansfield has spoiled his play and ruined his reputation. He declares that he never meant the play to be satirical, and that if rightly played Bluntschli would be one of the most pathetic and touching characters in the world.[13] Mr. Shaw apparently forgets that in London, where the play was played seriously, it was a dead failure, while in this country it was one of the season's successes. Undoubtedly Mr. Mansfield's irony made the play, and if it was a gratuitous invention of his own brain, then the greater Mansfield he. However, Mr. Shaw wrote the drama, and if it has succeeded beyond its deserts he has a right to object, though such a proceeding is somewhat unusual.

Things like this make one wonder how much of what we call the art of the world was intentionally so. I have always wondered just what Shakespeare would say if he could read the forbidding tomes of Shakespearean literature written in all languages, and I have always privately maintained the Browning commentaries and encyclopedias were largely instrumental in bringing about that gentleman's demise. It is queer what work the philosophers and critics make of artists anyway. If Shakespeare were alive today he probably could not answer the vexed Shakespearean questions. As Henry James says, he simply planted his genius and let it grow and he was not particularly responsible for or even concerned about the form it took.

Courier, August 24, 1895, p. 6.

13. Writing in the *New Review* for July 1894 ("A Dramatic Realist to His Critics"), Shaw called *Arms and the Man* a "comedy of disillusionment," and no burlesque. "I meant no mockery at all. The observation [that life is a farce] is made in the play in a manner dramatically appropriate to the character of an idealist who is made a pessimist by the shattering of his illusions." (*Shaw on Theatre*, ed. E. J. West [New York: Hill and Wang, 1958], pp. 33–34) By 1895 Shaw's quarrel with Mansfield was concerned more with delays in the proposed American production of *Candida*, but in November he wrote to Ellen Terry in America that "if that villain Mansfield plays 'Arms & The Man' anywhere within your reach, will you go & see it & tell me whether they murder it or not." (Bernard Shaw: *Collected Letters 1874–1897*, ed. Dan H. Laurence [New York: Dodd, Mead & Company, 1965], pp. 572, 494 ff.)

DRAMA CRITIC

Several times during her years as a dramatic critic in Lincoln, Willa Cather wrote on the nature of the critic's work. Although every audience was in effect a judge of the play, one who published his criticism had additional responsibilities. Since she was often involved in the broils that attend public figures who talk a lot in print, Willa Cather sometimes needed to restate and fortify a position, asserting her principles of personal duty and social conscience. At other times she attempted to define the sources, the means, and the intention of criticism itself. The aim of the dramatic critic, she always believed, was to capture the physical and emotional quality of a performance and make it real to the imagination; but more and more she added a kind of moral judgment—what ought to be as well as what is. In 1894 she was talking about feeling; in 1895, about standards.

The Gallery Gods

The first thing is to care about the stage—not the forms but the passions of the world beyond "that line of lights." In this respect, those who sat in the cheapest seats in the highest places of the theatre were sometimes the most honest critics. They usually liked action plays like the popular Monte Cristo, *or even* Richard III. Monte Cristo *was performed many times and in many variations, most recently in Lincoln by James O'Neill (March 11–12, 1892), Fred Felton (December 26, 1893), and Frank Lindon (May 10, 1893). Thomas Keene had played* Richard III *with vigor on September 19, 1890, and November 22, 1892. On the other hand, the gallery did not always like love scenes. One particularly inept performance in Lewis Morrison's adaptation of* Faust *on January 17, 1894, made critics of all the gallery gods.*

The most alert and observing, and certainly the most courageous and candid dramatic critics in Lincoln are the gods of the gallery. The actor has a right to be fond of the gallery folk and to get off his longest and most eloquent speeches for their benefit. They are always enthusiastic and always generous. If an actor repeats a noble sentiment, strikes a telling pose, they always applaud him. If he makes a pun they laugh at it just as though Noah had not rung a chestnut bell at that fun in his day. They are never cold and uncertain like the people downstairs, who are afraid of splitting their kid gloves if they applaud. They hold their breath when Monte Cristo makes his celebrated announcement concerning the world, and they are thrilled when Keene cries, "Lay on, Macduff," in *Richard III* just as much as if the lines belonged there.[14] The gallery folks enjoy a play instead of analyzing it. Perhaps one reason the actors like the gallery so well is that it is largely filled with small boys and they furnish most of the enthusiasm and genuineness of the world anyhow.

Yet, though the gallery is generous, it can also be terribly merciless, and when the gallery gods turn down their thumbs they never revoke their sentence of doom. Last Wednesday night the gallery rose nobly to the occasion. It found itself unable to endure the lovering part of *Faust*. The soul grew sick within it to see such protracted demonstrations of affection by a Faustus who would insist upon always keeping his mouth open and the guileless innocence of a Marguerite who was much older than Faust and more experienced in the ways of the world and who could doubtless have taught him many, many things. After the tenth minute of the twelfth embrace the gallery could stand it no longer, and those mighty ones who dwell on high began violently kissing each other, hundreds and hundreds of them. The reproach was unique and it could have been given by no one so effectively. The gallery deserves universal thanks.

Journal, January 21, 1894, p. 16.

The Highest Kind of Criticism

The question that is now agitating the critics of the two continents and the little island that feels larger than both those continents is, shall a first-night criticism be done on the night of the performance or at the end of the week? The arguments in favor of the latter method are that the critic has time to carefully reconsider his views, correct his judgment and polish his metaphors. If the people want a critic to determine the destiny of a play or to write literature, the weekly method is much the best. But it is very doubtful if the people want that. They want to see something that will speak their own sentiments for them or that will contradict their opinions and give them the satisfaction of defending their position against that blockhead of a critic. Of course a critic cannot always or even often

14. Just where the gallery held its breath at Monte Cristo's announcement is not clear. In James O'Neill's version of the play there are several possibilities (text and pagination are from *Favorite American Plays of the Nineteenth Century*, ed. Barrett H. Clark [Princeton: Princeton University Press, 1943]): Act I: *Dantès*. I would not give this hour of my life for all the riches of Peru [p. 84]; Act II: *Mercédès*. All is fortune and misfortune in this world [p. 85]. Act V: *Dantès*. Ah, Mercédès, we are both condemned in this world [p. 125]. The parallel to "Lay on, Macduff!" is Edmund Dantès' cry before the fight at the end of Act V: "Danglars, your time has come!" and again, "No, for Heaven fights on my side and nerves my arm! I tell you, Danglars, you are going to die" [p. 128].

speak the voice of the multitude. He is only one weak and erring man, who sees more poor plays than are good for him, and is likely to be a little embittered. Neither can he be perfectly fair; he can only be honest. His judgment is faulty, like every other man's; it is influenced more or less by what he had for supper. But the question is, is it not likely to be weakened more by six suppers than by one? Of course a week's consideration must improve the intellectual and critical element of his notice, but ten to one it weakens the emotional element, and that after all is the most precious and volatile element, the one that goes to the hearts of the people. A critic's first instincts are the best because they are the truest. He cannot listen to argument on a point, he must not reason with himself; he must take his impression as he gets it and rush it upon paper. He must take it before it becomes an opinion or freezes into a deduction; while it is an emotion, a feeling, imperfect and half formed perhaps, but living. That is the great object; to have a notice alive, to have the glare of the footlights and the echo of the orchestra in it. The highest art in a next morning's notice is to reproduce to some extent the atmosphere of the play, to laugh if it was funny, to weep a little if it was sad, to say plainly and frankly if it was bad. Some individual notice of the actor is necessary, but even there the object is to reproduce in writing as far as possible the faults or merits which make up his artistic personality. The man who, after last year's season of grand opera in Chicago, said that Nordica was Rhine wine, Eames ice water, Melba champagne, but Calvé was a whole drunk, was as great a critic as Mr. Barron himself. This ability to reflect the feeling, the pitch, the morale of a play has been the secret of the success of all great critics. It is not a matter of judgment, but of sympathy. A morning notice should be an echo of the play, an accompaniment played in the same time and key.

Journal, October 21, 1894, p. 13.

The Journal *Critic*

By the late fall of 1894, word was out that in Lincoln papers, and especially in the Journal, *plays were not so much reviewed as "roasted." For some theatrical companies, Nebraska had become enemy territory. Willa Cather, best of all roasters, defended herself.*

"Does *The Journal* roast every show that comes to town?" inquired an advance man clad in plaid trousers and a waxed moustache. Well, not every one, but most of them, this year. The facts and figures are that fourteen companies have received favorable notice and fifteen rather unfavorable. Even the most enthusiastic play-goers must confess that the theatrical attractions in Lincoln this year have been unusually flat, stale and unprofitable. Last season no one had any reason to complain. There were poor companies here, but there were also good ones. Seabrooke, Robert Mantell, Felix Morris, Frank Daniels, Clara Morris, Julia Marlowe, DeWolf Hopper, Marie Tempest, W. H. Crane, *The Black Crook*, Richard Mansfield and Alexander Salvini all played at the Lansing.[15] Mr. Church deserves very great credit and considerable gratitude from the people of Lincoln for the class of amusements here last year. There is small profit and considerable risk in handling such attractions. But all of these, with the exception of Felix Morris, who was not sufficiently known here, drew crowded houses, and Mr. Church certainly did not lose money on them. With perhaps three exceptions every company that has played at the Lansing this fall has come straight from the Fifteenth Street Theatre of Omaha, where they gave for 50 cents exactly the same performance that Lincoln pays a dollar to see. A critic who has any battered remnants of conscience left cannot avoid "roasting" such companies. It is impossible to pour glowing adjectives and to burn incense to Mr. Gustave Frohman's No. 13 company of boys and girls just out of a western dramatic school. No critic enjoys perpetually "roasting" performances. It grows desperately monotonous after a time. There is a limit to the harsh adjectives in the English language, and it becomes difficult as well as unpleasant, this "roasting" business. But any newspaper that bestows the same exorbitant praise upon a No. 13 *Jane* company that it humbly tenders Richard Mansfield puts itself in a very ridiculous position. There is only one standard of criticism, and that is justice; to pay respectful tribute to what is great, to gladly acknowledge what is good, no matter where it is found, to be gentle to what is mediocre, to be absolutely uncompromising toward what is bad. Charity, friendship, good nature, kindly feelings toward the house or toward the players have nothing to do with it. It is not a question of how great an actor's name is, of what some other critic has said, of what house plays him, of how hard the times are, but of what can this actor do.

Journal, November 18, 1894, p. 13.

15. The following dates all refer to the 1893–1894 season: Thomas Q. Seabrooke, *The Isle of Champagne*, October 23; Robert Mantell, *The Face in the Moonlight*, October 18; Felix Morris, *The Old Musician* and *The Major*, November 6; Frank Daniels, *Little Puck*, November 3; Clara Morris, *Camille*, November 22; Julia Marlowe, *The Love Chase*, February 28; DeWolf Hopper (and Della Fox), *Panjandrum*, April 6; Marie Tempest, *The Fencing Master*, April 3; W. H. Crane, *Brother John*, April 4; *The Black Crook*, April 2; Richard Mansfield, *Beau Brummell*, April 23; Alexander Salvini, *The Three Guardsmen*, May 3.

Six weeks later, Willa Cather again stated the duty of a critic: " The newspapers are supposed to represent, if not discrimination in art, at least self-respecting intelligence and have a right to disparage anything gross and vulgar and to keep the legitimate before the conscience of the people" (January 6, 1895). Perhaps both attacks and defense made a difference, for the Frohman companies noticeably improved in their Lincoln engagements the next month, and when Gustave Frohman himself stopped in Lincoln to see his company, he told Willa Cather in an interview that of course the critic is a benefactor of the stage. He represents artistic conscience, and must have " absolute, fearless and unswerving honesty." The critic, he said (in what must be pretty much Miss Cather's language), " must be always on his guard and never allow himself to lapse into carelessness or good natured pleasantry. If he shuts his eyes to faults once, he will find that accuracy of vision is permanently injured. If he lays aside for a single occasion the robes of his righteousness he will find when he assumes them again that they don't fit him. He has grown too small for them" (February 3, 1895). There was also some disillusionment for the Journal *critic. When she wrote of the Spooners in* The Buckeye, *"a self-respecting little play," she was glad for the adjectives " pleasing" and " acceptable," which one could use " without either raising a cyclone over one's head, or making further inroads upon an already well-worn conscience" (April 26, 1895). By the next year she observed that "critics cannot save a play—any more than they can damn it. In this country the drama is all a big game of chance" (January 12, 1896). But there was always the ideal, which like so many other good things came from France.*

The French Ideal

. . . It is not much wonder that French actors never like to play outside of Paris. Without doubt that is the grand theatre of the world. The very street gamins there have more intuitive knowledge of the drama than the supposedly intelligent people of other lands. The French have a talent for appreciation. In matters dramatic they have an unerring instinct. It is this nicety of the popular taste that makes the present high standard of dramatic criticism possible in France. In other countries the critics and the public are always at war. The honest critic has the public always against him. If he denounces a play the people put the mighty approval of their dollars upon it and it is more than great, it is successful. If he approves of a play ten to one the public find it stupid. But in France the critic and the public pull together; that is why they make only great plays and permit only great actors over there. Every man is a critic; his judgment is crude but just. Sarcey only says what all other Frenchmen think. Small marvel that French actors like French critics. Their critics are worth respecting, worth listening to, even. They understand perfectly all the technique of the drama, all the vocal and physical possibilities and perfections of the actor. They know where training stops and art begins, where the imitative verges into the creative, where endeavor becomes inspiration, where talent becomes genius. In America the critic is a sort of useless attaché of the press, at war with the stage, who is supposed to be flippant or gushing, as occasion demands. In Paris he is the mainstay and safeguard of the theatre, pronouncing just and wise judgments upon dramatic art, respected even by the people he condemns.

Journal, June 16, 1895, p. 12.

A ROUND OF REVIEWS

Reading the reviews of plays in the three seasons Willa Cather worked as a drama critic in Lincoln, one can sit somewhere in the world of fact but feel the real theatre, see real people out of another time—all fragmentary, of course, in glinting moments mixed and dreamlike. Sometimes the actors rise out of the language like figures on a stereopticon slide, in three dimensions of arrested motion, but arrested only a bright moment before they blend again into the color of the passing show. Perhaps even more vivid is the sense of someone real on this side of the footlights, absorbed into splendor or, on a bad evening, thrown back on her own irreverent resources. The reviews which follow (most of them excerpts) are only brief samplings from those Willa Cather wrote, often in haste, for tomorrow's paper. In most cases the routine opening is omitted (there are, after all, just so many ways to say "Last night at the Lansing"), as well as brief notices of minor actors, and details of the story (" The plot is soon told"). These accounts, taken together with the Shakespeare reviews on pages 286 ff. give a fair view of what one saw in the western theatre of the mid-nineties.

Clara Morris in Camille

Before playing in Camille, *Clara Morris had appeared in Lincoln in two other works adapted from the French: Sardou's* Odette *on January 15, 1891, and Belot's* L'Article 47 *on January 16, 1893. She was well known as a " suffering" actress of the French " emotional school."*

Nothing can be more natural than nature, more lifelike than life. There are heights beyond which even art cannot rise. Comment upon the wonderful power of Clara Morris' voice, upon the technical perfection of her acting are utterly unnecessary. One may comment upon excellencies of average acting, but when we find a perfect individual creation, we accept it as unquestioningly as we accept nature's work, and upon it we build a whole philosophy of art. To criticize the way in which Clara Morris dies in *Camille* would be as impertinent as to criticize any real death. One can only say of perfection that it is perfect; we have no adjectives which go any higher; we can only try to see what the great artist does with this creation of hers, and perhaps how she attains her perfection.

Clara Morris' acting certainly cannot be placed in the same class or viewed in the same light as that of Modjeska and Julia Marlowe in

Shakespearean productions. One is the high appreciation and complete sympathy with the great works of a great master, the other is a medley of passions and emotions so great, so boundless that even the most emotional plays of the most emotional age can scarcely give them room to vent themselves. Clara Morris acts by feeling alone. One can see her gestures and poses have never been practiced before a mirror. Sometimes they are almost grotesque in their violence, and her body writhes as though it were being literally torn asunder to let out the great soul within her.

Camille is an awful play. Clara Morris plays only awful plays. Her realism is terrible and relentless. It is her art and mission to see all that is terrible and painful and unexplained in life. It is a dark and gloomy work that has been laid upon more geniuses than one.

But after all is said there is so little said where so much is felt, so much reverenced. There is the terrible scene with Monsieur Duval, the last kiss upon Armand's forehead which was pure as a wife's, holy as a mother's, and the last embrace which was restrained, which are beyond all words, which we can only remember and shudder and suffer at the memory. Men cannot say where art gets its beauty, where power gets its strength. The greatest perfection a work of art can ever attain is when it ceases to be a work of art and becomes a living fact. Art and science may make a creation perfect in symmetry and form, but it is only the genius which forever evades analysis that can breathe into it a living soul and make it great.

Journal, November 23, 1893, p. 5.

The Signed Reviews

Each of Willa Cather's two signed reviews in the winter of 1893–1894 was published in the "Amusements" column of the Journal, *along with another more routine account of the same play, signed "S. J. P." The "W. C." note on Royle's* Friends *is an additional comment rather than a full evaluation; the review of Mortimer's* Gloriana *is more nearly complete. During the previous season* Friends *had played on January 24–25, 1893, and* Gloriana *on February 6, 1893. (See also the later review of another performance of* Friends, *page 272.) The titles of the two reviews given below are those used originally in the* Journal.

Friends is Purely Ideal

After the omnipotent public has spoken and spoken as loudly and enthusiastically as it did last night, very little is left to say. The work of the actors was so admirable that if much were said even a cynical critic would become as enthusiastic as did the audience, and enthusiasm is forbidden a critic. The play dealt with a situation that has been the temptation and tantalization of playwrights ever since Damon and Pythias and David and Jonathan set the idea going. *Friends* seems to be one of the strongest, perhaps the strongest drama that has ever been written on the subject. The only trouble with Mr. John Paden, Jr., and Mr. Adrian Karje is that they are too sweetly sentimental on each other. The great virtue of friendship is to keep itself to itself; if it imparts itself gratuitously to the unhappy object of affection it ceases to become friendship and becomes a bore. The delightful part about a sentimental friendship is that it can never have the pleasure of arresting its existence unless it wishes to be hopelessly and forever crushed. It is strange anyway that in this day of the world, when the individual is so loudly asserting his mightiness, any one should write a drama on one man's loving another man better than himself. It is a beautiful idea, perhaps, but it does not exist outside of girls' boarding schools. The advance notices state that Mr. Royle has planted his flower in the fresh soil of youth. We can agree that Mr. Royle has done an excellent job in his horticulture, but Mr. Royle's flowers are things of the past, like orange blossoms, and are so delicate that today even the "fresh soil of youth" cannot support them. The soil of youth today is careful as to its crop, and there is not money enough in flowery friendship. The fact is, we all love ourselves very much more than we do any other being on earth. We like other people as they administer to our vanity or amusement. If there is any deluded soul who does not believe he is the most charming and gifted man on earth, and who loves another man better than himself, I should like to see him; he is dangerous to society—or would be, only the other man never likes back. W. C. [*Journal*, December 14, 1893, p. 6]

Even the Servants Were Ideal

It is hard to say anything about *Gloriana* until one has got over the effects of laughing at it, and unfortunately one doesn't get over the effects of laughing at it until it is entirely too late to say anything. In this age of the world no playwright has audacity enough to attempt tragedies; everyone writes comedies. The author of *Gloriana* seems to have been more successful than most of his contemporaries because he has been more modest. He has made his cast a small one, but he has made every character unique. There are no parts written to fill up space or to set other parts off to advantage. Every character was created, developed and acted for itself. Mr. Mortimer has put some of his best work on the servants.

The conventional stage ladies' maid has become so trite that in these days she is taken for granted to possess remarkable personal charms or a make-up box of the first quality; it is seldom that an opera glass is raised in her direction. Certainly Miss Barnum as Kitty overthrew all one's ideas of ladies' maids. She resorted to neither personal charms nor bewitching grace, she had recourse alone to art and costume. Her realism was relentless, often cruel. That realism which calls up the shuddering memories of one's old housemaids is infinitely more brutal than that which recalls the sobs of old sweethearts or the pangs of one's first love.

Mr. Alf Hampton as Spinks lingers in one's memory. His lower jaw is, if natural, a gift from heaven; if artificial, an achievement of genius. His English dialect was a revelation. "Never man spake like this man before," especially the "Ow-w-w!" There is no reason why the heavy valet should not be as great a figure as the heavy father or the heavy villain.

The pleasant sense of novelty that one gets from the play is largely due to the character of Count Evetoff. The Russian has been introduced into English novels with great success, but this is his first appearance in English comedy and it is a new thing under the sun, or, what is infinitely rarer, behind the footlights. The Russian type is largely exaggerated, of course, but one goes to the theatre to see exaggerations if only they are neatly done. Moreover, the character of the count presents a new kind of dialect, and an altogether new shade of complexion and necktie, which are advantages that cannot be overestimated. W. C. [*Journal*, January 10, 1894, p. 6]

Plays with Craigen and Paulding

Maida Craigen as Lady Anne and Frederick Paulding as Henry VI had been with Thomas Keene's production of Richard III *(in Lincoln last on November 22, 1892). In their own company during the 1893–1894 season, they gave several performances at the Lansing: in Paulding's own play,* A Duel of Hearts, *on February 19; in two short plays,* The Setting of the Sun *and* The Dowager Countess, *on February 20; in* Romeo and Juliet *on March 12; and in* The Duel of Hearts *again on March 13, 1893.*

This is Miss Craigen's first starring season, but it is safe to say that it will not be her last. Artists of her stamp can lead more easily than they can follow. Few people would have recognized in the Lady Stanhope of last evening the actress who rather indifferently supported Keene last year. Miss Craigen has, in addition to the emotional faculty of a great actress, the power of control and composure which is remarkable in so young an actress. Most emotional actresses are so eager to show that they can be emotional that they begin their emotion in the first scene of the first act and continue in a straight course of methodic misery. Miss Craigen does not allow emotion to touch her in the first act, though in the scene with Louie she has opportunities to be melancholy that most actresses would give their eyes for. No one, not even on the stage, can be uplifted and transfigured by emotion until he or she has battled stubbornly against it. The great actor's tact and temptation is in repressing his emotion and keeping it under. He must always tame his highest flights and tone his loudest cries just as a litterateur must cut out the passages that are dearest to him. An actress cannot afford to be much more emotional on the stage than she would in a drawing room. Miss Craigen fights her emotional instincts for the first act and a half nobly, then the reaction sets in and great emotions, with all their benedictions of power, are hers. Miss Craigen is beautiful, but she reverses the usual order of theatrical impressions. She strikes you first as an actress, then as a beautiful woman. Her work in the insane scene was not so finished as that of the great Clara, but neither was it so painful. It is a question just how far realism ought to go in stage insanity, perhaps Morris might be better with a little less, Miss Craigen with a little more. However, the play might have made her insanity of such a very peculiar kind that perhaps the usual symptoms of insanity won't fit it. One longs to see Miss Craigen in a stronger play than *The Duel of Hearts*, in *Camille* or *Fédora* or something that would more fully test her power. She undoubtedly has a great future before her, for she has all those hundred spontaneous, unthought of little touches that are so much greater than the great things, and above all she has that power of moving and melting for which we can forgive and forget so much.

Mr. Frederick Paulding was Keene's leading man last year. The only fault anyone had to find with him was that he did not play the role of Richard III. Mr. Keene's mantle has certainly fallen upon very much broader and shapelier shoulders than his own. How Mr. Paulding could have played a whole season with Keene and still be the conscientious, rantless, self-respecting actor that he is, is the great wonder. That he remained uncontaminated is sufficient proof of his strength and intelligence. One would need strong superlatives to say how much better he is than Keene. That quiet, restrained anguish of his in the last act will not be soon forgotten by any of us. He sang like a good fellow, loved like a gentleman and suffered like a man. Indeed a quieter, decenter, better behaved pair of stars have not struck Lincoln for a long time, and we hope they will come soon again, for we are sick of this ranting, tearing "power" that can't even behave itself, much less move men and women to great emotion. Goethe said, "The highest cannot be spoken." Thank heaven it can't be and blessed are the actors who do not try.

Journal, February 20, 1894, p. 2.

. . . It gives one almost personal pain to see artists dabble in roles that are too little for them; it is even worse than seeing the very little Davids try to carry Saul's armor. Miss Craigen could do very little in *The Setting of the Sun*, because there was very little to be done. Somewhere in literature it has been said that you can't gather figs from thistles, neither can you gratuitously bestow figs upon thistles. An actor cannot put into a part greatness that does not belong there, and the actors last evening were too truly artists to attempt to. If Booth and Bernhardt were in the leading roles with Barrett and Mrs. Siddons and all the other mighty dead to help them out, *The Setting of the Sun* would still be hopelessly flat.

Journal, February 21, 1894, p. 3.

She

[Edward] Barbour's dramatization of Rider Haggard's *She* was presented to a weary and yawning audience at the Lansing Theatre last night. The play opened with a prologue in which the first Kallikrates, the "Original Jacobs" vacillated between the wily Egyptian and the Queen of Kor, and in which Amenartas stood pleading for the effervescent affections of her husband, who, when under Ayesha's charms, resembled butter that is subjected to the influence of solar rays. Finally the susceptible priest died from too much affection. The ladies, after a good deal of cursing, disappeared and at last the prologue was over. After an interval of one thousand four hundred and forty years the curtain rose again upon some very illegitimate and uncalled for comedy. When the reincarnation of Kallikrates appeared it was not hard to believe that he had lived for some hundreds of years. He showed traces of wear and looked as though after he quit the pulpit he spent most of his time acting in melodrama. Mr. Edwin Browne was an insufferable cad last night; in the prologue he was a Greek cad, in the drama he was an English cad, and he was a living illustration that cads are the same the world over. He was corpulent and stagy, he could not even read his lines intelligently. The lines Mr. Barbour meant to be funny this beefy Leo delivers in tones both tragic and tearful.

As to She herself, we saw very little of her. Because of the fearful and wonderful construction of the play she did not appear until the last part of the third act, when she did deign to grace the stage for a few moments. She was quite pretty—when she had her veil on. She likewise was utterly incapable of reading her lines. The only person in the cast who at all, either in make-up or acting, portrayed anything of Haggard's novel was Mr. Fred Summerfield as Horace Holly. He was not offensive. The whole performance was "one barren waste lit by no single star." One sat and longed for the Holdens and high art.[16]

The play is as awful as the people who play it. All the good situations were left out and the unimportant ones made use of. The scene in the catacombs of Kor was omitted and the pot dance treated trivially. A dramatized novel is generally a thing to be feared and distrusted. In this play all the weird suggestions of unknown lands and peoples, of mystery and awful age, of reckless daring and of careless love which lend Mr. Haggard's book its charms are lost. The effect of the performance was to disgust one with the world and make one long for the time

> When the Rudyards cease to Kipling,
> And the Haggards Ride no more.

Journal, April 20, 1894, p. 6.

Uncle Tom's Cabin

Adaptations of Harriet Beecher Stowe's Uncle Tom's Cabin *had been on the boards since 1853, and with various companies and changes of blood-hounds had become a stock attraction of the Lincoln theatres—three separate performances in the year of 1892–1893, for example. That she saw a good many of the Tom shows from childhood on is shown in Willa Cather's 1929 recollections of the early stage. The* Uncle Tom's Cabin *companies, she said, were "the very poorest of all, . . . but even they had living blood-hounds. How the barking of these dogs behind the scenes used to make us catch our breath! That alone was worth the price of admission, as the star used to say when he came before the curtain."[17] The spectacle grew. Advertisements for the performance of November 21, 1893, mentioned "40 people, 3 palace cars | 20 ponies, donkeys and burros | 8 original plantation*

16. A repertory company which played farces and comedies, usually during a week's stay.

17. "Willa Cather Mourns Old Opera House" (see note 1, above).

jubilee singers | A pack of man-eating Siberian bloodhounds, including Ajax,
the $5,000 championship beauty | Eva's golden chariot, costing $3,000.
Uncle Tom and his typical southern ox-cart. Two bands of music." Next
fall came the Rusco and Swift Company for a performance on September
29, 1894. Their advertisement read: "The acme of all such organizations,
introducing the only barefooted Topsy in the world, the prize pony of the
world's fair, the Egyptian donkey, imported expressly, and the prize-
winning silver cornet band. Street pageant at high noon." Perhaps in 1929
Willa Cather recalled their performance, and what she wrote about it.

The Rusco & Swift *Uncle Tom's Cabin* company played that classic
drama at the Lansing last night. All *Uncle Tom's Cabin* companies are bad,
this being one of the worst. The companies who play the immortal
production are usually made up of mongrel nondescript actors, a very
sleepy and sometimes very pretty little girl, and a few hungry-looking
curs that have become stage-struck and have left the ordinary walks of
life, cultivated a tragic howl and seek for glory on the histrionic boards.
These stage-struck dogs are peculiar creatures and are very much like all
other actors. They are generally of plebeian extraction, as their color, in
spite of all their paint and "make-up," always shows. On the stage they
are very fierce and courageous, but behind the flies they whine about the
manager with their tail between their legs and patiently submit to the
caresses of the soubrette. They are vain in the extreme and will go without their bone to wear a silver collar. They are pitiably fond of praise and
pitiably sensitive to censure. If the transmigration theory is true, then
surely in their previous incarnation these dramatic dogs wore checked
trousers and a red tie and diamonds and walked the Rialto.[18]

   Uncle Tom's Cabin is old, older than almost any other play, because
it never had enough vitality in it to keep it young. In point of construction
it is about the poorest melodrama on the American stage, and that is
saying a good deal. From a literary point of view the play is like the book,
exaggerated, overdrawn, abounding in facts but lacking in truth. The

18. A charming companion-piece for this vignette on the stage dog is the child Willa's
earliest signed and preserved essay, a pencil-written "debate" entitled "Dogs" which was
kept in the papers of her friends the Gere sisters and printed in part in *The World of Willa*
Cather, p. 196, and note, p. 254. Some of the sentences of "Dogs" have that recognizable
rhythm: "The nature of most dogs is kind, noble and generous, O! how different from the
snarling, spitting crul cat. . . . Did you ever see a tall massive dog with curly hair bright
eyes and a knowing air? Did you ever see a poor thin scrragy cat, with dirty hair dull
green eyes and drooping tail. If so I leave it to your common sense to answer for I know
you will say the noble majestic dog."

work of a woman who sat up under cold skies of the north and tried to write of one of the warmest, richest and most highly-colored civilizations the world has ever known; a Puritan blue-stocking who tried to blend the savage blood of the jungle and the romance of Creole civilization. The play is like the whooping cough or the measles, an experience that must be gone through with some time, and it is least painful in extreme youth.

The Rusco & Swift company is made up of an Uncle Tom who suffers from obesity, who also doubled for George Harris; an Eliza with a painful nasal twang, who also doubled for Miss Ophelia; a very wishy-washy St. Clair, a little Eva who was really very pretty and natural, and a very disgusting Topsy who wore her dresses above her knees and who must have been reading *Trilby*, as her feet and legs were very insufficiently clothed by a thin coat of black paint. I never realized until last night why Mr. Du Maurier's novel was immoral or what evil influence it could have, but that Topsy opened every eye. It is said that after the appearance of Rose in *Robert Elsmere* [by Mrs. Humphry Ward] all the young ladies in society at once began to play the violin. Now, if all the young ladies in society should begin to imitate Trilby's noted peculiarity in the matter of footwear, it would make matters awkward indeed. No, the shoe dealers cry out against the immorality of Trilby.

With these talented actors the play went along in the usual manner. Eliza crossed the river on floating ice to slow music, George Harris shot off a blank cartridge at the slave trader, Eva read Uncle Tom words of hope and comfort about the new Jerusalem out of a city directory, and promptly at 9:45 little Eva expired, and not being interested in funerals I departed.

Journal, September 30, 1894, p. 2.

Robert Downing *in* The Gladiator

Robert Bird's romantic tragedy The Gladiator *had been given before in Lincoln, September 3, 1892, with Robert Downing wearing the Roman fighting costume. He appeared again in* Virginius *on November 29, 1893 (see page 123).*

It is the most unpleasant task in the world to condemn or even to disparage any honest artistic endeavor. It is a most difficult task to disparage a performance in which there is no radical error, but which fails only in that it attempts the sublime and never reaches it, because it deals with great themes and yet never uplifts the audience by one thrill of trans-figuring emotion. An actor's impersonation may be good and yet be very far from great. It may please the eye and the ear, and yet never get any nearer to the soul, never penetrate the flesh and reach the spirit. In many ways Mr. Downing is admirably fitted for the role of Nero [Spartacus?], the Gladiator. His strength of voice and power of gesture and even his somewhat too robust physique are perfectly in harmony with the part. Mr. Downing gave a very conscientious rendering of the play last night. His first scene was perhaps his best. There he maintained much of the repose of tone and manner which characterized him when he traveled as Mary Anderson's leading man years ago, when greater things were hoped of him than he has ever achieved. His reading of many of his lines was strong and self-contained. His "Oh to crush the universe" was powerful by reason of its hopeless quiet. But Mr. Downing is no more a great tragedian than he was last year, or the year before. The best part of his career lies behind him. Just wherein he fails no one can say. Tragedy is a dangerous undertaking. There is seldom more than one tragedian in a generation. There is holy ground even in the theatre, and Mr. Downing cannot enter upon it because, like the sons of Aaron, he carries in his censer only earthly fire. No one can say why a man with everything in his favor has not commanding greatness, any more than they can say why a man with everything against him has it. Science has never told us the origin of genius.

Miss Eugenie Blair appeared as Neodamia. Miss Blair has an un-usually beautiful face, though she is growing rather stout and she has a most unfortunate pose of the head. Miss Blair does not rise to an emotion; she tumbles slouchily into it. Her intonation was at times moving, but her acting has the same willowy droop as her head and shoulders. No matter how classical her robes, Miss Blair is always a comfortable modern matron. There is nothing exalted or spiritual in her love, and it utterly lacks passion. She has neither the fine dignity nor the coarser emotions both of which are so necessary to a tragedienne. She is limited to the mediocre. Her love is the sort that might make a comfortable fireside, but cannot made a great tragedy. Her caresses made up in length and duration what they lacked in fervor. Her religion lacked the same intensity and exaltation as her love. The conflict between the higher aspirations of the soul and the human yearnings of the flesh which made the slave girl's sacrifice she did not bring out at all because she felt neither. She simply turned her emotion on and let it run and it came in a placid and untroubled streamlet. She never loved at all, she was simply sweet and affectionate.

Journal, October 2, 1894, p. 3.

Another Friends

When Mr. Royle first brought his new play out in New York several years ago, it was feared that the general public were not sufficiently interested in the private life of artists and singers to care for a play whose scenes were laid entirely within the coasts of Bohemia. But the public is interested in any play that is warmly human, whether it deals with artists or artisans. What saves Mr. Royle's play is that it is a play of action, not of epigrams, that his men and women are something more than wits. The construction of *Friends* is by no means faultless, the fainting scene is incongruous and done by any less gifted artist than Selina Fetter would be ineffectual. The last act is rather weak, and instead of being a climax is a decided descent. Karje's blindness is uncalled for and very stagy. But we can forgive bad construction on the American stage just now, because we have so little but construction. *Friends* gives us some large generous emotion and that by far outweighs any little flaws that it may have. It deals not with the transient evils of the world, but with the lasting good. It has not escaped from a hospital or a French dissecting table.

It has no purpose, moral or immoral, beyond being a good play, and it exalts emotion instead of analyzing it or sneering at it. The rather sentimental nature of the masculine friendship may be a little strained and unnatural, but it at least only belies nature by making it better than it is, which is rather refreshing in these days when most of the lying is done the other way.

The success of the play is very largely due to the talented woman who plays the leading role. Selina Fetter's work is always good. Indeed, her powers have scarcely opportunity to appear in their full scope in the character of Marguerite Otto. She is an exceptionally graceful and womanly actress and is capable of deep feeling. Bits of acting like that burst of sobbing at the piano are worth seeing and pleasant to remember. The second act is particularly her own, and she makes the conflict between the woman and the artist plausible and moving.

Mr. Henderson and Mr. Royle seem to improve as the years go on. They are less sentimental in their friendship than they were last year and have discontinued several fond embraces. They are all the better for it. Mr. Royle, particularly, now makes a strong and sustained distinction between sentiment and sentimentality.

Journal, November 6, 1894, p. 8.

Yon Yonson

Dialect comedies like Yon Yonson, *even with type characters, were interesting to westerners, who were much aware of national differences and immigrant peoples.* Yon Yonson *had been given previously on November 12, 1892, and on January 3, 1894 (the latter review signed "H. B.").*

The play *Yon Yonson* is not at all a bad one. While the plot is not new, it is a plot and it hangs together. The play tells a simple connected story without any dodgings of the corners. It was written by a man with some brains, a fair knowledge of the technique of the drama and a perfect insight into Swedish character.

Mr. [Gus] Heege's Yon can properly be dignified by the title of an impersonation. Apparently the raw man from Sweden is the only kind of character that he can handle, but that is neither here nor there, for he certainly can do that with success. He is the ordinary everyday Swede that we find all over the west. He plays the part truthfully and with consistent stolidity, without poetic or sentimental ornamentation. His Swede is slow to speak and quick to act, with more strength of arm than cleverness of tongue. He preserves perfectly the phlegmatic calm, unbroken by one gleam of enthusiasm, characteristic of those northern nations.

Journal, January 12, 1895, p. 6.

The Black Crook

Before The Black Crook *came to town in 1895, Willa Cather had written in her Sunday column of the once famous, now destitute Pauline Markham, who had starred in the play in "that glorious age of unlimited beauty and champagne," when New Orleans flung orange blossoms and diamonds in her path and she was loved by the learned Richard Grant White, "the scholar's lamp burning cheerfully among the footlights" (Journal, January 20, 1895). The Black Crook, like Pauline Markham, had been beautiful and prized when it opened at Niblo's Theatre in New York in 1866—a fantasy with spectacular transformations, scenery of great splendor, music, a ballet, a Faustian story (an alchemist who bargained with the Devil), and Gothic characters like Count Wolfenstein, Red Glare, and Dragonfin. But*

[273]

the real point was that The Black Crook *was a shocker: it had put on the stage for the first time a ballet of chorus girls with very scanty costumes, an innovation that was both scandalous and irresistible. Once before Willa Cather had commented on the history of the play: "For two years the theatre was filled. The moralist inveighed, the pulpits thundered, but all this served only to advertise the show" (Journal, April 1, 1894). Here she describes the latest Lincoln performance.*

The Lansing has always been singularly free from those performances which a lady cannot witness without displeasure, nor a gentleman without disgust. But accidents will happen in the best of well regulated theatres, and one happened last night. Not that *The Black Crook* itself is half so black as it's painted. O dear, no, it's only a very mild, old fairy tale clad in spangles and silver stars, bathed in calcium lights and lost in a glittering maze of whirling ballet. Unless one has romantic personal reminiscences of the ballet or some member thereof, there is nothing objectionable in *The Black Crook*. But last night's rendering, or rather rending of it, was a thing which it would be pleasant to forget.

In the first place there were the costumes—in spectacular plays they matter rather more than the people who wear them—they were cheap and dirty and much the worse for wear. They were old, old, as old as the women of the ballet, as old as the *Black Crook* itself.

The entire performance was cheapened and vulgarized. It robbed the play of all the hazy, spangled charm that has for years hovered about it. The dancing was done by tall, raw, graceless women, who succeeded in rousing the worst element of the audience, and apparently enjoyed the howls of the drunken negroes in the gallery. The performance was offensive because it was entirely without loveliness of any sort, and in plays of this sort ugliness is wicked—it is immoral.

The only excuse *The Black Crook* ever had for existing at all was that it did in a certain way appeal to the aesthetic instincts. Take away that one redeeming feature of aesthetic emotion and you have left only triviality and vulgarity. Last night the latter greatly predominated. Siren glances are only alluring when they come from sparkling eyes, otherwise they are wearisome, not even naughty, just disgusting.

So this shoddy, cheapened performance with its soiled costumes, jaded women and coarse interludes was once the glorious and triumphant *Black Crook* of the days of Pauline Markham and Lydia Thompson's blondes. The play that papas went to see when they had told their sons to stay at home with mamma, the play that made hundreds of men rich as princes, the play in which Pauline Markham used to be buried in roses and pelted with diamonds. The play which made learned men forget their reserve and old men their years and shrewd men their wisdom. And it has come to this! Well, times change and beauty grows old, and even the *Crook* is faded and tawdry and the "boys" of the '60's are boys no more.

Journal, April 18, 1895, p. 3.

The next fall The Black Crook *came again (October 30, 1895). The* Courier's *theatrical note called it "not at all a bad performance. In fact it was so much better than that disreputable herd that was here last year that it was really a pleasure to see" (November 2, 1895). Portions of the longer* Journal *account of this happier performance make a coda for the April review:*

The Black Crook is regal even in its decay, and even in its age it retains something of the charm which made it once successful beyond the maddest managerial dreams. . . . Of course the play has no justification whatever, save the flutter of spangled skirts, but it's a great old *Crook* just the same, and it's dear to the hearts of the men who were boys in the '60's. The American people lost their heads over it thirty years ago . . . . and the rare and radiant Pauline Markham was petted alike by the diamonds of the wealthy and the epigrams of the learned. It's rather hard for the youths of the rising generation to understand why their papas were so sheepish and so absent minded when the *Crook* is mentioned, but we will take their word for its ancient charm and the woodmen must spare this tree for the sake of the rosy past and of the ballet that was.

Journal, October 31, 1895, p. 2.

The Spooners *in* Inez

A family repertory company which played stands of a week or more in Lincoln, the Spooners were well known there and generally well received. They were better than the Dime Musée, but did not offer the kind of entertainment a reviewer would ever take very seriously.

The springtime and the Spooners have come again. The appearance of the Spooners about this time has become so regular that it might be hailed as the "Approach of Spring," with Edna May Spooner as Spring,

Cecil Spooner as a cherub, Mollie G. Spooner as Nature and B. S. Spooner as Father Time. The very sight of those Spooner bills suggests to all right-minded men a spring suit and a straw hat. Every year we see those bills just about the time we are changing off from whisky to beer *Inez*.

Last night they played to standing room at the Funke. It was a very solid audience, made up of people who do not go to the theatre very often, and how they did enjoy it. After all they are the people who really enjoy. Their pleasure is never marred by discrimination and it makes up in intensity what it lacks in comprehensiveness. They are not fazed by technicalities. So long as the lines of the play deal in virtue, patriotism and justice, the enraptured hearers are not dampened by the fact that they are spoken with a decided nasal tone and that they have been said several thousand times before.

The plot of *Inez* had all the features requisite for touching that highly susceptible organ, the popular heart. There is a Yankee whose business is apparently to go about the world protecting female virtue, generally a rather thankless and unremunerative occupation. While he is practicing his profession in Mexico he meets Inez, the dancing girl, who is beloved by Francisco, a sergeant, also by Don Florez, his captain. Inez, after the manner of all heroines, prefers the poorer man. The sergeant quarrels with his captain and is sent to prison. The captain bestows diamonds upon Inez, but she flings them in the dust and cries, "I despise, I defy you!" in tones that would cut a hotel beefsteak. Dancing girls always have such an aversion for diamonds, you know.

Then the captain has her carried off to his villa in the proper fashion and surrounds her with luxury, which in this case consisted mostly of numerous highly colored soft pillows. The obliging American releases Francisco from prison, and they arrive at the villa just in time to prevent Inez from cutting herself with a sharp little dagger while she calls upon heaven to "protect me honor." In the last act of course the good were rewarded and the guilty were punished.

The Spooners have most firm belief in the ultimate triumph of virtue. They not only see that it triumphs, but triumphs with a blare of trumpets.

Between the second and third acts Cecil did some very acceptable dancing. She has a trim little figure and can wear a coat and trousers with an air. Her dancing in boy's clothes is easy and graceful. In skirts she is sometimes a little jerky in her movements, but there is no doubt that Cecil can dance. Edna May's voice still preserves its old indescribable indistinctness. At a late hour, the audience, having certainly got their money's worth, gathered up their babies and chewing gum and feather fans and departed.

Journal, April 23, 1895, p. 5.

Roland Reed in The Politician

The Politician was a play written and acted by Roland Reed (also a comedian familiar to Lincoln audiences). The Journal *review said of him: " Mr. Reed is made for a politician. He is always a good deal of a farceur and farceurs are at home in politics. His brusqueness, that sometimes jars just a little in other roles, is particularly fitting in General Limber, and it is a pity that a man who can wear the corners of his mouth as Mr. Reed can should have been lost to politics." As usual, the later* Courier *review has the same point of view but discusses different subjects.*

It is strange that men will write burlesques when they might write comedies, and that they prefer to build upon the sand when the rocks are so many that one is always in danger of stumping his toe on them. *The Politician* is a good farce, much better than the run of them, but the same material refined and dignified by a little of that saving quality, the truth, would have made a comedy that would outdraw and outlive all the farces of the generation. Suppose, for instance, that something of the tone and quality of *The Senator* were given to it. Suppose that General Limber were made a possible character, a fellow considerably warped by the elevating methods of nineteenth century politics, but with humanity enough left to fall in love right in the middle of an exciting campaign; a humorist who dabbled in corruption with a sort of cynical indifference and an artistic appreciation of the situation. He might have been quite a man under those circumstances and above the game he played. When John T. Raymond played the same role years ago under the title *For Congress*, he put more of that spirit into it.

Suppose too that Miss Cleopatra had been made a possible new woman, such a one as would not be certainly taken up by the police, and just enough "advanced" to escape the patrol wagon. A real woman, but an undeveloped one and with all the disturbing impetus of new ideas, bicycles and bloomers. What a chance for a character actress of the dashing sort! The only question is, if this sort of change were made in the play, would it not be just a little beyond Mr. Reed's grasp and an inch or two over Miss Rush's blonde head? I fear so.

All the minor characters are the same in general tone. When "Sister" entered I drew a hopeful sigh and speculated upon the chances of an oasis; her appearance warranted it, but no. In the theatre hopes are born only to be dashed, and mine did not survive "Sister's" flirt scene. "Sister" was not the gentlewoman whose illusions and complexion were marvelously preserved by fifty years of country life. She was the same old spinster of the farces, disguised a little by a white wig. Sometimes she wears a red wig and sometimes a yellow one and sometimes little curls that bob about her face. But she is ever the same in all ages and all climes, and no disguise can ever remove her loathsomeness.

The most redeeming feature of the farce was that ensemble scene at the end of the third act when Limber returned from the convention hall attended by the brass band, and Cleopatra mounts a chair exultingly waving a banner and Mike wraps the fainting and exhausted form of Peter Wooley in the American flag. That is a spirited scene and someway it makes one remember for the minute the excited admiration he used to feel when he followed the flambeaux clubs through the streets, when the horns tooted and the rockets hissed and the sparks flew.[19]

Courier, September 7, 1895, p. 8.

Variations on Faust

In Lincoln theatres of the nineties, a dramatized Faust *was almost as familiar as* Uncle Tom's Cabin. *A particularly interesting series of performances in 1894 and 1895 began with Lewis Morrison's version of the play ("Morrison's Faust") on January 17, 1894. That was the night the gallery rose in protest (see page 257). In the spring, Manager Ed Church of the Lansing organized another company starring John Griffith ("Griffith's Faust," which was based on the old Henry Irving adaptation). This company, too, played around the country and gave a number of performances in Lincoln. In the* Journal *and the* Courier *together there are a dozen or more reviews and articles about the* Faust *plays in this period. Not all of the reviews are Willa Cather's work. Some are too scholarly—that of March 25, 1894, is signed by Laurence Fossler, a German teacher at the University; others, especially that of May 11, 1894, are too fatuous, obviously puffs for "Griffith's Faust." In the reviews that can be identified as hers, we catch vivid glimpses of actors and scenes. The Mephisto in "Morrison's Faust"*

19. "Political rallies were marked by torchlight parades. The marchers carrying torches wore rubber capes to protect them from sparks." Louise Pound, *Nebraska Folklore* (Lincoln: University of Nebraska Press, 1959), p. 189.

*(an expurgated adaptation, she complained) had "a properly malignant face
and his acting was forcible save for a species of giggle which seemed intended
for demoniac laughter." The lighting effects in the Brocken scene were so
thrilling that "the play seems to be a grand substitution of electricity for
ethics and red lights for dramatic art" (Journal, January 18, 1894). But
Morrison was to be outdone by the Griffith company. The advance notice
(May 5, 1894) promised a scale of grandeur seldom witnessed, plus the
Nuremberg choir. The "Revel on the Brocken" is "a marvel of stagecraft"
with its flashes of electricity and showers of fire. The difference between
Willa Cather's reviews and all others is strikingly shown in two accounts
of this new production of Faust. According to the review on May 11, 1894,
Olive Martin was "a beautiful and enchanting Marguerite," whereas when
the company returned in the fall, Willa Cather in her September 16 Sunday
column described Miss Martin as "an ungainly Amazon," and hoped that
Griffith's coming performance in Chicago would help the ranting Devil find
repose. She wrote again about Griffith a year later.*

Griffith's *Faust* opened at the Lansing last night to a limited house.
Manager Church has really improved the company a great deal. With
the exception of Mr. Griffith himself the cast is entirely new, and in almost
every case the new people are better than the old, that is in every case but
one. Mr. Lyman is a better Faust than the company has ever had before.
In the first and third acts he really displayed considerable force. Of course
in the second act, the garden scene, he was simply ludicrous, but that was
largely the fault of the scene itself. What man could do that scene and keep
his dignity? It goes well enough in the opera, but in the play it makes one
of the stupidest and most monotonous of all love scenes. There is absolutely no action, no obstacle to overcome, nothing to call out great
emotion, no great test, no great temptation. Nothing to do but promenade
and spoon and spoon and promenade around and around that eternal
electric flower bed. It's a sort of "Here we go 'round the gooseberry
bush." As the gallery boys say, it's "soft," and that's all there is to it. This,
with apologies to Goethe.

Miss Winston makes a fair and buxom Marguerite. She acquitted
herself very creditably in that difficult fountain scene.

Mr. Thayer is really a very manly and martial Valentine. He is well
made, has a resonant voice and speaks his lines with understanding. By the
way, he is the only Valentine that company has ever had who has possessed
a beard, real or artificial. All the others have solemnly pronounced the

line, "I sat and stroked my beard," with shaven chins. Of course they might argue that Valentine shaved when he left the army.

Mr. Griffith was not playing up to his best at all last night. Excepting occasional spurts his work lacked enthusiasm and his interest in his lines seemed forced, all of which was natural enough, considering that the audience was as cold as the weather was hot. Mr. Griffith's talents are genuine and stand undisputed, but he drops too often into the colloquial. Freytag[20] said that Mephisto is "a tragic conception treated in a comc vein." Let Mr. Griffith be careful not to treat it in a farcical vein. The humor of the spirit that denies should be quiet, satiric, biting humor, not jocose and good natured. Mr. Griffith has the demoniac abandon, the fury of fiendish hate, more than any Mephisto THE JOURNAL critic remembers having seen. He has a force which will not be overlooked. It is there and one must see it and acknowledge it. But whether he does not sometimes use it capriciously is a question.

Journal, September 11, 1895, p. 8.

I have seen *Faust* until I have sometimes longed for the Damnation of Faust, the musical one by Berlioz of course. It is not the model play of the world to start on. It deals with problems too abstract, too remote. The day has gone by when we delighted in dramas dealing with the strife between Gods and men. In days when there was a stronger belief in the supernatural the play was very well. As for its literary value, any English version produced in this country is so utterly unlike Goethe's original that it is all lost. Then there is that spoonful garden scene and that restive Fourth of July on the Brocken. Two such acts would slaughter any play. And there is Marguerite. I never yet saw a Marguerite whom I did not long and yearn to shake. I always want to lengthen her dresses and teach her to do her hair up on her head. It has always seemed to me that there was not enough of her to make a respectable tragedy. There is in the play one great character, a character unique and apart, Mephistopheles, the spirit that denies. A character as strange as Hamlet and as little understood, always shrouded in mystery and doubt.

The great difficulty in the enacting of such a character is that Mephisto is not mortal. Something must be done to convey the idea of supreme evil, of more than mortal hate. This cannot be done directly. It must be accomplished indirectly and by inference. If a man starts to swearing and

20. Gustav Freytag (1816–1895) was a versatile novelist, playwright, historian, and critic in Germany. His *Technique of the Drama*, translated by Elias J. Mac Ewan (Chicago: S. C. Griggs and Company, 1895), has a discussion of *Faust* and Mephistopheles.

reels off his whole repertoire, curses until he is black in the face, then you know just how much he can swear. But if he mutters only an oath or two and looks the rest you are in doubt. You wonder what he could do in that line if he laid himself out and the chances are you will greatly exaggerate his powers. The actor who plays Mephisto never shows his hand. He should awe his listeners rather than excite them. His power is in his inscrutable mystery.

The only fault that I have to find with John Griffith's Mephisto is that it lacks dignity, awfulness. I should not be afraid of that kind of a devil. His Mephisto is a thoroughly jolly fellow with occasional bursts of very bad temper. He is so jolly that he is humorous even when he is angry. I do not object to the comedy which Mr. Griffith introduces, but to the kind of comedy. It's too good natured, too undignified, the kind of fun one hears among good fellows who are cynical but bear no malice. It should be, I think, a deeper comedy than that, a humor that takes in all the great jests of this world and the next, the whole gigantic joke of the creation. It should be a humor that would make one's blood run cold. Mr. Griffith has such a peculiarly fortunate face for the part that he might leave unsaid much more than he does. If he knew how much his eyes tell, I think he would not strain his voice so. He has intensity enough, but he lets it out too much; as someone has said, like most young artists he wastes that which is most dear. That which, like sentiment, when sparingly used is beyond price, when expended lavishly, vulgar and maudlin.

Courier, September 14, 1895, p. 8.

The Wife

After a somewhat exhausting run of farce-comedy, Gustave Frohman's company in *The Wife* broke the monotony. Anyone who has seen *A Charity Ball* or *Men and Women* has virtually seen *The Wife*. They are more than similar, they are almost identical. Mr. Belasco's work is not to be despised. I have always wished he had written stories instead of plays and had them illustrated by Gibson and published in the *Century* along with Mrs. Burton Harrison's "Bachelor Maid" and "Sweet Bells out of Tune." They would be fitting and proper there and doubtless we would all read them and be greatly edified. That is the kind of literature we want in our periodicals and in our "homes" and all we demand of a national literature is that it shall not injure our "sweet young girls." But just because Mr. Howells and Mrs. Harrison have made American literature a sort of young ladies' illusion-preserver, I should like to see the American stage remain free from any such restriction. The sweet young girls will read, and we must manufacture our literature accordingly; but they need not go to the theatre; instead they can go down to the park and see the animals. Except in comedy, domesticity on the stage is always flat, stale and unprofitable. In fact, it is rather stupid in any art. Mr. Belasco's plays affect me like that touching domestic picture by [Thomas] Hovenden, "Breaking Home Ties." Nym Crinkle says we go to the theatre not to see what is, but what might be. Certainly we go to change our atmosphere, to get for a moment into the atmosphere of great emotions that are forbidden in our lives. I hope that the stage will [keep] its illusions, that the footlights will always be a boundary line beyond which men will deign to feel and dare to love. I want them to be the dead line of the practical. The dress circle, the parquet, the orchestra chairs—that is all the dead world of fact; but right beyond that line of lights are the tropics, the kingdom of the unattainable, where the grand passions die not and the great forces still work;[21] a land of Juliets, Othellos, Theodoras and Marguerite Gautiers. It's the only place on earth they have left now, those great and unhappy ones. They are like Heine's "Gods in Exile." Let them at least have the stage. To exile Narcisse, Mistress Clarkson, Hermione and Ruy Blas and put in their place Robert Gray, Paul Gilmore and Kitty Ives is a mistake, a great one, and it will react upon our heads some day. We will pay for it.

There were some promising young people in *The Wife* company. If Miss Wheeler had half a chance she would be an actress of merit. But she has not had the chance. She was a raw Kansas City girl, who had never even seen any of the greatest acting, put down to hard work just when she should have had time to develop and study. She puts great sincerity and tenderness into her words, but she is utterly crude and even her elocution is faulty. I wish Miss Wheeler had been born further east. Geography is a terribly fatal thing sometimes.

Courier, September 28, 1895, p. 8.

Fleur de Lis

In Willa Cather's signed review of the play The Wedding Day *for the* Pittsburgh Leader *(October 26, 1897), she recalls last seeing Della Fox in the opera* Fleur de Lis *and saying then that the brilliant part of Miss Fox's future lay behind her. The following is her 1896 account of that occasion.*

21. This passage was used in the unsigned article, "The Return of the Romantic Drama," in the *Home Monthly*, November, 1896, p. 12.

In the drama all good things come from France and in light opera a few of them come from the same place. Those Frenchmen carry plots in their vest pockets and they have them to burn. MM. Chivot and Duru are responsible for all that is good in *Fleur de Lis* and that is a very considerable part of it. There are two friends, a marquis and a count of unpronounceable names, and they are so fond of each other that they quarrel from sheer love and for the possession of a duchy of some ancient and defunct relative who left no will. Now when the curtain went up last night and while the lobby of the theatre was still packed with souls belated who were longing to get inside the house, Joseph the count was besieging Joseph the marquis in his castle. At this juncture Fleur de Lis turns up, an unrecognized daughter of the marquis' frisky youth who had been left in Paris until called for. Count Joseph's son sees her, and after the manner of operatic sons becomes affectionate and tuneful. Fleur de Lis is smuggled into the garrison of her father. A touching scene takes place between the reunited parent and Miss Fox in baby clothes, which awakens the dormant paternal instincts of her sire. She devises a means of escape for her father and finally finds the will which bequeaths him the duchy. The music is rather better than is common to light opera and that duo at the end of the first act is tuneful enough.

This opera is fortunate enough to contain an idea and an actor, a character part and a man who can enact it in a manner passing well. A production that introduces such a comedian as Jefferson de Angelis is made. On consideration there is very little of the part itself, its success is all due to the man who plays it. Mr. Angelis has made Joseph, the count, a royal character. One minute he is foaming with rage and the next he chortles in his joy. He alternates between chuckling glee and grinding wrath. From one emotion or the other his face is kept continually red and his elephantine physique continually vibrating. He is an old gentleman with a record, and all this is the actor, not the part. He has just character. He has put into it more spirit and consistency and finish than most men have put upon Falstaff. It is perfect comedy of its kind, consistent rather than exaggerated, and sincere rather than vulgar. . . .

And what shall be said of Della Fox, the ever jaunty, the ever jolly, the ever popular? She is still jaunty, but not so spontaneous; still dashing, but not so vivacious. She has still that funny, despairing vocal squeak, a sort of feminine De Wolf Hopper trick of vocalization, and the part of her that walks, ah, but they are still beautiful! But Della Fox is not the rollicking comedienne she was when she wore a white yachting suit and puffed a cigarette in *Wang*. She is not even what she was in *Panjandrum* three years ago. She is lighter in person, but her manner is heavier and sometimes mirthless. She sang less than ever and worse than ever; half of her numbers were cut out. Her success in comic opera was sudden, complete, glorious—and brief. She is a young actress with a brilliant past.

Journal, March 26, 1896, p. 2.

Richard Mansfield in A Parisian Romance

Willa Cather said in " The Passing Show" (Journal, April 12, 1896) that Feuillet's A Parisian Romance was "a highly unsatisfactory play," thoroughly unpleasant and trite, with characters both too wicked and too good, and a tacked-on last act. But, as always, a play could be redeemed by a master: "The Baron Chevrial was only a minor role until Richard Mansfield made him one of the great characters of histrionic art." The individual talent could always assert its strength.

Said Biff Hall: "There are three kinds of actors—good actors, bad actors, and Richard Mansfield." The last and most desirable kind was seen at the Funke last night. One spends so much time and energy trying to exalt that which is not exalted, and applying that much misused word of three letters to matter to which it does not belong, that when we occasionally come face to face with a real work of art there is very little to say about it. Of its kind it is perfect. He who could tell why or how would be an artist himself.[22] As to Feuillet's play, it is well known. There are four acts of it. That is, there are five acts of the play, but there are only four of Richard Mansfield, and only those count. It is full of concentrated agony, and not a character escapes its due amount of pain. The baron expiates, but he is not the only one who suffers, Henri suffers, too, but in his case it is not called expiation. By the way, Mr. Johnson's Henri suffers remarkably well. In the first act he was all that could be desired. In fact he not only can be miserable on the stage, but he can be happy and sensible and very much in love. Miss Cameron too, was rather at her best in the first act. She was scarcely strong enough to redeem the intrinsic unpleasantness of her part in the last act. Miss Cary made a most noble Madame de Targy, about whom it was easy to believe high things. She wore her life with dignity and her misfortune with courage. There was delicacy of sentiment in her every gesture.

22. Cf. the review of Clara Morris in *Camille*, three years earlier: "One can only say of perfection that it is perfect. . . . we can only try to see what the great artist does" (page 262).

But the man who most concerns the world was the Baron Chevrial. The part is not a pleasant creation, nor, in the limited sense, is it beautiful. It is not "instructive" or "inspiring," there is no exact evidence that it "uplifts and elevates the soul." It is simply art. Most art is useless, all art is without ethics, or if it happens to touch them one way or the other they are incidental effects; they have nothing whatever to do with the primary causes and impulses of artistic creation. The creative laws of art are as merciless, as savage, as blind to human good [as is] nature, their great prototype. The Baron Chevrial of last night was an artistic creation of that rare and perfect sort, so finished, so thorough, so exquisite in detail that they make one remember that the greatness and glory of the drama is not all a dead tradition, that it is worth believing in and working for still. The mere make-up was a work of art. There was that continual pallor that rouge could not hide, that leaden colorless lower lip that drooped when he was fatigued, those eyes that were worse than the eyes of a satyr and those terrible hands with their ceaseless trembling.

What other actor would care enough to keep that exhausting nervous agitation up for more than ten minutes? Mansfield plays all the tragedy there is in this "product of money and civilization." He gives him his due. The people who loathe him most when he mouths over Marcelle's hand at the end of the third act, must have a kind of admiration for him when he staggers up beside the banquet table at his "petit souper" and gasps, "Show the gentleman in." The Baron Chevrial is gruesome enough, but he is no craven. He has his fun and he pays for it, his expiation is terrible enough, but he stays it out. He feels that the game is up, but he sits among the ladies of the ballet and makes no sign. His last [toast?] is to Plutus, "God, whom we all worship," and to material things. Then his face grows whiter still, his hand trembles even more, the wine is spilled, he staggers back in the arms of the little opera girl, and the Baron Chevrial toasts no more. In three minutes this spare, ghastly, tremulous, livid old rake appears before the curtain a portly, elegant and rather florid gentleman, and "Richard's himself again."

Journal, March 29, 1896, p. 5.

SHAKESPEARE ON THE STAGE

Willa Cather was consistently firm about Shakespeare: He was the greatest of all the immortals; and he belonged most humanly on the stage for everyone's imagination, not in the library for scholars. In the same way, her accounts of Shakespearean productions combine what is most lyrical and what is most down to earth in her prose. For specific judgments she had good performances to measure by: in the 1892–1893 season, for example, there had been Thomas Keene in Richard III, *Margaret Mather in* Romeo and Juliet, *Julia Marlowe in* Twelfth Night, *Helena Modjeska and Otis Skinner in* Henry VIII. *She had also thought a good deal about the Shakespearean characters, who seemed to come bodily to the imagination. Hamlet was as real as Shakespeare, as she wrote of him in her 1891 essay, "Shakespeare and Hamlet" (see Appendix I). Juliet should be played with "the lithesome youth Shakespeare meant her to have" (Journal, March 13, 1894). And, she wrote, "We have our own conception of Prince Hal; a youth red of hair, blue of eyes, hot of temper, coarse of tongue, amorous and sensual, but having withal a blunt honesty and sturdy manlihood which lies somewhere at the root of every Englishman" (Journal, August 11, 1895). The person of Shakespeare, too, came vividly alive. He was the one highest genius, whose talent was the mark of God's favor to man, and for this there would be the rituals of devotion in the Kingdom of Art. But the real drama of Shakespeare was that like every god incarnate, he must understate divinity, be the man of least pretentions. When in April, 1894, The Hopkins Trans-Oceanic Specialty Company arrived (with Kara the juggler, Fulgora the great "transfigurator," and the man who played the piano with his nose), she wrote: "Mr. Hopkins' advance notices say it is too bad Shakespeare is dead, he would have enjoyed the Trans-Oceanics so; which statement shows that Mr. Hopkins knows more about the real William than many people who probably read* Hamlet *oftener than he does. However, Shakespeare probably saw lots of Trans-Oceanics in his day and may be having a steady course of them now, for all we know" (Journal, April 27, 1894). The next year in April, near his birthday, she wrote again of Shakespeare the man; and throughout 1895 she had other occasions to note how his plays were going.*

A Man of the Theatre

It will be here again in a few days, that old 23d of April, on which it is written down in the parish record of Stratford-on-Avon that a certain child was born. There has been a movement among some of the leading actors of the world to make that day a fete day in the theatres of all nations, to make it international, so that once a year all the peoples of the earth shall be brought to think of that man who was the emperor of literature. It is just enough that this movement should come from the actors of the world, not the litterateurs, for it is to them that he belongs, not to the world of letters; that is the great and crowning glory of the stage, its one weapon against the jeers of pedantry, its one high and holy tradition, its justification before the eyes of God, that William Shakespeare was an actor, a manager, an usher even. He was not even a good or a great actor, but merely a fellow who had the dramatic instinct and hung around the theatre all his life. Not a particularly learned man and by no means a man of letters. He never knew that he was creating the literature of the future. His merry evenings at the Mermaid's Inn were never spoiled by the knowledge that the greatest savants of all nations would exhaust their wisdom to find the secret of his power. He wrote for the present, for the stage of his own day. He wrote because the theatres needed new plays and because he could construct them easily and rapidly. Some one has said that genius is the art of not taking pains. Shakespeare's genius must have been of that kind—his whole life shows it. It is not likely that he set up a great ideal and struggled to attain it. He wrote easily and carelessly, perhaps between drinks, like Dumas *père*. His best work is no more studied and premeditated than the work of God is. He wrote the truth, and it was therefore beautiful. It is doubtful if the literary excellence of his plays troubled him much. The literary critics who insist that modern actors have not sufficient intelligence to interpret Shakespeare should remember that he wrote, not for the litterateur, but for a stage infinitely lower than ours of today, and for actors infinitely less cultured. All this talk about the degradation of Shakespeare by introducing and producing his plays in modern theatres is rank nonsense. Why, if Shakespeare were alive he would think the Lansing theatre a wonderfully fine house. He would spend days of ecstasy in admiring the drops and scenery of any modern theatre. He would honestly admire much of Sardou and Dumas, and if he were to see La Grande Sarah, well, he would have nervous prostration or something very much like it. No, if Shakespeare should come to Lincoln I do not think he would be found among those occupying a chair in any of the universities. He would probably manage the Lansing, it needs a manager badly enough, heaven knows. Part of the time he would be scribbling plays over in the box office, and the rest of the time he would probably be found over at his namesake's across the street.[23] He would possibly wear plaid trousers and a large cluster of fresh-water diamonds in his tie, just like other managers; he might even wear curly hair. Doubtless the police would run him in occasionally, just as they used to centuries ago. The cultured and the elite and the universities would know nothing at all about him, just as those of his own day knew nothing about him. Then in about two hundred years the savants the world over would begin to make pilgrimages to Lincoln and enter the Lansing on their knees.

Journal, April 21, 1895, p. 13.

Henry IV, *with Frederick Warde and Louis James*

Willa Cather had seen other history plays, but the performance of Henry IV *in January, 1895, was her first encounter with Falstaff and Prince Hal (see her later comments on Verdi's opera* Falstaff, *pages 214 ff.). Frederick Warde and Louis James were well known Shakespearean actors, both in New York and on the road. They had played* Othello *in Lincoln the year before, on April 17, 1893. James had also been seen in a non-Shakespearean role—as Sir Lucius in Joseph Jefferson's production of* The Rivals *on November 30, 1891.*

Frederick Warde and Louis James played *Henry IV* to a good house at the Lansing last night.

For many years Louis James was known only in tragic roles. Recently he has ventured into comedy from time to time, and this season is presenting for the first time his version of the immortal Jack Falstaff, king of Sack and monarch of Boar's Head Tavern.

If Mr. James has ever done such genuine and sustained acting in any

---

23. Lincoln newspapers of July 11, 1893, record the opening of "The Shakespeare," a refreshment cafe on 13th and P Streets, operated by Peter Kuhlman and W. H. Newburg. The Lansing was on the southwest corner of 13th and P Streets, but no directory seems to list the exact location of "The Shakespeare." At the opening on July 10, the interior of polished oak and plate glass was much admired, a German choir of twenty-five voices serenaded Mr. Kuhlman with "a number of joyful symphonies," and there were excellencies like a buffet lunch, Fremont beer, and "a large amount of that peaceful revelry." (See the Lincoln *Evening News* [p. 1] and the *Journal* [p. 6], both for July 11, 1893.) "The Shakespeare" was still popular in the fall of 1894, according to Willa Cather's review of *The Devil's Auction* in the *Journal* of September 28: "It was a glorious audience, downstairs and up. The kind of an audience that wears tuberoses and large canes and migrates between acts. It was a classical audience, the kind that can't stand a specialty performance without something elevating and classical, something Shakespearean from across the street."

other Shakespearean play it would be hard to recall it. There are some of us who were never overly fond of him in tragedy, who found his acting forced and his reading at fault. But as the knight o' the cup he is entirely satisfying. His conception of the part seems to be more naturally pitched than that of many of the Falstaffs of the past. He is coarse without being vulgar and his jollity does not become maudlin. He tempers Sir John's depravity with a certain corpulent courtliness and floods all his weakness with a glowing sunshine of generous good nature. For after all Falstaff was a knight, and had been—when he was thinner, a gentleman.

His one redeeming element was his ever ready, his irrepressible and unquenchable wit which rose smilingly after every rebuff, which could face an irate tavern hostess and stand unawed at the councils of kings.

The question of an actor "subduing his personality" is talked about a great deal more than necessary just now. Mr. James has certainly accomplished that feat to actual perfection. There was absolutely no trace of the tragic actor left in that rotund, rollicking, roistering product of fifty years of wine, women and song who stood before us last night. Mr. James' reading is by no means perfect yet, he halts in his lines sometimes and seems never to have thoroughly mastered Shakespeare's difficult prose.

Frederick Warde is a merry and vigorous Prince Hal. He is especially pleasing in his light and festive days in the first three acts when he fills the days and nights with revelry, knowing well the cares that wait upon the brows of kings. Mr. Warde is too dramatic and too conscious of the audience in his "Yet, herein will I imitate the sun" speech, but jesting with Falstaff he is as merry a prince as one could wish, and in his scene with his father he shows the spirit of his blood.

As for the play, though it holds a high place among the historical plays of Shakespeare, it is by no means one of his best, nor one of the most fitting for modern stage presentation. The masterly treatment of political situations, the wonderful penetration into the character of national heroes which made it mean so much to Englishmen of the days of Elizabeth is largely lost on a nineteenth century American audience.

The wonder is that a play so entirely historical should have any vital interest left at all. How much will be left of a *Shenandoah* or *Held by the Enemy* in three hundred years? One always wonders if the playwright knew, as he stood in the wings of the Globe theatre on his "first nights," that his work would outlive all the stately splendor of the royalty gathered before him. That in history the names of Touchstone and Sir Jack Falstaff would outlive those of dukes and earls, that the regal majesty of his queens should outlive the greatness of Elizabeth and all the glories of the Tudors and the Stuarts, that of all of the kings of England his king alone should have empire without limit, dominion without end.

Journal, January 18, 1895, p. 8.

Playing the Histories

If Willa Cather was very modern in her view of Shakespeare as a man of the theatre, she was also ahead of her time in considering how the history plays might be rearranged for production.

It is a grave question as to just how far the historical plays of Shake-speare are fitted for the modern stage. They were not the product of his highest thought or most spontaneous inspiration. They were written to please his public. The chief merits of the plays are their accuracy and deep understanding of political situations which were still living problems in England, and their echoes of great events with which the world still rang. Think what it meant to an English audience to see their great national history wrought out before them in all the glamour of chivalry, to see their heroes live again and speak to them in that rich sonorous flow of verse. When *Henry VIII* was played there were old men in the audience who had seen Henry himself, who remembered the proud old cardinal and who had been among the throng in Westminster Abbey at the nuptials of Anne Boleyn and the king.

The historical plays undoubtedly made for Shakespeare what little reputation he had in his own day. The tragedies were far above the intelligence of his average listeners. Their masterly treatment of English politics has never been surpassed in all the history of the country, and the greatest political speeches ever made in parliament have taken their texts from the historical plays of Shakespeare. No other nation has such a history as those ten great dramas. Any man might become a writer of English history by reading them. Yet with all their careful accuracy they are redeemed from dullness by the fervor of imagination which Shake-speare gave to all his plays. He took up the history of England in the same way that he took up a romance of Boccaccio, rejecting or amending as he saw fit, for he had within himself the types of truth which were more trustworthy than the chronicles.

All this and vastly more is true of the literary merits of the plays, but that does not at all prove their fitness for stage representation today. To play any one of them in its entirety would be of course impossible, as people do not go to the theatre to spend the night nowadays, for the very good reason that most of them have something to do the next day. Then comes the question of where and how to cut them, upon which scholars and actors differ very strongly. The truth is that as a rule they are not cut nearly enough. In point of construction they are much inferior to all other Shakespearean plays, in fact many of them have very little construction at all. They are merely chapters of English history. The length of the cast and number of characters involved is something formidable. In *Henry VI* there are thirty-five characters, in *Henry V* twenty-nine, in *Richard III* thirty-six and in *Henry VIII* thirty-five, and most of them are, according to our standards, entirely superfluous and inconsequential. In Shakespeare's day people went to the theatre to see a "show" in the most lurid sense of the word. They wanted something spectacular. The more lords and earls, the more suits of velvet and coats of mail, the better. Actors were cheap and it was hard to make the cast large enough. But in these days even poor actors demand $20 a week and a company with a cast of thirty odd would find it rather hard steering.

If the historical plays are to be played in the future, which is very doubtful, they must stand still more rigid amputation. *Henry IV*, as we saw it Tuesday night, has been trimmed down to about the right dimensions, but *Henry VIII* and *Richard III* still need rigorous overhauling. What right has Henry VI to take almost the entire first act of *Richard III* when he is straightway conducted to the tower and never heard of again? What business has Buckingham to take up a whole scene of *Henry VIII* in going to his execution and making his adieu when we know very little of him and care still less?

Journal, January 20, 1895, p. 13.

Cleopatra at the Funke

In the fall of 1895, Lillian Lewis—an actress of national reputation but inexperience in Shakespeare—came to Lincoln during her tour as Cleopatra. Miss Lewis was remembered as the star of a special week of plays celebrating the opening of the Lansing, November 23–28, 1891, a repertory of Credit Lorraine, As in a Looking Glass, *and* L'Article 47. *When Lillian Lewis played in* Antony and Cleopatra *on October 22, 1895, Willa Cather wrote at length about the performance.*[24] *The whole affair—cn stage and*

24. That Willa Cather wrote both the *Journal* and *Courier* pieces (and evidently with relish) is apparent in the style and comment. But as an example of interlocking identifications, there is also the give-away misspelling of the river Cydnus in the *Journal* piece. Miss

in print—can only be called a tour de force *in high jinks and low comedy. One of the differences between actress and critic, of course, was that Miss Cather knew what she was doing. But however low the work of Shakespeare had fallen through Miss Lewis's benighted handling, it was made of such stern stuff that one could take the shattered* Cleopatra *and return it, whole again, to the imagination.*

The serpent of old Nile uncoiled at the Funke last night before a large and amused audience. While the text was considerably mutilated in places, still the general outline of the play was recognizably Shakespearean. The fortune telling scene was put first and after that a barge drew up and from it descended a large, limp, lachrymose "Kleo-paw-tra," with an Iowa accent, a St. Louis air and the robust physique of a West England farmer's wife. This ponderous personage descended from the barge and perching upon the back of a stuffed tiger somewhat moth-eaten she began gleefully coquetting with Mark Antony, recently of Rome, whom she occasionally called "Me Anthony," which showed that she had been reading *The Prisoner of Zenda*.

Mark Antony, impersonated by Edward Collier, was the only piece of legitimate acting in the whole production. In spite of a decided tendency to continually declaim and fling the Shakespearean lines about like banners, he has the conventional intelligent conception of his part and that is something, nay, in this company it was much.

The Enobarbus of George Wessell was certainly as remote as possible from that of Shakespeare. The real Enobarbus was a gentleman somewhat more shrewd than frank, wise in wine and women and wiser still in war, low of voice and smooth of tongue. Mr. Wessell shouted like a free silver advocate and that beautiful description of Cleopatra on the Cyndus [Cydnus], that paragraph that is almost as full of delicate poetry as

Cather simply knew it as "Cyndus." Later in the year, for instance, she wrote in her *Journal* column of March 22, 1896, that "Cleopatra's draught on the Cyndus was not more costly than [Bohemia's] wine." And "Cyndus" it continued until George Seibel in a review of the 1903 *April Twilights* ("A Pittsburgh Poet's Volume of Verse," Pittsburgh *Gazette*, April 26, 1903) pointed out the misspelling in the title of one of the poems, which appeared in that edition as "On Cyndus." The *Courier* piece is in an especially characteristic style, as Willa Cather often wrote in this period: swinging, a little reckless, intense; here rising out of burlesque into poetry. The description of Bernhardt as Cleopatra is imaginative (and also characteristic), though the re-creation was based on the performance of *La Tosca* which Miss Cather did see in Omaha (see page 116), and perhaps on other accounts she had read or heard; the language used to describe her is the same that Willa Cather used several other times when she wrote of Bernhardt (see pages 116 ff., 126).

Mercutio's Queen Mab speech, he mouthed as though he was shouting "Spartacus the Gladiator."

The gorgeous stage settings were certainly all that could be asked of a one-dollar attraction, but the crops must have failed in Egypt that year. During the battle of Actium the audience was treated to stereopticon views. It only needed a lecture. It's not every production of *Cleopatra* that's embellished by magic lantern slides. The bare-footed ballet was there, with both feet, but even it did not bring relief to the weary souls who longed for it.[25]

And how was it with the rural, robust queen, the royal Kleopawtra? Miss Lewis walks like a milkmaid and moves like a housemaid, not a movement or gesture was dignified, much less regal. She draped and heaped her ample form about over chairs and couches to imitate oriental luxury. She slapped her messenger upon the back, she tickled Mark Antony under the chin. She fainted slouchily upon every possible pretext and upon every part of the stage. And it was no ordinary faint either, it was a regular landslide. When the messenger brings the tidings of Antony's marriage she treats him exactly as an irate housewife might treat a servant who had broken her best pickle dish. When she lavishes her affection upon Antony, she is only large and soft and spoony. To call her amorous would be madness, she was spoony, and it was large, 200 hundred pounds, matronly spooniness.

Her death scene was done in the modern emotional drama ten, twenty and thirty-cent carnival style. She took a few tears from *Camille*, a few from *Article 47*, a few from *Credit Lorraine*, a few from *As in a Looking Glass* and made a death scene. She sat down upon a cane bottom dining room chair, took her crown from a little sixteenth century oak table, sighed and wept and heaved her breast and then died from an imaginary serpent hidden in a ditch of lettuce after having worn most atrocious gowns and having drawn and quartered and mangled some of the greatest lines in all the poetry of the world. *Requiescat in pace.* Was ever Shakespeare in this fashion played?

Journal, October 23, 1895, p. 6.

I feel that I am not at all able to do justice to Lillian Lewis as the Egyptian lotus bud. I shall see her in my dreams, that coy, kittenish matron, bunched up on a moth-eaten tiger stroking Mark Antony's double chin. I never saw a less regal figure and carriage. I have seen waiters

25. The advertisements for *Cleopatra* promised "The Barefooted Egyptian Ballet."

in restaurants who were ten times more queenly. Her movements were
exactly like those of the women who give you Turkish baths in Chicago.
And ah! the giddy manner in which she buckled on his armor and the
fulsome way in which she gurgled,

> . . . but, since my lord
> Is Antony again, I will be Cleopatra.

I suppose that is what the learned Malaprop of the *Evening News*[26]
would call "cloyish abandon." And the queer little motions she made
when she put that imaginary snake in her bosom, it was so suggestive of
fleas. And her resounding faint when she saw a vision of Mark Antony
in his cunning little pink wedding tunic being married to Octavia.[27]

There was just [one] good thing about Lillian Lewis' Cleopatra, and
that was that, as hunger makes one dream of banquets, it recalled the only
Cleopatra on earth worth the seeing, the royal Egyptian of Sarah
Bernhardt. I could see it all again, that royal creature with the face of
flame, every inch a queen and always a woman. The bewildering reality
of that first scene with Mark Antony in which her caresses are few, fitful,
unexpected, light as air and hot as fire. The regal queenliness with which
she sends him from her back to Rome, when she touches his sword with

26. The colorful dramatic critic writing for the Lincoln *Evening News* was Julius
H. Tyndale, who signed himself "Toby Rex."

27. Since the tone of the article is more serious after this point, it might be appropriate
to note here as a check and a comparison another example of Willa Cather's "Cleopatra"
style. In her signed column of December 20, 1896—sent from Pittsburgh and published in
the *Journal*—she describes Frank Daniels in *Wizard of the Nile*: "As for Daniels, O, he's just the
same old Daniels. He comes within an inch of being beheaded by the king's headsman, and
he narrowly escapes becoming lunch for the crocodiles, and he woos the fair and unsophisticated Cleopatra in vain. By the way this Cleopatra is decidedly an anachronism,
for the play bills tell us that she "knows naught of love." The real lady is supposed to have
studied that subject pretty thoroughly while she was in bibs. But no matter. Mr. Daniels
has a gloriously funny little song all to himself. He draws up his chunky little body with
great dignity, and all decorated with honors and garlands of lotus buds until he looks like
a haughty sacrificial lamb, he sings in his queer froggy little voice—which isn't a voice at
all—

> 'O Angeline, my circus queen
> Why has't disturbed my mind serene;
> My human snake,
> My Angeline!'

And after the tenth encore he grows hautier still and sings it in French, hissing it in the
approved Yvette Guilbert manner:

> 'Serpente humane,
> Mon Angelaine!'

The effect is simply indescribable."

her lips and invokes the god of victory, and one feels that in her veins there flows the blood of a hundred centuries of kings. And the restlessness of her when he is gone. How she beats the heated pillows with feverish impatience and strains her eyes out across the glowing desert and the sleepy Nile. The madness of her fury when the messenger delivers his news, how her face became famished and hungry and her eyes burned like a tiger's and her very flesh seemed to cleave to her bones. How—but bah! it is not possible to describe it. It was like the lightning which flashes and terrifies and is gone. Through it all she keeps doing little things that you do not expect to see on the stage, things that make you feel within yourself how she loves and how she hates. She gives you those moments of absolute reality of experience, of positive knowledge that are the test of all great art. The thing itself is in her, the absolute quality that all books write of, all songs sing of, all men dream of, that only one in hundreds ever knows or realizes. It leaps up and strikes you between the eyes, makes you hold your breath and tremble. And this reminds me of what Plutarch says, that Cleopatra's chiefest charm was not in her beautiful face, nor her keen wit, nor her wealth of wisdom, but "in the immensity of what she had to give," in her versatility, her intensity, her sensitiveness to every emotion, her whole luxuriant personality.

I wish it had been Sardou's Cleopatra that Miss Lewis played, for, compared to Shakespeare's it is cheap and tawdry, it has less beauty to mar, less dignity to lose. There have been innumerable attempts to dramatize that greatest love story of the ages. They began with Virgil, who tried to do it in that dramatic fourth book of the Aeneid in the person of the *infelix Dido*. Since then poets and dramatists and novelists galore have struggled with it. But among them all the great William is the only man who has made a possible character of the Egyptian queen. Some wise men say, indeed, that he had a living model for it, and that his Cleopatra "with Phoebus' amorous pinches black and wrinkled deep in time" was none other than the Dark Lady of the sonnets. The more one reads the sonnets the more probable that seems, and yet I think he was great enough to have done it without a model. He had no model for Caesar or Brutus or Antony and certainly none for Juliet. His mind worked independently of any romances or tragedies in his own life. It, in itself, had loved all loves, suffered all sorrow, known all tragedies. I sometimes think that if there is anything in the theory of reincarnation he must have been them all, Troilus, Antony, Romeo, Hamlet. No personal experience in fog-clouded England, no love in dusky Elizabethan London could have brought to him the sun and languor of the south, the beauty and luxury and abundant life of the lotus land. It was amusing even while it was painful to see the childish way in which they played with his great purposes and mangled his great art the other night. "Father, forgive them, for they knew not what they did." The gleeful, irresponsible way in which they went through that first scene where Antony is down in Egypt kissing away kingdoms and provinces. But Cleopatra was one woman of the ages, one unique product of the centuries, she had more than mortal resources and the love she inspired was almost more than mortal. No ordinary woman could be expected to enact it. As Antony said, if she would set a limit to the love she made men feel she "must needs find out new heaven, new earth." Well, she found them. She was more than a woman, she was a realization of things dreamed. As that shrewd philosopher, Enobarbus, said to Antony when a repentant mood was on him, "O, sir, you had then left unseen a wonderful piece of work; which not to have been blest withal would have discredited your travel."

To know Cleopatra was then a sort of finishing touch to a great man's education. If a man was to be traveled and experienced he must see her, as today, he must see the pyramids. All the greatest Romans took post graduate work in Egypt.

The finest drinking scene in literature was cut out the other night, while a dozen trivial scenes were left in. The talk about the serpents of Egypt which takes place between Lepidus and Antony Miss Lewis and her versatile husband [Lawrence Marston] saw fit to have spoken by Lepidus and Enobarbus. Now the only purpose of that scene is to recall to Antony Egypt and that one queen of serpents, recall them until he drinks and drinks again, till his footsteps are unsteady and he finally goes out flushed and reeling, leaning on the steady arm of Caesar, the beginning of the end. They failed utterly to bring out the meaning of that scene where the fight is declared by sea, where the gods have first [made] mad he whom they would destroy and Antony cries, "By sea, by sea!"

I wonder if any other poet could have given to Antony the dignity and majesty that Shakespeare gives him in defeat. After Actium, when Antony meets the queen he says,

O, whither hast thou led me, Egypt?

. . . .

Thy full supremacy thou knewest, and that
Thy beck might from the bidding of the gods
Command me.

It is said with a simplicity and pathos that dignify even its weakness. And O, the greatness of him after the last defeat. Well does Enobarbus call him an old lion dying. When they tell him that the queen is dead, all the simple manliness in him comes out. "The long day's task is done, and we must sleep." When the ruse is confessed he is not angry, he is beyond all that now. The keynote of the whole tragedy, the grand motif rounds once again. He does what he has always done. He has always gone back to her, after every wrong, after every treachery. He has left kingdoms and principalities to go to her, thrown away half the world to seek her, and now of his old captain, he asks one last favor, that they carry him to her now that he cannot go himself anymore, and he goes, for the last time.

That last meeting, that awful scene in which Antony, bleeding and dying, is dragged up to the sides of the monument, Miss Lewis omits. Possibly because it is almost impossible to represent it on the stage, possibly because the play is long and something must be cut to give time to the barefoot ballet. At any rate to cut it is to divest the play of half its greatness. For the "moral" of the play, if there be one, is in the last line that Antony speaks before the mists cloud over him and he begins to wander back to the old days of empire and delight.

One word, sweet queen:
Of Caesar seek your honor, with your safety.

That he should have lived for her and died for her, lost the world for her and yet should have had to say that at the end! There is a tragedy for you, in its darkest melancholy. The tragedy of all such love and such relations, of everything on earth that hides shame at its heart, that is without honor and absolute respect. All the hundreds of French novels that have been written upon the *union libre* have told us nothing new about it after that. That one line has in it all the doubt and dark tragedy of the whole thing. We Anglo-Saxons have no need of a *Sapho* or of the numerous and monotonous works of M. Paul Bourget. That story has all been written for us once as it never can be again, by a master whose like no one world can bear twice, whose ashes one planet can carry but once in its bosom.

Courier, October 26, 1895, pp. 6–7.

Rosalind at the Lansing

In December of 1895, Lincoln had another chance to see an actress try to star in Shakespeare. Effie Ellsler had appeared before, but in plays such as The Governess, Miss Manning, Hazel Kirke, *and—most recently—*

Doris (*April 24, 1895*). *When she played Rosalind in* As You Like It, *it did not help her cause that Lincolnites had a previous performance for comparison—Modjeska's Rosalind, on March 23, 1892.*

Shakespeare is a strain upon the talent of the greatest actors. Why the rank and file of the profession ever attack him at all, and where they get their complacent temerity for the onslaught, is one of the unexplained mysteries. Effie Ellsler, whom the program announced as "America's greatest actress," appeared as a most pleasant and affable Rosalind at the Lansing last night. She plays that most complex and intricate of Shakespeare's lighter characters with the same regardless pleasantry which she displayed as the much married Doris last season. Certainly Miss Ellsler made a very good-natured and practical Rosalind, and certainly good nature has never been called upon to cover a greater number of artistic sins. Her voice is entirely conventional and colorless, and she continually uses that apologetic rising inflection. She chirps the most delicately shaded phrases as lightly and ineffectually and as unconscious of their significance as a sweet child of seven repeating Bible verses for butterscotch.[28] It is amusing when it is not offensive. To hear Miss Ellsler prattle, "O, coz, my pretty coz, didst thou but know how many fathoms deep I am in love!" is an experience. Miss Ellsler's "interpretation" of the role, whatever else it may be, is certainly original. God forbid that there should be more than one woman playing it so at one time. It is a new wrinkle to enact Rosalind in a soubrette fashion, and Miss Ellsler should have all the credit of her creation. There is only one other woman to whom any glimpse of any sort of feeling is more utterly impossible, and that is Caroline Miskel [Mrs. Charles Hoyt], the beautiful and impossible. Miss Ellsler's Rosalind should play tennis and ride a bicycle and do a skirt dance. Love is not her vocation. . . .

Having seen Lillian Lewis as Cleopatra and Effie Ellsler as Rosalind, life holds little more to be desired, and one's capacity for mad delight and lofty exultation is pretty well exhausted. After this all plays will be hollow and all players tame. Such things make one hope that Shakespeare's grave is wide and deep, and that his ghost does not walk by night.

Journal, December 6, 1895, p. 6.

Othello, *with Louis James*

Louis James's Othello *in December, 1895, inevitably recalled his previous performance in the play (with Frederick Warde) on April 17, 1893, a*

28. See Miss Cather's description of Effie Ellsler's voice in another context, page 139.

production which Willa Cather was still deploring in her Sunday column a year later: "We can all remember the burly negro they made of Othello here last year, and we all remember their Desdemona, ah! would that we could forget!" (March 11, 1894).

When a rendition of Shakespeare is not great, when it lacks the transcendent emotion, the inspired enlightenment, the complete majesty of the highest art, it may still be earnest, intelligent and dignified. Such a performance Louis James gave at the Lansing last night. Mr. James is not a great tragedian. His best work he does as Falstaff. He is an excellent actor and one of great discrimination, but he lacks the tragic force. Somehow his individuality is not large and powerful enough to hold the centre of the stage and draw all eyes toward himself. He is without those qualities of body and soul which enable men to wrestle with great emotions, to conceive of great passions. Indeed, Mr. James is rather too much of a gentleman to be a brilliant comedian [tragedian?] when he turned his attention to the legitimate.[29]

Mr. James' Othello was a dignified gentleman, who loved well and hated well, but who had a rather negative personality in spite of his very positive emotion. He was not the raging lion of the desert that Shakespeare tells us of, nor was his love the elemental, primitive, resistless force that scorched up the Moor's very blood within his veins, and the happiness in his heart. It was a consistent Othello, played with vigor, intelligence and discretion; it lacked only one thing—genius. Mr. James is too civilized; he cannot reach the intensity of those few simplified and terribly physical and direct emotions which make up [the] life of the barbarian. Mr. James is an experienced actor, but his Othello is entirely too well behaved. He would never love a woman to madness or hate a man to the death. He groans and writhes, but you feel that the blood in his veins is cold when it should flow like molten lava.[30]

Mr. James is more than fortunate in his leading man and lady. After

29. By "the legitimate" Willa Cather here means serious drama or tragedy. The miswriting of "comedian" in this sentence is explained by the restatement of her point in the second *Othello* piece, taken from her Sunday column. There she says that "the stage lost a brilliant comedian when he turned his attention to tragedy." The almost identical wording is another of the countless marks of authorship in these reviews and columns.

30. Willa Cather had stressed these same characteristics of Othello in her *Journal* column of March 31, 1895. In her account of the opera *Otello* which she had recently seen in Chicago, she mentions the "fiery passion" of Tamagno as the Moor. Emma Eames played Desdemona as "exactly the gentle sort of woman that a fierce barbarian from the south would have loved."

seeing so many a weak and weeping Desdemona Miss Alma Kruger was a delightful surprise. She was beautiful, sad and tender. Her sympathy is quick and responsive, and she gives the part so many of those little natural touches like the way her eyes roam about the council chamber until she finds Othello, and the way she closes her eyes when he first embraces her at Cyprus. She is a young woman whose beauty and talent should make her a future.

Guy Lindsey is a promising young actor. He seems to improve every season, and last night he played an Iago which many an older actor might envy. He was such a tender, sympathetic Iago in company, so grieved and oppressed by the sins of the world. Alone he was so exultant and gleeful in his malignity. He loved evil-doing as some men love drink. The thought of mischief was sweet to him. He varied the usual rendering by keeping up his reckless bravado and devil-may-care attitude to the very last and the effect is in every way strong and satisfactory. Even after he is bound he is just the same, and when he stands above the corpse of Othello the look of triumph and rampant deviltry, of joy and demoniacal exultation, were a fitting close for a play in a tragedy of the power of evil.

The play was considerably altered from the version which Warde and James played here a few years ago. The scene in which Othello strikes Desdemona before the ambassadors from Venice and the scene between Emilia and Desdemona at the beginning of the last act were omitted, which is unusual.

The theatre men are growing a little careless about their scenery and last night they got the "long results of time" a little mixed and made old Cyprus get a move on with a vengeance. For the street in Cyprus in which Iago and Roderigo talked had two healthy-looking street car tracks, a "Dago" banana stand, and a prosperous meat market with a dozen dressed Thanksgiving turkeys hanging on the outside. Now, those were not the kind of Turks that went to Cyprus.

Journal, December 14, 1895, p. 6.

Just why Louis James continues to stick to "the legitimate" is rather a mystery to his friends. He is a man with the keenest possible sense of humor and the stage lost a brilliant comedian when he turned his attention to tragedy. His Falstaff was much the best thing he ever did, for in that he [had] his own nature with him and not against him. For some unknown reason he has dropped Falstaff from his repertoire since he and Warde separated, but there are many people who will continue to think it the notable production of his life. Even when compared to that superb Falstaff of Victor Maurel's [see page 214 f.] it had virtues of its own. But if Mr. James will play tragedy, why, tragedy he will play, all the world to the contrary. James has had a somewhat peculiar career, anyway. When he used to be Laurence Barrett's leading man everyone expected the greatest things from him some day. Wagging gray beards solemnly proclaimed him the tragedian of the future. Under Barrett's strict discipline and the constant stimulation of his example James did excellent work. He made an admirable record, but he cannot play a lone hand. As soon as he began starring his friends were disappointed in him. He lacked the power to key himself and his fellow players up to the necessary pitch. He was easy and honest and affable. He was never great enough or passionately in earnest enough to fix the public attention or win the public love. People admire James and accept him, but no one is very enthusiastic about him. It is because he does not really feel the tragic forces he represents, because he utterly lacks inspiration. Everything is forced. Truth, the mighty and the convincing is not with him. In Falstaff it was otherwise and yet Louis James was one of the best leading men in this country. But between a leading man and a star there is all the difference that there is between a good orchestra musician and a virtuoso, between the man who leads and the man who is led. One requires genius, the other only intelligence, tact and docility.

Miss Alma Kruger, Mr. James' leading lady, played an exceedingly pretty and charming Desdemona last week. It is not an easy role to play, that sweet lady of Venice, with her sinless dreams, her great love and her pitiful want of tact. It's a sorry admission to make, but really, the wicked and wily Emilia would have managed Othello much better than Desdemona. She had the guile wherewith to meet his suspicions. Emilia, as usual, was poorly played. We would like to see Emilia played well once. It is a strong part, and one that has many counterparts in the living world. Emilia was not a model woman at all; like as not her husband had reason to be jealous. She had married a bad man and saw the bad side of the world, and believed there was no other, which, for people of her life, is a comfortable belief. She saw a good deal of high life there in Venice and knew all the gossip and scandal of the day. She knew the policy of the duke and the price of the senators, and she knew why certain gondolas slipped quietly under the windows of certain palaces at midnight and who waited with restless dagger in the shadow of the deep archway, and why the bodies of young Venetian nobles were sometimes found, dressed as troubadors, with a beribboned lute on their shoulders, floating in the unfrequented waterways. Emilia was wise in the ways of the world and she delighted in its wickedness. She had a witty tongue and fearless one, and she was a cynic after the manner of Enobarbus. She accepted her life with a sort of cynical superiority. Desdemona was the first good thing that came into her life. She did not believe in her at first. She told her naughty stories and tried to find the vulnerable spot in her. Probably at first she hated her. But when she found that Desdemona was really what she seemed to be, it restored to her a lost faith, gave back a lost ideal, changed the whole face of the world. It is one of the thousand contradictions of life, that reverence and fondness that a woman whose instincts are better than her life has for some woman she believes absolutely good. She will betray a hundred lovers to keep one such woman's love and trust. So when Desdemona was dead, a frenzy of despair and hatred of life seized her. She had only known one good thing in life. It was not only the grief of personal affection that drove her upon Iago's sword. It was the admiration for goodness, the "hunger and thirst after righteousness," that exists in most of us, however effectually we may disguise it. After she has her death wound she only asks them to lay her beside her lady, and she dies singing Desdemona's old "Willow, Willow" song of love betrayed. The redemption of Emilia through Desdemona's higher influence is one of those hundred beautiful minor points in which all Shakespearean tragedies are rich.

Journal, December 22, 1895, p. 9.

From the fall of 1891 when she was a freshman taking "Junior Shakespeare" at the University, Willa Cather spoke of Hamlet *as one of the greatest of all creations. Her essay on Shakespeare and Hamlet, published in the* Journal *on November 1 and 8, 1891, is more on the character than the play, however; and more on the nature of creativity than on either Shakespeare or his work (see Appendix I). Her view of Hamlet then was quite simple: he is not a reasoning, logical, intellectual, or philosophical man who can universalize ideas; nor is he a puzzle if one accepts him as a sensitive, intense young man, who felt more and suffered more than others, who followed the law of his own heart, who was probably mad rather than feigning madness, and whose tragedy was that grief killed the creative art in him. She summarized it with, "He was very sensitive, he felt intensely, and he suffered more than other people, that was all." In so describing Hamlet she was in effect insisting that a character in literature is created as a personal reality, not as a logical contrivance. He feels, he is—and he is human, like me.*

In later years Hamlet's reality became much more complex. As she grew to admire intellect and knowledge, saw thought and emotion as part of the same subjectivity, used "analytical" and "scholarly" without fear, she could herself say more about any actor's performance or any writer's work. But even with modifications, the central fact of Hamlet's character continued to be his subjective sensitivity. She was irritated to read of E. S. Willard's "sensible Hamlet": "Give Hamlet one grain of common sense and you have no play at all. Everything depends upon his being beautifully but unreasonably stupid. To put it more seriously, Mr. Willard tries to interpret Hamlet's actions as influenced by the world outside, whereas Hamlet was a wholly subjective character and everything came from within" (Journal, February 11, 1894). A year later she spoke of the excessive exaltation of Hamlet as an intellectual puzzle, and his tyranny over tragedy. Come the revolution in tragedy, she said, "The melancholy Dane must be pulled down from banqueting with Plato and Socrates and put over with Charles I and Prince Arthur and all the other princely failures." Tragedy "will not come stalking with a stage strut and a toga. Then Hamlet will no longer be played as a philosopher and the standing enigma of the ages, but as a princely gentleman, very sensitive and very miserable, who might just as well have lived today as then. The actor of the future will give to Hamlet neither profundity nor knowing irony, but romance and melancholy and an almost effeminate grace and charm" (Journal, March 10, 1895).

When Walker Whiteside came to Lincoln the next fall, in November, 1895, he was slight and earnest, grieving to despair, reflective, irresolute, poetic, a noble failure—quite a good Hamlet, the papers said. The review in the Journal *may seem at first to be a little unlike Willa Cather's early views of Hamlet, but it is of course a serious attempt to evaluate the whole performance, and by the winter of 1895 she had become enormously more skilled in both exact analysis and the use of critical language. The piece for the* Courier, *written with greater leisure and thoughtfulness, is more essay than review. It has the same tone of exalted devotion to greatness in art with which she had begun, four years earlier, in that first essay on Shakespeare.*[31]

31. Other interesting relationships: Both the *Courier* piece and the 1891 essay, "Shakespeare and Hamlet," use a Mount Sinai allusion, though in the earlier essay it was to Moses and the burning bush. Both *Journal* and *Courier* articles have "the bleak turrets of Elsinore." The last line of the *Courier* essay, "Other heights in other lives, God willing," also ends a piece on the death of George Du Maurier (*Home Monthly*, November, 1896)—not in itself a proof of authorship, but certainly a suggestion. And compare "the greatness of a man's soul may outlive the weakness of his arm" in the *Courier* with "the introspection that weakened the arm" in the *Journal* review, and both with the symbolism of Willa Cather's key statement on creativity—that perilous voyage from brain to hand (see page 417). The tragedy of Hamlet, she had said in 1891, was the killing of the creative art in him.

Hamlet, *with Walker Whiteside*

... In English-speaking lands a tragedian is measured by his Hamlet. It is
the one play which tests almost equally his imagination and his intellect,
his scholarship and emotional power. It is the measure of both things
native and things acquired. Sooner or later every tragedian puts his ear
to the lips of this sphinx and awaits his answer. To few men has the inner
text of Hamlet spoken more deeply and truly than to the young tragedian
who played before us last night. Mr. Whiteside seems especially fitted
by God and nature to play Hamlet. It is much the best thing he does. He
keeps the role keyed up to that point where grief turns to despair and
hatred to impotent loathing. From that first frenzied oath on the bleak
turrets of Elsinore to that last thrust at the king when death goads Hamlet's
arm to tardy vengeance, he gives the character a melancholy consistency.

He plays a monotonous Hamlet. The first act opens upon Hamlet's
grief, and scene by scene, grief follows him; from every quarter, from the
queen, the king, Ophelia, Laertes, from himself most of all. It closes over
him, settles down upon him, and every act is in the same minor key.
Mirth has a thousand masques, but sorrow has but one. It is always its
old monotonous self. That earnest, studious face of Mr. Whiteside's, even
his slight physique, suggest the reflective and irresolute nature of Hamlet.

In those long monologues he brings out all the introspection that
weakened the arm and the acute analysis that warped the will of that most
modern of Shakespearean characters.

Mr. Whiteside's scene with the queen is neither lachrymose nor
tearful; it is for the most part, strong, manly and self-contained. He feels
the awfulness of being his mother's judge; he controls her like a child, by
the sheer force of his will until he breaks her pride, then he kneels beside
her and reasons, pleads with her.

His scene with the players and his directions to them are rather
monotonous, but his "The play's the thing" was delivered with the rage
of one distraught. He makes a triumph of that line. His scene with
Ophelia was a little obscure and difficult but I believe that it contains his
most pregnant acting. He does not betray the exact state of Hamlet's
feeling toward Ophelia any more than Shakespeare does. How could he
when Claudius and her cackling father were listening behind the arras,
and once when he broke into real feeling and almost lost himself he saw
their heads? Mr. Whiteside has not passed judgment upon the situation,
he handles it in a noncommittal way, and yet very suggestively. That

way he has of putting his arms about Ophelia, holding her close and begging her to go her way to a nunnery, would be almost funny if it were not pathetic. Is humanity inconsistent? In the play scene Mr. Whiteside rises to the full stature of his power. The way he drags himself across the floor to the feet of the king, the terrible accusation of his fixed eyes, his bootless burst of rage when the guilty king starts to his feet and his vain thrusts into the empty throne—action that came too late—these are all the works of a talented actor and a deep Shakespearean scholar. I think he has the only true solution of the change of rapiers in the scuffle with Laertes. It is the only possible one I have ever seen, and it was daringly original, dignified and intensely dramatic. In that one look of his when he felt Laertes' thrust and saw that his own foil was tipped and harmless, you could see the whole treachery of the situation come upon him. He glances from the queen to the king and from the king to the courtiers, and he knows that he is alone. He sees the end and his only ally is his own desperation. He unarmed Laertes, set his foot upon [the sword] and thrust his own harmless weapon at his cringing opponent. Then he caught up Laertes' sword and drove [it] home. He made that scene the worthy climax of a great play. . . .

Journal, November 21, 1895, p. 6.

"*That Greatest Drama*"

Once, a great many centuries ago there was a camp in the weary wilderness of Sinai, the camp of a people who were journeying from a bad country of plagues and fleshpots and taskmasters, of dark religions and horrible rites and grim barbarism, journeying to an undiscovered country, they hoped a better one. In the midst of the camp was a tabernacle. Without that tabernacle was the court of the people, where the multitude came and went, and babbled and worshipped; tradesmen, bondmen, lepers, things unclean. Within was a court where only the priests came, where the Levites performed their holy offices. And within that there was still another chamber, where only the high priest might enter, who carried God's fire in his censer. And as it was then, so it is now. There is another people journeying by slow stages into something better, something dim and undefined, lying off yonder beyond the peaks of Sinai. And with us we carry all that has been most worthy in our race, the memory and work of the great, our tabernacle, and the rest we leave to perish by the wayside, and the sands blow over them and they are forgotten. And we have our Holy Thing, which no man may profane without swift vengeance from our hands or from heaven's. And this holy ground of ours is Elsinore. Our civilization is not a thoughtful or scholarly one, but in its own rough way it is loyal to *Hamlet*. That play and the Magna Charta are the two most worthy things that the Anglo-Saxon people has done from its beginning. Other nations have written great tragedies, tragedies of man's heart and of his passions, but we alone have this tragedy of the soul, and of man's divinity. For *Hamlet* is not a play of love or action or impulse, but of thought, and of those deep and secret motives which deal with the soul alone, which fix the relations between it and the man himself, which decree its doom, which "summons it to heaven or to hell."

When a young player appears in *Hamlet*, he is our natural enemy. We regard him as a thief and a robber until he has proved that he is mightier than we. It is not for us to prove that he cannot play Hamlet, but for him to prove that he can. Just how far Mr. Walker Whiteside proves this it would be impossible to say after hearing him only once. But of so earnest, poetic and noble a work as he presented Wednesday evening, I can find little harsh to say. I have not seen all the Hamlets of history as Mr. Whiteside's New York critics seem to have done. Probably Mr. Whiteside knows a great deal more about Hamlet than I, that is his business. I can only judge him by what he makes me feel and know about it, for that also is his business. To me Mr. Whiteside's Hamlet is original and all his own, not because it is unlike Booth's or Kean's or Irving's—whom I never saw,—but because if one scene of it is stolen, it is all stolen, every look, every gesture, every breath he draws in it. It is the work of one man; it is the suffering of one man.

Several people asked me Wednesday evening if I did not think there was a gloomy monotony about this particular Hamlet. There certainly was, but I think that gloom is necessary to Mr. Whiteside's conception of the part, and that if he varied it he would be false to the best artistic instincts within him. To me, personally, it is the only true way of playing Hamlet. I cannot see in Hamlet the sportive wit that Mr. Lowell saw. There is wit, certainly, but it is more gloomy than the spoken pathos; it is the terrible ghastly sort of wit that masks suffering. It is a gloomy play. In most plays the inciting circumstances of the tragedy occur after the play opens, but Hamlet's father was dead and his mother false to his memory before the play begins. As in *Macbeth*, the clouds of the tempest are already lowering when the curtain rises. From that oath in the glimmering dawn upon the bleak turrets of Elsinore, his own dark fate

CRITICAL STATEMENTS: DRAMA

is upon him. It follows him like the ghost, completely surrounds him, and locks down upon him, like the curse of the Nibelung ring in the Wagnerian operas. [*Words missing*] . . . [a] fine scholarly quality that is difficult to define. He emphasizes the shrinking, almost feminine delicacy of the Prince, which a more robust actor misses altogether. There are moments when his reading is not convincing, is mechanical and almost weak, like his reading of "The time is out of joint, O cursed spite/That ever I was born to set it right," which was light and melodramatic. I think he will make that line deeper and more prophetic in time. For in that moment, looking into the reddening east, Hamlet saw his destiny unrolled before him, laid bare by the retreating clouds of night; he saw his sacrifice, that he was to be the instrument of fate, that he was to suffer for wrongs not of his doing, live for ends not his own, carry upon his shoulders the sins of a whole court. In that moment of elemental spiritual conflict he saw that his own life and his own love were not for him, saw them go out forever, as the curtains of the tempest shut out a star. After that, no more of the fair Ophelia. For him that was indeed a momentous dawn.

Mr. Whiteside's Hamlet may be weak, but he is noble. When he died Horatio did not say, "Good night, sweet Prince," but we, who watched, said it for him. As a play, it seems impertinent to write of *Hamlet*, after all that has been written and said and sung of it before. But as long as every spring the primroses blossom in the fields of Avon, and every summer the wild thyme blows about Anne Hathaway's cottage, we may all of us turn to that sacred and greatest name of our race and do it reverence. To reverence is the privilege of the small, as well as of the great. We may turn in awe and wonder to that greatest drama, that polar star in the glittering firmament of art, whereby all men gauge their work, and by whose magnitude we measure all the distances of heaven. And it shines not only for that astronomer whose business is with the planets and worlds, but for the herdsman, that he may drive his flock aright through the night, and for the fisherman to steer by on the lonely deep. It is ours, as Christ is ours. I never see it but there comes back to me that overpowering sense of its gigantic moral and artistic scope. Take that one scene in which mad Ophelia metes out to Laertes and the king and queen their destiny in flowers, where else is there anything so delicate? And then that complete immolation of Hamlet's personal life and passion to the great demands of his soul, of ethical justice, that great struggle with the Titanic powers of fate. Beside that all the finished dramas of the

French seems the hollow work of clever pigmies. It took the Saxon mind to recognize soul needs like that. The French write cleverer plays, the Italians more impassioned ones, but all that is greatest and highest in Anglo-Saxon character is there, in Elsinore. It is the same power, the same over-soul that builded the Gothic cathedrals. Someway the artists of the north seem to get so much nearer God. They are not craftsmen, they have no law but inspiration, they are priests in verse and prophets in stone.

And yet they say that *Hamlet* is a study in failure. Well, it was failure that was greater than success. Whoso loseth his life shall find it. So did Giordano Bruno fail when he was burned in Italy, so did Huss fail when he was burned in Switzerland, so did Christ fail when he was crucified in Judea. Their kingdoms were not of this world, their lives did not save this world, but their memories have. They gave the world the ideals by which we live, for which we die. For sometimes even in this world where "good is oft interred with our bones," the greatness of a man's soul may outlive the weakness of his arm. After all good is good, eternal, triumphant over weakness, defeat, failure. The "unlit lamp and the ungirt loin" is not the end. "Other heights in other lives, God willing."

Courier, November 23, 1895, p. 8.

Literature

❧ ❧ ❧

An artist may be clever when he answers
you, he may be skilful when he pleases
your senses, but when he speaks to the
living soul within you, then and then only
is he great. Only a diamond can cut a
diamond, only a soul can touch a soul.

The work is everything. There is so little
perfection.

ROMANCE

*In the winter of 1894–1895, Willa Cather turned from watching the world
beyond the footlights to that other more personal realm of the imagination—the
life of books and the arts of language. It was not a sudden or complete change of
interest; it was simply that she began to have more to say about literature than
about any of the other arts. And first of all she chose to write about the books and
the writers of romance, what she would call a year later "the highest form of
fiction" and lift into a metaphor of absolute joy: "Children, the sea, the sun,
God himself are all romanticists."* [1] *This was the fiction she had first loved, the
world of the three musketeers and D'Artagnan; of David Balfour, Erling the
Bold, and Hereward the Wake. This world had seas and islands to explore from
Homer to Kingsley and Stevenson, and recently there were the new lands of
Kipling's India and Anthony Hope's Ruritania. Treasure Island and Troy were
in some ways more deeply real than Eleventh Street in Lincoln. Romance,
to Willa Cather, was never child's play in a trivial sense, or escape, or a denial
of life; it was an affirmation of the highest kind of reality, the god-like realm of the
creative imagination.*

1. Passages quoted here and in the following paragraph are from Willa Cather's
article of November 2, 1895, "On Nature and Romance" (see pages 231 ff.).

Characteristically, Willa Cather's columns were running accounts of the news, a kind of logbook of what seemed important to her, and why. Literary comment was in some ways a chronicle of deaths and expectations. The first article on romance lamented the death of Stevenson and looked for one who might succeed him. The two men she named—Rudyard Kipling and Anthony Hope—were then in their twenties, popular but not permanently established. A third possibility, Stanley Weyman, was under forty. These writers might help to determine the course of fiction, and perhaps serve in an even greater way. " We need young men like Rudyard Kipling and Anthony Hope," Willa Cather said in the fall of 1895, "not because of the greatness of their talent, but because of the sincerity of their motive, because the atmosphere of their work is one in which men may love and work and fight and die like men." Romance was a leitmotif, an accompaniment to the exercise of human greatness.

Stevenson: " The King and Father of them All"

Robert Louis Stevenson, who died on December 4, 1894, was to Willa Cather the great master and chief of the modern writers of romance, "the king and father of them all" (see page 319, below). Her feeling for some of Stevenson's work—the stories of the New Arabian Nights *(1882),* Treasure Island *(1883), and* Prince Otto *(1885) had roots in her childhood. But she liked him also for his engaging free style in his essays, his charm and directness of manner, the color and poetry of his material; she could read him on books, on places, on the hundred and one moving or curious details of humanity. Even his life, from Scotland to Samoa, had seemed a romance; and when some of his letters appeared in 1895 she felt the impact of his personal heroism. Because in later years Willa Cather so often referred to the influence of Henry James, it should be recalled that he, too, was devoted to Stevenson—was, in fact, a trusted friend named as one of two executors in Stevenson's will (published in McClure's, July, 1895). In an 1888 essay James called Stevenson " the bright particular genius" whose books all open windows to different views, and who had all the freshness of youth, the sophistication of real artistry, the interest in personal gallantry, the supreme skill in make-believe that form a great writer of romance.[2] Quite possibly Willa Cather read James's essay. But her attachment to Stevenson far pre-dated her interest in James, and it is even possible, in the inevitabilities of history, that the first great master led her to the next; in those who loved Stevenson, there was a community of spirit.*

2. "Robert Louis Stevenson," first published in the Century, April, 1888, and collected in Partial Portraits (1888).

CRITICAL STATEMENTS: LITERATURE

Early in the week [December 18, 1894], it was cabled to us across the sea that Robert Louis Stevenson was dead. News like that we can ill afford to hear in a time when there are so many who know, or think they know, and so few who make. For despite his gaunt frame and sunken cheeks, Stevenson gave us some of the most strong and vigorous literature produced by any man of our time. No one knows very much about him. He was a delicate, nervous boy, always trying to write a novel and always failing, making and destroying a score of them before he accomplished anything that the publisher would take notice of. His first book was not written until he was thirty-one, and long before that his friends and relatives had decided that he was a dreamer and a dilettante who would never support himself or his family. When his first book came it was only a sea story for boys, but it had in it a strength and simplicity, a power of imagination which promised better things to be. More than all, it gave the man confidence in himself and he settled down to his work for better or for worse. He did not remain long in Scotland. The climate was too severe for him and the people bothered him, so he went off to his little island in the Pacific. After that day the world knew less of him than ever, except now and then big bundles of manuscript, written in the most unintelligible hand, were sent over to England by occasional steamers that anchored at the little port.

Mr. Stevenson has left us very few books and very good ones. He was safely out of the civilization that kills more authors than it stimulates. Safely out of the reach of literary friends and advisors, of the futile blame and barren praise of the public, of tempting offers from the holiday magazines, of literary dinners and musicales and high teas. Free to change and polish and recast his work until it was without a blemish, until weariness and the sense within him told him to stay his hand. That, perhaps, is why he has left us a few perfect books rather than a great many brilliant, shallow ones, full of force never concentrated, of rich promise never realized. That, perhaps, is why he was never betrayed into writing novels on heredity, or divorce, or the vexed problems of society, seeing that his business was to make, not to analyze; literature, not social science. Living down there in the wealth and fragrance of unceasing summer, in the sunlight and starlight of tropic seas and meridian lands, with the heathen and nature, who is the greatest heathen of all, he wrote books of fancy, pure and simple. He gave the world an outlook beyond the rigid horizons of social life, of something new, fresh, unheard of, full of brilliant color and rugged life. Not that he was influenced by the glowing tropics to Oriental profuseness. He kept the quaint, quiet style that he brought with him from Scotland. His heroes are not showy or dashing men. They are manly fellows, with silent lips and strong arms, and they have something that is denied to most heroes in modern fiction—they act. That is the thing that will be longest remembered of Stevenson. In an age of conversational novels he wrote books full of action. In a generation when fiction is full of the futileness of effort and of flippant scorn for work, he wrote of the glory and the hope of effort and of the completeness which a man's work gives to his life. He could not conceive of a futile passion. He wrote sometimes of love that redeems, oftener of hate that destroys, always of ambition that achieves. His books were never hopeful ones, but they were never lazy ones. He told of the things men did, not of the things men said. Of wild adventures on land and on water, of buried treasure and encounters on the high seas, all with the vivid truths of poetic exaggeration. If Mr. Stevenson had been a strong man in the days when men acted he would have sailed the seas under the black flag with a cargo of wine and Spanish gold. As he was a weak man in the days when men reflect, he was a romanticist. Of one thing there is no doubt, that he was a man of pure invention whom the world could ill afford to lose, who lies up there on the topmost peak of Pola [Vaea?] mountain amid the undying blue of summer seas, under the Southern Cross.

It is probable that before the advancement of encroaching realism and "veritism" and all other literary unpleasantness Stevenson will be relegated to the children's book shelves, along with Scott and Cooper and the elder Dumas. Fortunately the children are not realists as yet and exult in the imagination their elders have lost. But there is one book of his which, though it is perhaps his most imperfect from a technical point of view, deserves a better fate. *Prince Otto* is so seldom mentioned by people whose business it is to mention books that it may be very bad taste to like it. But it has a few very staunch admirers and ought to have many more. It contains the best character work that Stevenson ever did, besides being full of the dramatic action, the charm of poesy and romance in which all his books abound. It is his best love story, and shows that he could do great things with passion when he wished. But love has come down to us so entwined with sentimentality, so disguised by sermons and so distorted by conventions that Mr. Stevenson, who liked unlimited freedom, hated to touch it at all. It contains, too, his only weak hero, and shows that he understood and sympathized with weakness and inertia, though he preferred strength and action. It is not the finished book that

The Master of Ballantrae, or *David Balfour* is, but anyone who has read and liked Daudet's *Kings in Exile* will find in *Prince Otto* deep and lasting pleasure.

Journal, December 23, 1894, p. 13.

Speaking of Stevenson, if you want to read some noble and manly literature, just glance over those letters of his in the November [1895] *McClure's.*[3] There you will find the modesty, the sad self-depreciation which belongs to the truly great, whose minds have so much more power to conceive than their hands ever have strength to execute, whose work is so far below the level of their dreams. In one of them he remarks, "I do not think it is possible to have fewer illusions than I. I sometimes wish I had more. They are amusing. But I cannot take myself seriously as an artist; the limitations are too obvious." No, it's the people like Sarah Grand and Beatrice Harraden,[4] who take themselves seriously. Men like Stevenson have other standards than themselves whereby they measure the world, and they judge themselves impersonally, along with the rest of imperfect humanity, from a perspective above and beyond. A great craftsman's taste is always so much more perfect than his work.

In another letter he says: "I wonder exceedingly if I have done anything at all good; and who can tell me? and why should I wish to know? In so little a while, I, and the English language, and the bones of my descendants, will have ceased to be a memory! And yet—and yet—one would like to leave an image for a few years upon men's minds—for fun."

He wondered if he had done anything at all good. Well, as Henry James says, "Our doubt is our passion and our passion is our task. The rest is the madness of art."[5] But the greatest thing that Stevenson says in those letters is not about himself or his work, but about things in general. "The inherent tragedy of things works itself out from white to black and blacker, and the poor things of a day look ruefully on. Does it shake my cast-iron faith? I cannot say that it does. I believe in the ultimate decency

3. Some of the *Vailima Letters* written to Sidney Colvin and collected in the edition published by Stone and Kimball in 1895. Quotations from Stevenson given in this article are, successively, from letters written in October, 1894; May, 1893; and August, 1893.

4. "Sarah Grand" was the pseudonym of Frances Elizabeth McFall, Irish novelist whose three-volume *The Heavenly Twins* (1893) brought her notoriety. Beatrice Harraden was an English novelist, author of *Ships that Pass in the Night* (1893) and frequent magazine stories.

5. From "The Middle Years," first published in *Scribner's,* May, 1893, and collected in *Terminations* (1895).

of things; ay, and if I woke in hell, should still believe it!" Stevenson never wrote a greater sentence. He was a desperately sick man, and one who had suffered enough to turn most men bitter. But his suffering could not convince him; Hell itself could not convince him. There's optimism for you, the kind of optimism that produces and creates and brings into being, that is the source of all life in art and all art in life, of character as well as of craft.

Courier, November 2, 1895, pp. 6–7.

... During his long residence in Vailima Stevenson kept a sort of diary which he sent in monthly instalments to his friend [Sidney] Colvin, and the volumes called *Vailima Letters* are made up of the last five years of the correspondence. If you want to know the man Stevenson just read those letters, and there is not a man in this generation whom it would have been a higher honor or a sweeter pleasure to know. We have had a good many diaries thrust upon us, the diary of Frederick Amiel, the diary of Marie Bashkirtseff[6] and various others, and though all good in their way, they have been pretty painful reading sometimes. But if you want something downright cheerful, something full of the higher hope and larger optimism, read the diary of this overworked invalid, this man who was all his life sick unto death and exiled to the South Seas. Not a jot of morbid introspection, not a shadow of pessimism, they have the strong healthful ring of the diaries men wrote when the world was some centuries younger than it is now. If ever fate gave a goodly measure of hard knocks to any one, it did to this man Stevenson, and yet in all these letters with their humorous reference to political, financial, personal and literary tribulations, there is never one despondent wail. He had the clean grit of the Scots certainly, if he did not have their robust physique. As you read these letters you feel vaguely what authorship means in the higher sense, and learn what certain gay and smooth-reading chapters in *David Balfour* and *Ebb Tide* cost the man who made them. It sets one to thinking to read how the poor fellow drafted and wrote and then destroyed and wrote again. It reminds one of what George Eliot said when some gushing friend asked her if she did not "love to write," and she replied cynically that she was always miserable when she wrote, but she was more miserable when she did not. Of all his critics Stevenson himself was the most

6. *Journal Intime* (1883–1884, in part) by Henri Frédéric Amiel, Swiss poet and philosopher; *Journal* (1890, in English) by Marie Bashkirtseff.

merciless. He generally refers to his work as "my damned literature" and calls some of it trash that most of us are unsophisticated enough to think most excellent. . . .

Mr. Colvin's epilogue is comforting, for just toward the last those letters grew a little downhearted. The man was very ill and he felt his craft deserting him and his work came hard and the axles grated and rubbed dry. He lamented his growing inability to work. He wishes he could be buried back in Scotland among the hills under the heather, that heather he loved so well, whined about so little. He mentions [Samuel] Crockett's dedication of *The Stickit Minister* to him—the prettiest things in Crockett's whole book, by the way—and quotes what Crockett says about "where about the graves of the martyrs the whaups are crying, his heart remembers how." And Stevenson himself adds, "Ah! by God, it does, it does."[7] The letters grew pretty sad at that point. But just before the man died all his ancient cunning of hand returned to him, and he died in the high tide of a great novel, producing magnificently, with his spurs on, as such a man should die. All his life he had supremely dreaded the death of an invalid, and feared that he would die a sick man in his bed. He did not. He dropped at his study table in the midst of his task, fresh from the greatest of his works. For that last tale of the Scottish moorlands, unnamed and uncompleted,[8] his critics say is the richest and ripest of all his work, the beginning of what would have been his era of mastership in fiction. Never was his style so enchanting, they say, his fancy so rich, his sympathies so acute. The work was growing into absolute perfection, when, suddenly one morning down there in Samoa, a blood vessel snapped in that great brain, and the sleeper was awakened from his dream, and the dream was left to us incomplete, undreamed forever. If there is anything that argues for an immortality, another chance, it is things like this. What has become of the rest of that novel, the part that was never written, of all the greatest part of Stevenson we never got? The universe is merciless, but it is economical, would it tolerate a waste like that? There are so many of us who are good enough to fertilize the soil when we go under ground, and are not good for much else. But what's the sense in putting

7. Correctly: "'where about the graves of the martyrs the whaups are crying. *His* heart remembers how.' . . . 'Ah, by God, it does!'" Letter of August, 1893; *Vailima Letters*, in the edition of *Robert Louis Stevenson* (New York: Charles Scribner's Sons, 1909), XVII, 262.

8. *Weir of Hermiston*, published in 1896. It ran serially in the *Journal*, beginning in March of that year.

THE KINGDOM OF ART

soul like that in a miserable consumptive wreck of a body unless it's to
have another show, sometime, somewhere?[9]

Journal, January 5, 1896, p. 9.

Go Back, Mr. Kipling

*It is hard to realize the excitement of Rudyard Kipling's leap to fame when
as a young man of less than twenty-five he came with songs and stories of
India in* Departmental Ditties, Plain Tales from the Hills, Soldiers
Three, The Story of the Gadsbys, *and half a dozen other books, all
published in England in 1890 (in India, 1888). He was the working
symbol of the exotic East, so refreshing that even before he married Caroline
Balestier in 1892 and settled down in Vermont, the world was determined
that he must not forget his muse. In November, 1891, a literary note in the
Lasso, the magazine Willa Cather helped to edit when she was a freshman
at the University, said that "Edmund Gosse, in his article on Rudyard
Kipling in the* November Century, *entreats Mr. Kipling to seclude
himself beyond the pale of civilization, lest his genius be conventionalized.
Mr. Kipling has promptly obeyed by sailing for the Cape of Good Hope .
. . ." A few years later in her* Journal *column of October 14, 1894, Miss
Cather spoke of the current war between China and Japan, "that mutual
extermination of barbarians that is going on in the Eastern hemisphere.
There hasn't been such a picturesque combat in the memory of many
generations." Mr. Kipling should go over and write up that war, she said.
"It's entirely in his line and there must be color enough to make another
'Gate of the Hundred Sorrows.'" When Stevenson died the next December,
she wrote at greater length about Kipling's future.*

Instinctively when one of the greater lights goes out we look about
us to see what candles we have left us to dispel our darkness. Some way
Mr. Stevenson suggests Mr. Kipling, though the similarity goes no further
than their choice of uncanny and unusual subjects. Mr. Kipling is a young
and strong man who gave us promise and who is not in any hurry to
fulfil it. Fame does not seem to be good for him. For the last five years,
since he first won international recognition, he has been living on his past.

9. Portions of this article and of Willa Cather's *Journal* columns of January 19, 1896
(the burial in Samoa), and March 22, 1896 (Stevenson's collaborations), were used in the
unsigned article, "Stevenson's Monument," in the *Home Monthly* for September, 1896. On
Stevenson's willingness to collaborate, she had said, "If some Samoan chieftain of dusky hue
and oiled foretop had requested the genial Robert Louis to collaborate with him, no doubt
he would have been obliging enough to consent. He had genius enough for a half dozen
and kindness enough for half a hundred" (*Journal*, March 22, 1896).

He is too young to do that and his past is not great enough to stand it. He first came to a standstill when he began to write in collaboration with Wolcott Balestier because of his exceeding affection for Balestier's sister. Now, when a mortal man who has been favored by one of the immortal, even if she is only a grimy newspaper nurse [muse?], yokes her along with another man's name for the sake of a mortal maiden he does an unwise and foolish thing, and according to the decree of the Olympian he shall not escape unscathed. Since then he has been trying to live a respectable Puritan life in Vermont and be a full-fledged family man. It would be more encouraging to hear that he had taken to opium or strong drink or that he had married a half-caste woman and was raising vermilion hades out in India. Go back to the east, Mr. Kipling; we and our world are not for you. Our life is not free enough for you and you are not strong enough for it. You have not the divine nature, the lofty ideal that can preserve you through the fire unsinged and unharmed. Don't hang about our cities to study our manners. They might broaden and deepen a greater man, but they will corrupt and fetter and belittle you. Don't strive to repeat our drawing-room gossip; it is empty and vapid and not worthy of repetition. Don't tell in petty stories of our own pettiness; we have enough little Harvard men to do that. Tell us of things new and strange and novel as you used to do. Tell us of love and war and action that thrills us because we know it not, of boundless freedom that delights us because we have it not. Go back to the land where you wrote "The Gate of the Hundred Sorrows" and "Without Benefit of Clergy" and "On the City Wall." [10] That is the country for you. Go back where there are temples and jungles and all manner of unknown things, where there are mountains whose summits have never been scaled, rivers whose sources have never been reached, deserts whose sands have never been crossed. "Back to the land where the great sun is born." You need fierce color and we have not got it to give you; you need wild action and you will not find it here. In your younger and better days, Mr. Kipling, you would not have missed this great war in the east. You would be doing something better than writing stories for the holiday magazines. You would be off in Asia giving us the romance and poetry and horror of that great upheaval. That war will pass out of romance into musty history because there is no poet to record it for us. You have missed the opportunity of centuries that you, above all men, yes, even above far greater men,

10. These stories appeared respectively in *Plain Tales from the Hills*, *The Courting of Dinah Shadd*, and *In Black and White*, all published in 1888/1890.

are fitted for. Ah, Mr. Kipling, it would be sad and tragical if it were not so laughable that you who wrote *The Story of the Gadsbys* should be the victim of matrimony. It has shorn the wings of your freedom, and your freedom was your art. So back to the east, flee out into the desert before it is too late. Write loosely, carelessly, as you used to do, so that you give us the old novel delight. If the climate is not good for Mrs. Kipling then remember that you were married to your works long before you ever met her. Alas! there were so many men who could have married Mrs. Kipling, and there was only you who could write *Soldiers Three*. Remember your own words, "It cripples a man's sword arm, and, oh, it plays hell with his notions of honor."

"Down to Gehenna or up to the throne, he travels the fastest who rides alone." [11]

Journal, December 23, 1894, p. 13.

Anthony Hope: Modern Times in Zenda

Although he had been publishing since 1891, the English writer Anthony Hope (Sir Anthony Hope Hawkins) had his greatest success in 1894 with The Prisoner of Zenda, *a book that evidently gave Willa Cather very great pleasure, for references to it appear often in the following years. Hope was a prolific writer, however, and as he continued to pour out stories and novels he lost the first fine careless rapture that charmed for everyone the views of the mythical contemporary kingdom of Ruritania, the castle of Zenda, and the adventures of Princess Flavia, Rudolph Rassendyll, and Rupert of Hentzau.*

In the last five years two young men of great promise have come to light in English fiction; Rudyard Kipling and Anthony Hope Hawkins. Two men who have not trod in the accepted paths nor walked in usual ways, nor shown any very great respect for the examples of the masters. They have preferred, it seems, to strike off through Bypath Meadow and take their chances, and leave the company of well-ordered pilgrims of fame to go rejoicing on their way to the Celestial City. They can afford to be original; they have talent rich and brilliant, unlike that of other men, and they have other things, youth, future and possibilities.

A few months ago Mr. Hawkins published *The Prisoner of Zenda*, a romance that was withal so realistic, so modern in tone and feeling that

11. Two lines from "L'Envoi," which appeared at the end of *The Story of the Gadsbys*. Correctly: "Down to Gehenna or up to the Throne / He travels the fastest who travels alone."

it made one see a new hope in fiction, made one dream for the moment that the world had not outgrown the possibilities of romance. We have had, God be thanked, even in this generation writers of pure romance; Doyle[12] and Weyman and the king and father of them all, Robert Louis Stevenson, whose harp is sounding now to finer ears than ours. But all these are romancers of the past. They dress their characters in hose and doublets and gird them with swords, give them the manners of other times and other people. Even the deeds and men in *Kidnapped* and *David Balfour* seem immeasurably distant and far away. But Rudolph of the Elphbergs is a man of our own world and of our time, like us a "victim of civilization," and the civilization that cost him his love is our own, our own cherished, complicated civilization that costs us so much, upon whose altar we lay half of all that is dearest to us, while every year we make its demands more cruelly exacting, its requisitions more impossible. Just as the Chinese have devoted their national existence to making a language so ponderous that their own scholars cannot learn it and a religion so intricate that their own priests cannot remember it. One wonders all the while one is reading the book just where in Europe the kingdom of Ruritania is, and feels as though some shrewd traveler might discover it. The illusion of intense modernness and presentness is never once dispelled. In that masterly last chapter I was afraid, horribly afraid, that Rudolph might gather his Princess up bodily and flee with her like the knights of old and make an old time romance after all, or that he might be weak enough to stay and love and spoil the whole chivalrous tone of the book. But Mr. Hawkins did not fail us; the impossibilities of our complicated life and the night train ended it. Not a ship or a fiery steed, but the night train. "Rudolph, Rudolph, Rudolph!" that was all. That to my mind is the real wonder of the book, that it put a romance into a dress suit, a real romance with war and blood and love and honor, like the romances of the Grail or the Holy Sepulchre. And all this comes about so naturally and simply that it seems as if it might happen to any of us. Only, instead of faith and fanaticism standing for the opposing element, the forbidding fate, there are all those hundred little precautions with which we have hedged ourselves about to make life easy, but which have in reality made it so hard, so hard to live, so hard to lay aside.

12. Willa Cather preferred Sir Arthur Conan Doyle's historical romances to his mysteries, mentioning *The White Company* (1891), *Micah Clark* (1889), and *The Mystery of Cloombers* (1889), which she said "is a sort of Anglo-Indian romance, and in spirit, lightness of style and strong scene painting is much the best novel of the three" (*Journal*, March 15, 1896).

Mr. Hope has written a new book. He calls it *A Change of Air* [1894]. In plot and purpose it is entirely unlike *The Prisoner of Zenda* which is encouraging, for it shows that his head is not turned by success and that he is too strong to repeat himself even when the public demands it. I do not like it quite so well, but that may be a matter of personal taste merely. It is certainly a study in life as it is lived. Dale Bannister, a revolutionary poet from London, goes to live down at Denborough, a quiet English town, and falls into the hands of the Philistines. Falls very much into their hands, indeed he falls in love with one of them. He has brought with him a little colony of Bohemians to solace his exile, but when he mingles with the townsfolk and the fair daughters of the townsfolk he wearies of his colony, the little singer and all, and wants to be rid of them. It is the old story of the eagle who plucks out his feathers that he may become a domesticated bird. And the strange and admirable part of it is that Mr. Hawkins does not lament the lost eagle and hold him up as a terrible example to all eagles and warn them to remain on their eyrie heights. He lets him pluck himself and says no more about it. Indeed, Mr. Hawkins seems to sympathize very little with his genius. His heart goes out to the common people, people less gifted and warmer hearted whom Dale Bannister makes supremely miserable; the poor little soprano who breaks her heart for him, and erratic Dr. Roberts who goes mad over Dale's apostasy. I suspect apropos of the sorrows of genius that Mr. Hawkins thinks those expensive gentlemen cause a good deal more suffering than they ever experience. The principal episode of the book is not up to its general standard. It seems impossible and far-fetched and melodramatic. Pistols are dangerous weapons to handle in fiction sometimes. And the ending of the book is undoubtedly careless, a mere resort to get the characters out of the way, an excuse to stop. It would have been more frank in Mr. Hawkins to have stopped without an excuse. But the book as a whole rings true and Philip Hale, the journalist, who acts as a sort of Greek chorus between the book and reader, never disappoints one. The dialogue is of course unusually fine, sometimes clever, sometimes still cleverer by reason of its stupidity, the kind of talk one likes to hear and the talk one is compelled to hear. It is the dialogue that makes Mr. Hawkins' characters seem so alive, for it is talk with which reasonable and reasoning beings might address each other. Then his characters are able to hold sweet converse upon other subjects than the grand passion, which is an unusual accomplishment in characters. The book is full of that delicate cynicism that we met in *The Prisoner of Zenda* and *The Dolly*

Dialogues [1894], and there is the same quiet gentlemanly way of telling the sad truth, as when Philip Hale tells Tora, "One can't even be kind in the way one likes best." No, that's the curse of it all, one can't. It's when we most want to give bread that we must give the stone and the serpent. Life would be much easier if it were otherwise.

Courier, September 14, 1895, pp. 6–7.

Those Zenda stories by Anthony Hope that are appearing in *McClure's*[13] are really very diverting, and they afford one an excellent opportunity to study the character, or rather the characteristics of the Princess Osra, for to her and to her various intangible love affairs they seem to be entirely devoted. Now the princess is somewhat of a Bohemian and thoroughly plucky. She visited Stephen, the silversmith, at an hour when it is not customary for ladies to call on gentlemen, and she masqueraded as a peasant girl for her social highwayman and afterward was considerate enough to give him her red stockings as a souvenir. She calmly stakes herself against the castle of Zenda and plays dice with Count Nikolas, and when we last heard of her she coolly went forth to woo the indifferent miller of Hofbau. The princess is enterprising or nothing. And the most wonderful thing about her is her versatility and her Catholic tastes. She was mildly in love with them all and did not deny it. She managed even to conjure up feelings of tenderness for the miller in his red cap. But all her flames are so impossible and intangible. A smith, a highwayman, a priest and a miller. Now there are to be six Zenda stories, so the princess has two more chances, and I am afraid in one of these rounds she may get the worst of it. She has almost exhausted the varieties of impossible men, unless she tries a married man and a tenor. She will have to do something like that, for it would be against Mr. Hope's principles to let anything definite come to pass. He never does. He never gives any particular reason why they should not, but he makes the conditions hostile, and his heroes and heroines are latter day folks and are never strong enough or foolish enough to fight existing conditions. So they never get anywhere. Neither will the Princess Osra. She will probably keep on having adventures until the end of time and die a respected spinster.

Courier, November 9, 1895, p. 6.

13. Six "Zenda stories" with the general title of *The Heart of the Princess Osra* ran in *McClure's* from August, 1895 through January, 1896. The November story, "The Indifference of the Miller of Hofbau," has an allusion in Willa Cather's short story, "Eric Hermannson's Soul," first published in *Cosmopolitan* in April, 1900. (Reprinted in CSF, pp. 368 ff.)

Mr. Anthony Hope's new novel, *Phroso*, which begins in the April
[1896] *McClure's*, is an outright and downright disappointment. But this
has been a year of disappointments and when men like Thomas Hardy
write "Cynical Judes" [*Jude the Obscure*], and [like] George Meredith
write *The Amazing Marriage*, we cannot wonder at the failure of new and
comparatively untried men. It must have been pleasant to live in the days
of Thackeray and George Eliot and Dickens when new fiction never fell
below the mark. It may be unfair to judge a story by the opening chapter,
yet if a book begins badly it seldom improves, and this *Phroso* starts out
in such an utterly characterless manner. The first two chapters leave no
distinct impression of anybody or anything. They contain almost no
characterization. Furthermore they are dull. With the mass of readers
workmanship does not count, interest is everything. But the fact is that
work poorly done is very seldom interesting. An impartial reader, even
a partial one, will find that they so far care very little about the new Lord
of Neopalia and his island and the wicked Lord Constantine. There is one
gleam of hope in the Lady Euphrosyne, she of the expressive shoulders.
Hope is rather clever with women folk, he doesn't attempt too much
analysis and leaves them sort of unsolved. She may be dashing enough to
redeem all these other uninteresting people. So far we have only seen her
at luncheon, and there she spoke in Greek, so we know very little about
her. George Meredith has pronounced Anthony Hope the cleverest
writer of dialogue living, but even the dialogue in *Phroso* is below par.
As dialogue it is good enough, but so far there has been nothing worth
talking about. In interest and general style the first chapter of *Phroso*
cannot be mentioned with *The Prisoner of Zenda*. . . .

Journal, April 19, 1896, p. 13.

Stanley Weyman: The Anglo-Saxon Manner

*Among the writers of romance, Stevenson and Kipling were themselves
world-wanderers, bringing distance strangely alive out of their own
experience; Anthony Hope made a new world inside the old; and Stanley
Weyman wrote novels of adventures in the France and England of earlier
times. If his touch was heavier, his popularity was nearly as great, and books
like The House of the Wolf (1890), A Gentleman of France (1893),
Under the Red Robe (1894), and The Man in Black (1896)—plus
a good many stories and plays that were never collected—swept serially
through the newspapers and magazines with scarcely a pause.*

Sometimes one has a peculiar weakness for plays and books that are not very great or very profound just because they have in them an atmosphere of adventure and romance that gratifies the eternal boy in us. We all have it for *Treasure Island* and for the books and plays of Dumas *père*. Porthos, Athos and D'Artagnan are just about the three best friends we ever made in this world, anyway; they never intrude and they stay by us longer. The man who does not meet those three in his youth goes through life deprived of a great deal. In these days of books that are so full of thought and analysis and general unpleasantness those books ringing with action are a blessed refuge. And if we will only acknowledge it, Mr. Stanley Weyman's tales are almost as refreshing. It is a good thing he wrote them and it is a good thing Richard Mansfield has had them dramatized and is going to play them.[14] They are very quiet, undemonstrative books, for all they are so full of blood and carnage and abductions, and Mr. Mansfield is a very quiet and undemonstrative actor. His action will in itself supply the calm and lucid way of telling awful things; that is Weyman's peculiar style and that will be largely lost in the dramatization. *The House of the Wolf* as a play will probably lose not one whit of its quaint style, for Mansfield's face and gesture and bearing will supply it. People accuse Weyman of affecting the French style because his plots are laid across the channel. Could any style be more thoroughly Saxon? In its straightforward simplicity, its quaint brevity and lack of exaggerated feeling it almost reminds one of *The Anglo-Saxon Chronicle*. Compare it with the style of *The Three Guardsmen*. We have all seen Alexander Salvini as D'Artagnan. Can you imagine him as the Sieur de Marsac?[15] What would he do with all his bubbling buoyancy, his effervescence of animal spirits? Weyman's heroes have French names, but they have English heads and English hearts. They are all slow and stern. They might any one of them be leaders of Cromwell's army; they are Puritans, all of them. There is never one glint of mirth or pleasure in all Weyman's books, only heroic actions undertaken from duty rather than recklessness, and of pent-up feeling subdued with an iron hand. There is never a note of Dumas' gaiety, the romances are as grave as *Pilgrim's Progress*, and they are as English.

Journal, August 11, 1895, p. 9.

14. One play was produced in the 1896–1897 season, an adaptation of Weyman's *Under the Red Robe* by Edward Rose.

15. Weyman's *A Gentleman of France* (1893) was subtitled, "Being the Memoirs of Gaston de Bonne, Sieur de Marsac."

Defense of Dumas

"Porthos, Athos and D'Artagnan . . . just about the three best friends we ever made in this world," Willa Cather had said. Some of the romances of Alexandre Dumas père she had certainly absorbed into her own imagination: The Three Guardsmen, The Man in the Iron Mask, The Count of Monte Cristo. *What struck her forcefully was the magnificent energy of Dumas, who could create without pause a whole generation of romances of unfailing quality. "Dumas was a Titan literally and no figure of speech about it," she wrote just before she left Nebraska. "He belonged to the heroic age. He came from a mysterious people and had the iron vigor and untiring strength of his savage ancestors, as well as their strangely fresh and vivid imagination" (*Journal, *May 10, 1896). As Dumas could define the best kind of drama—four boards, four walls, two characters, and one passion—so he represented most completely the whole vital stream of the imaginative, creative fiction that had been called romance.*

Emily Crawford has an excellent article on the elder Dumas in the last *Century*.[16] A sympathetic biography of Dumas is always good reading and has always much of that same charm that permeates *The Three Guardsmen*, for Dumas lived very much as he wrote and had in himself all the merits and all the weaknesses of his novels. A nature at once so rich and so weak is almost without a parallel, and to write understandingly of it the biographer should be a romancer as well. Miss Crawford seems, however, to dwell rather too seriously upon Dumas' slight jealousy of his son Alexandre. Of all the younger Dumas' critics none wrote so admiringly of his work as his father. It was not his son's success that grieved Dumas, but the tendency of his son's work. He saw that one great success of the sort Alexandre had made meant a score of imitators and the gradual overthrow of romance. He knew that the fall of romance meant the final elimination of the aesthetic element from literature. He foresaw Zola. But to his son he was a good father if a careless one. . . .

In the same article Miss Crawford says Dumas' works will not long survive him because they are not weighty enough, because he only "saw the pageantry of history and penetrated into none of its philosophy." Heaven preserve us! What business has a novelist with the philosophy of history? His business is to see the romance of history, not to delve after sociological causes and effects. His art is not to dissect the dead men of

16. "The Elder Dumas," in the *Century* for March, 1896.

old, but to vivify them, and that, Miss Crawford, is a greater art than to analyze a whole nation of buried heroes. Miss Crawford also states that Dumas' novels are not deep enough to bear the test of time, and that they "do not interest this analytical generation." A good many hard things have been said about this generation, but that is a charge too great to be borne patiently. Was Dumas ever more popular than he is now? *The Three Guardsmen* series are recognized classics, and so long as there is youth and hope and imagination in the world they will remain such. Dumas' influence has never ceased to be felt in England, if it has in France; and in a hundred years Dumas, the elder, will be greater than Dumas the son, even in Paris. For France will run analytical fiction to death as it does everything else, and will go charging back to romance, singing a new Marseillaise. The possibilities of analytical fiction are limited; it can go on until it has lost all poetry, all beauty, until it reaches the ugly skeleton of things, there it must stop. The human mind refuses to be dragged further even in the name of art. We will all sicken of it some day and go back to romance, to romance whose possibilities are as high and limitless as beauty, as good, as hope. Some fine day there will be a grand exodus from the prisons and alleys, the hospitals and lazarettos whither realism has dragged us. Then, in fiction at least, we shall have poetry and beauty and gladness without end, bold deeds and fair women and all things that are worth while.

Journal, March 15, 1896, p. 9.

FIELDS OF VISION

Willa Cather often stressed the individual talent, but she also said that the artist-creator must know all, experience all. Shakespeare was the great and unequalled example of the genius who was himself and all other things too. A beginning writer could learn comprehension and grandeur from him; from other lesser talents he could learn definition, focus, the plotting of boundaries. Any one thing—a book, a style, a point of view, a genre—well considered and defined might be a lesson of art, or simply an object to hold in the mind as the hand holds a stone, feeling texture and shape until finally it must be retained or discarded. Or each book and each style might be called the glass of a personal view: How else should one find the frame and direction of his own vision except by looking from every point and noting where he chooses to linger? In these selections from Willa Cather's observations of the particular qualities of writers and books, she comments on the versatility and sophistication of French writers; a sense of place and the uses of environment; the marks of personal bias on subject and style; the limitations of genres; and both the limitations and the revelations in work like that of the Scottish writers, which might be modified by a locality or the particular vision of the people who live there.

Coppée

We have been particularly blessed with noted foreigners in this country lately . . . and now we are to have François Coppée, who will lecture in the metropolitan cities on French literature. M. Coppée is one of the most musical of poets, the most delightful of story tellers.[17] He has done some of the most plaintive and charming sketches in the French language, and that is saying a good deal, for the French have reduced the short story to the most perfect artistic form that it has ever attained. They seem to have the knack of grasping the very heart of a situation and making the details look after themselves, of making one critical episode tell a life and analyze a character. Even their long novels have the short story conciseness and directness; their epigrammatic tendencies seem to result in that. What is *Les Misérables* but a series of perfect short stories? M. Coppée is best known in this country by his short stories, "The

17. Coppée (1842–1908) had published some seventeen volumes of poetry, a number of plays, and stories in both French and English. A very attractive little book was *Ten Tales of François Coppée*, translated by Walter Learned, with pen-and-ink drawings by Albert E. Sterner, and an introduction by Brander Matthews (New York: Harper and Brothers, c 1890).

Substitute," "Two Clowns," "The Captain's Vices" and his perfect little romance *The Rivals*, which appeared in *Harper's* several years ago [November, 1892]. He is a romanticist and does not pretend to be anything else, and his romance is not at all the romance of vice. His stories have a purity which is unusual in France, and a freshness which is unusual anywhere. It is a curious fact that though French authors so generally affect realism they are all, Zola excepted, romanticists at heart.

Authors are generally known by their most inferior work and it is true of Coppée. He is above all a dramatist and a poet and it is because his poetry is so much better that his stories are so good. They are all written in a minor key, painted in half lights and low tones, sad autumnal colors which blend with exquisite harmony, full of hazy melancholy and rich with the golden sadness of a poet's dreams. They are not stimulating, they do not beget energy in the reader, they neither leave him with a desire to go out and embrace humanity in general or to crush it beneath his foot. But they do leave him with a sort of vague impression that the world is not so bad after all, and that it is not such a supreme misfortune to live in it. They fill him with a mild content and a vague but lasting pleasure, which certainly is one of the higher purposes of art. To be beautiful, that is enough. . . .

M. Coppée has never lived in Bohemia nor dwelt in the tents of Shem, which proves that Bohemianism is no more necessary to greatness than it is fatal to it. A man is not great because he is an Englishman or because he is a Frenchman, because he drinks light wines or because he drinks heavy wines, but by the will of heaven and the grace of God.

Journal, February 17, 1895, p. 9.

Anatole France

So Anatole France [18] has made the [French] Academy at last, and richly does he deserve it. M. France is not an old man; he still lacks two years of reaching the half century mark; but he is one of the foremost of all the French giants of learning. He is a classical scholar and an eastern scholar and what not. Besides that, he has written some of the most graceful poetry and some of the most vivid and luxuriant fiction of

18. "Anatole France" was the pseudonym of Jacques Anatole François Thibault (1844–1924). *Le Crime de Sylvestre Bonnard* (1881) and *Thaïs* (1890) had several English translations: *The Crime of Sylvestre Bonnard*, translated by Lafcadio Hearn (1890); *Thaïs*, translated by A. D. Hall (1891) and Ernest De Lancey Pierson (1892). It is impossible to say whether Willa Cather read these and other French books in the original or in translation—probably both, at various times.

modern France. He is best known in America by his *Crime of Sylvestre Bonnard*. His novel, *Thaïs*, is a masterpiece of historic fiction. It is an episode in the life of an Egyptian monk, who tries to convert the most admired Greek courtesan of the time. The scene, of course, is laid in the days of the final decadence of the Roman empire, when old things, outworn and corrupt, were giving place to new, when nature was revenging herself for the sins of the past and those old anchorites, the sons of wrath, were subduing the whole empire of the flesh out in the caves of the desert. It is a book before which *Hypatia* grows rather dim and lifeless. . . .

Journal, March 15, 1896, p. 9.

. . . It is rather surprising to find such a book [*The Crime of Sylvestre Bonnard*] in French, it is so quiet, so modest and reflective, so thoroughly undramatic. It is a quaint story of an old bibliophile who dwells in the Quai Malaquais along the Seine in a library of ancient tomes which he calls the City of Books. . . .

In a brief review it is impossible to give any adequate idea of the quiet charm of the book. It is full of such poetic bits of description as this: "And there is a big bumble-bee who tries to force himself into the mouth of a flower, brutally. But his mouth cannot reach the nectar and the poor glutton strives in vain. He gives up the attempt and comes out of the flower all smeared with pollen." When Monsieur Sylvestre visits the tomb of his dead Clémentine he says: "I saw only the sloping stone on which was graven the name of Clémentine. What I then felt was something so deep and vague that only the sound of some rich music could convey any idea of it. I seemed to hear instruments of celestial sweetness make harmony in my old heart. With the solemn accord of a funeral chant there seemed to mingle the melody of a song of love, long forgotten."

Throughout the whole book there is a sweet and lofty sentiment almost German in its character. Running all through it there is a tender, child-like melody, embellished by the quaint philosophy of a scholar of seventy years. It is a truly remarkable book for a man to write in this most cynical of all ages, a book ·so good, so simple, so sincere, so full of sweet illusions. One does not wonder that they created the author a member of the Academy of France last month. For he is the master of more styles than one, and he can write a book of stress and passion with the best of them as his stormy *Thaïs* testifies. And the same man who wrote *Thaïs*, that burning rhapsody of the Egyptian deserts, wrote this idyl that is as tender as a spring twilight, as fresh and fragrant as the humid odor of violets.

Journal, April 12, 1896, p. 13.

Hall Caine

Hall Caine is on his way to this country and will arrive in New York early next week. For the last three years there has been a sort of exodus of "the great" to America. Englishmen of name and Frenchmen of renown have indulged in American tours, but among them all there has been no stronger or more vigorous writer.[19] Whatever may be said of Hall Caine's exaggeration, inconsistency and strained situations, the real force and power of the man remains undisputed. He is an island man. He is not a man of the world. He exaggerates like all men who are bounded by a narrow horizon. His work all lacks perspective. But the power of imagination is there. . . .

Courier, September 21, 1895, p. 6.

. . . The subtitle, "A Modern Saga," is the keynote of the story [of *The Bondman*]. Caine deals in the mystical, the improbable and the darkly tragical, and Iceland is the proper background for him. It is a country beyond the end of the world, dark and remote, where the impossible is possible. The story of *The Bondman* is tragic and intense, from the first page to the last. . . . [It] is a book of fate, that is Hall Caine's element. His characters have little to do with their own destiny, good or evil is thrust upon them and they stand like grim spectators and watch their lives play themselves out for better or for worse. He sees fate as the old Northmen saw it, a power personal and relentless, pursuing alike men and gods. Iceland is the proper place for such a story. It seems more probable there than it would in the world of railroads and telegraph and commonplaceness. Fate is natural enough there among the endless nights and the wintry seas and the volcanoes whose rumbling reminds the world that under us all there is still nature, uncontrolled, unsubdued, inexplicable. We have largely eliminated the element of fate from our lives, or think we have, but among the descendants of Erling the Bold it is otherwise. There is something about the book that occasionally reminds one of Hugo. Perhaps it is the inevitable horror and suffering. Then Hall Caine's

19. Thomas Henry Hall Caine (b. 1853) had spent part of his life on the Isle of Man and used that setting in some of his later work, especially *The Manxman* (1894), which Willa Cather had read. Among his earlier novels were *The Shadow of a Crime* (1885), *The Deemster* (1887), and *The Bondman* (1890).

mind is a little like Hugo's in its exaggerated idealism. It is the Valjean type that appeals to him.[20] His heroes are all Christs and he crucifies them all. He is not at home with the commonplace. He does not make heroic men, but heroes, sometimes just a little stupid in their excessive heroism. But after all in the generation when so many men do light things cleverly, it is a heaven-sent boon to have a man who is in desperate and deadly earnest. For when all is said that can be said in praise of comedy, even the finest romantic comedy, tragedy remains the highest form of art. It speaks most deeply to the soul of man. It is true that life is keyed rather too low for that sort of thing just now. Henry James and Du Maurier and even Mr. Hope seem more in tune with the existence we lead, more nearly within the range of the possible. Perhaps if the South American war[21] would materialize it might give us the heroic impulse again, and we could read *The History of a Crime* or *Sevastopol* or even the ancient *Les Misérables* and think them possible. Too much security and comfort in living begets a sort of apathy toward the heroic, and an unconsciousness of those shadowy ideals that watch us out yonder in the big dark.

Journal, January 12, 1896, p. 9.

James Lane Allen

There is a remarkably agreeable story [*The Butterflies*] running in the *Cosmopolitan* just now by Mr. James Lane Allen.[22] It is certainly one of the best serial stories that the *Cosmopolitan* ever got hold of. It is a story of Kentucky farm life and manages to be true without being coarse and just without being offensive. The characters most involved are a young girl who has been brought up under the iron restrictions of the provincial church, and a young farmer whose impulses are rather too much for the church and the elders thereof. He is a sort of rustic Burns, a fellow with vivid imaginary powers, considerable personal vanity, an irresistible thirst for pleasure and a jubilant exultation in his youth, qualities sadly out of place in the country. In town there are a thousand things to gratify such tastes, above all there are books and music and the theatre. But in the country such a youth is likely to bring considerable trouble upon himself

20. Much of the preceding part of the review was used in the "Old Books and New" column by "Helen Delay" (a Cather pseudonym), in the *Home Monthly* for July, 1897.

21. Possibly referring to the boundary disputes between Argentina and Brazil (1895), and between Chile, Bolivia, and Peru (1894–1900). Venezuela was also in the news.

22. James Lane Allen (b. 1849) is perhaps better known for his *A Kentucky Cardinal* (1894). *The Butterflies*, subtitled "A Tale of Nature," ran in *Cosmopolitan* from December, 1895, to March, 1896.

and others. The body of the tale is cast between him and the girl who likes him rather more than he deserves, but certainly not more than is natural under the circumstances. So far, the girl is getting decidedly the worst of it, but whoever reads the tale will continue to like the boy just the same. What the young man needs is to fall into the hands of a world-wise and experienced flirt and be thoroughly and systematically quenched for a time. But such lads never get their dues, even the coquettes are tempted to be a bit easy with them. For the rest, Mr. Allen's story is a study in environment, an idyl of a southern summer. It could not have happened in winter, it could not have happened in town. In the country June is a stirring appeal to return to nature. Strange things happen in a country summer, even to city folks. Nature comes out renewed from her tipsy slumber and shakes off lightly the hundred centuries of her past, asserting herself like the reckless old pagan that she is. The birds sing "Hymen, Hymenus"[23] from every hawthorne hedge and the whole glittering green world shouts, "Evoe, evoe"; the old cry that calls youth to life. And a thousand hearts awake and say: "What does it matter, what does anything matter, but just this?" We are all pagans in the summer time. Bacchus will never lack followers while there is spring, nor while there is June will the daughters of the sea foam be forgotten. Mr. Allen's story is a sort of duo between the richness and joyousness of nature, the prodigal delight of all things truly hers, and the torturing sternness and barrenness of certain creeds and certain men who have tried to rob the sunlight of its meaning and steal from the breath of summer its sweetness. The whole tale so far is remarkably well done, done so well that one is not afraid of its suddenly becoming weak and disappointing. It has that subtle, allusive poetry and sympathy that makes even the most prosaic and commonplace tale beautiful. It is just the sort of thing that poor Hamlin Garland is always trying and always failing to do. And the reason thereof is that Mr. Allen has just two things that Mr. Garland has not, imagination and style. No man ever tried his hand at fiction and persisted in the vain attempt who so utterly lacked these essential things as Mr. Garland. Art is temperament and Hamlin Garland has no more temperament than a prairie dog.[24]

Journal, January 26, 1896, p. 9.

23. Perhaps an echo of Whitman's poem "O Hymen! O Hymenee"? See also the Whitman essay and notes 35–37, below.

24. The work of Hamlin Garland in *Main-Travelled Roads* (1891) and in many magazines (for example, "My Grandmother of Pioneer Days" in the *Ladies' Home Journal* for April, 1895) irritated Willa Cather for a number of years. She thought it was flat and commonplace.

Eugene Field

... Eugene Field [25] was only a journalist. The American newspaper was his task and his curse, as it has been of so many brilliant men. Journalism is the vandalism of literature. It has brought to it endless harm and no real good. It has made an art a trade. The great American newspaper takes in intellect, promise, talent; it gives out only colloquial gossip. It is written by machines, set by machines, and read by machines. No man can write long for any journal in this country without for the most part losing that precious thing called style. Newspapers have no style and want none. A newspaper writer should have no more individuality than those clicking iron machines that throw the type together. Eugene Field had been bound to the press from his youth, the bond slave of that great, roaring, grimy *deus ex machina*. For a man who was compelled to write so much it was wonderful that he wrote so well.

Courier, November 9, 1895, p. 7.

Eugene Field all his lifetime was a cheerful sort of a fellow, and everything he wrote bore the marks of his cheerful and genial personality. But the cheeriest of all his work was not published until after his death. It appeared only a few weeks ago under the title *The Love Affairs of a Bibliomaniac*. It is only fair to this book to say at the outset that it is nothing whatever like the *Literary Passions* of William Dean Howells in which that gentleman informs the astonished world that Dumas was a romanticist and discusses in an authoritative manner the charms of Tolstoi. It has nothing whatever of the pedantic, autocratic, exclusive flavor of Mr. Howells' work.[26] If ever a volume was filled with a genuine, humble, reverent love of the very leaves and covers and odors of books it is this

25. A well-known midwestern journalist, Field (b. 1850) had died on November 4, 1895. His *Love Affairs of a Bibliomaniac* was published posthumously in 1896. Willa Cather liked the book so much that she gave it to friends who would also enjoy it. One gift was to George and Helen Seibel, two of her earliest and best friends in Pittsburgh.

26. *My Literary Passions* by William Dean Howells ran in the *Ladies' Home Journal* in the winter of 1894–1895. Willa Cather's comment here is related to an outburst the previous summer when she wondered why it was necessary for Howells to state so importantly what a good many other people already knew (*Journal*, July 14, 1895). She could speak with some assurance, for one of these other people was Willa Cather herself. As a case in point, Howells had written in the *Ladies' Home Journal* for March, 1895, that Tolstoi was better as an artist than as a teacher; that his best books were *The Cossacks*, *War and Peace*, *Ivan Ilyitch*, and *Anna Karenina*; and that the story "Polikushka" was one of Tolstoi's best. Willa Cather had said the same things when she was a University freshman, three and a half years before (see pages 377–378).

little chronicle of Field's love affairs. It is not strictly biographical, it is not critical, and from cover to cover the word "art" does not once occur! It is not an analysis of the power of books, but rather a humble expression of their charms. He does not write of them constructively from the inside, but objectively from the outside. He does not write of books as "art," but as personalities. He does not see them as studies in environment or character, but as trusty companions, and he speaks of them as "a plain, blunt man who loves his friends" might speak. In this century books and women have been subjected to a most painful system of analysis. Every youngster before he is out of kilts announces that he likes in such a woman this trait, and in such a book that feature. It's a downright comfort to come across a man who loves a book *in toto*, with a personal affection, and who feels its charms without insisting upon dissecting it. This little book is so brimming with downright affection for all printed things that when you open it you lose your bearings for a moment and fancy that you are reading some old fellow of Goldsmith's or De Quincey's time before the fashion of analysis came over from France.

Eugene Field was a queer fellow; he was a man of letters of the old school, yet he lived in Chicago; he was a man who loved the classics and read them daily, yet he was a journalist, a strange and, unfortunately, rare anomaly. His *Love Affairs* is a sort of autobiography of his tastes. It is supposedly written by an old bookworm whose first flame was *The New England Primer* which he read in the company of a demure little Puritan maiden, Captivity Waite. In this they read of the burning of old John Rogers and many another cheerful incident and learned this sound maxim, which in after years the old bibliomaniac had engraved on his book plates:

My books and heart
Must never part.

The primer was followed by *Robinson Crusoe*, and as an explanation the old gentleman says: "I shall not say that *Robinson Crusoe* supplanted the primer in my affections. I prefer to say what is the truth; it was my second love." Here again we behold another advantage which the lover of books has over the lover of women. If he be a genuine lover he can and should love any number of books, and this polybibliophily is not a disparagement to any one in that number. The old bibliophilite recalls certain periods of his life by the books that then enamored him. . . .

Journal, February 23, 1896, p. 9.

Amélie Rives

So Amélie Rives is married again and to a Russian prince.[27] Princess Troubetzkoy, that will look well under the title of her next sensational novel. In spite of the fact that her divorce from Mr. Chanler is not many moons old, her friends are fondly hoping that she will become domesticated, and a few of her literary admirers think that she will settle down to steady work and produce something worth while. Amélie Rives comes of a family whose women have been models of propriety and social grace for generations. To have been born of one of the first families of Virginia is in itself a heritage. It gives one traditions. If Amélie Rives has not yet learned how to live, the chances are that she will never learn. Life is easy for Virginia women. Virginia chivalry has made it so. There is only one demand made of them, only one command laid upon them. Amélie Rives has not kept the faith; she has made herself ridiculous and has made her name common property among trashy and ignorant people the world over. That, in Virginia, is the unpardonable sin. She retained her position socially even after the publication of her erotic and irretrievably silly fiction, for the Virginians grant the privilege of free thought and the expression of it even to their women. But her personal adventures have been too much for them, and when she actually wrote a novel about the difficulties of her married life she outraged every tradition they held sacred.

As to Miss Rives' literary prospects, they are considerably worse than nothing and it is doubtful if she will ever rise above writing tales for *Town Topics*. Her first book, *The Quick or the Dead?* [1888], was trashy enough to make a sensation and it contained some glimmerings of talent, but its style was essentially weak and overwrought, and it contained the greatest of all literary faults, it was thoroughly and entirely unnatural. There is no remedy for that; if one does not see at least a few things as they are by the time one is twenty, then one never sees them at all and goes through life with distorted vision. If one does not stumble upon

27. Novelist and playwright Amélie Rives (1863–1945) married John Armstrong Chanler in 1888, divorced him and married a Russian, Prince Pierre Troubetzkoy in 1896. These marital rearrangements caused much comment in the papers, possibly because both her fiction and her opinions were startling enough to keep Miss Rives in the news. In an earlier article Willa Cather had called her work "trashy fiction" and had described her as "the eloquent apostle of the small winged god, Amélie whose books are upon one everlasting subject, whose adjectives all have one taste, whose descriptions all tend toward one end, and whose harp has but one fervid string . . ." (*Courier*, October 19, 1895).

jovial robust old nature before a certain age, then the time for an introduction is past. The literature of passion is either very great art or very
great rot. When it is subjective it is usually the latter. Amélie Rives tried
to write the most difficult sort of fiction in the world and she did it
passing poorly. And in all her strained, exaggerated pages there was never
one touch of human humor to give hope for the future. She evinced all
of Ouida's absurdities and trashy propensities without any of that misguided lady's undisputable talent. In short the princess of the unpronounceable name is utterly without the blessed quality of common sense, and it
is impossible to either live or write decently without it.

Journal, March 8, 1896, p. 13.

Mystery Stories

When you come to look over your category of remembered pleasures
you will not find very many mystery stories among them. The reason thereof is that in such a story everything depends upon plot; it's the plot first
and the truth afterward or never at all. Human nature is wronged and
exaggerated and distorted and belittled all for the sake of keeping the
wires sufficiently tangled. The characters, where any attempt is made at
characterization, are made to say and do things as absurd as the puppets of
a Punch and Judy show. So for the most part these stories of mystery are
read and thrown aside and forgotten as quickly as a puzzle that is solved,
for they contain none of the elements of lasting satisfaction. Of course
there are notable exceptions. In the first place there is Dickens' *Mystery of
Edwin Drood*, which is a classic instance that that sort of thing can be done
well. Then there is Conan Doyle's *The Sign of Four* and *The Mystery of
Cloombers* that have established their author's reputation for fiction that is
highly sensational and yet by no means devoid of good workmanship and
literary skill. Then there is a queer compound of undeniable brilliancy and
very patent trashiness, *Dead Man's Rock*, the first and very uneven production of Mr. [Arthur] Quiller-Couch's early youth. That indeed,
despite its palpable errors, its amazing weakness and its misguided power,
would be a very good example of a successful mystery tale if only that
absurd middle part about Tom and Tom's ridiculous drama and the
actress were left out. It's about as much out of place in that kind of a tale
as the interlude of the Tenor and the Boy was in the late lamentable
Heavenly Twins [by Sarah Grand]. Still, with its great ruby and the epi-
sodes in Ceylon and the mutiny at sea and Simon Colliver and his
unearthly song it is a tale thrilling enough to read twice if you are a

[335]

person of leisure. It really makes you chilly and that's an experience worth looking for in a book and all its abominable technical faults do not prevent the thing from holding your attention. There is a certain youthful fervor in it that tells.

But of all the stories of mystery, old and new, give us *The Wrecker*, by that master of the art of telling a good tale, Robert Louis Stevenson. It is the most human, the most manly, the most thrilling of them all. It can actually hold you in breathless anticipation from dawn till twilight, and if you have any traditional respect for the allotted hours of slumber, never start on that book late in the day. If you have half the imagination of a tadpole you will hang on till cock crow.

In his epilogue to the painter Will H. Low, Mr. Stevenson states that his purpose in the story was to make it at once sensational and human, to make possible and sensible human agents the wires of his plot. As it is a plausible nineteenth century tale of modern instances and modern interests, it is of course commercial, and the great money quest is at the bottom of it. The great end [of] modern endeavor and the goal of the knight-errantry of fortunes is money, just as literally as it was once the holy sepulchre. It is for that end that crimes are done and ventures made, so of course Stevenson took as romantic a form of it as he could find and from that made his plot. And with a would-be-sculptor to see the whole thing with an artistic eye and find in it an artistic significance, it makes a tale that is a tale. It would be hard to find a more exciting situation than the auction of the wreck in San Francisco, or a more weird idea than that voice at the telephone. The beauty of it is that the whole thing is carried out by modern means exclusively. There are no legends, no rubies, no pirates, no ghosts. It is all done with the ordinary commercial equipments of a business man, and the ordinary tendencies of that most modern of all productions, the professional art amateur. . . .

Journal, March 22, 1896, p. 9.

Children's Books

Now that Thomas Hughes is dead and everyone is thinking of him and his life work,[28] it seems strange that a man who wrote two such thoroughly good books as *Tom Brown's School Days* and *Tom Brown at*

28. Thomas Hughes (1822–March 22, 1896) was primarily a jurist and reformer, though remembered best for his accounts of life at Rugby and Oxford in the *Tom Brown* books.

Oxford should have written so little else worth reading. For undoubtedly these two books, especially the first one, are about the most stirring, honest and manly boys' books that English lads of today can find in their own tongue. So many boys' books are written for little Lord Fauntleroys who are supposed to spend their youth dreaming in their nurseries. Fortunately for us we have very few such boys. The English and the American boy are alike in this, that as a rule they are neither dreamers nor embryo poets, and they care more for football than all the classics put together. There are plenty of books for the mopey children who are averse to physical exertion, but for the real live boys who eat and sleep and fight and dig and will one day be deans and judges, merchants and soldiers, there is not so much literature as one might think. The whole category of child literature is largely a farce anyway. Generally it is read much more devotedly by their sentimental mammas than by the boys to whom it is presented. As soon as a boy is old enough to read at all he is old enough to read the classics; unless he is not a boy of the reading kind, and in that case it is useless to thrust a lot of weak literature upon him, he had much better be playing shinney. The whole Lord Fauntleroy system has been an injury to the highest interests of literature. It dissipates the interest and natural vigor of a child's mind and gives him a life-long bias in favor of light fiction. The boy who is a confirmed devotee of the *Youth's Companion* and the child authors at ten will slight his Virgil and at twenty he will probably be reading Captain Charles King and Marie Corelli.[29] Things were much better in the old days when a boy read only *Pilgrim's Progress* and *The Holy War* and Foxe's *Book of Martyrs* and was pounded through a dozen books of the *Aeneid*. He had the foundation then of a pure and classical literary taste. He had the roughest part of literature mastered at the beginning, and the rest, if he chose to pursue it, was one long play day for him. If he did not choose he was at least not weakened by the sentimentality of so-called child fiction, and is left practical and unimaginative as nature meant him to be. For of all pitiful and laughable beings there is none quite so ridiculous as an essentially unliterary mind that has been coddled by artificial methods into believing itself literary. It is no crime not to be literary; why should people think it necessary to wheedle and pamper and coax children to read feeble books

29. Captain Charles A. King wrote many popular stories of army life (*Foes in Ambush*, *Under Fire*, etc.). Marie Corelli was also a popular novelist, especially with Queen Victoria (see pages 189 ff.).

that only amuse him in a most unliterary way. If a boy will read Bunyan and Goldsmith in his youth, say when he is ten years old, it signifies much; it means that his mind goes out to that sort of thing, that he has the real instinct of scholarship and that wild horses cannot drag him from his books. If he reads Louisa Alcott or some kindred spirit it signifies absolutely nothing. Who are these writers of child literature anyway? Generally people who have ingloriously failed in every other line of authorship. Of course there are a few exceptions to this rule and Thomas Hughes was one of the most notable among them. There is nothing in *Tom Brown* that could offend the most correct literary taste. Hughes wrote the strong spirited English of other days. Defoe and Smollett could have read him without being shocked. It is all good, clean, strong English without a suspicion of namby-pamby sentimentality. It is the boys' loss that he did not write more. But Judge Hughes was an energetic, independent man, and it is small wonder that the career of an author had small attraction for him. Authors, players, painters, musicians, all artists whatsoever are forever at the mercy of the public caprice. From Homer down they have all, in a sense, eaten the bitter bread of charity. It is a bitter task, that of living by one's wits and amusing the public, and none too inviting to a strong man's spirit. For by the active practical men of the world all their followers of vague callings are patronized, regarded as Pericles regarded Aspasia.

Journal, April 12, 1896, p. 13.

Scottish Novelists: A Limited Landscape

The Scotchmen seem to be the gods of the hour among the devotees of ephemeral literature just now, and the gentlemen who were last year wearing Trilby neckwear are cultivating bonnie brier bushes in their coat lapels. Mr. Ian Maclaren and Mr. [Samuel] Crockett[30] have written some very fresh and satisfactory stories. They are all in dialect, which is a great advantage, as the reader, not understanding them, will not recognize their faults and will take their virtues for granted. Seriously, though, they have virtues and very pronounced ones. They are simple and they are direct. They are full of the quaint pathos of a sad people and the dim landscapes of a bleak country. But pathos in itself is not greatness. There are some

30. "Ian Maclaren" was the pseudonym of John Watson (1850–1907), clergyman, novelist, and lecturer, best known for *Beside the Bonnie Brier Bush* (1894) and *Days of Auld Lang Syne* (1895). Samuel Crockett (1860–1914) was also a minister and novelist. Some of his very Scottish books were *The Stickit Minister* (1893), *The Raiders* (1894), *Mad Sir Uchtred of the Hills* (1894), *The Men of the Moss-Hags* (1895), and *Bog-Myrtle and Peat* (1895).

facts and conditions that are in themselves pathetic, such as poverty, loneliness and death. A mere newspaper account of them is pathetic. That Crockett and Maclaren handle this element of pathos simply and without becoming maudlin, is greatly to their credit, but I doubt if it gives them any very high rank in literature. I doubt if local color alone ever gave real greatness to any man. There is a sameness and monotony about the work of these two Scotchmen that all too plainly asserts their limited powers and limited imagination. Apparently, living has taught them but a few lessons, that life is sad, that the world is Scotch and that creation is made up principally of heather and bonnie brier bushes. Local color, as Kipling once remarked, is a dangerous weapon. It is the element of women, they seldom write about anything else. The greatest artists, like Turgeneff, have always used it with an almost niggardly care. There are places in Turgeneff's novels where you can fairly feel him refraining from assisting himself by somber Russian landscapes and the threadbare, pathetic Russian peasant. Certainly Mr. Maclaren's most ardent admirer cannot call him versatile. One likes to read about sound, active, healthy men of the world sometimes, and not always about a collection of melancholy freaks. There is a wearisome sameness about the romances of old men and old women and boys and spinsters, who should have married and did not. The world is really not responsible for age or celibacy and gets tired of having the romances of these sad old people thrust forever in its face. And then in these plaintive Scotch romances the men are always preachers. I wonder if the population of Scotland is entirely made up of preachers? One thing these Scotch story tellers will certainly do, they will supply the Sunday school libraries for generations to come.

Neither Mr. Crockett nor Mr. Maclaren have, so far as I know, successfully handled a long story. Stevenson said that he did not consider that he had really done anything in literature until he had written a long story. That any clever person could write a sketch, but that it took considerable ability and tact to write even a poor novel. Certainly this is true. A short story is merely a mood, an impression. The chances are that it will have genuineness and continuity like any burst of feeling. But a novel requires not one flash of understanding, but a clear, steady flame and oil in one's flask beside. Not a mood, but a continuous flow of feeling and thought and a vast knowledge of technique and of the artistic construction of the whole. Many a man can fashion an arch or design a spire or carve a gargoyle, but to build a cathedral is quite another matter. Then I object to Mr. Maclaren's everlasting sadness and to everybody "dying at the end." Pierre Loti once wrote a book of such melancholy stories, but he frankly called it *The Book of Death and Pity* [*Le livre de la pitié et de la mort*, 1891] and his readers were forewarned and forearmed.

Of course everyone dies, but there is no use in inviting the whole world to the funeral obsequies of the entire population of Scotland. Death is not the especial privilege of the Scotch, sometimes English men die, occasionally even Americans. There are tragedies in life much greater than death, if one insists upon being tragic. There are short stories and short stories. The short story is a great art in its way; it should leave one vivid impression. It should have a vital point, or it should atone for the lack of such a point by beauty of language and quality of style, or else it should be pleasant. Now, Kipling's short stories are good reading because they are so various in theme and treatment. They are full of real men, young men, active and able bodied, pleasant fellows whom you can chat with and laugh with and forget. But I object to being introduced to a sombre character merely to attend his funeral six pages after I have met him. I don't believe in sadness in six entrees with a funeral for dessert. To be persistently sad is as narrow as to be persistently frivolous.

There was a really strong Scotch novel published a few years ago, though it seems to have been already forgotten by the changeful worshippers of Scotch fiction of the day. I speak of Barrie's *Little Minister* [1891].[31] That at least was a whole novel, not a book of sketches. Of course it was about a minister, being Scotch, but this minister was enterprising and he did something else than die. Indeed, he did so unfuneral a thing as to get married. It was quite a trick for Mr. Barrie to bring about that marriage too, it was no easy thing to manage a love affair between a staid and studious clergyman and a reckless, creedless gypsy. That scene between Babbie and Gavin at the well and the scene of Gavin's danger and Rob Dow's sacrifice were well done. Now Mr. Crockett, I imagine, would have taken old Nannie, who did not want to go to the poorhouse, and old Margaret, who had a "past," and old Ogilivy who had loved Margaret in his youth, and old Rob Dow who died to rescue the minister who had saved his soul, and any other aged and infirm persons who were handy, and made a separate story of each one because he has not the patience or craft to weave them all into one strong consistent novel that has both major and minor strains, and that is brave and cheerful and fair

31. Before 1895, James M. Barrie (1860–1937) had also written *Auld Licht Idylls* (1888), *A Window in Thrums* (1889), *Sentimental Tommy* (1895), and the play *The Professor's Love Story* (1895). He continued to be one of Miss Cather's favorite authors.

to both sides of human life. These chroniclers of woe seem to delight only in telling old women's tales of the hardships they have seen and the wakes they have attended. There is a merry side to life and a funny side to poverty; men are young once, and rejoice in their youth; they love sometimes and they often smile, they exult in the perfection and loveliness of the things that are, Mr. Crockett and Mr. Maclaren to the contrary. There are pleasure gardens in the world as well as graveyards, waltzes as well as funeral marches, living men as well as dead, young women as well as old, sonnets as well as epitaphs.

Courier, November 30, 1895, pp. 6–7.

Burns and Others

They are making great preparations over in Edinburgh to celebrate Burns' centenary. Scotch literature has, during the last decade, achieved that anticlimax of real advancement, "popularity." A hundred years ago and more when the peasant plowboy infused new life into English verse there was, with the exception of those fine old Scottish lyrics and ballads, no Scotch literature worth the name. The Scotch have always been scholars and students of literature, but they have been slow to produce. Indeed Scottish scholarship, unrivalled in its thoroughness, has given the world very little literature beyond learned commentaries and theological works that no one reads. The literature of Scotland has been made by an unlettered plowboy and a half a dozen men of this generation whose activity has been stimulated by foreign influence and the venturesome atmosphere of this fiction-devouring generation. The last twelve years have done more than made Scotch fiction popular; the productive advance has been great and rapid in every way, both as to matter, manner and quality. Twenty-five years ago who ever talked of Scottish fiction? The last generation produced a band of story [strong?] young men in Scotland, men clever of hand and sound of heart. There is Stevenson and Barrie and Crockett and Mr. Watson of *Brier Bush* fame. Yet it is hardly proper to class these men together, for decidedly Stevenson belongs to another "school" than the latter three, being, in a literary sense, more of a "citizen of the world" than they. The present living writers of Scottish fiction are intensely and excessively local, and to their "local color" and the quaint pathos of the dialect they owe the greater part of their success. For these successful writers of Scottish fiction are really more the children of opportunity than of genius. Of course, it has been said that genius is merely the power to grasp the opportunity. [In a] true worldly sense,

[341]

measuring worth only by success, that is so, but in the artistic sense genius means a higher thing; it means to be before one's time, to reveal further than the world can see, and many of its sons have been born generations before their opportunity was come, and have worked out their problem unaided and unencouraged in the waste places of the earth. If ever the world was ripe for Scottish fiction of the quaint, homely sort these men are giving us, it is now. The world is tired; this century has lived too much and too fast. We are born in a century already old; it has done so much it has run the whole course of emotions, it is exhausted by pleasure and caprice and gone back to the simple, restful sentiments of childhood, that second childhood that has innocence without joy, quiet without hope. Since the nineteenth century came in, strong and glad, the child of revolution and change, we have had every kind of life and every kind of literature. First we had the literature that pleased, then for the most part the great confident power that produced it died out, and now we have only the literature which amuses. Melodramatic literature has been overdone until we are weary of blood and passion, realism has been pushed to its last limit until we are sick of the barnyard and gutter, and as for the weird and fantastic—heavens, is there one more nerve left in us that has not been jangled and jarred by these craftsmen of the impossible? *Vive la bizarrerie!* is the literary watchword; we have studies in color, studies in environment, studies in heredity, studies in sex, studies in anything but common sense. Anything that is odd, unheard of, unnatural "goes." We translate from other languages not what is good, but what is bizarre. Even the strong men who guard and keep the honor of English literature, men like Hardy and George Meredith, cannot refrain from adding occasionally to this literary curiosity shop. As for the stage, it has gone mad over psychology and absurdities and "problems" and general woe. And the result of it all is, we are tired, both bored and exhausted, weary unto death. There comes a time when the gayest and most dissipated worldlings want to get off in some quiet place in the country and drink spring water and go to bed with the robins, and—forget. Forget pleasures that are impossible, forget the sorrows that are inevitable, the supreme delight never to be found, the commonplace discomfort never to be avoided. We are at that state now; jaded, exhausted, satiated we have come back to nature acknowledging that she is best, amid the wrecks of an old life we are beginning anew. The Scotch fiction of this decade is the cry of this new childhood in us. We want the stiff winds of the heather, the storms the mountains, the cold raindrops; we want to feel the fresh wind of the hills upon our cheeks once again. We want plain people; people who know nothing of problems or of tragedies or of grand passions; people who love their children and read their Bibles and believe in God. We want an author who can say with Robbie Burns,

My heart's in the Highlands,
My heart is not here,
My heart's in the Highlands
A-chasing the deer.

The present Scottish fiction, nearer than anything else we have, satisfies this feeling. If literary taste generally were more healthful and vigorous it would scarcely do so, for it is altogether too melancholy, most of it, and lacks that note of hopeful joy that is at the bottom of all thoroughly healthful literature. Scotland seems to have forgot how to laugh since Burns died. But now we want not joyous activity so much as rest. We want to be single and we want to be pure. Reeling home from its nocturnal orgies which no longer amuse, our Bacchanal civilization has heard this sweet, austere note from the Highlands "where about the graves of the martyrs the awks are crying," [32] and has yearned toward it. It is like the pilgrim's song after the Venus music in the *Tannhauser* overture. We have seen purple and gold unto blindness, ah, we want the gray, cold skies of Scotland! Barrie, Crockett and Watson have taken the sentiment and quiet pathos that have lain for years in the old Scotch ballads, and will lie forever in the breast of the Scottish people, and given it to the world when the world most needed it. That is their work. Sometimes they have done it well, sometimes ill, certainly they have done it without much variety or versatility. But it has gloriously served its turn. If we would only go back a century, we would find sentiment quite as pure and beautiful handled in a better manner, but we will not read old books, that is an axiom in the reading world, which has all the Athenian avidity for something new. Nevertheless, *The Little Minister*, and the countless ministers of *The Bonnie Brier Bush* have given us pleasure of the nobler sort and that we needed bitterly.

And yet, who would not give all of these books for "The Twa Dogs," or "The Cotter's Saturday Night," or "Holy Willie's Prayer," or anything else by that "blithe spirit," Burns the poet, by that sad wreck,

32. From the dedication to Stevenson in Crockett's *The Stickit Minister* (see page 315), and also Stevenson's poem "To S. R. Crockett." The word "awks" used here should be "whaups" (curlews).

Burns the man, who Stevenson says "died of being Robert Burns?" There was purity for you, and beauty, with joy and hope and healing in its wings. How queer it was that just when English verse was most stiff and stilted, when literature consisted of the sparkling artificiality of the wits of Queen Anne's day, when men wrote of heaven without reverence and of hell without fear, there should awaken out in the fields of Ayrshire that glorious voice, sweet as a thrush's throstle, singing songs to [a] pink-tipped daisy and a field mouse run down by the plow. Just a plow-boy, singing because the sun shone and maids were fair, and yet, with those spontaneous metres which the larks taught him, he gave new life to English verse, and with that joyous humor which God taught him he gave new hope to English hearts. By the grace of heaven he did just that, rustic, human, naughty Bobby Burns. Of course he died in poverty and was buried by charity, and the songs that have made the world glad for a century did not get their author bread enough to eat nor shelter for his dying head; for the work that is done for eternity is only paid in eternity, and yet, if God is just, it must draw heavy interest indeed. The pity is not that little men should prosper, but that great men should starve. Poor Burns made a sad mess of his life, they say, but he never bungled in his song—and it was to sing that the Lord made him. Even the songs like "Wandering Willie," and "Bruce's Address at Bannockburn" ["Scots, Wha Hae"], that he wrote in those last bitter days of poverty and shame, retain all his peculiar grace of expression and genuineness of sentiment. But God's was the gain; they bought Robert Burns neither glory nor a coat to his back. No, the world is not cruel, it is only stupid. It does not know. One day it woke up—and built him a monument. Burns called himself once "but a younger son of the house of Parnassus," so he will ever be, the child heart of them all, youngest and most joyous of all the sons of fame. All his sins and all his virtues, all his weakness and all his might, are best summed up in that verse which the muse of Scotland spoke to him in his dreams:

> "I saw thy pulses maddening play,
>   Wild-send thee Pleasure's devious way,
>   Misled by Fancy's meteor-ray,
>   By passion driven;
>   But yet the light that led astray
>   Was light from Heaven." [33]

Journal, May 24, 1896, p. 13.

33. Words of the Muse in Burns's "The Vision," stanza xviii.

POETS

Throughout the prose of Willa Cather's journalistic years runs a veining of phrases and lines of poetry (usually quoted from memory) and allusions to poets and their work as if it were all a common body of reference like Shakespeare, the Bible, or Greek and Teutonic mythology. Separate articles on poets and poetry are rare; most of the comment appears in other contexts, like the essays on Poe, Byron, and Verlaine (see pages 380 ff.) which focus on the totality of life and art. Articles were usually written because of what she read in the papers and periodicals —a death, a monument, an honor given or denied, occasionally a new book she liked. With so many fragments and omissions (and because Willa Cather's first published book would be a volume of poems in 1903, April Twilights) her critical views of poetry are doubly interesting. Uses of the English past are mostly from poets of her own century: Shelley, Keats, Byron, Arnold, Browning, Tennyson, Thomas Moore, Burns, the Rossettis, with fewer references to the Americans, Poe and Whitman principally. In other languages her current favorites were Alfred de Musset and Heine, with elements of Lamartine, Béranger, Villon, and Gautier; there were also Homer, Sappho, Anacreon, Virgil, Dante, and Goethe. We find, too, a miscellany of FitzGerald's Rubáiyát, old French songs, English and Scottish ballads, a few references to Milton and Wordsworth. Shakespeare, of course, is always at hand. The principal choices among contemporaries are clear: Swinburne in England, Verlaine in France, Kipling wherever he was. (Yeats and Housman would come later.) From works of the immediate past, she had read two of particular interest: James Thomson's The City of Dreadful Night *and Whitman's* Leaves of Grass. *If she knew Whitman, did she also know Emily Dickinson, whose poems first appeared in the early nineties? Perhaps. Certainly somebody on the* Courier *liked Emily, for while Willa Cather helped to edit the paper in the fall of 1895 "Success Is Counted Sweetest" appeared in two issues. Most logically this was the choice of her co-editor Sarah B. Harris, who had written an article on Dickinson the previous spring (Courier, April 6, 1895). And someone also selected a poem by Ella Wheeler Wilcox, whom Miss Cather called "that drivelling writer of shoddy and sentimental verse" (Journal, March 8, 1896). At twenty-one, Willa Cather was not quite sure that women poets amounted to much. This was her theme in early 1895, when she wrote of the death of Christina Rossetti and added notes on Sappho and Elizabeth Barrett Browning—her first important discussion of poetry.*

Christina Rossetti

The article on Christina Rossetti is especially important because in it Willa Cather quotes and comments on the poem "The Goblin Market," from which she took one of the epigraphs for her first book of short stories, The Troll Garden (1905): "We must not look at Goblin men,/We must not buy their fruits;/Who knows upon what soil they fed/Their hungry thirsty roots?" These lines, which come early in the poem, suggest the Circe-like fascination and enslaving power of the Goblins' mysterious, forbidden fruit. The second epigraph on the title page of the 1905 Troll Garden is composed of phrases from Charles Kingsley's parable on the fall of Rome, in his book The Roman and the Teuton (trolls in a troll-garden and the forest children outside): "A fairy palace, with a fairy garden; . . . inside the trolls dwell, . . . working at their magic forges, making and making always things rare and strange." If one reads Kingsley (see Appendix III), the essay "On Nature and Romance" (see pages 231 ff.), the complete "Goblin Market," and the following excerpts from the article on Christina Rossetti, he will have Willa Cather's first-hand comment on The Troll Garden.

On December 30 [1894] Christina Rossetti died at her home in London. Miss Rossetti had the misfortune to be the lesser light of a family richly endowed with genius, and the simple music of her poetry is almost drowned by the loftier themes and deeper cadences of her brother. His greatness threatens to absorb hers altogether, as Dante's did Sordello's. "So doth the greater glory dim the less." But although Christina Rossetti's poetry is neither vital nor potent enough to greatly influence or guide the poets of the future, nor fervid and impassioned enough to claim immortality, she wrote some very natural and beautiful verse, which is more read in England than it is here. There is no better proof that she possessed something of the real gift of song than that her poetry is so different from that of her brother and all the pre-Raphaelite school. It must have taken considerable individuality of thought and inspiration to withstand the constant influences of so winning a personality and so enchanting a style as Gabriel Rossetti's. Her themes and her treatment of them are in most cases diametrically opposite from his. Her favorite themes were religious, while his poetry is entirely that of sentiment and the earthly passions. While in poetry religious subjects always run the risk of being commonplace and prosy, they are better than imitations of passions or forced sensuousness. She wrote the best sacred poetry of this century, of that there can be no doubt. Never sinking to moralizing, never yielding to accepted forms, she wrote with the mystic, enraptured faith of Cassandra, which is a sort of spiritual ecstasy, and which is to the soul what passion is to the heart.

It was given to Christina Rossetti to write one perfect poem, one poem pregnant with deep meaning, yet so melodious that it does not depend on its significance for its beauty, a poem which is vivid enough to delight a child, profound enough to charm a sage. It is her famous "Goblin Market." In its weird mysticism it reminds one of the elfland scenes in *Peer Gynt*, in the quaint grotesqueness of the rhythm and imagery it recalls the lyrics of the Japanese. Morning and evening the Goblin merchantmen wander crying their wares.

> "Our grapes fresh from the vine.
> Pomegranates full and fine,
> Dates and sharp bullaces,
> Rare pears and greengages,
> Damsons and bilberries,
> Taste them and try:
> Currants and gooseberries,
> Bright-fire-like barberries,
> Figs to fill your mouth,
> Citrons from the South,
> Sweet to tongue and sound to eye;
> Come buy, come buy."

[*Other sections of "The Goblin Market" which Miss Cather quoted have been omitted throughout the summary of the story.*]

Lizzie and Laura are filling their pitchers at the brook in the evening. Lizzie stops her ears to the goblin song, but "sweet tooth Laura" listens. Lizzie flees home at the sound of their approach, but Laura crouches in the reeds and gazes longingly at the fruit as the swart misshapen goblin men come trooping by. . . . The goblins pile their wares about her and she buys the fruit with one of her golden curls. Then she "Sucked their fruit fair or red . . . ." Then she goes home, sated with the goblin fruit and yet longing for more. In the morning the two sisters waken, Lizzie "warbling for the mere bright day's delight," Laura longing for night and the goblin fruit. At nightfall she hurries to the brook and listens; Lizzie hears the cry of the goblin men and sees their coming shadow, but Laura cannot hear them, cannot see them. . . . Day by day she goes hungering and thirsting for the goblin fruits, dreaming of them, longing for them, her life is "Thirsty, cankered, goblin-ridden." But once tasted the goblin fruit gives only hunger, not satisfaction; only desire, not fulfillment. At last Lizzie takes all her hoard and goes to the goblins to buy their fruit for her wretched sister. But one may not buy from the goblin folk with gold, they take only the gold of one's heart and they sell only to who will eat. They beat and mock her but she will not taste, and they squirt the juice of their pomegranates in her face. She hurries home with the juices dripping on her face. . . . But when Laura tastes the poison juices on the good face of her sister they turn to wormwood in her mouth and she raves with remorse and loathing until tired out . . . . In the morning she wakes and the goblin's thirst is forgotten . . . . Never has the purchase of pleasure, its loss in its own taking, the loathsomeness of our own folly in those we love, been put more quaintly and directly.

Christina Rossetti's life and career were not happy. She realized too well the narrowness of her limitation and the futileness of much of her work. She had indeed the desire to fly, but not the strength of wing. Her heart was one of those in which the laurel had not taken root kindly, the divine fire was not given to her lavishly, there was not enough of it to warm her to great creation, only a spark which wasted the body and burnt out the soul.

It is a very grave question whether women have any place in poetry at all. Certainly they have only been successful in poetry of the most highly subjective nature. If a woman writes any poetry at all worth reading it must be emotional in the extreme, self-centred, self-absorbed, centrifugal. Generally it is confined either to reverence or love. Christina Rossetti possessed the true artistic consciousness of her limits. She attempted neither epics nor dramas, but confined herself to the simplest lyrics. Learning and a wide knowledge of things does not seem to help women poets much. It seems rather to cripple their naturalness, burden their fancy and cloud their imagination with pedantic metaphors and vague illusions. Learned literary women have such an unfortunate tendency to instruct the world. They must learn abandon. The women of the stage know that to feel greatly is genius and to make others feel is art. The women of literature have still to realize that. A woman has only one gift and out of the wealth of that one thing she must sing and move with song. An old Greek, who knew more of the world than Plato by a great deal, said that when Zeus made the world he gave to the horse swiftness and to the bull strength and to the fishes the power of swimming and to the birds wings and to man reason. When he came to woman he had nothing of that kind left to give, so he gave to her the power of loving, as a weapon against all strength and steel and fire. Out of the fullness of that power a woman must do her work. They have tried other weapons, but they have used them awkwardly or at best only "fenced by the book." A woman can be great only in proportion as God put feeling in her.

Journal, January 13, 1895, p. 13.

Sappho

There is one woman poet whom all the world calls great, though of her work there remains now only a few disconnected fragments and that one wonderful hymn to Aphrodite. Small things upon which to rest so great a fame, but they tell so much. If of all the lost richness we could have one master restored to us, one of all the philosophers and poets, the choice of the world would be for the lost nine books of Sappho. Those broken fragments have burned themselves into the consciousness of the world like fire. All great poets have wondered at them, all inferior poets have imitated them. Twenty centuries have not cooled the passion in them. Sappho wrote only of one theme, sang it, laughed it, sighed it, wept it, sobbed it. Save for her knowledge of human love she was unlearned, save for her perception of beauty she was blind, save for the fullness of her passions she was empty-handed. She was probably not a student of prosody, yet she invented the most wonderfully emotional meter in literature, the sapphic meter with its three full, resonant lines, and then that short, sharp one that comes in like a gasp when feeling flows too swift for speech. She could not sing of Atrides, nor of Cadmus, nor of the labors of Hercules, for her lyre, like Anacreon's, responded only to a song of love.

Journal, January 13, 1895, p. 13.

Swinburne

The following comment on Swinburne was written at a time when English poets were much in the news—the arguments on who should fill the laureateship, vacant since the death of Tennyson (see pages 192 ff.), and the reports through 1895 of Oscar Wilde's trial and imprisonment.

... Undoubtedly Mr. Swinburne is the greatest living English poet indeed, since his brother in Apollo is picking oakum in prison, he is the only one left us now. Swinburne is a great lyric poet, perhaps he is almost too much of a poet. Sometimes the matchless completeness of his rhythm almost drives one to distraction. English ears were not meant for much rhythm. What with his rhythm and rhyme and alliteration, his meaning is frequently quite subordinated. He repeats his pet rhymes over and over, just as Homer takes those great thundering lines and hurls them at you again and again for very delight in his own thunder. Swinburne is thoroughly a Greek, in his thought and treatment, as well as in his theme. The Greek tendencies are discernible in every detail of his verse, even in his indomitable love of joining an adjective and a verb to merely do the work of an adjective. It's the old trick of Homer's "loud-sounding sea." Sometimes I think Swinburne himself quite forgets his meaning in the delight of his measure. He can do anything with poetic measures. He has even imitated the Sapphic measures perfectly in stubborn, unyielding English syllables. He is intoxicated with melody and drunk with sound. He is like a bacchant singing himself hoarse and scourging himself with rods at the Eleusinian mysteries. And yet he is a mighty singer. As Oscar Wilde said of him:

> And he hath been with thee at Thessaly,
>   And seen white Atalanta fleet of foot
> In passionless and fierce virginity
>   Hunting the tusked boar, his honeyed lute
> Hath pierced the cavern of the hollow hill,
> And Venus laughs to know one knee will bow before her still.
>
> And he hath kissed the lips of Proserpine,
>   And sung the Galilaean's requiem,
> That wounded forehead dashed with blood and wine
>   He hath discrowned, the Ancient Gods in him
> Have found their last, most ardent worshipper,
> And the new Sign grows grey and dim before its Conqueror.[34]

Courier, November 30, 1895, p. 6.

Whitman

Willa Cather's essay on Whitman is significant not only because it establishes a very early reading of Leaves of Grass *but because it shows the writer almost in the process of working out her attitudes, and so obviously torn between the mental predilection toward order and the emotional pull*

34. From "The Garden of Eros" in *Poems* (1881).

toward "the joy of life." Whatever directions that argument took in the years that followed 1896, we know that Whitman stayed with her until his line appeared as the title, and perhaps more, of O Pioneers! *in 1913. Perhaps it is worth noting that both her first book of short stories and the first novel in the style that pleased her took their titles from strongly affirmative writers—*The Troll Garden *from Kingsley, who wrote of romance and the sweep of history and myth;* O Pioneers! *from Whitman, poet of the cosmos and the earth's body.*

Speaking of monuments reminds one that there is more talk about a monument to Walt Whitman, "the good, gray poet." Just why the adjective good is always applied to Whitman it is difficult to discover, probably because people who could not understand him at all took it for granted that he meant well. If ever there was a poet who had no literary ethics at all beyond those of nature, it was he. He was neither good nor bad, any more than are the animals he continually admired and envied. He was a poet without an exclusive sense of the poetic, a man without the finer discriminations, enjoying everything with the unreasoning enthusiasm of a boy. He was the poet of the dung hill as well as of the mountains, which is admirable in theory but excruciating in verse. In the same paragraph he informs you that, "The pure contralto sings in the organ loft," and that "The malformed limbs are tied to the table, what is removed drop horribly into a pail." [35] No branch of surgery is poetic, and that hopelessly prosaic word "pail" would kill a whole volume of sonnets. Whitman's poems are reckless rhapsodies over creation in general, sometimes sublime, sometimes ridiculous. He declares that the ocean with its "imperious waves, commanding" [36] is beautiful, and that the fly-specks on the walls are also beautiful. Such catholic taste may go in

35. From "Song of Myself," section 15, lines 1 and 14–15. The latter quotation should read: "The malform'd limbs are tied to the surgeon's table, / What is removed drops horribly in a pail." Texts for this and the following Whitman quotations are from the 1891–1892, or deathbed, edition as printed in Walt Whitman, *Complete Poetry and Selected Prose*, edited by James E. Miller, Jr. (Riverside Edition; Boston: Houghton Mifflin Company, 1959).

36. I do not find this particular phrase in Whitman, but if it is from Willa Cather's memory of "In Cabin'd Ships at Sea" the implications are indeed interesting. In that poem are two lines which might have been telescoped: "The boundless blue on every side expanding, / With whistling winds and music of the waves, the large imperious waves." And the metaphor of book, ship, and voyage in the poem ("Speed on my book! spread your white sails my little bark athwart the imperious waves") might be compared with Willa Cather's metaphor of the writer's art, the perilous voyage between brain and hand (see page 417).

science, but in poetry their results are sad. The poet's task is usually to select the poetic. Whitman never bothers to do that, he takes everything in the universe from fly-specks to the fixed stars. His *Leaves of Grass* is a sort of dictionary of the English language, and in it is the name of everything in creation set down with great reverence but without any particular connection.

But however ridiculous Whitman may be there is a primitive elemental force about him. He is so full of hardiness and of the joy of life. He looks at all nature in the delighted, admiring way in which the old Greeks and the primitive poets did. He exults so in the red blood in his body and the strength in his arms. He has such a passion for the warmth and dignity of all that is natural. He has no code but to be natural, a code that this complex world has so long outgrown. He is sensual, not after the manner of Swinburne and Gautier, who are always seeking for perverted and bizarre effects on the senses, but in the frank fashion of the old barbarians who ate and slept and married and smacked their lips over the mead horn. He is rigidly limited to the physical, things that quicken his pulses, please his eyes or delight his nostrils. There is an element of poetry in all this, but it is by no means the highest. If a joyous elephant should break forth into song, his lay would probably be very much like Whitman's famous "Song of Myself." It would have just about as much delicacy and deftness and discrimination. He says: "I think I could turn and live with the animals. They are so placid and self-contained, I stand and look at them long and long. They do not sweat and whine about their condition. They do not lie awake in the dark and weep for their sins. They do not make me sick discussing their duty to God. Not one is dissatisfied nor not one is demented with the mania of many things. Not one kneels to another nor to his kind that lived thousands of years ago. Not one is respectable or unhappy, over the whole earth." [37] And that is not irony on nature, he means just that, life meant no more to him. He

37. "Song of Myself," section 32. The correct reading of the 1891–1892 edition is as follows:

I think I could turn and live with animals, they're so placid and self-contain'd.
I stand and look at them long and long.

They do not sweat and whine about their condition,
They do not lie awake in the dark and weep for their sins,
They do not make me sick discussing their duty to God,
Not one is dissatisfied, not one is demented with the mania of owning things,
Not one kneels to another, nor to his kind that lived thousands of years ago,
Not one is respectable or unhappy over the whole earth.

CRITICAL STATEMENTS: LITERATURE

accepted the world just as it is and glorified it, the seemly and unseemly, the good and the bad. He had no conception of a difference in people or in things. All men had bodies and were alike to him, one about as good as another. To live was to fulfil all natural laws and impulses. To be comfortable was to be happy. To be happy was the ultimatum. He did not realize the existence of a conscience or a responsibility. He had no more thought of good or evil than the folks in Kipling's *Jungle Book*.

And yet there is an undeniable charm about this optimistic vagabond who is made so happy by the warm sunshine and the smell of spring fields. A sort of good fellowship and whole-heartedness in every line he wrote. His veneration for things physical and material, for all that is in water or air or land, is so real that as you read him you think for the moment that you would rather like to live so if you could. For the time you half believe that a sound body and a strong arm are the greatest things in the world. Perhaps no book shows so much as *Leaves of Grass* that keen senses do not make a poet. When you read it you realize how spirited a thing poetry really is and how great a part spiritual perceptions play in apparently sensuous verse, if only to select the beautiful from the gross.

Journal, January 19, 1896, p. 9.

Carman and Hovey

In the spring of 1896 Willa Cather noticed and liked the work of two poets, Bliss Carman and Richard Hovey. Her comments on their Songs from Vagabondia *are curiously reminiscent of what she had said about Whitman the previous fall—a rugged, unfinished style, but also the joy of life, "that glad pleasure at the mere existence of things." Once before (November 11, 1894) she had written unfavorably on some poems by Carman (she thought the name must be a* nom de plume *and spelled it "Carmen"). A year and a half later she knew more about him, and she also found Hovey's* Taliesin, *published in two issues of* Poet Lore *(February and March, 1896), an exciting and lyrical dramatic poem. Carman and Hovey brought together two elements about which Willa Cather felt deeply: the poetry of earth and the noble passion of the Greek world.*

A recent periodical remarks that there is not one young man in the United States who writes verse of extraordinary merit. When you come to consider the matter, it would be rather difficult to put your finger on one. There has not been a volume of poetry worth reading twice put out by a native of these states for ten years or more. Yet the muse has not

entirely deserted the continent. There are two young writers of verse in
Canada who seem destined to become poets. It seems that in early youth
they found each other out as Coleridge and Wordsworth did, and their
first, or, at least, one of their first, volumes of verse was issued together
under the title, *Songs from Vagabondia,* by Bliss Carman and Richard
Hovey.[38] That was first published in 1894 and was republished again last
year [second and third editions, 1895]. While the lyrics therein could
scarcely be called evidences of genius, they were so fresh, so untrammelled,
so free from any flavor of imitation, that they proved conclusively that
up in Canada two young men were finding out nature for themselves.
They were two so strikingly antagonistic to the heavy pessimistic verse
that was then and is now being produced at such an alarming rate. Here
were evidently two young men who wrote with infectious joy of bees
and flowers and butterflies and yet in a manner thoroughly manly and
abundantly virile. The verses were sometimes rugged in form, often lacking in finish, sometimes so capricious that they were absolutely undignified.
But poetic form seems to be almost common property when compared
to the rarity of poetic feeling. And poetic feeling in a somewhat crude
state, these verses undoubtedly had. Above all, they had that joyousness,
that glad pleasure at the mere existence of things that seems to be the
bottom of a poet's nature and the active causal force of his song. . . .

All of these verses are out-of-door poetry. So much of the verse that
is written now is about wine and unkind maidens, boudoir poetry. Or
else it takes nature in an exaggerated mood and sings of unearthly storms
and all uncanny things. But these two fellows seem content to take the
genial old world just as it is, and love it with all its unkindness. They are
young men of a contented spirit and unsophisticated enough to like the
sun just because it shines. . . .

Journal, April 26, 1896, p. 13.

It is dangerous business to predict a new poet, for with poets the
story of the Ugly Duckling is so often reversed and what promised fair,
falls outdone at midday. It is not easy in the beginning to tell a star from
a glow-worm. But the last two numbers of *Poet Lore* have published a

38. At this time William Bliss Carman (1861–1929), a Canadian, had several other
volumes of verse, including *Low Tide on Grand Pré* (1893) and *A Sea-Mark* (1895), and had
frequently published critical articles in American magazines. Richard Hovey (1864–1900)
was an American, author of the poetic drama *Launcelot and Guenevere* (1891) and *Seaward*
(1893). In the two articles above, the spelling of Bliss Carman's name has been corrected.
Miss Cather continued to write it "Carmen."

poem called *Taliesin: A Masque,* that seems to breathe a higher and purer spirit of poetry than anything that has appeared since Browning's last poems and Swinburne's "Atalanta in Calydon." It has been a long time since any poetry fallen into a magazine has had much strong lyric impulse in it. Here is an extract that a youth sings as he stands upon the summit of Mount Helicon amid the muses:

> Below
> The city waits with garlands and I go;
> The city waits with garlands like a bride.
> Now with the joy still in that book of hers,
> I must go to her. Not a sea breath stirs
> Across the garden where she waits and dreams
> Of one whose coming shall be like the tide
> Of day, flooding the marsh-long loops and gleams
> Of sunrise heavens in midsummertide.
> I am her lover; it is I she waits.
> Farewell, I go like summer to her gates.[39]

There is the pure lyric quality in those verses, the poetry absolute and the sort of high noon meridian ecstasy that Keats and Shelley knew how to breathe into song. They are without Swinburne's copious loquaciousness, strong and clear and Greek, like the outline of white marble against a blue Attic sky. Later on as the youth springs down from the mountain he sings:

> O word, O life, O City of the Sea!
>   Hushed in the hum
> Of streets; a pause is on the minstrelsy,
>   I come, I come!
> The sunlight of thy garden from afar
>   Is in my heart.
> A girl's laugh dropt from heaven like a star,
>   Tells where thou art.

You can see him kick the clouds from under him as he descends. There is nothing studied or diffuse in those lines, they have the true

---

39. In this and the following passage from *Taliesin,* punctuation has been corrected but words left as they were printed. Variants are as follows: In the first quotation, l. 4, for *book* read *look*; l. 6, for *garden* read *gardens*; l. 7, for *the tide* read *a tide*. In the second quotation, l. 1, for *word* read *World*.

joyous, poetic impulse that shoots straight as an arrow. If Mr. Richard Hovey can go on writing verse like that, fame holds for him a crown such as men of old wore. Unfortunately the whole poem is not quite so good, some of the choruses are weak. But the blank verse has a rhythm that few living Englishmen can equal and the figures are rich and natural.

Journal, March 1, 1896, p. 9.

NOVELS AND NOVELISTS

*The chronicle of Willa Cather's attention to novels and novelists in her writing
begins in the winter of 1894. It accelerates especially after January, 1896, when
she was mostly at home in Red Cloud and had more time to consider thoughtfully
and work out in writing some of the guiding principles of fiction, the certain range
in the Kingdom of Art which was becoming clearly her own. She tried her hand
at full-scale book reviews—the kind that appeared in most of the better magazines
—for they were much like the play reviews which by then she could write with
professional skill. Writing on books, she became in general more impersonal and
restrained; but just as she had done in the theatre, she kept a steady watch on the
current literary scene, reacting with fury at the usually mindless stream of words
that babbled through the magazines, or turning with deep and serious delight to
the few great books and writers that had the absolute authority of truth.*

*When they are viewed from a calmer distance of fifty or a hundred years, the
choices the artist makes from the center of his own present are often curiously out
of proportion, like figures in a primitive painting. But in the confusion of the
moving present it is hard indeed to select and arrange all things in order. Willa
Cather at twenty or twenty-two evaluated the novelists of her day better than we
have a right to expect. "George Meredith, Thomas Hardy, and Henry James
excepted," she said in 1895, "the great living novelists are Frenchmen" (Journal,
May 5, 1895). That meant Daudet, Zola, Pierre Loti. And from Russia she
chose the Tolstoi of* Anna Karenina. *She liked some very popular books, Du
Maurier's* Trilby *especially; but it is quite clear that she never confused Trilby
with Anna. In discussing contemporary novelists, she had the strength of some
high standards derived from their forerunners. Among the English novelists of the
past, she was most faithful to Thackeray, and above all to Henry Esmond. Next,
perhaps, would come George Eliot, though in various contexts she also admired
Jane Austen, Richardson, Smollett, and Fielding. Among French writers, there
were Dumas père for his storytelling, Hugo for* Les Misérables, *and George
Sand, Balzac, Maupassant. Contrary to everyone's expectation, Flaubert is rarely
mentioned. In fact, one statement shows unequivocally that at least in May, 1895,
Flaubert was not in her charmed circle of French masters: Mark Twain had asked
what the French sensualists could teach the American people about novel writing or
morality, and Willa Cather remarked that "it would not seriously hurt the art of
the classic author of* Puddin'head Wilson *to study Daudet, De Maupassant,
Hugo and George Sand, whatever it might do to his morals" (Journal, May 5,
1895). Among the Russians of the past Willa Cather admired Turgenev most,
Dostoevski in passing. In America, it was Hawthorne.*

But even measuring the new by the old did not make criticism easy. In 1895–1896 one had to sort out and evaluate writers like Hardy, James, Howells, and Mark Twain who were in the middle of their own action; no one knew the end. If Willa Cather was right about Hardy and James, and moderately so about Howells (a great figure and a dull writer), she was also wrong about Mark Twain, whose humor did not appeal to her and whose ignorance of French history and literature, as demonstrated in the currently serialized Personal Recollections of Joan of Arc, *seemed appalling. (Although* Joan of Arc, *which began in* Harper's *in April, 1895, was published pseudonymously as "by the Sieur Louis de Conte," Willa Cather's remarks in the* Courier *during that fall show that she had no difficulty in recognizing the author.) Eventually, of course, she liked Mark Twain for other reasons, and the proportions changed. But when the scene is caught at that particular moment and viewed now with the wisdom of hindsight, our interest is less in what writers she picked than in what she selected to praise or blame in them. For it would be hard to believe that in the winter and spring of that last year in Nebraska Willa Cather was not trying some fiction of her own. What she said then about another writer is surely some sign of the road she had started to take.*

Hardy

To readers who had observed Thomas Hardy's development in twenty years from the charm of Under the Greenwood Tree *(1872) or* A Pair of Blue Eyes *(1873) to the power of* Tess of the D'Urbervilles *(1891), the English novelist's new book was at least puzzling. Serialized in* Harper's *Magazine beginning in December, 1894, it was called* The Simpletons *in the first installment; this was changed to* Hearts Insurgent *in the next issue, and under that title it continued to disturb and disappoint a good many of Hardy's admirers. Willa Cather was very outspoken about it. Like others, she thought it was full of absurd melodramatic claptrap and intellectual pretensions, with a completely unrestrained plot. Somewhat revised, the book was published later in the year as* Jude the Obscure. *It should be said, however, that in spite of* Jude *Miss Cather did not desert Hardy, and especially her favorite* Tess.

There is [in *Harper's Magazine*] that crowning piece of arrant madness and drivelling idiocy, *Hearts Insurgent*. I admire Thomas Hardy; I admire the lofty conception of *Tess of the D'Urbervilles*, the finished execution of *A Pair of Blue Eyes*, the beautiful simplicity of *Far from the Madding Crowd*. But for *Hearts Insurgent* I have no forgiveness. If Mr. Hardy ever had any serious purpose or intention in writing the thing, I suppose he meant to show what idiots a little learning makes of people of the downright plebeian stock. Analytical powers are a great misfortune to working people, for they take them too seriously, as children take Byron and Carlyle. But on the whole I doubt whether Mr. Hardy ever had any purpose at all. Like the brook, he simply goes on forever, from one madness into another. That whole tale is one series of epileptic fits, or whatever kind of fits those are in which people continually fall down. He absolutely runs the gauntlet of all possible relations between men and women. If there is any possible combination in this line that he has left undone I should like to know it.[40]

Courier, October 5, 1895, p. 7.

The few of Thomas Hardy's many admirers who clung with the tenacity of growing despair to his last midsummer madness, *Hearts Insurgent*, while it was capering madly through *Harper's Magazine*, will be dumfounded by the changes that the author has made in it before publishing it under its new title *Jude the Obscure*. In *Hearts Insurgent* the central theme of the story—if it could be accused of having a central theme at all—is the stubborn and platonic relationship between Jude and Sue. Now in *Jude the Obscure* Mr. Hardy insists upon the unplatonic nature of this relationship and dwells upon the details thereof in a manner worthy of Zola himself. He even makes her the mother of the unaccounted for child which crept so strangely into *Hearts Insurgent* for the express purpose of hanging its precocious self. Nay, he makes her the blooming mother of three children. O, if ever there was a mixed-up, insane tale it is this same *The Simpletons*, alias *Hearts Insurgent* alias *Jude the Obscure*. Certainly the first title, *The Simpletons*, and the last, *The Obscure*, fit it, for no mortal mind can at all remember its plot nor follow its absurd analysis nor fathom its medley of Christian and pagan philosophy. If you want, just by way of experiment, to be more baffled and puzzled and disgusted than you were when you finished *Hearts Insurgent* just read *Jude the Obscure* and there you have it. It will take several decent ordinary novels to bring you to your senses again. Yet in the preface of *Jude the Obscure* Mr. Hardy states with that charming inconsistency which characterizes him throughout

40. Cf. one of the answers in the *Courier's* "Notes and Queries" column for August 31, 1895, in response to a question on what would happen next in Hardy's *Hearts Insurgent*: "If there is left undone any one mad act of insanity which the charming characters have not already committed, we suppose they will joyfully proceed to do it. More than this we know not nor wish to know."

the tale, that the book is "practically the same as when first written." The public differs with him. It thinks that three children make considerable difference. It is no wonder that out of respect for childhood Mr. Hardy hesitated to give the infants in question two such hysterical and generally erratic parents, but even that would be less alarming than spontaneous generation. Now the question is, did Mr. Hardy withhold their shocking details out of consideration and respect for that high and holy organ of respectability, *Harper's Magazine*, whose fair fame *Trilby* has already sullied?[41]

Journal, February 2, 1896, p. 9.

James

Although we cannot be sure when Willa Cather discovered Henry James, it is clear from her own later statements that she read his work with the attention a student gives a master. Yet she wrote very little about James in the period before June, 1896; when she did, her tone was firm and confident but in no sense idolatrous. Her references to James are noticeable only in her last year in Nebraska. In the fall of 1895 she said that the career of F. Marion Crawford was a sad thing—he was rich, successful, and well-published, but he had not treated his talent with reverence. "I have always thought he suggested Henry James' melancholy 'Lesson of the Master,'" she wrote. "It hits him much harder than the expurgated part of Trilby *ever hit Whistler" (Courier, September 21, 1895). James's passage at the end of "The Middle Years"—"Our doubt is our passion and our passion is our task. The rest is the madness of art"—is quoted or alluded to in pieces on Stevenson (November 2, 1895), Poe (published October 12, 1895, but written in the previous spring), and Mary Anderson (May 3, 1896). There are other allusions, of course, including some references to particular titles. But so much of James was published in the periodicals of the day that she might have seen a good many miscellaneous pieces before they were collected. One wonders how much she did read in James's articles on literature and the theatre, his portraits of people and places, the early novels. But however far Willa Cather explored, it was still the early Henry James she read at this time, when his sentences were as lucid and easy as light, their movement inevitable.*

Their mania for careless and hasty work is not confined to the lesser men. Howells and Hardy have gone with the crowd. Now that Stevenson

41. At this time Willa Cather apparently did not know that serialized novels were often cut by magazines to fit available space. Such editing could account for differences between the *Harper's* version and the final published form of *Jude*.

is dead I can think of but one English-speaking author who is really keeping his self-respect and sticking for perfection. Of course I refer to that mighty master of language and keen student of human actions and motives, Henry James. In the last four years he has published, I believe, just two small volumes, *The Lesson of the Master* and *Terminations*,[42] and in those two little volumes of short stories he who will may find out something of what it means to be really an artist. The framework is perfect and the polish is absolutely without flaw. They are sometimes a little hard, always calculating and dispassionate, but they are perfect. I wish James would write about modern society, about "degeneracy" and the new woman and all the rest of it. Not that he would throw any light on it. He seldom does; but he would say such awfully clever things about it, and turn on so many side-lights. And then his sentences! If his character novels were all wrong one could read him forever for the mere beauty of his sentences. He never lets his phrases run away with him. They are never dull and never too brilliant. He subjects them to the general tone of his sentence and has his whole paragraph partake of the same predominating color. You are never startled, never surprised, never thrilled or never enraptured; always delighted by that masterly prose that is as correct, as classical, as calm and as subtle as the music of Mozart.

Courier, November 16, 1895, p. 6.

It is strange that from *Felicia* [by Fanny N. D. Murfree, 1891] down, the stage novel has never been a success. Henry James' *Tragic Muse* [1890] is the only theatrical novel that has a particle of the real spirit of the stage in it, a glimpse of the enthusiasm, the devotion, the exaltation and the sordid, the frivolous and the vulgar which are so strangely and inextricably blended in that life of the greenroom. For although Henry James cannot write plays he can write passing well of the people who enact them. He has put into one book all those inevitable attendants of the drama, the patronizing theatre-goer who loves it above all things and yet feels so far superior to it personally; the old tragedienne, the queen of a dying school whose word is law and whose judgments are to a young actor as the judgments of God; and of course there is the girl, the aspirant, the tragic muse who beats and beats upon those brazen doors that guard the unapproachable until one fine morning she beats them down and comes into her kingdom, the kingdom of unborn beauty that is to live through her.

42. *The Lesson of the Master* was published in 1892, *Terminations* in 1895. Perhaps Willa Cather missed *The Real Thing* in 1893.

It is a great novel, that book of the master's, so perfect as a novel that one does not realize what a masterly study it is of the life and ends and aims of the people who make plays live. . . .

Journal, March 29, 1896, p. 9.

Du Maurier's Trilby

George Du Maurier's Trilby *began as a serial in* Harper's *in January, 1894, and by the time it appeared in book form the public was already Trilby-mad, perhaps because of the charm of the girl herself, or the evil fascination of Svengali the hypnotist who controlled her, or both the glamor and the daring of artists' life in the Latin Quarter. Though some said* Trilby *was immoral, Willa Cather liked and defended the book.*

She has come to us at last in book form—Trilby the much talked of, Trilby the well-beloved. There has not been a heroine made for years that people have taken into their hearts and lives, and loved as they have Trilby. Critics say "Thackeray, Thackeray," but Thackeray's heroines are not lovable, though his heroes are. Thackeray never made a woman whom one could love. Of course there have been noble women enough in fiction, indeed almost too many "noble women." There is even Charles Dudley Warner's "Edith of the Golden Home,"[43] concerning whom we are all anxiously awaiting further intelligence. O yes! there are plenty of admirable heroines, perfect Minervas and Hermiones, but some way poor little Trilby seemed to need love so and everybody gave it to her. The merchant in his country home, the broker at his desk, the painter at his easel, the actor in the flies, we all of us loved her so dearly that she was an experience in our lives. The strange part of it was that it was the good people who loved her the most. The people who were really and greatly good like Little Billee loved her just as he did. The world has been just to Trilby; it has loved her and not been ashamed to say so. For six months the English-speaking peoples have talked of little else. It may be unreasonable, but it is true that this little studio girl, who posed for the "altogether," with her pretty foot, her army coat and taint of Bohemia, will go to her place in literature and on our book shelves more beloved than all the righteous and cultured Evadnes and Bernardines and Marcellas which these fretful times have called forth.

Journal, September 16, 1894, p. 13.

43. Edith Delancy was the long-suffering wife and heroine in Charles Dudley Warner's *The Golden House*, serialized in *Harper's*, July-November, 1894. Her home was called the "Golden House" because it was so colored by the sunset light.

The originals of the illustrations of *Trilby* are now being exhibited in New York and the dear critics are deciding that Du Maurier cannot draw, as they have already decided that he cannot write and knows nothing whatever of music. What a storm of rage and jealous disapproval that book has raised among the litterateurs of this country. The classicists have found fault with its colloquial style, the realists with its romanticism, the romanticists with its realism, and the moralists with its morals. The book's greatest fault is that it has met with unqualified success, success that the classicists and romanticists and realists, and even the moralists, would give their two eyes for. It is true that poor books have been widely read and sold through several editions. Everyone read *The Heavenly Twins*, because it was atrocious, and laughed at the book and themselves when they were through with it. Most people read *The Kreutzer Sonata* because they knew they should not, and even Haggard's *She* was universally read because the world has not yet outgrown the liking for fairy tales. Very many books are widely read through curiosity, but very few are widely read and reread through real liking. That is Du Maurier's unpardonable crime; he is popular among the many and also among the few. He has become popular not through shocking or amusing people, but by appealing to them, warming them, going straight to their hearts. It is certainly inconsistent that today, when Balzac and *Tess of the D'Urbervilles* [are] in all the public libraries, there should be objections to *Trilby*'s appearance in *Harper's Magazine*. It is doubly inconsistent that people who can read unflinchingly Sarah Grand and Iota,[44] with their cheap, vulgar, ignorant discussions of questions that should not be touched outside of a medical clinic, should shudder at the clean, dainty pages of Du Maurier's latest novel.

There has been no book published for years which is more free from the fleshly and sensual than *Trilby*. It is full of the spirit of humor and good-fellowship, but of the grossness of passion there is not a touch. That is one reason why a young man could not have written *Trilby*. It is the work of a man whose heart is still young and tender, but whose blood has lost the mad impetuosity of youth. It is the most gentle and fatherly of books. You never have the uncomfortable sensation that the man is venting his lower nature in his work; that he is making his ideal mistress of Trilby. He treats her tenderly and sadly, as an old man might treat a foolish child for whom he cared. Always you feel behind the book the strong, tender personality of a man who has seen much of love and sin and suffering and who has not at all solved the riddle of it all. That is the

44. For Sarah Grand, see note 4, above. "Iota" was Mrs. Kathleen Mannington Caffyn, author of *Yellow Aster* (1894) and *Children of Circumstance* (1894).

great charm of the book, the wise, gentle, sympathetic man, whom every sentence brings you closer to.

And *la petite* Trilby herself, is she so shockingly bad as people pretend she is? The trouble is that she is not bad enough. If she had become utterly depraved and consumed a great deal of bad gin, people would consider her a proper character for a book and even for that fifth gospel, *Harper's Magazine*. We do not particularly object to people who are utterly bad within and without; we call them "lessons," for they give us the "holier than thou" feeling. But we insist that if a woman sins once she shall be utterly and irredeemably bad, whereas in the real world it does not always happen that way. It is hard to see what makes some people so bitter on this poor little model from the studios of Paris. She suffered enough, God knows. If Du Maurier had allowed her to sin and then become a perfectly happy and respected woman, then the wise men would have a right to object. It would have been an error of both art and ethics. In books, at least, one cannot sin with impunity, and retribution should follow swift upon the steps of crime. Surely Du Maurier has meted out punishment to his heroine. She loses everything, love and home and happiness, even friendship. True he does not punish her harshly, as a younger man would have done, but gently, as a man who has seen so much hopeless pain in the world that he cannot bear to dwell upon it long, much, perhaps, as Dumas would have punished Camille had he written the book at sixty instead of one and twenty.

Of course *Trilby* wasn't written for children or to be published in *St. Nicholas*. It doesn't ever come in misses' sizes. Du Maurier states in the beginning that it was not meant as an accompaniment for nursing bottles. People who are shocked had better stop right there and confine themselves to the Rollo books. Perhaps the book isn't artistic, but it would be hard to find a more graceful and unobtrusive touch of art than Trilby's last confession to Mrs. Bagot, where she says the meanest thing she ever did was to deprive poor little Jeannot of that buggy ride. There are a good many of us who have not quite learned to read that passage with dry eyes yet. Perhaps, after all, Trilby was right, and meanness and selfishness is the one sin for which even God has no forgiveness. The great good about the book is that it moves us so unselfishly. It is not that we envy Trilby's life or covet Trilby's world that makes us read the book three times over. It is our love and pity for her as she is. It makes us want to go right out and find her and comfort and help her. It is worth reading a very long novel to feel that way once. Whether the book is artistic or not matters very little. It has done what art and correct style frequently cannot do; it has appealed to the human in humanity; it has won for itself a place in the hearts of the people. Most of us would write books if we could do that.[45]

Journal, December 23, 1894, p. 13.

Pierre Loti's The Romance of a Spahi

By the spring of 1896 Willa Cather was familiar with most of the important French writers, but she had a special feeling for the style and themes of Pierre Loti (pseudonym of Julien Viaud, b. 1850). If she came upon The Romance of a Spahi *(Le Roman d'un spahi)* late, she might have already seen *Propos d'exil (1887),* Fantôme d'Orient *(1892), or* Madame Chrysanthème *(1887)—certainly* Pêcheur d'islande *(1886).[46] Although* Le Roman d'un spahi *first appeared in 1881, the University of Nebraska library copy was the 1893 Calmann-Lévy edition. Also available was the 1890 English translation by M. L. Watkins (Chicago and New York: Rand, McNally & Company).* The Romance of a Spahi *is a book of sun and desert silences ("the Sahara, the great 'sea without water'") and deep jungle mysteries.*

I picked up another book by Pierre Loti the other day. It is called *The Romance of a Spahi*, and it is just the kind of a book that Loti always writes and that no other man on earth can write. The story is simple and soon told. Jean Peyral was drafted for a soldier and taken away from his mother and little betrothed and his mountain village, up in the Cévennes, and taken to Africa, to old Saint Louis of the Senegal. He was only a boy from the mountains and life in the tropics told on him, the heat and the homesickness, the glaring lights and the eternal flatness of the desert. He had an affair with a mulattress, the wife of a trader, a woman who had lived in Paris, who was at once violent and cunning, as wise as Europe, as cruel as Africa. She betrayed him and he was sent to the hospital. It was his first experience, and he had it hard. When he was well again the loneliness was worse than ever and he took to the blacks and the devil. He took a black slave girl to live with him, a girl with big eyes and shapely

45. Portions of the second and fourth paragraphs of this article were used in the unsigned piece, "Death of George Du Maurier," in the *Home Monthly* for November, 1896.
46. Mrs. George Seibel has told me of Willa Cather's fondness for the works of Pierre Loti, and how in Pittsburgh, in 1896, she got Mrs. Seibel to read *Pêcheur d'islande* in French. When Miss Cather returned from abroad in 1902, one gift she brought the Seibels was a portrait-sketch of Pierre Loti which she had purchased somewhere on Paris's Left Bank.

arms and lips like a red cactus flower, one of the most beautiful women of the Senegal. She was a little captive from the land of Gallam, the land of ivory and gold.[47]

He grew to be a model soldier, this Jean, brave and prompt, and a man of honor, but his connection with a black woman forever shut him from all chance of promotion. At last one day toward the close of his exile, his regiment was ordered to Algeria, that meant one step nearer home, freedom from the black woman and a visit to the old peasant father and mother, who, up in their mountain village, were growing old with waiting for their boy. But just before they took boat an old comrade rushed in and begged Jean to let him go in his place. The black woman begged and there was a scene, and Jean gave it up. Africa had done its work, had wrought the fatal destruction that the tropics always brings upon men from the mountains. He was bound to this desert land that he hated, to this woman he despised. She had charmed him with her amulets, thrown a spell over him by her savage chants. This is the climax of the book, the tragic force, then everything clears for the catastrophe, for even in their novels the French are dramatic. Things go from bad to worse; the slave girl sells Jean's old watch that his father gave him the day he marched away with the other village boys, singing bravely to keep back the tears. He drives her away, but she comes back as they always do, and he takes her back, as they always do, for with her she brings a little child, half white, that has Jean's eyes and that never smiles.

Just before the time of Jean's home-going there is a battle. The night before the encounter he dreams of his mother and the mountains and of his betrothed, who has married another man. For he is only a little peasant of the Cévennes masquerading in a fez and red uniform, who is living wrongly because France has put him where nature did not intend him to be. Next day he was killed, run through the breast, and dragged himself under the shade of a tamarind tree to die. When the slave girl hears that he has "gained paradise," she goes out among the dead and finds him. She strangles his child by filling its mouth with sand, and stretching herself upon his body, takes a poison she had bought of an

47. Pierre Loti's description of the girl Fatou-gaye's homeland of Gallam suggests the book's characteristic style: "Old sacred land, of which she dreamed for hours with closed eyes! The land of gold and ivory, in whose warm waters sleeps the alligator in the shadows of the lofty mangroves, and where the heavy foot of the elephant is heard striking the ground as he rushes through the forest solitudes." (*The Romance of a Spahi*, translated by M. L. Watkins [Chicago and New York: Rand, McNally and Company, 1890], pp. 170–171).

African priest, and dies. In his hand the man held a silver image of the Virgin, his parents had tied about his neck in far away France; in her hand the woman held the amulet of leather her black mother had given her when she was carried away a captive from Gallam. "Guard them well, O precious amulets!"

At night the watchers came, the only watchers who ever sit by the dead who fall in the Soudan; first the jackals, then the vultures, then the winds and the bleaching sands of the desert.

That is all there is of the story, all the rest is description, environment. But ah, such description! All English description is odious. Careful, accurate, burdened with irrelevant detail, lifeless, leaving no picture in the reader's mind. But with the French it is a different matter. They write as they paint, to bring out an effect. All through this book one can smell the aroma of the tropics, see the palms and the tamarinds and the old white mosques, and the burning sandy water of the Senegal, hear the sound of the tom-tom and the epic chants of the griots.[48] The language is simple, simple as the savage life it pictures, intense as the savage emotions it portrays. It is a tragedy of environment and the bitterness of exile.

"War hath three daughters—Fire, Famine and Death—and yet the nations grovel before her, and kiss the red dust at her feet."

I like to think of Pierre Loti, soldier, sailor and artist, sailing among his green seas and palm-fringed islands, through all the tropic nights and orient days. Anchoring at white ports and talking with wild men, now on the high seas and now on the desert, which the ancients quaintly called a sea. We see too much of civilization, we know it all too well. It is always beating about our ears and muddling our brains. We sometimes need solitude and the desert, which Balzac said was "God without mankind."[49] Loti is a sort of knight-errant to bring it to us, who gives to [us] poor cold-bound, sense-dwarfed dwellers in the North the scent of sandalwood and the glitter of the southern stars.

Courier, November 9, 1895, pp. 6–7.

Zola's The Fat and the Thin

Willa Cather first wrote about Zola in her Journal *column of December 30, 1894, as "a landmark in the gradual waning of the realistic school," a*

---

48. The griots, or wandering musicians, compose romances, heroic songs, and marches for the warriors.

49. The conclusion of Balzac's "A Passion in the Desert" ("c'est Dieu sans les hommes").

writer who is "great, misguided, miserable" because he cannot see beauty
and is without joy. Even in his skill and seriousness (which must be admired),
he fails to vivify. He writes of flowers like a botanist, not a poet: "Out of
all his mass of floral detail you never catch a whiff of fragrance or a flash of
color." When in February, 1896, she wrote the following book review of
The Fat and the Thin, *a translation of Zola's* Le Ventre de Paris (1873)
by Ernest Alfred Vizetelly, she was more sympathetic. The review itself,
with only minor changes, was used again in her signed "Books and Maga-
zines" column in the Pittsburgh Leader, May 27, 1898.

One of the latest translations from Zola is published under the unpleasant title *The Fat and the Thin.* The French title, *The Market of Paris,*
is certainly much more dignified and it is hard to see why the American
publishers made the change, unless it is because in this country Zola's
readers are generally rather vulgar people and like coarse titles.[50] The
book is one of Zola's best, and what is more to the point one of his most
decent and endurable. It is painful, certainly, and a book that no one could
read for pleasure, but it is clean and powerful, sometimes almost beautiful.
The story is soon told; Florent was a law student in Paris when his old
mother at Le Vigan died. He returned home and found that she had
literally died from overwork and that his little half-brother, Quenu, had
been almost starved to pay his expenses in Paris. He took the boy back
to the capital with him, gave up his law studies and went to work to
support his brother. During the *coup d'état* of 1851 he was knocked down
by the mob and a woman beside him was shot. In endeavoring to lift
her he got blood on his hands. He was found by the soldiers and because
of his suspicious appearance was tried and transported. Years afterward
he returned penniless and hungry and rode into Paris on the vegetable

50. Willa Cather is no doubt thinking of the earlier English version of the book,
called *The Markets of Paris,* a translation by John Stirling (Philadelphia: T. B. Peterson and
Brothers, c1879), for the literal translation of *Le Ventre de Paris*—"The Belly of Paris"—
would be no more elegant than "The Fat and the Thin." (Even farther afield was the new
title of the Stirling version when it was reissued in 1882—*La belle Lisa; or, The Paris Market
Girls.*) The Vizetelly translation which Willa Cather reviews was originally published in
America by F. T. Neely in 1895; pagination used here, however, is to the 1908 edition published by Chatto and Windus, London. The quotations above are as they appeared in the
Journal, but there are numerous variations from the Vizetelly text. For example, in the first
quotation (from p. 5), for *at length he* read *he at length;* for *seemed to wear* read *seemed to him to
wear.* A sentence has been omitted between "angry at his return" and "As he crossed." In
the second quotation (from pp. 31–32) the last sentence should read: "The uproar was akin
to that of colossal jaws." In the third quotation (from p. 26), for *neighboring shop* read
neighboring streets. See also note 51, below.

cart of a kindly peasant woman. "When at length he reached Courbevoie the night was very dark. Paris, looking like a patch of star-sprent sky that had fallen upon the black earth, seemed to wear a forbidding aspect as though angry at his return. As he crossed the Neuilly bridge he sustained himself by clinging to the parapet, and bent over and looked at the Seine, rolling inky waves between its dense, massy banks. A red lamp on the water seemed to be watching him with a sanguineous eye" [p. 5]. After wandering about hungry among the markets, he found that his brother had become a well-to-do pork butcher. His brother had been fond of him, and he and his wife received poor Florent kindly, if not gladly. He got work in the fish market and was favored by a handsome fish wife who smelt always of herrings. Then he got mixed up in politics, became a mild sort of socialist, was arrested, tried, and again transported. So much for Florent, a rather colorless character in spite of his exaggerations. Zola is not strictly successful with characters of the Jean Valjean type. But the bulk of the book and the charm of it are the incidental descriptions of the markets of Paris. Those markets into which all the delicacies of the world are poured, that are "like some huge central organ beating with giant force and sending the blood of life through every vein of the city. The uproar of them is akin to that of mighty jaws" [pp. 31–32]. One can fairly see it, that great stronghold of plenty in the midst of want, that storehouse of food that is set up in the midst of aching poverty for an eternal temptation. You can feel in some of the descriptions the freshness of the morning. You can see the sunrise over the markets. "The luminous dial of Saint Eustache was palling as night light does when surprised by dawn. The gas jets in the wine shops in the neighboring shop went out one by one as stars extinguished by the brightness. And Florent gazed at the vast markets now gradually emerging from the gloom, from the dream-land in which he had beheld them, stretching out their ranges of open palaces" [p. 26]. He manages without too great a burden of detail to get it all before you, the piles of fragrant greenery, the heaps of flaming carrots with the black soil still clinging to their roots, the gray shimmer of the dripping fish-counters, the roses in their glass cases and the booths of fresh picked violets. And all about them the frugal bartering of hungry people and the roar and clamor of Paris. The description is quite equal to that of Zola's greatest descriptive novel, *The Transgression of the Abbé Mouret.*

As for the rest of the *dramatis personae*, there is the fat butcher and his wife, whose complexion is like fresh pork. Then there is La Normande, the queenly fish wife, who befriended poor Florent, and there are Cadine and Marjolin, two children brought up by an old market woman. The boy and girl lived in the markets, eating what they could steal, selling flowers when they were not too idle, loving each other by way of a pastime, lunching in empty cellars, clambering over the roofs in the moonlight, happy as the sparrows that twittered about the towers of St. Eustache, and just as good for nothing. The most cheerful figure in the book is the young painter, Claude, who never had enough to eat and wore an old streaked overcoat to hide his lack of other clothing. He hung about the markets day and night, wild with enthusiasm over the profusion of colors, never vexed save when the seductive odors of the food made him hungry, and tightening his belt that his empty stomach might not inter- fere with the satisfaction of his eyes. He used to go down every morning to watch the effect of the sunrise upon the rows of bullock's lights. "And when a ray of sunshine fell upon the lights and girdled them with gold, an expression of languorous rapture came into his eyes, and he felt happier than if he had been privileged to contemplate the Greek goddesses in their sovereign nudity or the chatelaines of old romance in their brocaded robes" [p. 187]. It was he, too, who said: "Do you know the battle of the Fat and the Lean? Cain was certainly one of the fat, Abel one of the lean. Ever since the first murder there have been rampant appetites which have drained the life-blood of the smaller eaters. It's a continual preying of the stronger upon the weaker; each swallowing his neighbor and getting swallowed in turn. Beware of the Fat, my friend!" [pp. 217–218].[51]

In spite of its unquestionable merit, of its undeniable power, this book is only a novel of the butcher shop with a fish wife for a heroine. And once again Zola has only written a book full of repulsive odors, about another kind of unhappiness. Of all men under the skies, the most pitiful is this Zola, the miserable, this Émile the unhappy. One could almost sell his soul to know for one minute the dreams that Shakespeare or that Dante saw, but who for all his fortune and for all his fame would be Zola? Better be a day laborer whistling in the sun than this man who has

51. This passage should read as follows: "Do you know the 'Battle of the Fat and the Thin'? . . . Cain . . . was certainly one of the Fat, and Abel one of the Thin. Ever since that first murder, there have been rampant appetites which have drained the life-blood of the small eaters. It's a continual preying of the stronger upon the weaker; each swallowing his neighbor, and then getting swallowed in his turn. Beware of the Fat, my friend." The book's epigraph from *Julius Caesar*—on Cassius and his "lean and hungry look"—probably carried over into the text.

mastered all the craft of his art only to find that its soul is unattainable to him forever. For beauty is the only justification of any art and when that is lacking what remains is worthless. All this massive work of Zola's is like one of those terrible granite bulls unearthed from Nineveh, it lacks the impress of a human soul. Its life is sluggish, like the blood that flows in reptiles, you never feel in it that thrill as of a soul that wakens and expands before the sun. You may heap the details of beauty together forever, but they are not beauty until one human soul feels and knows. That is what Zola's books lack from first to last, the awakening of the spirit. An artist may be clever when he answers you, he may be skilful when he pleases your senses, but when he speaks to the living soul within you, then and then only is he great. Only a diamond can cut a diamond, only can a soul touch a soul. All this question of art is just another version of Bunyan's siege of the town of Mansoul.[52] All the creators in the world have sent out their armies to rouse that sleeping king; when for a moment they can command his high attentions, immortality is theirs. Émile Zola is one of the strongest craftsmen of his time, but he cannot accomplish that which is the end of craft. He is like a miser who has gathered all the treasures of the world, but who has lost the capacity to enjoy. And again, "What shall it profit a man if he gain the whole world and lose his own soul."

Journal, February 16, 1896, p. 9.

Mrs. Burnett and Thackeray

Mrs. Frances Hodgson Burnett (b. 1849) was English, but she had lived in the United States since 1865. She was known particularly for Little Lord Fauntleroy *(1886), and a series of quiet domestic books like* Editha's Burglar *(1888),* Sara Crewe *(1888), and* Little Saint Elizabeth *(1890). A* Lady of Quality *(1896) was her first attempt at a more complex handling of history and character. Willa Cather liked historical novels, but an eighteenth-century story would have to be measured by the very high mark set by Thackeray's* Henry Esmond. *That model had come up before in her note on Richard Mansfield in* Beau Brummell: "*The whole play was like a chapter from* Henry Esmond, *in some way it was entirely Thackerayesque. It was saturated with the spirit of the time and people that Thackeray loved to deal with*" (Journal, April 29, 1894). *When she thought about historical plays or novels, the contemporary writer who best fulfilled her expectations was George Meredith. Historical novels must first*

52. In Bunyan's *The Holy War.*

of all "vivify," as she had said of Dumas; they must bring the past to life, and that would take both knowledge and creative skill.

After devoting herself for some ten years to children's stories, Mrs. Burnett decided to give us something serious again, and certainly to her belongs the credit of a great attempt. The story of *A Lady of Quality* is written in a most difficult key and purports to be written by Isaac Bickerstaff of *The Tatler*. Mistress Clorinda is a lady of quality, born and brought up under the most adverse circumstances. The scene of her advent into a world which, on the whole, used her very well, is one of the best in the book. She was the ninth girl child whom her mother had had the misfortune to bear her boisterous, indignant old husband. The poor lady died after the baby's birth, and if she had won her way the baby would have died with her. Mistress Wildairs had no very high opinion of the happiness allotted to a woman in this world, and she thought that rather than to live a woman, it would be better not to live at all. Her last dying strength was spent in struggling to stop her baby's breath. But Clorinda had a strong talent for living and getting all out of life that there is in it, so she lived. She grew up in her father's hall among the grooms and stable boys and servants, hunting with her father in boys' clothes and the comrade of his rowdy companions. She was always unjust and selfish, especially toward her two poor, pale sisters, who were neither brilliant nor beautiful. As to Clorinda's beauty Mrs. Burnett is never weary of describing it. On her fifteenth birthday Clorinda puts aside her stable boy manners and boy's attire forever, and becomes outwardly the pink of propriety, because, as she very candidly confessed, she wants to make a good match, and her rough ways would go against her. Indeed, Miss Clorinda is a very outspoken young person and singularly frank in her somewhat bold, ethical views. When her father is bringing her home from a ball one night, and tells her to be as wild as she will, so that she never disgraces the family, she says frankly: "There thou mayest trust me; I would not be found out." That is about the keynote of the young lady's character—not to be found out. Young Sir John Oxon, a London rake, comes out into the country and, while seeming to treat him coldly, Clorinda commits some very rank indiscretions. Finally, she marries Lord Dunstanwolde, but on the very evening of her betrothal to him, meets his kinsman, the Duke of Osmonde, and falls violently in love with him. She has at bottom, however, a rough idea of justice, and we are informed that during the old lord's very brief life she made him a model wife.

After he falls dead at a ball nothing seems to stand between her and the adoring Osmonde, when suddenly John Oxon, desperate from debt, appears upon the scene as a suitor for her hand. She refuses him, and he threatens to tell all the story of her past escapades with him to Osmonde. In a heated interview with him, she strikes him with her loaded riding whip and kills him. She carries him down into the old wine cellar of her London house and buries him and then has the cellar walled up. Then she marries the Duke of Osmonde and Mrs. Burnett proceeds to make her a saint among women.

What a strange book for Mrs. Burnett to write, modest, womanly, little Mrs. Burnett of *Lord Fauntleroy* fame. There never was a more inconsistent book. As though a vain and selfish woman would not be vain and selfish still, even if she did love the Duke of Osmonde. It is not possible to put aside one's part. One is one's part; it is a part of one's body and soul; it is ever living in one's blood. If Mrs. Burnett had been content with making her wilful heroine merely a good wife to the Duke of Osmonde, one might believe her; but she must make her the poor man's friend, the benefactor of hundreds. Even to the sympathetic lover of the wonderful in fiction, this must seem a bit overdrawn.

Mrs. Burnett insisted in telling the story in the eighteenth century style, she does not do it satisfactorily. That eighteenth century prose is strongest, and, in some respects, the best in the language. To attempt to imitate it puts an author in direct competition with Smollett and Steele and Fielding, and among such mighty warriors of the pen what must become of the gentle author of *Little Lord Fauntleroy*? As some critic has said, it also puts her book in direct comparison with that ever unassailable masterpiece of English prose, *Henry Esmond*. That alone would be fatal to any novel brought forth in these days of pigmies. Then Mrs. Burnett does not take kindly to the atmosphere of the past century; she is always forgetting and dropping the mark; the sentiment and feeling of the whole book are too vivid, too modern; the characters only masquerading, and you feel that all the time. It is all acting. A few obsolete words and a satin waistcoat and powdered wig cannot give a picture of the last century. Comparisons may be odious in art, but they are the only means of keeping your taste pure and inviolate. People who never make them have no stability of judgment. And this book fairly clamors for comparison with *Henry Esmond*. Compare it, and all there is left of it is a wraith, a shadow, an attempt that failed. By the side of *Esmond* it is mere light opera, mock heroic. Thackeray allows Beatrix Esmond no repentance, no "change of heart." A selfish nature is selfish always. She is always the same Trix from the day she puts on her red stockings to captivate little Harry Esmond until she is an old, selfish woman, struggling in her delirium to enter the boudoir of a prince that has been closed to her, muttering of old Harry Esmond, dead and buried beyond the sea, whom she was not brave enough to follow. She was in love with him hard enough, no doubt of that; but she was herself first and her personality was her destiny. She served herself diligently all the days of her life and enjoyed it, regretting nothing, all the while vaguely wanting Henry Esmond. But the want was not strong enough to cope with the other demands of her nature. It was more easily stifled than vanity. She was made for power and conquest, as some men are, but then women conquered in another way. She could have no more gone to live on a tobacco plantation in Virginia than Napoleon could have settled down and raised potatoes in a granite gorge in Corsica, because he loved some Corsican girl. Destiny is stronger than we, and our necessities are so much stronger than our desires. We so seldom can allow ourselves to take what we want. If we are for evil, if the devil has won the toss for our souls, evil we must do, and our power to love works woe as well as our power to hate. People call Thackeray bitter because he is so true. Beside him what wonder that motherly little Mrs. Burnett and her undeserving heroine make a poor showing? For there were two King Williams in England, the great William of verse, and the great William of prose, and their reign is as supreme and as undisturbed as the serenity of the north star.

Journal, June 14, 1896, p. 13.

Mrs. Humphry Ward and George Eliot

Willa Cather seems to have read a good many of the novels of the English writer Mrs. Humphry Ward (b. 1851), for scattered through the columns are allusions to Miss Bretherton *(1884),* Robert Elsmere *(1888),* David Grieve *(1892),* Marcella *(1894), and eventually the new* Sir George Tressady *which ran in the* Century *from November, 1895, to October, 1896. Mrs. Ward, a niece of Matthew Arnold, was a cut above the other popular lady novelists of the day, but she did lean to social comment (for one thing, she was an opponent of women's suffrage), and according to Willa Cather's most fundamental principles these concerns were for tracts, not novels. There is one earlier comment on Mrs. Ward in Willa Cather's columns. She says that Mrs. Ward and Elizabeth Barrett Browning made "the same respectable blunder": with study and intel-*

lectuality they achieved "merit without greatness" (Journal, *January 13, 1895*). *There is no extended comment on George Eliot, but Willa Cather regularly classed her with the great ones: "The feminine mind has a hankering for hobbies and missions, consequently there have been but two real creators among women authors, George Sand and George Eliot"* (Journal, *September 23, 1894*).

Is Mrs. Humphry Ward a George Eliot? That is the question which the reviewer seems never tired of asking and answering. What rank nonsense! As well ask, was Thackeray a Dickens? Of course Mrs. Ward is not George Eliot and of course she is herself. She has very little in common with *La Grande* George except that she is the only other woman of her nation who has shown the power to write a really important novel, and to do it not once but again and again. Mrs. Ward is really a very wonderful woman; she has the power to construct and mass a novel with perfect harmony and proportion as to its parts, never losing sight of her main end, a power that is becoming rare in these days of the apotheosis of the short story. And she always has an end; she reaches it not by a sudden turn of the scale, not by a happy chance or through the outbursting of a pent-up fire, but slowly, in the old orthodox fashion, by gathering all the threads of her plot into one strand and bringing external forces to bear on the destiny of her men and women. With an exception [*Miss Bretherton*] her novels are all unusually long and events happen slowly; she takes plenty of time and space and good language to bring things to pass. She is fond of analyzing and has a strong gift for it; not for analyzing emotions so much as mental attitudes, which are, indeed, responsible for most of our emotions.

From the first half of any one of her novels one ought to be perfectly able to tell just about what the characters will do in the second half, she diagrams their mental possibilities and impossibilities so clearly. The mental attitude of her characters is everything. You can wager they will be consistent to that in the end, no matter what little outbreaks of temporary inclination may intervene; and they are all admirable people; one must always respect them even if one does not love them mightily. Her descriptive powers are great, almost too great; she has a perfect grasp of detail and can particularize ad infinitum. But the power to make a whole picture stand out by a few masterly strokes she has not. Detailed description has its disadvantages in fiction. In painting, where the eye can see all at a glance, it is very well; but on a printed page it is likely to overtask the memory somewhat and blur the ultimate clearness of the picture. It certainly does with Mrs. Ward. In short, Mrs. Ward has the gift of appealing to one's intelligence rather than to one's sympathies, and writes admirable books rather than lovable ones. But hers is a most entertaining and well bred intelligence and very much more satisfactory and dependable than the uncertain gifts of her more lively contemporaries; and her cold-blooded premeditation is less provoking than [the] scrambles of those clever young Englishmen who sometimes hit and sometimes miss. When she at last finishes a novel, it is always a skilful and a solid work, if not a vivid one.

George Eliot had what Mrs. Ward has not, "the red blood of common life." Of course, Mrs. Ward can write of the common people. The first part of *David Grieve*, and even *Marcella*, contain some excellent work of that art; but she can't be one of them. George Eliot could. There is no corner in Mrs. Ward's well regulated heart where that hot, imperious blood of the street beats and throbs and battles for its rights. She understands it, but she can never know it. The author of *Adam Bede* could lay all her own traditions aside and at will confine herself to those simple, elementary emotions and needs that exist beneath the blouse of a laborer, as well as under the gown of a scholar. Mrs. Ward can write of these people kindly and seriously, but the important events in her books are brought about only by Oxford graduates. That element of refinement and culture must be there; she cannot work without it. She is at home in but one world. George Eliot was a naturalized citizen of both. She could take a common laborer and a girl who had never read Ruskin or Carlyle and have them love and hate "for a' that, and a' that." To her the fundamental principles and actuating needs of life were the same the world over, whether in the Florence of Lorenzo the Magnificent or in the shop of a village carpenter, unintensified by learning and untamed by thought.

A long time ago when she was not half the skilful novelist that she is now, Mrs. Ward wrote a light, sketchy little romance called *Miss Bretherton*. It was not a remarkably clever book at all and Miss Bretherton herself was rather a failure, but one learned to know some nice people in it. There is no picture of married life anywhere that is quite so satisfying as that of Marie and Paul. It's quite great, the feeling those two wise and witty and yet single people had for each other, and the way they met and satisfied each other's needs, big and little. One hopes that Mrs. Ward learned that beautiful affection near at home. The book, rough and sketchy as it is, shows Mrs. Ward's mental policy. The heroine is a young actress, a raw, ignorant girl from Australia, with great talent and personal charms, but totally without education or artistic conceptions. The hero is a novelist who loves her well enough, but cannot forgive her crudeness and wounds her cruelly by telling her so. She goes off to Italy and the novelist's sister, Marie, takes her in hand and puts her through a course of Shakespeare and French, and then the novelist can love her altogether. Alas, when they find a girl as pretty as Miss Bretherton, even novelists seldom wait for the French and Shakespeare; they might be happier if they did. But just that is Mrs. Ward's limitation; she cannot conceive of a high affection without a high mental affinity.

Journal, May 31, 1896, p. 13.

Tolstoi

Some of Willa Cather's highest praise for a single novel was given to Anna Karenina, *which like other novels of Tolstoi's early period—*War and Peace, Sevastopol, *and* Ivan Ilyich—*was a living body created by the master who had "inimitable craft and power unlimited." Her continued protest against fiction as social argument certainly links these 1896 notes on Tolstoi with a paragraph in the* Lasso *for November, 1891, when as one of the editors Willa Cather left her unmistakable mark on the literary column. The* Lasso *praises Tolstoi's story "Polikushka" (in* The Invaders, *translated by Nathan Haskell Dole, 1887): "In this sketch Tolstoi does not reason, nor argue, nor attack anything nor anybody, nor go into social or moral ethics. He just tells a little commonplace story very simply and very effectively. Had he contented himself with the simplicity of 'Polikushka,' or with the freshness and vigor of* The Cossacks, *or even with the irony of* The Death of Ivan Ilyich, *and not been seized by the fatal idea that it was his especial mission to reorganize society and reconstruct the universe, Tolstoi would be a happier man and a better writer" (pp. 20–21).*

In the second item below, Willa Cather is referring to an article in the Independent *for February 20, 1896—"The Turning of the Tide" by Maurice Thompson, who had several times called Tolstoi, Flaubert, Dumas fils, Ibsen, Hardy, and others "unclean." Mr. Thompson was speaking of "a fiction keyed in adultery and depending upon illicit passion for its tone and its imaginative appeal. The gamut of* Madame Bovary, Anna Karenina, Tess *and the rest, has been achieved, and has been tipped and pointed with the Sarah Grand performance." But as Willa Cather had said many times, the only immorality in art is bad art.*

Tolstoi is writing a new novel. Heaven grant that it is not another *Master and Man,* and yet the deluded old man once wrote *Anna Karenina*! He may not have been so good a man when he wrote for the pleasure of mankind as now when he writes for the glory of God, but the saints themselves would confess he was a better novelist. He possessed all the great secrets of art once, an inimitable craft and power unlimited, but after his first attack of asceticism he branded all these as vanity and flung them to the winds, destroying his great unfinished novel written in the *Karenina* vein. Then he began to write for a "moral purpose." Now art itself is the highest moral purpose in the world, and when a man deserts it for another he pays money for that which is not bread and gets the worst of the bargain. The world of letters could ill afford to lose Tolstoi, the novelist, and it is doubtful if the Russian peasants are any happier or more grateful for the efforts of Tolstoi, the philanthropist. If God is at all a literary God *Anna Karenina* will certainly do more toward saving its author's soul than all the prosy tracts he has written since, from *The Kreutzer Sonata* of Wanamaker memory [53] down to the *Master and Man.* When Count Tolstoi lived in the world and was, as he assures us, a wicked man, he wrote one of the greatest novels of his country. Now that he lives like a recluse and makes pea soup for Russian peasants he writes some of the most wearisome stuff that is published. "Be good and you will be clever" as the old copy books said.

Journal, May 17, 1896, p. 13.

In a recent number of the *Independent,* Mr. Maurice Thompson makes his semi-annual condemnation of realistic fiction and arraigns *Madame Bovary* and *Anna Karenina* along with the rest. In a gentleman of Mr. Thompson's very modest and rather insignificant literary attainments such sweeping assertions seem rather daring. He may perhaps have a right to condemn the masterpieces of other nations, for this is a free country, but his taste in so doing is rather questionable. From Henry James or even Mr. Howells such statements would command respect, for they have done something on the other side of the question; they have not only avoided being offensive, but have given pregnant and powerful illustrations of their theories as to the delicacy and decency of literature. But Mr. Thompson has nothing to show for himself but some very inferior and short-lived stories and his narrow and arrogant opinions. It is a precarious

53. In 1890 Postmaster-General John Wanamaker kept *The Kreutzer Sonata* out of the United States mails.

undertaking to denounce a great book just because it does not appeal to your personal tastes. It's too much like the man who denounced Doctor Johnson because he did not make a good neighbor. A great book is a creation, like a great man; you can acknowledge its power and influence without cherishing any personal fondness for it. Many a great book and many a great man would be "ill to live with," as Carlyle's mother frankly said of her mighty son. But their greatness remains just the same and commands respect, not because it is good or bad, in the moral sense, likeable or unlikeable, but because it is mighty, a force, like the sea or a cataract, and thousands of other things that are not measured by their ethics or their amiability. The world could better afford to lose all of Mr. Thompson's harmless tales and even all his lofty, ethical opinions, than to part with twenty pages of *Anna Karenina*.

Journal, March 22, 1896, p. 9.

THE LIFE, THE ART

With the young Willa Cather there was always the problem of how to join the two selves of artist and person. The question took her through many turns of emphasis and belief, and perhaps it would be a while before she could settle it to her satisfaction. It seemed surely that the quality of the mind, what a person was, must affect his art; a person of a certain temperament, like Byron perhaps, would make an artist of a particular kind. Yet it became painfully clear that what the world—or Philistia—might call good or bad in a man's life might have little to do with any absolute judgment of his art, for the qualities of genius are so complex that there are no rules of thumb to measure them by. Always distinctions, individualities, the pull of conflicting judgments—even in herself. With Poe, one could promptly blame society; not so with Wilde and Verlaine. But she had modified her view of Wilde from June, 1894, to the fall of 1895—would she also change her mind about Verlaine? We live in doubleness, she seems to say often in this period, and some clear-cut truth, like those Ionian marbles against the bright blue ancient sky, grows in time so much more difficult to trace. In all art there was the inextricable mingling of the creator with the created, the consuming of elements to make one greater thing.

Poe

The essay on Poe, as it reads from the second paragraph on, is obviously the one Willa Cather read at the joint meeting of the University of Nebraska literary societies on June 8, 1895 (see pages 21 f.). Because it was designed for oral presentation, it has a few more oratorical flourishes than do most of her journalistic articles of the period. But Poe was one whose life and art formed contradictions that could easily arouse impassioned speech. One of the few masters of "pure prose," one of the few important American poets, his distinction in art was balanced by that archetypal tragedy of the unfulfilled genius, best described by Shelley in Adonais*—though above all, as Shelley said, "the immortal stars awake again."*

My tantalized spirit
    Here blandly reposes,
Forgetting, or never
    Regretting, its roses,—
Its old agitations
    Of myrtles and roses.

For now, while so quietly
   Lying, it fancies
A holier odor
   About it, of pansies—
A rosemary odor,
   Commingled with pansies.—
With rue and the beautiful
   Puritan pansies.[54]

Edgar Allan Poe

The Shakespeare society of New York, which is really about the only useful literary organization in this country, is making vigorous efforts to redress an old wrong and atone for a long neglect. Sunday, September 22, it held a meeting at the Poe cottage on Kingsbridge Road near Fordham, for the purpose of starting an organized movement to buy back the cottage, restore it to its original condition and preserve it as a memorial of Poe. So it has come at last. After helping build monuments to Shelley, Keats and Carlyle we have at last remembered this man, the greatest of our poets and the most unhappy. I am glad that this movement is in the hands of American actors, for it was among them that Poe found his best friends and warmest admirers. Some way he always seemed to belong to the strolling Thespians who were his mother's people.

Among all the thousands of life's little ironies that make history so diverting, there is none more paradoxical than that Edgar Poe should have been an American. Look at his face. Had we ever another like it? He must have been a strange figure in his youth, among those genial, courtly Virginians, this handsome, pale fellow, violent in his enthusiasm, ardent in his worship, but spiritually cold in his affections. Now playing heavily for the mere excitement of play, now worshipping at the shrine of a woman old enough to be his mother, merely because her voice was beautiful; now swimming six miles up the James River against a heavy current in the glaring sun of a June mid-day. He must have seemed to them an unreal figure, a sort of stage man who was wandering about the streets with his mask and buskins on, a theatrical figure who had escaped by some strange mischance into the prosaic daylight. His speech and actions were unconsciously and sincerely dramatic, always as though done for effect. He had that nervous, egotistic, self-centered nature common to stage children who seem to have been dazzled by the footlights and maddened by the applause before they are born. It was in his

54. From "For Annie."

blood. With the exception of two women who loved him, lived for him, died for him, he went through life friendless, misunderstood, with that dense, complete, hopeless misunderstanding which, as Amiel[55] said, is the secret of that sad smile upon the lips of the great. Men tried to befriend him, but in some way or other he hurt and disappointed them. He tried to mingle and share with other men, but he was always shut from them by that shadow, light as gossamer but unyielding as adamant, by which, from the beginning of the world, art has shielded and guarded and protected her own, that God-concealing mist in which the heroes of old were hidden, immersed in that gloom and solitude which, if we could but know it here, is but the shadow of God's hand as it falls upon his elect.

We lament our dearth of great prose. With the exception of Henry James and Hawthorne, Poe is our only master of pure prose. We lament our dearth of poets. With the exception of Lowell, Poe is our only great poet. Poe found short story writing a bungling makeshift. He left it a perfect art. He wrote the first perfect short stories in the English language. He first gave the short story purpose, method, and artistic form. In a careless reading one cannot realize the wonderful literary art, the cunning devices, the masterly effects that those entrancing tales conceal. They are simple and direct enough to delight us when we are children, subtle and artistic enough to be our marvel when we are old. To this day they are the wonder and admiration of the French, who are the acknowledged masters of craft and form. How in his wandering, laborious life, bound to the hack work of the press and crushed by an ever-growing burden of want and debt, did he ever come upon all this deep and mystical lore, this knowledge of all history, of all languages, of all art, this penetration into the hidden things of the East? As Steadman says, "The self-training of genius is always a marvel."[56] The past is spread before us all and most of us spend our lives in learning those things which we do not need to know, but genius reaches out instinctively and takes only the vital detail, by some sort of spiritual gravitation goes directly to the right thing.

Poe belonged to the modern French school of decorative and discriminating prose before it ever existed in France. He rivalled Gautier, Flaubert and de Maupassant before they were born.[57] He clothed his

55. Frederick Amiel, in his *Journal*.

56. Probably Edmund Clarence Stedman, critic and anthologist, who did write on genius. However, William Stead was the author of the famous *If Christ Came to Chicago* (1893).

57. Only partially true, unless one thinks of accomplishment as birth. Poe's prose was being published in the 1830's when Flaubert was in his teens and Théophile Gautier in his twenties. Judith Gautier, however, was born in 1850, Maupassant in the same year.

tales in a barbaric splendor and persuasive unreality never before heard of in English. No such profusion of color, oriental splendor of detail, grotesque combinations and mystical effects had ever before been wrought into language. There are tales as grotesque, as monstrous, unearthly as the stone griffins and gargoyles that are cut up among the unvisited niches and towers of Notre Dame, stories as poetic and delicately beautiful as the golden lace work chased upon an Etruscan ring. He fitted his words together as the Byzantine jewelers fitted priceless stones. He found the inner harmony and kinship of words. Where lived another man who could blend the beautiful and the horrible, the gorgeous and the grotesque in such intricate and inexplicable fashion? Who could delight you with his noun and disgust you with his verb, thrill you with his adjective and chill you with his adverb, make you run the whole gamut of human emotions in a single sentence? Sitting in that miserable cottage at Fordham he wrote of the splendor of dream palaces beyond the dreams of art. He hung those grimy walls with dream tapestries, paved those narrow halls with black marble and polished onyx, and into those low-roofed chambers he brought all the treasured imagery of fancy, from the "huge carvings of untutored Egypt" to "mingled and conflicting perfumes, reeking up from strange convolute censers, together with multitudinous, flaring and flickering tongues of purple and violet fire." Hungry and ragged he wrote of Epicurean feasts and luxury that would have beggared the purpled pomp of pagan Rome and put Nero and his Golden House to shame.

And this mighty master of the organ of language, who knew its every stop and pipe, who could awaken at will the thin silver tones of its slenderest reeds or the solemn cadence of its deepest thunder, who could make it sing like a flute or roar like a cataract, he was born into a country without a literature. He was of that ornate school which usually comes last in a national literature, and he came first. American taste had been vitiated by men like Griswold and N. P. Willis until it was at the lowest possible ebb.[58] Willis was considered a genius, that is the worst that could possibly be said. In the North a new race of great philosophers was growing up, but Poe had neither their friendship nor encouragement. He went indeed, sometimes, to the chilly salon of Margaret Fuller, but he was always a discord there. He was a mere artist and he had no business

58. Rufus Wilmot Griswold (1815–1857), critic, anthologist, Poe's literary executor who (it is said) stole his copyright from Mrs. Clemm; and Nathaniel Parker Willis (1806–1867), magazine editor, one time employer and publisher of Poe, author of miscellaneous light prose such as *Pencillings by the Way* (1844), *Dashes at Life with a Free Pencil* (1845), etc.

with philosophy, he had no theories as to the "higher life" and the "true happiness." He had only his unshapen dreams that battled with him in dark places, the unborn that struggled in his brain for birth. What time has an artist to learn the multiplication table or to talk philosophy? He was not afraid of them. He laughed at Willis, and flung Longfellow's lie in his teeth, the lie the rest of the world was twenty years in finding.[59] He scorned the obtrusive learning of the Transcendentalists and he disliked their hard talkative women. He left them and went back to his dream women, his Berenice, his Ligeia, his Marchesa Aphrodite,[60] pale and cold as the mist maidens of the North, sad as the Norns who weep for human woe.

The tragedy of Poe's life was not alcohol, but hunger. He died when he was forty, when his work was just beginning. Thackeray had not touched his great novels at forty, George Eliot was almost unknown at that age. Hugo, Goethe, Hawthorne, Lowell and Dumas all did their great work after they were forty years old.[61] Poe never did his great work. He could not endure the hunger. This year the Drexel Institute has put over sixty thousand dollars into a new edition of Poe's poems and stories. He himself never got six thousand for them altogether. If one of the great and learned institutions of the land had invested one tenth of that amount in the living author forty years ago we should have had from him such works as would have made the name of this nation great. But he sold "The Masque of the Red Death"[62] for a few dollars, and now the Drexel Institute pays a publisher thousands to publish it beautifully. It is enough to make Satan laugh until his ribs ache, and all the little devils laugh and heap on fresh coals. I don't wonder they hate humanity. It's so dense, so hopelessly stupid.

Only a few weeks before Poe's death he said he had never had time

59. From his first review of Longfellow's *Ballads and Other Poems* in *Graham's Magazine*, April, 1842, Poe quarrelled with the New England poet in print, accusing him of plagiarism and other literary sins. Perhaps Willa Cather's judgment of Longfellow should be recorded here: "There seems to be a peculiar fatality about the story of Miles Standish. He doesn't seem to work up well in prose or verse. Probably Mr. Longfellow killed him thoroughly some years ago, along with English hexameter" (*Journal*, February 11, 1894).

60. In the stories "Berenice," "Ligeia," and "The Assignation."

61. Generally true. George Eliot's first important novel, *Adam Bede* (1859), was published when she was forty. Hugo published *Hernani*, *Notre Dame de Paris*, and *Ruy Blas* before he was forty, but the great novels *Les Misérables* (1862) and *Histoire d'un Crime* (written 1852, published 1877) came after. Goethe was fifty-nine when *Faust* appeared. Hawthorne had published only *Twice-Told Tales* before he was forty. Some of Lowell's major poems were published earlier, but his career as editor and critic began at thirty-eight. It is true for Dumas *père* (*Les Trois Mousquetaires* and *Le Comte de Monte Cristo* were published at forty-one) but not Dumas *fils*.

62. The story appeared in *Graham's Magazine*, May, 1842.

or opportunity to make a serious effort. All his tales were merely experiments, thrown off when his day's work as a journalist was over, when he should have been asleep. All those voyages into the mystical unknown, into the gleaming, impalpable kingdom of pure romance from which he brought back such splendid trophies, were but experiments. He was only getting his tools into shape, getting ready for his great effort, the effort that never came.

Bread seems a little thing to stand in the way of genius, but it can. The simple sordid facts were these, that in the bitterest storms of winter Poe seldom wrote by a fire, that after he was twenty-five years old he never knew what it was to have enough to eat without dreading tomorrow's hunger. Chatterton had only himself to sacrifice, but Poe saw the woman he loved die of want before his very eyes, die smiling and begging him not to give up his work. They saw the depths together in those long winter nights when she lay in that cold room, wrapped in Poe's only coat, he, with one hand holding hers, and with the other dashing off some of the most perfect masterpieces of English prose. And when he would wince and turn white at her coughing, she would always whisper: "Work on, my poet, and when you have finished read it to me. I am happy when I listen." O, the devotion of women and the madness of art! They are the two most awesome things on earth, and surely this man knew both to the full.

I have wondered so often how he did it. How he kept his purpose always clean and his taste always perfect. How it was that hard labor never wearied nor jaded him, never limited his imagination, that the jarring clamor about him never drowned the fine harmonies of his fancy. His discrimination remained always delicate, and from the constant strain of toil his fancy always rose strong and unfettered. Without encouragement or appreciation of any sort, without models or precedents he built up that pure style of his that is without peer in the language, that style of which every sentence is a drawing by Vedder.[63] Elizabeth Barrett and a few great artists over in France knew what he was doing, they knew that in literature he was making possible a new heaven and a new earth. But he never knew that they knew it. He died without the assurance that he was or ever would be understood. And yet through all this, with the whole world of art and letters against him, betrayed by his own people,

63. Elihu Vedder (1836–1923), American painter and illustrator. Among the books of the Cather family is a copy of FitzGerald's translation of the *Rubáiyát* of Omar Kháyyám, "With an Accompaniment of Drawings by Elihu Vedder" (Boston: Houghton Mifflin and Company, 1886).

he managed to keep that lofty ideal of perfect work. What he suffered never touched or marred his work, but it wrecked his character. Poe's character was made by his necessity. He was a liar and an egotist; a man who had to beg for bread at the hands of his publishers and critics could be nothing but a liar, and had he not had the insane egotism and conviction of genius, he would have broken down and written the drivelling trash that his countrymen delighted to read. Poe lied to his publishers sometimes, there is no doubt of that, but there were two to whom he was never false, his wife and his muse. He drank sometimes too, when for very ugly and relentless reasons he could not eat. And then he forgot what he suffered. For Bacchus is the kindest of the gods after all. When Aphrodite has fooled us and left us and Athene has betrayed us in battle, then poor tipsy Bacchus, who covers his head with vine leaves where the curls are getting thin, [holds] out his cup to us and says, "Forget." It's poor consolation, but he means it well.

The Transcendentalists were good conversationalists, that in fact was their principal accomplishment. They used to talk a great deal of genius, that rare and capricious spirit that visits earth so seldom, that is wooed by so many, and won by so few. They had grand theories that all men should be poets, that the visits of that rare spirit should be made as frequent and universal as afternoon calls. O, they had plans to make a whole generation of little geniuses. But she only laughed her scornful laughter, that deathless lady of the immortals, up in her echoing chambers that are floored with dawn and roofed with the spangled stars. And she snatched from them the only man of their nation she had ever deigned to love, whose lips she had touched with music and whose soul with song. In his youth she had shown him the secrets of her beauty and his manhood had been one pursuit of her, blind to all else, like Anchises, who on the night that he knew the love of Venus, was struck sightless, that he might never behold the face of a mortal woman. For Our Lady of Genius has no care for the prayer and groans of mortals, nor for their hecatombs sweet of savor. Many a time of old she has foiled the plans of seers and none may entreat her or take her by force. She favors no one nation or clime. She takes one from the millions, and when she gives herself unto a man it is without his will or that of his fellows, and he pays for it, dear heaven, he pays!

The sun comes forth and many reptiles spawn,
He sets and each ephemeral insect then

> Is gathered unto death without a dawn,
> And the immortal stars awake again.

Yes, "and the immortal stars awake again." None may thwart the unerring justice of the gods, not even the Transcendentalists. What matter that one man's life was miserable, that one man was broken on the wheel? His work lives and his crown is eternal. That the work of his age was undone, that is the pity; that the work of his youth was done, that is the glory. The man is nothing. There are millions of men. The work is everything. There is so little perfection. We lament our dearth of poets when we let Poe starve. We are like the Hebrews who stoned their prophets and then marvelled that the voice of God was silent. We will wait a long time for another. There are Griswold and N. P. Willis, our chosen ones, let us turn to them. Their names are forgotten. God is just. They are,

> Gathered unto death without a dawn,
> And the immortal stars awake again.

Courier, October 12, 1895, pp. 6–7.

Wilde

Willa Cather's first comment on Oscar Wilde was in a signed review of a performance of Lady Windermere's Fan *on June 4, 1894. Her eventual judgment of the play, after another performance on December 17 of that year, modified her first reaction a little—the play was more amusing and less irritating than at first, but still "hopelessly artificial," without imagination and sincerity. By the following spring, Wilde had been accused and brought to trial (on April 27, 1895). Willa Cather's comment in May still referred to the faults she had traced in* Lady Windermere's Fan—*thin cleverness and insincerity—but by September she had looked at the case with a larger view and could feel that Wilde had at least the possibilities of an artist. Perhaps she had read more of his poetry, for she quotes it as if by memory in the last article on Wilde, and again later in the fall when she talks of Swinburne. One might guess, too, that she had read some of the many articles in the local papers recalling that Wilde had lectured in Omaha and Lincoln in March of 1882, and that in spite of his sunflowers and knee breeches he had made a good deal of sense. Even the nonsense had a kind of imaginative color and charm.*[64]

64. Among the articles recalling Wilde's visit was one in the *Journal* column of a Nebraska newspaperman, Walt Mason, who had found in his scrapbook an account of an interview with Wilde. The reporter had asked the visitor when he would return to England. "I can't say," said Wilde. "I want to travel over your country, (I suppose it is yours),

[387]

Lady Windermere's Fan

... As a play *Lady Windermere's Fan* is very poorly constructed. There is almost no action in the first two acts. There is no justification for anything. Why should Lady Windermere yield to a temptation so weak it did not deserve even the name of temptation? Mr. Wilde deigned to give no reason either ethical or artistic. As a piece of literature the play is exceedingly clever. The lack of dramatic interest is almost atoned for by the brilliant play of repartee. The dialogue was sharp and spirited, and clever epigrams flashed back and forth like keen foils in the hands of skilful fencers. Mr. Wilde's English is always exquisite; in this play it is particularly so. He has a color sense of words unequalled outside of France. He handles words as though they were tints, and shades his sentences as though each were a picture.

As a rule even wicked novels and plays allow their most "realistic" characters passions—that is not considered a virtue as yet and may be used without bringing the charge of prudishness against a playwright. Mr. Wilde does not even allow Lady Windermere that; he gives her only vanity covered by an insufficient garment of innocence and pride. She does not know what love means. Leaving ethics as entirely out of the question as Mr. Wilde does, and judging the case from an ordinary French novel standpoint, love that can be tempted deserves to be trampled upon. Virtue and indifference may be tempted, but love never. Lady Windermere had no pretext for her desertion, not even that pitiable, shabby pretext of passion. Her plea for leaving her husband was that she was degraded, and she willingly stepped into a degradation infinitely blacker.

The theme of Mr. Wilde's play is motherhood, a thing which no man can ever realize, which a man of Mr. Wilde's ethics and school and life cannot even conceive. To hear Mr. Wilde on that subject is like hearing

---

thoroughly before I go back home. I would mount the fiery coyote and chase to his lair the fierce and bloodthirsty broncho. I would seat myself in a poncho, with a swarthy and picturesque Mexican at my side, and float down the silvery Rio Grande where the myriad lariats which fringe the stream send forth their sweet fragrance. I want to see the untamed savage surrounded by his kind, unfettered by the follies of a garish world, and ungirded by the bonds of frivolous fashion. Clad in the skins of the chase, and adorned with primary colors from nature's laboratory, the claybank, I want to listen to him chant the tepee or walk through the sinuous mazes of his wild wampum." Walt Mason commented, "It seems a pity that a man who could get off such a string as that, which would have given a boom to any comic paper, had to lose his grip in the end and be immured in a pestilential prison with a life-long lock" (*Journal*, May 19, 1895).

one of the very little satans philosophizing on Calvary. Some of Mr. Wilde's touches are very good. The third act, in which Mrs. Erlynne finds her heart, in which she suffers all the agony of childbirth over again, and after twenty years the anguish and ecstasy of motherhood come even to her, is beautiful. That in the last act she could leave her child with the truth untold, is powerful. These are old situations, Mr. Wilde did not invent them. But that Lady Windermere could go out of her home to another man without saying one word of her child was barbarous. I know no name to call it by, it was worse than savagery. If she had said her child was hateful to her because it was her husband's, a mark of her own degradation and the lie she believed her marriage to be, we could have forgiven her. But she never speaks of it, never thinks of it until her own mother pleads for it to her. Truly, "she is a better woman than I." No, women do not do such things. Our world is bad enough, God knows, but it is not that bad.

Lady Windermere's Fan is not a bad play; it is only drivelling. Mr. Wilde is afraid to be coarse, so he is insinuating. His play is no better than the very bad plays of the world, only sillier. He does not want to defend evil, he is too cold to wish to defend evil. He tries ethics merely as a convenience for art. He does not attempt to apotheosize filth, he plays with it because he likes it when it is pretty. His philosophy is so contemptible, so inane, so puny that even with all its brilliant epigrams the club talk in the third act is wearisome. The most drivelling character in the play, that little puppy Cecil Graham, Mr. Wilde has chosen as his especial mouthpiece, and through him vents all his unwholesome spleen and his pitiable smallness, as Shakespeare poured out through his chosen Mercutio his clean humor and wondrous wit, and all the infinite wealth of his warm great heart. W. C. [*Journal*, June 5, 1894, p. 1]

The Aesthetic Movement

The downfall of the leader of the aesthetic movement pre-figures the destruction of the most fatal and dangerous school of art that has ever voiced itself in the English tongue. It is the beginning of a national expiation for national art that is artificial and insincere, for the school which claims that nature imitates art. We will have no more such plays as *Lady Windermere's Fan*, no more such stories as *The Portrait of Dorian Gray*.[65] We can do without them. They were full of insanity. It is a peculiar fact that the aesthetic school which has from the beginning set

65. Correctly: *The Picture of Dorian Gray*.

out to seek what was most beautiful has ended by finding what was most grotesque, misshapen and unlovely. Overwrought senses like overwrought reason end in madness, chaos and confusion. A man who founds his art upon a lie lives a lie, it matters not what form his sins may take. He has in him the potentiality of all sin, the begetter of all evil—insincerity. He thwarts the truth and tricks it, buys it and sells it until he loses all perspective, moral and artistic. He cries out like Pilate, "What is truth?" When *Lady Windermere's Fan* went through the west last season praise of it was almost universal. But there were a few who would not be blinded by its cleverness, who felt in it that falseness which makes the soul shudder and revolt. It had in it no one especially objectionable situation, no one especially objectionable line, but the whole play was a lie, a malicious lie upon human nature. It was stamped through and through with insincerity, the sin which insults the dignity of man, and of God in whose image he was made.

This school and all its atrocities grows naturally enough out of the artificial way in which men and women are living. It is a legitimate consequence of the hurried, hectic life of the end of the century. Every century or so society decides to improve on nature. It becomes very superior and refined indeed, until right through its surface there breaks some ghastly eruption that makes it hide its face in shame. Then we grow wiser for a little time. We put on sackcloth and go back to our father's house and become again as little children. Then it is that human endeavor becomes bold and strong and that human art is charged with new life. For it is while we are in that child-like mood of penitence that nature opens her arms to us and God tells to us the secrets of heaven. [*Journal*, May 19, 1895, p. 12]

Hélas!

To drift away with every passion till my soul
Is a stringed lute on which all winds can play,—
Is it for this that I have given away
My ancient wisdom, and austere control?
Methinks my life is a twice-written scroll
Scrawled over on some boyish holiday
With idle songs for life and virelay
Which do but mar the secret of the whole.
Surely there was a time I might have trod
The sunlit heights, and from life's dissonance

Struck one clear chord to reach the ears of God.
Is that time gone? lo! with a little rod
I did but touch the honey of romance
And must I lose a soul's inheritance?[66]

Oscar Wilde

I did not know whether to give the name of the author of that lament or not, for he has made even his name impossible. He wrote it a year ago[67] when he was a young man, a first honor man from Oxford, the most lionized of all young English lions, the wittiest of young wits, petted by all the great ladies of the kingdom, but it was a foreshadowing of doom. One wonders if he knew then how true it was. One wonders if he remembers it now in his prison. As poetry it is not bad, and he did others much better. He wrote dramas that will be models to English playwrights of the future. He might have been a poet of no mean order, he might have been one of the greatest living dramatists, he might have been almost anything, but he preferred to be a harlequin. I am not speaking of his crimes against society, which all men know. I am speaking of his crimes against literature, which came much earlier, which only a few saw and lamented. We are told that there is only one sin for which there is no forgiveness in Heaven, no forgetting in Hell. That is the sin against the holy spirit, not the holy spirit of the Trinity, but the holy spirit in man. The sins of the body are very small compared with that. To every man who has really great talent there are two ways open, the narrow one and the wide, to be great and suffer, or to be clever and comfortable, to bring up white pearls from the deep or to blow iris-hued bubbles from the froth on the surface. The pearls are hard to find and the bubbles are easy to make and they are beautiful enough on a sunny day, but when a man who was made for the deep sea refuses his mission, denies his high birth-right, then he has sinned the sin. What evil he does after that belongs to the police records, to psychology, to what you will, but not to literature. His name is "Marked with a blot, damned in the book of Heaven." This man was not only a comedian, he was a buffoon. He used the holiest things for ends the basest. He made the ark of the covenant a trick box, the anointed

66. "Hélas" appears as the epigraph to *Poems* (1881). The wording here has two variations from Wilde's text: Line 4 should read "Mine ancient wisdom ..." and line 12 "Is that time dead? ..."

67. A misstatement, of course. It is possible that Willa Cather saw the poem (or at least the statement that Wilde was an honor man from Oxford "a year ago") in some reprint of an 1882 article without noticing the context.

spear a harlequin's wand; he took the tapers from the altar for festival lights and brandished them in the wild melee of a carnival night. So little would have changed it all, a little sincerity, a little reverence for his own gift, and as he himself once wrote:

> And the mighty nations would have crowned me,
> Who are crownless now and without a name,
> And some orient dawn had found me kneeling
> On the threshold on the Home of Fame.[68]

O the pity of it, the irony of it!

And yet, as Howard Pyle said in a fairy tale, "Naught that has died can ever live, naught that has lived can ever die."[69] The author of "Hélas" is in prison now, most deservedly so. Upon his head is heaped the deepest infamy and the darkest shame of his generation. Civilization shudders at his name, and there is absolutely no spot on earth where this man can live. Cain's curse was light compared with his. About him are men of lesser crimes than his, men who stole perhaps because they were hungry. And yet, suppose through those prison walls a great song should echo, suppose through those prison windows a great sunset should flame, what soul there would know and understand, would thrill with that rapturous appreciation which, whatever the creeds may say, is the very ecstasy of prayer? Who but this man most shamed of all, who is, in spite of himself, spite of the world, an artist still? You cannot kill it, that heavenly birthright, that kingly dower which makes men akin to the angels and to see the visions of paradise. You cannot give it to women, nor drown it in wine, nor stultify it with vice. You may belittle it, stunt it, distort it, but it is of God and it knows not death.

The Orientals sometimes make rings in the form of a serpent, and in the serpent's head they set a gleaming jewel. They have a legend about such rings. When Satan fell from Heaven he became a serpent and every mark of his holiness and high estate departed from him save one; the jewel, blessed of God, which had adorned his angel's crown sank deep into

68. From Wilde's "Flower of Love." The lines, almost certainly quoted and arranged from memory, should read as follows: "And the mighty nations would have crowned me, who am crownless now and without name, / And some orient dawn had found me kneeling on the threshold of the House of Fame." (*Poems of Oscar Wilde* [London: Methuen and Company, 1908; from the edition of 1881], pp. 231–232)

69. A paraphrase of a passage in Howard Pyle's *Otto of the Silver Hand* (New York: Charles Scribner's Sons, 1888), p. 47. Brother John is reporting what the Angel Gabriel said to him: "'Nothing that has lived,' said he, 'shall ever die, and nothing that has died shall ever live.'"

his flat head and became embedded in the flesh. The serpent in rage would mangle his head against the rocks, but the stone was harder than adamant. He would bury himself in the slime and cover it with mud, but filth could not dim the luster of the jewel. That is Satan's eternal torment, that he cannot be wholly evil or wholly lost, that through every baseness and every degradation he must carry the birthmark of heaven, the signet of the Sons of God.

When one looks out over the chaos and confusion of wasted life and wasted talent, one wonders whether Oscar Wilde, and all the rest of us for that matter, will not have another chance. Another chance to try our tools, for after all that is all that matters, that we do our work, our best work, until our tools break in our hands. Another chance where the toys and dear delights that distract us in our youth, and the vanities and falsehoods that mislead us in our age will not allure us nor perplex us any more. Where we can look at white light without shrinking and not long for the flare of gas lamp nor the glow of firesides. Where the soul can feel as here the senses do, where there will be a better means of knowing and of feeling than through these five avenues so often faithless, that alike save and lose us, that either starve us or debauch us. Perhaps.

> Blot out his name then, record one lost soul more,
> One more task declined, one more footpath untrod,
> One more devil's triumph and sorrow for angels,
> One more wrong to man, one more insult to God.[70]

Courier, September 28, 1895, p. 6.

Verlaine

One of the most thoughtful and carefully articulated of these early critical statements, Willa Cather's essay on Verlaine binds together some of the miscellaneous strands of her comment and attitudes on the artist, music, language, history, myth, romance, character, the physical world, Philistia, beauty, humanity, and the morality of art.

Death has been busy among the great of France this winter. January 8 [1896] Paul Verlaine died in Paris. From the Café du Soleil there is missed a ragged, dirty old man with high cheek bones and slanting eyes, who used to sit there with his glass of absinthe and read the newspaper, jotting down fragments of poetry upon the margins. A profligate, a vagabond, a

70. Browning, "The Lost Leader." Line 4 should read: "One wrong more to man...."

criminal. From French literature there is missed one of the greatest poets of modern France; an artist in words, a colorist in phrases, the originator of a new school of poetry. The whole of Nordau's ponderous and on the whole rather stupid volume on degeneration[71] is not enough to explain Paul Verlaine, though it fits him exactly. He was without an exception the strangest paradox of a paradoxical age. Imagine a satyr converted to the most ecstatic form of ascetic Christianity and there you have Verlaine, the grossest of sensualists, the most exalted of the devotional mystics. Heine, in his *Gods in Exile*, tells of a lot of fauns and satyrs who were converted to the early church and who became abbots and monks. Every night, powerless against the entreaties of the river gods and the nightingales, they went forth and held high carnival with the nymphs and dryads and crowned Bacchus and Aphrodite anew. Then, when the cock crew they stole back to their monastery and miserable and penitent crept up the altar stairs to their bleeding god and wept and worshipped and did bitter penance until they heard again the call of the nightingale.[72] This double life was the existence of Paul Verlaine. Both moods were exaggerated, violent, insane even, but both were perfectly sincere. Most artists are victims of only one form of insanity, he was cursed with two. He was imprisoned again and again for unmentionable and almost unheard of crimes, but he wrote some of the most beautiful and devout religious poetry in any tongue. He was a practicer of every excess known to man, yet if ever inspiration and spiritual rapture came from a human pen it is in his verses on the Christ. This is all disease you say; certainly it is, but we all gather the pearls fast enough in this world and nobody troubles himself much about the disease of the oyster which produced it. Oysters do not grow pearls under normal conditions nor do men write great poems. The finest things in this world do not always grow like cabbages. Things like Verlaine's *Poèmes Saturniens* need conditions of their own. And yet this man was respectably born into a commonplace world and

71. Among Willa Cather's books from her university and Lincoln years is a copy of Max Nordau's *Degeneration*, the translation published by D. Appleton and Company in 1895. She has written her name on the flyleaf. There is a small penciled check on page 119 at the beginning of Nordau's discussion of Verlaine, in which he calls the French poet the most admired model of the Symbolists, a man who has "all the physical and mental marks of degeneration," who is a dipsomaniac, an Impulsivist, a vagabond, a repulsive degenerate, a dreamer, a mystic, and a dotard.

72. *The Gods in Exile*, first published in 1836 (the French version in the *Revue des Deux Mondes*, 1853), is a portion of Heine's *Germany*, a two-volume collection translated by Charles Godfrey Leland (London: William Heinemann, 1892), II, 295 ff. See also the story of the Nightingale of Basle in *Germany*, I, 12 ff.

was well brought up by his old mother in the Batignolles, and he went to the university and became a bachelor of arts and became engaged to a good woman and tried hard enough to live the life of a respectable citizen. But nature, who needs the tiger as well as the ox, "Who with the Eden didst devise the snake," had other uses for him, and his doom was decreed. He spent his life like Villon, vagabonding about the highways and byways of France, sometimes reduced to robbing a peasant's hen roost. He had but three homes, the street, the hospital and the prison. He did not write in a study and he had no books. He wrote in jail or in the open fields, from quite another reason than Bunyan's.

It is difficult to tell in English what Verlaine has done in French. To do that one should use his own flexible and fanciful tongue. Many of his adjectives have no equivalent in English, and the beauty of his rhythm and the incomparable grace and movement of his verse are of course entirely lost in translation. He is harder to translate than Heine, or even than Gautier. Miss Gertrude Hall has done some of them fairly well, though after reading the original they seem paltry and futile enough. . . .

[*Here are printed "L'Amour par terre," "Colloque Sentimental," and "Streets," from* Poems of Paul Verlaine, *translated by Gertrude Hall (Chicago: Stone and Kimball, 1895).*]

These sound rather more like Heine in translation than they do in French, for in the tongue in which they were written they have a quality which Heine's verse did not. Verlaine's verse is definite only through its vagueness. Facts and incidents count for nothing, it is all the mood. He does not write of a night or a woman or a passion, but of a sensation. His care is not so much the theme as for his words, every poem of his is a set with gleaming jewels like the tiara of an eastern princess from which all the colors of the changeful skies shimmer; warm lights of morning, high lights of glaring noon, sad lights of evening, cold lights of windy days. They are more like jewels than anything else, emeralds that are green as stormy seas, rubies that are red as heart's blood, diamonds that glitter like the starlight and like them they are cold, beautiful and strangely unhuman. His verses are like music, they are made up of harmony and feeling, they are as indefinite and barren of facts as a nocturne. They tell only of a mood. He called one of his greatest volumes *Romances Without Words*, and indeed they are almost that. He created a new verbal art of

communicating sensations not only by the meaning of words, but of their
relation, harmony and sound.

Let it not be understood that this is any attempt to justify Verlaine's
life or his own personal vileness. Once a fine lady said to a great artist
who was swearing while he painted: "Could you not paint just as well if
you did not swear?" He replied, simply: "I always swear when I paint."
In cases like that of Paul Verlaine we might be Christ-like for once and
forgive, especially as we can understand him so little. Compared to the
greatness of his work the weakness of his life is of small moment. Until
we can write his verses and be respectable citizens at the same time we have
small right to enter protests. Not that it is necessary for a man to be
wicked to write good poetry, but that the poet's chief concern is not
with his life, but his work. Life in itself is a great task and to live it well
or even decently is an art. God knows we poor, commonplace citizens
find that at times it takes all our intelligence and thought and endeavor
just to live respectably well, to know the right thing and to do it. What
if we had all the infinite cares and struggles and perplexities of an artist
heaped on top of the ordinary woes of life? One or the other must suffer,
not from evil intent, but from neglect, from an inability to do two
things well at once, from our very finiteness and the limitations of human
capacity. One cannot at the same time build in brick and marble. Now to
these strange beings who create, not because they want to create, mind you,
but because they are doomed and destined to it by nature, a sonnet
matters more than a deed. They care more for the purity and perfection
of their dream character than their own, more for the excellence of their
work than of themselves. To them a faulty line is a more grievous sin
than an unpaid debt, a heroine imperfectly drawn and awkwardly handled
of more importance than a living woman's virtue and happiness. They
cannot help it; they are made so. If there was not that selfish instinct of
art preservation there would be no art. Now, when a man has this double
task of living and working laid upon him, one or the other must suffer
in proportion as the tasks are great and he is weak. If his work suffers we
hoot him and say he is an impostor; if his life suffers we damn him and
say he is a degenerate, but we hoard his achievements away in our
treasuries of beauty.

But, you say, could we not have a great company of artists who are
both conventional and great? Try it, and you will have a throng, not of
Shakespeares and Shelleys and Goethes, but of Wordsworths, Tennysons
and Alfred Austins. But, the Philistines tell us, such erratic geniuses are

enemies of society, a state of them would go to destruction. Never fear. A state of artists? Why, a nation does well indeed if it produces a beggar's [baker's?] dozen of them throughout its whole history. If the world were all Mount Aetnas it would be uninhabitable, but one serves to relieve the monotony and there is no use in everlastingly quarreling with it because it is not peaceable and well conducted like other mountains. The world will never have genius enough to destroy it, the human race will perish one day and be food for worms, but not from poets any more than from love. But since these erratic gentlemen are few and far between, it behooves us to be charitable, and to remember that if their feet stumble it is because they watch the stars. When Childe Harold is roaming the wide deep and bringing us home the trophies of the unseen world we might forgive him that "wild weeds are growing on his wall," since a man cannot practice poetry and horticulture at the same time. The Philistine who lives uprightly and well and who provides properly for his family is not ashamed that he knows little of pictures and nothing of music and has not read the romances of Flaubert. His citizenship was his first duty and it took his time and strength. Now the artist must do all these things that the Philistine has left undone, he is bound to do them, he was made and created for it. Need he be so horribly ashamed if he has neglected some of the estimable virtues of the Philistine? He approves of them, yearns for them, but God has given him other duties that come first, and he has only three score years to do them in. Why, if you want orthodox authority, Christ Himself encouraged the meditative Mary against the reproof of her domestic sister, Martha. You cannot judge an artist by ordinary standards because his duty is to do extraordinary things. Even the Philistines hoot an ordinary artist. Paul Verlaine's life was tragic, a black tragedy, but we have all the profit and he had all the misery, we can afford to be generous. Sometimes, in thinking it all over, one wonders why this race of miserable, sensitive, unhappy followers of the beautiful was ever created at all, for when all is said it is only a vain endeavor, a pursuit of the impossible. But that is a question for a higher oracle, like so many others.

> O thou, who man of baser earth did'st make,
> Who with the Eden did'st devise the snake,
> For all the sin wherewith the heart of man is blackened,
> Man's forgiveness give—and take![73]

Journal, February 2, 1896, p. 9.

73. This stanza is number LVIII in the first version of FitzGerald's *Rubáiyát* (*Poetical and Prose Writings of Edward FitzGerald*, collected and arranged by George Bertham [Variorum

Byron

It seems that Byron is to have a revival like Napoleon and Poe, and just now, to understand current literary allusions, one must take up the thumb-marked volume of his youthful days and run over *Childe Harold* and *Sardanapalus*. There is ultimate justice in the world of letters, and just as surely as the stars move in their appointed places, does a man settle at last into his place. Once Byron was altogether too much exalted. Of late years he has been altogether too much forgotten. He and Tom Moore were the last of a certain class of poets. Singers, rather than poets, they were the last of those merry and tuneful gentlemen whose task was not to labor or to think very much, but only to live and sing, who were exempt, or at least considered themselves exempt, from all the sterner duties of living, who lived on the crest of the wave, were always and forever in love, sang strong and virile songs, full of unparalleled imagery and poetic gladness, as totally lacking in conscience or a sense of responsibility as the bards of Greece. They went gaily through life, loving in a song and forgetting in a sonnet, like the sunlight that both quickens and kills, not knowing that they were "bohemians," worshipping beauty, but never formulating their worship into a creed. They were the last of their school; the world has grown graver since then. But nevertheless, Byron has again become the fashion, and if you want to get at the real Noel, Lord Byron, the place to do it is in his letters. In Byron's day letter writing was still an art, and not a painful duty. Byron's letters are among the best that have come down to us; they have the real cheerful, witty gentleman, full of vanity about his curls and his conquests, but never about his work. . . .

In his letters to Shelley he says he cannot understand the shrinking, sensitive spirit of Keats when he broke and died under the heartless criticism of his bigoted countrymen. His own feeling under such circumstances was one of anger merely, and his answer was *English Bards and Scotch Reviewers*. He frankly confesses to Shelley that he cannot greatly admire Keats' verse; and no wonder, for Keats was a poet of a new and spiritual school that could move Byron no more than it could the dark-eyed Turkish girls he loved. Byron could see the beauty of action or of an

---

edition; New York: Doubleday, Page and Company, 1902], I, 28). It is printed in that edition as follows:

> Oh, Thou, who man of baser Earth didst make,
> And who with Eden didst devise the snake;
> For all the sin wherewith the Face of Man
> Is blacken'd, Man's Forgiveness give—and take!

active passion, but of the higher verse of fancy and spiritual harmony he knew no more than the fervid Arabian poets of the desert. Like them he was a poet only of nature, of nature that is simple, primitive, violent, glorious; that cares but for one thing. Like them, he was blinded by the glare of orient noons and intoxicated by the languor of orient nights, wherever there was free action. Wild land, wide seas, sunlight and beauty; there Noel Byron was at home and there he was a poet. He was the poet of nature and of sense, of nature that is sense. But the still voice that Keats awakened was not of nature, not of the whirlwind nor the earthquake, but of another world.

Byron's poetry is some of it very gloomy, but he was fair enough to inflict his gloom upon his public and not upon his friends. His letters are always cheerful and never introspective. To Moore he does once say that pleasure does not give what it promised, that the game is not worth the cost, and in his own case the sword is wearing out the scabbard. But for the most part his epistles are gay and racy enough. You can see him enduring every hardship in uncivilized lands, eating the most unsavory dishes and sleeping in a cow house or on a mountain side, braving all sorts of dangers and risking his neck among the brigands simply because a country was fair to look upon. He was no ninny, this man, if he was a dandy. Once back in civilization again, and he was again starving himself and swimming unheard of distances to reduce his flesh. Toward the last when he was growing tired of all the world and contemplating a simple soldier's life among the Greeks, he was forever pursued from Venice to Rome and from Rome to Florence by amorous dames—alas, they were always dames!—who wanted to flee to the end of the earth with him, while he, poor fellow, was too tired to flee anywhere and only wanted to die quietly and respectably. He did finally escape them and got off to Greece where he was a brave man and a valiant soldier, and promised to be a still better poet, had not the end come, as it always comes, at the wrong time....

Journal, March 8, 1896, p. 13.

Ruskin

Reading the last of Willa Cather's long articles written in the winter and spring of 1895–1896, one thinks of "Ruskin" in relation to "Carlyle"—that first essay of five years before. Her theme in 1896 is still an appreciation of the individual artist and a feeling for the drama of his life. But there is a change, and it might be described in terms at least parallel to her statement on how Ruskin outstripped his master Carlyle: "He has taken the wild and stirring

*strains of the peasant philosopher and set them to delicious harmony, over
the rugged vision of the sage he has diffused the effulgent glory of a poet."*

News has come across the sea that John Ruskin, the greatest living
master of pure English prose, is near his end.[74] His death will probably
call public attention to him, and we will glance again through the enchanted pages of *The Stones of Venice* and wonder at their melody. Not
that we will any of us read much or deeply, or do more than in a hurried
way admire it as literature. Fate has measured out its full share of irony
to Ruskin, though it has never warped his reverent spirit with bitterness.
He has never wished to be identified as a man of letters; he wrote only to
defend certain theories of art, yet in his own lifetime he is accounted one
of the greatest of English stylists, while his views on art are considered
wholly visionary and unpractical. Perhaps this is just enough, perhaps it is
said in the same spirit in which the old Jews said of their prophet who cried
out day and night against their iniquity, "He is only a poet." Be that as it
may, this man has certainly produced some twelve or fifteen volumes of
the most perfect prose of our generation. Ruskin has asserted that in the
matter of style Carlyle was his master. But he outstripped him as Raphael
and Leonardo and many another man has his master. He has taken the
wild and stirring strains of the peasant philosopher and set them to
delicious harmony, over the rugged wisdom of the sage he has diffused
the effulgent glory of a poet.

But Ruskin's work, great as it is, is a little thing compared to the
mind that produced it. To have lived so pure, so intense, so reverent a
life as his is greater than to have written *Modern Painters*. For Ruskin is
perhaps the last of the great worshippers of beauty, perhaps the last man
for many years to come who will ever kneel at the altar of Artemis, who
will ever hear the oracle of Apollo, his is perhaps the last head on which
the failing light of the Renaissance has lingered. This man's life has been
one act of worship. He has mastered all tongues to read their songs,
visited all lands to study their temples, loved all people who had among
them any of the beautiful things done by man. He could never have
beauty enough; he has studied art from its primer, "ransacked the ages,
spoiled the climes," worshipped in ancient temples, found tongues in

74. Ruskin did not die until 1900; however, his work had been completed. In general,
Willa Cather shows particular knowledge of Ruskin's defense of Turner and views of art
in the volumes of *Modern Painters* (1843–1860), *Seven Lamps of Architecture* (1849), *The
Stones of Venice* (1851–1853), *Sesame and Lilies* (1865), and *The King of the Golden River*
(1851).

oracles long dumb, made the sea give up its dead and the earth them which slept. There was not enough in all the treasuries of art to glut this man's passion; he must even go to the sculptured bulls of old Assyria and the frescoes of old Egypt to appease somewhat his love for color and form.

It is not Ruskin the savant or Ruskin the political economist or even Ruskin the essayist that is most noble to contemplate, but Ruskin the simple worshipper of beauty, journeying from place to place, from ruin to ruin, catching from sculptured stone and painted canvas every impress the spirit of beauty had left through all the world's history, as the patient pilgrims of long ago sought for the footsteps of their Lord up the mount of Calvary. He could stand a day before a single fresco in Florence, he could spend hours on a ladder before an old church in Venice, holding to a stone projection with his left hand, and with his right drawing some detail of sculpture. Of all the poets and painters who have felt the charm of Venice, none felt it more deeply than he. Venetian art never had so warm an interpreter among Englishmen. Whenever he spoke of it he fell into unconscious poetry. "That scarlet cloud may, indeed, melt away into paleness of night, and Venice herself waste from her islands as a wreath of wind-driven foam from their beach; that which she won of faithful light and truth shall never pass away. Deiphobe of the sea, the Sun God measures her immortality to her by its sands. Flushed, above the Avernus of the Adrian lake, her spirit is still seen holding the golden bough; from the lips of the sea sibyl men shall learn for ages to come what is most noble and most fair; and, far away, as the whisper in the coils of a shell, withdrawn through the deep hearts of nations, shall sound forever the enchanted voice of Venice."[75] Who can write such English now?

His erudition alone would have entitled Ruskin to a high place in his country. But he himself scorned erudition; he knew that to know is little and to feel is all. He was a linguist, yet he despised rhetoric and etymology as trivial and artificial; he was a scientist, yet his creed was not of science.

75. From the close of "The Hesperid Aeglé," *Modern Painters*, V, Part IX ("Of Ideas of Relation"), Chapter XI, pp. 423–424. All textual and page references in this and the following notes are to the named volumes in Ruskin's *Works* (Boston: The Aldine Publishing Company, 1910). In the passage from "The Hesperid Aeglé" quoted here, Ruskin is comparing Turner and Giorgione, whose ruined frescoes, ten years before, were "yet glowing, like a scarlet cloud, on the Fondaco de Tedeschi." Willa Cather omitted a portion of the next sentence, in which Ruskin had inserted Zanetti's comment on the frescoes: "And though that scarlet cloud (*sanguigna e fiammeggiante, per cui le pitture cominciarono con dolce violenze a rapire il cuore delle genti*) may, indeed, melt away. . . ." Other variations in wording: for *foam from their beach* read *foam fades from their weedy beach*; for *sands* and *boughs* read *sand* and *bough*; for *learn for ages* read *learn for ages yet*; for *a shell* read *the shell*.

His creed, to express it roughly and somewhat vaguely, was this: That beauty alone is truth, and truth is only beauty; that art is supreme; that it is the highest, the only expression of whatever divinity there may be in man. That the highest end of an individual life is to create, or, at least, to see and feel beauty; that the only true measure of a nation's worth is the art of that nation; that a people who left behind it greater monuments of art was a great people; that a people who left none was sordid and lived in vain; that all the spiritual force of a nation immortalizes itself with the spirit of beauty forever; that by the decree of God there is no better channel it can take; that a nation barren of art had built with straw and bits of glass, had built upon the sand and should perish utterly from the face of the earth; that beauty and its handmaiden, art, were the only things worthy of the serious contemplation of men, the only things which could satisfy the "immortal longings" within them. All sciences, discoveries, systems, which did not tend to increase the aggregate sum of beauty could not increase the sum of human happiness. They were merely wheels within wheels, like the prophet's vision. Beauty was God revealed, he said; man's business was to find God.

Yes, actually there is an Englishman of the nineteenth century who believes this, who has lived it and shouted it day and night into the deaf ears of his countrymen. All his lectures on political economy are simply to justify this theory, to induce men to live more simply that they may live more beautifully. He worked ten years on *Modern Painters* merely to defend Turner. Did ever one man take up such a task for the sake of another? And the strangest feature of it is that his personal friendship for Turner really had very little to do with it. That the work of one great man should go unappreciated was to him the greatest and saddest of national crimes. When England was busy with buying and selling, with traffic and corn markets, with troubles in Ireland, he wrote: "This century has caused every one of its great men, whose hearts were kindest and whose spirits most perceptive of the works of God, to die without hope— Scott, Keats, Byron, Shelley, Turner. Great England of the iron heart now, not of the lion heart; for these souls of her children an account may one day be required of her."[76] To him these crimes seemed the blackest of the century—of more moment than foreign policy or home rule or the British dominion in India. Is this the maddest folly or the deepest wisdom? If our standard be true, and power and money be indeed the things worth

76. *Modern Painters*, Part IX, Chapter XII ("Peace"), p. 438. The opening sentence begins: "So far as in it lay, this century...."

striving for, what a madman! If, perchance, that other standard be the true one, and faith and gentleness and a knowledge of God be the work of life, what a prophet.

Surely this Ruskin has ever been the most impractical of men. He is out of sympathy with all our much talked of inventions and directly opposed to what we call the progress of civilization. He hated railroads because they are not beautiful nor conducive to an appreciation of scenery. He hated the great iron traffic of England because the metal is put to ignoble uses and not moulded into beautiful shapes; he hated newspapers because they corrupted literary taste. He wanted the English army to interfere with the military power of Austria because the Austrian guns were set against Venice and pointed directly at the palace containing the most beautiful pictures in the world. Imagine the English army, Kipling's English army, out afighting for Titians and Tintorettos!

In one of his greatest essays written years ago he said, "You have put a railroad bridge over the fall of Schaffhausen, you have tunnelled the cliffs of Lucerne by Tell's chapel, you have destroyed the Clarens shore by Lake Geneva; there is not a quiet valley left in England which you have not filled with bellowing fire; there is no particle of English earth into which you have not trampled coal dust."[77]

To him this denunciation seemed as sweeping and as terrible as that of the Lord to the heathen queen, "You have burned My altars with fire and My prophets you have slain with the sword."

Yes, this man would have travelled on foot rather than see the country palled in the black smoke of the "road of iron," he would have foregone the "luxuries of civilization" to hear the nightingales sing as they did once among the oaks of Galba. Mad son of art, to sleep, to sleep! You will be happier so, last of the lovers of Italy!

He belonged to the age of epics and Ionian columns, of marble and fine gold, not to this papier-mâché civilization. He is old and silenced now, and near his death, this preacher of truth in a world of vanity, last of the priests of Artemis, last of the mourners of art. The world may go on in its chosen course now, no voice will distrust its sophistries any more. Engines will thunder through the cliffs of Lucerne, the frescoes of

77. *Sesame and Lilies*, Lecture I ("Of Kings' Treasuries"), p. 62; in *Works*, IV. The quotation has a number of variations from the Ruskin text, which reads as follows: "You have put a railroad bridge over the fall of Schaffhausen. You have tunnelled the cliffs of Lucerne by Tell's chapel; you have destroyed the Clarens shore of the Lake of Geneva; there is not a quiet valley in England that you have not filled with bellowing fire; there is no particle left of English land which you have not trampled coal ashes into . . . ."

Giorgione will crumble away bit by bit in the old churches of Venice, no one will notice or care. Dust to dust. The past is past. The violets grow over the last great English poet down in Rome. We have Whistler and Yvette Guilbert and the *Yellow Book*, the natural and inevitable products of our shallow thoughts and sordid lives. *Vive la bagatelle*!

> Spirit of Beauty, tarry yet awhile
>   Although the cheating merchants of the mart
> With iron roads profane our lovely isle,
>   And break on whirling wheels the limbs of Art,
> Ay! though the crowded factories beget
> The blindworm Ignorance that slays the soul,
>   O tarry yet![78]

Or as Alfred de Musset said, though it is impossible to translate him in half his beauty,

> Your world is superb, your men are perfect,
> The mountains are levelled, the plains flash with light;
> Wisely have you pruned the tree of life,
> Everything is swept before your roads of iron,
> All is grand, all is beautiful, but the soul dies in your air.
> You have invented great words,
> They float afar in tainted winds,
> They have destroyed the terrible idols of old,
> But they have also frightened away the birds of heaven.
> Hypocrisy is dead, we no longer believe in priests,
> But virtue is also dead, and we no longer believe in God.[79]

Journal, May 17, 1896, p. 13.

78. Oscar Wilde, "The Garden of Eros."
79. From *Rolla*, Part IV. Probably Willa Cather's own translation. The following text of the original is from Alfred de Musset, *Poésies Complètes*, edited by Maurice Allem (Paris: Librairie Gallimard, 1951), p. 294.

> Votre monde est superbe, et votre homme est parfait!
> Les monts sont nivelés, la plaine est éclaircie;
> Vous avez sagement taillé l'arbre de vie;
> Tout est bien balayé sur vos chemins de fer,
> Tout est grand, tout est beau, mais on meurt dans votre air.
> Vous y faites vibrer de sublimes paroles;
> Elles flottent au loin dans des vents empestés.
> Elles ont ébranlé de terribles idoles;
> Mais les oiseaux du ciel en sont épouvantés.
> L'hypocrisie est morte; on ne croit plus aux prêtres;
> Mais la vertu se meurt, on ne croit plus à Dieu.

Improvisations Toward
a Credo, 1894–1896

✤ ✤ ✤

It is an awful and a fearsome thing, that
short voyage from the brain to the hand,
and many a gleaming argosy of thought
has gone down in it forever.

*Recalling the years in the early 1900's when she first knew Willa Cather, Miss
Edith Lewis remarks, "I think it is her talk that I remember best," her talk that
was "sometimes more brilliant than her writing; for it had the freer quality of im-
provisation. Thought and language seemed simultaneous with her. . . ."* [1] *There
is no better way to describe the special quality—and even the form—of the separate
articles that sometimes developed in Willa Cather's newspaper columns. They are
improvisations—free movements from object to observation to a more intense conviction, all with the immediacy of a human voice and the drama of a person who
speaks from the center of his own discoveries. Several of Willa Cather's improvisations are toward a credo: they show her in the process of finding out what she
believed about art—her art. One of the earliest is in a column of September, 1894,
from which E. K. Brown, in his biography of Willa Cather, quoted the last paragraph as the "most explicit statement of her conception of art."* [2] *The larger portion
of that column reprinted here supplies something of the context of that first statement and also is a point of comparison for the three important articles of 1895–1896.
One can see the same hand at work in all four pieces. But it is even more satisfying
to find that by the spring of 1896 when she wrote the two final statements—so much
richer, more subtle, and more complex than that one of 1894—Willa Cather could
recognize clearly the emerging form of the artist-self she had been seeking, and
with it the individual talent in which all credos must begin.*

1. *Willa Cather Living: A Personal Record* (New York: Alfred A. Knopf, 1953), p. xvi.
2. *Willa Cather: A Critical Biography*, completed by Leon Edel (New York: Alfred A. Knopf, 1953), p. 66.

COMMITMENT

The Superfluous Woman is a better book than *The Heavenly Twins*,[3] but it has no real excuse for existing at all. The heroine is a superfluous character in literature. There is in all the dreary waste of paper no one strong situation, no one flash of truth that gives the book a right to be. In a work of art intrinsic beauty is the *raison d'être*. Any piece of art is its own excuse for being. Art, like wisdom, is born full-armed without the will or consent of man. He cannot say it yea or nay. . . . No man, or woman, is ever justified in making a book to preach a sermon. It is a degradation of art. Browning says that the glory and the good of art is that it can teach indirectly, that it need never preach. Every great work of art should teach, but never preach. It should not sit in the high place in the temple and lay upon men's shoulders burdens that it would not lift with its finger; it should go down into the fields and the streets and toil and love and suffer with men and teach them the sweetness of its endurance and the greatness of its affection, like that greatest of teachers whom the Pharisees despised. An artist should have no moral purpose in mind other than just his art. His mission is not to clean the Augean stables; he had better join the Salvation Army if he wants to do that. . . .

The mind that can follow a "mission" is not an artistic one. An artist can know no other purpose than his art. A book with a direct purpose plainly stated is seldom the work of a great mind. For this reason *Uncle Tom's Cabin* will never have a place in the highest ranks of literature. The feminine mind has a hankering for hobbies and missions, consequently there have been but two real creators among women authors, George Sand and George Eliot.

In these days of purposes and vexed moral problems it is hard for an author to keep himself untainted by the world. It is hard to hold fast to art pure and simple. One reason we all loved Trilby so was because she didn't have any mission or any purpose, and taught us nothing except to love her. She didn't talk Herbert Spencer or Darwin or Humboldt[4] at us,

3. *The Superfluous Woman* was published anonymously in 1894, the author since identified as Emma Frances Brooke. *The Heavenly Twins* (1893) was by Madame Sarah Grand, English novelist and feminist, whose books often "sermonized." (See also note 4 in "Literature," above.)

4. A German scientist and physical theorist, Alexander von Humboldt (1769–1859) wrote the notable *Kosmos* (1845–1862) in which he described the universe as a functioning organic unit. In another work of 1849 he studied the variations of nature "in different lands and different climates."

but just sang "Alice, Ben Bolt" very badly. An author is not an artist until he can create characters that we love not for their goodness or their character or their "cause," but for themselves. An artist has nothing to do with how much wine we may drink at dinner or how low we may wear our ball dresses. His business is to make men and women and breathe into them until they become living souls.

Kipling and Richard Harding Davis, who make very little men of very common clay, are better and truer artists than Madame Grand and "Iota,"[5] who make colossal monstrosities. If one cannot make great men and make them real men, as Thackeray and Balzac did, then it is better to make very common little men in sack coats as Howells does. The main requisite is that they live.

The further the world advances the more it becomes evident that an author's only safe course is to cling close to the skirts of his art, forsaking all others, and keep unto her as long as they two shall live. An artist should not be vexed by human hobbies or human follies; he should be able to lift himself up into the clear firmament of creation where the world is not. He should be among men but not one of them, in the world but not of the world. Other men may think and reason and believe and argue, but he must create.

Journal, September 23, 1894, p. 13.

5. Of these popular writers, Willa Cather at this time admired Kipling, tolerated Richard Harding Davis (journalist and writer of much popular magazine fiction), disliked Sarah Grand, and mentioned the pseudonymous "Iota" as a curiosity.

THE DEMANDS OF ART

The other day I saw an elevator boy intently perusing a work of literature. I glanced at it and saw that it was Ouida's *Under Two Flags*. I could remember when I first met that book and read it quite as intently as the elevator boy was doing, and I was inclined to be patient with him when he took me to the wrong floor, for I knew that he was envying Bertie Cecil his beautiful boots or that he was pondering upon the peaches of great price that Bertie used to throw at the swans to please his sweetheart, and it struck me that it is rather tragic that one of the brightest minds of the last generation should descend to become food for elevator boys.[6] Sometimes I wonder why God ever trusts talent in the hands of women, they usually make such an infernal mess of it. I think He must do it as a sort of ghastly joke. Really, it would be hard to find a better plot than is in that same *Under Two Flags*, and the book contains the rudiments of a great style, and it also contains some of the most drivelling nonsense and mawkish sentimentality and contemptible feminine weakness to be found anywhere. Preachers have cried out against the immorality of "Ouida," and mammas have forbidden their daughters to read her, and gentlemen of the world have pretended to shudder at her cynicism. Now the truth of the matter is that her greatest sins are technical errors, as palpable as bad grammar or bad construction, sins of form and sense. Adjectives and sentimentality ran away with her, as they do with most women's pens. And then she lacked all sense of humor and will never know how magnificently ridiculous her melancholy heroes and suffering women are. It's a terrible curse to lack a sense of humor, for it reacts on one and makes one gratify the humor of every other living creature. Ouida is Nordau's "degenerate" incarnate.

And the worst of it is that the woman really had great talent. No less a person than John Ruskin advised all his art students to read *A Village Commune* and said it was the saddest and most perfect picture of peasant life in modern Italy ever made in English. There is poetry enough in *Pascarel* for a dozen novels. There is some wonderful work of mythology and historical association in *Ariadne*. There is some matchless description in *Wanda*. There are great passages in *Friendship*, but in them all there is

6. The many volumes of English novelist "Ouida" (Marie Louise de la Ramée, 1839–1908) began to appear in the mid-1860's. *Under Two Flags* (1867) is a story of Guardsman Bertie Cecil (and others) in the fashionable life of England and France during the time of Wellington.

not one sane, normal, possible man or woman. I hate to read them. I hate to see the pitiable waste and shameful weaknesses in them. They fill me with the same sense of disgust that Oscar Wilde's books do. They are one rank morass of misguided genius and wasted power. They are sinful, not for what they do, but for what they do not do. They are the work of a brilliant mind that never matured, of hectic emotions that never settled into simplicity and naturalness. They are the product of one who was too early old, too long young. Of one who was misled into thinking that words were life, who was tempted by the alluring mazes of melodrama. Of a life that only imagined and strained after effects, that never lived at all; that never laughed with children, toiled with men or wept with women; of a lying, artificial, abnormal existence. Ink and paper are so rigidly exacting. One may lie to one's self, lie to the world, lie to God, even, but to one's pen one cannot lie. You may talk brilliantly and still be very much of a fool. But when one comes to write, ah, that is different! Every artificial aid fails you. All that you have been taught leaves you, all that you have stolen lies discovered. You are then a translator, without a lexicon, without notes, and you are to translate—God. You have then to give voice to the hearts of men, and you can do it only so far as you have known them, loved them. It is a solemn and terrible thing to write a novel. I wish there were a tax levied on every novel published. We would have fewer ones and better.

I have not much faith in women in fiction. They have a sort of sex consciousness that is abominable. They are so limited to one string and they lie so about that. They are so few, the ones who really did anything worth while; there were the great Georges, George Eliot and George Sand, and they were anything but women, and there was Miss Bronte who kept her sentimentality under control, and there was Jane Austen who certainly had more common sense than any of them and was in some respects the greatest of them all. Women are so horribly subjective and they have such scorn for the healthy commonplace. When a woman writes a story of adventure, a stout sea tale, a manly battle yarn, anything without wine, women and love, then I will begin to hope for something great from them, not before.

Courier, November 23, 1895, p. 7.

THE ARTIST'S LIFE

There is a play with a history running at the Empire in New York just now. It is called *Bohemia*, and the present version was written by that very talented young man, Clyde Fitch, the author of *Beau Brummell*. But this is not the first time a drama has been made from Henri Murger's book. Dion Boucicault made a play of it years ago, but for some reason or other its days were short in the land.[7] Mr. Fitch's play is decidedly a comedy, but Boucicault's had a decidedly tragic trend, perhaps that was the trouble, it was too serious. But at any rate it had much more of the real spirit of Murger's book, which in spite of its spirit and wit, its merry escapades and youthful adventures, is one of the saddest of books. Not that it is avowedly or even intentionally sombre, but the inherent consequences of its very theme are among the most tragic that darken life.

There have been many books professedly written on the alluring topic of the life of artistic Bohemia under the empire, but in reality there is only one, the *Scènes de la vie de Bohème*, by that Florizel of Bohemia, Henri Murger. Murger is little known in this country, even among the people who zealously affect French fiction. He was a litterateur who flourished in Paris in the famous days of the '40's. He was the son of a tailor who had little patience with his son's artistic vagaries, and Henri was driven into the ranks of those defiant young disciples of art who hated all orthodox power, all recognized authority, and who called themselves Bohemians because they did not care to call themselves outcasts. Most of them were not bad fellows at heart, but they had to contend against a hopeless poverty until all standards of pecuniary honor were pretty well lost among them. For despite all sentimental notions to the contrary, Bohemia was the result of an absence of money rather than an absence of morals, and not one of its many celebrated inhabitants dwelt there a day longer than his income compelled him to.

Murger was a hack, like most of his fellows. He could do good work, but he had to live and to do that he edited a fashion paper and a hatter's magazine. It was not until he published *The Bohemians*, in 1848, that he achieved any considerable success. But even then his finances were but little improved and when M. Barrière, a young dramatist, called on Murger to propose turning the book into a play he found him in

7. The history of book and plays began with Henri Murger (1822–1861) and his *Scènes de la vie de Bohème* (1848). Murger and Théodore Barrière collaborated on a play, *La Vie de Bohème* (1849), which was in turn adapted into the English play *Mimi* by Dion Boucicault in 1873. The adaptation by Clyde Fitch called *Bohemia* played in New York in 1896, starring Viola Allen. Also in 1896 came Puccini's version, the opera *La Bohème*.

bed in the middle of the afternoon because he had lent his trousers to a friend and had no others. But a play they made of it, and it was produced at the Variétés in '49 with phenomenal success. Then Murger, like most of his successful brethren, at once left the Latin Quarter and Bohemia, though even in his respectable home in the Rue Notre Dame de Lorette he always kept upon his wall a velvet mask, a woman's glove and a faded bouquet, souvenirs of Mimi and the old days in the Quarter. After this change he began to write in what he called his second style and used to say of *The Bohemians*, "That devil of a book will always stand between me and the Academy." Although Murger considered his second style his best, the fact remains that *The Bohemians* is the strongest and most important of his works. Perhaps because his peculiar strain of talent was only at its best in Bohemia, more probably because in the quicksands of that fair and treacherous land he had lost that which makes men do good work.

The preface of Murger's work is an eloquent defense of Bohemianism. He claims that it is as old as genius and inseparable from it. "In ancient Greece, to go no further back in the genealogy of Bohemianism, there existed a celebrated Bohemian, who lived from hand to mouth round about the fertile country of Ionia, eating the bread of charity and halting in the evening to tune beside some hospitable hearth the harmonious lyre that sang of the lover of Helen and the fall of Troy." But even he admits that the Bohemia of Paris was full of misguided young men, allured by the romantic starvation of Chatterton and Moreau,[8] who suffered needlessly and had much better been making an honest living. He defines Bohemianism as "a stage in artistic life, the preface to the Academy, the Hôtel-Dieu, or the morgue." More frequently to the latter two, if there is anything in statistics. For when all is said Bohemia is pre-eminently the kingdom of failure, at least it is the province of non-success.

For a young man it may be a temporary abiding place whose skies are not altogether hopeless, a land where a prince may wed a shepherdess and Autolycus sings his ribald songs, a land of youth where he tarries but a moment and from which the serious business of life will call him away.[9] But an old man who is still hanging about the outskirts of Bohemia is a symbol of the most pitiful failure on earth. Alphonse Daudet, the most

8. Hégésippe Moreau (1810–1838), French poet who died in a poorhouse shortly after the publication of his one book *Myosotis* (1838).

9. Like Shakespeare's sea-coast kingdom of Bohemia in *The Winter's Tale*, Murger's Parisian Bohème has an almost mythical appeal as the bittersweet land of youth and possibilities. But Murger's final point is exactly as Willa Cather states it. He says in his first chapter, which prefaces the stories of Bohemia, that these sketches are "in reality studies of manners, and their heroes belong to a class misjudged up to now, whose greatest fault is

unprejudiced of all the modern French novelists, a man whose views are totally uninfluenced by personal weaknesses, tells a story of an old man who used to haunt the Latin Quarter. In his youth he had broken away from a respectable family and devoted himself to the gay pursuits of literary Bohemia. He married a woman who habitually dressed in a carter's costume and smoked a pipe, and he dwelt in a vineyard on a hillside overlooking St. Ouen. Once, in his early youth, he wrote an article on Muscat grapes which was accepted by the *Figaro*. That was the beginning and end of his literary career. He spent the rest of his life in being a Bohemian and trying to get into the mood to write again. Every evening he came into Paris and drank and made epigrams to forget the low woman in the hideous carter's costume which he had thought so fascinating when he had first seen it at a mask ball. To forget that he had neither talent nor appreciation, had none of the virtues of genius and all its vices, that his one work on Muscat grapes had been published and forgotten years ago. He tried to hang himself, but they cut him down. Finally he threw himself from one of the barricades that surrounded Paris and lay there all night with his ribs crushed in and his thighs broken. When he was picked up and put in an ambulance he remarked quietly: "They will speak of me as a man who always missed the mark." After five days of terrible agony he died. He was consistent in his failure even to the end. Daudet says with a shudder: "I shall never forget him." 10

---

disorder; and yet they can give as an excuse for this same disorder—it is a necessity which life demands from them." In the "Epilogue to the Love Affair of Rudolph and Mimi," Marcel and Rudolph talk with nostalgia of the fragrant years that are ended, but Marcel sees that finally "we have had our days of fun, of carelessness and of paradox. All that is very fine; a good novel could be made of it; but this comedy of mad love affairs, this wasting of days with the prodigality of people who believe that they have all eternity to throw away, all that must come to an end." For, he says, "it isn't possible to go on living for a long time on the edge of society, on the margin of life, almost." One of his final observations returns to what Murger said in the preface: "Poetry doesn't exist alone in a disorderly existence, in unforeseen pleasure, in love affairs which last as long as a candle, in more or less peculiar rebellions against prejudices which will always be the rulers of the world . . . ." (For convenience, I have quoted from a modern edition, *Latin Quarter: Scènes de la vie de Bohème* by Henri Murger, translated by Elizabeth Ward Hugus, with an introduction by D. B. Wyndham Lewis [New York: Dodd, Mead and Company, 1930], pp. 31, 285–286. Because Willa Cather used *The Bohemians* as the title, she may have seen the English version called *The Bohemians of the Latin Quarter*, illustrated with ten etchings from designs by Montader [London, 1883].)

10. "La Fin d'un pitre et de la bohème de Murger," in *Trente Ans de Paris* (Paris: Flammarion, n.d.), pp. 229–256. An English version is "The End of a Mountebank and of Murger's Bohemia," in *Thirty Years in Paris* (New York: Fred Defau and Company, n.d.), pp. 149–164.

One such character is enough to teach the unpleasant lessons of responsibility to a whole generation.

In its essence Bohemianism is a rebellion against all organized powers, and that in itself is defeat, for victory is with the organized powers of the universe. A man begins by defying the accepted standards of art; if he is a great man he will stop there, and if he is a very great man he will revolutionize art. If he is a weak man and can accomplish nothing by his objections generally he goes further and defies the accepted standards of social government; even there he may go scatheless, for there are such things as artistic anarchists. He may even go further and defy the accepted ethical standards without utter destruction for sometimes the wicked do prosper. But if he goes so far, he never stops there. He takes the last inevitable step and defies nature; then he goes out like a candle in a whiff of wind. He does not even leave a smoke, a name, a memory. He attains absolute annihilation and the cycle of Bohemianism is completed.

The guides can point out the dwellings of some great men in Bohemia; of Thackeray, of de Musset, of Master Daudet himself, but they are all empty dwellings, and their famous tenants did not occupy them long. Artists have never been close observers of the conventionalities of life because it requires too much time and that way lies an artificial regularity. But to openly defy the accepted conventionalities of any generation requires an even greater expenditure of time and that way lies anarchy. For the business of an artist's life is not Bohemianism for or against, but ceaseless and unremitting labor. The man who writes of great men's feats has little time to set at them, and what with hunting for rhymes and polishing his verses a poet has little time to gather violets for his *chère amie.* François Coppée says that a poet's life consists of ink and reams of paper. Ah, the poet's work has so little to do with his life and often his life has so little poetry in it. Poor Heinrich Heine when he was making divine verses of love and youth during those nine long years he lay helpless with spinal disease in the Rue d'Amsterdam wrote, "What does it avail me that enthusiastic youths and maidens crown my marble bust with laurel wreaths, if meanwhile the shrivelled fingers of an aged nurse press a blister of Spanish flies behind the ears of my actual body? What does it avail me that all the roses of Shiraz glow and bloom so tenderly for me? Alas! Shiraz is two thousand miles from the Rue d'Amsterdam, where in the dreary solitude of my sick room I smell nothing, unless it be the perfume of warmed napkins." 11 If you would know how poets live, read Browning's "How It Strikes a Contemporary." He tells the same story.

We are always trying to see in a man's life the cause for his work, to trace in his blood and environment the reason for his genius. That has so little to do with it. No man can find any explanation for the fanciful caprices of Our Lady of Beauty. At one time she favors a vagabond in the streets of Paris, at another a praying tinker in Bedford jail. The rest of us might be vagabonds or tinkers forever without moving her to one smile. She is as fanciful as Cleopatra and as unscrupulous; her favorites run the whole gamut from slaves to kings, and upon them she showers all the golden favors that the rest of us may beg without avail until we die. For her, the rest of the world does not exist. Who will ever know why or how this goddess of created things moulds a man to her will? Perhaps, when he is a baby sleeping in his cradle, she lays upon his head her fragrant fingers, perhaps, when he is in the first turbulent slumbers of his young manhood she kisses him in his dreams. And the why of it surely no man knows. Perhaps, being a woman, she has caprices unexplicable; perhaps, being a goddess, she has wisdom unfathomable.

Journal, April 5, 1896, p. 16.

11. From Heine's *Confessions* (1854). This passage may be found in a slightly different translation in *Poetry and Prose of Heinrich Heine*, selected and edited with an Introduction by Frederic Ewen (New York: Citadel Press, 1948), pp. 488–489. According to that version, the nurse applies "cantharides" behind the ears.

A MIGHTY CRAFT

Novels on the Christ and the Christ period have been rather a fad for the last twelve years. Of course they have all failed more or less, for the Christ ideal is higher than it has yet been given any writer of fiction to reach, and of all men modern novelists should be the last to attempt to do what even modern painters have not accomplished. Since the days of the Florentine and the Italian school, no art—music which is essentially modern excepted—has ever attuned itself perfectly to sacred subjects. Novelists have tried time and again to build up the proper background about the "pale Galilean." But someway all their profuse descriptions and the splendor of their oriental settings only detract from that grave central figure which is most beautiful in its simplicity, and no account of Him ever written now can equal the plain and childlike one set forth in the gospel of the New Testament. On this one subject the greatest modern artists stand baffled and outdone before those four fishermen of Galilee. For the fishermen had that which art cannot give nor genius simulate; faith, blind and unquestioning. As Alfred de Musset said in his verses on the Christ, "We have been born too late into a world too old."[12]

Among these many novels of old Palestine there is one little read and of considerable merit by Mr. Edgar Saltus; he calls it *Mary Magdalen*.[13] Mr. Saltus tried to write a novel of a period, an eastern symphony in prose which should have in it the very life of old Palestine as Flaubert's *Salammbô* has of old Carthage.[14] Of course he failed to do this; failed simply because he is not great enough. But despite its weaknesses of plot and purpose he produced a book both readable and beautiful. The first part

---

12. From *Rolla*, Part I: "Je ne crois pas, Ô Christ! à ta parole sainte: / Je suis venu trop tard dans un monde trop vieux." Alfred de Musset, *Poésies Complètes*, edited by Maurice Allem (Paris: Librairie Gallimard, 1951), p. 282.

13. *Mary Magdalen* was first published in 1891; a new edition came out in 1896. Willa Cather had previously written on the work of American novelist and essayist Edgar Saltus (1855–1921) in her *Journal* column of July 14, 1895. His new novel that summer, *When Dreams Come True*, had, she said, the old vigor of style and vivid, unusual use of words as in the early days when he wrote *The Truth about Tristrem Varick* (1888)—a "daring and original novel . . . full of subtle description, clear characterization, strong situations . . . It was and is one of the strong pieces of American fiction. It is one of our few books which from the intricate beauties of its language could not be translated into another tongue." Saltus also wrote books on metaphysics: *The Philosophy of Disenchantment* (1885) and *The Anatomy of Negation* (1886).

14. Flaubert's *Salammbô* was published in 1862. One English version, with the same title, was translated by M. French Sheldon (New York: Lovell, Coryell & Company, 1886).

of it, laid in Herod's palace at Jerusalem, is done in his best style. And there are few American writers who have more of this precious quality of style than Mr. Saltus. He uses a peculiarly fervid and ardent English that is all his own, and it is one of the greatest pities among the many pitiful things in this world that he has nothing better to say in it. In spite of all the preaching of the Philistines—to whom he gives honor and glory for their good intentions—there are very few artistic careers wrecked from the lack of manhood. But Mr. Saltus is one of the unfortunate few. Generally if a man have the temperament, that is if he have the artist in him, his ideals and his human worth will be found stowed away in him somewhere. For art is not so much the conception of lofty things, but the telling of them. But Mr. Saltus, apparently, is a "lost soul" whose name the Philistines may write triumphantly upon their banners forever, and who would furnish a text for more sermons than the world would ever listen to. He writes as perfect and musical English as any man of his generation. His style has that inestimable quality of freshness, as you read him you keep thinking that his thought came to you with all the coloring of his mood still on you. He has a clear and powerful intellect, a discerning intelligence which has enabled him to write several valuable books on metaphysics. But the truth is that Mr. Saltus' "soul"—it's too bad we have no word but that to express a man's innermost ego—is completely lost among his many accomplishments and rattles feebly about among them like a dried pea in a bladder. He absolutely does not possess the power of idealization. All his books abound in the most effective and alluring descriptions, in characters strongly drawn and cleverly treated that would make excellent subordinates in a great novel, but you may look all night for the dominant character, the man or woman who shall embody the purpose of the book and justify its creation, and you never find him. Mr. Saltus has never made one character whom it would be a pleasure or a profit to know. It is said that in New York Mr. Saltus' personal reputation is so bad that no one will rent him apartments. With one or two exceptions it would be equally difficult for any of his characters to find a landlord.

Yet, for all this, technically considered Mr. Saltus has the literary gift, the craft of exquisite speech for which all men long and few attain. But it is as though Melba should sing "Sweet Marie" and "The Band Played On." It is such pitiful waste of power. For in literature as in song just that native ability means so much, and, alas! it cannot be cultivated, even by the most worthy, nor acquired even by the most industrious. There are a thousand people who see in *Carmen* all that Calvé does.

There are a thousand who have dreamed *Alastors* and *Endymions*, but, ah, to sing it, to say it! It is an awful and a fearsome thing, that short voyage from the brain to the hand, and many a gleaming argosy of thought has gone down in it forever. Great thoughts are not uncommon things, they are the property of the multitude. Great emotions even are not so rare, they belong to youth and strength the world over. Art is not thought or emotion, but expression, expression, always expression. To keep an idea living, intact, tinged with all its original feeling, its original mood, preserving in it all the ecstasy which attended its birth, to keep it so all the way from the brain to the hand and transfer it on paper a living thing with color, odor, sound, life all in it, that is what art means, that is the greatest of all the gifts of the gods. And that is the voyage perilous, and between those two ports more has been lost than all the yawning caverns of the sea have ever swallowed. Today it seems that many people have lost sight of the mighty craft there is in literature and there is a general conception abroad that who thinks may write. Nordica writes and Mary Anderson writes and ex-President Harrison and Mrs. Ward Beecher and Odette Tyler all write. There is a popular crusade in the direction of literature. But it is not a thing to be troubled over, time will adjust it. There were other crusades many centuries ago, when all the good men who were otherwise unemployed and their wives and progeny set out for Palestine. But they found that the holy sepulchre was a long way off, and that there was no beaten path thereto, and the mountains were high and the sands hot and the waters of the desert were bitter brine. So they decided to leave the journey to the pilgrims who were madmen anyway, without homes; who found the water no bitterer than their own tears and the desert sands no hotter than the burning hearts within them. In the kingdom of art there is no God, but one God, and his service is so exacting that there are few men born of woman who are strong enough to take the vows. There is no paradise offered for a reward to the faithful, no celestial bowers, no houris, no scented wines; only death and the truth. "Thy truth then be thy dower."

Journal, March 1, 1896, p. 9.

APPENDICES
A NOTE ON THE EDITING
BIBLIOGRAPHY
INDEX

❖ ❖ ❖

The 1891 Essays

❉ ❉ ❉

CONCERNING THOMAS CARLYLE

The first important published work by Willa Cather, an essay on Thomas Carlyle, came out simultaneously in the Nebraska State Journal *and the* Hesperian *on March 1, 1891. It appeared in the* Journal *on page 14 under the heading, "Concerning Thos. Carlyle," and was signed "W. C." In the* Hesperian *it ran in the "Literary" column on pages 4 and 5, and was unsigned. It is impossible to know which publication technically came first, or exactly by what route in each case the essay arrived in print. The two versions have slight differences in wording and punctuation, suggesting that some editing had been done by either the papers or Willa Cather or both. The same spelling errors appear in both printings (Marsellaise for Marseillaise, Bastile for Bastille, Thebiad for Thebaid), and each one has an occasional omitted word. When there are differences that show editorial handling—deliberate re-punctuation or changes in wording—it is usually the* Hesperian *version that seems closer to Willa Cather's characteristic manner. The* Journal *version is more rigidly punctuated and trimmed; the* Hesperian *version often has longer sentences, more rhythmical and fuller phrasing. For example:*

p. 422, l. 26–27	*H*: as no other man ever has	*J*: as no other man has
p. 422, l. 45	*H*: the gist of the whole matter	*J*: the gist of the matter
p. 423, l. 14	*H*: against the stormy red sunset	*J*: against the stormy, red sunset
p. 423, l. 29	*H*: and indeed it must have been	*J*: and, indeed, it must have been
p. 424, l. 18	*H*: and it was a terrible thing to him that it was so	*J*: and it was terrible to him that it was so

In two instances the Journal *version distorts the meaning. In paragraph two (page 422), an entire phrase (or column line) has been omitted from the next-to-last sentence:*

H: He said but little of the great vices of the time or of the wrongs which he himself suffered.

J: He said but little of the wrongs which he himself suffered.

In the last sentence of the essay, the punctuation changes the sense:

H: He dreamed always in life great, wild maddening dreams

J: He dreamed always in life; great, wild maddening dreams

The essay printed here is the Hesperian *version, partly because it is more accurate, partly because the style seems to be closer to an original version, but also because the* Hesperian *is much less accessible than is the* Journal. *The article is reproduced as it was printed except for the correction of spelling and typographical errors and adjustments to printing conventions.*

Perhaps no man who has ever stood before the public as an English author was [so] thoroughly un-English as Thomas Carlyle. His life, his habits, and his literature were most decidedly German. The mansion on Piccadilly, the sedate tea parties, the literary clubs, and even the coveted tomb in old Westminster, so dear to the heart of every Englishman, were things of no moment to Carlyle. He was a recluse, not that he had any aversion for men, but that he loved his books and loved Nature better. He saw little of society; yet, though he never bent his knee to it, he never trampled upon its laws. He was merely indifferent to it, for he was one of the few men who can live utterly independent of it, while those who condemn it most severely, cling to it as the only thing which can give them zest or ambition enough to live. He respected social laws, for they are the outgrowth of man's honest sentiments of what is best to be done in his conduct toward his fellows. He revered any production of the hand or of the mind of man, be it some old rune cut upon stone in an English forest, or a social code which allotted to his higher, stronger nature and passions the same sphere of action as to every coal heaver on the streets of London. He said but little of the great vices of the time or of the wrongs which he himself suffered. He bore no sense of enmity toward any one; he only pitied,—with all the strength of his great heart,—pitied everything that lived.

Carlyle posed but poorly as a political economist. His love and sympathy for humanity were boundless, and he understood great minds and earnest souls as no other man ever has. In this lay his power as a biographer and as a historian. He could understand how the Marseillaise might set men's hearts on fire; the storming of the Bastille, and the revolt of the women [were] pictures after his own heart, in which the hot blood of the old sea kings still raged. The passions and the sincerity of the French revolution made it sacred to him. But of the liberals of his own country, men who demanded rights but never shed one drop of honest blood in defense of them; whose revolts were mere riots, instigated neither by principle nor by patriotism, but by sullen anger; whose aspirations rose from an ale glass, and found their tomb therein—of these he understood nothing; they were dark enigmas to him; he was "above them all, alone with the stars." Moreover, Carlyle was not a practical man. He knew, for instance, that education is the right of every man, and that it is the most potent factor in the suppression of crime. But when the English liberals rushed upon him, asking whether education should be compulsory; at what age this compulsory education should begin; at whose expense; and whether the schools should be sectarian, he was utterly aghast. He was only an awkward fellow, born a peasant, and a peasant always, with a great genius, and a soul sincere as truth itself. He could handle the most profound problem in metaphysics delicately enough, but he was dull and bungling when he tried to grasp political theories. Perhaps the gist of the whole matter was, that he was always looking for a cause, or for its effect in everything, both of which are somewhat difficult to find in modern English politics. He was always dreaming too, one half his heart was always in Valhalla. The best traits of [his] character, and the strongest powers of his mind belonged to other times and to other people.

He went far out into one of the most desolate spots of Scotland, and made his home there. There among the wild heaths, and black marshes, and grim dark forests, which have remained unchanged since the time of the Picts and the Saxons, he did his best work. He drew his strength from those wild landscapes; he breathed into himself the fury of the winds; the strength of the storm went into his blood. Carlyle was the greatest painter in England. His pictures were not wild sketches of imagination, but were photographs from nature.

Like Scott, he lived much in the open air, and might be seen evening after evening striding the heath, or climbing the rocky hills, his tall, angular figure, braced to the wind, standing out sharply against the stormy red sunset.

It is well known that Carlyle's married life was not strictly a happy one, and that Mrs. Carlyle sometimes complained bitterly of his indifference to her. The wife of an artist, if he continues to be an artist, must always be a secondary consideration with him; she should realize that from the outset. Art of every kind is an exacting master, more so even than Jehovah. He says only, "Thou shalt have no other gods before me." Art, science, and letters cry, "Thou shalt have no other gods at all." They accept only human sacrifices. There are few women who love an abstract ideal well enough to see this, fewer still who [,] like Mary Shelley, will honor it, and submit to such treatment without jealousy. It is very likely that Carlyle used violent language when interrupted in one of the soliloquies of Teufelsdröckh to be informed that his coffee was ready. Very likely Mrs. Carlyle was much hurt and grieved; she certainly made excellent coffee. She would have liked it better if he had lived in London, and put on a white tie and a dress coat, and gone to the receptions. She hated this solitude which was her husband's inspiration, and indeed it must have been very unpleasant for her. The lack of harmony in their conjugal relations was due to the faults of neither, but was merely a very unfortunate circumstance.

Carlyle's was one of the most intensely reverent natures of which there is any knowledge. He saw the divine in everything. His every act was a form of worship, yet it was fortunate that he did not enter the ministry. He would have been well enough in the pulpit, though he would have preached on Scandinavian mythology, and on the Hindoo, as well as on the Hebrew faith; but he could never have smiled benignly at the deaconess' tea parties, nor have praised the deacon's stock, nor have done the thousand other little things requisite for success. The minister of today should be as shrewd a wire-puller as the politician. He would have gone to the kirk with the very best intentions, and, being suddenly struck with some idea while ascending his pulpit stairs, would have made an eloquent and powerful address upon the doctines of Buddha, at which his audience would either have gone to sleep, or have been shocked, as they happened to feel listless or irritable. He was too passionately, too intensely religious to confine himself to any one creed. He could never see why Saint Peter's and the Coliseum should always frown at each other as they stand there in Rome, with the graves of two faiths between; one dying, one long since dead: he loved them both so well. Even the scars of barbarian swords upon the polished marble he half revered; they were honest arms which struck those blows.

This reverential seriousness of disposition was characteristic of him in literature, as in everything else. He never strove to please a pampered public. His genius was not the tool of his ambition, but his religion, his god. Nothing has so degraded modern literature as the desperate efforts of modern writers to captivate the public, their watching the variation of public taste, as a speculator watches the markets. When Orpheus sings popular ballads upon the street corners, he is a street singer, nothing more. The gates of hell do not open at his music any more, nor do the damned forget their pain in its melody. Carlyle went out alone into the solitude and wrestled with his great ideas, finding them difficult to express in words, so great, so ungainly were they. He little cared whether his books were popular, whether they were even read. He wrote only that which was in him and which must be written. In vain his publishers groaned over his "terrible earnestness"; he would not laugh for them. He was always down in the chamber of the fates, at the roots of Ygdrasil, the tree of life, which the Norns water day and night, one with honey and two with gall, and it was a terrible thing to him that it was so. Milton says that the lyric poet may drink wine and live generously, but the epic poet, who sings of the descent of the gods to men, must drink water out of a wooden bowl. He is the last poet who has thought so, and he is the last poet who has given us an epic.

Carlyle's was one of the most unhappy temperaments. He never saw things as others did; his wild fancy and bad digestion distorted everything. In writing, he does not willfully exaggerate; he only portrays things as they seemed to him. Like the old Anchorites of the Thebaid, he kept upon his knees within his narrow cell until the outside world looked supernatural to him. The little difficulties of his life were to him actual demons and powers of darkness sent to torment him. His dyspepsia was an actual Tophet. How far his ill health may have influenced his writings is not known. Certainly not so far as some critics claim, who assert that "Sartor Resartus" is but the result of a year of miserable health, the morbid fancies of a sick man. If so, it is a new and pleasing feature of bad gastronomy.

He was proud to the extreme, but his love was predominant even over his pride. He, himself, would suffer any privation rather than sacrifice an ideal; but for his brother's sake he wrote for money. It seemed to him like selling his own soul. He wrote article after article for reviews, and cut up his great thoughts to fit the pages of a magazine. No wonder he hated it; it was like hacking his own flesh, bit by bit, to feed those he loved.

Throughout his entire life he was tormented by interference. He was not the kind of a man to be popular, for he was unwise enough to stand aloof from all sects and all parties. None defended him. No one creed nor the doctrines of any one sect were broad enough to hold him. Like the lone survivor of some extinct species, the last of the mammoths, tortured and harassed beyond all endurance by the smaller, though perhaps more perfectly organized offspring of the world's maturer years, this great Titan, son of her passionate youth, a youth of volcanoes, and earthquakes, and great, unsystematized forces, rushed off into the desert to suffer alone.

He died as he lived. Proudly refusing a tomb in Westminster, as did one other great English writer, he was buried out on the wild Scotch heath, where the cold winds of the North Sea sing the chants of Ossian among the Druid pines. He lies there on that wild heath, the only thing in the British Isles with which he ever seemed to harmonize. He dreamed always in life great, wild, maddening dreams: perhaps he sleeps quietly now,—perhaps he wakes.

SHAKESPEARE AND HAMLET

This essay appeared in two parts in the Nebraska State Journal *on successive Sundays, November 1 and 8, 1891 (p. 16 and p. 11). The first installment was not signed. The second installment concluded with the initials, " W. C." The article as it is reprinted here has been lightly edited to correct quotations and printing errors (see A Note on the Editing, page 453).*

It is generally conceded that into no other one of his plays did William Shakespeare put so much of himself and of his own soul's life as into *Hamlet*. Perhaps this fact will in some measure account for the stress which is laid upon the play and the importance which is given to it in English literature. To the student of Shakespeare the play has proved to be a better key to the real character of the man who wrote the greatest dramas in the English language than the cryptogram of Mr. [Ignatius] Donnelly. True, it does not tell his name, but it is time, in this age, that we should at least begin to care very little about the bodies and bones of the promulgators of our great faith and the founders of our great organizations. They, themselves, were more careful of their truths than of their persons. Relic worship and the war for the holy sepulchre are supposed to have ended with the Middle Ages.

The cause for the various current opinions upon the character of Hamlet, and the root of many of the dissensions and controversies is that many of the best scholars and critics try to make of Hamlet a much grander, more learned and more intellectual personage than the author of the play ever intended him to be. I don't think Shakespeare had any definite purpose even in writing *Hamlet*. It was not like him to plan a play which should be a puzzle for all time to come. He probably read the legend and felt sorry for the young prince, and as an expression of his sympathy wrote about him. He probably had no intention of giving the drama any more of himself than he gave to any other of his plays. The Danish prince had nothing in common with him except that both were misunderstood, and both suffered. He gradually grew into the play as he wrote it, without any special reason. Perhaps outside matters bore more heavily upon him than usual. It may be his feeling and individuality were wrought up intensely, and crept out into the play which he happened to be writing.

Hamlet was certainly not the philosopher, the intellectual monstrosity which he is often represented to be. He was not even the strong, broad-minded, world-worn statesman which Edwin Booth makes him. In years, Hamlet was but a boy who pounded at Virgil down at the old university at Wittenberg, and wrote love letters and bad verses to Ophelia. He was galloping about the court yard on Yorick's back only a few years ago. We are given no glimpse of his personal character before his great sorrow came upon him, but even through it some of his old boyish habits cling to him. His illustration of this is very prominent in the unsophisticated way in which, after his first meeting with the ghost, he pulls out his note book to note the fact that, "one may smile and smile and be a villain." Had Hamlet known the world a little better, or had he been a few years older, he would not have thought it necessary to make a note of that fact every time he was brought to a realization of it, or all Denmark could not have furnished him tablets enough. One can almost imagine the contents of that note book. Notes on the old classics, made at Wittenberg, raptures on everything in nature from the moon to roses, and vague effusions respecting his passion for Ophelia.

In the first act, his soliloquy is one of the most simple, touching passages in literature. His cry, "Frailty, thy name is woman!" is no cynical observation on the daughter of Eve. A cynic would have couched the thought in very different language, and would have somewhat enjoyed saying it. This is a boy's first glimpse of a thing that he shudders at. It is no light matter to him that women are fickle: his mother is a woman, and Ophelia is one. His, "Oh Soul! a beast that wants discourse of reason would have mourned longer," is no rhetorical flourish; it is positively piteous. During the first act, Hamlet learned many bitter lessons from experience, his best, perhaps his only teacher. But his experience also drove him mad and killed him. Suffering, though it embittered Hamlet's nature, could not poison it. In the second and third acts, his replies to fawning, scraping Rosencrantz and Guildenstern are certainly cynical. It is the tenderest, deepest feeling that, when once it is embittered, becomes most acrid. That man who has never hoped, never dreamed, never loved, never suffered, is never a cynic. But in the scene with the queen, Hamlet forgets his cynicism and becomes Gertrude's son again.

Hamlet had not the first element of the intellectual or of the philosophical in him. He was never able for a moment to lay aside that intense personality of him and view himself as one individual of a great species, a type of a race. He could not see Gertrude merely as a woman, committing an error common to women of her day, but always as "My mother." That the prince should have done much logical reasoning during that period of his life which the play covers, is improbable. Throughout the entire play he was under an intense nervous strain; his feelings were wrought up to the highest possible pitch. Logical reasoning and intense feeling are directly antagonistic. The Egyptian priests knew this when they demanded of a candidate that he first sacrifice his passions and his affections. A man who would be born unto knowledge must indeed become dead to the world. None of his great soliloquies are premeditated; all are perfectly spontaneous. The famous "to be, or not to be," does not look toward a universal affirmation; it is merely a chance remark. It is not very likely that at that particular time Hamlet would undertake a discussion of human destiny. He had at length determined upon a course by which to touch the king's conscience; but as he reflected upon the consequence, the confusion, the turmoil, the exposure of his mother's guilt, the dishonor to the state, he was almost tempted to take the easy way out of it, and— rest. Then the question came to him, as it has come to many another. If it is applicable to anyone else, I suppose Hamlet would not object; but at that particular moment he was thinking entirely too much about my Lord Hamlet to be devoting very much attention to humanity in general.

He is a poor philosopher, for he never reasons, he only suffers. He has premises, hundreds of them, and he jumps from major to minor, and from minor back to major, but he stops there; [the] syllogism ends with his premise; he never draws a conclusion. From the first act to the last, he makes but one absolute statement, one assertion of whose truth he is absolutely sure. That he makes when leaping into the grave of his loved Ophelia throwing his arms above his head, at Laertes, his white face glaring, he cries, "This is I, Hamlet the Dane!" In the last act, he even doubts his identity; he doubts everything. His dying words, "the rest is silence," are wonderfully in keeping with his character.

If we refuse to recognize intellect as the cause of that wonderful strength of Hamlet's, and lay it aside, we must substitute something, for we must acknowledge with Polonius, "Though this be madness, yet there is method in't." The keynote of Hamlet's character is merely this: He was very sensitive, he felt intensely, and he suffered more than other people, that was all. The intellectual school insist upon putting props under Hamlet because they do not understand him; for the first instinct of the intellect is to analyze, and you can only sympathize with Hamlet. They attempt to see in his every word a "means" to produce certain "dramatic effects," to account for his every act, when in reality they cannot account for them any more than Hamlet could. Goethe, more aspiring than the rest, but with better sense than most of them, brings his great German capacity to bear upon the subject, and in *Wilhelm Meister* mildly suggests that to rectify this shocking lack of art the whole plot be changed, the whole play be revolutionized, so that every cause may have its perceptible effect and every effect its perceptible cause. He advises, in short, that *Hamlet* be made dramatic! The intellectual school realize the importance of the play, but they never quite like it; they always prefer *Macbeth*, claiming that there is more art in it. This may be so; in *Hamlet* certainly we have "more matter with less art." Sometimes I wonder if Shakespeare would have quite known what was meant, if art, or the art purposes in his plays, had been mentioned to him. The emotional and intentional plane of life is infinitely higher than the intellectual. It is the source of every great purpose, of every exalted aim. It is not attained by study; it is not seen through a telescope, nor reached by mastering the pages of a Latin grammar. This upper world is only trodden by those who have reached it through suffering. Some men are born in it, and we call them geniuses. Some attain, but they must travel the old path to paradise, which leads down through hell. What is conceived and written in this rare atmosphere can be appreciated, estimated or judged only by men who breathe the same air.

Hamlet has been accorded the place of the greatest masterpiece of the greatest master, not by literary critics, but by popular taste. The critics themselves, preferring other of Shakespeare's plays, would spend little enough time on it were it not for the constant demand of the public. On the boards it has been presented oftener, and more successfully than any other Shakespearean drama. In the schools and colleges it is now indispensable, and by the great "unpopular public" it is more read than any other play in the English language. You will find a worn, marked copy in the office of almost every country doctor, lawyer or tradesman. Among the everyday men of the everyday world *Hamlet*, by a broad sort of metonymy, has come to mean Shakespeare. The play is a living, vital force in a living age, a part of the spiritual life of the nineteenth century. The critics have been forced to study it. This they do from a wholly intellectual standpoint, and so see in it only the intellectual. The light streaming in through the stained glass of a cathedral window turns even the marble virgin's face to the color of blood. The critics have no other light than the intellectual, for they have declared that the emotions and intentions are not to be trusted. The altar lights they have called *ignis fatui*, and have put them out. They analyze the play in a scientific manner, and do it most skilfully. They take a microscope and see all the beauty of the cell organization, a field which men of the emotional school never enter. They say, "This caused life," or "This resulted from life," but life they never find. They think they have all, and indeed they have much; the massive framework, the delicate nerve structure, and all the perfectly formed organism upon which the eye of the anatomist loves to dwell. But they never feel the hot blood riot in the pulses, nor hear the great heartbeat. That is the one great joy which belongs exclusively to those of us who are unlearned, unlettered, to those of us who have nothing else. The critics laugh at us and say, of course there is emotion in *Hamlet*, but it is merely one of the primary elements of the play, that we have never advanced far enough to appreciate the more finished art. So be it. We can answer them only as an Indian prince answered an English astronomer when reproved for sun worshipping. The old prince patiently heard the man of science through and then lifted his eyes toward the murky London skies, dull and dark with the smoke of traffic and of commerce, and said: "Oh, my Lord, if you could but see the sun."

So much for the critic and for the intellectual students of literature. To a young author with his first book under his arm, who has had a great truth to tell, and has told it ill, they seem very strong and very terrible, these scribes and pharisees, who are so spotless in the observance of literary law, and the forms of their religions. Still, they are not so strong as they appear. They did their worst to Keats, and they only killed his body. They tried to change him, to polish him, to conventionalize him, and when he repulsed them and went his own way, they hated him as the Thracian maiden hated Orpheus. But their darts were powerless so long as the world stood spellbound at his music. So they raised a great cry through the *Edinburgh Review*, and drowned the music's voice with their clamor. Drunken with the brutal rites of their god, they rushed upon him and tore him limb from limb, and stained with his blood the rocks that were moved and melted by his music. But the lyre by chance fell into a great river, and it floated on past the old cities and the vineyards and the olive-crowned hills, silencing the nightingales and waking the soft Italian night with its music. And the children playing under the myrtle trees listened and wondered, and ceased playing, and were children no more. And the women who had trodden the wine press all day heard wearily, and their life seemed not so hard and they were less ashamed, and the red upon their feet seemed not so much like blood as it had seemed yesterday. Yet they murmured, "We will tread the press no more, we will be better tomorrow." And the shepherds far away on the hills, keeping their flocks by night, heard it, and they arose and their hearts grew strong and they whispered, "It is the annunciation; a new Christ comes." Then the lyre floated on, until Zeus, the son of Kronos, took it and placed it among the stars, where it lies,

> borne darkly, fearfully, afar;
> Whilst shining through the utmost veil of heaven [1]
> The soul of Adonais like a star
> Beacons from the abode where the Eternal are!

1. The line is actually: "Whilst burning through the inmost veil of heaven" (*Adonais*, l. 439).

And the Thracians say, "We put it there." So it is with all literature which reaches the hearts of the people, where it finds its noblest, surest immortality. The critics may kill the author, they may attack his productions and rend their structure to pieces, and declare the style imperfect; but the soul they never touch, for they have never reached it; the soul they never kill, for they have never seen it.

The position in which Hamlet was placed would not have been so terrible to anyone else. It would have been a very simple matter to Laertes indeed when Polonius was killed, and Ophelia driven mad. Laertes was not much burdened by a sense of filial or of fraternal obligation. He tried to throttle Hamlet, and then went through the duel more as a matter of form than anything else. It is not often that a northern country produces such a character as Hamlet. He would have been more natural, perhaps, as a lad of Venice or of Verona. To him it seemed that he was born for one end, to avenge his father. Foreign and repugnant as the touch [task ?] was to his nature, he took it upon him as a sacred mission, a call from God, and broke his great heart upon it. He says himself,

> The time is out of joint; O cursed spite
> That I was ever ever born to set it right.[2]

He never faltered in the execution of his terrible oath to the ghost in the first act. He did indeed wipe everything from his mind; books, art, ambition—yes, even love. He gave himself entirely and completely to his work. Perhaps the saddest part of his great self-sacrifice was his parting from Ophelia. He spoke not a word to her; what could he say? Ophelia loved the queen and would have thought him mad had he mentioned the ghost. She would have been sorry for Hamlet, but she could not have understood the sacredness of his mission nor why he must leave her. She could not have understood, no one could. Ophelia's description of it is one of the most touching things in the play.

> He took me by the wrist and held me hard,
> Then goes he to the length of all his arm,
> And, with his other hand thus o'er his brow,
> He falls to such perusal of my face
> As he would draw it. Long stay'd he so;
> At last, a little shaking of mine arm,
> And thrice his head thus waving up and down
> He rais'd a sigh so piteous and profound
> As it did seem to shatter all his bulk
> And end his being. That done, he lets me go,
> And, with his head over his shoulder turn'd,
> He seem'd to find his way without his eyes;
> For out o' doors he went without their help,
> And, to the last, bended their light on me.

Anyone else would have married Ophelia, used a little discretion and finally ruled Denmark and Norway. It would have been an infinitely more sensible proceeding, but Hamlet took the most difficult solution of the problem because it seemed to him the right one. He followed no written or spoken law, but the

2. Correctly: "That ever I was born to set it right" (I. v. 189–190).

law of his own heart, and just in proportion as it was more delicately organized than the hearts of other men, so the law was more stringent and his conception of honor higher, purer and more intensely vivid. He had infinite charity for everyone else, but none for himself. No wonder Goethe is puzzled to find an explanation for his acts; no wonder that the entire court thought him mad. He was like a man whose eyes are stronger than the eyes of other mortals, and who sees some great star upon the horizon that beckons him, and he followed it. Because other men do not see it they say to him: "Thy sight is false," or, with the queen say they see "nothing at all, yet all that is I see." The far-sighted eye is as much diseased as the near-sighted one, and it may be as great a flaw in perfect vision to see more than other men as it is to see less than other men.

Some prominent writers upon *Hamlet* have, with the keenest possible insight into Hamlet's character, and the strongest possible soul sympathy with Hamlet's suffering, after many learned discussions with infinite analysis of motive, decided that Hamlet feigned madness. Poor Hamlet! "Oh to love so, he loved, yet so mistaken!" The very cause of his trouble was that he could not feign anything, as he tells the queen, "Seems, madam! Nay, it is; I know not 'seems.'"

The madness of Hamlet is the highest point in tragedy which Shakespeare ever reached. Here he attains his greatest end by no trick of introducing witches, or dagger or blood stain. The tragedy of the play does not lie in the fact that a file of corpses covers the stage in the last scene. The real tragedy of the play is [the] breaking of Hamlet's heart fiber by fiber, muscle by muscle. The final snap of the last quivering cord merely closes the tragedy. Hamlet died at the very close of the play, but he has been dying ever since the first act. Some students of the play have said that it would have been bad taste in Shakespeare to have made his first character a monomaniac. Evidently the gentlemen who take this view of the case have not forgotten their childish longing to have all the stories "end right," and the hero "live happily forever after." True tragedy is something more than bloodshed. Suppose Hamlet to have been really mad; suppose him to have suffered until that delicately balanced mind was the seat of dire confusion, "like sweet bells, jangled out of tune and harsh." And suppose that he had not fallen in the duel, but that the great artist had left him a hopeless maniac. Suppose, on the other hand, Hamlet had eaten, drunk, slept and read as usual, and feigned madness as a matter of convenience, a mask under which he might successfully plot to possess himself of the throne, and to avenge his father. To feign madness was, under the circumstances, the most politic thing Hamlet could have done. It would have made him master of the situation. The only wonder is that with such shrewd diplomacy to start with, he did not succeed better. Perhaps he did not play his little part skilfully enough, was not earnest enough about it. Suppose, I say, that the prudent, well balanced, exemplary Hamlet should have finally been so unfortunate as to have Laertes' sword run through him; now which, I ask, is the higher tragedy, Hamlet mad or Hamlet dead? It is perhaps a sad thought that with such strength there should be such weakness; yet then Shakespeare took his greatest, grandest character, and, like Apollo to the priestess he loved, gave unto him the divine speech, never to be understood; the divine prophecy, never to be believed; which is at once the curse and the highest heritage of genius.

Hamlet feigning madness would have been something of an Iago, grand and beautiful, noble and upright, a character as Iago certainly is, and pure and elevated as is the taste of those who admired him above all other Shakespearean characters. Shakespeare could not, even had he wished it—as he doubtless did—have given to each and every one of his several thousand characters the ennobling characteristics of Iago without producing an effect, almost of monotony. [November 1, 1891, p. 16]

In Mr. [Edward] Bulwer-Lytton's novel *Zanoni*, he describes as one of the elementary steps to a higher order of manhood, a manhood which shall defy death, fathom space, sovereign the stars, that the candidate be first rendered susceptible to sensations other than those which the flesh is heir to, that he hear music in silence, see light in darkness, and the sunlight becomes a sort of external *elixir vitae* to him. But at the same time he suffers intolerable pain from the millions of larvae with which the air and water are peopled and trembles in agony at things which fall upon the rest of mankind as humdrum and unnoticed as light falls upon the lids of a sleeper. Hamlet had to contend with the realities not only of this world, but of a world of his own.

Shakespeare has drawn no friendship, not even the friendship of Anthony and Caesar, which is more beautiful than the friendship of Hamlet and Horatio. One especially revolting feature of Goethe's proposed revision of *Hamlet* is that it degrades the friendship of the prince and Horatio, makes it vulgar and self-interested, gives a reason why Hamlet and Horatio should love each other. He would make Horatio son of the vice regent of Norway, and would have Hamlet give his dying voice to him instead of to Fortinbras, so substituting a political intrigue for the love that sprung up between two men in their old free student life at Wittenberg; that came unbidden, grew unforced, until it was stronger than the men themselves and was only broken at the end with Horatio's "Good night, sweet prince," perhaps not even then. He had come down from the university to be near his friend in his sorrow. When he found the extent of Hamlet's grief he would not return, but stayed with Hamlet, letting his work and his ambitions go. If we may judge from his own conversation and from remarks let fall by Hamlet he was a scholar, probably a much better one than Hamlet ever was, and Hamlet was proud of it. He was the one man who understood or rather appreciated Hamlet and he never doubted him an instant. It was to him that Hamlet poured out his anguish, to him that he wrote and confided the story of the king's treachery. He was with him in the ghost scene, protecting him and curbing his rashness; he was with him at the play, and at Ophelia's grave; and in the duel he was at his side. He was with him where a woman's love failed him. He studied, planned and dreamed with him in their old days; now he suffered and would have died with him had it not been for Hamlet's last request, "Horatio, I am dead, thou liv'st. Report me and my cause aright to the unsatisfied." So the one, Hamlet's other self, lived and worked out the work they had planned to do together. The one was not quite dead while the other lived. Reason for the friendship of Hamlet and Horatio: What is the reason for gratification, the cause of chemical affinity? Hamlet himself gives the only reason he knew:

Nay, do not think I flatter;
For what advancement may I hope from thee
That no revenue hast but thy good spirits
To feed and clothe thee?...
Since my dear soul was mistress of her choice
And could of men distinguish, her election
Hath seal'd thee for herself; for thou hast been
As one, in suffering all, that suffers nothing,
A man that fortune's buffets and rewards
Hast ta'en with equal thanks; and bless'd are those
Whose blood and judgment are so well commingled
That they are not a pipe for fortune's finger
To sound what stop she please. Give me that man
That is not passion's slave and I will wear him
In my heart's core, ay, in my heart of heart,
As I do thee.

It is not often that two souls are delicately joined enough to experience a friendship like that of Hamlet and Horatio. It is hardly covered by the word friendship; it is an almost awful thing. Old Damon and his Pythias knew it, and Julius and his Anthony. I think if Julius had gotten up from his tomb and "gone down into Egypt" again, that Anthony would have given him Cleopatra, just as he gave him everything else. He must even have been glad that Julius had loved her for it seemed to draw him closer to his dead hero.

Had Hamlet's first sorrow not have been so heavy that it crushed him, he might have been a great artist of some kind. These strained, exaggerated natures sometimes focus themselves in this way. Had he had a few more years with Horatio down in the silence of Wittenberg, he might have been a genius; as it was he was only very miserable. It is strange how delicate is the distinction between miserable men and great men. Through all its existence the charcoal feels within its black breast every throb, every aspiration of the kindred gem. It feels its very being throb and break with light, light quiver through its every atom, but it is all latent, men do not see it. For lack of some crowning touch of the great chemist, it lies always in the dark, and can give back the light which the great sun locked up in it centuries ago, only in one way, through fire, by its own consumption. The gem shines on a thousand years uninjured, shimmering in its own light. The charcoal gives light too, but it dies in giving light birth. Hamlet's grief killed the creative art in him, and left him only the "bad dreamer." Poor fellow! he lived hard, and he died hard. "The rest is silence."

It was upon this prince, perhaps the least powerful and awe inspiring of all Shakespearean heroes, that William Shakespeare exhausted the greatest treasure of his genius, and into whose life he breathed his own. I think that this is all Shakespeare meant Hamlet to be, a man who suffered. To Macbeth he gave the most finished characteristic art in the world; to Julius Caesar he gave his masterpiece of oratory; to Lear he gave the strongest pathos in literature; Hamlet he pitied, and he gave him the legacy of his love. In a certain way Shakespeare is as much misunderstood as his masterpiece. We try to make him the intellectual giant of the ages, when in truth I do not suppose he was half so intellectual as Newton. He was no great scholar; he took rather to the soul than to the technique of learning. He had little Latin history and more Greek mythology.

The great secret of Shakespeare's power was supreme love, rather than supreme intellect, supreme love for the ideal in art, and for the real in it too, which is but a form of the ideal after all. There have been other men with as much ability, as much talent, but they have contented themselves with being men of letters, rather than creators of thought. They hold a very prominent position in society, they are the presidents of the great literary clubs, they are editors of the leading magazines, they are sought out at every reception. It is a pleasant career, their penning of pretty pieces of literature, and there is fame in it; but it is a very different thing from thought creations, from thought birth, the agony in which all the forces of body, brain and soul are drawn to one vital center in the effort of one life to give individuality to a greater life, the agony of the Doric women who bore the sons of the gods. Modern authors admire the great creations of thought, oh yes, and they would like well enough to produce them, but they are unwilling, either for the sake of the idea itself or for the sake of the truth which inspired it, to undergo the pain, the suffering, the separation from other men, the solitude and the loneliness which thought learning involves. They each love; they are not strong enough for the sacrifice, so they say "we will serve both, men and art." They serve the one, but the other they prostitute. They do not intend this, it comes upon them gradually. They forget that an artist should be unlike other men, for he should be a revelation to other men. They forget that conventionalism of art is the death of art. Yet we have conventionalized everything, men and the cities of men. When was it that the gods left Rome? Was it when it was sacked and pillaged, and bought and sold? Ah, no; but when the first locomotive rumbled across the trestle bridge over the Tiber. The railroad did what time, and fire, and steel could not do, made Rome like other cities. The fauns and the nymphs started in terror when they heard that first shrill whistle, and they wept all day in the fountains and at night they said farewell to the tombs along the Via Appia, and left Rome forever. Now we go there and turn away disappointed, sick at heart. The strength we look for is gone. We go to see the death we envy, we find the life we live.

The artist begins with earnestness and devotion enough, but the sirens sing his praises, and he listens to them. He busies himself with the lighter vein of his art because it is the pleasantest and easiest for the time; but when he seeks his old power it is gone, he knows not whither. He anxiously calls upon his God, but it responds no more. After that he may clasp his knees in desperate entreaty, he may cry and cut himself with sharp stones, and cause his children to pass through the fire before it, but it is of no avail, once silenced, it is silenced forever. Today all artists see too much of the world, they are alone too little. He who walks with the crowd is drawn to its level. The law of maternal impression is true in the mental as well as in the physical world, and every thought is more or less colored by the atmosphere in which it is conceived. Thought born in a crowd gives men nothing better than they have already, and they soon tire of it. If an artist does any good work he must do it alone. No number of encouraging or admiring friends can assist him, they retard him rather. He must go off alone with his own soul and they too must labor and suffer together, with none seeing but the stars. It was only after Moses had left all the luxury, the learning, and the culture of the Egyptian court, and had fled into [the] Midian desert and dreamed for years in the sand hills, that the bush burned before him and was not consumed. Long afterward, when he went up Mount Sinai to receive the great revelation of the law, at the foot of the mountain he left his people, farther up he took Aaron and Hur and the elders, still further up he left even Joshua, and went alone—to God. The oracle did not speak in the crowded streets of Athens, nor yet in the schools of Plato, but out in the solitudes of Delphi.

It is not an easy thing, this separation from the world. Authors are not made of marble or of ice, and human sympathy is a sweet thing. There is much to suffer, much to undergo: the awful loneliness, the longing for human fellowship and for human love. The terrible realization of the soul that no one knows it, no one sees it, no one understands it; that it is barred from the perception of other souls; that it is always alone. It is a hard thing to endure, and only love can endure it, a love as deep and as serene as the eternal force of the universe Shakespeare loved.

It seems strange that many literary men who have so much should yet lack so much, that with all their correctness and elegance of form, they fall so far short of some men who had neither. Their learning burdens rather than aids them. It is just as it was long ago when the model young man came to Christ and said, "Lord, what good thing shall I do that I may inherit eternal life?" And Christ said, "Thou knowest the law and the prophets." And he said, "All these have I kept from my youth up." And Christ looked upon him, and loved him, for there was promise in him, and he said, "One thing thou lackest. Thou hast gained great wealth through observance of the law, and it was well gained. Now go and take all this which is rightfully thine, and sell it and give unto the poor. Give all, and follow me out into the desert and the waste places, and over the rugged mountain sides, and among the publicans and sinners, and over to Calvary." And the youth went away sorrowful, for he had great possessions. "Will of Avon" gave all, he was only an English country lad, and had not much to give, and went out into the wilderness with the fishermen, while the rest of us stay and worship properly at Jerusalem. Ingersoll says he is glad that Shakespeare never went to Oxford, and took a degree, and became a fellow, and taught Alpha, Beta to the young Englishmen. For myself, I am glad that he was not an ambitious man or a learned man, or a popular man, or even a very good man; but just Will Shakespeare, writer of plays; that he did not know many languages, but saw rather more in English than other writers; that he was not even travelled, and had never seen the lands he worshipped in his dreams, except as he saw the world float by him in the London fogs. He did not want to be studied; he just wanted to be loved. He did not write to make men think; he wrote to make men feel. We insist upon viewing him exclusively in the intellectual sense, we discern the dramatic power in *Macbeth* and the art purposes in the balcony scene. Probably Shakespeare had no more art purposes in writing the balcony scene than Romeo had when he swung himself up by the balustrades of Capulet's balcony, and lifted his lips to Juliet's. There is no art in the balcony scene, it's all heart. There are under all our forms and fashions, a few fundamental principles which are alive in us all. The different castes of society would almost become different species were it not for those few common touches of nature which make the whole world kin. Shakespeare was master of these few elementary emotions which are the keystone of life. Upon their strength he gathers art, history, poetry, science, philosophy and dramatic law, just as the great ocean surges sweeping up over the rocks gather pebbles, sand, sea wreck, starfish, driftwood and fling them back into the sea. W. C. [November 8, 1891, p. 11]

APPENDIX II

An Uncollected Story

"The Elopement of Allen Poole," which appeared in the Hesperian *on April 15, 1893, pages 4–7, is the first published story, so far as is presently known, in which Willa Cather made use of her memories of Virginia. Miss Cather was at this time the literary editor of the* Hesperian, *which may explain why the story was not signed. For a discussion of its identification as her work and of its connection with her later fiction, see pages 104 ff.*

THE ELOPEMENT OF ALLEN POOLE

I

"Seein' yo' folks ain't willin', sweetheart, I tell yo' there hain't no other way."

"No, I reckon there hain't." She sighed and looked with a troubled expression at the thin spiral of blue smoke that curled up from a house hidden behind the pine trees.

"Besides, I done got the license now, an' told the preacher we was comin'. Yo' ain't goin' back on me now, Nell?"

"No, no, Allen, of course I hain't, only—" her mouth quivered a little and she still looked away from him. The man stood uneasily, his hands hanging helplessly at his side, and watched her. As he saw the color leave her cheeks and her eyes fill up, he began to fear lest he might lose her altogether, and he saw that something must be done. Rousing himself he went up to her, and taking her hand drew himself up to the full height of his six feet.

"See here, Nell, I hain't goin' to make yo' leave yo' folks, I hain't got no right to. Yo' kin come with me, or bide with 'em, jist as yo' choose, only fo' Gawd's sake tell me now, so if yo' won't have me I kin leave yo'."

The girl drew close to him with that appealing gesture of a woman who wants help or strength from some one, and laid her face on his arm.

"I want yo', Allen, yo' know that. I hain't feelin' bad to go, only I do hate to wear that dress mighty bad. Yo' know Pap bought it fo' me to wear to the Bethel camp-meetin'. He got real silk ribbon fo' it, too, jist after he sold the sheep, yo' know. It seems real mean to run away in it."

"Don't wear it then, I kin get yo' plenty o' dresses, wear what yo' got on, yo' surely purty enough fo' me that way."

"No, I must wear it, cause I ain't got nothin' else good enough to marry yo' in. But don't lets talk about it no mo' dear. What time yo' goin' to come tonight?"

"Bout ten o'clock I reckon. I better not come too early, yo' folks might hear me. I lay I won't go fer away today, them revenue fellers is lookin' fo' me purty sharp."

"I knowed they would be, I knowed it all along. I wish yo' wouldn't still no mo'. I jist am scared to death now all the time fo' fear they'll ketch yo'. Why don't yo' quit stillin' now, Allen?"

"Law me, honey! there hain't no harm in it. I jist makes a little fo' the camp-meetin's."

"I don't keer 'bout the harm, it's yo' I'm feerd fo'."

"Don't yo' worry 'bout me. I kin give 'em the slip. I'll be here tonight at ten o'clock if all the revenue officers in the country are after me. I'll come down here by the big chistnut an' whistle. What shall I whistle, anyhow, so yo' kin know it's me?"

"'Nelly Bly,' course," she whispered, blushing.

"An' yo'll come to me, sho?"

Her only answer was to draw his big, blonde head down to her and hold it against her cheek.

"I must go now, Allen, mammy will be lookin' fo' me soon." And she slipped from his arms and ran swiftly up the steep path toward the house.

Allen watched her disappear among the pines, and then threw himself down beside a laurel bush and clasping his hands under his head began to whistle softly. It takes a man of the South to do nothing perfectly, and Allen was as skilled in that art as were any of the F. F. V.'s who wore broadcloth. It was the kind of a summer morning to encourage idleness. Behind him were the sleepy pine woods, the slaty ground beneath them strewn red with slippery needles. Around him the laurels were just blushing into bloom. Here and there rose tall chestnut trees with the red sumach growing under them. Down in the valley lay the fields of wheat and corn, and among them the creek wound between its willow-grown banks. Across it was the old, black, creaking foot-bridge which had neither props nor piles, but was swung from the arms of a great sycamore tree. The reapers were at work in the wheat fields; the mowers swinging their cradles and the binders following close behind. Along the fences companies of bare-footed children were picking berries. On the bridge a lank youth sat patiently fishing in the stream where no fish had been caught for years. Allen watched them all until a passing cloud made the valley dark, then his eyes wandered to where the Blue Ridge lay against the sky, faint and hazy as the mountains of Beulah Land.

Allen still whistled lazily as he lay there. He was noted for his whistling. He was naturally musical, but on Limber Ridge the mouth organ and jews harp are considered the only thoroughly respectable instruments, and he preferred whistling to either. He could whistle anything from "Champagne Charley" to the opera airs he heard the city folks playing in the summer at the Springs. There was a marvelous sweet and mellow quality about that chirp of his, like the softened fire of the famous apple brandy he made from his little still in the mountains. The mountain folk always said they could tell Allen Poole's whiskey or his whistle wherever they found them. Beyond his music and his brandy and his good heart there was not much to Allen. He was never known to do any work except to pour apples into his still and drink freely of the honied fire which came out of the worm. As he said himself, between his still and the women and the revenue officers he had scarcely time to eat. The officers of the law hated him because they knew him to be an incorrigible "moonshiner," yet never could prove anything against him. The women all loved him because he was so big and blue-eyed and so thoroughly a man. He was happy enough and good natured enough; still it was no wonder that old Sargent did not want his daughter to marry the young man, for making whiskey on one's own hook and one's own authority is not a particularly safe or honorable business. But the girl was willing and Allen was very much so, and they had taken matters into their own hands and meant to elope that night. Allen was not thinking very seriously about it. He never took anything very seriously. He was just thinking that the dim blueness of the mountains over there was like her eyes when they had tears in them, and wondering why it was that when he was near her he always felt such an irresistible impulse to pick her up and carry her. When he began to get hungry he arose and yawned and began to stroll lazily down the mountain side, his heavy boot heels cutting through the green moss and craunching the soft slate rock underneath, whistling "My Bonnie Lies Over the Ocean" as he went.

II

It was about nine o'clock that evening when Allen crossed the old foot-bridge and started down the creek lane toward the mountain. He kept carefully in the shadow of the trees, for he had good cause to fear that night. There was a little frown on his face, for when he got home at noon he found his shanty in confusion; the revenue officer had been there and had knocked the still to pieces and chopped through the copper worm with an ax. Even the winning of his sweetheart could not quite make up for the loss of his still.

The creek lane, hedged on either side by tall maples, ran by a little graveyard. It was one of those little family burying grounds so common in the south, with its white headstones, tall, dark cedars, and masses of rosemary, myrtle and rue. Allen, like all the rest of the Mountain men, was superstitious, and ordinarily he would have hurried past, not anxious to be near a graveyard after night. But now he went up and leaned on the stone fence, and looked over at the headstones which marked the sunken graves. Somehow he felt more pity for them than fear of them that night. That night of all nights he was so rich in hope and love, lord of so much life, that he wished he could give a little of it to those poor, cold, stiff fellows shut up down there in their narrow boxes with prosy scripture text on their coffin plates, give a little of the warm blood that tingled through his own veins, just enough, perhaps, to make them dream of love. He sighed as he went on, leaving them to their sleep and their understanding.

He turned aside into a road that ran between the fields. The red harvest moon was just rising; on one side of the road the tall, green corn stood whispering and rustling in the moonrise, sighing fretfully now and then when the hot south breeze swept over it. On the other side lay the long fields of wheat where the poppies drooped among the stubble and the sheaves gave out that odor of indescribable richness and ripeness which newly cut grain always has. From the wavering line of locust trees the song of the whip-poor-will throbbed through the summer night. Above it all were the dark pine-clad mountains, in the repose and strength of their immortality.

The man's heart went out to the heart of the night, and he broke out into such a passion of music as made the singer in the locusts sick with melody. As he went on, whistling, he suddenly heard the beat of a horse's feet upon the road, and silenced his chirping.

"Like as not it's them government chaps," he muttered.

A cart came around the bend in the road, Allen saw two men in it and turned aside into the corn field, but he was too late, they had already seen him. One of them raised his pistol and shouted, "Halt!"

But Allen knew too well who they were, and did not stop. The officer called again, and then fired. Allen stopped a moment, clutched the air above his head, cried "My Gawd!" and then ran wildly on. The officer was not a bad fellow, only young and a little hot headed, and that agonized cry took all the nerve out of him, and he drove back toward town to get the ringing sound out of his ears.

Allen ran on, plunging and floundering through the corn like some wounded animal, tearing up stalk after stalk as he clutched it in his pain. When he reached the foot of the mountain he started up, dragging himself on by the laurel and sumach bushes. When his legs failed him he used his hands and knees, wrenching the vines and saplings to pieces and tearing the flesh on [his] hands as he pulled himself up. At last he reached the chestnut tree and sank with a groan upon the ground. But he rose again muttering to himself: "She'd be skeered to death if she seen me layin' down."

He braced himself against the tree, all blood and dirt as he was, his wedding clothes torn and soiled, and drawing his white lips up in the old way he whistled for his love:

> ·Nelly Bly shuts her eye when she goes to sleep,
> But in the morning when she wakes then they begin to peep.
> Hi Nelly! Ho Nelly! listen unto me,
> I'll sing for you, I'll play for you a charming melody.

He had not long to wait. She came softly through the black pines, holding her white dress up carefully from the dewy grass, with the moonlight all about her in a halo, like a little Madonna of the hills. She slipped up to him and leaned her cheek upon his breast.

"Allen, my own boy! Why yo' all wet, Oh it's blood! it's blood! have they hurt yo' honey, have they hurt yo'?"

He sank to the ground, saying gently, "I'm afeerd they've done fo' me this time, sweetheart. It's them damned revenue men."

"Let me call Pap, Allen, he'll go fo' the doctor, let me go, Allen, please."

"No, yo' shan't leave me. It ain't fo' many minutes, a doctor won't do no good. Stay with me Nell, stay with me, I'm afeerd to be alone."

She sat down and drew his head on her knee and leaned her face down to his.

"Take keer, darlin', yo' goin' to git yo' dress all bloody, yo' nice new frock what yo' goin' to wear to the Bethel picnic."

"Oh Allen! there ain't no Bethel picnic no more, nor nothin' but yo'. Oh my boy! my boy!" and she rocked herself over him as a mother does over a little baby that is in pain.

"It's mighty hard to lose yo', Nell, but maybe it's best. Maybe if I'd lived an' married yo' I might a' got old an' cross an' used to yo' some day, an' might a' swore at you an' beat yo' like the mountain folks round here does, an' I'd sooner die now, while I love yo' better'n anything else in Gawd's world. Yo' like me, too, don't yo' dear?"

"Oh Allen! more'n I ever knowed, more'n I ever knowed."

"Don't take on so, honey. Yo' will stay with me tonight? Yo' won't leave me even after I'm dead? Yo' know we was to be married an' I was to have yo' tonight. Yo' won't go way an' leave me the first night an' the last, will yo' Nell?"

The girl calmed herself for his sake and answered him steadily: "No, Allen. I will set an' hold yo' till mornin' comes. I won't leave yo'."

"Thank yo'. Never mind, dear, the best thing in livin' is to love hard, and the best thing in dyin' is to die game; an' I've done my best at both. Never mind."

He drew a long sigh, and the rest was silence.

APPENDIX III

From

The Roman and the Teuton

The following selection from Charles Kingsley's The Roman and the Teuton: A
Series of Lectures Delivered Before the University of Cambridge *(London and New
York: Macmillan and Co., 1891), pages 1–5, is given here as a point of reference for both
the statements in* The Kingdom of Art *and the fiction Willa Cather wrote throughout
her career. As the source of one of the epigraphs for* The Troll Garden, *Kingsley's
parable has unusual significance; but it is no less revealing when taken in conjunction with
Willa Cather's numerous references to Rome, the Teutonic tribes, the Goths, the Barbarians,
the movements of history in nations or families, the psychological contrasts of innocence
and experience. See particularly the critical statements in "A Sense of History," pages
220 ff.; "Christina Rossetti," pages 346 ff.; and the discussion on pages 93 ff.*

THE FOREST CHILDREN

I wish in this first lecture to give you some general conception of the causes which
urged our Teutonic race to attack and destroy Rome. I shall take for this one
lecture no special text-book: but suppose you all to be acquainted with the
Germania of Tacitus, and with the 9th Chapter of Gibbon. And I shall begin, if
you will allow me, by a parable, a myth, a saga, such as the men of whom I am
going to tell you loved; and if it seem to any of you childish, bear in mind that what
is childish need not therefore be shallow. I know that it is not history. These lectures
will not be, in the popular sense, history at all. But I beg you to bear in mind that
I am not here to teach you history. No man can do that. I am here to teach you
how to teach yourselves history. I will give you the scaffolding as well as I can; you
must build the house.

Fancy to yourself a great Troll-garden, such as our forefathers dreamed of
often fifteen hundred years ago;—a fairy palace, with a fairy garden; and all around
the primaeval wood. Inside the Trolls dwell, cunning and wicked, watching their
fairy treasures, working at their magic forges, making and making always things

rare and strange; and outside, the forest is full of children; such children as the world had never seen before, but children still: children in frankness, and purity, and affectionateness, and tenderness of conscience, and devout awe of the unseen; and children too in fancy, and silliness, and ignorance, and caprice, and jealousy, and quarrelsomeness, and love of excitement and adventure, and the mere sport of overflowing animal health. They play unharmed among the forest beasts, and conquer them in their play; but the forest is too dull and too poor for them; and they wander to the walls of the Troll-garden and wonder what is inside. One can conceive easily for oneself what from that moment would begin to happen. Some of the more adventurous clamber in. Some, too, the Trolls steal and carry off into their palace. Most never return: but here and there one escapes out again, and tells how the Trolls killed all his comrades: but tells too, of the wonders he has seen inside, of shoes of swiftness, and swords of sharpness, and caps of darkness; of charmed harps, charmed jewels, and above all of the charmed wine: and after all, the Trolls were very kind to him—see what fine clothes they have given him—and he struts about awhile among his companions; and then returns, and not alone. The Trolls have bewitched him, as they will bewitch more. So the fame of the Troll-garden spreads; and more and more steal in, boys and maidens, and tempt their comrades over the wall, and tell of the jewels, and the dresses, and the wine, the joyous maddening wine, which equals men with gods; and forget to tell how the Trolls have bought them, soul as well as body, and taught them to be vain, and lustful, and slavish; and tempted them, too often, to sins which have no name.

But their better nature flashes out at times. They will not be the slaves and brutes in human form, which the evil Trolls would have them; and they rebel, and escape, and tell of the horrors of that fair foul place. And then arises a noble indignation, and war between the Trolls and the forest-children. But still the Trolls can tempt and bribe the greedier or the more vain; and still the wonders inside haunt their minds; till it becomes a fixed idea among them all, to conquer the garden for themselves and bedizen themselves in the fine clothes, and drink their fill of the wine. Again and again they break in: but the Trolls drive them out, rebuild their walls, keep off those outside by those whom they hold enslaved within; till the boys grow to be youths, and the youths men: and still the Troll-garden is not conquered, and still it shall be. And the Trolls have grown old and weak, and their walls are crumbling away. Perhaps they may succeed this time—perhaps next.

And at last they do succeed—the fairy walls are breached, the fairy palace stormed—and the Trolls are crouching at their feet, and now all will be theirs, gold, jewels, dresses, arms, all that the Troll possesses—except his cunning.

For as each struggles into the charmed ground, the spell of the place falls on him. He drinks the wine and it maddens him. He fills his arms with precious trumpery, and another snatches it from his grasp. Each envies the youth before him, each cries—Why had I not the luck to enter first? And the Trolls set them against each other, and split them into parties each mad with excitement, and jealousy, and wine, till, they scarce know how, each falls upon his fellow, and all upon those who are crowding in from the forest, and they fight and fight, up and down the palace halls, till their triumph has become a very feast of the Lapithae, and the Trolls look on, and laugh a wicked laugh, as they tar them on to the unnatural fight, till the gardens are all trampled, the finery torn, the halls dismantled, and each pavement slippery with brothers' blood. And then, when the wine is gone out of them, the survivors come to their senses, and stare shamefully and sadly round. What an ugly, desolate, tottering ruin the fairy palace has become! Have they spoilt it themselves? or have the Trolls bewitched it? And all the fairy treasure —what has become of it? no man knows. Have they thrown it away in their quarrel? have the cunningest hidden it? have the Trolls flown away with it, to the fairy land beyond the Eastern mountains? who can tell? Nothing is left but recrimination and remorse. And they wander back again into the forest, away from the doleful ruin, carrion-strewn, to sulk each apart over some petty spoil which he has saved from the general wreck, hating and dreading each the sound of his neighbour's footstep.

What will become of the forest children, unless some kind saint or hermit comes among them, to bind them in the holy bonds of brotherhood and law?

This is my saga, gentlemen; and it is a true one withal. For it is neither more nor less than the story of the Teutonic tribes, and how they overthrew the Empire of Rome.

APPENDIX IV

Early Interviews

After Willa Cather became a public figure, she rarely talked about the art of writing and her own relationship to it. In later years, published interviews and articles about the increasingly famous novelist continued to use certain of her biographical and critical state-ments but with diminishing context and personal detail. The following early interviews—both relatively unknown—are therefore invaluable for their frank, detailed, and responsive personal comment on Willa Cather's work and art. More warmly and authentically than many later published statements—like the old game of Gossip, repetition and selection tended to distort the facts—they bring us the person of the working novelist who twenty years earlier spoke so freely in the Kingdom of Art. The first interview, published in the Philadelphia Record with a New York dateline, took place in the summer of 1913, just after the warm critical reception of O Pioneers!; *it may be called the "mother lode" from which countless later stories on Miss Cather were derived. It is reprinted here from a clipping kept by the Cather family. The second interview (reprinted in part) occurred in Lincoln in the fall of 1915, after the appearance of* The Song of the Lark.*

Janus-like, the 1913 and 1915 interviews look both ways. Though memory has fused and foreshortened some details (the authors Willa Cather remembers liking best, for instance, were more properly from the period following 1896), the continuity of her ideas about art is clearly shown. Those familiar with the 1893–1896 articles will recognize the reiterated principles of feeling, sincerity, the personal relationship, simplification, indi-viduality; themes of the artist's untiring effort and devotion to his art, the loss of the woman in the artist, the beauty of language and the individuality of speech, the distance between the artist and the near-artist, the futility of reform; the interest in national character, the sense of the old world in the new; the importance of a "good ear," of subject matter found in human life, of both observation and sympathy. For a biographical reference, we have Willa Cather's plain statement of her newspaper work "in college and immediately after graduation." She has also made some choices: Dumas' kind of writing ("the games that live forever") is not forgotten; but Willa Cather, too, has "recognized her limitations"—or her genius—and knows the kind of writing she must do: She has chosen a more stripped, exacting style and submerged some of the color—in part, the "purple flurry" that maturity sees in youth. Joining past and future, her remarkable description in 1913 re-creates that first ride into Nebraska thirty years before: the feeling of a land that erased personality, the motif of the larks' "splendid notes," and the personal experience of nostalgia and courage that throughout her work became transmuted into many forms. And what she said of Sarah Orne Jewett in 1913 may still be Willa Cather's best description of her own way of working—to try out character and themes over and over until they are realized on the page, "that honest endeavor to tell truly the thing that haunts the mind."

In another kind of continuity, the interviews also remind us that for twenty years before she was a novelist, and for some years after, Willa Cather was an exceedingly efficient, knowledgeable, and successful woman-journalist and woman-editor in a highly competitive publishing world.

WILLA CATHER TALKS OF WORK

Special Correspondence of the [Philadelphia] Record   New York, August 9 [1913]

Miss Willa Sibert Cather, whose new novel, *O Pioneers!* has just placed her in the foremost rank of American novelists, began to do newspaper work on the *Nebraska State Journal* while she was still an undergraduate in the University at Lincoln. From Lincoln Miss Cather came East as far as Pittsburgh, to go on the regular staff of the *Daily Leader*.

Leaving the newspaper life, while still very young, Miss Cather then accepted a position to teach, first Latin and afterward English, in the Pittsburgh High School. It was during this time that she wrote the verse and short stories which secured her the post of associate editor of *McClure's Magazine* and took her finally to New York.

Miss Cather's new novel, *O Pioneers!* is of special interest to Philadelphians— this magnificently grave and simple and poetic picture of early days on the uplands of Nebraska—if only for the strong influence of Whitman which the writing shows. There is the wise, clean-earthed philosophy of Whitman in the selection of the book's theme, too, and Miss Cather quotes her title direct from our superb white-bearded old lover of the world.

Though Miss Cather no longer spends all her time in the McClure Publications offices, on Fourth Avenue (she was managing editor of *McClure's Magazine* for four years), she is still connected with that publishing house; and I was eager to have her opinion of modern short-story writing in the United States.

"My own favorite American writers?" said Miss Cather. "Well, I've never changed in that respect much since I was a girl at school. There were three great ones I liked best then and still like—Mark Twain, Henry James and Sarah Orne Jewett."

"You must have read a lot of work by new people while you were editor of *McClure's*?" I suggested.

"Yes," smiled Miss Cather, "I suppose I read a good many thousand stories, some good and some bad."

"And what seemed to you to be the trouble with most of the mediocre ones?"

"Simply this," replied Miss Cather unhesitatingly, "that the writer had not felt them strongly enough before he wrote them. Like everything else in the world, this is a question of—how far. No one person knows much more about writing than another. I expect that when people think they know anything about it, then their case is hopeless. But in my course of reading thousands of stories, I was strengthened in the conclusion that I had come to before; that nothing was really worth while that did not cut pretty deep, and that the main thing always was to be honest.

"So many of the stories that come into magazines are a combination of the genuine and the fake. A writer has really a story to tell, and he has evidently tried to make it fit the outline of some story that he admires, or that he believes has been successful. You can not always tell just where a writer stops being himself and begins to attitudinize in a story, but when you finish it, you have a feeling that he has been trying to fool himself. I think a writer ought to get into his copy as he really is, in his everyday clothes. His readers are thrown with him in a personal relation, just as if they were traveling with him; and if he is not sincere, there is no possibility of any sort of comradeship.

"I think many story writers try to multiply their ideas instead of trying to simplify them; that is, they often try to make a story out of every idea they have, to get returns on every situation that suggests itself. And, as a result, their work is entertaining, journalistic and thin. Whether it is a pianist, or a singer, or a writer, art ought to simplify—that seems to me to be the whole process. Millet did hundreds of sketches of peasants sowing grain, some of them very complicated, but when he came to paint 'The Sower,' the composition is so simple that it seems inevitable. It was probably the hundred sketches that went before that made the picture what it finally became—a process of simplifying all the time—of sacrificing many things that were in themselves interesting and pleasing, and all the time getting closer to the one thing—It.

"Of course I am talking now about the kind of writing that interests me most —I take it that is what you want me to do. There is *The Three Guardsmen* kind, which is, perhaps, quite as fine in its way, where the whole zest of the thing is the rapid multiplication of fancies and devices. That kind of writing, at its best, is like fencing and dancing, the games that live forever. But the other kind, the kind that I am talking about, is pretty well summed up in a letter of Miss Sarah Orne Jewett's, that I found among some of her papers in South Berwick after her death:

"'Ah, it is things like that, which haunt the mind for years, and at last write themselves down, that belong, whether little or great, to literature.'

"It is that kind of honesty, that earnest endeavor to tell truly the thing that haunts the mind, that I love in Miss Jewett's own work. Reading her books from the beginning one finds that often she tried a character or a theme over and over, first in one story and then in another, before she at last realized it completely on the page. That wonderful story, 'Martha's Lady,' for instance, was hinted at and felt for in several of her earlier stories. And so was the old woman in 'The Queen's Twin.'

"I dedicated my novel *O Pioneers!* to Miss Jewett because I had talked over some of the characters in it with her one day at Manchester, and in this book I tried to tell the story of the people as truthfully and simply as if I were telling it to her by word of mouth."

"How did you come to write about that flat part of the prairie west, Miss Cather, which not many people find interesting?"

"I happen to be interested in the Scandinavian and Bohemian pioneers of Nebraska," said the young novelist, "because I lived among them when I was a child. When I was eight years old, my father moved from the Shenandoah Valley in Virginia to that Western country. My grandfather and grandmother had moved to Nebraska eight years before we left Virginia; they were among the real pioneers.

"But it was still wild enough and bleak enough when we got there. My grandfather's homestead was about eighteen miles from Red Cloud—a little town on the Burlington, named after the old Indian chief who used to come hunting in that country, and who buried his daughter on the top of one of the river bluffs south of the town. Her grave had been looted for her rich furs and beadwork long before my family went West, but we children used to find arrowheads there and some of the bones of her pony that had been strangled above her grave."

"What was the country like when you got there?"

"I shall never forget my introduction to it. We drove out from Red Cloud to my grandfather's homestead one day in April. I was sitting on the hay in the bottom of a Studebaker wagon, holding on to the side of the wagon box to steady myself—the roads were mostly faint trails over the bunch grass in those days. The land was open range and there was almost no fencing. As we drove further and further out into the country, I felt a good deal as if we had come to the end of everything—it was a kind of erasure of personality.

"I would not know how much a child's life is bound up in the woods and hills and meadows around it, if I had not been jerked away from all these and thrown out into a country as bare as a piece of sheet iron. I had heard my father say you had to show grit in a new country, and I would have got on pretty well during that ride if it had not been for the larks. Every now and then one flew up and sang a few splendid notes and dropped down into the grass again. That reminded me of something—I don't know what, but my one purpose in life just then was not to cry, and every time they did it, I thought I should go under.

"For the first week or two on the homestead I had that kind of contraction of the stomach which comes from homesickness. I didn't like canned things anyhow, and I made an agreement with myself that I would not eat much until I got back to Virginia and could get some fresh mutton. I think the first thing that interested me after I got to the homestead was a heavy hickory cane with a steel tip which my grandmother always carried with her when she went to the garden to kill rattlesnakes. She had killed a good many snakes with it, and that seemed to argue that life might not be so flat as it looked there.

"We had very few American neighbors—they were mostly Swedes and Danes, Norwegians and Bohemians. I liked them from the first and they made up for what I missed in the country. I particularly liked the old women, they understood my homesickness and were kind to me. I had met 'traveled' people in Virginia and in Washington, but these old women on the farms were the first people who ever gave me the real feeling of an older world across the sea. Even when they spoke very little English, the old women somehow managed to tell me a great many stories about the old country. They talk more freely to a child than to grown people, and I always felt as if every word they said to me counted for twenty.

"I have never found any intellectual excitement any more intense than I used to feel when I spent a morning with one of those old women at her baking or butter making. I used to ride home in the most unreasonable state of excitement; I always felt as if they told me so much more than they said—as if I had actually got inside another person's skin. If one begins that early, it is the story of the man-eating tiger over again—no other adventure ever carries one quite so far."

"Some of your early short stories were about these people, were they not?"

"Yes, but most of them were poor. It is always hard to write about the things that are near to your heart, from a kind of instinct of self-protection you distort them and disguise them. Those stories were so poor that they discouraged me. I decided that I wouldn't write any more about the country and people for which I had such personal feeling.

"Then I had the good fortune to meet Sarah Orne Jewett, who had read all of my early stories and had very clear and definite opinions about them and about where my work fell short. She said, 'Write it as it is, don't try to make it like this or that. You can't do it in anybody else's way—you will have to make a way of your own. If the way happens to be new, don't let that frighten you. Don't try to write the kind of short story that this or that magazine wants—write the truth, and let them take it or leave it.'

"I was not at all sure, however, that my feeling about the Western country and my Scandinavian friends was the truth—I thought perhaps that going among them so young I had a romantic personal feeling about them. I thought that Americans in general must see only the humorous side of the Scandinavian—the side often presented in vaudeville dialect sketches—because nobody had ever tried to write about the Swedish settlers seriously.

"What has pleased me most in the cordial reception the West has given this new book of mine, is that the reviewers in all those Western States say the thing seems to them true to the country and the people. That is a great satisfaction. The reviews have concerned themselves a good deal more with the subject matter of the story than with my way of telling it, and I am glad of that. I care a lot more about the country and the people than I care about my own way of writing or anybody else's way of writing."

F. H.

THE VISION OF A
SUCCESSFUL FICTION WRITER

by ETHEL M. HOCKETT

[*Lincoln Daily Star*]   [October 24, 1915]

For the benefit of the many young people who have literary ambitions and to whom the pinnacle of success attained by this Nebraska novelist appears as the most desirable thing to be gained in the world, Miss [Willa] Cather was persuaded to give the time from her busy hours in Lincoln of living over school days with old acquaintances, to give a number of valuable suggestions from her rich fund of experiences.

"The business of writing is a personal problem and must be worked out in an individual way," said Miss Cather. "A great many people ambitious to write, fall by the wayside, but if they are the discourageable kind it is better that they drop out. No beginner knows what he has to go through with or he would never begin.

"When I was in college and immediately after graduation, I did newspaper work. I found that newspaper writing did a great deal of good for me in working off the purple flurry of my early writing. Every young writer has to work off the 'fine writing' stage. It was a painful period in which I overcame my florid, exaggerated, foamy-at-the-mouth, adjective-spree period. I knew even then it was a crime to write like I did, but I had to get the adjectives and the youthful fervor worked off.

"I believe every young writer must write whole books of extravagant language to get it out. It is agony to be smothered in your own florescence, and to be forced to dump great carloads of your posies out in the road before you find one posy that will fit in the right place. But it must be done, just as a great singer must sacrifice so many lovely lyrical things in herself to be a great interpreter."

Miss Cather is pre-eminently qualified to give advice to young writers, not only from her own experiences in traveling the road which led her to literary success, but because she has had opportunities to study the writings of others from the viewpoint of a buyer.

After she had worked on Lincoln newspapers, one of which was edited by Mrs. Sarah Harris Dorris whom she visited last week, Miss Cather went to Pittsburgh where she worked on a newspaper for several years. She tired of newspaper work and became the head of the English department in the Allegheny high school in Pittsburgh where she remained three years. It was while teaching that she wrote the verses which appeared in the book *April Twilights*, and the stories which made up the book *The Troll Garden*. These stories and verses were published by McClure's, most of them appearing in the *McClure's* magazine. A year after their publication, Mr. McClure went to Pittsburgh and offered Miss Cather a position on his magazine which she accepted. Exceptional opportunities were shortly afterward afforded Miss Cather, as Miss Ida Tarbell, Mr. Philipps, Mr. Baker and several other prominent writers, left *McClure's* and bought the *American* magazine.

Within two years, therefore, Miss Cather was managing editor of *McClure's*. She held that position for six years.[1] Although life as managing editor was stimulating, affording Miss Cather opportunity for travel abroad and in this country, she could do no creative work, so left in order to produce the stories pent up in her mind. She says the material used in her stories was all collected before she was twenty years old.

"Aside from the fact that my duties occupied much of my time, when you are buying other writers' stuff, it simply isn't the graceful thing to do to do any writing yourself," she said.

Leaving *McClure's*, Miss Cather moved to a suburb of New York and wrote *Alexander's Bridge* and *The Bohemian Girl*. She went to Arizona for the summer and returned to New York to write *O Pioneers!*

Miss Cather's books all have western settings, in Nebraska, Colorado and Arizona, and she spends part of each year in the west reviewing the early impressions and stories which go to make up her books.

"No one without a good ear can write good fiction," was a surprising statement made by Miss Cather. "It is an essential to good writing to be sensitive to the beauty of language and speech, and to be able to catch the tone, phrase, length of syllables, enunciation, etc., of persons of all types that cross a writer's path. The successful writer must also be sensitive to accomplishment in others.

"Writers have such hard times if they just have rules and theories. Things that make for integrity in writing are quite as unnameable as the things that make the difference between an artist and a near-artist in music. And it is the longest distance in the world between the artist and the near-artist.

"It is up to the writer and no one else. He must spend thousands of uncounted hours at work. He must strive untiringly while others eat and sleep and play. Some people are more gifted than others, but it takes brains in the most gifted to make a success. Writing has to be gone at like any other trade. One trouble is that people aren't honest with themselves; they are awfully unfrank about sizing themselves up. They have such queer ways of keeping half-done things stored by and inconsistently saying to themselves that they will finish them after a while, and never admitting they shrink from that work because they are not qualified for it.

"One trouble with young writers is that they imitate too much, often unconsciously," said Miss Cather. "Ninety-nine out of every hundred stories received by magazines are imitations of some former success. This is a natural mistake for young people to make. The girl or boy of 24 or 25 is not strong enough to digest experiences in the raw, therefore they take them pre-digested from things they read. That is why young writing does not as a rule amount to much. These young writers can sometimes give cries of pain and of rapture and even the cry from a baby sometimes moves.

"Young writers must care vitally, fiercely, absurdly about the trickery and the arrangement of words, the beauty and power of phrases. But they must go on and on until they get more out of life itself than out of anything written. When a writer reaches the stage where a tramp on a rail pile in Arizona fills him with

1. This biographical outline is generally true, but some details have been omitted.

as many thrills as the greatest novel ever written, he has well begun on his career.

"William Jones once expressed this idea well when he told me great minds like Balzac or Shakespeare got thousands and thousands more of distinct impressions and mental pictures in every single day of life than the average man got in all his life.

"I can remember when Kipling's *Jungle Tales* meant more to me than a tragic wreck or big fire in the city. But I passed through that stage. If I hadn't again grasped the thrills of life, I would have been too literary and academic to ever write anything worth while.

"There are a great many young people who like good literature and go to work on a magazine or newspaper with the idea of reforming it and showing it what to print. It is all right to have ideas, but they should be kept locked up, for the beginner should do the things in his employer's way. If his ideas are worth anything, they will come out untarnished; if they are not, they will get mixed up with crooked things and he will be disillusioned and soured.

"I have seen a great many western girls and boys come to New York and make a living around magazines and newspapers, and many rise to very good positions. They must be wide awake, adaptable and not afraid to work. A beginner can learn a lot about magazine requirements and style by proof-reading, or doing other jobs other than writing the leading editorials. Every magazine has its individual style.

"Most people have the idea that magazines are like universities—existing to pass on the merits of productions. They think if stories and articles are accepted, it is an honor, and if they are refused, it is a disgrace. They do not realize the magazine is in the business of buying and selling.

"The truth is that many good stories are turned down every day in a magazine office. If the editor has twenty-five children's stories in the safe and a twenty-sixth good children's story comes in with one poor adventure story, he must buy the poor adventure story and return the good children's story. It is just like being overstocked in anything else. The magazine editor must have variety, and it is sometimes maddening the way the stories come in in flocks of like kinds.

"The young writer must learn to deal with subjects he really knows about. No matter how commonplace a subject may be, if it is one with which the author is thoroughly familiar it makes a much better story than the purely imaginational.

"Imagination, which is a quality writers must have, does not mean the ability to weave pretty stories out of nothing. In the right sense, imagination is a response to what is going on—a sensitiveness to which outside things appeal. It is a composition of sympathy and observation."

Miss Cather makes the comparison between learning to write and learning to play the piano. If there is no talent to begin with, the struggler can never become an artist. But no matter what talent there is, the writer must spend hours and years of practice in writing just as the musician must drudge at his scales.

Miss Cather laughed merrily as she said that her old friends in Lincoln insist on dragging up what she pleased to call her "shady past," and reminding her of her rhetorical and reformative flights of her youth. It was recalled by one friend that she led the last cane rush in the university, that she wore her hair cropped short and a stiff hat and that the boys among whom she was very popular, called her "Billy." Miss Cather graduated from the University of Nebraska in 1895.

A Note on the Editing

✳   ✳   ✳

The texts of the newspaper articles reprinted in "Critical Statements" and Appendix I have been kept as close to the original printed versions as possible without perpetuating typographical errors, misspellings, and garbled sentences. In a sense, for newspaper writing of this kind there is no primary text, proofread by the author, and demanding exact reprinting. Possibly Willa Cather checked the articles in the *Courier* during the time she was an editor, or she might have seen the Sunday columns in the *Journal* when they were set, but it is unlikely that she could have proofread the *Journal* reviews. Printing errors did occur, perhaps more often in the Lincoln newspapers of the 1890's than in contemporary papers (the first linotype did not arrive at the *Evening News* until 1895, and the papers were often at the mercy of itinerant typesetters, or "tramp printers"). The quality of the typesetting in the Lincoln newspapers also varied greatly during that time. When Willa Cather's first essays appeared in the *Journal* in 1891, printing errors occasionally reached a surrealist level, as the examples from "Shakespeare and Hamlet" given below will illustrate. In the 1893–1896 period, however, the printing was generally clean, with only occasional difficulties.

The articles in this collection have been lightly edited, primarily to remove typographical errors or their resulting confusions. Misspelled words have been corrected. The spelling of proper names and of words which appear frequently ("Shakespearean" and "theatre") have been generally regularized. When omissions have been noted, words supplied by the editor are enclosed in brackets. When an error is suspected in the primary text, a variant reading with a question mark follows, enclosed in brackets. When there is a reasonable doubt as to whether a detail is printer's chance or author's intention, it has usually been left unchanged. For example, a phrase in the review of *Faust* (*Courier*, September 14, 1895) appears as "restive Fourth of July." Though "festive" would be more usual, there is no absolute reason to consider "restive" a typographical error and it should remain. Punctuation and usage are often individual matters in Willa Cather's newspaper writing, and there has been no attempt to regularize them or to make them consistent throughout. Some usages are printer's style. The *Journal* in the 1890's followed "short punctuation" (omitted commas), "down style" (capitals only for proper names), and "short spelling" (see *Printing Comes to Lincoln*, Lincoln: Woodruff Printing Co., 1940, p. 42). But on the whole there are habits of marking that seem to be more personally related to sentence rhythms, meaning, and emphasis; punctuation has therefore been kept as irregular and casual as it was. In a few instances, commas or semicolons have been adjusted when the sentence would be otherwise difficult or confusing to read. Quotations have been regularized according to standard texts when it is clear that the errors have no personal significance: for example, errors might suggest that the passage was quoted from memory, or slight word changes might reveal a particular turn of thought.

"Shakespeare and Hamlet" (Appendix I) has been edited more thoroughly than other selections in the book, for it had an extraordinary number of typographical errors. As a matter of historical, literary, and journalistic interest, here is a record of some of the lines as Willa Cather first read them in print in the *Journal*, Nov. 1 and 8, 1891.

Page 427, ll. 10–11. *The line intended to read:* His, "Oh, Soul! a beast that wants discourse of reason would have mourned longer," is no rhetorical flourish *appeared as:* His, "Oh Soel! a heart that wants would have mourned longer." Discourse of reason, is no rethorical flourish.

Page 427, l. 15. *What should have been:* his replies to fawning, scraping Rosencrantz *appeared as:* his replies to Fauriny, scraping Rosencrantz.

Page 428, l. 7. *Intended:* "Though this be madness, yet there is method in't." *In print:* "Though this be madmen, yet their method isn't."

Page 429–430. *Intended:*
> The soul of Adonais like a star
> Beacons from the abode where the Eternal are!
And the Thracians say, "We put it there."
> *In print:*
> The soul of Idonair like a star
> Beacons from the abode where the eternal are;
> And the Thracians say, "We put it there."

Page 431, l. 9. *Intended:* yet all that is I see. *In print:* yet all that is free.

Page 433, ll. 13–16. *Intended:* Give me that man / That is not passion's slave and I will wear him / In my heart's core, ay, in my heart of heart, / As I do thee. *In print:* Give me that man who is not passion's slave and / I will in my heart's care, ay, in my heart of / heart, ween him I do thee.

Also: tha *for* the, moom *for* moon, Poloniur *for* Polonius, attach *for* attack, mark *for* mask, ended *for* bended, stand *for* stayed, touch *for* task.

Bibliographical Note

Willa Cather's miscellaneous publications during her early Nebraska years (to June, 1896) include both signed and unsigned items in almost all categories: fiction, poetry, articles, news stories and notes, editorials and comment, sketches, reviews, essays. A study of her critical attitudes and statements might involve anything identifiable as hers; however, I have restricted my material to a core of semi-official newspaper writing: drama reviews and weekly columns published in the Lincoln papers after 1893. The bulk of the material written from the fall of 1893 to the end of June, 1895, has long been identified as Willa Cather's, even though most of it was unsigned. I have been able to locate and identify some 120 additional items, including more than 75 published between July 7, 1895, and June 14, 1896 (see below). As I have determined the material for *The Kingdom of Art*, it includes Willa Cather's critical and personal writing selected from (1) reviews of plays and other entertainment in the *Nebraska State Journal* (hereafter cited as *Journal*) and the *Courier*; and (2) unsigned weekly columns of theatrical, literary, and personal comment in the *Journal* and the *Courier*: "One Way of Putting It," "Between the Acts," and "With Plays and Players" (1893–1894), "Utterly Irrelevant" and "As You Like It" (1894–1895), and "The Passing Show" (from July, 1895). I have made incidental use of unsigned fiction, verse, and editorial or feature matter from publications (*Lasso, Hesperian, Courier*) with which Willa Cather had an official connection.

For the purposes of this book, I have been concerned not with compiling a complete bibliography of Willa Cather's writing during 1893–1896, but with giving a checklist that shows as accurately as possible the extent and nature of her critical statements, especially those on art and the artist. The principal task, of course, is to identify unsigned material. In the case of Willa Cather, the work of checking unsigned pieces is infinitely more complicated than with other writers, for she wrote in quantities that now begin to resemble the production of a Dumas *père*. On the other hand, the task is much simpler, for her own statements and those of her contemporaries, as well as the announcements of the papers themselves, provide us public directives. If a paper says that Willa Cather will contribute her weekly columns as of a certain date, when they appear we have no choice but to believe that she wrote them. Or if a paper says that Willa Cather *is* its drama critic (or *has been* for "more than two years," as the *Journal* stated in June, 1896), we can assume that she is (or has been) writing the drama criticism. The burden of proof is therefore the other way around: Show us why she is *not* the author of a piece, we might well say. These directives are fairly clear, at least by March, 1894 (see "Writer in Nebraska," and notes in the checklist below). Nevertheless, the items must also be examined individually and reasons determined for their attribution and inclusion. Here the very continuity of

Miss Cather's newspaper writing is an advantage. In some ten years of continuous writing, there are many signed pieces by which to test the unsigned. It was also her nature to link, repeat, and develop variations on a theme, so that in both style and content the total work is a unit. While the items included here have been checked independently, I have had the enormous help of the initial selections made by the late Flora Bullock, whose bibliography of Willa Cather's writing to 1895, though unpublished, has been indispensable for Cather scholars. Because I have changed and extended those listings, some account of the circumstances should be given.

Miss Bullock, a fellow-student of Willa Cather at the University of Nebraska in the 1890's, was asked by Benjamin D. Hitz in 1943 to compile a bibliography of Miss Cather's newspaper and other writing during her Lincoln years. Miss Bullock completed the work in late 1945. The annotated bibliography is in the Hitz collection of Cather material at the Newberry Library; a copy is on microfilm at the Nebraska State Historical Society. Miss Bullock described some of her findings in "Willa Cather, Essayist and Dramatic Critic: 1891–1895," in *Prairie Schooner* (Winter, 1949), and the story of her search is in her letters to Benjamin Hitz, also in the Newberry collection. Miss Bullock's bibliography is not complete, nor was it intended to be definitive. Her correspondence with Hitz shows that she researched the primary material in the newspapers with intelligence, care, sensitivity, even excitement. But she was then in her seventies and often delayed by illness, hot weather, the handling of heavy newspaper volumes; eventually she became eager to finish her task. We also learn from the letters that although Miss Bullock knew the general pattern of Willa Cather's newspaper writing during their student days, she did not remember the details. Her listing was therefore made exactly as any other scholar might attempt such a task—from the inside, proceeding from known attributions to related items. She began with the signed columns of "The Passing Show" which had appeared in the *Courier* from the fall of 1897 to early 1900. She also knew of items identified as Willa Cather's in a scrapbook kept by Will Owen Jones, managing editor of the *Journal*, presumably while he was teaching journalism at the University in 1894. (Though this book is not now available, the Jones identifications are listed in an unpublished portion of the M.A. thesis by James R. Shively, "Willa Cather's College Years" [University of Nebraska, 1949]; and at the University of Nebraska Library, in notes kept by the late Clara Craig, at one time reference librarian.) With these clear-cut identifications and the signed columns in the *Courier*, Miss Bullock worked out a system of cross-references and verifications both in style and in content. That there are omissions must also be recognized. Some are the results of timing. Miss Bullock did not remember exactly when Miss Cather began her dramatic criticism, and it was not until she was almost finished that a friend suggested the period when they had taken the journalism class taught by Jones. Miss Bullock placed this in the first semester of 1893–1894, but in actuality the course—for which both Miss Bullock and Miss Cather were enrolled—was given the second semester. Thus, the 1893 items were selected late in the work of compilation. Miss Bullock did overlook a signed review on December 14, 1893; and, though I begin with the date she established, I believe that the listings before 1894 are still incomplete. After January, 1895, the listings of reviews are extremely sketchy (one letter to Hitz notes that she lost some pages of her notes for 1895)—and this we find is in the period when Miss Cather was professionally established as "the *Journal* critic." For example, even though they are very characteristic in style and have cross-references with earlier established pieces (including one of Jones's identifications), reviews of *The Fencing Master* (Mar. 3, 1895) and *Our Flat* (May 14, 1895) are omitted. Passages from both reviews reappear in Miss Cather's later signed work. Moreover, Miss Bullock assumed incorrectly that all of the newspaper writing stopped with Willa Cather's graduation in 1895, or at least in the range of her task she did not check further. Her listing of items in 1893–1895 is therefore a remarkable beginning for the Cather bibliography, but—like the present collection—by no means an end.

In establishing the material for this book, I have continued the method used by Miss Bullock—checking for relationships with identified writing. (I have also studied signed work by other Lincoln writers of 1890 ff. to verify differences.) By now the break between June, 1895, and October, 1897, has been filled in, first by the noting of Willa Cather's signed columns of "The Passing Show" sent from Pittsburgh to the *Journal* from December 6, 1896, to the summer of 1897, and then by the recognition of play reviews and book notes signed "Sibert" in the Pittsburgh *Leader*, October, 1897, to 1900. These references were given by Harry Finestone in his unpublished doctoral dissertation, "Willa Cather's Apprenticeship" (University of Chicago, 1953) and by John P. Hinz in "Willa Cather in Pittsburgh," in the *New Colophon*, III (1950). ("Sibert" is established as Miss Cather's signature not only because she eventually used it as a middle name—Willa Sibert Cather—but because the *Leader* reviews and the columns of "The Passing Show" published at nearly the same time in Lincoln papers are closely related, sometimes carrying identical material.) There are, then, chains of repeated material beginning with the Lincoln writing before 1896, through the "Sibert" articles in the *Leader*, and into other work signed "Willa Cather." I have discovered further that the columns and reviews did continue in the Lincoln papers from June, 1895, to June, 1896, and also that Miss Cather published signed play reviews in the *Leader* as early as November, 1896 (see the checklist). The hitherto overlooked group of 1896–1897 *Leader* reviews, with much repeated material from the Lincoln reviews, has been particularly valuable in affirming authorship. In all, we have an uninterrupted flow of Cather material through the early years, signed and unsigned; a great, defined network of interrelated newspaper writing, with linkages and repetitions so numerous and complicated that it is impossible to do more than suggest the kinds of relationships.

In identifying the Cather material used in *The Kingdom of Art*, I have followed a rule of testing by three elements, all of which must be present: (1) *circumstance*—the writer must be at hand, in a logical position to be doing the work; (2) *style*; and (3) *reference*—the work must relate to other writing by direct statement ("As I said in . . ."), repetition, or a variation on the content. Examples:

(1) For all of the columns and reviews listed here there are numerous public statements, particularly in the newspapers, to affirm that during the period in which they appeared Miss Cather was identified as the author of the columns and the writer of dramatic criticism for the paper. I have not used play reviews unless there is proof that Miss Cather is in town.

(2) In checking style, habits of phrasing and sentence rhythms are eventually apparent to the ear. Sometimes parallels are obvious. In the following examples, the first of each pair of expressions is from an unsigned review, the second from a later signed piece: "His step is light and his laugh is light" (review, *Journal*, Jan. 26, 1895); "His laugh is light and his step is light; he plays a staccato part from first to last" (signed review, *Leader*,

May 25, 1897). "Not that it is any better than any other audience, O, no, but it likes to hear coarseness boldly stated . . ." (review, *Journal*, Sept. 28, 1894); "You don't hear Davenport's placid accents, O no, you hear another voice swift as the wind . . ." (signed, "The Passing Show," *Journal*, Jan. 31, 1897). "Her death scene was done in the modern emotional drama ten, twenty and thirty-cent carnival style. She took a few tears from *Camille*, a few from *Article 47*, a few from *Credit Lorraine*, a few from *As in a Looking Glass* and made a death scene" (review, *Journal*, Oct. 23, 1895); "She plays it after the 'modern emotional' manner, the ten, twenty, and thirty cent *Kameel*, *Article 47*, *As In a Looking Glass* manner" (signed, "The Passing Show," *Journal*, Mar. 7, 1897). Some stylistic identifications are more complicated, but perhaps more absolute than simple parallels. In Willa Cather's essay on Shakespeare and Hamlet (*Journal*, Nov. 1 and 8, 1891), occur the phrases "strained, exaggerated natures" and "intellectual as Newton." Possibly she reread the piece several weeks before Walker Whiteside was due to arrive in a production of *Hamlet* (Nov. 21, 1895), for her review of *The Colonel's Wives* (*Journal*, Nov. 7) calls it an odious play: "The intellect of a Newton could not follow it." And she says of one good actor: "in that strained, impossible play he was never guilty of an unnatural gesture or intonation." The accents are often unexpectedly personal: though one might doubt it at first, Willa Cather did use slang like "rot" and expressions like "Bah!" even in her later signed pieces.

(3) There are numerous sequences of closely related pieces that restate comments, re-use passages or phrases, and run from the first listings by Miss Bullock, through the new material I have added from 1895–1896, to *Leader* reviews by Sibert, and to those signed Willa Cather. The following examples will give an idea of these sequences (names in brackets here and in the checklist identify the first listing of the item):

(*Sequence 1*)
"They are insensible to any odor milder than musk and any play tamer than melodrama."—Review, *Police Patrol*, *Journal*, Apr. 6, 1894. [Bullock].

"Their nostrils have become so vitiated by musk that they are absolutely insensible to any milder perfume."—Review, *The Passport*, *Journal*, Feb. 14, 1895. [Slote].

"After one has smelled musk the odor of violets is not perceptible."—"The Passing Show," *Courier*, Mar. 12, 1898. Signed Willa Cather. [Bullock].

(*Sequence 2*)
"There are some people, first rate people, who do not think Hoyt funny."—"As You Like It," *Journal*, Feb. 10, 1895. [Bullock].

"Let's see; DeWolf is six feet seven in his stockings with a big thundering voice that sounds like a whole bowling alley in action, a princely pair of legs and such irrepressible good humor that he can make you laugh by merely standing still. Well, he may do. I should not be greatly surprised if he made an excellent Falstaff. Besides he has seen Maurel play Verdi's Falstaff and that's a whole Shakespearean education in itself."—"The Passing Show," *Courier*, Aug. 24, 1895. [Slote].

"And then of course there was DeWolf. DeWolf the tall, of the talented legs. No one has ever been able to say quite what it is that makes Hopper so funny. . . ."—Review, *Wang*, *Journal*, Oct. 25, 1895. [Slote].

"There are plenty of people of good taste who do not find DeWolf Hopper excruciatingly funny, and it is rather difficult to say just what there is about him that makes one feel so cheerful. I am inclined to think that it is not so much anything that he does, as he himself, his big, genial personality."—"The Passing Show," *Courier*, Nov. 2, 1895. [Slote].

Albert Hart in *Wang* is not Hopper but "he makes up for it in the plentifulness of his legs and the limitless possibilities of his laugh."—Review, *Wang, Journal*, Jan. 31, 1896. [Slote].

"It's hard to say just what makes Mr. Daniels so funny. More than likely it is his diminutiveness just as the secret of DeWolf Hopper's comedy is in his bigness."— Review, *Wizard of the Nile, Leader*, Dec. 15, 1896. Signed Sibert. [Slote].

"I have never been able to decide just what it is that makes DeWolf Hopper so funny. . . ." [Here is used a passage revised from the review of *Wang*, Oct. 25, 1895].—Review, *El Capitan, Leader*, Mar. 23, 1897. Signed Sibert. [Slote].

"DeWolf Hopper, the merry giant, is with us . . . . There are plenty of sane and well balanced people who do not find Hopper funny at all."—"The Passing Show," *Journal*, Apr. 4, 1897. Signed Willa Cather. [Hinz, Finestone].

Out of context such lists of repetitions make habits of speech more obvious than they are. In the work, they become glancing signatures without a name.

Fiction and poetry, as I have indicated above, are not included in the checklist. The most complete bibliography of Willa Cather's early fiction is in *Willa Cather's Collected Short Fiction, 1892–1912* (Lincoln: University of Nebraska Press, 1965), pp. 583 ff. To it I can add one unsigned item: "The Elopement of Allen Poole," *Hesperian* (Apr. 15, 1893), pp. 4–7. For a discussion of the reasons for attribution, see pages 104–106. The most complete bibliography of Willa Cather's early poetry is in *April Twilights (1903)*, edited by Bernice Slote (Lincoln: University of Nebraska Press, 1962), pp. 59 ff. Two pieces of light verse, both unsigned, may be tentatively added: "He Took Analytics," *Hesperian* (Dec. 1, 1893), p. 12; and "With Prophetic Promptings" [*Count Gismond*], *Hesperian* (Dec. 19, 1893), p. 3. For a discussion, see page 18.

Some general sources used in determining the checklist and establishing biographical and historical facts:

This study has been based almost entirely on primary material. First of all, the newspapers, 1890 ff.: *Nebraska State Journal, Courier, Evening News, Daily Call, Weekly Herald, Independent, Vanity Fair*—all published in Lincoln; Omaha *World-Herald*, Omaha *Bee*, Beatrice *Weekly Express*, Beatrice *Express*, Red Cloud *Chief, Webster County Argus*, Pittsburgh *Leader* (1896 ff.). The Pittsburgh magazines: *Home Monthly* (1896 ff.), *Library* (1900). University of Nebraska publications: *Lasso* (1891–1892 only), *Hesperian* (1890–1896), *Nebraskan* (1892–1896), *Sombrero* (1892, 1894), *Nebraska Literary Magazine* (four issues only: May, Nov., 1895; Feb., June, 1896). Collections: The Benjamin D. Hitz Collection of Willa Cather material, Newberry Library; the Abbott, Pound, and Gere collections of manuscripts and papers, Nebraska State Historical Society; vertical files of the University of Nebraska Libraries, Nebraska Alumni Association, Nebraska State

Historical Society; Lincoln City Library; Pennsylvania Room, Carnegie Library, Pittsburgh. Nebraska State Historical Society picture and map collections. Material at the Willa Cather Pioneer Memorial, Red Cloud. Interviews with Mrs. George Seibel, Mrs. Frank Watson (Olive Latta), Charles Cather, Mr. and Mrs. Philip Southwick (Helen Cather), Merle C. Rathburn, John Richard Meyer; and those who, when living, had talked to me of Willa Cather and the days of the 1890's: Miss Elsie Cather, Professor Louise Pound, Miss Olivia Pound, Mrs. Gretchen Beghtol Lee.

Also for accounts of Willa Cather's early years: Mildred R. Bennett, *The World of Willa Cather* (New edition with notes and index; Lincoln: University of Nebraska Press, 1961); E. K. Brown, *Willa Cather: A Critical Biography*, completed by Leon Edel (New York: Alfred A. Knopf, 1953); Edith Lewis, *Willa Cather Living* (New York: Alfred A. Knopf, 1953); Elizabeth Shepley Sergeant, *Willa Cather: A Memoir* (Lincoln: University of Nebraska Press, 1960); James R. Shively, "Willa Cather's College Years": M.A. thesis, University of Nebraska, 1949, reprinted in part as *Willa Cather's Campus Years* (Lincoln: University of Nebraska Press, 1950).

Also for Lincoln, the University: Histories of Nebraska and Lincoln say little about the 1890's, and again I have used the newspapers as a principal source. Standard books on Nebraska are James C. Olson, *History of Nebraska* (Lincoln: University of Nebraska Press, 1954); Addison Erwin Sheldon, *Nebraska: The Land and the People* (3 vols.; Chicago: Lewis Publishing Co., 1931); also Sheldon's *History and Stories of Nebraska* (Chicago and Lincoln: University Publishing Co., 1914) and *Nebraska: Old and New* (Chicago and Lincoln: University Publishing Co., 1937); Federal Writers' Project, *Nebraska: A Guide to the Cornhusker State* (New York: The Viking Press, 1939). Everett N. Dick, "Problems of the Post Frontier Prairie City, as Portrayed by Lincoln, Nebraska, 1880–1890," *Nebraska History* (April–June, 1947), 132–143, was helpful in determining a fair population of Lincoln to replace the padded 1890 U.S. Census figure of 55, 154. Also: *Pen and Sunlight Sketches of Lincoln* (Chicago: Phoenix Publishing Co., n.d. 1893 ?); Andrew J. Sawyer, *Lincoln, The Capital City* (2 vols.; Chicago: S. J. Clarke Publishing Co., 1916); Lloyd Shaw, *The City of Lincoln and State of Nebraska* (Lincoln: State Journal Co., 1890); E. P. Brown, *The Prairie Capital* (Miller and Paine: The Fiftieth Year, 1930); Cherrier's *Lincoln City Directory* (Lincoln: State Journal Co.), vol. I (1890), and Hoye's *City Directory of Lincoln* (Lincoln: State Journal Co.), vols. I (1891)–VI (1896); Charles G. Dawes, *A Journal of the McKinley Years* (Chicago: R. R. Donnelly & Sons Co., 1950), esp. pp. 4–46 for 1893 in Lincoln; *Inventory of Lincoln Newspapers* (Lincoln, 1958); Writers' Program, Works Projects Administration in the State of Nebraska, *Printing Comes to Lincoln* (Lincoln: Woodruff Printing Co., 1940). University of Nebraska yearbooks, the 1892 and 1894 *Sombrero*, have excellent information; also the University Catalogs, 1883–1891, 1891–1898; *University Board of Regents: Biennial Report* for the years 1890–1896; *Alumni Directory:* Graduates, 1869–1912 (Lincoln: Lincoln Printing Co., 1912); Semi-Centennial Anniversary Book: *The University of Nebraska, 1869–1919* (Lincoln: By the University, 1919); *Ellen Smith: Registrar of the University of Nebraska, 1877–1902* (Lincoln: By the University, 1928); and I have been permitted to study the accession books of the University of Nebraska Libraries and early records of the Registrar.

Checklist

University Publications

Lasso

Willa Cather contributed to this magazine at least during the period she was an associate editor (Oct., 1891–Feb., 1892). No material is signed. No definite attributions can be made at this time, though judging by style she was probably the author of art and literary notes, possibly some drama notes later in the year.

Hesperian

1891   Untitled essay on Carlyle. Mar. 1, 1891, pp. 4–5. Unsigned. [Slote]. Generally the same essay published in the *Nebraska State Journal* on the same date. Several variations in style.

1892–1893 Numerous paragraphs in editorial and feature columns show Willa Cather's hand during the period she was Literary Editor. Probably hers are the following unsigned paragraphs (titles supplied): From the column "Executive Excerpts"—"Audiences" (Feb. 15, 1893) and "On the Passing of Great Men" (Mar. 1, 1893). From the column "Waste-Basket Waifs"—"Shakespeare" (Apr. 1, 1893) and "Puns" (Apr. 15, 1893). Editorial paragraphs appropriate to the Literary Editor, such as the defense of *Hesperian* poetry (Mar. 1, 1893). Selections attributed in this book include the following:

Students counting words. Mar. 15, 1893. Editorial. Unsigned. [Slote].
The Lansing curtain. Mar. 15, 1893. Editorial. Unsigned. [Slote].

1893–1894 In this year Willa Cather was managing editor of the *Hesperian*, and the publication shows her hand throughout. Specifically attributed in this book:
"Salutatory." Sept. 27, 1893, pp. 1–2. Unsigned. [Slote].
    Editorial statement of policy.
Waste-Basket Waifs. Talker in Shakespeare. Oct. 16, 1893, pp. 9–10.Unsigned. [Slote].
Waste-Basket Waifs. Football. Nov. 15, 1893, p. 9. Unsigned. [Slote].
Dramatic Notes. Walker Whiteside in *Richelieu*; Clara Morris in *Camille*. Dec. 1, 1893, pp. 5–6. [Attributed by Flora Bullock in "Willa Cather, Essayist and Dramatic Critic: 1891–1895," *Prairie Schooner* (Winter, 1949)].

Defense of writing. Dec. 19, 1893, p. 3. Editorial. Unsigned. [Slote].

Pastels in Prose. An Alumnus on Charter Day. Mar. 10, 1894, p. 4. Unsigned. [Slote].

"The Student and the Stage." Apr. 2, 1894, pp. 5–6. Unsigned. [Slote].

Thanks to the staff. June 9, 1894, p. 3. Editorial. Signed Willa Cather. [Jones].

Newspapers

Following is a chronological annotated checklist of Willa Cather's critical and personal writing in the *Nebraska State Journal* (1891–1896) and the *Courier* (1895), including signed essays of 1891, and columns and selected reviews of 1893–1896. While it lists all pieces used in *The Kingdom of Art* and a representative sampling of other items, it is not intended to be complete.

1891

Mar. 1   "Concerning Thos. Carlyle." *Journal*, p. 14. Article. Signed W. C.

Nov. 1   "Shakespeare and Hamlet." *Journal*, p. 16. Article. First of two parts. Unsigned.

     8   "Shakespeare and Hamlet." *Journal*, p. 11. Article. Second of two parts. Signed W. C.

1893

Nov. 5   One Way of Putting It. *Journal*, p. 13. Sketches. [Bullock].

     12   One Way of Putting It. *Journal*, p. 13. Sketches. [Bullock].

     19   One Way of Putting It. *Journal*, p. 9. Sketches. [Bullock].

     22   Walker Whiteside in *Richelieu*. *Journal*, p. 6. Review. [Bullock].

        Actors "ought at least to play an expurgated edition of it in which the mightiness of the pen and the 'brightest lexicon of youth' were left out." Cf. review of *Monte Cristo*, January 26, 1894.

     23   Clara Morris in *Camille*. *Journal*, p. 5. Review. [Bullock].

        Related comments in "One Way of Putting It," Nov. 26, 1893; "Between the Acts," Mar. 25, 1894.

     26   One Way of Putting It. *Journal*, p. 10. *Camille*, Clara Morris, sketches. [Bullock].

     30   Robert Downing in *Virginius*. *Journal*, p. 6. Review. [Slote].

        Consistent with other comments on Downing in "One Way of Putting It," Dec. 3, 1893; reviews of Oct. 2, 1894 and Nov. 24, 1895.

Dec. 3   One Way of Putting It. *Journal*, p. 13. Sketches, Robert Downing. [Bullock].

     14   *Friends*. *Journal*, p. 6. Review. Signed W. C. [Slote].

        The first signed review. One of two reviews of the play in this issue of the *Journal*, the other signed S. J. P.

     17   One Way of Putting It. *Journal*, p. 13. Sketches, Funke Theatre curtain. [Bullock].

1894

Jan. 10   *Gloriana*, with Emily Bancker. *Journal*, p. 6. Review. Signed W. C. [Bullock].

        One of two reviews of the play in this issue of the *Journal*, the other signed S. J. P.

     18   Morrison's *Faust*. *Journal*, p. 5. Review. [Bullock].

        Actually two reviews, separated by a rule. The first is probably Willa

[1894]   Cather's. Cf. related comments on the performance in "One Way of Putting It," Jan. 21, 1894.

20   Hoyt's *A Trip to Chinatown. Journal*, p. 3. Review. [Slote].
       The first in a sequence of related or repeated comments on Hoyt's plays. See reviews and columns in the *Journal* for Nov. 1, 4, 1894; Feb. 7, 10, Oct. 10, 1895; and review of *A Milk White Flag*, signed Sibert, in the Pittsburgh *Leader*, Dec. 1, 1896.

21   One Way of Putting It. *Journal*, p. 16. Lansing Theatre curtain, stage pronunciation, architecture, musée band, performance of *Faust*. [Bullock].

26   James O'Neill in *Monte Cristo. Journal*, p. 6. Review. [Slote].
       "As the Count he was—well, he was James O'Neill as the Count of Monte Cristo." The same sentence rhythm appears in later work: "As to Mr. Goodwin, himself, well, he is just Mr. Goodwin . . ." (*Journal*, Dec. 4, 1894); "As to Mr. Goodwin, well, he is just himself, just jolly, clever, easy-going Nat Goodwin" (review, signed Sibert, *Leader*, Mar. 9, 1897). The following repeats a statement in the review of *Richelieu* (Nov. 22, above): "For the role of the romantic actor we wish such trite and choice bits of rhetoric as 'the pen is mightier than the sword' . . . would be stricken from the plays they burden and make ludicrous."

28   One Way of Putting It. *Journal*, p. 13. Prize fight, Lansing curtain, the state capitol, other sketches. [Bullock].

Feb. 7   The Kendals in *The Ironmaster. Journal*, p. 3. Review. [Bullock].
       Related accounts in "Plays and Players," Feb. 11, 1894.

9   *The Spider and the Fly. Journal*, p. 6. Review. [Bullock].

11   "The Critic's Province." *Journal*, p. 12. Editorial. [Bullock].
       Plays and Players. *Journal*, p. 13. Audiences, the Kendals, the Gerry Society and education of actresses. Signed Deus Gallery. [Jones, Bullock].

13   *Fantasma. Journal*, p. 5. Review. [Bullock].

17   "The Curtain Falls." *Journal*, p. 5. University production of Greek and Latin plays. [Jones, Bullock].

20   *A Duel of Hearts*, with Craigen and Paulding. *Journal*, p. 2. Review. [Jones, Bullock].

21   *The Setting of the Sun* and *The Dowager Countess*, with Craigen and Paulding. *Journal*, p. 3. Review. [Jones, Bullock].
       Comparison of Maida Craigen and Clara Morris.

22   *In Old Kentucky. Journal*, p. 5. Review. [Bullock].

24   The Greek and Latin plays. *Journal*, p. 6. Review of second performance. [Bullock, Abbott].

25   With Plays and Players. *Journal*, p. 9. Greek tragedy, realism, Modjeska. [Jones, Bullock].

Mar. 1   Julia Marlowe in *The Love Chase. Journal*, p. 3. Review. [Jones, Bullock].

2   *The Ensign. Journal*, p. 3. Review. [Bullock].
       Comments on lovemaking on the stage relate to review, Mar. 14, 1894.

4   With Plays and Players. *Journal*, p. 13. Julia Marlowe, Steele Mackaye, Bernhardt, Olive May. Signed Deus Gallerie. [Jones, Bullock].

[1894]11   With Plays and Players. *Journal*, p. 13. Modjeska, Maggie Mitchell, Warde and James, Booth's successor, English critics. [Jones, Bullock].

13   *Romeo and Juliet*, with Craigen and Paulding. *Journal*, p. 2. Review. [Bullock].

14   *A Duel of Hearts*, with Craigen and Paulding. *Journal*, p. 2. [Bullock].

16   *The White Squadron. Journal*, p. 3. Review. [Bullock].

17   *The Idea. Journal*, p. 3. Review. [Bullock].

22   *The Voodoo. Journal*, p. 6. Review. [Bullock].

23   Lewis Morrison in *Richelieu. Journal*, p. 3. Review. [Slote].

Characteristic comment and style: "His acting is quiet and forcible, but it is elocutionary. He never pains one, but he never surprises one, his Richelieu utterly lacks spontaneity. In the correctness of his elocution he too often forgets to feel. . . . Miss Florence Roberts . . . narrowly escaped being beautiful and she narrowly escaped acting, but she did not quite get anywhere. . . . In short, her acting is graceful, smileful, tearful and utterly heartless. Her melancholy does not move one, her love is only stage love. She seems to have all the necessary requirements of an actress, but the spark that quickens art to life is absent." Compare "Morrison stops just where elocution ends and acting begins," in the Sunday column two days later (Mar. 25, 1894); on Henry James: "You are never startled, never surprised . . . always delighted" (*Courier*, Nov. 16, 1895); and comments on Julia Marlowe and Clara Morris throughout the spring of 1894.

25   Between the Acts. *Journal*, p. 13. Defense of criticism, Clara Morris, romance and realism, Lewis Morrison and mediocrity. [Bullock].

30   Herrmann the Magician. *Journal*, p. 8. Review. [Bullock].

Apr. 1   Between the Acts. *Journal*, p. 13. Theatrical handouts and advertising. Not characteristic. [Bullock; doubtful].

3   *The Black Crook. Journal*, p. 5. Review. [Bullock].

4   Marie Tempest in *The Fencing Master. Journal*, p. 5. Review. [Jones, Bullock]. Related comment in review of *The Fencing Master* (Mar. 3, 1895) and "As You Like It," May 26, 1895.

5   William H. Crane in *Brother John. Journal*, p. 6. Review. [Bullock]. Passage used in review of *Shore Acres*, signed Sibert, in the *Leader*, Dec. 29, 1896. Compare also "As You Like It," Dec. 9, 1894.

6   *Police Patrol. Journal*, p. 6. Review. [Bullock]. Related passages in review of *The Passport* (Feb. 14, 1895) and "The Passing Show," signed Willa Cather (*Courier*, Mar. 12, 1898).

7   DeWolf Hopper in *Panjandrum. Journal*, p. 2. Review. [Bullock]. Similar comment and style in review of *Wizard of the Nile*, signed Sibert (*Leader*, Dec. 15, 1896).

8   Between the Acts. *Journal*, p. 13. Plays of the preceding week, the actor's art, Mounet-Sully's classic art, mediocrity, Marie Tempest. [Bullock].

15   Between the Acts. *Journal*, p. 13. Mrs. Kendal, Gilbert and Sullivan, story of Rider Haggard's *She*. [Jones, Bullock].

18   Minstrel show. *Journal*, p. 3. Review. [Bullock].

[1894]20   *She. Journal*, p. 6. Review. [Bullock].
            Related material in "Between the Acts," Apr. 15, 22, 1894.

22   Between the Acts. *Journal*, p. 13. Dramatization of novels, Sousa's band, Richard Mansfield, Buffalo Bill and Katherine Clemmons, comments on actors and playwrights. [Jones, Bullock].

24   Richard Mansfield in *Beau Brummell. Journal*, p. 5. Review. [Jones, Bullock].

26   *The District Fair. Journal*, p. 5. Review. [Bullock].
            Old spinster type, corkscrew curls: compare review of *The Politician* (*Courier*, Sept. 7, 1895).

27   The Hopkins Trans-Oceanic Specialty Company. *Journal*, p. 6. Review. [Bullock].

29   Between the Acts. *Journal*, p. 13. Mansfield in *Beau Brummell*, Shakespeare's birthday. [Jones?, Bullock].

May 4   Alexander Salvini in *The Three Guardsmen. Journal*, p. 6. Review. [Bullock].
            Similar comment and styles in "The Passing Show," signed Willa Cather, *Journal*, Dec. 27, 1896, and review of *A Soldier of Fortune*, signed Sibert (*Leader*, Jan. 12, 1897).

5   Sousa's Band [afternoon program]. *Journal*, p. 2. Review. [Bullock].
     Fred Emerson Brooks, California Poet-Humorist [evening program]. *Journal*, p. 2. Review. [Slote].
            Characteristic comment: "Mr. Brooks is an odd genius. He has strength and virility and just enough awkwardness to free his work from the elocutionary curse. . . . He is successful because he is strong and original and awkward and has something to say. . . . [The pianist's success] was solely on account of her enthusiasm and her determination to conquer all obstacles. The piano, which should have responded to every touch like a living thing, was noticeably and persistently deficient." Compare descriptions of Margaret Mather's voice "like the warmth of a living touch" ("The Passing Show," *Courier*, Oct. 19, 1895) and Melba's as "an individual living thing" ("As You Like It," June 9, 1895).

18   Blind Tom. *Journal*, p. 6. Review. [Bullock].

June 5   *Lady Windermere's Fan. Journal*, p. 1. Review. Signed W. C. [Bullock].

7   *The Chimes of Normandy. Journal*, p. 2. Review. Signed W. C. [Bullock].

Sept. 13   Roland Reed in *The Woman Hater. Journal*, p. 5. Review. [Bullock].
            Similar passages in reviews of Roland Reed in *The Politician* (*Journal*, Sept. 5, 1895) and review of *My Friend from India*, signed Sibert (*Leader*, Jan. 26, 1897).

14   The Royal Entertainers in Vaudeville. *Journal*, p. 6. Review. [Slote].
            Interviews with two members of the company and knowledgeable statements about performances are included in "Utterly Irrelevant," Sept. 16 and 23, 1894. This is the most characteristic and interesting of the several reviews which appeared during the company's stay. "What that company most needs is professional backbone in the management." (It claims to be professional, but it is a little amateurish to begin at 8:45 and string out for several hours. Specialties should go off like a fire-cracker. Acts wander in at their own sweet will and stop to take a nap

[465]

[1894]   when tired. The production should have the vivacity of a gallop or a waltz, but has all the slowness of a minuet with none of its dignity.) Variations of the last metaphor are used frequently in later reviews. (See *Jane*, Nov. 14, 1894.)

16   Utterly Irrelevant. *Journal*, p. 13. Art at the State Fair, interview with magician William Zanetti of the Royal Entertainers, *Trilby*. [Bullock].

Underground. *Journal*, p. 3. Review. [Slote].

Style relates to review of *The Ensign* (Mar. 2, 1894).

23   Utterly Irrelevant. *Journal*, p. 13. Libraries, Tenth Street, Annie Kenwick of the Royal Entertainers, Marion Manola, death of Major Hastings, book agents, *The Superfluous Woman* by Madame Grand, the way of the artist. [Bullock].

28   *The Devil's Auction*. *Journal*, p. 3. Review. [Bullock].

Characteristic material and style: "The only way to define the limits of the plot is to say that it deals with the works of nature and that the scene is laid in the universe." The description of actors and actresses at liberty— "On the Rialto"—has a parallel version in the review of *The Newest Devil's Auction* (*Journal*, Dec. 13, 1895). See below for a comparison of the passages.

30   *Uncle Tom's Cabin*. *Journal*, p. 2. Review. [Bullock].

Utterly Irrelevant. *Journal*, p. 13. Eating in theatre boxes, concert or stage, Sieveking's recital, Salvation Army. [Bullock].

Oct. 2   Robert Downing in *The Gladiator*. *Journal*, p. 3. Review. [Bullock].

Related comments in "Utterly Irrelevant," Oct. 7, 1894.

5   *The Derby Winner*. *Journal*, p. 6. Review. [Bullock].

The worst of the plays by illiterate writers this season. Reference in "As You Like It," Jan. 6, 1895.

7   Utterly Irrelevant. *Journal*, p. 13. McKinley, French and English public, Robert Downing in *The Gladiator*, the baseball boy and the athletic girl, church music and beauty in the world, theatrical news. [Bullock].

9   *Gloriana*. *Journal*, p. 2. Review. [Bullock].

Relates to previous review of *Gloriana* (Jan. 10, 1894).

12   *Charley's Aunt*. *Journal*, p. 5. Review. [Bullock].

14   *Rush City*. *Journal*, p. 6. Review. [Bullock].

Utterly Irrelevant. *Journal*, p. 13. Bernhardt and Duse, egotism of the University, Oliver Wendell Holmes, war in China, the right kind of teacher, theatrical comment, *Vanity Fair* in Lincoln. [Bullock].

21   Utterly Irrelevant. *Journal*, p. 13. Local concerts, Queen Victoria, actors and managers, the best kind of drama criticism. [Bullock].

25   *The Hustler*. *Journal*, p. 2. Review. [Slote].

"Mamie Mayo in her song, the 'Bowery Girl,' was altogether refreshing." Cf. Oct. 28, 1894, below [Utterly Irrelevant], and references to "Mamie Mayo the other night."

28   Utterly Irrelevant. *Journal*, p. 13. Writing of novels, audience response to Mamie Mayo and Anna Boyd [of last year's *A Trip to Chinatown*], newspaper gossip, Lincoln women's clubs, interview with an actor in the penitentiary. [Bullock].

[1894]30   Fowler's Players in *A Wife's Honor. Journal*, p. 2. Review. [Slote].
        Related to the following review. Plays compared.

31   Fowler's Players in *Married for Money. Journal*, p. 6. Review. [Bullock].
        A comedy, better for the company than the play of the preceding night:
        "Miss Maggie Miller as Simpkins was much more pleasing as a soubrette
        than as the erring wife of the night before. Once a soubrette, always a
        soubrette. It is a fatal mistake to transpose her into the serious, and a
        clever soubrette is worth twenty erring wives anyway."

Nov. 1   Hoyt's *A Trip to Chinatown. Journal*, p. 2. Review. [Bullock].
        Relates to sequence of comments on Hoyt (see above, review of Jan. 20,
        1894). The play is not perfect without "the matchless Anna Boyd."
        See other comments in Sunday columns of Oct. 28, Nov. 4, 1894.
        Passage on Hoyt and American humor used in review of *A Milk White*
        Flag, signed Sibert (*Leader*, Dec. 1, 1896).

4   More or Less Personal [a head for a regular editorial column, probably a
        compositor's error]. *Journal*, p. 12. Hoyt, *The Green Carnation*, the State
        Penitentiary, Owen on Bacon and Shakespeare, Duse's privacy. [Bullock;
        title error noted].

6   *Friends. Journal*, p. 8. Review. [Slote].
        Relates to signed review of *Friends*, Dec. 14, 1893.

The two following reviews and that of Jane (*Nov. 14, 1894*) *illustrate the kind of*
"meatax" criticism for which Willa Cather became famous in this season and which
brought theatrical managers like the Frohmans to respond.

7   *Hot Tamales. Journal*, p. 5. Review. [Slote].
        The play has old jokes, a "heavy villain whom nature has cursed with
        the mad delusion of thinking he can sing bass," and a quartet "that
        cannot find the key even once. It is indeed 'moss covered' and should be
        left to requiescat in pace. Also in this day of enlightenment the bass
        villain should find something else to do with his few quavering tones
        than rocking them in the Cradle of the Deep."

9   Charles A. Loder in *Oh, What a Night. Journal*, p. 6. Review. [Slote].
        "Mr. Loder is as repulsive as ever."

10   *Pinafore. Journal*, p. 6. Review. [Slote].
        Refers directly to comments made in the signed review of another local
        talent production, *Chimes of Normandy* (June 7, 1894). Characteristic
        style and comment: She had "just that little dash of assertiveness which is
        to the comedienne what soul is to the tragedienne."

11   As You Like It. *Journal*, p. 13. Nethersole, private libraries, Bliss Carman,
        ministers and Pauline Hall, French hero worship, church music, student
        recitals, *Vanity Fair*. [Bullock].

14   *Jane* and *The Great Mogul* ["Gustave Frohman's Company No. 13"]. *Journal*,
        p. 2. Review. [Bullock].
        "*Jane* is written in the neatest kind of waltz time and it was played last
        night in can can measure. . . . If Mr. Gustave Frohman wishes to engage
        farce comedy people he should give them farces to play. There was a
        time when the Frohman name insured the merit of a play, when of

[1894]   anything with the Frohman name attached we could say, 'It is good,' but time has changed this very much for the worse. The Frohmans are wealthy enough now to sell their name and it is just so much worse for the confiding public." See interview with Frohman, "As You Like It," *Journal*, Feb. 3, 1895.

18   As You Like It. *Journal*, p. 13. Defense of roasting, egotism of artists, theatrical news, magazines, University library. [Bullock].

21   Pauline Hall in *Dorcas*. *Journal*, p. 2. Review. [Slote].
        Related to other comments on light opera, actresses. See "As You Like It," Nov. 25, 1894, July 14, 1895.

25   As You Like It. *Journal*, p. 13. "Jolly" Pauline Hall [see above, Nov. 21], light opera, theatrical news, Rubinstein's death. [Bullock].

Dec. 2   As You Like It. *Journal*, p. 13. Football, marriage and actors, pronunciations, failure of actors, theatrical news. [Bullock].

4   Nat Goodwin in *A Gilded Fool*. *Journal*, p. 8. Review. [Bullock].
        Comments on Goodwin and Carleton's *A Gilded Fool* and other plays continue throughout the newspaper writing. See "As You Like It," Dec. 9, 1894. A passage from this review is used in the review of Goodwin in *An American Citizen*, signed Sibert (*Leader*, Mar. 9, 1897).

5   *A Summer Blizzard*. *Journal*, p. 5. Review. [Bullock].
        Reference in "As You Like It," Jan. 6, 1895.

8   Katie Emmett in *Killarney*. *Journal*, p. 2. Review. [Slote].
        "All stars need not be brilliant, but they should twinkle a little and should possess a marked adaptability for some one thing, whether walking the slack wire or high tragedy. Commonplaceness is not a crime, but is sometimes decidedly tiresome." Similar comments in the summary of a speech by Willa Cather (see "Writer in Nebraska," page 27); "As You Like It," Dec. 16, 1894; and throughout the writing.

9   The Tavary Grand Opera Company in *Il Trovatore*. *Journal*, p. 4. Review. [Bullock].
        Reviews of Dec. 9, 10, and "As You Like It," Dec. 16, 1894, are closely related in style and comment. See also numerous later references to Mme. Helena von Doenhoff of this company.
        As You Like It. *Journal*, p. 13. Nat Goodwin and comedy, William Crane in *Brother John*, Lillian Russell, "living pictures." [Bullock].

10   *Il Trovatore*, with Helena von Doenhoff. *Journal*, p. 8. Review. [Slote].

14   Thomas Q. Seabrooke in *Isle of Champagne*. *Journal*, p. 6. Review. [Slote].
        Related comment in "The Passing Show," *Journal*, Aug. 11, 1895 and Feb. 2, 1896, concerning Seabrooke's wife.

15   Daniel Sully in *O'Neil*, Washington, D.C. *Journal*, p. 2. Review. [Bullock].

16   As You Like It. *Journal*, p. 13. Comedians playing Shakespeare and classic comedies, stage realism, actors and society, interview with Helena von Doenhoff, Madame Tavary's dog. [Bullock].

18   *Lady Windermere's Fan*. *Journal*, p.2. Review. [Bullock].
        Comments relate to signed review of June 5, 1894.

20   *In Old Kentucky*. *Journal*, p. 3. Review. [Slote].

[1894]   Related to review of previous production of the play, Feb. 22, 1894. Compares actresses, comments on southern accent and appearance, recalls *The Ensign* (Mar. 2, 1894).

23   As You Like It. *Journal*, p. 13. Stevenson, Kipling, *Trilby*. [Bullock].

30   As You Like It. *Journal*, p. 13. Zola, Bernhardt. [Bullock].

1895

Jan.   4   Sol Smith Russell in *The Heir at Law. Journal*, p. 6. Review. [Bullock].

6   *The Charity Ball. Journal*, p. 6. Review. [Bullock].
A Belasco play by a Frohman company. References continue throughout.
As You Like It. *Journal*, p. 13. The Haydon Art Club exhibit, Sol Smith Russell's curtain speech, defense of roasting [reference to plays through the fall].

8   *Thro' the War. Journal*, p. 2. Review. [Bullock].
"Miss Olive Martin played the southern heroine with prayers and tears and groans and poses illustrating all the angles in plane geometry. [She] could hardly be called a southern type. . . ."

11   *A Jolly Good Fellow. Journal*, p. 8. Review. [Bullock].
References to *Charity Ball* (Jan. 6) and *Gloriana*.

12   *Yon Yonson. Journal*, p. 6. Review. [Slote].
Cora Macy a "monotonous heroine," a term frequently used (Walker Whiteside a "monotonous Hamlet" in review of *Hamlet, Journal*, Nov. 21, 1895).

13   As You Like It. *Journal*, p. 13. Christina Rossetti, E. B. Browning, Sappho. [Bullock].

18   *Henry IV*, with Frederick Warde and Louis James. *Journal*, p. 8. Review. [Slote].
Direct reference in "As You Like It," Jan. 20, 1895. Earlier comment on their work in tragedy, "With Plays and Players," Mar. 11, 1894. *Henry IV* is recalled in "As You Like It," June 2, 1895.

20   As You Like It. *Journal*, p. 13. Historical plays of Shakespeare, Julia Marlowe in the wrong plays. [Bullock].

22   *Men and Women. Journal*, p. 8. Review. [Bullock].
Relates to Jan. 6, 27; Feb. 3; Sept. 25, 1895.

23   Recital by George R. Williams [elocutionist] and Bertha Davis [violinist]. *Journal*, p. 6. Review. [Slote].
The soloist in a "fortunate mistake."

26   J. K. Emmett in *Fritz in a Madhouse. Journal*, p. 6. Review. [Bullock].
Characteristic comments: glides along in waltz time, does the natural thing with children. Passage repeated in review of *Rosedale*, signed Sibert (*Leader*, May 25, 1897).

27   *The Girl I Left Behind Me. Journal*, p. 6. Review. [Slote].
Frohman attended the play. See especially the interview, "As You Like It," Feb. 3, 1895; also references to Belasco plays and Frohman companies throughout.
As You Like It. *Journal*, p. 13. Three Belasco plays in January, interview with Bernice Wheeler, marriage of Helena von Doenhoff, Dumas, Nat Goodwin. [Bullock].

Feb. 1   "Sweetie" Corinne in *Hendrick Hudson. Journal*, p. 5. Review. [Slote].
[1895]   Homely chorus girls—so awfully moral.

     2   *Charley's Aunt. Journal*, p. 6. Review. [Slote].
             Reference to previous performance (review of Oct. 12, 1894) and compares. Style: Hurries along to gallop time (compare reviews of Sept. 14, Nov. 14, 1894; Jan. 26, 1895).

     3   As You Like It. *Journal*, p. 13. Interview with Gustave Frohman, theatrical news. [Bullock].

     7   Hoyt's *A Temperance Town. Journal*, p. 6. Review. [Slote].
             Relates to other Hoyt plays and comments. See "As You Like It," Feb. 10, 1895.

    10   As You Like It. *Journal*, p. 13. *A Temperance Town* and Hoyt's comedy, Mendelssohn concert. [Bullock].

    14   Sadie Martinot in *The Passport. Journal*, p. 2. Review. [Slote].
             References in Sunday columns of May 26, 1895; Jan. 12, 1896. Stylistic repetitions in later work.

    17   As You Like It. *Journal*, p. 9. Coppée and French fiction. [Bullock].

    22   Eddie Foy in *Off the Earth. Journal*, p. 8. Review. [Slote].
             Comments on Louise Montague as a "fly and flippant comedienne"; Foy disappointing: his mirth had no special novelty or individuality of its own. The cloud drop "needs a little attention from the celestial architects. There is a decided rift in heaven which would be very much better for a strip of court plaster."

    24   As You Like It. *Journal*, p. 13. Julia Marlowe, lecture by Max O'Rell, French drama, good and evil in acting. [Bullock].

    26   *The New "Paul Kauvar." Journal*, p. 6. Review. [Bullock].

Mar. 2   Clay Clement in *The New Dominion. Journal*, p. 6. Review. [Bullock].

     3   As You Like It. *Journal*, p. 13. Clay Clement. [Bullock].
         The Fencing Master. Journal, p. 8. Review. [Slote].
             This production compared with that of last year (see review, Apr. 4, 1894): Dorothy Morton's movements heavy, Marie Tempest's fascinating though artificial. Characteristic comments: "American music is like American wines. They both lack body, richness, age, traditions—everything that wine and music should have." Passage used in review of *Wizard of the Nile*, signed Sibert (*Leader*, Dec. 15, 1896).

    10   As You Like It. *Journal*, p. 13. Clay Clement as an actor, Modjeska's dignity, Hamlet, Mrs. James Potter. [Bullock].

Willa Cather attended the opera in Chicago during the week of March 10, and was ill for a period after her return. She resumed her Sunday column on March 31, and though some of the reviews at the end of March may be hers, the first to suggest definite relationships with other work is that of April 2. The Nebraskan *on April 5 noted that Miss Cather was around again.*

    31   As You Like It. *Journal*, p. 13. Verdi's *Falstaff*, Emma Eames in *Otello*. [Bullock].

Apr. 2 Griffith's *Faust. Journal*, p. 8. Review [probable]. [Slote].
[1895] Style and content relate to reviews of Apr. 17, 1895 (men learning how to carry shoulders); Sept. 11, 14, 20, 1895.

7 As You Like It. *Journal*, p. 13. Private life of actors, Paul Potter's version of *Trilby*. [Bullock].

14 As You Like It. *Journal*, p. 13. A play called *Nebraska*, Beerbohm Tree's lecture at Harvard. [Bullock].

17 *Shenandoah. Journal*, p. 5. Review. [Bullock].
Characteristic comment: More to do than to say. One character should learn how to carry his shoulders (see review of Apr. 2, 1895).

18 *The Black Crook. Journal*, p. 3. Review. [Slote].
Related to "As You Like It," Apr. 21, and review, Oct. 31, 1895.

21 As You Like It. *Journal*, p. 13. Shakespeare, French dramatic criticism, episode at performance of *The Black Crook*. [Bullock].

23 The Spooners in *Inez. Journal*, p. 5. Review. [Slote].
Style and content related to numerous other reviews of the Spooners. See Sept. 10, 14, 1895.

25 Effie Ellsler in *Doris. Journal*, p. 8. Review. [Slote].
See review, Dec. 6, 1895. Style and content characteristic (the play flabby and melodramatic in its construction).

26 The Spooners in *The Buckeye. Journal*, p. 8. Review. [Slote].
A self-respecting little play, abounding in innocence and unsophistication. Reference to critic's own habit of raising cyclones.

28 As You Like It. *Journal*, p. 14. Theatrical news, Marie Wainwright and southern families, nature as ruler of the world. [Bullock].

May 5 As You Like It. *Journal*, p. 14. Bernhardt, Salvini, controversy between Max O'Rell and Mark Twain. [Bullock].

12 As You Like It. *Journal*, p. 12. Clara Morris, Mansfield, Salvini, magazines, Magruder's *Princess Sonia*. [Bullock].

14 *Our Flat*, with Emily Bancker. *Journal*, p. 6. Review. [Slote].
Comparison with *Gloriana*. Emily Bancker's "special forte of doing perfectly atrocious things in an entirely guileless manner." See note on relationships in style, above; and use of passage in review, Nov. 26, 1895.

19 As You Like It. *Journal*, p. 12. Actresses as writers, Wilde and *Lady Windermere's Fan*. [Bullock].

26 As You Like It. *Journal*, p. 12. Marie Tempest, Chicago *Chap Book*, maturity in writers. [Bullock].
Specific recollections of Marie Tempest (in *The Fencing Master* last season), Sadie Martinot (in *The Passport* last winter), and comment by Mme. Doenhoff (Dec. 16, 1894).

June 2 As You Like It. *Journal*, p. 9. *Trilby* tableaux in Beatrice, theatrical news, Warde and James recalled in *Henry IV*. [Bullock].

7 The Oriole Opera Company in *Girofle-Girofla* and *Chimes of Normandy*. *Journal*, p. 6. Review [probable]. [Slote].
Style ("a wordy Viennese opera with scant melody and abundant dialogue"); Alfred de Musset quoted, a characteristic reference throughout.

[1895] 9   As You Like It. *Journal*, p. 12. *Princess Sonia*, Melba, theatrical news. [Bullock].

16   As You Like It. *Journal*, p. 12. Duse and the isolation of the artist, French critics. [Bullock].

30   As You Like It. *Journal*, p. 12. Theatrical news, Rubinstein, *Outre Mer*, Queen Victoria, Patti and Melba. [Bullock].

July 7   As You Like It. *Journal*, p. 9. William Winter as critic, Katherine Fisk's "emotional intelligence," Lillian Russell on a bicycle. [Slote].

14   As You Like It. *Journal*, p. 9. Edgar Saltus' novel *When Dreams Come True*, Howells and reading, Bernhardt. [Slote].

The Sunday column now took over permanently the name "The Passing Show." It had been used on June 16 and 23, 1895, as the head on a column of political comment by W. O. Chapman.

21   The Passing Show. *Journal*, p. 9. Dumas *fils*, Bernhardt, Zola, Mary Anderson's book, comments on Clara Morris recalled. [Slote].

Aug. 4   The Passing Show. *Journal*, p. 9. Henry Guy Carleton as playwright, *A Gilded Fool* compared with Belasco plays, Olive May Carleton in Beatrice. [Slote].

11   The Passing Show. *Journal*, p. 9. Grave of Madame Carvahlo in Père-Lachaise, America buying as Rome did, books of romance, Stanley Weyman, reference to comment on Seabrooke's wife (review, Dec. 14, 1894). [Slote].

24   The Passing Show. *Courier*, pp. 6–8. Includes theatrical handout material, notes from Omaha theatres. [Slote].

31   The Passing Show. *Courier*, pp. 6–8. Felix Morris and the starring system, theatrical announcements. [Slote].

On August 3 the Courier *had announced that " Miss Willa Cather who for the past two years has been the dramatic critic and theatrical writer for the* Journal, *will become a member of the* Courier *staff. . . ." That she wrote reviews of the same play for both the* Journal *and the* Courier *may be seen in some of the comments: On the Flints' exhibition of hypnotism: "About the genuine quality of the exhibition there was no doubt" (*Journal, *Sept. 3); " Their work is beyond a doubt genuine" (*Courier, *Sept. 7). On The Buckeye: " Cecil Spooner has the grace and ease of motion that no dancing teacher can touch" (*Journal, *Sept. 10); " She can dance, dance with a natural grace and ease which can never be taught or acquired by practice, which must be born with one, and is born with very few" (*Courier, *Sept. 14).*

Sept. 3   The Flints in an Exhibition of Hypnotism. *Journal*, p. 6. Review. [Slote].
"A rotund svengali with taffy mutton chops of a dusky hue. . . ."

5   Roland Reed in *The Politician*. *Journal*, p. 2. Review. [Slote].
Relates to review of *The Woman Hater* (Sept. 13, 1894).

7   The Passing Show. *Courier*, pp. 6–7. Developing actors in America, dramatizing *Romola*, Calvé, Isadore Rush in *The Politician*, Mascagni. [Slote].
Roland Reed in *The Politician*. The Flints. *Courier*, p. 8. Reviews. [Slote].

[1895]10   The Spooners in *The Buckeye. Journal*, p. 8. Review. [Slote].
            Relates to review of Apr. 26, 1895.

11   Griffith's *Faust. Journal*, p. 8. Review. [Slote].
            Relates to review of Apr. 2, 1895, and others on *Faust*.

14   The Passing Show. *Courier*, pp. 6–7. Writers of romance, the Dovey sisters.
            [Slote].
            Griffith's *Faust*. The Spooners. *Courier*, p. 8. Reviews. [Slote].

21   The Passing Show. *Courier*, pp. 6–7. Hall Caine, Duse, Nordica, Irving,
            actors and literacy, F. Marion Crawford and American literature. [Slote].

24   *The Hustler. Journal*, p. 8. Review. [Slote].
            The play has deteriorated since last year; not a classic then but a "very
            neat, clean little farce." See review and comment, Oct. 25, 28, 1894.

25   *The Wife. Journal*, p. 3. Review. [Slote].
            Relates to reviews of Jan. 6, 22, 27, 1895; "As You Like It,". Jan. 27,
            Feb. 3, 1895. "Let us at least have the much abused 'grand passions' in
            the theatre, they are perfectly safe there and can't hurt us. They are
            impossible and improper in life. We all admit that and we have cheer-
            fully banished them from a world that is not big enough. But they are not
            dangerous across the footlights." Compare the review of *The Wife* in the
            Courier, Sept. 28, 1895.

27   *Rush City. Journal*, p. 8. Review. [Slote].

28   The Passing Show. *Courier*, pp. 6–7. Wilde, Gautier, Lussan. [Slote].
            The Wife. Courier, p. 8. Review. [Slote].
            Passage on the stage ("the kingdom of the unattainable, where the grand
            passions die not") used in "The Return of the Romantic Drama,"
            unsigned article in the *Home Monthly*, Nov., 1896.
            Untitled article in "Man and Woman / A Symposium." *Courier*, p. 10. Signed
            Willa Cather. [Jones].

Oct.   2   *Too Much Johnson. Journal*, p. 3. Review. [Slote].
            A comedy "with a stick in it." Compare the review of *The Wife* in the
            Journal, Sept. 25, 1895 ("give us either guileless comedy or give us
            emotional drama with a stick in it").

5   *Too Much Johnson. Courier*, p. 8. Review. [Slote].
            The Passing Show. *Courier*, pp. 6–7. Paganini, Hardy. [Slote].

10   Hoyt's *A Contented Woman. Journal*, p. 5. Review. [Slote].
            Relates to a sequence on Hoyt (see the note, above). "He is an American,
            as American as a cocktail, and he has the monumental pluck and nerve of
            his people." Compare the comment on Hoyt in "The Passing Show,"
            signed Willa Cather, *Journal*, Jan. 3, 1897 ("no more nerves than a
            cocktail").

12   The Passing Show. *Courier*, pp. 6–7. Edgar Allan Poe. [Slote].

15   *Human Hearts. Journal*, p. 6. Review. [Slote].
            Characteristic style and comment: Hal Reid has "intensity and homely
            dignity . . . he does the lofty, scornful act well; his lips have a sort of
            Byronic curl to them that was made for scorn." "Nebraska governors
            sit around on store boxes and cry 'Heigho' for diversion, but not so with

[1895]   the governor of that centre of civilization, Arkansas. He was guarded like a king in his castle, like a sultan in his palace, like the pet pug of an opera singer."

17   "The Dovey Sisters at the Funke." *Journal*, p. 2. Review. [Slote].

19   The Passing Show. *Courier*, pp. 6–7. Amélie Rives-Chanler, Margaret Mather as Juliet, Cora Potter the gentlewoman. [Slote].

23   Lillian Lewis in *Cleopatra*. *Journal*, p. 6. Review. [Slote].

25   DeWolf Hopper in *Wang*. *Journal*, p. 6. Review. [Slote].
       Relates to a sequence on Hopper and *Wang* (see Note, pp. 458 f.). Passage from this review revised and used in review of *El Capitan*, signed Sibert (*Leader*, Mar. 23, 1897).

26   The Passing Show. *Courier*, pp. 6–7. Lillian Lewis and *Cleopatra*, the child prodigy and the artist. [Slote].

30   *The Globe Trotter*. *Journal*, p. 6. Review. [Slote].

31   *The Black Crook*. *Journal*, p. 6. Review. [Slote].
       Relates to review, Apr. 18, 1895.

Nov. 2   The Passing Show. *Courier*, pp. 6–7. DeWolf Hopper, nature and romance, Stevenson's letters, Nat Goodwin. [Slote].
       The Globe Trotter. *The Black Crook*. *Courier*, p. 8. Reviews. [Slote].

7   *The Colonel's Wives*. *Journal*, p. 3. Review. [Slote].
       Stylistic relationships (see Note, p. 458).

9   The Passing Show. *Courier*, pp. 6–7. Zenda stories, Pierre Loti's *Romance of a Spahi*, Dumas' *Route de Thèbes*, death of Eugene Field, *The Colonel's Wives*. [Slote].

16   The Passing Show. *Courier*, pp. 6–7. American authors. Henry James. [Slote].

21   *Hamlet*, with Walker Whiteside. *Journal*, p. 6. Review. [Slote].

23   The Passing Show. *Courier*, pp. 7–8. Ouida, women in fiction, *Hamlet*. [Slote].

24   Robert Downing in Sardou's *Helena*. *Journal*, p. 3. Review. [Slote].
       "Sardou is never bad, he is seldom great, he is always the same wonderful master of stage effects."

26   *Our Flat*, with Emily Bancker. *Journal*, p. 6. Review. [Slote].
       Miss Bancker is assisted by "the faithful Bella, the willowy Psyche, and red stockings," though not quite the highly excitable and emotional Bella that Miss Lee Jervis played last year. Compare the review of May 14, 1895: "none shone like the faithful Bella, Bella of the psyche and the scarlet hose, Bella with the feather in her hair."

30   The Passing Show. *Courier*, pp. 6–7. Swinburne, Scottish writers. [Slote].

Dec. 6   Effie Ellsler in *As You Like It*. *Journal*, p. 6. Review. [Slote].
       Relates to review of Effie Ellsler in *Doris* (Apr. 25, 1895).

The *Journal* announced on December 8 that Miss Cather would "begin her regular contributions to the Sunday Journal" on December 15.

13   *Newest Devil's Auction*. *Journal*, p. 3. Review. [Slote].
       A dance of the Follies of all nations. The ballet appeared in the usual Folly costume in all shades and colors. Reference to the production of last season and a revised version of one passage in the earlier review. The

[1895]   first version (Sept. 28, 1894): "There was the old tragedienne in her faded velvets and faded complexion and faded hair, and the plump soubrette and the leading man in his battered silk hat . . . ." In the present one: "There was the pale, careworn tragedian, in his frayed black Prince Albert, the stately tragedienne, in her colorless hair and weary smile and faded velvets. There was the rollicking soubrette, the heavy villain . . . ."

14   Louis James in *Othello. Journal*, p. 6. Review. [Slote].

15   The Passing Show. *Journal*, p. 9. Dumas *fils*, the Heine statue, Paderewski, the intermezzo from *Cavalleria Rusticana*. [Slote].

22   The Passing Show. *Journal*, p. 9. Louis James and *Othello*, Mansfield, the Charity Concert. [Slote].

1896
Jan. 5   The Passing Show. *Journal*, p. 9. Stevenson's letters, art and athletics, Calvé, Clay Clement, Max Alvary in Omaha. [Slote].

12   The Passing Show. *Journal*, p. 9. Hall Caine's novels, Campanini, *The Passport* and Sadie Martinot, *Ladies' Home Journal*. [Slote].
Passages used in "Italo Campanini," unsigned article in the *Home Monthly*, Jan., 1897.

19   The Passing Show. *Journal*, p. 9. Yvette Guilbert, Alfred Austin as Laureate, monument to Stevenson, Walt Whitman. [Slote].

26   The Passing Show. *Journal*, p. 9. James Lane Allen, Bernhardt, Pearl Etynge as woman and artist. [Slote].

31   *Wang*, with Albert Hart. *Journal*, p. 6. Review. [Slote].
Relates to a sequence on *Wang* (see Note, pp. 458 f.).

Feb. 2   The Passing Show. *Journal*, p. 9. Verlaine, Hardy's *Jude the Obscure*. [Slote].

4   The Holdens in *Roxy, the Waif. Journal*, p. 6. Review [probable]. [Slote].
Style: "The stars might flicker and fade away and the firmaments be rolled together in a scroll, but the Holdens would continue to play to large and rapturously interested audiences in Lincoln just the same." The play is "a breezy, well-written little comedy with little plot and lots of nonsense to it."

9   The Passing Show. *Journal*, p. 9. England's Laureate, Dumas *fils*, Russian art, Ingersoll, the Chicago Sappho. [Slote].

16   The Passing Show. *Journal*, p. 9. Zola's *The Fat and the Thin*, Bernhardt. [Slote].
The Zola piece, with slight revisions, was reprinted in the "Books and Magazines" column, signed Sibert, *Leader*, May 27, 1898. See also "As You Like It," *Journal*, Dec. 30, 1894.

23   The Passing Show. *Journal*, p. 9. Eugene Field and *Love Affairs of a Bibliomaniac*, Duse, Hammerstein's *Faust*, writing dialogue, Corelli's novels. [Slote].

Mar. 1   The Passing Show. *Journal*, p. 9. Edgar Saltus, the kingdom of art, Ambroise Thomas and Père-Lachaise, *The Globe Trotter* recalled, Richard Hovey. [Slote].

8   The Passing Show. *Journal*, p. 13. Byron revival, the American theatre, Amélie Rives. [Slote].

[1895]15   The Passing Show. *Journal*, p. 9. Conan Doyle's stories, defense of Dumas *père*, Nordau on Alfred Austin, Anatole France and the Academy. [Slote].

22   The Passing Show. *Journal*, p. 9. Duse, mystery stories and Stevenson's *The Wrecker*, death of a model, Alfred Austin, defense of *Anna Karenina*. [Slote].

26   *Fleur de Lis. Journal*, p. 2. Review. [Slote].
    Comment on Della Fox in this review recalled in review of *The Wedding Day*, signed Sibert (*Leader*, Oct. 26, 1897).

29   Richard Mansfield in *A Parisian Romance. Journal*, p. 5. Review. [Slote].
    The Passing Show. *Journal*, p. 9. James's *The Tragic Muse* and stage novels, Sol Smith Russell in *Mr. Valentine's Christmas* and *An Everyday Man* reviewed. [Slote].

Apr. 5   The Passing Show. *Journal*, p. 16. Bohemianism, death of Mrs. Jennie Kimball. [Slote].

12   The Passing Show. *Journal*, p. 13. Anatole France, *A Parisian Romance* recalled, Thomas Hughes and children's literature. [Slote].

19   The Passing Show. *Journal*, p. 13. Anthony Hope's *Phroso*, magazine stories, The *Chap Book*, Sir Richard and Lady Burton, Chicago *Record* story. [Slote].

26   The Passing Show. *Journal*, p. 13. Carman and Hovey, Bernhardt, hats in theatres. [Slote].

May 3   The Passing Show. *Journal*, p. 13. Mary Anderson, Paderewski's gifts to composers. [Slote].

10   The Passing Show. *Journal*, p. 13. *The Rivals*, Marion Crawford and Dumas *père*. [Slote].

17   The Passing Show. *Journal*, p. 13. Ruskin, Tolstoi. [Slote].

24   The Passing Show. *Journal*, p. 13. Burns and Scottish writers. [Slote].

31   The Passing Show. *Journal*, p. 13. Mrs. Humphry Ward and George Eliot. [Slote].

June 7   The Passing Show. *Journal*, p. 13. Clay Clement, Daudet's characters. [Slote].

12   Boston Comic Opera Company in *Olivette. Journal*, p. 6. Review [probable]. [Slote].

14   The Passing Show. *Journal*, p. 13. Mrs. Burnett's *A Lady of Quality*, foreign artists, death of Clara Schumann. [Slote].
    Passage on foreign artists used in "Prodigal Salaries to Singers," unsigned article in the *Home Monthly*, Oct., 1896.

Addendum: The Pittsburgh *Leader*

The following signed play reviews appeared in the Pittsburgh *Leader* during the 1896–1897 season. Because they are so close in time and content to the Lincoln reviews of the preceding three seasons, they are especially valuable in the identification of Miss Cather's work, and in what they show of its continuous, closely related, and multiple nature.

1896
Nov. 24   The Hollands in *A Superfluous Husband* and *Colonel Carter of Cartersville*. Signed Willa. [Slote].

Dec. 1   Hoyt's *A Milk White Flag*. Signed Sibert. [Slote].
[1896]   Passage used from review of *A Trip to Chinatown* (*Journal*, Nov. 1, 1894).
      8   *Thoroughbred*. Signed Sibert. [Slote].
     15   Frank Daniels in *Wizard of the Nile*. Signed Sibert. [Slote].
             Passage used from review of *The Fencing Master* (*Journal*, Mar. 3, 1895).
             Statements repeated from reviews of *Panjandrum* (*Journal*, Apr. 7, 1894)
             and *Wang* (*Journal*, Oct. 25, 1895).
     22   "Beautiful Anna Held." Signed Sibert. [Slote].
     29   *Shore Acres*. Signed Sibert. [Slote].
             Passage used from review of *Brother John* (*Journal*, Apr. 5, 1894).
             Other references in style and content.

1897
Jan. 5   *Robin Hood*, with the Bostonians. Signed Sibert. [Slote].
             References in style and content.
     12   Otis Skinner in *A Soldier of Fortune*. Signed Sibert. [Slote].
             References to Dumas, Salvini, other topics and style related to Lincoln
             reviews.
     19   Fanny Davenport in *Gismonda*. Signed Sibert. [Slote].
             Related to comments on Sardou and *Helena* (*Journal*, Nov. 24, and
             Courier, Nov. 30, 1895). Statements related throughout.
     26   *My Friend from India*. Signed Sibert. [Slote].
             Passages used from reviews of *The Woman Hater* (*Journal*, Sept. 13, 1894)
             and *Our Flat* (*Journal*, May 14, and Nov. 26, 1895).
Feb. 9   *Puddn' Head Wilson*. Signed Sibert. [Slote].
     23   Margaret Mather in *Cymbeline*. Signed Sibert. [Slote].
             Related to previous comments on Mather, Shakespeare.
Mar. 2   *The Sporting Duchess*. Signed Sibert. [Slote].
      9   Nat Goodwin in *An American Citizen*. Signed Sibert. [Slote].
             Related in style, comment.
     16   Nethersole in *Carmen*. Signed Sibert. [Slote].
     23   *El Capitan*. Signed Sibert. [Slote].
             Passage used from review of *Wang* (*Journal*, Oct. 25, 1895) and other
             comments on DeWolf Hopper.
Apr. 6   John Drew in *Rosemary*. Signed Sibert. [Slote].
     20   Richard Mansfield in *Merchant of Venice*. Signed Sibert. [Slote].
May 25   Lizzie Hudson Collier in *Rosedale*. Signed Sibert. [Slote].
             Passage used from review of *Fritz in a Madhouse* (*Journal*, Jan. 26, 1895).
June 1   *The People's King*. Signed Sibert. [Slote].
             Reference to *A Parisian Romance* (*Journal*, Mar. 29, 1896).
          Also identifiable as Willa Cather's are the following unsigned *Leader* reviews,
          which will be discussed elsewhere: Roland Reed in *The Wrong Mr. Wright*
          (Sept 22, 1896), Sol Smith Russell in *A Bachelor's Romance* (Oct. 13, 1896),
          Joseph Jefferson in *Rip Van Winkle* (Nov. 10, 1896), Julia Marlowe in *Romeo
          and Juliet* (Feb. 2, 1897), *Lohengrin* (Mar. 4, 1897), *Tannhauser* (Mar. 6, 1897).
          A note to the review of *Tannhauser* says that it was written by "A lady who
          wields a trenchant pen."

Index

The titles of books belonging to Willa Cather and her family do not appear in the following index, but a description of some of the volumes may be found on pages 38–40. See also the Index Supplement (following the index) for the location of passages from Part II ("Critical Statements") which are quoted in Part I ("First Principles").

Abbott, Keene, 17
Abbott, Ned, 20 f.
Adam Bede, 376, 384 n.
Adams, Maude, 68, 243
Adonais, 62, 380
Aeneid, 295, 337
Affaire Clémenceau, L', 248
Aïda, 165
Alastor, 76, 78, 417
Alcott, Louisa, 338
Alexander, Hartley Burr, 9
Alexander's Bridge, 100 f., 109 f., 451
Alfred the Great, 47, 193
Allen, James Lane, 330–31
Amiel, Frederick, 314, 382
Anacreon, 349
Analytics of Literature, 18
Anderson, Mary, 48, 70–71, 89 n., 150, 154–59, 187 f., 207, 209, 271, 360, 417
Angelis, Jefferson de, 283
Anna Karenina, 38, 65, 187, 357, 377–79
Antigone, 216 n., 220
Antonia, 85
Antony and Cleopatra, 291–97
April Twilights, 106, 292 n., 345, 450
Archer, Jane, 186. *See also* Harris, Sarah B.
Ariadne, 194 n., 408
Arms and the Man, 254 f.
Arnold, Matthew, 32, 36, 40 f.

Art of Fiction, The, 40
Article 47, L', 53 n., 262, 291, 293
As in a Looking Glass, 291, 293
As You Like It, 298
Ashmore, Ruth, 188 f.
Austen, Jane, 357, 409
Austin, Alfred, 189, 192–93, 194
Axtell, Charles, 29

Bach, J. S., 44, 177
Ballad-Monger, The, 196
Balzac, Honoré de, 90, 153 f., 167 f., 181, 357, 363, 367, 407, 452
Barbour, Edward, 267 f.
"Barrack Room Ballads," 192
Barrie, James M., 340 f., 343
Barrière, Théodore, 410 f.
Barron, Elwyn A., 129, 154, 209–10, 258
Bashkirtseff, Marie, 314
Bates, Herbert, 9, 13, 28
Baxter, Richard, 178
Beau Brummell, 121, 130, 236, 245, 259 n., 371, 410
Beecher, Mrs. Henry Ward, 188, 417
Beethoven, Ludwig van, 44, 60, 177, 188
"Before Breakfast," 91–92
Behrens, Charlotte, 151–52

Belasco, David, 58, 83, 236, 237–40, 244 ff., 281 f.

Bernhardt, Sarah, 46 f., 54, 75, 78, 80, 86, 115–21, 126, 138, 140 f., 154 f., 157, 160, 203, 209, 216, 220, 292 n., 294–95

Besant, Walter, 254

Beside the Bonnie Brier Bush, 338 n., 331, 343

Bible, 35, 36, 43, 60

Bixby, A. L., 13, 21

Bizet, Georges, 163, 167

Black Crook, The, 259, 273–75

Blair, Eugenie, 271–72

Blouet, Paul, *see* O'Rell, Max

Boccaccio, Giovanni, 161

"Bohemian Girl, The," 101 f., 106, 451

Bohemians, The, 410 ff.

Bonaparte, Napoleon, 55, 168, 224, 229

Bondman, The, 329

Book of Death and Pity, The, 340

Book of Martyrs, 337

Booth, Edwin, 70, 216 n., 224, 426

Bothwell, 192

Boucicault, Dion, 410

Bourget, Paul, 226, 297

Boyd, Anna, 184 f.

Brand, 135

Brodie, Steve, 202 n., 203

Brother John, 58, 62 n., 259 n.

Brown, E. K., 95, 105, 405

Brownell, W. C., 127, 136 n.

Browning, Elizabeth Barrett, 70, 345, 374, 385

Browning, Robert, 32, 36, 64, 78, 205, 255, 393, 406, 414

Bryan, William Jennings, 19, 25, 28

Buckeye, The, 260

Buffalo Bill, *see* Cody, William F.

Bulwer-Lytton, Edward, 432

Bunyan, John, 55, 78, 338

Burnett, Frances Hodgson, 371–74

Burns, Robert, 78, 341, 343–44

Burton, Lady Isabel, 185–86

Burton, Sir Richard, 185–86

Butterflies, The (Allen), 330–31

Byron, George Gordon, Lord, 34, 36, 186, 398–99, 402

Caffyn, Kathleen Mannington, *see* Iota

Caine, Hall, 107, 204, 329–30

Calvé, Emma, 68 f., 76, 134, 197, 258, 416

Camille, 8, 53 n., 73, 79, 117, 120, 187, 246 ff., 262–63, 293

Campanini, Italo, 8, 44, 165–67, 183

Campbell, Mrs. Patrick, 191

Campbell, Thomas, 41

Canfield, Dorothea, *see* Fisher, Dorothy Canfield

Captivi, 216 n., 220

Carleton, Henry Guy, 131, 236, 243–46

Carlyle, Thomas, 10, 34, 36, 40, 42, 86, 222, 399 f., 421–25

Carman, Bliss, 222, 353–54

Carmen, 76, 133, 163, 167, 416

Carvalho, Marie Miolan-, 161–62

Cavalleria Rusticana, 162 f., 182 ff.

Celeste, Mlle., 139

Century, 7, 32, 281, 316, 324, 374

"Chance Meeting, A," 89, 99

Change of Air, A, 320

Chap Book, The, 32

"Charge of the Light Brigade, The," 212

Charity Ball, The, 237, 240, 244, 281

Charm, The, 254

Chatterton, Thomas, 385, 411

Chimmie Fadden, 210

Christus, 160–61

Church, Ed, 259, 278 f.

City of Dreadful Night, The, 162 f., 345

"Clemency of the Court, The," 59

Clement, Clay, 121, 124–25

Cody, William F. (Buffalo Bill), 188, 221 n.

Collins, Lottie, 200

Colvin, Sidney, 313 ff.

Consuelo, 210

Contented Woman, A, 240

Cooke, John Esten, 41–42, 136 n.

Coppée, François, 71, 326–27, 413

Corbett, James J., 182, 188, 207

Corelli, Marie, 189, 193–94, 337

Corwin, Charles, 218

Cosmopolitan, 254, 330

Cossacks, The, 332 n., 377

Count of Monte Cristo, The, 38, 63, 139, 172, 256 f., 324, 384 n.

"Count of Crow's Nest, The," 42, 84, 92

Courier, 12 ff., 22 ff., 148, 173, 275, 277 f., 291 n., 292 n., 303, 358

Craigen, Maida, 265–67

Crane, Stephen, 19–20

Crane, William H., 44, 58, 62 n., 259

Crawford, Emily, 324–25

Crawford, F. Marion, 360

Credit Lorraine, 291, 293

Crime of Sylvestre Bonnard, The, 328

Crinkle, Nym, 282

Critic, The, 32

Crockett, Samuel, 52, 315, 338–41, 343

Crouch, Frederick Nicholls, 168–69

Daily Call (Lincoln), 12, 24

Daly, Augustin, 246

Dame aux camélias, La, 209, 247

Daniels, Frank, 259, 294 n.

Daudet, Alphonse, 31 f., 36, 38, 60, 63 f., 84–85, 138, 245, 357, 411–13

Davenport, Fanny, 126

David Balfour, 313 f., 319

David Garrick, 129 f.

David Grieve, 374, 376

Davis, Richard Harding, 222, 407

Dead Man's Rock, 335

Death Comes for the Archbishop, 45, 110 ff.

"'Death in the Desert, A,'" 67 n., 96

Decameron, The, 248

De Koven, Reginald, 187

Demi-Monde, Le, 187 n., 246 ff.

Dickens, Charles, 335

Dickinson, Emily, 345

Doenhoff, Helena von, 86, 131–32, 149

Dolly Dialogues, The, 254, 320–21

Don Caesar de Bazan, 121

Donnelly, Ignatius, 426

Doris, 139, 298

Dorris, Mrs. Alvin, *see* Harris, Sarah B.

Dovey, Alice, 145–48

Dovey, Ethel, 145–48

Dowager Countess, The, 265

Downing, Robert, 123, 270–71

Doyle, Sir Arthur Conan, 319, 335

Drew, John, 7, 243

Duchess, The, *see* Hungerford, Margaret Wolfe

Duel of Hearts, A, 265 f.

Dumas, Alexandre, *père,* 31 f., 36, 38, 63 f., 79, 83 f., 87, 162, 246–49, 323, 324–25, 357, 372, 384, 445

Dumas, Alexandre, *fils,* 38, 209, 227, 246–49, 324, 364, 384

Du Maurier, George, 142, 270, 303 n., 330, 357, 362–65

Duse, Eleonora, 55, 116–19, 150, 152–54, 203

Eames, Emma, 133, 197, 258, 299 n.

Earthen Chariot, The, 138

Ebb Tide, 314

Edgren, A. H., 8

Edinburgh Review, 429

Elektra, 216 n., 320

Eliot, George, 36, 50, 64, 70 f., 158, 314, 357, 374–77, 384, 406, 409

Eliot, T. S., 92 f.

Ellsler, Effie, 139, 297–98

"Elopement of Allen Poole, The," 104 ff., 437–41

Emerson, Ralph Waldo, 34, 36, 40, 42, 211 n., 222

Emmett, J. K., 139–40

"Enchanted Bluff, The," 99 f., 103, 109

Endymion, 76, 98, 100, 417

England's Darling, 193

"Eric Hermannson's Soul," 92, 94 ff., 99, 231 n., 321 n.

"Escapism," 83

Étrangère, L', 247 f.

Evans, Augusta J., 181, 194

Evening News (Lincoln), 12, 13, 18, 24, 26, 294

Express (Beatrice), 23, 27

Eytinge, Pearl, 70

Falstaff, 131, 214–15

Far from the Madding Crowd, 358

Fat and the Thin, The, 367–71
Faust, 202–3, 256 f., 278–81, 384 n.
Fédora, 117, 191, 266
Felicia, 361
Femme de Claude, La, 227, 247
Fencing Master, The, 136 f., 259 n.
Few Memories, A, 155 ff.
Field, Eugene, 48, 332–33
Fielding, Henry, 223, 357, 373
Fisher, Dorothy Canfield, 9, 37, 108
Fiske, John, 32
Fitch, Clyde, 245, 410
Flacke, Henri, 216
Flaubert, Gustave, 31, 37, 60, 90, 98, 138,
    357, 382
"Flavia and Her Artists," 96–97
Fleur de Lis, 282–84
For Congress, 277
Fortunio, 138
Fox, Della, 134, 282 ff.
Foy, Eddie, 196–97
France, Anatole, 327–29
Francillon, 247
Fremstad, Olive, 86
French Poets and Novelists, 40
French Traits, 127, 136 n.
Freytag, Gustav, 280
Friends, 14, 263–64, 272–73
Friendship, 408
Fritz in a Mad House, 139
Frohman, Gustave, 17, 259 f., 281
Fyles, Franklin, 237

"Garden Lodge, The," 96
"Garden of Eros, The," 350, 404
Garland, Hamlin, 218, 222, 224, 331
Gautier, Judith, 138–39, 382 n.
Gautier, Théophile, 61, 138, 246, 352, 382,
    395
Georgics, 101
Gere, Charles H., 12
Gere, Mariel, 23 n., 28 f., 269 n.
Gerwig, George W., 15, 29
Gilded Fool, A, 128, 131, 216, 243 f., 246
Giorgione, 401 n., 404
Girl I Left Behind Me, The, 237 f.

Gladiator, The, 270–72
Gloriana, 263, 264–65
"Goblin Market, The," 93, 95, 346 ff.
"Goddess Diana, The," 101–2
Godefroi and Yolande, 79
Gods in Exile, The, 35, 37, 98, 101, 394
Goethe, Johann Wolfgang von, 38, 65,
    151, 202, 267, 279 f., 384, 428, 431 f.
Golden Age, The, 192
Goldsmith, Oliver, 254, 338
Goodwin, Nat, 44, 56, 127, 128–31, 216,
    243 f.
Gosse, Edmund, 316
Grand, Sarah (Frances Elizabeth McFall),
    313, 335, 363, 377, 406 n., 407
Green Carnation, The, 135
Griffith, John, 278–80, 281
Grimm, Jacob, 36, 86
Griswold, Rufus Wilmot, 383, 387
Grout, Madame, 89–90
Guilbert, Yvette, 225–26, 404

Haggard, H. Rider, 209, 267 f., 363
Hall, Gertrude, 395
Hall, Pauline, 134
Hamlet, 90–91, 105, 286, 302–8, 426–36
Hammer and Rapier, 41, 136 n.
Hammerstein, Oscar, 202–3
Hardy, Thomas, 32, 322, 342, 357, 358–60
Harper's, 327, 358 ff.
Harraden, Beatrice, 313
Harris, Sarah B., 13 n., 23 ff., 27 f., 186,
    345, 450
Harrison, Benjamin, 187 f., 224, 417
Harrison, Mrs. Burton, 222, 281
Hawkins, Sir Anthony Hope, *see* Anthony
    Hope
Hawthorne, Nathaniel, 222, 357, 382, 384
Heart of Ruby, 138
"Heart of the Princess Osra, The," 321
Hearts Insurgent, 358–60
Heavenly Twins, The, 313 n., 335, 363, 406
Heege, Gus, 273
Heine, Heinrich, 32, 35, 37 f., 64, 98,
    100 ff., 204, 394 f., 413

"Hélas!," 390 ff.
Hendrick Hudson, 252
Henry IV, 288–90, 291
Henry V, 291
Henry VI, 291
Henry VIII, 102, 286, 290 f.
Henry Esmond, 48, 130, 357, 371, 373–74
Herald (Lincoln), 12, 16
Hernani, 246, 384 n.
Heroes and Hero Worship, 36, 40, 86
Hesperian, 10 ff., 14, 16 ff., 104, 173, 421 f., 437
Hichens, Robert, 135
Histoire de ma vie, 210
History of a Crime, The, 330, 384 n.
Hockett, Ethel M., 450
Hofmann, Josef, 148–49
Hole in the Ground, A, 240, 242
Holmes, Mary J., 181, 193–94
Holy War, The, 337
Home Monthly, 3 f., 29, 145, 166 n., 195
Homer, 35, 212, 249, 350
Hope, Anthony, 63 f., 222, 232, 254, 309 f., 318–22, 330
Hopper, DeWolf, 55, 140, 259, 283
House of the Wolf, The, 210, 322 f.
Hovenden, Thomas, 282
Hovey, Richard, 168 n., 353–56
"How They Brought the Good News from Ghent to Aix," 212
Howard, Bronson, 236, 246
Howells, William Dean, 33, 62, 64, 180, 186, 203, 204 n., 245, 281, 332, 358, 360, 378, 407
Hoyt, Charles H., 56, 236, 240–43, 246, 252
Hughes, Thomas, 336 ff.
Hugo, Victor, 38, 60, 63, 246, 249, 329–30, 357, 384
Huguenots, Les, 52 n., 53, 131, 214 n.
Hungerford, Margaret Wolfe ("The Duchess"), 188, 193
Hunt, Ebenezer, 10
Hustler, The, 177, 184
Hypatia, 328
Hyperion, 86

Ibsen, Henrik, 32, 38, 62, 83, 134 f., 236
Iliad, 100 n.
Inez, 275–77
Ingersoll, Robert G., 177, 210–11, 435
Inter-Ocean, 129, 209
Iota (Kathleen Mannington Caffyn), 363, 407
Irving, Sir Henry, 44, 79, 189–91, 202 n., 278
Ivan Ilyitch, 332 n., 377
Izeyl, 120

James, Henry, 18, 31, 40, 64, 74 f., 78 n., 80, 211, 245, 255, 310, 313, 330, 357 f., 360–62, 378, 382, 447
James, Louis, 52, 288–90, 298–301
"Jameson's Ride," 192
Jane, 259
Jefferson, Joseph, 7, 44 n., 187 n., 288
Jerome, Jerome K., 186, 222
Jewett, Sarah Orne, 103, 446 ff.
Johnson, Alvin, 8 f.
Jolly Good Fellow, A, 252
Jones, Will Owen, 12 ff., 20 f., 452
Joseph and His Brothers, 90
Journal, see *Nebraska State Journal*
"Joy of Nelly Deane, The," 103
Jude the Obscure, 322, 358–60
Julius Caesar, 370 n.
Jungle Book, The, 353, 452

Kant, Immanuel, 179 f.
Keats, John, 5, 36, 45, 62, 64, 65, 86, 98, 108, 198 f., 249, 355, 398 f., 402, 429
Keene, Thomas, 57, 123, 256, 265 f., 286
Kettler, Fred, 175
Kháyyám, Omar, 385 n.
Kidder, Katharine, 150 n.
Kidnapped, 319
King, Captain Charles, 337
Kings in Exile, 63, 313
Kingsley, Charles, 36, 93, 95 f., 230, 346, 351, 442
Kipling, Rudyard, 13, 32, 55, 57, 63, 192, 232, 309 f., 316–18, 322, 339 f., 407, 452
Kreutzer Sonata, The, 65, 363, 378
Kruger, Alma, 300, 301–2

Ladies' Home Journal, 176, 187–89, 207
Lady of Quality, A, 48, 371–74
Lady of Venice, The, 321–22
Lady Windermere's Fan, 79, 179, 387–90
Lang, Andrew, 222
Langtry, Lily, 166, 228
Lasso, 10, 15, 316, 377
Lawrence, D. H., 43
Leader (Pittsburgh), 4, 282, 368, 447
Leaves of Grass, 345, 350, 352 f.
Lees, James T., 8 f.
Lehmer, D. N., 9
Lesson of the Master, The, 360 f.
Lewis, Edith, 405
Lewis, Lillian, 291–97, 298
Library, The, 20 n., 77–78
Lindsey, Guy, 300
Lion's Mouth, The, 243, 246
Little Lord Fauntleroy, 371, 373
Little Minister, The, 340, 343
"Locksley Hall," 151
Locrine, 193
Longfellow, Henry Wadsworth, 36, 322, 384
Lorenz, Richard, 218
Lost Lady, A, 102 f., 110
"Lost Leader, The," 393
Loti, Pierre (Viaud, Julien), 32, 38, 60, 64, 77, 107, 340, 357, 365–67
"Lou, the Prophet," 59
Love Affairs of a Bibliomaniac, The, 48, 332–33
"Love Among the Ruins," 159
Love Chase, The, 53 n., 236
Lowell, James Russell, 36, 222, 382, 384
Lucy Gayheart, 112
Lussan, Zélie de, 86, 131, 133

Mabie, Hamilton Wright, 36
Macbeth, 326, 428
McClure's, 32, 310, 313, 321 f., 447, 450 f.
McFall, Frances Elizabeth, *see* Grand, Sarah
Mackaye, Steele, 236
Maclaren, Ian (John Watson), 52, 338–41, 343

Madame Bovary, 31, 89–90, 377 f.
Madonna of the Future, The, 64
Mann, Thomas, 90
Mansfield, Richard, 7, 121, 122–23, 126, 130, 172, 216 n., 224, 254–55, 259, 284–85, 323, 371
Mantell, Robert B., 144, 151–52, 259
Marcella, 374, 376
Markham, Pauline, 273 ff.
Marlowe, Julia, 7, 44, 53 f., 80, 140, 186 f., 209–10, 259, 262, 286
"Marriage of Phaedra, The," 96
Mary Magdalen, 415
Martin, Olive, 279
Mascagni, Pietro, 162–63, 183
Mason, Walt, 13, 16 f., 24, 27–28, 387 n., 388 n.
Massenet, Jules, 162, 248
Master and Man, 378
Master of Ballantrae, The, 313
Mather, Margaret, 7, 48, 86, 140, 144, 286
Maude, 180
Maupassant, Guy de, 32, 60, 135, 357, 382
Maurel, Victor, 55, 197, 214 f., 301
Mayo, Mamie, 184 f.
Melba, Nellie, 48, 86, 132, 187 f., 195, 197, 207 f., 214 n., 258, 416
Men and Women, 237–38, 239 f., 244, 281
Mendelssohn, Felix, 216
Meredith, George, 123, 180 f., 188, 194, 322, 342, 357, 371
"Middle Years, The," 360
Millet, Jean François, 218, 448
Misérables, Les, 238, 326, 330, 357, 384 n.
Miskel, Caroline, 240 n., 298
Miss Bretherton, 374 ff.
Modern Painters, 400, 402
Modjeska, Helena, 7, 54, 79 n., 102, 140, 186, 262, 286, 298
Moore, Thomas, 34, 41, 398 f.
Moreau, Hégésippe, 411
Morris, Clara, 8, 53 f., 57, 140, 186, 259, 262–63, 266
Morris, Felix, 195–96, 259

Morris, William, 192

Morrison, Lewis, 51, 256, 278–79

Morton, Dorothy, 136 f.

Mounet-Sully, Jean, 127–28, 203

Mozart, Wolfgang Amadeus, 44, 74, 149, 177

Murfree, Fanny N. D., 361

Murger, Henri, 171, 410–11

Murphy, Tim, 196

Musset, Alfred de, 35, 37 f., 64, 153, 404, 415

My Ántonia, 36, 85, 106 f., 109, 239 n.

My Literary Passions, 332

My Mortal Enemy, 102–3, 110

Mystery of Cloombers, The, 319 n., 335

Mystery of Edwin Drood, The, 335

Navarro, Mme. Antonio de, *see* Anderson, Mary

Nebraska, 223–24

Nebraska Editor, 26

Nebraska Literary Magazine, 21, 28

Nebraska State Journal, 4 n., 10, 12 ff., 172 f., 182, 214 n., 216 n., 241, 251, 258, 263, 275, 277 f., 291 n., 292 n., 299 n., 302 f., 316, 421 f., 426, 447

Nebraskan, 11 n., 18, 22

Nethersole, Olga, 79 n., 120, 136 f.

New Dominion, The, 121, 124

New England Primer, The, 333

News, see Evening News

"Night at Greenway Court, A," 28, 41–42, 59

Noble, Thomas, 218

Nobody, 253

Nordau, Max, 192, 195, 223, 394, 408

Nordica, Lillian, 8, 53, 86, 183 f., 188, 197, 258, 417

Norma, 102

Norse Stories, 36

"Novel Démeublé, The," 4, 80, 83 f.

Nuit de Cléopâtre, Une, 138

O Pioneers!, 100 n., 103–4, 106, 351, 445, 447 f.

Oedipe Roi, 127

"Old Beauty, The," 112

"Old Mrs. Harris," 38

Old Musician, The, 196

"On the Divide," 25, 59, 94 ff., 105, 107

One of Ours, 12, 60, 85, 109

O'Neil, Washington, D.C., 250–51

O'Neill, James, 123 n., 171, 256 f.

Orefice, Gaetano, 210

O'Rell, Max (Paul Blouet), 136, 137–38

Orpheus and Eurydice, 87

Ostrovsky, Aleksandr, 134 f.

Otello, 53, 163–66, 214, 299 n.

Othello, 84, 288, 298–302

Ouida (Marie Louise de la Ramée), 194, 335, 408

Our Flat, 55, 68

Overland Monthly, 25

Paderewski, Ignace, 188, 195

Paganini, Nicolò, 149, 164–65

Pair of Blue Eyes, A, 358

Panjandrum, 259 n., 284

Parisian Romance, A, 121, 216, 284–85

Parkhurst, Charles, 188

Pascarel, 408

"Passing Show, The," 13, 23, 25 f., 125 f., 284

Pater, Walter, 36, 40

Paul Kauvar, 236

Paulding, Frederick, 265–67

Pauline, 161

"Paul's Case," 96 f.

Payton, Corse, 177, 248 n.

Peattie, Elia W., 26

Pêcheur d'islande, 365

Peer Gynt, 347

Père Goriot, 154

Père-Lachaise, 34, 160 ff., 167 f.

Perjured Padulion, A, 11

Pershing, John J., 9

Personal Recollections of Joan of Arc, 358

"Peter," 59

Petschnikoff, Alexander, 225

Pettitt, Henry, 198 f.

Phèdre, 154, 158

Phillpotts, Eden, 84

Phroso, 322

Picture of Dorian Gray, The, 389

Pilgrim's Progress, 35, 43, 323, 337

Pinero, Sir Arthur Wing, 83–84, 236

Plain Tales from the Hills, 316 f.

Plutarch, 295

Poe, Edgar Allan, 21, 36, 63 f., 79, 360, 380–87

Poèmes saturniens, 394

Police Patrol, The, 127

"Polikushka," 332 n., 377

Politician, The, 4 n., 277–78

Pollock, Sir Walter Herries, 254

Poor Relation, The, 79

Pound, Ezra, 92 f.

Pound, Louise, 3, 9 ff.

Pound, Olivia, 9, 22 n.

Pound, Roscoe, 9, 18

Prince Otto, 310, 312–13

Prisoner of Zenda, The, 63 f., 67 n., 210, 231, 292, 318–20, 322

Professor's House, The, 13, 110

Puvis de Chavannes, Pierre, 78

Pyle, Howard, 392

Quick or the Dead?, The, 334

Quiller-Couch, Arthur, 335

Rachel, 54, 86, 88 n., 154, 158, 225 f.

Ramée, Marie Louise de la, *see* Ouida

Rascoe, Burton, 50

Record (Des Moines), 14

Record (Philadelphia), 445

Red Badge of Courage, The, 20

Reed, Roland, 4 n., 57, 277

Rehan, Ada, 246 n.

Réjane, 70

Republican (Omaha), 24

Reszke, Jean de, 197 f., 114 n., 115

Richard III, 123, 256, 265, 286, 291

Richardson, Samuel, 357

Richelieu, 236

Rivals, The (Coppée), 327

Rivals, The (Sheridan), 44, 186 f., 236, 288

Rives, Amélie, 334–35

Road to Thebes, The, 248

Robert Elsmere, 270, 374

Robinson, Theodore, 217–18

Robinson Crusoe, 333

Rolla, 35, 404, 415 n.

Roman and the Teuton, The, 93, 98, 230, 346, 442–44

Romance of a Spahi, The, 107, 365–67

Romances without Words, 395

Romeo and Juliet, 48, 98, 151, 157, 265, 286

Roméo et Juliette, 131, 145, 162, 208 n., 214 n.

Romola, 209–10

Rossetti, Christina, 70, 93, 96, 345, 346–49

Rossetti, Dante Gabriel, 192, 346

Royle, Edwin Milton, 263 f., 272–73

Rubáiyát, 345, 385 n., 397 n.

Rubinstein, Anton, 72, 160–61, 183

Ruskin, John, 32, 34, 36, 40, 42, 65, 70, 173, 175, 179, 186, 399–404, 408

Russell, Lillian, 134, 208

Saints' Everlasting Rest, The, 178

Salammbô, 31, 37, 90, 94, 98 ff., 103, 415

Saltus, Edgar, 76, 415–16

Salvini, Alexander, 63, 121–22, 125–26, 172, 220, 247, 259, 323

Sand, George, 38, 54, 60, 70 f., 85, 158, 170, 210, 357, 375, 406, 409

Sapho, 38, 297

Sapphira and the Slave Girl, 104 ff., 112

Sappho, 33, 71, 158, 345, 349

Sarcey, Francisque, 235, 260

Sardou, Victorien, 150 n., 162, 247, 262, 287, 295

Sartor Resartus, 40

Savonarola: A Tragedy, 192

Scalchi, Sofia, 8, 162, 183

Scènes de la vie de Bohème, 171, 410

Scented Garden, The, 185

Schubert, Franz, 59

Schumann, Clara Wieck, 169–70

Schumann, Robert, 169–70

Scott, Sir Walter, 402

"Sculptor's Funeral, The," 96

Seabrooke, Thomas Q., 259

Second Mrs. Tanqueray, The, 231

Seibel, George, 37, 60, 292 n., 332 n.
Seibel, Helen, 22, 37, 60, 332 n., 365 n.
Senator, The, 277
Serao, Matilde, 153
Sergeant, Elizabeth Shepley, 60 n., 85
Sesame and Lilies, 400 n., 403 n.
Setting of the Sun, The, 265, 267
Sevastopol, 330, 377
Shadows on the Rock, 45, 60, 91, 110 ff.
Shakespeare, William, 33, 36, 44, 52, 55, 57, 60, 166, 193, 211, 236, 246, 255, 286–88, 326, 389, 426–36, 452
"Shakespeare and Hamlet," 105, 426–36
Shakespeare Up to Date, 11
Shaw, George Bernard, 32, 254–55
She, 209, 267–68, 363
Shelley, Percy Bysshe, 32, 36, 40, 43, 64, 108, 153, 355, 380, 398, 402
Shenandoah, 236, 253, 289
Sherman, Lucius A., 13, 18, 28
Shore Acres, 236
Sign of Four, The, 335
Simpletons, The, 358–60
Sir George Tressady, 374
Skinner, Otis, 7, 286
Smith, W. Morton, 12, 23 ff., 28, 173
Smollett, Tobias George, 223, 338, 357, 373
Sohrab and Rustum, 41
Soldiers Three, 63, 316, 318
Sombrero, 11
"Song of Myself," 352
Song of the Lark, The, 86–89, 98 n., 110, 112, 155, 445
Songs from Vagabondia, 353 f.
Sons of the Morning, 84
Sordello, 161, 180
Sorrows of Satan, The, 193 f.
Sousa, John Philip, 198, 199–201, 243
Spencer, Herbert, 32
Spender, Stephen, 160
Spider and the Fly, The, 252
Spooner, B. S., 276
Spooner, Cecil, 56, 140, 276
Spooner, Edna May, 140, 275 f.
Spooner, Mollie G., 276

Staël, Madame de, 206
Stedman, Edmund Clarence, 382
Stevenson, John, 253
Stevenson, Robert Louis, 13, 31, 36, 40, 63 f., 73, 77, 98, 100 f., 169 n., 188, 194, 232–33, 309–16, 319, 322, 336, 339, 341, 343 n., 344, 360
Stickit Minister, The, 315, 338 n., 343 n.
Stones of Venice, The, 400
Story of the Gadsbys, The, 316, 318
Stowe, Harriet Beecher, 268
"Success Is Counted Sweetest," 345
Sully, Daniel, 249–51
Summer Blizzard, A, 252
Superfluous Woman, The, 406
Swinburne, Algernon Charles, 40, 189, 192 f., 349–50, 352, 355, 387

"Tale of the White Pyramid, A," 11 n.
Taliesin: A Masque, 168 n., 353, 355
Tamagno, Francesco, 52–53, 195, 214 n., 215, 299 n.
Tanner, Cora, 140
Tavary, Marie, 86, 131–32
Temperance Town, A, 240 f.
Tempest, Marie, 134, 136 f., 259
Tennyson, Alfred, Lord, 36, 180, 189 f.
Terminations, 361
Tess of the D'Urbervilles, 358, 363, 377
Teutonic Mythology, 36, 86 n.
Texas Steer, A, 196 n., 240
Thackeray, William Makepeace, 36, 44, 64, 130, 180, 188, 222, 254, 357, 362, 371, 373–74, 384, 407
Thaïs (France), 327 n., 328–29
Thaïs (Massenet), 248
Thirty Years in Paris, 84
Thomas, Ambroise, 167–68
Thompson, Maurice, 377 f.
Thomson, James, 163 n., 345
Thousand Nights and a Night, The, 186
Three Guardsmen, The, 38, 63, 121, 247, 323 ff., 448
Thunderstorm, The, 134–35
Toby Rex, *see* Julius H. Tyndale
Tolstoi, Leo, 31, 64 f., 73, 212, 357, 377–79

Tom Brown at Oxford, 336–37
Tom Brown's School Days, 336
Tosca, La, 46, 117, 120, 126, 292 n.
Town Topics, 334
Tragic Muse, The, 89 n., 361

Transgression of the Abbé Mouret, The, 369
Treasure Island, 63, 310, 323
"Treasure of Far Island, The," 65 n., 99
Tree, Sir Herbert Beerbohm, 191, 196
Trilby, 18, 56, 142, 270, 357, 360, 362–65
Trip to Chinatown, A, 184 f., 240 ff.
Troll Garden, The, 92 f., 95–97, 109, 230, 346, 351, 442, 450
Trovatore, Il, 131 f., 145 f.
Turgenev, Ivan, 13, 38, 72, 339, 357
Turner, Joseph, 186, 400 n., 401 n., 402
Twain, Mark, 241, 357 f., 447
Twelfth Night, 53, 286
Tyler, Odette, 208, 417
Tyndale, Julius H., 14 f., 17, 26, 294 n.

Uncle Tom's Cabin, 268–70, 278, 406
Under Two Flags, 194 n., 408

Vailima Letters, 313 n., 314
Vanity Fair (Lincoln), 58
Vedder, Elihu, 385
Ventre de Paris, Le, 368
Verdi, Giuseppe, 163, 165 f., 214–15
Verlaine, Paul, 32, 37, 38, 73, 380, 393–97
Viaud, Julien, *see* Loti, Pierre
Victoria, Queen, 189 ff.
Village Commune, A, 408
Virgil, 35, 101, 295
Virginia Bohemians, The, 42
Virginius, 123, 222, 236, 270
Vizetelly, Ernest Alfred, 368
Voodoo, The, 251

Wagner, Richard, 186, 222
"Wagner Matinee, A," 96
Wainwright, Bishop, 229–30
Wainwright, Marie, 229–30

Walküre, Die, 88
Wanda, 408
Wang, 55, 140, 284
War and Peace, 332 n., 377
Ward, Mrs. Humphry, 50, 270, 374–77
Warde, Frederick, 288–90, 298, 300
Warner, Charles Dudley, 362
Waste Land, The, 93
Watson, John, *see* Maclaren, Ian
Wedding Day, The, 282
Weekly Express, see Express
Weekly Herald, see Herald
Westermann family, 12, 14
Westermann, William, 9
Weyman, Stanley, 63, 310, 319, 322–23
Wharton, Edith, 50–51
Wheeler, Bernice, 240, 282
When Bess Was Queen, 209
Whistler, James McNeill, 53, 186, 404
White Squadron, The, 253
Whiteside, Walker, 303–5
Whitman, Walt, 40, 74–75, 80, 345, 350–53, 447
Wife, The, 83, 281–82
Wiener, Mr. and Mrs. Charles, 38
Wilcox, Ella Wheeler, 345
Wilde, Oscar, 7, 33, 47, 57, 135, 236, 349 f., 380, 387–93, 404 n., 409
Willard, E. S., 127, 303
Willis, Nathaniel Parker, 383 f., 387
Winter, William, 117
Winter's Tale, The, 157, 411 n.
World-Herald (Omaha), 19, 26
Wrecker, The, 336
Wycherley, William, 210

Yellow Book, 32, 404
Yon Yonson, 273
Youth's Companion, 337

Zangwill, Israel, 222
Zanoni, 432
Zola, Émile, 38, 49, 62, 64, 116, 181, 327, 357, 367–71

INDEX SUPPLEMENT

Key: Pages on which quotations from Part II ("Critical Statements") or the Appendices appear are indicated by parentheses and boldface type. Pages on which the quotations may be found in context follow in standard type.

(32) 410 ff. (34) 222, 403, 398 (35) 404 (38) 323 (43) 417, 392, 124 (43–44) 177 (44) 308, 374, 190, 165, 382, 386, 163, 163, 161 (45) 330 (45–46) 348 (46) 401, 120, 258, 324–325, 262, 262, 285 (47) 126, 193, 331, 388 (48) 407, 373, 379, 333, 132, 157 (49) 117, 271, 347, 132, 371 (50) 376 (51) 261 (52) 299, 299, 186, 187, 338–339, 133 (54) 120 (55) 119, 192–193 (56) 130, 129, 243, 365 (57) 391, 334–335, 390 (58) 244, 175, 244, 209 (60) 177, 330, 271 (61) 260, 245, 162, 138 (62) 232–233 (63) 448, 122, 312, 319, 330, 317, 385 (64–65) 312 (65) 149, 233, 267, 152, 402, 217, 378 (65–66) 402 (66) 217, 187 (66–67) 282 (67) 334–335 (68) 282, 338 (69) 282, 423, 407 (70) 210, 400, 156–158 (71) 158, 413, 414 (72) 143, 183, 238, 239 (73) 144, 208, 314, 246, 383, 395–396, 247, 378 (74) 360 ff., 350 ff. (75) 226, 120–121 (76–77) 417 (77) 417, 313 (78) 354, 344, 121 (79) 157, 249, 326, 375, 216 (82) 177 (83) 249, 237 (90) 305 ff. (91) 331 (93) 230 (93–94) 232 (94) 328, 231 (98) 169 (107) 365 ff., 329–330, 218, 331 (108) 355, 225